Routledge International Handbook of Outdoor Studies

The 'outdoors' is a physical and ideological space in which people engage with their environment, but it is also an important vehicle for learning and for leisure. The *Routledge International Handbook of Outdoor Studies* is the first book to define and survey the multidisciplinary set of approaches that constitute the broad field of outdoor studies, including outdoor recreation, outdoor education, adventure education, environmental studies, physical cultural studies and leisure studies. It reflects upon the often haphazard development of outdoor studies as a discipline, critically assesses current knowledge in outdoor studies, and identifies further opportunities for future research in this area.

With a broader sweep than any other book yet published on the topic, this Handbook traces the philosophical and conceptual contours of the discipline, as well as exploring key contemporary topics and debates, and identifying important issues in education and professional practice. It examines the cultural, social and political contexts in which people experience the outdoors, including perspectives on outdoor studies from a wide range of countries, providing the perfect foundation for any student, researcher, educator or outdoor practitioner looking to deepen their professional knowledge of the outdoors and our engagement with the world around us.

Barbara Humberstone is a Professor of Sociology of Sport and Outdoor Education at Buckinghamshire New University, UK. Her research interests include: embodiment and nature-based sport, and wellbeing and outdoor pedagogies. She co-edited *Whose Journeys? The Outdoors and Adventure as Social and Culture Phenomena* (2003); *Seascapes: Shaped by the Sea: Embodied Narratives and Fluid Geographies* (2015), and has published papers in a variety of journals. She is Editor-in-Chief of the *Journal of Adventure Education and Outdoor Learning* and was Chair of the European Institute for Outdoor Adventure Education and Experiential Learning (2004–2008). She is a keen windsurfer, walker, swimmer and yogini.

Heather Prince is Associate Professor of Outdoor and Environmental Education in the Department of Science, Natural Resources and Outdoor Studies at the University of Cumbria. UK. She designs, develops and teaches on many undergraduate and postgraduate courses in outdoor studies, and is interested in pedagogic practice in outdoor education, and ecology. She is a member of the Editorial Board of the *Journal of Adventure Education and Outdoor Learning*, a Principal Fellow of the Higher Education Academy, UK, and loves adventuring in wild places on foot and by boat.

Karla A. Henderson is Professor Emeritus in the Department of Parks, Recreation and Tourism at North Carolina State University, USA. Her research interests include women and social justice, physical activity, and research methods as they pertain to the outdoors and other leisure experiences. She has been published in a number of journals and served as a founder for the Coalition for Education in the Outdoors and of the American Camp Association's Committee for the Advancement of Research and Evaluation. She enjoys hiking in the mountains, travelling and playing her trumpet.

Routledge International Handbook of Outdoor Studies

Edited by Barbara Humberstone,
Heather Prince and Karla A. Henderson

Routledge
Taylor & Francis Group

LONDON AND NEW YORK

First published 2016
by Routledge
2 Park Square, Milton Park, Abingdon, Oxon OX14 4RN

and by Routledge
711 Third Avenue, New York, NY 10017

Routledge is an imprint of the Taylor & Francis Group, an informa business

British Library Cataloguing-in-Publication Data
A catalogue record for this book is available from the British Library

Library of Congress Cataloging in Publication Data
Names: Humberstone, Barbara, editor of compilation. | Prince, Heather, editor of compilation. | Henderson, Karla A., editor of compilation.
Title: Routledge handbook of Outdoor Studies / edited by Barbara Humberstone, Heather Prince and Karla Henderson.
Description: New York : Routledge, 2016. | Includes bibliographical references and index.
Identifiers: LCCN 2015019457| ISBN 9781138782884 (Hardback) | ISBN 9781315768465 (eBook)
Subjects: LCSH: Outdoor recreation—Study and teaching. | Outdoor education. | Environmental education. | Leisure—Study and teaching.
Classification: LCC GV191.6 .R68 2016 | DDC 796.5—dc23
LC record available at http://lccn.loc.gov/2015019457

ISBN: 978-1-138-78288-4 (hbk)
ISBN: 978-1-315-76846-5 (ebk)

Typeset in Bembo
by Swales & Willis Ltd, Exeter, Devon, UK

Contents

List of figures   x
List of tables   xi
Foreword   xii
Notes on contributors   xvi
Acknowledgements   xxix

Introduction   1
Barbara Humberstone, Heather Prince and Karla A. Henderson

PART 1
Constructs and theoretical concepts   5

Introduction   7
Heather Prince

1 Foundation myths and the roots of adventure education in the Anglosphere   11
   Andrew Brookes

2 From 'Erlebnis' to adventure: a view on the German Erlebnispädagogik   20
   Peter Becker

3 Environmental concerns and outdoor studies: nature as fosterer   30
   Johan Öhman and Klas Sandell

4 Outdoor studies and a sound philosophy of experience   40
   John Quay and Jayson Seaman

5 Healing the split head of outdoor recreation and outdoor
   education: revisiting Indigenous knowledge from multiple perspectives   49
   Philip Mullins, Gregory Lowan-Trudeau and Karen Fox

6 Health and wellbeing benefits of activities in the outdoors   59
   Cathryn Carpenter and Nevin Harper

Contents

7 Shifting perspectives on research in the outdoors   69
   Emily Coates, Alan Hockley, Barbara Humberstone and Ina Stan

PART 2
Formal education in outdoor studies   **79**

   Introduction   81
   Heather Prince

8 The primacy of place in education in outdoor settings   85
   Greg Mannion and Jonathan Lynch

9 Scandinavian early childhood education: spending time in the
   outdoors   95
   Ellen Beate Hansen Sandseter and Trond Løge Hagen

10 Supporting early learning outdoors in the UK: culture clash and concord   103
   Sue Waite

11 Curricular outdoor learning in Scotland: from practice to policy   113
   Beth Christie, Pete Higgins and Robbie Nicol

12 Teaching trainee teachers about outdoor education   121
   Erik Backman

13 Pedagogic practice in higher education in the UK   131
   Tim Stott

14 Formal curricular initiatives and evaluation in the UK   141
   Heather Prince and David Exeter

PART 3
Non-formal education and training in/for/about outdoor studies **151**

   Introduction   153
   Karla A. Henderson

15 Careers in the outdoors   159
   Linda Allin and Amanda West

16 Beyond training for tolerance in outdoor experiential education:
   more than just leadership   168
   Mary Breunig and Elyse Rylander

17 Professional accreditation in the UK outdoor sector   178
    Heather Brown, Ian Harris and Su Porter

18 Certification in outdoor programmes   189
    Aram Attarian

19 Ethical considerations in outdoor studies research   198
    Letty Ashworth, Lucy Maynard and Karen Stuart

20 Adventure education: crucible, catalyst and inexact   207
    Jim Sibthorp and Dan Richmond

21 Challenge course programming: on the rise or in compromise?   217
    Mark Wagstaff

22 The camp experience: learning through the outdoors   227
    M. Deborah Bialeschki, Stephen M. Fine and Troy Bennett

23 Sail training   236
    Ken McCulloch

24 Forest School in the United Kingdom   244
    Sara Knight

25 Developing therapeutic outdoor practice: adventure therapy   251
    Kaye Richards

26 Reviewing and reflection: connecting people to experiences   260
    Roger Greenaway and Clifford E. Knapp

PART 4
International voices and cultural interpretations   269

    Introduction   271
    Karla A. Henderson

27 The inclusion of outdoor education in the formal school curriculum:
    Singapore's journey   277
    Susanna Ho, Matthew Atencio, Yuen Sze Michelle Tan and
    Chew Ting Ching

28 Friluftsliv: nature-friendly adventures for all   288
    Kirsti Pedersen Gurholt

Contents

29 Turistika activities and games, dramaturgy, and the Czech
    outdoor experience   297
    Andrew J. Martin, Ivana Turčová and Jan Neuman

30 Outdoor studies in Japan   307
    Taito Okamura

31 Using outdoor adventure to contribute to peace: the case of Kenya   316
    Shikuku W. Ooko and Helen N. Muthomi

32 Outdoor activities in Brazilian educational camps   325
    Marcelo Fadori Soares Palhares and Sandro Carnicelli

PART 5
Social and environmental justice and outdoor studies   **333**

    Introduction   335
    Barbara Humberstone

33 Race, ethnicity and outdoor studies: trends, challenges and
    forward momentum   341
    Nina S. Roberts

34 Equality and inclusion in the outdoors: connecting with nature
    from an Indian perspective   351
    Di Collins and Latha Anantharaman

35 Gender in outdoor studies   360
    Karen Warren

36 Age and the outdoors   369
    Mike Boyes

37 Disability and the outdoors: some considerations for inclusion   378
    John Crosbie

38 Spirituality and the outdoors   388
    Paul Heintzman

39 Outdoor education, environment and sustainability: youth,
    society and environment   398
    Geoff Cooper

40 Land management and outdoor recreation in the UK   409
    Lois Mansfield

PART 6
Transdisciplinary and interdisciplinary approaches to understanding and exploring outdoor studies   419

    Introduction   421
    Barbara Humberstone

41 Experiential learning: towards a multidisciplinary perspective 425
    Colin Beard

42 Enskilment and place-responsiveness in outdoor studies: ways of life 435
    Mike Brown and Brian Wattchow

43 Outdoor education, safety and risk in the light of serious accidents 444
    Andrew Brookes

44 Challenges in adventure sports coaching   455
    Loel Collins and Dave Collins

45 Adventure tourism   463
    Paul Beedie

46 Ecotourism: outdoor pedagogy at the periphery   472
    Patrick T. Maher

47 Bourdieu and alpine mountaineering: the distinction of high
    peaks, clean lines and pure style   482
    John Telford and Simon Beames

48 The archaeology of the outdoor movement and the German
    development: in the beginning was the curiosity about the sublime 491
    Peter Becker

49 Surfing, localism, place-based pedagogies and ecological sensibilities
    in Australia   501
    Rebecca Olive

Index   *511*

Figures

3.1 The main themes in the development of modern environmental concern 31
4.1 Being, doing and knowing are whole in aesthetic experience 44
6.1 Socio-ecological health and wellbeing domains 60
10.1 An ecological model of cultural influences 104
10.2 Illustrating pedagogical possibilities: micro-level interactions in the context of different cultural densities 109
14.1 Tree of outstanding outdoor learning 145
16.1 A continuum of social relationships among human groups 170
16.2 The experiential learning cycle 171
16.3 Epistemological lens 175
17.1 Signposts to a profession 179
17.2 Outdoor continuous professional development framework 183
20.1 Likelihood of costs and benefits of adventure education and adventure recreation 209
21.1 Challenge course programme continuum 221
27.1 A framework to guide the teaching and learning of OE in PE 280
27.2 Findings on areas of professional development needs of teachers: key challenges of curricular reform 284
29.1 *Turistický* club marked paths 301
29.2 The dramaturgy wave 303
38.1 Outdoor activities and spirituality 388
41.1 An evolving multidisciplinary modelling of the human experience 431
46.1 Priest's model of outdoor education 474
46.2 Outdoor education as a blend of subject areas 476

Tables

3.1 The relationship between the selective traditions of environmental
    education, outdoor studies and environmental concern   36

6.1 Six dimensions of psychological wellbeing   62

12.1 A model of theoretical orientations within PETE   127

13.1 UK higher education undergraduate programmes with the words
    Outdoor or Adventure in their title   132

13.2 Examples of typical fieldwork investigations used in one UK HE
    outdoor programme   135

18.1 Certification opportunities for outdoor leaders in the USA   190

34.1 Characteristics of the people who participated in the interviews   354

38.1 Role of introspection/spirituality in satisfaction with park experience
    by activity participated for the most time while at the park   392

43.1 OE ski-slope fatalities, worldwide   445

43.2 OE falls, Australian fatalities   446

43.3 OE avalanche multiple fatalities, worldwide   448

43.4 OE open-water small craft multiple fatalities, worldwide   449

43.5 OE adverse weather multiple fatalities, worldwide   452

Foreword

I have just said farewell to the undergraduate *friluftsliv* (outdoor studies) students at the end of their one-year course at the Norwegian School of Sport Sciences. Six months ago, I said farewell to a group of international exchange students who had spent a semester studying alongside their Norwegian counterparts. For the past four years I have taught these two classes together, and each year I faced the challenge of having too little reading material that could stimulate discussion across the various national and cultural boundaries represented in the classroom and, importantly, across the disciplinary divides within outdoor studies itself. This Handbook goes a long way to easing that challenge and I feel honoured to have been asked to write this Foreword.

The editors of the *Routledge International Handbook of Outdoor Studies* have chosen a timely theme that responds to contemporary needs in university-level outdoor programming and research. The key word in the title, in my view, is 'international'. For some years now, outdoor studies has been internationalising, mainly with exchanges of students in bachelor and master's degree programmes, but also with staff moving from one employment position to another globally. I am an example of the latter, a New Zealander who moved to Norway to further develop my professional knowledge and experience while sharing my expertise with new colleagues. At the same time as university students and staff have been moving around the globe seeking opportunities to explore outdoor practices beyond their home territories, there has also been a steady increase in the diversity of nations represented among outdoor studies scholars, at conferences, in journal publications and in online communities. These scholars are engaged in an increasingly global conversation around outdoor studies. The need for literature that supports internationalised and internationalising scholarship in this field is well nigh and this Handbook contributes significantly to meeting that need.

Barbara Humberstone, Heather Prince and Karla Henderson are a powerful team, whose capability to deliver scholarly work is clearly demonstrated through their joint editorship of this book. I first met Barbara at an outdoor education conference more than 20 years ago, and have admired her energetic and industrious commitment to the field of outdoor studies ever since. She combines scholarship with practice, both teaching practice and recreational activity practice, with apparent ease. At conferences, I usually manage to catch up with her only after she has returned from kayaking or windsurfing with colleagues. Heather is another lively talent in the UK, an international research collaborator and cross-disciplinary scholar. Karla's professional work has been part of the body of literature in outdoor recreation that I have consulted since my own student days. While I have not had the pleasure of meeting Karla in person, she has been one of my 'go to' authors for many years. Between them, through a variety of earlier publications, the editors individually have done much to open up outdoor studies to new perspectives, including those on gender, social and cultural diversity, field-based pedagogy and much more.

I began writing this Foreword from a *hytte* (cabin) deep in the *Oslomarka* (forest), near a lake called *Gjerdingen*, on 17 May, Norway's national day. The coincidence of being in such a place, on that particular day of the year, provided great incentive to reflect on this new publication and its role in positioning outdoor studies as a very contemporary and international phenomenon. After arriving in Norway, I adopted the term 'outdoor practices' to encapsulate the field of study in which I am engaged. In New Zealand, I had taught local and international students, all of whom understood the terms 'outdoor education', 'environmental education' and 'outdoor recreation' in sufficiently similar ways to allow them to share classrooms and field experiences relatively unproblematically. In Norway, the wider mix of cultures and languages among students and staff necessitated linguistic innovations. Outdoor practices seemed to me to encapsulate the different human services – such as education, recreation, environmental care, therapy, tourism, youth development and so on – that rely upon, and are based in, outdoor spaces. Using the term 'outdoor practices' opened up space for discussion about commonalities and differences in approach to the 'outdoors' and the meanings that people in Scandinavia, the various regions within Europe, North America and the Antipodes attach to the outdoors. These were the areas of the world within which most of my students located their homes; drawing on personal experiences and research, we also discussed practices in some Asian and African lands. The term outdoor studies also reflects the same diversity and openness that has been my aim and I applaud the linguistic choice. I heartily congratulate the editors for drawing the diverse sub-fields of outdoor studies towards one other. It is an orientation that will undoubtedly propel the field in interesting new directions.

At the *hytte*, I sat on the top bunk, writing with my laptop on my knees. Beside me was the book I was then reading, about cabins in Norwegian culture. The author of that book pointed out the deep significance of cabins in Norwegian outdoor practices, while at the same time also making clear that the meanings and practices associated with cabins have changed considerably over time and will continue to change. I had travelled to the *hytte* mainly by car, but walked the final kilometre or so because the road was still too deeply buried in snow for ordinary vehicles to pass. Notably, I had not skied, biked or walked there, as per the so-called 'traditional' views of *friluftsliv* and outdoor recreation. My friends and I collected water for our needs from the lake, some 50 metres from the cabin door, and we boiled it on an Ulefos wood-burner. We had electricity and internet, and used both of them during the hours we were not outside, in the forest, around the lake. Our outdoor practices were an amalgam of past and present, old technologies and new, underscoring the complexity of the field today. In any one culture, or nation, such complexity is apparent to those who care to look for it, and that makes a book such as this – focusing as it does on the nuances and complications in the conceptual and theoretical tools available for understanding outdoor practices – highly relevant in a multitude of educational contexts. The first and last sections are particularly innovative in this regard. This is a handbook to be used within nations as well as across nations.

The comprehensiveness of this volume stands it in good stead to become a future classic. Each of the six sections provides a set of readings suitable for supporting a particular scholarly focus, such as formal education or informal learning and leisure. For these reasons, in addition to those already highlighted, this is a book that every serious scholar of outdoor studies will want. I look forward to the scholarship and educational developments it provokes.

Dr Pip Lynch
Professor in Friluftsliv, Norwegian School of Sport Sciences, Oslo, Norway
4 June 2015

★ ★ ★

Merriam Webster's New World Dictionary defines 'international' as 'of, relating to, or involving two or more nations'. It defines a 'handbook' as a 'concise reference book covering a particular subject'. Finally, it defines 'outdoor studies' as . . . well, no it does not. 'Outdoor studies', it seems, is too large a notion for *Merriam Webster's* definitional grasp. So, I am left to my own devices to introduce the reader to the *Routledge International Handbook of Outdoor Studies*.

On the face of it, the book's title reveals a multinational exploration of outdoor studies that can serve as a handy reference for anyone interested in this particular subject matter. So far so good. The 'international handbook' part of things is self-explanatory. The book is replete with chapters written about outdoor studies by a variety of people from a variety of academic disciplines from a variety of countries across the globe. This makes for a rich mixture of interesting readings drawn from an equally interesting mix of individuals from different races, ethnicities and countries of origin. At the same time, what unites the book's 49 chapters is a focus on the outdoors from six different vantage points: (1) constructs and theoretical concepts; (2) formal education in outdoor studies; (3) non-formal education and training in/for/about the outdoors; (4) international voices and cultural interpretations; (5) social and environmental justice in outdoor studies; and (6) transdisciplinary and interdisciplinary approaches to understanding and exploring outdoor studies. Having reflected on the book in its entirety, I can say with confidence that all six vantage points lead to novel and engaging perspectives on outdoor studies. At the same time, the reader's challenge is how best to approach the book. How best to orient oneself to its multicultural and multinational flavour? How best, in sum, to make sense of the *Routledge International Handbook of Outdoor Studies*?

For me, the way I got to grips with the book was through its wide-ranging exploration of humankind's relationship with the outdoors. In this regard, the book challenged my parochial view of things. For example, in the United States of America, where I live, we still tend to view the outdoors as a backdrop for the human drama. We see the outdoors as but a stage on which our individual comedies and tragedies unfold. If the outdoors has value, it is mainly instrumental. The idea of the outdoors having intrinsic value is still largely beyond us. When it comes to the *Bible's* 'Book of Genesis', we are strict constructionists. We take the idea of humankind's dominion over the Earth literally.

But there are other ways of interpreting humankind's relationship with the outdoors, and one of the best things about the *Routledge International Handbook of Outdoor Studies* is that it gives voice to these other perspectives. As I have written elsewhere (see 'The gift', in Clyde Butcher, *Nature's Places of Spiritual Sanctuary*. Ochopee, FL: Window of the Eye, Inc., 1999), one might think of this book as a multinational response to the following set of questions: Do we see the outdoors as separate and distinct from us, as if we are superior to it? Or do we see ourselves as intimately connected with the outdoors, as if we are but a small part of it? Do we value the outdoors merely as a storehouse of raw materials for human exploitation? Or do we value the outdoors as the miraculous ground of our being from which all blessings flow? What do we teach about the outdoors and what does the outdoors teach us? Is our relationship with the outdoors secular or sacred? Do we move the earth, or does the Earth move us? How, in the final analysis, should we conceive of our relationship with the outdoors?

The primary value of this book for me was that it nudged me out of my intellectual comfort zone by introducing me to perspectives on our relationship with the outdoors that I had not considered before. The book forced me to expand my limited worldview by introducing me to refreshing ideas that had not crossed my mind. When those ideas differed from my own, I had to reduce my resulting cognitive dissonance by either enlarging my worldview to accommodate the new perspectives or dismissing the new perspectives as not being persuasive. By the time I reached the end of the book, I felt like I had sampled from a cross-cultural intellectual smorgasbord. The content was filling while simultaneously making me hunger for more.

The *Routledge International Handbook of Outdoor Studies* left me wondering what distinguishes our species from all others. What makes us unique? What is our special gift that we alone can offer the rest of the world? People who think deeply about these questions conclude that it is our human capacity to step outside ourselves, to be self-reflective, to be self-aware, that makes us special. We can think our thoughts and then ponder that very thought process. We can act on our thoughts and then ponder the consequences of those very actions. Unlike other species, we have the ability to be self-monitoring, self-regulating beings.

Self-awareness is both a blessing and a curse. The blessing lies in the opportunity self-awareness affords us to choose how we live. The curse lies in the obligation self-awareness demands of us to answer for the way we live. Opportunity and obligation. Together they constitute our freedom. History will judge us by the use we make of this freedom. Nowhere will that judgement reveal more about our species than in the way we treat the outdoors – our fundamental ground of being.

I am moved by the thought that humankind may be Nature's way of keeping track of itself. That Nature has evolved self-monitoring, self-regulating beings who can step outside themselves, take a good look around and, when necessary, mend the errors of their ways, is a wonderful way to think about our gift as a species. Because we are human, we make mistakes. Because we are human, we have the capacity to learn from our mistakes and act accordingly. Therein lies the hope for this book and the outdoors it celebrates.

Daniel L. Dustin PhD
Department of Parks, Recreation, and Tourism,
University of Utah, Salt Lake City, USA

Please address all correspondence to Daniel Dustin PhD
Department of Parks, Recreation, and Tourism
College of Health
University of Utah
250 South 1850 East Room 200
Salt Lake City, Utah 84112-0920
(801)-585-7560
email: daniel.dustin@health.utah.edu

Contributors

Linda Allin PhD is a University Teaching Fellow in the Department of Sport, Exercise and Rehabilitation at Northumbria University, UK. Her PhD explored Women's Career Identities in Outdoor Education. From 2007–2012 Linda was co-editor of the *Journal of Adventure Education and Outdoor Learning* with Professor Barbara Humberstone and she remains on the Editorial Board. Her main outdoor adventures involve kayaking and playing on white water.

Latha Anantharaman BA is an environmentalist, writer, editor and translator. She began writing about rural life in a column called 'Village Diary' in India and then in a book, *Three Seasons*, which has now been published. She also writes on literature, books, rural issues and travel for a variety of periodicals.

Letty Ashworth MPhil is a Research Teaching Assistant in the Department of Science, Natural Resources and Outdoor Studies at the University of Cumbria, UK. She has worked with marginalised young people in informal outdoor education settings though practice and research. Her research areas are informal outdoor learning, outdoor curricula and youth development. She teaches across postgraduate and undergraduate outdoor courses in areas such as Personal Development and Therapeutic Applications of the Outdoors, Social Issues, and Research Methods. She is a mountaineer and canoeist, and enjoys outdoor journeying.

Matthew Atencio PhD is an Assistant Professor with the California State University – East Bay, USA, in the Department of Kinesiology. He is a former Assistant Professor at the National Institute of Education (Singapore) and he has also worked at the University of Edinburgh in Scotland. He has published extensively in the areas of youth sport, 'informal' physical activity and outdoor education; his work often examines teaching, coaching and mentoring practices within these contexts. Dr Atencio enjoys playing football/soccer and travelling, and has combined both of these interests for the past 20 years.

Aram Attarian PhD has been involved in adventure education and outdoor leadership for more than 40 years. He is an Associate Professor Emeritus in the Department of Parks, Recreation and Tourism Management at North Carolina State University, USA. His teaching and research focused on outdoor leadership, adventure recreation, climbing resource education and management, and visitor safety. He co-edited *Technical skills for Adventure Programming* (2009) and published *Risk Management in Outdoor and Adventure Programs: Scenarios of Accidents, Incidents, & Misadventures* (2012). He enjoys climbing, hiking and spending time outdoors.

Erik Backman PhD is a Senior Lecturer in Educational Sciences at The Swedish School of Sport and Health Sciences, Stockholm, Sweden. His research includes outdoor education (*friluftsliv*), physical education, teacher education and issues of assessment. He has co-edited two Swedish anthologies, *Friluftssport och äventyrsidrott-utmaningar för lärare, ledare och miljö i en föränderlig värld* [Outdoor sport and adventure – challenges for teachers, leaders and environment in a changing world] (2011) and *I takt med tiden? Perspektiv på idrottslärarutbildning i Skandinavien* [In line with the times? Perspectives on physical education teacher education in Scandinavia] (2013), and has published papers in a variety of journals. After hosting the European Institute for Outdoor Adventure Education and Experiential Education (EOE) seminar 2013 in Stockholm, he has co-edited *Urban Nature: Inclusive Learning Through Youth Work and School Work* (2014). Erik enjoys different kinds of skiing and boating.

Simon Beames PhD is a Senior Lecturer at the Moray House School of Education, University of Edinburgh, UK. His research focuses on educational expeditions, using social theory to examine outdoor education practice and learning outside the classroom.

Colin Beard PhD is a Professor of Experiential Learning at Sheffield Business School, Sheffield Hallam University, UK. He is a UK National Teaching Fellow and Fellow of the Royal Society of Arts. He originally trained as a zoologist, though his work now covers both the natural and social sciences. He has published widely, in books and journal articles, on the topic of experiential learning.

Peter Becker PhD is an Emeritus Professor of Sociology and Anthropology of Sport at Philipps University of Marburg, Germany. In 1996 he co-founded the European Institute for Outdoor Adventure Education and Experiential Education (EOE) of which he was the Chair from 1996 to 2004. His academic interests are in the body and movement as instruments of social youth work, youth work and school, early education, history of Erlebnispedagogy, theoretical fundamentals of adventure pedagogy and transcultural aspects of European outdoor education.

Paul Beedie PhD is a keen active adventurer (a member of the Association of Mountaineering Instructors) and has been involved in teaching and researching adventure tourism for many years. His research has been driven by an interest in adventure and includes explorations of risk, identity and community. He is currently working at the University of Bedfordshire, UK, and together with colleagues in the UK and internationally is playing a central role in establishing the Adventure Tourism Research Association.

Troy Bennett is a graduate assistant in Parks, Recreation, and Tourism at the University of Utah, USA, specialising in outdoor recreation programs for youth. He brings 20 years of practical experience leading youth recreation programmes in non-profit organisations and has served as the director of a municipal parks and recreation department. Research interests include investigating the cumulative influence of recreation experiences, helping practitioners to improve programme delivery and outcomes, and promoting conservation, sustainability and healthy lifestyles through a connection to nature. He enjoys camping with his family, skiing fresh Utah powder, whitewater rafting and working in the garden.

M. Deborah Bialeschki PhD is the Director of Research for the American Camp Association and a Professor Emeritus from the University of North Carolina Chapel Hill, USA, after 20 years of faculty service in the Department of Recreation and Leisure Studies. Deb's research interests include youth development, the value of outdoor experiences, gender perspectives and evaluation. She contributes to her community through varied volunteer activities, loves sports and outdoor activities, enjoys time with friends and family (including the four-legged furry ones), and still finds time to play trumpet in the community band.

Mike Boyes PhD is an Associate Professor in Outdoor Education at the School of Physical Education, Sport and Exercise Sciences at the University of Otago, Dunedin, New Zealand. He has published widely in outdoor education journals, made numerous conference presentations, regularly obtains research grants and supervises a large number of postgraduate students. He has held a number of outdoor instructor awards, is the Chairman of the New Zealand Mountain Safety Council research committee and serves on the Executive of Education Outdoors New Zealand.

Mary Breunig PhD is an Associate Professor of Recreation and Leisure Studies at Brock University, Canada and Past-President of the Association for Experiential Education. Her scholarship focuses on social and environmental justice in Outdoor Experiential Education. She is co-author of *Outdoor Leadership: Theory and Practice*. She is a research consultant, former Outward Bound Instructor and a National Outdoor Leadership School Instructor. She is an outdoor enthusiast and urban flaneur.

Andrew Brookes PhD is Associate Professor in Outdoor and Environmental Education, La Trobe University, Australia.

Heather Brown MA is a Project Manager for the Institute for Outdoor Learning (IOL, UK). Her background includes teaching to master's level, outdoor management development and course design of the Telstra (Australian equivalent of BT) MBA. When not working for IOL she facilitates leadership and change management workshops for clients in the corporate and voluntary sector, and coaches a range of professionals. She enjoys sailing and hill walking and, in 2013, took part in a charity walk into the Australian desert.

Mike Brown PhD is a Senior Lecturer in the Faculty of Education, The University of Waikato, New Zealand. He is co-author of *A Pedagogy of Place: Outdoor Education for a Changing World* (2011) and co-editor of *Seascapes: Shaped by the Sea* (2015). He is interested in how place-responsive approaches to teaching and learning shape understandings of the physical and social worlds we inhabit. He teaches undergraduate students and supervises a range of postgraduate research projects. He is a keen sailor, mountain bike rider and occasional skier.

Sandro Carnicelli PhD is a Programme Leader for BA (Hons) Events Management and BA Tourism Management at the University of the West of Scotland, UK, with academic interests in sport tourism, adventure tourism, serious leisure, volunteering and emotional labour. Sandro has published articles in journals including *Annals of Tourism Research* and *Tourism Management*. He is also a member of the International Academy for the Development of Tourism Research in Brazil, on the Advisory Board of the *Annals of Leisure Research*, and Treasurer of the Leisure Studies Association. Sandro is personally interested in hiking and water-based sports.

Cathryn Carpenter PhD has implemented outdoor experiential programmes in secondary and tertiary settings as well as within commercial organisations for more than 30 years. She is currently working at Victoria University, Australia, as a Senior Lecturer in the Bachelor of Youth Work. Her PhD researched outdoor health and wellbeing programmes designed for young people experiencing the consequences of difficult lives and substance abuse issues. Cathryn has been a council member and past president of the Victorian Outdoor Education Association, and a member and past chair of the International Adventure Therapy Committee. She is currently balancing the challenging demands of work or telemark skiing adventures, developing an ecologically sustainable garden, and staying healthy.

Chew Ting Ching is currently heading the Character and Citizenship Education department in Assumption English School in Singapore. She holds a Master's in Counselling from Monash University and continues to have an interest in how the outdoors could promote student reflection and positive changes. Her personal interests include cycling and kayaking. She has even brought her personal foldable kayak overseas for paddling.

Beth Christie PhD is a Lecturer in Outdoor and Environment Education at the Moray House School of Education, University of Edinburgh, UK. She is Programme Director for the MSc Learning for Sustainability, teaches on a range of postgraduate and undergraduate programmes and supervises PhD and MSc students' and replace with 'and her research interests include the philosophy, theory and practice of outdoor learning and learning for sustainability and the broader social ecology surrounding the developing policy landscape in Scotland in relation to those pedagogical approaches and the 3–18 curriculum. She is Associate Editor of the *Journal of Adventure Education and Outdoor Learning*, a reviewer for *Journal of Experiential Education*, and an active member of the European Institute for Outdoor Adventure Education and Experiential Learning.

Emily Coates was awarded her PhD in 2012 from Buckinghamshire New University/Brunel University, UK. Her thesis is entitled 'A fine balance: stories of parents who climb'. While completing her PhD, Emily served as part of the Leisure Studies Association Committee. After her PhD Emily continued down a route in education, she completed a TeachFirst PGCE with Leicester University in 2013 and currently works in a primary school in Leicester. She continues to enjoy climbing.

Dave Collins PhD has more than 200 peer review publications and 40 books/book chapters published. He is professor of coaching and performance at University of Central Lancashire, UK. Current research interests include performer and coach development, cognitive expertise, and the promotion of peak performance across different challenge environments. He has worked with more than 60 world or Olympic medallists, as well as professional teams, dancers, musicians and executives. As a performer, Dave was excessively average at rugby, American football, martial arts and adventure sports. He is a Director of the Rugby Coaches Association, iZone Driver Performance, a Fellow of the Society of Martial Arts, ZSL, BASES, Associate Fellow of the British Psychological Society and an ex-Royal Marine.

Di Collins MSc is a Leading Practitioner of the Institute for Outdoor Learning in the UK. She was awarded a Churchill Fellowship to travel to Australia to explore making connections with nature and the outdoors. She has worked as an outdoor, youth and community education facilitator and consultant, and a lecturer on outdoor education, youth work and community development degree courses. She has also taught in primary and middle schools, and is currently director of Journeying Gently, UK. She is now developing her love of the outdoors through photography and writing.

Loel Collins D.Prof teaches at the University of Central Lancashire, UK, on the Outdoor undergraduate degree programmes and the postgraduate degrees within the Institute of Coaching. His research interests lie in the understanding of professional judgement and decision making, and the education of adventure sports leaders, coaches and teachers. He has taught extensively in outdoor education and has more than 30 years of experience in a range of organisations around the world. He is the author of books, book chapters and peer-reviewed papers on a range of related outdoor subjects. In his own time, he is an active whitewater and sea kayaker, canoeist and telemark skier.

Geoff Cooper MA worked as a teacher, teacher trainer and for the Peak National Park before developing Wigan Council's two residential outdoor education centres in the Lake District, UK. He has organised workshops on outdoor and environmental education for teachers and leaders in the UK and across the rest of Europe. Author of *Outdoors with Young People*, he chairs the Adventure and Environmental Awareness Group, is a mentor for outdoor professional development, a Board member of EOE and a Fellow of the Institute for Outdoor Learning. Geoff enjoys slower journeys on foot, by paddle or sail, which allow time to meet people, share stories and appreciate nature.

John Crosbie PhD has been involved in the development of outdoor activities and outdoor education for people with disabilities for most of his career. He holds high-level awards in a variety of outdoor disciplines, has managed a specialist outdoor centre for people with disabilities (Lake District Calvert Trust, UK) for 17 years and has advised other outdoor centres as well as a number of National Governing Bodies on inclusion issues. His PhD examined the benefits of outdoor education for people with disabilities. John is currently chair of the Institute for Outdoor Learning, UK.

David Exeter MSc is Director of Outdoor Learning at Macmillan Academy and a leading outdoor educator in the UK. He is known for his strategic vision and leadership on learning outside the classroom and his in-depth operational knowledge of school-based outdoor education, learning and adventure. David has a substantial track record of senior management experience and operational delivery of adventure-based learning programmes. He has extensive experience of risk management, organisational development and system leadership within the education sector, with a specific focus on adventure in education.

Stephen M. Fine PhD graduated from the University of Toronto, Canada. He is a curriculum specialist, and founder and co-director of The Hollows Camp in Canada, a year-round outdoor learning centre and summer camp. As both a youth development professional and an independent researcher, Stephen's interests include intra-group dynamics, learning in context, global citizenship, and stewardship of natural lands. Additionally, he coordinates research endeavours for the International Camping Fellowship and the Canadian Camping Association. He lives year round on-site at The Hollows, and enjoys canoeing and kayaking, as well as Nordic and alpine skiing.

Karen Fox PhD is a Professor at the Faculty of Physical Education and Recreation at the University of Alberta, Canada. She began her scholarly career in outdoor recreation and education with a focus on environmental ethics. Questions of Indigenous worldviews, environmental ethics and ecological health shape her research about theories of leisure, Indigenous perspectives of 'leisure', and the importance of embodiment and sensoria in leisure. She is an avid bicycle tourer, whitewater kayaker and photographer.

Roger Greenaway PhD trained and worked as a teacher of English and outdoor education in the UK. His doctorate was a study of management learning outdoors. Roger first encountered reviewing at Brathay – a development training centre where he worked with young people, managers and trainers. In the 1990s, Roger's handbooks about reviewing activities (see http://reviewing.co.uk) kick-started his current occupation as a worldwide provider of trainer-training workshops in active and creative reviewing. Roger serves on the board of the *Journal of Adventure Education and Outdoor Learning*. He claims that reviewing plays a key role in his sporting achievements in windsurfing and ultra running.

Kirsti Pedersen Gurholt DrScient is a Professor of *friluftsliv* and pedagogy at the Norwegian School of Sport Sciences, Norway. Her research interests include historical, cultural and pedagogical analysis of *friluftsliv* and physical education. She co-edited *Nature and Identity. The Culture of Nature* (2003) and *Aktive Liv* (2010), and has published in Norwegian and English-speaking journals. She is in authority of the Norwegian involvement in the *Erasmus+* Joint Master's degree programme Transcultural European Outdoor Studies (2011–2017) and was chair of the European Institute for Outdoor Adventure Education and Experiential Learning (2008–2012). She is a skier, mountaineer and dancer.

Trond Løge Hagen is an Assistant Professor in the Department of Physical Education at Queen Maud University College of Early Childhood Education (QMUC) in Trondheim, Norway. His primary research focus is on outdoor play, children's physical play on playgrounds and the use of nature as learning environments, resulting in several publications in a variety of journals and books.

Nevin Harper PhD has been combining his passions for wilderness travel, experiential learning and group development as a guide, trainer, researcher, author and adventurer since 1991. His doctoral research focused on adolescent wilderness therapy; he holds a master's degree in Leadership and remains a qualified trainer and leader in the outdoor adventure industry in Canada. He co-chairs the Adventure Therapy International Committee, instructs for the Outdoor Council of Canada and 'Paddle Canada', Chairs Sport Management at Camosun College and the National Research Coordinator for Outward Bound Canada.

Ian Harris MA is the Director of the School of Sport, Tourism and Languages at Southampton Solent University, UK, having previously been a PE, outdoor education and mathematics teacher in secondary schools. He teaches at the university, and mentors and assesses practitioners progressing through the Institute for Outdoor Learning (IOL) accreditation scheme, and Chairs the IOL Higher Education special interest group. He is a member of the SkillsActive outdoor employers group, and undertakes centre inspections for the British Activity Providers Association, Adventure Mark and Learning Outside the Classroom provider accreditation schemes.

Paul Heintzman PhD is a Professor of leisure studies at the University of Ottawa, Canada. He worked in the recreation, environmental and social service fields before completing his PhD in Recreation and Leisure Studies at the University of Waterloo, with a thesis on leisure and spiritual wellbeing. His teaching and research areas include leisure and spirituality, parks, outdoor recreation and education, and the philosophy and ethics of leisure. He is author of *Leisure and Spirituality: Biblical, Historical and Contemporary Perspectives*. In 2003 he received the Society of Park and Recreation Educators (SPRE) Teaching Innovation Award. He enjoys various outdoor activities.

Karla A. Henderson PhD is Professor Emeritus in the Department of Parks, Recreation and Tourism at North Carolina State University, USA. Her research interests include women and social justice, physical activity, and research methods as they pertain to the outdoors and other leisure experiences. She has published in a number of journals and served as a founder for the Coalition for Education in the Outdoors and of the American Camp Association's Committee for the Advancement of Research and Evaluation. She enjoys hiking in the mountains, travelling and playing her trumpet.

Peter Higgins PhD is Professor of Outdoor and Environmental Education at the Moray House School of Education, University of Edinburgh, UK, teaching academic and practical elements of outdoor, environmental and sustainability education. He is Dean of Students in the College of Humanities and Social Sciences, and Director of the United Nations University Regional Centre of Expertise in ESD (Scotland). He is a board member of several UK trusts, national and international panels and advisory groups, chaired the Scottish Government's Learning for Sustainability Advisory Group and co-chairs the Government Implementation Group. He is Scottish representative on the UNESCO programme 'Reorienting Teacher Education to Address Sustainable Development'.

Susanna Ho PhD is one of the pioneers who started the outdoor education department in the Ministry of Education in Singapore. As a Senior Specialist, she provides leadership in the outdoor education curriculum in Singapore schools. Her research interests and efforts are focused in the areas of curriculum and assessment in physical and outdoor education. She is part of an Economic and Social Research Council (ESRC) study team, comprising researchers from the UK, Denmark and Australia, which examines the impact of outdoor learning on the wellbeing of children. She is an editorial board member of the *Journal of Experiential Education*. In her leisure time, she enjoys exploring the island-wide park connectors on her foldable bicycle and volunteers in wildlife conservation projects.

Alan Hockley PhD was awarded his doctorate in 2011 from Buckinghamshire New University/ Brunel University, UK, after a career in events management and then a BA (Hons) in Outdoor Education and Adventure Recreation. His thesis is an investigation into how landscape is interpreted through the approach of walking, considering how relationships with it and place are established and developed through this practice. It takes account of the storied character that inhabits both. Alan continues to teach at Buckinghamshire New University as a Senior Lecturer with the Learning Development Unit and as an Associate Lecturer in Sport, Leisure and Event Management.

Barbara Humberstone PhD is a Professor of Sociology of Sport and Outdoor Education at Buckinghamshire New University, UK. Her research interests include embodiment and nature-based sport, social and environmental injustice and wellbeing and outdoor pedagogies. She co-edited and edited a number of publications including; *Seascapes: Shaped by the Sea. Embodied Narratives and Fluid Geographies* (2015) and has published papers in a variety of journals. She is Editor-in-Chief of the *Journal of Adventure Education and Outdoor Learning* and was Chair of the European Institute for Outdoor Adventure Education and Experiential Learning (2004–2008). She is a keen windsurfer, walker, swimmer and yogini.

Clifford E. Knapp PhD is a passionate teacher, writer, reader, wood carver, naturalist and family man. He retired from Northern Illinois University, USA, in 2001 and remains active as a consultant in place-based education. He taught undergraduate and graduate courses in environmental ethics, outdoor education, Indigenous cultures, arts and crafts, and other outdoor curriculum-related topics. He has published books, articles and book chapters on reflection, solos, environmental ethics, humanising environmental education, experiential education and other subjects. In his twilight years he teaches about waging peace instead of war, loving instead of hating, and cultivating a sense of wonder in nature instead of indifference.

Sara Knight has just retired as a Principal Lecturer in Education at Anglia Ruskin University, UK. She has contributed to the development of Forest School in the UK, publishing academic papers and textbooks on this subject, and has been a keynote speaker at conferences in the UK, Europe, Asia and Canada. Originally a kindergarten teacher, she still loves working with very young children in outdoor spaces. She enjoys hiking, travelling and gardening, and works voluntarily at her local theatre, where she also performs and directs.

Gregory Lowan-Trudeau PhD is a Métis scholar and educator. He is currently an Assistant Professor in the Werklund School of Education at the University of Calgary and an Adjunct Professor in the Department of First Nations Studies at the University of Northern British Columbia, Canada. Childhood journeys on the lakes, rivers, trails, mountains and coastal waters of western Canada, exposure to cultural teachings, and family stories inspired him to pursue a career as a land-based educator. Over the past 15 years, Greg has combined academic study with professional practice and travel across Canada and around the world. His current research interests include Indigenous science and environmental education, land use planning and ecological activism.

Jonathan Lynch is a Senior Lecturer in Outdoor Studies at the University of Cumbria, UK. 'His contribution in this text is informed by his current PhD research: teachers' considerations of place in curriculum planning of outdoor learning. He is especially interested in place-responsive pedagogy that includes the more-than-human and socio-ecological orientations to outdoor learning and education.

Patrick T. Maher PhD is an Associate Professor in the Department of Community Studies at Cape Breton University, Canada. He is an Associate of the Transcultural European Outdoor Studies consortium and was a Visiting Scholar based at the Norwegian School of Sport Sciences in 2012. Dr Maher has played a critical role in founding the International Polar Tourism Research Network, and is the project lead for the University of the Arctic's Thematic Network on Northern Tourism. He is a Fellow of the Royal Canadian Geographical Society, editor of the *Journal of Experiential Education* and convener of the 7th International Outdoor Education Research Conference in 2016.

Greg Mannion PhD works as a Senior Lecturer in the School of Education, University of Stirling, UK. His research brings together understandings of the links between nature and culture to consider the way places – particularly places other than classrooms – can be sites of learning and participation. Currently, his research considers the way schools might harness natural places and community into outdoor and environmental education, education for sustainability, place-based education and intergenerational citizenship.

Lois Mansfield PhD is a geographer and a Principal Lecturer in Upland Management at the University of Cumbria, UK. Her research interests focus on the sustainable use of upland resources with respect to integrated land management. Her most recent project involves the production of a book designed as a toolkit to help communities and land managers find integrated solutions to conflicts of interest in upland areas. As a lecturer, she is particularly keen on the application of theory through fieldwork for students.

Andrew Martin PhD is an Associate Professor in the School of Sport & Exercise, Massey University, Palmerston North, New Zealand. His fascination with the Czech way of outdoor education led to the book *Outdoor and Experiential Learning*, which focuses on the outcomes and educational process of courses involving the Czech dramaturgy method and *turistika* activities. He is actively involved in coaching, organising and participating in a wide variety of sports, including triathlons.

Lucy Maynard PhD is Head of Research at Brathay Trust, a youth development charity in Cumbria, UK. Professionally, Lucy uses a participatory action research approach to bring together theory and practice. This approach supports participants, practitioners and organisations to develop deeper understandings of experiences, facilitate change and support good practice. Lucy's work focuses on empowerment and critical pedagogy, stemming from her 2011 doctorate studies into experiences of outdoor youth development. Personally, Lucy enjoys walking and running with her dogs, road cycling that takes in mountain passes, and recently developed a passion for cycle touring.

Ken McCulloch PhD is a Senior Lecturer in the Institute for Education, Community and Society at the University of Edinburgh, UK. His academic interests are in work with young people in non-school settings, including youth work and outdoor education, particularly sail training. His publications include articles on sail training, which was the topic of his PhD thesis in 2002. This work arose from involvement in sail training as a practitioner. As recreation, he is a part-owner of a cruising yacht based on the west coast of Scotland.

Philip M. Mullins PhD is an Associate Professor of Outdoor Recreation and Tourism Management at the University of Northern British Columbia, Canada. His research interests include wilderness and the Western nature–culture dichotomy, phenomenology and skill development, and outdoor education for sustainability. In addition to other articles, he has published 'Living stories of the landscape: perception of place through canoeing in Canada's north' (2009) in the journal *Tourism Geographies*, as well as 'The commonplace journey methodology: exploring outdoor recreation activities through theoretically informed reflective practice' (2014) in the journal *Qualitative Research*. He is an editor of the *Journal of Experiential Education*. Phil enjoys canoe travel and Canadian winters.

Helen N. Muthomi PhD is a Lecturer in the Department of Recreation Management and Exercise Science in Kenyatta University, Kenya. Her research interests include aquatic sports and activities, leisure, counselling and change management, exercise adherence, sports and fashion, team building and conflict management, and outdoor adventure pursuits and leadership. She is the coordinator of Kenyatta University Adventure and Leadership Park (KUALEP), and a founder board member of the Association of Adventure, Outdoor and Experiential Learning – East Africa. Her hobbies include mountain climbing, bungee jumping, jogging and cooking.

Jan Neuman PhD is an Associate Professor and former head of the Department of Turistika, Outdoor Sports and Outdoor Education, Faculty of Physical Education and Sport, Charles University, Prague, Czech Republic. He is one of the leading Czech experts in the field of outdoor experiential education. He is actively involved in a range of outdoor activities and programmes with tertiary students across the Czech Republic.

Robbie Nicol PhD is a Senior Lecturer in Outdoor and Environmental Education and Head of the Institute for Education, Teaching and Leadership at the Moray House School of Education, University of Edinburgh, UK. He has authored more than 50 articles, is a co-opted board member of the European Institute for Outdoor Adventure Education and Experiential Learning, a member of Cairngorms National Park Outdoor Access Forum, a member of the Advisory Panel for the Wilderness Foundation and a regular reviewer for various academic peer-reviewed journals.

Johan Öhman PhD is Professor of Education at Örebro University's School of Humanities, Education and Social Sciences in Sweden. Among other things, he is one of the scientific leaders of the research group SMED, director of the graduate school UVD, member of the international advisory board of Environmental Education Research, and convener of the network Environmental and Sustainability Education Research at the ECER conference. His area of research is ethical and democratic issues within the sphere of sustainability, environmental and outdoor education, and he is the author and co-author of several research papers, book chapters and textbooks, both in Swedish and in English, on these themes. In his spare time he is a devoted skier in the Swedish mountains.

Taito Okamura PhD is the CEO of Backcountry Classroom, Inc., a provider of outdoor education programmes for companies, sports teams, schools and communities. He researches the cause and effect of outdoor experiences, and developed the software, Experiential Education Evaluation Form, to identify causal relationships. He was on the faculty at Nara University of Education and the University of Tsukuba, Japan, for ten years, and has served as a trustee in the Japan Outdoor Education Society. He founded the Wilderness Education Association Japan in 2013. Further, he has directed Camp Hanayama, sponsored by Yoshonen Camp Society since 1969.

Rebecca Olive PhD is a Postdoctoral Research Fellow at The University of Waikato, New Zealand. She has published about sport and physical cultures, gender power relations, feminist theory, social media and ethnographic methods in journals including *International Journal of Cultural Studies, Sport, Education & Society* and *Sociology of Sport Journal*. In particular she is interested in how cultural change is produced through individual relationships, ethics and pedagogies.

Shikuku W. Ooko is a Wilderness Emergency Medical Technician and registered with the USA National Registry of EMT. He is the founder of Janam Peace Building Foundation in Kenya, and conducted a three-year Pathways to Peace project using outdoor adventure between 2010 and

2012, following the 2007–2008 post-election violence in Kenya. He previously worked with the National Outdoor Leadership School both as an instructor and an administrator. He is a founder board member of the Association of Adventure, Outdoor and Experiential Learning – East Africa, and a member of the World Leisure Organization Educational Services Committee. His hobbies include mountain hiking, snorkelling and playing his saxophone.

Marcelo Fadori Soares Palhares MSc completed his MSc in 2014 at the São Paulo State University (UNESP), Brazil. He is a leisure researcher studying the relationships between leisure, sport and sociology. Marcelo is a member of the Laboratory of Leisure Studies of the São Paulo State University and a member of the organising committee of the 1st International Congress in Adventure Activities (Rio Claro, Brazil). His personal interests include surfing and whitewater rafting.

Su Porter MA is Programme Leader for the BA (Hons) Outdoor Adventure Education programme at the University of St Mark and St John, UK. She is a qualified teacher who has extensive experience as an outdoor practitioner, including stints with Outward Bound in the UK and abroad, freelance instruction and development training. She mentors and assesses practitioners progressing through the Institute of Outdoor Learning (IOL) accreditation scheme. Su continues her practical professional involvement as an active MIA, MTUK Course Director and leading practitioner of IOL. Su is a mountaineer who enjoys taking part in any outdoor adventure that she can share with friends.

Heather Prince PhD is Associate Professor of Outdoor and Environmental Education in the Department of Science, Natural Resources and Outdoor Studies at the University of Cumbria, UK. She designs, develops and teaches on many undergraduate and postgraduate courses in outdoor studies, and is interested in pedagogic practice in outdoor education, and ecology. She is a member of the Editorial Board of the *Journal of Adventure Education and Outdoor Learning*, a Principal Fellow of the Higher Education Academy, UK, and loves adventuring in wild places on foot and by boat.

John Quay PhD is a Senior Lecturer in the Graduate School of Education at the University of Melbourne, Australia. He taught outdoor education in schools in Victoria, Australia, for ten years, before making the shift to a university career. His main research interest involves bringing philosophical perspectives to educational issues, including those of outdoor studies but also considering education more broadly. He is author of *Education, Experience and Existence: Engaging Dewey, Peirce and Heidegger* (2013) and co-author, with Jayson Seaman, of *John Dewey and Education Outdoors: Making Sense of the 'Educational Situation' Through More Than a Century of Progressive Reforms* (2013), while publishing papers in a range of journals associated with outdoor studies. He enjoys cycling to keep fit and skiing to have fun.

Kaye Richards PhD is Senior Lecturer in Outdoor Education at Liverpool John Moores University, UK, and a Chartered Psychologist of the British Psychological Society. She has worked in the outdoors for more than 20 years, with a specialist area in adventure therapy, and counselling and psychotherapy. This has included working at the British Association for Counselling and Psychotherapy, being a longstanding member of the Adventure Therapy International Committee, and Chair of the Institute for Outdoor Learning (UK) specialist interest group in Outdoor and Adventure Therapy. She is a member of the editorial board of the Journal of Adventure Education and Outdoor Learning and has published across all these areas. Her personal interests include expedition leadership, running and mountain art.

Dan Richmond is a PhD student and the National Outdoor Leadership School Research Fellow at the University of Utah, USA, in the Department of Parks, Recreation, and Tourism. His research interests include instructor effectiveness, group dynamics, leadership education and non-cognitive skill development. Prior to returning to school, Dan worked in public media where he managed projects related to programme evaluation, programme development, fundraising and volunteer training. Dan is a field instructor for the National Outdoor Leadership School (NOLS), and enjoys good books, great beers, long runs in the mountains and road trips.

Nina S. Roberts PhD is a Professor of Recreation, Parks & Tourism at San Francisco State University and Director of the Pacific Leadership Institute. A Fulbright scholar, her research interests include community engagement, constraints to park visitation, youth development, and race, class and gender issues in outdoor recreation. Her work provides managers in outdoor recreation, natural resource management and environmental education with ideas/resources needed to respond more effectively to changing demographics, as well as cultural shifts and trends. She has been professionally active with a variety of boards, including the Association for Experiential Education, National Parks Promotion Council, Center for Park Management, Yosemite Institute and Healthy Parks Healthy People, Bay Area network. With a mixed-race background she is constantly inspired to both speak and write about the value of cross-cultural connections and parks. She loves hiking, biking, camping, boating, flying kites on the beach and playing Taiko (Japanese drumming) during her leisure time.

Elyse Rylander is at Prescott College, USA, where she is earning a master's degree by studying the relationship between the lesbian, gay, bisexual, transgendered and queer (LGBTQ) community and outdoor experiential education. Elyse is also the Executive Director of OUT There Adventures, a Seattle-based outdoor leadership organisation that works specifically with LGBTQ identified youth and their peer allies. She has spent years sharing her passion for the outdoors with others as a paddling guide, instructor and challenge course facilitator. She enjoys hiking with her dog and cheering on her favourite sports team, the University of Wisconsin Badgers.

Klas Sandell PhD is Professor of Human Geography at Karlstad University, Sweden. His research interests include outdoor recreation, nature-based tourism, public access, landscape perspectives, views of nature and outdoor pedagogies. He is a member of the board for the National Centre for Outdoor Education and the advisory group for the Swedish Centre for Nature Interpretation. Besides scientific articles and book chapters, he has co-edited several books in Swedish, e.g. *The History of Outdoor Recreation – from 'The Hardy Outdoor Life' to 'Ecotourism and Environmental Education'*, *The Pedagogy of Outdoor Life* and *Outdoor Sport and Adventure Sport*. He is building his own kayaks to paddle in the archipelago where he lives.

Ellen Beate Hansen Sandseter PhD is an Associate Professor in the Department of Physical Education at Queen Maud University College of Early Childhood Education (DMMH) in Trondheim, Norway. Her primary research focus is on children's physical play, outdoor play and risky/thrilling play among children in Early Childhood Education and Care (ECEC) institutions. She has cooperated with early childhood researchers from both England and Australia to study cultural differences in provision of outdoor – and risky – play in ECEC settings. Recently she has been involved in a study of Norwegian children's experiences of participation and wellbeing in Norwegian ECEC institutions, as well as project mapping all child accidents and injuries in Norwegian ECEC institutions.

Jayson Seaman PhD is Associate Professor of Kinesiology and Affiliate Associate Professor of Education at the University of New Hampshire, USA. After starting his career as a high school English teacher, Jayson worked to implement various types of 'experiential' school reforms at the local, state and national levels. His research focuses on cultural socialisation and identity processes in learning, which he pursues by critically examining the historical foundations of 'experiential' reforms and through empirical studies of concept formation and social identity using qualitative sociolinguistic methods. He has published in journals such as *Education and Culture, Educational Studies* and the *International Journal of Qualitative Methods*, and is the author with John Quay of *John Dewey and Education Outdoors: Making Sense of the 'Educational Situation' Through More Than a Century of Progressive Reforms* (2013). Jayson is professionally active in whitewater paddlesports instruction, and is an avid triathlete and telemark skier.

Jim Sibthorp PhD is a Professor at the University of Utah, USA, in the Department of Parks, Recreation, and Tourism. He teaches courses on youth programming, outdoor education, and research design and analysis. Jim's current research focuses on youth development through outdoor and adventure programming. Through his work with both the American Camp Association and the National Outdoor Leadership School, Jim continues to design, implement and translate studies that bridge research and practice. His personal outdoor pursuits include river trips, skiing, hiking and anything on, or in, the ocean.

Ina Stan PhD was awarded her doctorate in 2008 from Buckinghamshire New University/Brunel University, UK. The research was carried out between 2004 and 2008. She then went on to work as a postdoctoral research assistant Buckinghamshire New University, on the wellbeing and outdoor pedagogy project, doing ethnographic research on the wellbeing of primary children in the outdoors. She has been working as a part-time lecturer teaching research methods, sport sociology, English for academic purposes, and personal and professional development at Buckinghamshire New University.

Tim Stott PhD is Professor of Physical Geography and Outdoor Education at Liverpool John Moores University, UK, where he has taught and carried out research for 20 years, prior to which he was a secondary geography teacher and field centre geography tutor. Tim's research interests are mainly in fluvial geomorphology. He has carried out fieldwork in Iceland, Svalbard, Greenland, the French and Swiss Alps, British Columbia and Ladakh. His research interests also include e-learning in HE, with a particular interest in online learning and assessment, virtual field guides, fieldwork and expeditions, and is co-founder of Expedition Research. He is a member of the Editorial Board for the *Journal of Adventure Education and Outdoor Learning* and a reviewer for several international academic journals. He has been an external examiner at nine HE providers of outdoor/adventure programmes in the UK over the past two decades.

Karen Stuart PhD is Director of her own consultancy company, Kaz Stuart Ltd, in the UK. From a participative action research approach, Kaz works to understand people's lived experiences to give voice to those most silenced, as well as to evidence impact and develop practice. Kaz's research interests focus on agency and critical pedagogy. She has worked in the outdoors with adults and young people as an instructor, guide and expedition leader. Kaz was New Zealand Paragliding Champion in 1995 and the Women's World Champion Paraglider in the First World Air Games in 1997. She now hikes, climbs, cycles, mountain bikes and is an open water swimmer.

Yuen Sze Michelle Tan PhD is a Postdoctoral Research and Teaching Fellow in the Department of Curriculum and Pedagogy at the University of British Columbia, Canada. She was formerly a research fellow at the National Institute of Education in Singapore. Her research interests include curriculum innovation and reform, collaborative teacher inquiry and teacher professional development. She is passionate about integrating the outdoors with teaching instruction. She has published in the areas of teacher education, outdoor education and science education. Her personal interests include hiking, botanical drawings, and playing the piano and electric organ.

John Telford PhD is a Lecturer at the Moray House School of Education, University of Edinburgh, UK. He is a keen climber and mountaineer. His research interests include using social theory to critically analyse outdoor education, the development of outdoor learning within mainstream education, and the contribution of outdoor education to environmental/sustainability education.

Ivana Turčová PhD is a Lecturer in the Department of Turistika, Outdoor Sports and Outdoor Education, Faculty of Physical Education and Sport, Charles University, Prague, Czech Republic. Her doctoral thesis examined the diversity in outdoor language in relation to Czech and British English. She is actively involved in a range of outdoor activities.

Mark Wagstaff EdD is Professor of Recreation, Parks, and Tourism at Radford University in the USA. He currently teaches challenge course programming classes and conducts research within the industry. In addition to research papers and book chapters, he has co-authored and co-edited adventure-based texts including *Introduction to Outdoor Leadership*, *The Backcountry Classroom*, *Technical Skills for Adventure Programming* and *Controversial Issues in Adventure Programming*. Mark is a former Outward Bound instructor, Wilderness Education Association instructor and professional raft guide. He is passionate about international travel and experiencing other cultures.

Sue Waite loves walking that allows her to look closely at the natural world. She is Associate Professor (Reader) at the Institute of Education, Plymouth University, UK, where she co-leads the outdoor and experiential learning research network (oelres.net). She researches and writes about outdoor learning in relation to social justice, affective and wellbeing issues. She has conducted studies that consider the role of natural environments such as woodlands and national parks in enhancing young people's lives and the provision of outdoor learning in mainstream schooling, leading an Economic and Social Research Council (ESRC) study to explore how outdoors might smooth transition from early years to primary education. Current projects include an ESRC international partnership network with colleagues in Australia, Denmark and Singapore, and the Natural Connections Demonstration Project to embed and evaluate curriculum learning outside the classroom in natural environments across primary, secondary and special schools.

Karen Warren PhD teaches courses in experiential education, outdoor leadership, wilderness studies and social justice at Hampshire College in the USA. She also serves as a Graduate Program Advisor at Prescott College in Prescott, AZ. Her books include *Women's Voices in Experiential Education*, *The Theory of Experiential Education* and *Theory and Practice of Experiential Education*. Based on her research on race, gender and class-sensitive outdoor leadership, Karen has written and spoken extensively on gender and social justice issues in experiential education. She is also interested in student-directed learning communities, outdoor accessibility, transgressive teaching, and paddling and exploring in remote areas of the world.

Brian Wattchow is a Senior Lecturer in Outdoor Education in the Faculty of Education, Monash University, Australia, and has more than 30 years' experience teaching, guiding and researching in outdoor education. In 2010, he completed a 2500 km canoe descent of River Murray and published his first collection of poetry, titled *The Song of the Wounded River* (Ginninderra Press, 2010). He co-authored *A Pedagogy of Place: Outdoor Education for a Changing World* (Monash University Publishing, 2011) and recently edited a new book titled *The Socio-ecological Educator: A 21st Century Renewal of Sport, Physical, Health, Environment and Outdoor Education* (Springer, 2014).

Amanda West PhD is Head of the Department of Sport and Exercise Sciences at the University of Sunderland, UK. Her PhD examined how risk mediated rock climbers' identities and reasons for climbing, and she has published research about risk and gender in sports and outdoor environments, as well as approaches to the assessment of university students. Her main outdoor adventures involve Munro bagging and some gentle rock climbing.

Acknowledgements

We would like to thank all contributors for making this book possible and also our family and friends for their support. Heather would like to thank her family, Ivan, Angus and Hal Walsh, for their support and encouragement.

Barbara, Heather and Karla would like to acknowledge their reciprocal thanks to each other in the editing of this Handbook and for the professional dialogue and growth that has developed over the course of this project.

We are indebted to Taylor and Francis for inviting us to take on this project and to their team with whom we have enjoyed working.

Introduction

Barbara Humberstone, Heather Prince and
Karla A. Henderson

This international compilation brings together current leading scholars in outdoor studies from a variety of disciplines to bring to readers principal ideas and leading-edge developments. We also draw together the strands of outdoor studies into one volume, making the important connections among key threads including education, leisure, physical culture, sport, the outdoor environment and practice.

During the last decades research into outdoor studies has grown significantly, yet haphazardly and erratically. This text examines and reflects upon these developments and draws upon scholars from a variety of disciplinary backgrounds to consider the accomplishments and opportunities for future research and perspectives. Mapping this discipline, such that the relevant connections are emphasised and emergent research is highlighted, is timely.

This *Routledge International Handbook of Outdoor Studies* draws together what may have been viewed as disconnected dimensions in the past. This volume is not only a review of outdoor studies, but aims to provide a coherent framework through providing greater engagement among the contributing dimensions and by making cutting-edge, interdisciplinary research available. It provides a resource for researchers, policy makers, lecturers, and graduate and undergraduate students undertaking research and applying research to practice. This Handbook brings together and summarises the current core body of knowledge in outdoor studies, and offers guidance for the future.

Outdoor studies has its roots in the late 1990s, when the education assignment of the term outdoor education was felt, by some academics and practitioners, to be too limiting because it did not cover the full range of study and practice in the outdoors, which was then perceived not to be of an educational nature. In some countries this concern also coincided with an increasing marginalisation of the outdoors in school curricula as well as a widening expanse of opportunities and understanding of its potential range and breadth worldwide. Many professionals held an underlying and emerging desire to capture an understanding of outdoor environments through environmental education and human–nature interactions drawing upon interpretative and reflexive approaches.

One definition of outdoor studies used in the UK is:

> a discipline which includes the study of perceptions and responses to the natural environment, personal and environmental philosophy, environmental knowledge and outdoor skills. Using direct experience, it seeks to raise environmental awareness and encourage personal development within a framework of individual and group values and safety. (UCSM, 1998, p. 1)

Outdoor studies, we suggest, is the term that fruitfully encompasses a broad range of approaches, foci and methods such as, but not limited to, experiential learning, adventure education, organised camps, environmental education, outdoor leadership, nature-based sport and wilderness therapy. Terminology in any sphere, and not least in this book, is governed by culture, policy drivers and history, with political, temporal, institutional, chronological and marketing determinants. We maintain agreement that:

> The 'outdoors' may be perceived, in one sense, as an ideological space where people alone or together engage actively or passively with their 'environment' . . . In another sense, the 'outdoors' is perceived as a vehicle for learning as well as leisure . . . As such, it is formally constituted by a number of groupings looking towards recognition and the development of outdoor profession(s) . . . Thus the outdoor sector provides, makes available or engages with, outdoor adventure experiences for a variety of purposes, including education, youth and social work, management development, therapy, leisure and recreation. Consequently, diverse outdoor traditions have emerged not only in relation to specific geographical landscapes, but also as a consequence of particular cultural, social and political contexts. (Humberstone, Brown & Richards, 2003, p. 7)

A significant development in the last 20 years has been in the socio-cultural and socio-environmental study of outdoor recreation, leisure and sporting activities. These areas provide the medium through which formal, non-formal and informal education and learning have been made available and accessible mainly, but not only, to young people. Emerging from particular schools of sociological thought, these types of activity have been identified for the purposes of social and/or cultural analysis as sports including lifestyle, alternative, extreme, and adventure (e.g. Lyng, 1990; Rinehart & Sydnor, 2003; Wheaton, 2004; McNamee, 2007; Thorpe & Rinehart, 2010) or for socio-environmental analyses, nature-based sport/sport in nature (Vanreusel, 1995; Humberstone, 1998), and more recently, action sport (see Thorpe, 2014).

Initially, research analyses and writings around adventurous and extreme sports from sociology of sport perspectives, for example, tended to be concerned with theorising the notion of voluntary risk taking or being 'on the edge' in Western society. From an educational perspective, Turčová, Martin and Neuman (2005) highlighted the variations and ambiguities in the ways outdoor and adventurous activities have been identified. Furthermore, some educators tend to refer to these educational media as outdoor or adventurous activities (see Allin & Humberstone, 2010) or, in Scandinavian contexts, *friluftsliv* (Gurholt, 2008).

Although these diverse interpretations and terminologies provide rich bounty for analysis, they also point to tensions among different schools of thought, and significant potential for discourse, and in particular the notion of outdoor physical cultures as sports. For example, more than four decades ago, outdoor educator and mountaineer Drasdo (1972) asked:

Is mountaineering anything to do with sport? Despite some affinities, the answer is no. It is impossible to find a definition of sport which will include all the values of mountaineering without also including all manner of activities which are manifestly not of a sporting nature. (p. 33)

These variations in terminology and thinking across disciplines and countries are worth discussing today. The chapters in this Handbook represent thinking from across disciplines and from authors in more than a dozen countries throughout the world. The authors of these chapters describe what outdoor studies means in their contexts, and highlight the underlying, and oft times unspoken, differences and hegemonies among the viewpoints and perspectives.

The intention of this Handbook is to draw upon this internationally and interdisciplinarily varied picture of the field that incorporates outdoor areas such as education, learning, recreation, activities, sport and adventure, including combination sub-sets of physical education, environmental education and categorisations within those areas. We present this picture from a Western-oriented pivot, using the English language as its tool. Texts in other languages besides English are likely to highlight a richer interpretation of this field. A pluralistic approach including transdisciplinarity as it runs through outdoor studies, however, is presented with critical framing, with the emphasis on professional practice through historical, social, cultural, ethical, methodological and political lenses. The Handbook is necessarily selective in cultural representations, choice of emphasis and topic areas. However, paradoxically, it fulfils a niche area, and has international and transdiscipline appeal.

This *Routledge International Handbook of Outdoor Studies* is organised into six parts. The first, 'Constructs and theoretical concepts', defines and explores the structural and philosophical underpinning of the discipline in key areas and through multiple perspectives with a flavour and sense of internationalism and culture. The next part, 'Formal education in outdoor studies', focuses on the training of teachers and formal curricula within as well as outside physical education, in addition to more specialised aspects such as outdoor play, outdoor learning, environmental education, outdoor education, and outdoor and adventurous activities. The third part, 'Non-formal education and training in/for/about the outdoors', addresses structured out-of-school outdoor settings with designated leadership, such as after-school programmes, community-based organisations and summer learning environments. Non-formal opportunities provide a means to combine education and leisure/outdoor recreation in highly complementary ways. The fourth part concentrates on 'International voices and cultural interpretations', and centres on hearing cultural and historical backgrounds and perspectives aside from the dominant British-American discourses. These cultural assessments allow traditional as well as emerging ideas to come forward based on varying cultural interpretations of outdoor studies. The fifth part explores 'Social and environmental justice and outdoor studies'. Outdoor studies cannot be complete without consideration of social and environmental thought, and the diverse frameworks that illustrate contradictions, complexities and webs of connection. The final part of this Handbook, 'Transdisciplinary and interdisciplinary approaches to understanding and exploring outdoor studies', aims to describe how researchers and practitioners from different disciplines work jointly to create new conceptual, theoretical, methodological and translational processes that move beyond discipline-specific approaches to promote outdoor studies.

This Handbook signposts future participatory research, through the continued involvement of providers, participants and other stakeholders. The chapters converge on understanding and potentially transforming human interaction within and with the environment or non-human world. At the educational level, co-construction in outdoor learning increasingly is seen as a process of developing best practice to make a difference to people and to the environment. While, at a cultural level, participatory research in diverse nature-based physical cultures may uncover the practices that may lead to increasing ecological sensibilities and praxis.

In this Handbook, we present a range of viewpoints from authors from different disciplines and geographical areas. A value of this book is that it raises questions and challenges to consider in the future related to research and to practice in the outdoors. Chapters in this book highlight the broad range of contexts, understandings and approaches that make up outdoor studies. Nevertheless, mapped across all of these dimensions is the significance of the dynamic, fluid human–environment/nature interactions and the importance that outdoor pedagogies of diverse kinds may have in promoting ecological sensibilities among young and not so young, and within various outdoor educational and physical cultures.

References

Allin, L. & Humberstone, B. (2010). Introducing 'journey(s)' in adventure and outdoor learning research. *Journal of Adventure Education and Outdoor Learning, 10*(2), 71–76.

Drasdo, H. (1972). *Education and the Mountain Centres.* Tyddyn Gabriel: Welsh Universal Press.

Gurholt, K. (2008) Norwegian *friluftsliv* and the ideal of becoming an 'educated man'. *Journal of Adventure Education and Outdoor Learning, 8*(1), 55–70.

Humberstone, B. (1998). Re-creation and connections in and with nature: Synthesizing ecological and feminist discourses and praxis? *International Review for the Sociology of Sport, 3*(4), 381–392.

Humberstone, B., Brown, H. & Richards, K. (2003). *Whose Journeys? The Outdoors and Adventure as Social and Cultural Phenomena.* Barrow-in-Furness, UK: Fingerprints.

Lyng, S. (1990). Edgework: A social psychological analysis of voluntary risk taking. *American Journal of Sociology, 35*(1), 851–886.

McNamee, M. (Ed.) (2007). *Philosophy, Risk and Adventure Sports.* Oxford: Routledge.

Rinehart, R. & Sydnor, S. (Eds) (2003). *To the Extreme: Alternative Sports, Inside and Out.* Albany, NY: State University of New York Press.

Thorpe, H. (2014). *Transnational Mobilities in Action Sport Cultures.* London: Palgrave Macmillan.

Thorpe, H. & Rinehart, R. (2010). Alternative sport and affect: Non-representational theory examined. *Sport in Society, 13*(7/8), 1268–1291.

Turčová, I., Martin, A. & Neuman, J. (2005). Diversity in language: Outdoor terminology in the Czech Republic and Britain. *Journal of Adventure Education and Outdoor Learning, 5*(2), 101–118.

UCSM (University College of St Martin) (1998). *Development Plan.* Lancaster: unpublished.

Vanreusel, B. (1995). From Bambi to Rambo: Towards a socio-ecological approach to the pursuit of outdoor sports. In O. Weiss & W. Schulz (Eds.) *Sport in Space and Time.* Vienna: Vienna University Press.

Wheaton, B. (Ed.) (2004). *Understanding Lifestyle Sports, Consumption, Identity and Difference.* London: Routledge.

Part 1
Constructs and theoretical concepts

Introduction

Heather Prince

The breadth, depth and diversity of applications and professional practice in outdoor studies are widely acknowledged. This section seeks to define and explore the structural and philosophical underpinning of the discipline in key areas and through multiple perspectives, with a flavour and sense of internationalism and culture.

As in other parts of this Handbook, the choice of conceptual frameworks and areas of focus is necessarily selective but includes critical perspectives that we consider to be foundational to outdoor studies. These are established not only from the 'Anglosphere' – Australia, Canada, the USA and UK – but also from Sweden and Germany with specific cultural constructs (e.g. the German *Erlebnispädagogik* and *Bildung*, described by Becker, and Indigenous knowledge, by Mullins, Lowan-Trudeau and Fox). The authors describe different philosophical perspectives with a range of outcomes through experiential, adventure, recreational and educational approaches, historical roots and meanings, environmental concerns, health and wellbeing, and research. We recognise that these constructs might be seen as time specific and that, were this book being written in a different decade, the prioritisation of contributions might be different, nevertheless they all present conceptualisations that have rigour and application, and influence practice.

Our intention is not to focus on semantics or definitions but to note that the foundations and direction authors take within the scope of outdoor studies is interesting. Brookes and Becker derive current propositional meanings from adventure, Öhman and Sandell, and Mullins *et al.*, focus on the connections with nature for environmental concern and environmental education, and for outdoor recreation and outdoor education, respectively. Experiences in the outdoors and experiential education and learning are the concepts discussed by Quay and Seaman, and Carpenter and Harper (for health and wellbeing). Coates, Hockley, Humberstone and Stan acknowledge this multifaceted nature of outdoor studies through examining research paradigms, and suggest that cross-disciplinary research could be of value in supporting all areas of outdoor studies and in extending the reach of the field.

Two different approaches are taken in the discussion of the emergence, explanation and interpretation of current practice and rhetoric. Brookes focuses on the inspiration, influence and contribution of single individuals, and hagiographic interpretations of these figures to explain outdoor practice and discourse, acknowledging that myths probably overemphasise the influence of individuals, which are also subject to multiple and contested interpretations. He examines the influence of militaristic and masculinist tendencies within a historical perspective on the understanding of contemporary adventure education.

Becker discusses frameworks, processes and pedagogies that have influenced the interpretation of adventure in Germany, and the relative importance of these in its conceptual understanding. He argues that *Erlebnispädagogik* is a pedagogy that is now transcending schools but does not have a theoretical foundation, and introduces *Erlebnisse* (and variants) as emotional states of awareness as outcomes of this and other processes. More important to outdoor studies is *Bildung* to overcome challenges, tensions or crises, following the objective hermeneutics work of Oevermann (2004). The adventurous 'being on the way' is a cultural pattern that can support Bildung.

Environmental education is a specific and engendered component of outdoor studies with the rich pedagogic tradition of using nature as a fosterer, as outlined by Öhman and Sandell. Similarly, Mullins, Lowan-Trudeau and Fox emphasise Indigenous knowledge as relational where reciprocity is important, with nature fostering deep connections to place. Encounters with nature are crucial to both these perspectives, but are interpreted differently.

Öhman and Sandell focus on the possible implication of nature encounters for environmental concern as the contemporary manifestation of an historical process of development through 'nature protection', 'nature conservation' and 'environmental control', to the current tensions between 'alternative' and 'sustainable development'. They argue that what constitutes outdoor studies has shifted concomitantly with the traditions and pedagogy of environmental education to a position of pluralism. Suggested potentials for future ways in which outdoor studies might expand perspectives on the environment and a sustainable future have clear parallels to other chapters in this section: experiential, relational, existential, human ecology, ideological and spatial.

The positioning of outdoor studies in deconstructing experience is clear and understood in practice but the theoretical conceptualisation of experiential education and experiential learning is still a challenge. Quay and Seaman examine this close connection between experience and education, combining the philosophies of Dewey and Heidegger to articulate a theory of experience that embraces being, doing and knowing. They posit that outdoor educators have a good awareness of the inherent connection between these elements, but that theoretical frameworks and the manifestation of these in practice are not well developed. They advocate that a sound philosophy of experience that views traditional and progressive forms of schooling through the same lens should be the way forward.

The knowing and being elements identified as key to experiential learning in outdoor studies reflect Indigenous ways. Indigenous knowledge that is mythic, sacred and locally ecological (Marker, 2006), and its practical application or embodiment, is highly valued. The Western dominant conceptualisation of land as a space to be conquered, occupied and visited but not inhabited, and of culture as place-independent, is challenged by Mullins *et al.*, with Indigenous knowledge providing alternative ways of thinking and doing outdoor recreation and outdoor education. In their chapter, the authors attempt to disrupt the nature–culture dichotomous thinking with its foundational paradigms situating humans within or outside the natural world (the inherited epistemological position of Cartesian rationality critiqued by Nicol, 2003) upon which much outdoor recreation and outdoor education theory is structured. They suggest ways in which cross-cultural understanding can be enhanced through different outdoor experiences with critical self-reflections and creativity informed by Indigenous perspectives. Interestingly, ways of knowing have been identified previously as a framework for holistic understanding into which outdoor and environmental education might more broadly sit as an alternative pedagogy (Nicol, 2003).

Connections to the natural world for communities as well as the individual are framed in the multidimensional (socio-ecological) approach advocated by Carpenter and Harper for promoting health and wellbeing. Conceptually, the individual is shown as being nested within their community and environment as in Indigenous cultures. This approach has generally been focused on the built environment or human-centric places, but the model suggests that more natural areas have benefits. The social dimensions of the group context to promote health and wellbeing are important in the experiential process as they enable individuals to look beyond themselves. The authors propose a 'dose of Nature' as the minimum time exposure people should be in the outdoors to have benefit, and also highlight 'numinous' components (Otto, 1958), which contribute to the spiritual or existential qualities of outdoor experiences as suggested by Öhman and Sandell.

All these chapters suggest a shifting landscape in the understanding and extent of outdoor studies mirrored by shifting perspectives on research in the outdoors described by Coates *et al.* The range of constructs and conceptualisations within this section illustrates the need for a range of research paradigms and methodologies. These are mainly, but not exclusively, qualitative in nature and the authors here provide examples of socio-cultural and spatial research towards the understanding of the outdoors as social phenomena. The match to the wealth and diversity of content within this section is good, but if outdoor studies is going to establish itself further, and gain credence, meaning and impact across other disciplines, then research methods and approaches also need to have extended and valid reach.

Outdoor studies, with all its constituent parts, focuses on situated learning with a strong focus on historical, cultural and social aspects (Brown, 2010). Many of these authors derive meanings and understanding from other perspectives and subject areas. They follow the implicit thinking that, rather than develop eclectic new theories, researchers should seek to understand the efficacy of practice through established frameworks in other disciplines (Houge Mackenzie, Son & Hollenhorst, 2014). The contextualisation of outdoor studies within epistemological pluralism will better define it for international understanding.

Outdoor studies is a young and emerging discipline not without issues of identity, particularly in a global context. This section describes and examines critically the tensions, challenges and dichotomies in understanding theory and practice, as well as potential and possible future solutions. Although this approach could be construed as a disorganised position for the development of the discipline, it illustrates a clear drive to recognise its contribution as vibrant, exciting, stimulating and pedagogically important to individuals, groups, communities and society.

References

Brown, M. (2010). Transfer: Outdoor adventure education's Achilles heel? Changing participation as a viable option. *Australian Journal of Outdoor Education, 14*(1), 13–22.

Houge Mackenzie, S., Son, J.S. & Hollenhorst, S. (2014). Unifying psychology and experiential education: Toward an integrated understanding of why it works. *Journal of Experiential Education, 37*(1), 75–88.

Marker, M. (2006). After the Makah whale hunt: Indigenous knowledge and limits to multicultural discourse. *Urban Education, 41*(5), 482–505.

Nicol, R. (2003). Outdoor education: Research topic or universal value? Part three. *Journal of Adventure Education and Outdoor Learning, 3*(1), 11–28.

Oevermann, U. (2004). Adorno als empirischer Sozialforscher im Blickwinkel der heutigen Methodenlage. In A. Gruschka & U. Oevermann (Eds.) *Die Lebendigkeit der kritischen Gesellschaftstheorie* (pp. 189–234). Wetzlar: Büchse der Pandora.

Otto, R. (1958). *The Idea of the Holy.* New York, NY: Oxford University Press.

1

Foundation myths and the roots of adventure education in the Anglosphere

Andrew Brookes

La Trobe University

The field of outdoor studies has its share of foundation narratives, including some focused on the inspiration and efforts of admired founders. Examples in the Anglophone world include Lord Baden-Powell and Kurt Hahn, both of whom, with good reason, are credited with great influence. As might be expected in the case of organisations framed as popular movements, it is not difficult to find somewhat heroic accounts, and even the most hagiographic interpretations of influential figures can help explain elements of outdoor practice and discourse. Foundation myths, Rippin and Fleming (2006) point out, are not only at the heart of Western civilisation but often central to organisational culture. While myths, by definition, probably overemphasise the influence of a single individual, read critically they can help explain and interpret current practice and rhetoric.

Advocates of more than one approach to organised outdoor education attribute philosophies or ascribe current practice to a founder, usually male. Lord Baden-Powell is one obvious founding figure, if one accepts that the Scouting Movement has contributed directly and indirectly to at least some forms of current outdoor education. Kurt Hahn, a founder of the Outward Bound movement is also a contender. The style of programme he introduced has long attracted adherents and also the attention of critics (see, for example, Drasdo, 1972). Introducing the most-cited outdoor education article published in the last twenty years, Hattie and colleagues (1997) take an adherent line:

> *Most researchers trace the origin of modern adventure education to Kurt Hahn (1957).* In 1941 Hahn devised the first Outward Bound program for the Blue Funnel Shipping Line to reduce the loss of lives due to sinkings of their ships in the Atlantic Ocean. A month-long course was designed to accelerate the development of independence, initiative, physical fitness, self-reliance, and resourcefulness. The success of these programs led Hahn to support the establishment of Outward Bound schools in England and then throughout the world; by 1995 there were 48 schools on five continents. In addition, Hahn set up many other schools . . . and helped to establish the Duke of Edinburgh Awards and the network of United World Colleges. These schools emphasize the role of character, service, challenge,

and physical endeavor, and many have adopted the theme espoused by William James (1967) in his search for the 'moral equivalent of war.' Hahn claimed that the aim of Outward Bound was to 'enthral and hold the young through active and willing Samaritan service, demanding care and skill, courage and endurance, discipline and initiative.' (p. 44, my emphasis)

Hahn has undoubtedly influenced some approaches to adventure education, although even within the Anglosphere different influences on outdoor (and adventure) education have manifested themselves in different regions at different times, resulting in a diversity of approaches and philosophies (Lynch, 1999; Brookes, 2002).

Not all that is attributed to Hahn is supported by historical evidence (Veevers & Allison, 2011), although far less has been written at length about Hahn than about Lord Baden-Powell and the Scouting Movement. In the case of Baden-Powell, scholarship has been both extensive – Jeal's (2007) definitive biography runs to more than 600 pages – and somewhat contested, particularly around themes of militarism, imperialism, masculinity, homophobia and racism (Macleod, 1983; Rosenthal, 1986; Springhall, 1987; Summers, 1987; Salzman, 1992; Dedman, 1993; MacDonald, 1993; Pryke, 1998). Scouting emerged earlier than Outward Bound, at the beginning of the 20th century in the context of British imperial struggles in Africa. It would be surprising if its origins did not reflect beliefs and values of the time. Outward Bound's formation, shaped by concerns about survival of merchant marine crews in lifeboats during the Second World War, was somewhat different, reflected in its use of courses of a set length rather than ongoing involvement in a social movement. While the early emphasis of Scouting rhetoric was on instilling character, Outward Bound tended to emphasise character as an emergent by-product of self-actualisation (Millikan, 2006).

An early film about the original Outward Bound School, *The Blue Peter* (Rilla, 1954), exhibits elements of Outward Bound absent or overlooked in Hattie *et al.*'s (1997) introduction. Although from the merchant marine rather than the military, staff are uniformed and addressed by rank. The boys are required to 'fall out, on the double'. Important characters are defined by wartime experience. There is laughter at a foreign name. A boy who enquires about visitor days is asked if he can't get along without his mother. Women appear on the margins, but the courses are male only and run by males. Rosenthal (1986) has pointed out that the evident success of Scouting for boys can be explained by its appeal rather than its achievements. *The Blue Peter* shows the extent to which Outward Bound, by accident or design, appealed to prevailing beliefs.

Foundation narratives become myths when they over-attribute to one individual aspect of programmes contributed to by hundreds of individuals with diverse motivations and beliefs, which over time depart significantly from the original vision. Moreover, as Hoberman (1995) observed:

The Olympic (1894), Scouting (1908), and Esperanto (1887) movements . . . have all benefitted from benign myths of origin rooted in reverential attitudes toward the personal qualities of their respective founding fathers and the salvational doctrines they created. One result of such cults of personality is a 'halo effect' that can confer on such movements a degree of immunity to critical examination. (p. 3)

Scouting has seen its share of criticism since those comments were made, but the value of critical examination remains, with less emphasis on uncovering what a founding figure believed (cf. Jeal, 2007; Veevers & Allison, 2011) than on what influence they have had. In this chapter, I explore two examples of how insights from historical studies can point to potentially enlightening critiques of contemporary programmes or rhetoric, first, through militaristic influences and, second, in the role anxieties play about youth and masculinity.

Militarism in contemporary outdoor programmes

Some forms of outdoor education are undoubtedly used as part of military training, but most outdoor education is not overtly militaristic. The Scouting Movement adopted some military trappings, such as uniforms. Dedman (1993) argued it was less militarily conceived than popularly supposed, but Summers (1987) contended that, at grass-roots level, it was more militaristic than its founders intended. Both Scouting and Outward Bound have changed over time. Freeman (2010) describes shifts, albeit contested, within Outward Bound as it moved away from a Hahnian legacy:

> [T]he movement combined some older aspects of muscular Christianity with more historically specific concerns, rooted in the experience and aftermath of war. The faith of the movement's early leaders in the promotion of character and leadership ensured the maintenance of training programmes based on exposure to challenging and potentially dangerous situations, and the explicit promotion of 'Character Training Through Adventure'. However, by the mid-1960s, the language of character and leadership, and other aspects of the Hahnian educational vision, had come under sustained challenge from both outside and within the organisation, and the rhetoric of character-training was gradually abandoned, replaced with an emphasis on the 'softer' aims of 'self-discovery' and 'personal growth'. (p. 23, in-text citations omitted)

Changes in emphasis notwithstanding, 20th century Anglo societies are so steeped in historical military influences (Howard, 2001 orig. 1977) that their elimination from adventure education may be partial: '[militarism is] simply an acceptance of the values of the military subculture as the dominant values of society: a stress on hierarchy and subordination in organization, on physical courage and self-sacrifice in personal behaviour, on the need for heroic leadership in situations of extreme stress . . . ' (p. 109).

A distinctive form of militarism shaped Anglosphere outdoor education. The modern experiences of land war of those nations were almost entirely on foreign soil (Bourne, 1997; Dyer, 2004). In earlier times irregular war, or small-scale local wars, have characterised almost all human societies (Dyer, 2004). Adventure education, a sub-section of outdoor education, borrowed ontological and epistemological frames from expeditionary military adventures: through a presumption that environments will be unfamiliar and by using an assumption that leadership requires skills and personal qualities – the right stuff – rather than local knowledge. The British (Schools) Exploring Society application form for leaders, for example, does not emphasise local knowledge and experience (British Exploring Society, 2014). The idea of the transformative journey into the unknown is, of course, a universal template in popular culture (Vogler, 2007; Smelser, 2009), no doubt contributing to acceptance of adventure education, but it does not explain why leaders should not have a good knowledge of their workplace.

These historical influences can partly explain specific programme elements, such as map-reading exercises, which use topographical maps, rather than wayfinding based on familiarity and landmarks. One reason to examine to consider alternatives, since women are now included in many of these programmes, is that females do better at landmark-based way finding than the more geometric military style (Schmitz, 1999).

The venture-into-the-unknown model has consequences for curriculum aims and purposes, particularly understandings of place, but it also has a material effect on safety and safety planning, particularly when programmes define leadership responsibilities around personal qualities and skills rather than local knowledge. Following a tragedy on the Mangatepopo River in New Zealand in which six students and one teacher drowned, the Independent Review Team reported: '[the] programs emphasized skills, adventure, and group processes more than environmental understanding through outdoor activities . . . programs focussed on environmental knowledge and understanding are inherently more likely to be attentive to environmental circumstances and hazards' (Brookes, Corkill QC & Smith, 2009, p. 36). Following the death of a student on a World Challenge Expedition in Vietnam, the leader reportedly: 'wouldn't have chosen that route if [he] had known what it was like . . . [the leader] who had led expeditions to Malaysia, Kenya and Madagascar, had not taken an expedition up the 9,800ft (3,000m) Fansipan mountain before' (Judd, 2001). Many other examples of failures due to lack of local environmental knowledge have been reported (Brookes, 2011).

A second implication of militarism in outdoor education derives from Dyer's observations about military training (2004):

> [T]he armed forces of every country can still take almost any young male civilian and in only a few weeks turn him into a soldier with all the right reflexes and attitudes. Their recruits usually have no more than twenty years' experience of the world, most of it as children, while the armies have had all of history to practise and perfect their techniques. (p. 31)

He points out that the principal focus is on changing values and loyalties. The almost unmatched effectiveness of military training, particularly in comparison to most education, is reason to consider what power outdoor education programmes derive from militaristic methods even when no militaristic ends are evident, some signs of militarism are absent, and foundation myths direct attention elsewhere.

Boot camp programmes for young offenders obviously borrow from military training, but programmes that seem to eschew military influences might still be understood as working in much the same way. The *Brat Camp* series of TV shows (Whittaker & Abood, 2005), versions of which have aired around the world, focused not on induction into a military organisation, but on US-based programmes intended to be therapeutic for troubled teens. A report by the United States Government Accountability Office on deaths in such programmes (Kutz & O'Connell, 2007) should be required reading for anyone studying such programmes, but here I consider only whether there are elements of military training in programmes that superficially eschew it. In the first series of *Brat Camp*, staff are referred to by (lower case) monikers such as rhythm otter, bright dragon, mountain spirit, silver heart and stone bear. Staff appear never to raise their voices. Staff do not wear uniforms, and look more like the hippies who protested the Vietnam war than the soldiers who fought it. There appear to be no military drills. In short, there is a distinct – perhaps deliberate – absence of the visible signs of boot camp. Nevertheless there is a form to the experience portrayed that fits with some essential elements of military boot camp, including the strangeness of the situation for participants; complete lack of any alternative courses of action for the participants (other than compliance), control by staff of the explanatory frameworks and language, and complete dependence of participants on staff for material needs and comfort. A ritual removal of jewellery, distinctive clothing, and other symbols of individual personality parallel boot camp, as does the lack of contact with the outside world. Physical hardships, daily routines and exercise, insistence on attention to detail and a steady diet of small triumphs are also features of military training (Dyer, 2004), and involve, to an extent, devices not available to those conducting everyday schooling or even parenting. None of these observations is definitive, of course, and in any case they are based on what the filmmakers were allowed to film and what they chose to include in the programme, but they point firmly in the direction of militaristic methods, particularly those that employ what are now understood as coercive or persuasive social situations (see, for example, Ross & Nisbett, 1991; Zimbardo, 2007).

Playing on anxieties in the community

Outward Bound and, especially, the Scouts were conceived and gained traction from anxieties about perceived 'declines' in youth, particularly in masculinity. Neither programme relied on or required what would count today as evidence in the social sciences for the problems they constructed or the solutions they advanced, but instead appealed very successfully to popular beliefs and concerns:

> It may be, however, that masculinity is always in crisis, at least in the United States during the twentieth century . . . the decade preceding the introduction of Outward Bound to the United States was marked by a high level of anxiety about the disappearance of manly virtue . . . [l]ike the Boy Scouts, Outward Bound was but one of many responses to a crisis of masculinity . . . [m]agazine articles that introduced the Outward Bound idea to the America public bore titles such as 'Is Our Youth Going Soft?', 'Character, the Hard Way', 'Marshmallow Becomes a Man', 'Outward Bound: How to Build a Man the Hard Way' and 'Rugged Camps Turn Boys in Iron Men'; clearly articulating Outward Bound as a method for shoring up American manhood. (Millikan, 2006, pp. 842–843)

Citing a speech made by Hahn in 1960, McKenzie (2003) records that he saw physical fitness, self-discipline, craftsmanship and service as necessary because of 'declines of a diseased civilization' (p. 9). Freeman (2010) observes that, in the early years, the Outward Bound movement 'combined some older aspects of muscular Christianity with more historically specific concerns, rooted in the experience and aftermath of war' (p. 23), echoing, he noted, earlier Edwardian concerns about the declining character of young men.

A great deal has been written about the connections between the Scout Movement's foundation and ideas of manliness. According to Baden-Powell, 'God made men to be men . . . We badly need some training for our lads if we are to keep up manliness in our race instead of lapsing into a nation of soft, sloppy cigarette suckers' (cited by Warren, 1800, p. 203).

Anxieties about youth recur every generation, which makes them a natural focus for educational rhetoric of any stripe. Winton (2008) has argued that more recent popular arguments for character education gained adherents in spite of 'conceptual problems and a limited knowledge base' because the rhetoric character education appealed to 'Canadian and American insecurities about social cohesion, academic achievement, economic competitiveness, civic engagement, personal safety, moral decline, and the loss of a common culture' (p. 307).

On the face of it, specific anxieties about manliness have receded. Both Scouting and Outward Bound have moved away from gendered rhetoric. Here I consider what role contemporary anxieties about youth might have in driving support for outdoor programmes, and whether those concerns remain gendered.

Gill's (2007/2008) *No Fear: Growing Up in a Risk Averse Society* is one contribution to popular literature and community debates about risk and adventure in childhood, particularly in the UK. There is no hint of concerns about manliness in the book, and very little gendered language. Gill's work is cited approvingly on the website of *The Campaign for Adventure* (Campaign for Adventure, 2005), and in other blogs, news reports and websites, although it has also been cited in the scholarly literature. Another contribution to overall debate about childhood, from the USA, Louv's (2008) *Last Child in the Woods: Saving Our Children From Nature Deficit Disorder* reworks and modernises the anxiety theme. The use of the term 'deficit' foregrounds an implicit theme in earlier youth movement rhetoric, similarly linked to a movement (the Children and Nature Network), and also contributing to community debate. Nature deficit disorder is not a recognised medical condition, but is a registered trademark. Louv is a journalist, and does not represent his work as scholarly or peer reviewed, but it has nevertheless been cited more than 2000 times in the scholarly literature. It is not overtly gendered; indeed, references to boys and girls, mothers and fathers, are balanced.

In both works and the debates associated with them, traditional anxieties about youth have been reworked into anxiety about overprotectiveness, in effect anxiety about over-anxiety, in communal discourse that has laid the groundwork for outdoor programmes that purport to offer adventure or even risk. Neither publication focuses overtly on gender, but parental overprotectiveness has gendered connotations. Gill's book, immediately on publication, prompted a BBC headline, 'Do we mollycoddle our children?' (Croft, 2007), and was cited in more than 100 blogs and news reports that used the term 'mollycoddle'. Numerous responses to Louv's book used the same term, which derives from 'moll' meaning girl or prostitute, and as a noun (mollycoddle) means an effeminate man or boy, synonymous with terms such as nancy-boy, milksop or mummy's boy (Oxford Dictionaries, 2014). Gill's book refers to 'the nanny-state', another gendered term frequently teamed with the more neutral terms bubble-wrap kids and helicopter parent. Concerns about over-regulation and parental overprotectiveness are not one and the same, of course, but both persist with connotations of the overprotective *mother* (producing a generation of *sissies*, another synonym for mollycoddle). Articles such as 'Are we suffering from mollycoddlitis?' (Mayhew, 2007), which argues that risk aversion is damaging individual children and is itself a risk to society, appear to be whistling the overprotective mother tune.

The solution to a lack of manliness has consistently been removal of boys from maternal care and into male institutions. Maternal overprotectiveness appears in the scholarly literature as a condition, albeit a contested one (Gerard, 1944). I could find ten times the number of scholarly references to maternal overprotectiveness than to paternal overprotectiveness. A search on the exact phrase 'overprotective mother' produced three times as many hits as a search for 'overprotective father', consistent with the gendered roots of terms such as paranoid parents and bubble-wrap kids.

Simplistic appeals to old biases about mothering impede careful debate about real dilemmas around risk, safety and opportunity. Zelizer (1985) points out that, in the USA, typical families in the 17th and 18th centuries would experience two or three child deaths under ten. Indeed, overt mourning for child deaths tended not to occur at all until child health improvements in the late 19th century greatly improved child mortality. However, in the early 20th century an epidemic of child deaths in New York resulted from the introduction of railways, trolley cars, cars and trucks on to roads and streets that had hitherto been children's playgrounds. By 1927 in New York State more than 20,000 were killed or injured annually – nearly three times the cause of death for 5 to 14 year olds than any single disease, and these deaths were not accepted in the way deaths in earlier centuries had been.

Mothers were blamed, not for overprotectiveness but for neglect: '[m]others were urged to 'take the burden of death of the shoulders of the Lord', by accepting that their children's accidents had preventable causes' (Zelizer, 1985, p. 44). Lower-class deaths were blamed on mothers. One writer in 1922 opined: 'women so often neglect or refuse their obvious duty . . . until a limp crushed body has been put in their arms' (Zelizer, 1985, p. 47). Children lost the contest for public space and were moved indoors. Summer camps were attractive because children would be safe (Van Slyck, 2006). The neglectful mother has not vanished; indeed, there is at least an implication in more recent public discussions that the overprotective mother is, in effect, neglectful.

Generalised attitudes towards risk and overprotectiveness provide no useful guidance in making any particular decision about what a child should or should not do in any given situation, and can be implicated in seriously unsafe and unnecessary choices (Brookes, 2011). Putting the words of a paranoid parenting song to an overprotective mother tune appeals to old prejudices, and potentially interferes with legitimate debate about risk and safety.

Final comments

Summers (1987) and Perry (1993) have shown that, to understand the Scouting Movement, it is necessary to move beyond the organisation and the founder, and investigate what took place on the ground under the influence of myriad leaders and communities. Van Slyck (2006) has made a similar point about the influence of individuals on summer camp programmes in the USA. Too much can be made of foundational narratives. By the same token, too much can be made of critiques of those narratives. Programmes on the ground might be inadequately represented by generalised accounts, and inaccurately portrayed by generalised critiques. My purpose is not to replace one set of generalisations with another, but to open lines of enquiry that foundational narratives might close off as somehow disrespectful, improper or disloyal.

Programme choices between treating the outdoors as a dangerous unknown or learning to feel safe, and at home, in the outdoors are important. If the power of outdoor programmes can be better understood by examining parallels with military training, then that question should be explored. If old prejudices about removing boys from their mothers are being repackaged with gender-free labels, any implications should be reviewed. In each case the purpose of critique is to improve the field, even if it means reconsidering cherished narratives.

References

Bourne, J. (1997). Total war I. The Great War. In C. Townsend (Ed.) *The Oxford Illustrated History of Modern War* (pp. 100–119). Oxford: Oxford University Press.
British Exploring Society (2014). Leading with British Exploring. Retrieved from: www.britishexploring. org/explore-with-us/lead-with-us.aspx.
Brookes, A. (2002). Lost in the Australian bush: Outdoor education as curriculum. *Journal of Curriculum Studies, 34*(4), 405–425.
Brookes, A. (2011). Preventing fatal incidents in outdoor education. Lessons learnt from the Mangatepopo tragedy. *New Zealand Journal of Outdoor Education, 2*(6), 7–32.
Brookes, A., Corkill, QC, B. & Smith, M. (2009). Report to Trustees of the Sir Edmund Hillary Outdoor Pursuit Centre of New Zealand. Mangatepopo Gorge incident, 15 April 2008. Turangi: OPC Trust. Copies available on request.
Campaign for Adventure (2005). Campaign for Adventure. Retrieved from: www.campaignforadventure.org.
Croft, I. (2007). Do we mollycoddle our children? Retrieved from: www.bbc.co.uk/blogs/legacy/world-haveyoursay/2007/10/do_we_mollycoddle_our_children.html.
Dedman, M. (1993). Baden-Powell, militarism, and the 'invisible contributors' to the Boy Scout scheme, 1904–1920. *Twentieth Century British History, 4*(3), 201–223.

Drasdo, H. (1972). *Education and the Mountain Centres*. Tyddyn Gabriel, Denbighshire: Frank Davies.

Dyer, G. (2004). *War: The Lethal Custom* (2nd edn). New York: Carroll and Graf Publishers.

Freeman, M. (2010). From 'character–training' to 'personal growth': the early history of Outward Bound 1941–1965. *History of Education, 40*(1), 21–43.

Gerard, M.W. (1944). Maternal overprotection by David M. Levy. *Social Service Review, 18*(1), 115–117.

Gill, T. (2007/2008). *No Fear: Growing Up in a Risk Averse Society*. London: Calouste Gulbenkian Foundation.

Hattie, J., Marsh, H.W., Neill, J.T. & Richards, G. E. (1997). Adventure education and Outward Bound: Out-of-class experiences that make a lasting difference. *Review of Educational Research, 67*(1), 43–87.

Hoberman, J. (1995). Toward a theory of Olympic internationalism. *Journal of Sport History, 22*(1), 1–37.

Howard, M. (2001 orig. 1977). *War in European History*. Oxford: Oxford University Press.

Jeal, T. (2007). *Baden-Powell: Founder of the Boy Scouts*. London: Yale University Press.

Judd, T. (2001). Heavy rucksack blamed for girl's fatal plunge, *The Independent* (UK), 11 December.

Kutz, G.D. & O'Connell, A. (2007). *Residential Treatment Programs. Concerns Regarding Abuse and Death in Certain Programs for Troubled Youth*. Washington, DC: United States Government Accountability Office.

Louv, R. (2008). *Last Child in the Woods: Saving Our Children From Nature-deficit Disorder*. New York: Algonquin Books.

Lynch, P.M. (1999). Enterprise, Self-help and cooperation: A history of outdoor education in New Zealand schools to 1989. PhD, University of Canterbury, Christchurch.

MacDonald, R.H. (1993). *Sons of the Empire: The Frontier and the Boy Scout Movement 1890–1918*. Toronto: University of Toronto Press.

Macleod, D.I. (1983). *Building Character in the American Boy: The Boy Scouts, YMCA and their Forerunners 1870–1920*. Madison, WI: University of Wisconsin Press.

Mayhew, J. (2007). Are we suffering from mollycoddlitis? *The Safety and Health Practitioner, 25*, 39–42.

McKenzie, M. (2003). Beyond 'the outward bound process': Rethinking student learning. *Journal of Experiential Education, 26*(1), 8–23.

Millikan, M. (2006). The muscular Christian ethos in post-Second World War American liberalism: Women in Outward Bound 1962–1975. *International Journal of the History of Sport, 23*(5), 838–855.

Oxford Dictionaries (2014). Mollycoddle: Retrieved from www.oxforddictionaries.com/definition/english/mollycoddle.

Perry, E.I. (1993). From achievement to happiness: Girl Scouting in Middle Tennessee, 1910s–1960s. *Journal of Women's History, 5*(2), 75–94.

Pryke, S. (1998). The popularity of nationalism in the early British Boy Scout movement. *Social History, 23*(3), 309–324.

Rilla, W. (writer) (1954). *The Blue Peter*. H. Mason (producer), Group 3 Limited.

Rippin, A. & Fleming, P. (2006). Brute force: Medieval foundation myths and three modern organizations' quests for hegemony. *Management & Organizational History, 1*(1), 51–70.

Rosenthal, M. (1986). *The Character Factory: Baden-Powell and the Origins of the Boy Scout Movement*. London: Collins.

Ross, L. & Nisbett, R.E. (1991). *The Person and the Situation. Perspectives of Social Psychology*. New York: McGraw-Hill.

Salzman, A. (1992). The American scene: The Boy Scouts under siege. *The American Scholar, 61*(4), 591–597.

Schmitz, S. (1999). Gender differences in acquisition of environmental knowledge related to wayfinding behaviour, spatial anxiety, and self-estimated environmental competencies. *Sex Roles, 41*(1/2), 71–93.

Smelser, N. (2009). *The Odyssey Experience: Physical, Social, Psychological, and Spiritual Journeys*. Oakland: University of California Press.

Springhall, J. (1987). Baden-Powell and the Scout movement before 1920: Citizen training, or soldiers of the future? *English Historical Review, 102*(October), 934–942.

Summers, A. (1987). Scouts, Guides and VADs: A note in reply to Allen Warren. *English Historical Review, 102*(October), 943–947.

Van Slyck, A.A. (2006). *A Manufactured Wilderness: Summer Camps and the Shaping of American Youth, 1890–1960*. Architecture, Landscape and American Culture series. Minneapolis: University of Minnesota Press.

Veevers, N. & Allison, P. (2011). *Kurt Hahn: Inspirational, Visionary, Outdoor and Experiential Educator*. Rotterdam: Sense Publishers.

Vogler, C. (2007). *The Writer's Journey: Mythic Structure for Writers*. Studio City, CA: Michael Wiese Productions.

Warren, A. (1800). Popular manliness: Baden-Powell, Scouting, and the development of manly character. *Manliness and Morality: Middle-class Masculinity in Britain and America, 1940*, 199–219.

Whittaker, S. & Abood, T. (writers) (2005). *Brat Camp*, Episode 1, Season 1. J. Isaacs (producer), Channel 4.

Winton, S. (2008). The appeal(s) of character education in threatening times: Caring and critical democratic responses. *Comparative Education, 44*(3), 305–316.

Zelizer, V.A.R. (1985). *Pricing the Priceless Child: The Changing Social Value of Children*. New Jersey: Princeton University Press.

Zimbardo, P. (2007). *The Lucifer Effect: How Good People Turn Evil*. London: Rider.

2

From 'Erlebnis' to adventure

A view on the German Erlebnispädagogik

Peter Becker

PHILIPPS UNIVERSITY OF MARBURG

I

After the period of National Socialist rule with its singular promotion of youthful, racially pure bodies, fast as greyhounds, tough as leather and hard as Krupp steel (Hitler, 1935), 'Erlebnispädagogik' in Germany had been publicly discredited, but it has been able to recover remarkably fast since the 1970s. By this time it had become a solid and attractive component of youth work and youth welfare. Where 'Erlebnispädagogik' was once educational 'dynamite' and a new approach to reforming the Wilhelmine school system, today it has largely left the sphere of the school. Besides youth work it is located in in-company training, and further and early education. Although at present there is only one academic university qualification, there are additional qualifications provided by *Fachhochschulen* (technical colleges) and a large market offering further education. There are tentative indications for the subject to spread more widely into the academic field.

Despite its confirmed position and the widespread acceptance of its practices, neither a proper systematic reappraisal of the full one-hundred-year history of this pedagogical subcategory can be found nor can one perceive a noteworthy academic discourse within the field dedicated to its theoretical analysis or its normative orientation. By omitting to do this, the discipline of 'Erlebnispädagogik' renounces the establishment of a self-determined position from which its own developmental tendencies could be viewed critically. This deficiency becomes apparent especially in the uncritical way US outdoor programmes are adopted, which drives 'Erlebnispädagogik' forward in three directions.

1   *Tendency towards standardisation*: As the words 'programme' and 'programming' indicate, the language imported together with models suggests that educational processes can be standardised. However, these processes elude any logic of subsumption since they are always unique. This standardisation endeavour misunderstands the human education process as a technical industrial production process in which standardised and economically viable procedures guarantee the production of always identical products.

2   *Tendency towards economisation*: The introduction of contracts and objective agreements into the pedagogical action context likewise fails to recognise the nature of the educational

process. This contract-mindedness remodels educational developments along the principles of the exchange of equivalents in which the parties involved are monitored and in which any contraventions have to be sanctioned. Contracts introduce suspicion and threat into the agreements; they destroy the participants' voluntary dedication to the matter; above all they destroy the trust between the parties that is necessary to carry out the activities and to overcome crisis situations. The upshot of this is that it is not about an individual who undergoes an educational experience but a consumer who knows how to gain his or her advantage in the marketplace through the possession of a contract.

3 *Tendency towards 'therapeutisation'*: The increasing use of 'Erlebnisse' for therapeutic ends perceives people as self-absorbed individuals focused mainly on finding, developing and extending their own selves. Unfulfilled needs and any difficulties are given a pathological veneer. What is reinforced and catered for is the desire for psychological growth through experiential and adventure therapies. This therapeutic quest for happiness leads to irresponsible misjudgement of emotional suffering and of well-qualified therapy, and inappropriately extends the therapeutic discourse into normal everyday life.

The explanation for the current boom of 'Erlebnispädagogik' can be found especially in this last point, with its tendency to renounce discipline and asceticism. Advanced industrial nations are confronted with the 'decline in the significance of industrial labour' (Honneth, 1994). This also means that the value patterns of Protestant ethics that have been the mainstay of working life are losing their orientation-giving power. Parallel to this decline, there is growth in another direction of a consumption-related hedonist range of values, which attaches more significance to the techniques of self-growth, to the quest for ever new sources of experience and thrill, and expressive aesthetic self-styling. In this context, the quest for 'Erlebnisse' does not only embrace the field of pedagogy but also extends into other areas of life, as reflected by new compound terms such as the German 'Erlebniswelten', 'Erlebnisgastronomie', 'Erlebnismilieu', 'Erlebnisreisen', 'Erlebnispaket' and 'Erlebnistage' – all promising adventure, excitement, entertainment, amusement and thrilling experiences while eating, travelling, holidaying, having a day out and so on.

The consumption-driven self-seekers and post-modern souls must be served. New industries are developing; outdoor markets and markets catering for psychological needs make enormous profits. The outdoor 'look' fits to any situation in life, in the same way as the rucksack, which goes with nearly every dress code. However, this consumption-driven self-realisation lacks the socially integrative bonding power of a meta-narrative, which might serve to generate mutual recognition between individuals. Although working always means doing something for others and producing surplus to benefit others, consumption does not have any significance that goes beyond the individual consumer (Honneth, 1994; Voswinkel, 2013).

II

It is not the first time in German cultural history that 'Erlebnis' is causing considerable excitement and irritation. The term, which is practically untranslatable into English, emerged in the rising field of life philosophy during the 19th century, before it was discussed systematically towards the end of the century by Dilthey while laying the foundations of the humanities and of literary theory. It became a central diagnostic term of the period at the beginning of the next century. The essential characteristic of 'Erlebnis' is its direct, pre-conceptional perception of a certain part of reality in which the subject that is experiencing and perceiving the situation is not yet separated from the object that is being experienced and perceived. Subject and object are still a whole. It is only in its conception that the subject is separated from the object, which in turn dissects the holistic physical-psychological unity of the 'Erlebnis' into its individual parts. The emotional intensity that is connected with 'Erlebnis' does not only reinforce this unity, which makes 'Erlebnis' stand out from ordinary experiences, but also endows it with direction-giving developmental power, which strives to be expressed and which then, in this form, through re-experiencing and emotional exploration, becomes the basis of understanding (Schnädelbach, 1983; Neubert, 1990).

In its popularised form, 'Erlebnis' became a buzzword and a battle cry in the early 20th century. Its pre-conceptional, irrational basic hue, which perceived the mind to be a threat to life, corresponds to the culture-critical, anti-rational mentality of that period. For its proponents it became a means to fight against cultural decline. For its critics, however, it was only an expression of the inevitable modernisation process. Immediately after the war, Max Weber (1995) saw the 'Erlebnis' as a false god who was pervading all street corners, magazines and journals. He said people went to great lengths to have 'Erlebnisse', because no 'Erlebnis' meant no personality. Those who did not get any pretended they did. In the end, it did not matter what kind of 'Erlebnis' it was, it only mattered that one had it. Weber, however, held that personality was formed not through chasing irrational 'Erlebnisse' but through patient and disciplined dedication to a matter outwith oneself. He saw the intensive hunt for 'Erlebnisse' as a regression representative of the self-destructive potential of the modern age. This would make the 'Erlebniskultur' a counter-reaction to the rational demystification of the world.

Walter Benjamin also views the increasing significance of 'Erlebnis' sceptically, partly because it goes along with the devaluation of experience. While experience always seeks the same, he says, 'Erlebnis' seeks the unique and sensational (Benjamin, 1991, p. 198). This comparison indirectly refers to the two poles of modernisation and tradition. While experience is based on tradition and assures its continued existence, 'Erlebnis' is practically the inevitable result of, and enforced by, the modern fragmented lifestyle, which is intensified in big cities. The increased speed of life, the growing anonymity through lack of bonding with others, the ceaseless sensory shock waves from escalating traffic and noise, screaming neon signs and overflowing window displays do not give people peace, time or space to deal with what is happening to them. Given the huge scale of these stimuli, their volatility and randomness, they do not penetrate into people's memory. They remain on the surface and are not transformed into a deeply anchored experience (Makropoulos, 1989).

In defiance of this sociological stance, proponents used genuine 'Erlebnisse' in their fight 'against an intellectualistic civilisation that has become hostile to life, against an education that is shackled by conventions and is alien to life, and for a new awareness of life' (Schnädelbach, 1983, p. 172). The Wilhelmine school system, for example, was also regarded as solidified and alien to life. Progressive pedagogy tried to revitalise schools by means of this empathic 'Erlebnis' (Oelkers, 1992, 1993; Hofer & Oelkers, 1998). It became the synonym for modern pedagogy, albeit revivalists' ideas differed. While one demanded 'that every school lesson be an 'Erlebnis', another lamented that 'nobody knows what "Erlebnis" actually means', because without understanding of what it meant it was impossible to say what its importance was for the school system (Neubert, 1990, p. 11).

The many schools of the progressive education movement at the time could use 'Erlebnis' more freely than regular state schools. Against the backdrop of life philosophy and bourgeois cultural criticism 'Erlebnis' was experimented with, and used as an argument against, the old styles of teaching, i.e. against textbooks and syllabi, against 'chalk and talk' teaching, against repetition and too much reflection, in favour of using more imagination, more creativity and a greater focus on the children. The shining light of the Outward Bound movement, Kurt Hahn, also drew inspiration from the pool of ultra-conservative cultural criticism when he founded his first school. His pedagogical goal was not enlightenment, but he wanted to heal children and society, remedy the physical decay, the loss of care, initiative and sympathy by means of 'Erlebnisse' (Stübig, 2007).

At the foundation of Salem, this therapy through 'Erlebnisse' was subordinated to the revisionist goal of the 'political re-establishment of the [German Empire]' (quoted in Machtan, 2013, p. 483). Through progressive educational methods Salem was developed into a 'stronghold and fortress in the ideological battle against the democratic system of the Weimar Republic . . . ' (ibid. p. 483), because, as Hahn wrote to the historian Hans Delbrück, if Germany were to 'get back on the path to being a world power', it was dependent 'on finding a more worthy generation than the one in 1914 if such an hour were to occur' (quoted in Machtan, 2013, p. 483).

This representation of the first heyday of 'Erlebnis' would be incomplete without mentioning the youth movement 'Wandervogel', the foundation of which was also a reaction to the authoritarian drill structure of the Wilhelmine grammar school. In contrast to the culture of adults, young people, for example, went on self-organised short or long tours at the weekends or during the school holidays, at home or abroad. They did not use 'Erlebnis' for any specific pedagogical purpose, they just followed their urge to go on tour, but evidence shows that these tours remained forever in the memory of these young people as exciting, beautiful, sad, unique or moving 'Erlebnisse'. What becomes apparent here is what is often overlooked by 'Erlebnispädagogen'. 'Erlebnisse' are by-products, beyond pedagogical planning and direction giving, which can come about in the course of implementation. They are emotional states of awareness that follow different laws than those of pedagogy that is focused on methodical rationality.

III

The pedagogy of National Socialism, following that of the Weimar Republic, also was not without 'Erlebnis'. While progressive education introduced 'Erlebnis' into school, the Nazis used it to design their camps, which constituted the second pillar of education besides school. They also easily adapted and integrated activities of the Wandervogel that went beyond pure walking with their own activities. The campfire and other fire rituals, cross-country games, dances and physical exercises, singing accompanied by the guitar, and marching were used in combination with indoctrination in racist and national ideology as propagated by the Führer to form closely knit National Socialist communities. Understandably, post-war Germany at first looked with scepticism at the instrumentalisation of 'Erlebnisse' and at the communities that had played a principal role in its formation. The state school system, as part of the administrated world, remains suspicious of the pedagogically unwieldy term with its associations of spontaneity, irrationality, holism, immediacy and authenticity. The 'Erlebnispädagogik' was, however, finally denazified through Kurt Hahn's therapeutic version, who, in the early 1950s, brought together selected apprentices and grammar school students for four-week courses in the schools he had founded.

IV

Until today, 'Erlebnispädagogik' has never reconnected with the argumentative spirit of its early days. Maybe this theoretical deadlock could be overcome by turning away from the level of consciousness of 'Erleben' and 'Erlebnis' towards the action level, focusing on those activities that are generally connected with 'Erlebnispädagogik' today. Such a change in perspective would lead not only to different theoretical connections, but would also open up a different view of possible educational processes.

The physical practices that are of interest in this respect are, for example, hiking, climbing, sailing, canoeing or rowing. They involve going to landscapes, such as forests, mountains, rivers, lakes and the sea, and spending a number of days there. The point of setting out from home marks two realities at the same time: one is the reality that is left behind, the other is the reality that is visited.

One leaves behind a reality that tries to be a reliable provider of a trouble-free everyday life. This reality is ordered by tried and tested routines, which largely ensure that there are no surprises or disturbances. Here things happen as a matter of course, are familiar and the unfamiliar and uncertainties are avoided. Emotions such as astonishment or fear, which might obstruct action, have therefore lost their significance (see Blumenberg, 2010, on the world of everyday life).

Those who set out to encounter unknown natural spaces need to move away from this way of life. They cross over into another reality, which is full of surprising events. Pieces of equipment may get lost or damaged, storms or thunder storms arise unexpectedly, paths differ from the map, sudden, overwhelming views and prospects occur, group dynamics go crazy, emotions block action and change one's perceptions, there are unknown animals or plants, somebody is injured, etc. What the routines of everyday life manage to hold at bay now become normal occurrences. Reality reveals a host of new possibilities and opportunities, and can be very unpredictable. When reality becomes so temporary or provisional, individuals become uncertain of how to deal with it;[1] they are at the mercy of this reality.

Why should one exchange a comfortable, certain reality for such an uncertain, strenuous one? In the first sentence in his Metaphysics, Aristotle points out that human beings by nature seek understanding and knowledge. This means they are curious and take an interest in the unknown. Curiosity causes disquiet in the individual, which can be relieved only by the unfamiliar. The unfamiliar can be gained only by giving up the familiar and certainty. In return, curiosity and departure hold the promise of a better future, which is characterised by greater knowledge and experience. Until recently, there was a close elective affinity between acquiring knowledge and undergoing an adventure. The complete title of the 'Alpine Journal' reads: 'A Record of Mountain Adventures and Scientific Observation'.

The departure, or the packing of the rucksack, is an indication that the individuals have already let go of the familiar and act in imaginative anticipation of what the future will bring. Packing for the departure into the unknown means choosing between necessary and unnecessary items, and therefore it is not routine. Rather it can be classified as belonging to the ascetic tradition of self-scrutiny. In order to be able to make decisions about what to take in the face of the available space in the rucksack, individuals have to gain a clear understanding about their present way of life and about their uncertain future way of life. Who am I at the moment and who do I want to be in the future? The fully packed rucksack is the symbolised answer. It is the expression of the ascetic choice to do without, and of the ensuing principle of 'Omnia mea, mecum porto'. The material restrictions make greater demands on the individual's self-confidence in being able to manage tricky situations with the minimal amount of resources. For this self-confidence, the sociologist Oevermann (1998) has coined the functional term of structural optimism, which ensures that in critical situations individuals do not lose the confidence that things will turn out well even when it seems that all bad things are happening together – in case of doubt, it will turn out well. Equipped with structural optimism it will be easier to confront the future that has become open and uncertain; it can be perceived as a challenge rather than a threat.

V

The curious individual turns into an individual of 'Bildung',[2] an individual who cannot be content with what he or she is and who, therefore, needs help from the outside to gain knowledge and promote self-development. Once s/he has set out, s/he receives this support from the as yet unknown obstacles hidden in the new reality that reveal themselves. The interruptions provoked by these events demonstrate that the tried-and-tested routines are no longer useful and that individuals must confront and deal with the obstacles to continue the action. This break-down of routines Oevermann describes as crisis provoking since there are no tried-and-tested routines available for an immediate solution of the problem that has arisen.[3] This is why the interruptions divert the individual's attention to the unique quality of the situation. The events grip the individuals who cannot extract themselves from them. They are forced to deal with the situation. They are obliged to leave the security of their routines.

Following the crisis system developed by objective hermeneutics (Oevermann, 2004a), one can categorise the great variety of unexpected events that can occur on adventurous tours into three crisis types, as follows.

1   The decidedly most common crisis that occurs when passing through unknown natural spaces is the *traumatic crisis* caused by obstacles arising from outer or inner nature. Feelings of pow-erlessness in the face of mighty nature, aching joints and blistered feet, the overwhelming sensation of happiness after a successful ascent, the warmth of the camp fire, strong tailwinds or headwinds, not only bring home to individuals the very physical nature of their existence, from which they cannot escape, but also show them the limits that nature has set for them. The 'brutal facts' of inner and outer nature forces them to adopt an attitude that might, on the one hand, lead to a dietetic of 'being on the way'[4] and, on the other hand, to a practice of respectful and mimetic treatment of nature.

2   The second type of crisis is caused by events that demand decision making. When being on the way such events frequently occur when reorientation becomes necessary or when sudden changes in weather require individuals to seek different destinations. Decision-making breaks the reflex arc. It creates distance and gives individuals time to deal with the approaching future. Now there is space to think up and play out hypothetically different possibilities. The structurally critical nature of the situation is that, for the selection of one of these, there are no routines that relieve individuals of the need to make a decision and that, at the same time, a decision has to be made. In this decision-making process the myth of modern individuals who are open to the world, who can prove themselves and who are able to take charge of their own future, is re-enacted.

3   If landscapes and their geology, flora and fauna are meant to be more than just the back-drop, the necessary stage for paddling, sailing or hiking, or if views, valleys, mountains, trees, clouds, soaring eagles, the sound of running water or wind, birdsong, the starry night sky, and the feelings and moods these phenomena arouse, are also to be contemplated for their own sake, one must interrupt the course of the activities. Only when freed from practical neces-sities and worries, unhurried and exclusively, will unbiased reflection and appreciation of the phenomena become possible, and new and unexpected aspects of them can be discovered. In turn, the landscape will become open for aesthetic and sensual appreciation only if it is freed from being instrumentalised for specific purposes – for example, hikers cease to assess the ter-rain in terms of how strenuous or easy it will be. Only when the fruit of the apple tree is not seen any more solely as edible, will the tree set free its play of colours, its forms and scent, and unlock its mythological associations.[5] In the practice of being on the way, traumatic crises and decision-making crises are inevitable. They are constitutive ingredients of adventure. Leisurely contemplation within adventure is somewhat of an antithesis for which time and space are not always available.

The critical situations in adventure are not over on arrival at the destination. They live on, at night, in the tales told in the hut, at the camp fire, or in tents and in wilderness huts. The more conscious the crisis has been, the more urgently it needs to be told. As St Matthew (12, 34) says, 'for out of the abundance of the heart the mouth speaketh'. In the pressure-free mode of the practice, the crises that have been lived through can be put at a distance and in the interplay between narrative and listening, questions and answers can be reproduced cognitively and can be understood. The new experience can be reinforced and integrated in the existing store of routines. This kind of narrative reflection does not take place during an artificially contrived meeting, but develops in a practical way naturally from the intensive events.

VI

Thus it becomes clear that the structural core of the adventurous being on the way is an inter-play between crisis and routine. While the tried and tested reproduces itself in routines until it is called in to question by the sudden intervention of an event, dealing with the ensuing crisis must produce something new to restore the power of routine. In this process the individuals do not only experience something new about the obstructive part of the material world they are confronted with, they also experience something about themselves because when resolving a crisis they are not only confronted with the world but also with themselves. They experience something about how they dealt with the crisis and about how they accepted and engaged with a suddenly open future, whether they reacted hesitantly, fearfully, with help, level-headedly, self-confidently, etc. Experience with the outside world may always also be a form of self-enlightenment. However, this is not the aim but a by-product. The primary focus remains the confrontation with the material world. This dual aspect of gaining experience also means that the experiences individuals have are always specific to themselves, they cannot be transferred as a whole to other individuals. What can be transferred is only a propositional share, which must be separated from the subjective, personal share (Oevermann, 2002).

Since the crisis is an event in which something new is formed, which forces the established to transform itself, it is also the place where individuals undergo their 'Bildung'. It needs something strange, obstructive, something that is not identical with their usual routines, to promote their 'Bildungs' process. It takes the intrusion of strangeness to shake up what is familiar and taken for granted, to bring forward objections against the established and to prevent its confirmation. The self-confident individual who ultimately emerges has freed him/herself from the initial fright of the sudden and unexpected intrusion of the event and has autonomously and successfully over-come the crisis that ensued. S/he may not be totally independent from the recognition of others but is not dependent on them because of this sureness and self-confidence.[6]

VII

In contrast to 'Erlebnis', which in the end is a phenomenon of excitement that occurs practically automatically at unusual events, the adventurous being on the way is a cultural pattern, a playful social practice of dealing with curiosity, thirst for knowledge and 'Bildung' through experience. As a cultural action model it belongs to the sphere of the objective mind. It is a form of practice in which all obstacles turn the world into a puzzle that has to be solved, because otherwise self-determined goals cannot be reached. Causing disquiet in this way puts pressure on individuals' routines to prove themselves and stimulates the 'Bildungs' process. Embracing this action pattern is a habitus that sees the uncertain and open future of life not as a risk but as a chance to deal with obstacles, uncertainty and the unfamiliar with an open mind and with the confidence of being able to find a solution.

At first glance, neither adventure nor 'Erlebnis' seem to have any real significance or function for the continuity of the community or society, quite in contrast to challenges in working and family life. However, if one looks at it from the point of view of how necessary it is for society to create normative bonds to curb disintegration, adventure belongs to those cultural practices that produce surplus benefits that hold the community together. The attitudes and values of the adventurous being on the way represent an action model that is most attractive for modern societies. Every adventure confirms and demonstrates direction and action patterns. Its political dimension, as a function of values and orientation, takes place practically unconsciously, behind the individuals' backs.

Finally, although being on the adventurous way, as a playful frame for the interplay between crisis and routine, is a place of 'Bildung', it cannot be used as a pedagogical tool and neither can 'Erlebnis'. This is partly because the prescribed curricular framework of education largely suppresses any individual act of goal setting, and also that traumatic crises caused by the brutal facts of inner and outer nature cannot be avoided. However, to demand traumatic crises as a pedagogical component of being on the adventurous way, as in the Klotzmärsche of the Wandervogel – as violence against and domination over inner nature – would turn pedagogy into a black art.

The physical aspects of adventure overtly push the fundamental dilemma of violence and pain into the foreground when something new emerges from nature. Suffering that stands before the fulfilment of a promise is also the theme of one of the original scenes of the concept of 'Bildung', the exodus (Boenicke, 2000). The three-phased nature of being on the adventurous way, departure, proving one's worthiness in crises and fulfilment of the promise, corresponds to the three biblical phases of the exodus from Egypt, the many long years in the desert and the arrival in the promised land. The metaphor of 'desert' contains the ideas of the actual hardship and suffering, and also the constantly present temptation to give up the abstract promise of freedom and 'Bildung', which still lie in a far distant future.

The phase of proving oneself not only entails making great efforts in order to learn, it also requires the possibly hurtful understanding that, in addition to effort, 'Bildung' and autonomy are dependent on something that is unknown and non-identical.

Notes

1　Activities which deal with these conditions of reality in a playful way are generally called adventure. The Latin root of the term, 'advenire', comprises the meaning of approach as well as that of befalling.

2　The German language makes a difference between 'Bildung' and 'Erziehung' (education). 'Bildung', like 'Erlebnis', can be translated into English only with great difficulty, if at all. With reference to Herder, who was influenced by Shaftesbury in his ideas of 'Bildung', one could translate the term possibly by 'self-formation'. The difference between the two terms could be exemplified by the two recommendations 'become who you can be' for 'Bildung' and 'become who you are supposed to be' for education. Education subsumes its recipient under assumptions imposed from the outside. The direction 'become who you are', which is probably to be attributed to Pindar, also subordinates the individual under a predetermined destiny, one that comes not from the outside but from inside. (All individuals can do is fulfil their destiny.) Erziehung contains the word 'Zucht' (discipline), which points to strict subordination to something predetermined (Meyer-Drawe, 1999). To ensure the realisation of this predetermined goal is the reason for the development of the whole educational apparatus: school, curriculum, lesson plans, exams, punishments, etc. While the methodological and didactic shaping of education accepts the condition of the restricted time frame at school and is designed to ensure that pupils can absorb their subject matters smoothly and without interruptions, 'Bildung' takes its orientation from the 'timeless', leisurely pursuit of, i.e. from the unhurried, crisis-related (about crisis, see note 3) devotion to the matter that needs deconstructing. One last point about the difference: in German one can say that children and dogs are 'wohl erzogen' (well educated), but not that dogs are 'wohl gebildet'.

3　The related pair of terms of crisis and routine and their connection with the process of 'Bildung' has been taken from the theory and research programme of objective hermeneutics (see Oevermann, 1991, 1998, 2001, 2004a).

4　'Being on the way' (Unterwegssein, in German) is in contrast to 'Reise' (journey), which generally leads to associations with tourism. People follow prescribed categories that impede their own initiative, such as travel destination, travel itinerary, travel guide, travel programme, etc. 'Being on the way' is meant to direct attention to the more fundamental anthropological situation of transition that the human being as 'homo viator' finds him/herself in. It is an uncertain time, which points to the process of Bildung but also to the mythical narrative of Bildung of the exodus, especially to the arduous crossing of the desert.

5   If one is at leisure things not only open themselves to aesthetic-sensual perception. Contemplating the biological, physical and geographical laws of the objects also needs to be done (Oevermann 2004a). Atmospheric contexts are interesting in this respect, such as dusk and dawn, sunrise and sunset, the full moon behind moving clouds, thunderstorms and storms, a stream meandering through a valley, which make up a considerable part of the attraction of being on the way. They are particularly well suited to exemplify how both approaches, the conceptual perception and the reconstruction of the laws of natural sciences, on the one hand, and the sensual perception that stimulates the imagination, provokes emotions and changes moods, on the other, can be joined and intensified into a comprehensive understanding of landscape and nature.

6   From an ontogenetic point of view, adventurous undertakings are particularly attractive for children and young people because they are a playful expression of a part of their lives. Both developmental stages can be understood as moratoria that are still free from the seriousness of life and in which the individuals can prepare for adult life without disturbance. While increasingly fewer surprises break in to the continuum of actions when getting older, interruptions in the form of crises are common in the everyday life of children and young people. Therefore, fictitious and real adventures are opportunities to deal in a playful way with the interplay between crisis and routine. Children practically live in the mode of adventure since everything is new for these newcomers to the world. As a matter of principle, at birth their futures became open and the strange and unfamiliar have become irrevocable facts of their lives. A retreat to the original form of connection with their mother is not possible any more. In order to change their situation they have to follow their curiosity and explore their unfamiliar surroundings, they have to move towards the places where they can build and accumulate experience, where they undergo physically based experiences. Since in this exploration traumatic crises are inevitable, there is the danger of being over-protected, which may hinder the development towards more independence (Oevermann, 2004b). In the 'in-between-land' of youth between childhood and adulthood, adventure and the character of the hero represent the ontogenetic material of experience of this developmental stage, such as leaving the familiarity and security of the family, the departure into an unknown future, the trying out of alternative life plans, the change to relying on their own self-responsible performance. (About the function of adventure during childhood and youth, see Becker, 2010, 2013.) In adulthood being on the adventurous way can serve as a self-induced ascetic test of authenticity and lifestyle routines.

Acknowledgement

Translated by Gudrun Vill-Debney.

References

Becker, P. (2010). By the campfire and on tour. Unpublished manuscript.
Becker, P. (2013). Frühe Bildung in Zeiten ihrer Ökonomisierung und unter dem Druck der pädagogischen Kompetenzwende. In Ders. (u.a.) *Abenteuer, Natur und frühe Bildung* (pp. 131–189). Opladen: Barbara Budrich.
Benjamin, W. (1991). Die Wiederkehr des Flaneurs. In Ders. (u.a.) *Gesammelte Schriften*. Bd.III, Frankfurt/M: Suhrkamp.
Bischof, N. (n.d.). *Das Kraftfeld der Mythen*. München o.J: Piper.
Blumenberg, H. (2010). *Theorie der Lebenswelt*. Berlin: Suhrkamp.
Boenicke, R. (2000). *Bildung, absoluter Durchgangspunkt*. Weinheim: Beltz.
Hofer, C. & Oelkers, J. (Eds.) (1998). *Schule als Erlebnis*. Braunschweig: Westermann.
Honneth, A. (2004). *Desintegration*. Frankfurt/M: Fischer.
Machtan, L. (2013). *Prinz Max von Baden*. Berlin: Suhrkamp.
Makropoulos, M. (1989). *Modernität als ontogenetischer Ausnahmezustand*. München: Fink.
Meyer-Drawe, K. (1999). Zum metaphorischen Gehalt von 'Bildung' und 'Erziehung'. *ZfPäd 45*, 161–175.
Neubert, W. (1990). *Das Erlebnis in der Pädagogik (1930)*. Lüneburg: Ziel.
Oelkers, J. (1992). Kann 'Erleben' erziehen? *Zeitschrift für Erlebnispädagogik*, 3–13.

Oelkers, J. (1993). 'Erlebnispädagogik': Ursprünge und Entwicklungen. In Homfeldt, H.G. (Ed.) *Erlebnispädagogik* (pp. 7–26). Hohengehren: Schneider.

Oevermann, U. (1991). Genetischer Strukturalismus und das sozialwissenschaftliche Problem der Erklärung der Entstehung des Neuen. In S.Müller-Dohm (Ed.) *Jenseits der Utopie*, (pp. 267–336). Frankfurt/M.: Suhrkamp.

Oevermann, U. (1998). *Vorläufiges Résumée über: 'Gemeinsamkeiten und Differenzen von religiöser,* ästhetischer *Natur- und Leiberfahrung'.* Unpublished manuscript.

Oevermann, U. (2001). Die Philosophie von Charles Sanders Peirce als Philosophie der Krise. In H.-J. Wagner (Ed.) *Objektive Hermeneutik und Bildung des Subjekts* (pp. 209–246) Weilerswist: Velbrück.

Oevermann, U. (2002). Wissen, Glauben, Überzeugung – Ein Vorschlag des Wissens aus krisentheoretischer Sicht. Unpublished manuscript.

Oevermann, U. (2004a). Adorno als empirischer Sozialforscher im Blickwinkel der heutigen Methodenlage. In A. Gruschka & U. Oevermann (Eds.) *Die Lebendigkeit der kritischen Gesellschaftstheorie* (pp. 189–234). Wetzlar: Büchse der Pandora.

Oevermann, U. (2004b). Sozialisation als Krisenbewältigung. In D. Geulen & H. Veith (Eds.) *Sozialisationstheorie interdisziplinär: Aktuelle Perspektiven.* Stuttgart: Lucius & Lucius.

Schnädelbach, H. (1983). *Philosophie in Deutschland 1831–1933.* Frankfurt/M: Suhrkamp.

Stübig, H. (2007). Kurt Hahn und seine Erlebnistherapie. In P. Becker (u.a.) *Abenteuer, Erlebnisse und die Pädagogik* (pp. 99–114). Opladen: Barbara Budrich.

Voswinkel, S. (2013). Gekaufte Wertschätzung. In A. Honneth (Ed.) *Strukturwandel der Anerkennung* (pp. 121–154). Frankfurt/M: Campus.

Weber, M. (1995). *Wissenschaft als Beruf.* Stuttgart: Reclam.

3

Environmental concerns and outdoor studies

Nature as fosterer

Johan Öhman

ÖREBRO UNIVERSITY

Klas Sandell

KARLSTAD UNIVERSITY

Outdoor studies has long been regarded as an important tool for public environmental concern (e.g. Hammerman, Hammerman & Hammerman, 2001; Place, 2004; Sandell & Öhman, 2010). In the last decade several studies have been conducted on the relationship between outdoor experiences and environmentalism, with an emphasis on the effect that participation in outdoor education has on environmental knowledge, pro-environmental attitudes and behaviour, and their interconnection (see Sandell & Öhman, 2013).

The aim of this chapter is to discuss the evolvement – roots and changes – of outdoor studies involving nature encounters and their possible implications for environmental concern. This has been, and still is, one the major themes in the very rich pedagogic tradition of using nature as a fosterer. In the outline of the chapter we first focus on the subtleties of environmental concern with the aid of an environmentally historic model of how care for nature and environmental protection has gradually developed over the last century. We continue by giving a brief overview of the development of nature as fosterer in general. In this overview we specifically focus on the role of outdoor studies within environmental education. Finally, we deepen this perspective and look ahead by suggesting six potentials of outdoor education as an environmental pedagogy.

The evolvement of the current distanced relation to nature

'Environmental concern' can mean many different things. One way of acquiring a deeper understanding of the different social perspectives of environmental issues with regard to what being 'environmentally concerned' means is to give a brief environmentally historic review of today's urbanised industrial societies.

One of the most striking changes to be highlighted by such a review is that in industrial countries during the 20th century the general public's everyday encounters with nature gradually changed from being direct to indirect. Only a century ago a large part of the population made their living from agriculture, forestry and fishing, with concrete daily and 'bodily' experiences of weather and wind, animals and plants. In addition, even if they did not work on the land, the vast majority of people had to chop and carry their wood and water, make do with an outside dry toilet, empty the slops, etc. A 'through-the-wall' society gradually developed in the industrial countries, which eventually spread to other parts of the world. This is a society where all the important parts of the ecosystem go 'through the wall' in the form of wires, cables and pipes for lighting, heating, water and sewage. This has taken place in parallel with urbanisation and while employment has changed from being based on the land, via industrial production, to service and communication. The fact that we often regard 'society' and 'nature' as two separate clear-cut entities says a great deal about our current perceptions (see Sandell, Öhman & Östman, 2005, including a discussion about the concept of nature).

In parallel with other forms of modernisation and the changed relationship to the landscape, a discussion has arisen about the consequences that this development will have on nature and the environment, and the responsibility of society for these consequences. In short, it is a discussion that has gone from *nature protection*, via *nature conservation*, towards post-war *environmental control*, to the current buzz words around *sustainable development* and climate change, which includes the ongoing tension concerning the need to also include more radical perspectives with '*alternative*' development ideals (see Figure 3.1).

This process has been characterised by a successive widening and deepening. Initially, around the turn of the 20th century, it was mainly about deciding where particularly valuable forms of nature and animal species were situated, and then protecting them from industrialisation by means of national parks and protection orders (*nature protection*). Later, through a more nuanced picture of the interplay between nature and culture in the landscape, it became increasingly important to decide which landscape values to take care of (*nature conservation*). Due to post-war ecological

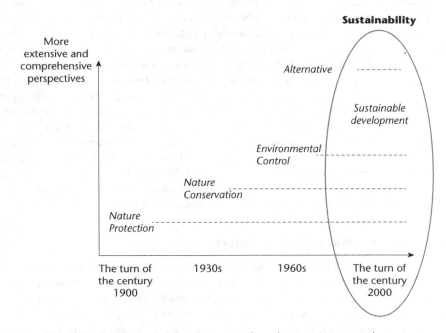

Figure 3.1   The main themes in the development of modern environmental concern

Note: even though these perspectives can largely be associated with specific periods of time, some sources of inspiration go further back in time and, as shown in the illustration, have an influence on later periods (Sandell *et al.*, 2005)

insights that society as a whole had to be included, the perspective was then widened from nature to environment. In these environmental discussions about exploitation of raw materials and the increased use of poisonous substances, the links between social development, consumption and the relationship to nature became much more obvious (*environmental control*). In today's discussions about *sustainable development,* in principle all aspects of society are relevant. This applies to everything from ethical approach, the economy and global relations to private consumption and lifestyle, all of which are communicated and discussed in the media to the extent that in every affluent person's living room and computer the entire world is both immediate and tangible. Today's discussions about the climate, where city-dwelling, internet-connected service workers might worry about melting inland ice, can be seen as an illustration of how much society has changed compared with the concerns of farmers, fishermen and foresters in the early 20th century, who instead worried about how the weather would determine whether or not food would appear on the table.

Of special interest with regard to the social and pedagogic aspects of the modern environmental debate is the criticism of mainstream development that arose during the 1970s. This was when radical environmental groups began to demand '*alternatives*', which initially represented a negation of the then conventional development strategy, but which is now a recurrent theme with regard to energy, food, trade, and so on. It is noteworthy that, in general, the other themes of environmental concern fail to question the fundamental values and principles of modern development and instead focus on the symptoms.

A good illustration of the friction that exists within the current aspirations for sustainability is Norwegian philosopher Arne Naess's (e.g. 1989; cf. Reed & Rothenberg, 1993) differentiation between 'shallow' and 'deep' ecology. He describes shallow ecology as combating pollution, and striving for a more efficient distribution of resources and a stabilising of the global population. He points out that advocates of this approach tend to offer narrow technical and scientific explanations. According to Naess, in addition to the requirements of the shallow movement, the deep ecological movement represents a large number of much more radical perspectives, such as a classless society, autonomy, decentralisation, self-support, protection of all cultures, respect for life, etc.

An important overall intellectual construction of the historical process described above is the tension between rational development in the name of modernisation and an alternative progress related to Romanticism's critique of civilisation, and the pointing out of its sordid materialism and blind belief in technology. This is why we now have a situation where 'being environmentally engaged' can be said to consist of elements of all the main themes that we have described as characteristic of a growing environmental engagement. So, when we speak about the consensus-like concept of 'sustainability', it actually hides important ideological tensions between 'sustainable development' – solutions within the system – and 'alternative progress' – a change of system. This historical displacement from direct to indirect encounters with nature, and the parallel widening and deepening of the nature conservation and environmental debate, is the actual framework – the rationale – for the relation between outdoor studies and environmental concern that is the focus of this chapter.

Outdoor studies using nature as fosterer

Outdoor studies, and especially pedagogical encounters with nature, can be said to have developed partly as a reaction to, and partly as a reflection of, the environmentally historical development and discussion outlined above. Outdoor studies can be said to form part of the experience-based and action-oriented tradition that has its philosophical roots in Aristotle's empiricism and ideas about experience as the basis for learning. The above-named Romanticism was also an important framework for the establishment of outdoor life, nature-tourism and outdoor education some 100–150 years ago. Jean-Jacques Rousseau's formative idea of natural learning through direct physical experience has been a particularly important source of inspiration, as have other thinkers, such as Henry David Thoreau and Aldo Leopold.

When outdoor life and nature-based tourism became more clearly established at the end of the 19th century, the interest in experiences in nature was also often clearly linked to pedagogical ambitions. The activities of the tourist associations that began with the establishment of the Norwegian tourist association in 1868 can be seen as an illustration of this. At that time the idea was that instructions, information, cabins, etc. would facilitate the experience of nature and culture – on site – in the landscape. During the 20th century, the theoretical starting points of this action- and experience-based tradition were developed further by educationalists who advocated the benefits of practical knowledge. In short, it can be said that this method and theoretical tradition has been about moving from the classroom into the natural and cultural landscape in order to enrich teaching and learning. The fundamental idea has been to use the outdoor environment as a way of learning directly from reality, where phenomena appear in their natural contexts, in order to increase awareness about the environment and life (see e.g. Hammerman *et al.*, 2001; Ogilvie, 2005). Important motives have also been the strengthening of pupils' own motivation and making teaching more effective.

An example of how this so-called 'reform pedagogics', with contact with nature as a vital element, is put in to practice is the setting up of the Scout Movement around 1900 with the aim of educating young people in 'citizenship', outdoor life and nature encounters ('woodcraft'). Experiences, education and behaviour were linked, such as: 'By continually watching animals in their natural state, one gets to like them too well to shoot them' (Baden-Powell, 1910, p. 20). Another important source of inspiration in the early Scout Movement – also illustrating the above-mentioned tension between modernisation and alternative progress – was Ernest Thompson Seton (1906/1902). From his 'Woodcraft Indians', inspired by the North American indigenous population, Seton was more radical and saw outdoor life more as a goal in itself rather than just a method.

Also in school and within education, outdoor education in the landscape has long been advocated. In his *Didactica Magna* (1657/1907), Johan Amos Comenius (1592–1670) draws attention to the fact that 'Men must, as far as possible, be taught to become wise by studying the heavens, the earth, oaks, and beeches, but not by studying books; that is to say, they must learn to investigate things themselves, and not the observations that other people have made about the things' (p. 150). With regard to this interest in 'hands on'-education, we can also see that biological and geographical excursions have historical roots that stretch back to the days of Carl Linnaeus in the 18th century. In the early 20th century, progressive educationalists, inspired by John Dewey's pragmatic philosophy, talked about the importance of concept formation in school by having direct contact with the studied phenomena (Quay & Seaman, 2013). This alternative educational tradition, where knowledge is sought in encounters with a reality outside school, can be seen as a criticism of the theoretical, abstract and linguistic ideals that dominated schools in the Western cultural sphere. From this perspective, learning in nature can be regarded as a compensatory form of knowledge and a complement to theoretical learning (Dahlgren & Sczcepanski, 1998). One talked about the 'extended classroom' and learning came to be seen as a process, of which problem solving was an integral part and where the pupils' emotional, physical, aesthetic and cognitive sides would be stimulated.

The role of outdoor studies within three traditions of environmental education

Already in the early 1900s the expressed aims of the outdoor education offered in school can be seen to reflect environmental education. At first it was mainly about fostering a consideration of nature so that pupils would develop a love of animals and could be in nature without polluting it or destroying it – ambitions that reflect what is described above as *nature protection* and *nature conservation*. The role that outdoor studies has and has had within environmental education has also changed in line with the changes that have taken place over the decades in environmental education.

In order to deepen our understanding of the various environmental education perspectives that outdoor studies can have today, we will place them relative to three so-called selective traditions that have taken shape within environmental education over the past forty years. By selective tradition we mean the regular patterns of choice of content, and ways of working that have been created over time in a specific educational activity (Williams, 1973). Empirical studies of environmental education show three such selective environmental education traditions: a *fact-based*, a *normative* and a *pluralistic* (Sandell *et al.* 2005; Öhman, 2008; Table 3.1). These traditions have been developed in succession, although all three can be found in today's environmental education. The traditions that are accounted for here are based on Swedish studies, although similar traditions have also been identified in countries with similar education systems (Sund, 2015).

Fact-based environmental education

At the beginning of the 1970s outdoor education became a more obvious part of the developing environmental education (Quay & Seaman, 2013). The first selective environmental education tradition to take shape can be called *fact-based*. Here, a lack of knowledge was seen as the most important cause of the environmental problems of the day – it was considered that the general public knew very little about how nature worked and the impact that modern society had on ecosystems. The main task of environmental education was thus to communicate scientific facts and models that could provide increased insights into the environmental problems of the day. In this tradition, values were generally regarded as belonging to the private sphere.

With regard to the outdoor education aspects of this tradition, the science of ecology played an important role. It meant learning through direct inquiry about nature and how humans influenced and altered the system. There are clear links here to the wider environmental engagement of *environmental control*. Here, studies in nature are seen as a way of creating effective and more in-depth learning. An argument for this is that when pupils have a direct encounter with, and can study different phenomena in, a natural setting, they gain a better understanding of and have deeper insights into the complexity of the ecosystem than is possible by simply studying simplified diagrammatic models in textbooks. Another reason is that studies in the outdoors lead to more effective learning – knowledge about nature and the environment becomes more tangible and lasting if you have examined things at first hand. Outdoor studies also means that all the senses can be used, which in turn means that the experience of a phenomenon has several dimensions. In short, this environmental education tradition builds on the supposition that if pupils know how nature and humans interplay with nature, they will act in environmentally friendly ways (examples of research that highlight the relations between nature experiences and environmental knowledge are Bogner, 1998; Eaton, 1998; Bradley, Waliczek & Zajicek, 1999).

Normative environmental education

At the end of the 1970s and beginning of the 1980s environmental education features were radicalised. Outdoor education became an education *in*, *about* and *for* the environment, where 'for' meant 'understanding the relationship of natural resources to world survival'

(Ford, 1981, p. 13). The developing environmental movement grew stronger, as did public opinion and criticism of the industrial society's market economy and the lifestyles that this generated. Many blamed society's basic structure, production system and values for environmental problems, in accordance with the environmental involvement referred to above as *alternative*. The *normative* tradition that developed during this period maintains that the environmental problems are largely due to the lifestyle that has developed in the industrialised and post-industrialised countries. Environmental education therefore aimed to influence pupils so that they developed more environmentally friendly attitudes and values, which in turn could lead to changes in behaviour. This change is seen as both self-evident and essential.

Here, outdoor studies is regarded as an important platform for these changes. Rich and positive experiences of nature, its diversity, beauty and complexity, are expected to lead to nature becoming something that people will want to protect and care for. In this way, outdoor studies also leads to people wanting to change their everyday habits and approaches in ways that reduce the burden on nature and the environment (see Hansson, Öhman & Östman, 2015). The use of outdoor studies within the normative tradition thus builds on a strong belief in the connection between experiences of nature, care for nature and an environmentally friendly way of acting (examples of research linked to this perspective are Ewert, Place & Sibthorp, 2005; Smith-Sebasto & Cavern, 2006; Chawla & Flanders Cushing, 2007).

Pluralistic environmental education

In the last decades of the 20th century the understanding of the nature of environmental problems gradually changed from local to more global and diffuse. This revealed a need to coordinate a more enduring social, economic and ecological development, at the same time as alternatives to the market economy became more remote (Sandell *et al.*, 2005). The complexity that resulted made it more difficult to find obvious solutions to the problems. As already indicated, a tension appeared between those who considered that the problems could be solved within the framework of the present economic system and its prioritised values, and those who thought that a radical change of system was necessary.

The *pluralistic* environmental education tradition can be seen as a consequence of this change of perspective. In this tradition, environmental and sustainability problems are seen as ideological conflicts between different values, approaches and interests. There is also a reluctance to privilege any particular party in these conflicts. The focus is instead on a critical examination of and discussion about the different alternatives that are available (Gough & Scott, 2007; Schinkel, 2009; Öhman & Öhman, 2013).

The education is pluralistic in so far as it highlights as many different points of view as possible in order to create a firm foundation for the pupils' own standpoints. The aim of the education is that the pupils will be competent enough to take an active part in the democratic debate about sustainable development. Important frames of reference are significance to the democratic approach and a multicultural globalised world, where efforts towards a preferential right of interpretation in terms of what is 'right' sustainability can often be challenged (Jickling, 2003).

What role, then, can outdoor studies play in a pluralistic approach? Given that the sustainability problem has become more conflicting, the pedagogical discussion has instead centred on a more complex management of the entire educational situation with regard to environmental fostering in nature (see Lugg, 2007). Here, the focus has been on what is necessary for a more long-term and radical change of people's living patterns and relationships to nature.

This discussion has considered aspects such as the knowledge content, how the encounter with nature takes place, what this looks like and what the starting points for the activity are.

We maintain that direct encounters with nature could have an important role in pluralistic environmental education in that they can create different perspectives of nature, society and our lifestyles than those we usually come up against. However, the perspectives that are created or further developed in these encounters with nature do not necessarily give a 'true' picture of the problem (according to the fact-based tradition) or the 'right' answers to our questions (according to the normative tradition). From a pluralistic environmental education tradition, the whole point of encounters with nature is rather that they open up more possibilities to think about the environment and sustainable development and what this might mean. In this way, the pedagogics could increase the number of voices in the discussion about a sustainable future and anchor these voices in concrete, physical experiences that surpass traditional book-knowledge. The pedagogical encounter with nature would thus play an important democratic role. In Table 3.1 we have summarised the relationship between the role of outdoor education in different selective traditions of environmental education and their connections to the themes of environmental concern described in Figure 3.1.

Six potentials of outdoor education as an environmental pedagogue

To conclude, we will describe in more depth how we believe outdoor studies can contribute to the most recently developed environmental education tradition – the pluralistic. We do this by looking ahead and suggesting six different environmental education potentials that we think direct encounters with nature can have within such an educational context. These potentials are inspired by our previous studies of Swedish outdoor education and environmental history, and are developed in more detail in Sandell and Öhman (2010) (see also Sandell & Öhman, 2013).

1. An experience-based knowledge of nature

When we learn about nature through a direct encounter we also involve ourselves in knowledge. In this way nature is not reduced to facts but can also have aesthetic, moral, practical or

Table 3.1 The relationship between the selective traditions of environmental education, outdoor studies and environmental concern

Selective tradition	Purpose	Role of outdoor studies	Theme of environmental concern
Pre-environmental education (ee)	Respect for nature	Establish nature-friendly norms	Nature protection and Nature conservation
Fact-based ee 1970–	To transfer scientific facts	Deepen ecological knowledge	Environmental control
Normative ee	To change attitudes and behaviour	Rich nature experiences- Care for nature- Environmentally friendly behaviour	Alternative development
Pluralistic ee 1990–	Critical examination of different alternatives	Expanding the perspectives	Sustainability (Alternative –Sustainable development)

emotional implications. This kind of knowledge is important, partly because it broadens the perception of nature and partly because it creates a relationship to nature that can have significance for future judgements and decisions (see also Bonnett, 2007).

2. A relational ethics

The experiences that people have in connection with outdoor education can form the basis for a relational ethics, where people's emotional and existential experiences lay the foundation for ethical reflections (see Kronlid & Öhman, 2013). In an educational activity that involves direct encounters with nature, a number of situations can arise that lead to a spontaneous care for animals and plants, where people identify themselves both with the individual creature or plant and with nature as a whole (Andersson & Öhman, 2015). We think that discussions about, and reflections on, such experiences can have considerable significance for young people's environmental moral development and environmental ethical awareness.

3. An existential perspective

We have already indicated that the complexity of environmental and sustainability problems requires measures that involve ecological, economic and social perspectives. In our view, the encounter with nature can play an important role by the addition of a fourth, *existential*, perspective (see Quay, 2013). The complexity of sustainable development in its full breadth asks for depth in its underpinnings, and here the feelings of peace and contentment that can arise in connection with longer periods in nature, e.g. hiking or canoeing trips (Isberg & Isberg, 2007), could be important sources of inspiration for existential perspectives. For example, such experiences can lead to an ethical position where caring about nature is not only a matter of securing future human generations' material standards but that connectedness to nature can be a quality of life involving so many other creatures.

4. Human ecology in practice

In the introduction we drew attention to the fact that most people in the industrialised world live a life that at least at a superficial level is completely separated from nature (see also Louv, 2011). Outdoor studies can be said to represent a reconnection to nature. Pedagogical encounters with nature enable people in a modern urban society an opportunity to directly and tangibly – and with your own body – experience affinity with nature and our dependence on nature in order to meet our basic needs (Sandell *et al.*, 2005).

5. 'Rich life with simple means'

Outdoor studies can play an important ideological role by offering a position from which the everyday life, the modern lifestyle and society's development can be observed critically (see Nicol, 2014). This position is based on the idea that long sojourns in nature can offer an alternative and valuable experience – 'a rich life with simple means', where meaningfulness, quality of life and pleasure are not linked to consumption, material standards or economic reward after basic needs are fulfilled, but to physical and mental freedom, community and encounters with nature (Henderson & Vikander, 2007; Isberg & Isberg, 2007). Thus, this is illustrative that proximity to nature can encourage and influence a decrease in pressure on natural resources.

6. Spatial relations

Our dependence on place is a basic feature in all sustainability discussions and here outdoor studies can serve as an important reminder (Tuan, 1974/1990; Massey & Jess, 1995). For example, this can happen when people are able to practically experience and use local, traditional and tried-and-tested knowledge that is adapted to the specific characteristics of the landscape – how different places use the landscape. These can serve as pedagogic illustrations of people's ongoing spatial relationship to the environment (e.g. Greunewald & Smith, 2008; Hill, 2013).

The connections between sustainable development, mobility and spatial relation can also be said to have a deeper meaning in terms of democracy. From a democratic perspective, the general public's perceptions, motivation and initiatives are crucial for the long-term acceptance and impact of environmental policy. Here, personal experiences in the landscape play an important role – personal landscape relationships that give human ecological references to people's dependence on the environment and how we, in a responsible way, ought to deal with that which is 'common' so that a more sustainable future can be created.

References

Andersson, K. & Öhman, J. (2015). Moral relations in encounters with nature. *Journal of Adventure Education and Outdoor Learning.* DOI: 10.1080/14729679.2015.1035292.

Baden-Powell, R.S.S. (1910). *Scouting for Boys: A Handbook for Instruction in Good Citizenship* (revised edn, 3rd impression). London: Arthur Pearson Ltd.

Bogner, F.X. (1998). The influence of short-term outdoor ecology education on long-term variables of environmental perspective. *Journal of Environmental Education, 24*(4), 17–30.

Bonnett, M. (2007). Environmental education and the issue of nature. *Journal of Curriculum Studies, 39*(6), 707–721.

Bradley, J.C., Waliczek, T.M. & Zajicek, J.M. (1999). Relationship between environmental knowledge and environmental attitude of high school students. *Journal of Environmental Education, 30*(3), 17–21.

Chawla, L. & Flanders Cushing, D. (2007). Education for strategic environmental behaviour. *Environmental Education Research, 13*(4), 437–452.

Comenius, J.A. (1657/1907). *Didactica Magna.* London: Adam and Charles Black.

Dahlgren, L.O. & Szczepanski, A. (1998). *Outdoor Education: Literary Education and Sensory Experience: An Attempt at Defining the Identity of Outdoor Education.* Linköping: Linköping University, Sweden.

Eaton, D. (1998). *Cognitive and Affective Learning in Outdoor Education.* Toronto: Department of Curriculum, Teaching and Learning, University of Toronto.

Ewert, A., Place, G. & Sibthorp, J. (2005). Early life outdoor experiences and an individual's environmental attitudes. *Leisure Sciences, 27*, 225–239.

Ford, P.M. (1981). *Principles and Practices of Outdoor/Environmental Education.* New York: Wiley.

Gough, S. & Scott, W. (2007). *Higher Education and Sustainable Development: Paradox and Possibility.* Abingdon: Routledge.

Gruenewald, D.A. & Smith, G.A. (2008). *Place-based Education: In the Global Age.* New York: Lawrence Erlbaum.

Hammerman, D.R., Hammerman, W.M. & Hammerman, E.L. (2001). *Teaching in the Outdoors.* Danville, IL: Interstate Publishers.

Hansson, P., Öhman, J. & Östman, L. (2015). Reading the outdoors – an analysis of the Swedish outdoor environmental and sustainability education discourse-practice. In P. Hansson (Ed.) *Text, Place and Mobility. Investigations of Outdoor Education, Ecocriticism and Environmental Meaning Making.* Uppsala: Acta Universitatis Upsaliensis.

Henderson, B. & Vikander, N. (Eds.) (2007). *Nature First: Outdoor Life the Friluftsliv Way.* Toronto: Natural Heritage Books.

Hill, A. (2013). The place of experience and the experience of place: intersections between sustainability education and outdoor learning. *Australian Journal of Environmental Education, 29*, 18–32.

Isberg, R. & Isberg, S. (2007). *Simple Life 'Friluftsliv': People Meet Nature.* Victoria, Canada, and Oxford, UK: Trafford Publishing.

Jickling, B. (2003). Environmental education and environmental advocacy. Revisited. *Journal of Environmental Education, 34*(2), 20–27.

Kronlid, D. & Öhman, J. (2013). An environmental ethical conceptual framework for research on sustainability and environmental education. *Environmental Education Research, 19*(1), 21–44.

Louv, R. (2011). *The Nature Principle: Human Restoration and the End of Nature-deficit Disorder.* Chapel Hill, NC: Algonquin Books of Chapel Hill.

Lugg, A. (2007). Developing sustainability-literate citizens through outdoor learning: Possibilities for outdoor education in higher education. *Journal of Adventure Education & Outdoor Learning, 7*(2), 97–112.

Massey, D. & Jess, P. (Eds.) (1995). *A Place in the World? Places, Cultures and Globalization.* Oxford: Open University.

Naess, A. (1989). *Ecology, Community and Lifestyle: Outline of an Ecosophy* (trans. and revised by Rothenberg, D.). Cambridge: Cambridge University Press (original: Økologi og filosofi, Oslo, 1973).

Nicol, R. (2014). Entering the fray: The role of outdoor education in providing nature-based experiences that matter. *Educational Philosophy and Theory, 46*(5), 449–461.

Ogilvie, K.C. (2005). *Leading and Managing Groups in the Outdoors* (2nd rev. edn). Penrith: Institute for Outdoor Learning.

Öhman, J. (2008). Environmental ethics and democratic responsibility: A pluralistic approach to ESD. In J. Öhman (Ed.) *Values and Democracy in Education for Sustainable Development: Contributions from Swedish Research,* (pp. 17–32). Malmö: Liber.

Öhman, J. & Öhman, M. (2013). Participatory approach in practice: An analysis of student discussions about climate change. *Environmental Education Research, 19*(3), 324–341.

Place, G. (2004). Youth recreation leads to adult conservation. *National Recreation & Park Association, 39*(2), 29–36.

Quay, J. (2013). More than relations between self, others and nature: Outdoor education and aesthetic experience. *Journal of Adventure Education & Outdoor Learning, 13*(2), 142–157.

Quay, J. & Seaman, J. (2013). *John Dewey and Education Outdoors: Making Sense of the 'Educational Situation' through more than a Century of Progressive Reforms.* Rotterdam: Sense Publishers.

Reed, P. & Rothenberg, D. (Eds.) (1993). *Wisdom in the Open Air: The Norwegian Roots of Deep Ecology.* Minneapolis and London: University of Minnesota Press.

Sandell, K. & Öhman, J. (2010). Educational potentials of encounters with nature: reflections from a Swedish outdoor perspective. *Environmental Education Research, 16*(1), 113–132.

Sandell, K. & Öhman, J. (2013). An educational tool for outdoor education and environmental concern. *Journal of Adventure Education and Outdoor Learning, 13*(1), 36–55.

Sandell, K., Öhman, J. & Östman, L. (2005). *Education for Sustainable Development: Nature, School and Democracy.* Lund: Studentlitteratur.

Schinkel, A. (2009). Justifying compulsory environmental education in liberal democracies. *Journal of Philosophy of Education, 43*(4), 507–526.

Seton, E.T. (1906/1902). *The Birch-bark Roll of the Woodcraft Indians.* New York: Doubleday, Page & Company.

Smith-Sebasto, N.J. & Cavern, L. (2006). Effects of pre- and post-trip activities associated with a residential environmental education experience on students' attitudes toward the environment. *Journal of Environmental Education, 37*(4), 3–17.

Sund, P. (2015). Experienced ESD-schoolteachers' teaching – an issue of complexity. *Environmental Education Research, 21*(1), 24–44.

Tuan, Y.-F. (1974/1990). *Topophilia: A Study of Environmental Perception, Attitudes, and Values.* New York: Columbia University Press.

Williams, R. (1973). Base and superstructure in Marxist cultural theory. *New Left Review, 82*, 3–16.

4

Outdoor studies and a sound philosophy of experience

John Quay

UNIVERSITY OF MELBOURNE

Jayson Seaman

UNIVERSITY OF NEW HAMPSHIRE

Experience and outdoor studies

Scholars in outdoor studies have long engaged with the notion of experience in education. This effort is necessitated by its status as a 'field based' endeavour, one that often attempts to challenge educational orthodoxy. The construct of experience offers a possible way through the thicket of educational questions entailed within any programme of reform, but its interpretation remains an unresolved issue.

Any focus on experience draws education together with philosophy, as the two are intimately entwined. John Dewey – widely regarded as the chief architect of experience in education – argued, 'if we are willing to conceive education as the process of forming fundamental dispositions, intellectual and emotional, toward nature and fellow-men [*sic*.], philosophy may even be defined *as the general theory of education*' (1916, p. 383). In this chapter we build on Dewey's pragmatism to outline an account of experience for outdoor studies, crafted also from Martin Heidegger's phenomenology.

Why 'experience'?

Scholars have reason to take up experience in the field of outdoor studies. Many of the initiatives under this title began as 'progressive' alternatives to more traditional classroom-based forms of education, ranging from nature study, to school camps, to adventure programming, to environmental education, to place-based education (see Quay & Seaman, 2013). Such reforms typically emerged in response to problems perceived with indoor studies, such as a moribund curriculum and flagging student motivation.

This historical origin created difficulties because it usually positioned outdoor studies as a reaction *against* traditional education – and in the eyes of critics, was concerned *only* with experience. When questions about the nature of progressive reforms (like outdoor studies) arise, the answer often entails some version of what they are *not* – traditional, indoor, classroom-based education; versions of outdoor studies were often justified throughout the 20th century because they were the opposite, educationally speaking, of the indoor classroom.

A consequence of this dichotomy is that outdoor studies are often associated with the catchphrase 'learning by doing' (Roberts, 2011). The doing vs thinking dichotomy has recently been sustained in part by heavy reliance on constructivist models derived from the human potential movement, which characterise experiential learning as an action–reflection cycle (Fenwick, 2003; Seaman, 2008). We do something (experience) then we reflect on it (thinking); 'experience' is a necessary precursor to how educators plan for and facilitate the thinking. As one popular article maintains, 'experience alone is insufficient to be called experiential education, and it is the reflection process which turns experience into experiential education' (Joplin, 1981, p. 17). Encoded in such models is a persistent and unfortunate hierarchy: experience – provided through means like outdoor studies – is the poor cousin to thinking.

Historical accounts of experience in outdoor studies thereby express what Dewey described as 'educational confusion' (1931, p. 1). This confusion reflects the ongoing conflict between opposing viewpoints in education, where 'the opposition . . . tends to take the form of contrast between traditional and progressive education' (1938, p. 17). Another way Dewey described this confusion/conflict is as 'the case of the child *vs.* the curriculum' (1902, p. 5). Both renditions highlight the dichotomy between outdoor and indoor studies: one is more concerned with the interests of the child or young person, the other with knowledge contained in the curriculum.

The most obvious path out of this problem would seem to be through some compromise between the two, a '*via media*' (1938, p. 5), as Dewey put it (although he advocated a different solution). This middle way is, in effect, what usually happens, resulting in a subtle mixing of the two – teaching for student interest some of the time, and for knowledge acquisition at other times – thereby leaving both viewpoints intact and mollifying each side to a degree. The action–reflection cycle is one version of this compromise. Yet attempts at compromise or balance do not offer a way out of educational confusion, they simply reproduce it.

For Dewey, the perpetual battle between opposing 'sects' (1902, p. 4) represented a serious misunderstanding of education – if not philosophy – itself. He wrote: 'It is the business of an intelligent theory of education to . . . indicate a plan of operations proceeding from a level deeper and more inclusive than is represented by the practices and ideas of the contending parties' (1938, p. 5). Going to a level deeper requires development of 'a coherent theory of experience' (p. 30) or a 'sound philosophy of experience' (p. 91) that illuminates 'Education itself' (p. 6) rather than some -ism of education. Rather than balancing experience with thinking, experience must be understood more broadly to encompass both.

Outdoor studies will benefit from revisiting Dewey's call for a 'coherent theory of experience'. Illuminating 'a new order of conceptions leading to new modes of practice' (p. 5) in this way will help reconcile perceived dichotomies between various sub-disciplines while making outdoor studies, writ broadly, a more potent source of educational and ecological reform (see e.g. Knapp, 1997; Priest, 1986).

Reflective experience

A major contribution Dewey makes to a philosophy of experience is to insist that thinking is also experience: 'reflective experience' (1929, p. 7). This repositions experience as more than just doing. Experience now holistically embraces life itself, or vice-versa: 'we use the term "life" to denote the whole range of experience' (1916, p. 39). More than thirty years later, Dewey reiterated that he had always intended experience 'to designate, in a summary fashion, all that is distinctively human' (1981, p. 331). Living experience comprises both reflective experience and another mode of experience, referred to (from within the perspective of reflective experience) as 'pre-reflective' (1933, p. 106) or 'post-reflective' (p. 107). Pre-reflective and post-reflective are the 'two limits of every unit of thinking', and can be described in more detail as 'a perplexed, troubled, or confused situation at the beginning' of reflective thinking, and 'a cleared-up, unified, resolved situation at the close' (p. 106). In between are the 'general features of reflective experience':

> They are (*i*) perplexity, confusion, doubt, due to the fact that one is implicated in an incomplete situation whose full character is not yet determined; (*ii*) a conjectural anticipation – a tentative interpretation of the given elements, attributing to them a tendency to effect certain consequences; (*iii*) a careful survey (examination, inspection, exploration, analysis) of all attainable consideration which will define and clarify the problem in hand; (*iv*) a consequent elaboration of the tentative hypothesis to make it more precise and more consistent, because squaring with a wider range of facts; (*v*) taking one stand upon the projected hypothesis as a plan of action which is applied to the existing state of affairs: doing something overtly to bring about the anticipated result, and thereby testing the hypothesis. (Dewey, 1916, p. 176)

While organised in a series of steps, these features of reflective experience 'do not follow one another in set order' (1933, p. 117). Pre-reflective experience can be seen in Dewey's account of reflective experience at point (i). Beyond this point, 'two types' (1916, p. 169) of reflective experience emerge, which can be discerned 'according to the proportion of reflection found in them'. The less reflective type involves steps (ii) and (v), meaning that steps (iii) and (iv) can potentially be disregarded. Following (ii) and (v), 'we simply do something, and when it fails, we do something else, and keep on trying till we hit upon something which works' (p. 169). Dewey referred to this as 'trial and error' (p. 170).

But trial and error does not always work, and if such efforts do not resolve the issue, a more 'regulated' (1929, p. 7) type of reflective experience might be required, which means embracing steps (iii) and (iv): 'it is the extent and accuracy of steps three and four which mark off a distinctive reflective experience from one on the trial and error plane. They make *thinking* itself into an experience' (1916, p. 176). Here we think more carefully about the problem and we call on knowledge gleaned elsewhere. Dewey, however, recognised a trap with such thinking: it may become disconnected from practical situations in life – '"abstract" when that word is used in a bad sense to designate something which exclusively occupies a realm of its own' (1929, p. 9). In order to guard against this, Dewey stressed that we must always return from this regulated type of reflection back to concrete trial and error – to try out our newly formed ideas in practice, otherwise it remains abstracted. 'We never get wholly beyond the trial and error situation. Our most elaborate and rationally consistent thought has to be tried in the world and thereby tried out' (1916, p. 177).

The implication for outdoor studies is to view thinking as a 'mode of experience' (1929, p. 19) – reflective experience – which occurs as movement between a range of possible reflective options that fall into two broad types: a practically oriented type (which could be called *absorption in practice*) and an abstract theoretical type (which could be called *the practice of thinking* in the way 'thinking' is conventionally understood – see Lave, 1988; Quay, 2003). However, and importantly, these types do not simply offer a choice – rather, the practical type of reflective experience is always the base from which the abstract type emerges and returns, if it is engaged at all – and *both* are reflective experience.

Aesthetic experience

Reflective experience alone offers very little about the 'pre-reflective' or 'post-reflective' states we occupy in life, from which reflective experience emerges and returns. Just as the more abstract type of reflective experience is rooted in a more practical type, so the more practical type of reflective experience is rooted in a mode of experience that is not reflective: *aesthetic experience*. For 'cognitive experience must originate within that of a non-cognitive sort' (Dewey, 1929, p. 23).

> [A]esthetic experience is experience in its integrity. Had not the term 'pure' been so often abused in philosophic literature, had it not been so often employed to suggest that there is something alloyed, impure, in the very nature of experience and to denote something beyond experience, we might say that [a]esthetic experience is pure experience. For it is experience freed from the forces that impede and confuse its development as experience; freed, that is, from factors that subordinate an experience as it is directly had to something beyond itself. *To [a]esthetic experience, then, the philosopher must go to understand what experience is.* (Dewey 1934, p. 274; Italics added)

Based on Dewey's claims, aesthetic experience is a crucial mode of experience to grasp. A key characteristic of aesthetic experience is that it concerns 'experience as it is directly had' – which is different than reflective experience. In its Latin roots, reflect means to bend back, and reflective experience bends experience back on itself, looking back at things that have happened, or projecting ideas forward to things yet to come. But, as bending back, it cannot grasp the present moment. This is what aesthetic experience is – experience of what is going on in the immediate present.

Understanding aesthetic experience, however, is more difficult than understanding reflective experience. Perhaps the main reason for this is our familiarity with reflective thinking – as in the action–reflection cycle – such that thinking of experience (or learning) in a way that is not reflective seems impossible. But, ironically, we are doing it all the time, without really noticing. This is the mode of thinking Dewey called 'qualitative thought' (1930, p. 18) or 'affective thinking' (1926, p. 3). Merely because aesthetic experience is not reflective experience does not mean no thinking is occurring, just a different mode of thinking – an immersive awareness of the present.

Qualitative affective thinking is of experience as it is directly had: aesthetic experience. It is, in contemporary language, thinking *in* practice rather than thinking *about* practice. Moreover, Dewey uses words like *aesthetic, affective* and *qualitative* because he is referring to something emotional. Thinking *in* practice is a felt awareness of the immediate present: a felt awareness as you are living it, not bending back on itself as in reflective experience. Importantly, aesthetic experience is where we usually live: in the present. It is also where the problems and issues emerge that induce us to engage with reflective experience, and where we return to after reflective experience. Just as aesthetic experience is a mode of thinking, it is a mode of doing, but in a different way to reflective experience. Martin Heidegger's philosophy helps in understanding this difference, particularly his early work and the notion of *being*.

Being, doing and knowing

Reflective experience incorporates two emphases. First is *regulated* reflection, which is concerned mainly with knowing things, with knowledge about practice. Second is concrete doing, or thinking as working in practice. Both types of reflective thinking are important, and both work together; their distinction can never be clear-cut.

Of course, thinking about how something will work and then organising resources to increase the chances of success is one way of understanding concrete doing. But doing is more than just working things out; much of doing in life occurs as getting on with things in the present, in aesthetic experience, where there is no 'breakdown' that needs addressing (Koschmann, Kuutti, & Hickman, 1998). In aesthetic experience, both doing and knowing disappear as specific, separable emphases; they are 'submerged' (Dewey, 1934, p. 274) in aesthetic experience. (The narrower concept of 'flow' might help grasp this notion – see Csikszentmihalyi, 1990.) This submersion is an essential quality of aesthetic experience. In Heidegger's terms this character is best understood as simplicity, which here means holistic: no separable parts. And, if aesthetic experience is simple, then reflective experience is multiple. Being simple, aesthetic experience never involves separating the whole into parts – the whole is primary. The multiple, in contrast, deals with the relations between parts as separable things/concepts/ideas – now the separate things are primary and we contemplate their relations with one another.

When something is declared to be simple, this often is thought to mean 'easy'. But not so with aesthetic experience. Heidegger stresses the difficulty in comprehending the simple. 'The simple . . . is our name for what is inconspicuously the most difficult, which, when it occurs, appears to everyone immediately and ever again as the easiest and most accessible; yet it remains incontestably the most difficult' (1994/1937–38, p. 13). This difficulty, as stated earlier, relates to the seeming naturalness of thinking as reflection, as the bending back of experience so as to be focused on it, scrutinising it – where we see a multiplicity of separate parts in relation with one another. It is much easier to think about separate and multiple things: 'the multiple is the easy – even where concern over it seems toilsome. For progress from one thing to another is always a relaxation, and it is precisely this progress that is not allowed by the simple' (p. 13). Thinking qualitatively, affectively – a feeling awareness of the simple whole – is so different that it is more difficult to comprehend.

One way Heidegger described this simple whole of experience is as 'being-in-the-world' (1996/1927, p. 49). This is where we actually live, in the moment. With this awareness we can then reflect on experience more generally and see that life comprises 'various ways of being' (1985/1925, p. 295). In this sense we sometimes talk about multiple identities being available – but this representation tends to objectify being-in-the-world to the extent that we lose sight of living experience. Referring to *ways of being*-in-the-world conveys the holistic nature essential to understanding aesthetic experience. All aspects that are discernible in reflective experience are – in Dewey's terms – submerged in aesthetic experience to the extent that we are not aware of them, like *self*, *others* and *nature* (Quay, 2013a). This means that each way of being-in-the-world has its associated ways of doing and ways of knowing, which are then discernible through reflective experience. But in aesthetic experience, being-in-the-world, the whole is primary; doing and knowing merge and are never separated out as they are in reflective experience (see Figure 4.1).

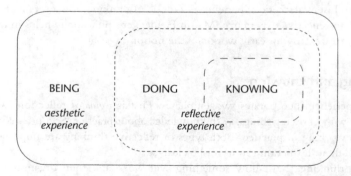

Figure 4.1 Being, doing and knowing are whole in aesthetic experience

Experiential learning and experiential education

So what does this mean for outdoor studies? Integrating Deweyan pragmatism, which has never been seriously explored in outdoor studies, with Heidegger's phenomenological notion of *being* offers a theory of experience which possesses a coherency that can further illuminate two of the core beliefs in outdoor studies: one concerning experiential learning, the other experiential education. First, it opens up commonly accepted models of experiential learning centred around action–reflection cycles. It offers 'a new order of conceptions' (Dewey, 1938, p. 5) that provides a different way of comprehending what happens *in experience* – that is, as immersed in various kinds of practice including reflective practice. Second, this new order of conceptions – a new way of comprehending doing – should lead to 'new modes of practice' (p. 5). This is not to suggest wholesale change, rather some realignment of current applications, based on shifting understanding.

Experiential learning

The more coherent theory of experience offered here is premised on two basic modes of experience, aesthetic and reflective: both are essential to learning. This represents two key advances: (1) reflection *is* experience, rather than being other than, or coming after, experience; and (2) experience *always* involves thinking, with aesthetic and reflective experience espousing different modes of thought. These advances, in our view, place a special premium on returning to 'experience' – i.e. to doing – as a core educational concern, rather than privileging 'reflection' as the source of learning. This said, a further development is awareness of a distinction between two connected types of reflective experience: a more concrete type focused on *doing* and a more abstract type focused on *knowing*. This belies the representation of reflection as a simple cycle by proposing that a more precise description requires both types, each with its own variations shifted between in myriad different ways. This movement is premised on the notion that abstract reflection is itself rooted in concrete reflection, otherwise it becomes disconnected and is then abstract in the negative sense that Dewey recognised – a kind of self-absorption.

A further key advance is the identification of aesthetic experience. No longer is experience just doing (as in the action–reflection cycle). Now it can be understood to embrace *being*, as being-in-the-world. Experience is being, doing and knowing. Doing and knowing become explicit in reflective experience, their relation being the object of thought. Yet doing and knowing are rooted in being; they are submerged in aesthetic experience, or being-in-the-world. We can comprehend this reflectively by saying that knowing is rooted in doing, which is rooted in being (see Figure 4.1). Change to any one is a change to all three. In this sense ways of being are ways of doing are ways of knowing.[1]

Experiential education

The purpose of reflective experience is to change being; it is not just knowing and doing that are altered. This change is learning (again, in contemporary terms, this means learning necessarily entails changes to identity – see Seaman & Rheingold, 2013). But learning through being-in-the-world involves more than an individual mind; it involves self, others and environment submerged in holistic aesthetic experience (Quay, 2013a). In reflective experience, self, others and environment are categories that can be rearranged to fix some problem or issue; the ways these issues are culturally organised for encounter by young people is *education* – by 'experience in education', Dewey (1938) means for us to consider the way experience, as we have discussed it here, is situated in the context of *being* as it is organised culturally.

In his 'technical definition of education' (1916, pp. 89–90) Dewey describes education as 'that reconstruction or reorganization of experience which adds to the meaning of experience, and which increases ability to direct the course of subsequent experience'. In other words, education involves reflective experience that reconstructs or reorganises being. This change to aesthetic experience should have consequences for subsequent experience (the problem is resolved and if a similar situation is encountered again it may no longer present as a problem). This process of perpetual change defines Dewey as a progressive educator.

With this definition, any experience that involves resolution of an issue could be described as experiential learning and experiential education. However, Dewey highlights the important distinction between learning and education. He notes: 'experience and education cannot be directly equated to each other' (1938, p. 25). For Dewey, education is associated with growth in a much broader sense than just physical growing. 'Any experience is mis-educative that has the effect of arresting or distorting the growth of further experience' (p. 25). Growth is growth of further experience – and that is what education supports.

Two important factors concerning the connection Dewey draws between growth and education are significant for outdoor studies. (1) The growth of further experience requires more than just specialisation in one or other ways of being, as if ways of being can be treated separately and compartmentalised. (2) The 'further experience' Dewey speaks of is not the remote future of adult life. Instead it is the future within aesthetic experience, the expansion of possibilities for performance *within* a particular way of being – the transformation of future practice. These two factors have implications for asserting new modes of practice (as Dewey put it), or at least reinforcing the best of what professionals within various kinds of outdoor studies are already doing.

Outdoor studies – written broadly – is well positioned to problematise being and facilitate its reorganisation. Outdoor studies historically have reflected diverse concerns in and out of formal schools (Quay & Seaman, 2013). The rich array of contemporary practices can enable interrogation of many different ways of being: being a bushwalker, being a field geologist, being a woman in the hypermasculine world of high-altitude mountaineering, being a member of an indigenous community. Outdoor studies shares concerns with, and can educationally craft, these ways of being such that issues may arise that draw received ways of being into question.

The second factor, concerning 'further experience', is made forcefully when Dewey connects the notion of mis-educative experience with traditional forms of schooling. 'Young people in traditional schools do have experiences,' he acknowledges. 'The trouble is not with the absence of experiences, but their defective and wrong character – wrong and defective from the standpoint of connection with further experience' (1938, p. 27). The problem is that the further experience typically defined within traditional schooling is to achieve a job in adult life: education then becomes career preparation – and this preparation takes the form of knowledge (knowing) acquisition and skill (doing) development, while ignoring being.

Yet this future, while able to be abstractly anticipated (reflected upon) by young people, does not often play a significant role in their immediate, aesthetic experience. In other words, while adult jobs are in the future, this future is so remote that it does not strongly influence the present – it is unavailable as a way of *being*. Dewey points out that goals must be tangible, otherwise they are literally outside the field of view. He thus speaks of how we always work towards 'ends-in-view, or purposes of which we are aware' (1933, p. 17). These purposes – seen from *within* young people's experience – must characterise aesthetic experience in order to possess educative potential.

Even in traditional forms of schooling, the ends-in-view of aesthetic experience are not adult jobs, but rather the assessments (assignments/exams) by which students are measured.[2] These can only characterise various ways of being a student (for example, in science or history) aimed at preparation for adult life beyond school. However preparation of this sort is so focused on knowing and (less so) doing that being is ignored, resulting in the creation of student ways of being that do not connect well to the growth of further experience – in the lives of young people. Thus Dewey declared: '"preparation" is a treacherous idea' (1938, p. 47).

Outdoor studies has an advantage in this regard, because, as a field-based enterprise, it is inherently much more attuned to aesthetic experience. Educators involved with outdoor studies seem to have a much better awareness of the inherent connection between being, doing and knowing. But this awareness, while visible in practice, has not become a well-developed facet of outdoor education theory or practice, partly because of impoverished models of learning and its relation to experience.

Conclusion

Outdoor studies prominently engages with the notion of experience, whereas in science, mathematics or the humanities subjects it is scarcely considered. And, when it is, it usually involves attempts at making disciplinary studies more relevant, trying to connect abstract theory with concrete practice. Yet *being* remains systematically overlooked – as if it can be deferred until young people leave school. Outdoor studies is far ahead of these traditional forms of schooling in that it inherently recognises being, but up to now has lacked the conceptual framework through which to convey this understanding. As a consequence, in distancing themselves from traditional forms of schooling, outdoor educators have unwittingly reproduced the educational confusion that has plagued reforms for many years (Quay & Seaman, 2013). The way forward and out of this confusion lies in a sound philosophy of experience, which will enable viewing traditional and progressive forms of schooling through the same lens – and so to further development of outdoor studies, and education more generally.

Acknowledgement

We would like to acknowledge Martin Lindner, Martin Vollmar, Peter Becker and Ralf Westphal at the University of Marburg, who influenced the formulation of the ideas addressed in this chapter.

Notes

1   Dewey speaks of these as occupations, accounts of which are accessible in Quay (2013b, 2015), Quay and Seaman (2013), and Seaman and Nelsen (2011).
2   As such they can be classified as misrepresentations of mature disciplines (Popkewitz, 2007).

References

Beames, S. & Atencio, M. (2008). Building social capital through outdoor education. *Journal of Adventure Education and Outdoor Learning, 8*(2), 99–112.
Csikszentmihalyi, M. (1990). *Flow: The Psychology of Optimal Experience*. New York: Harper & Row.
Dewey, J. (1902). *The Child and the Curriculum*. Chicago, IL: University of Chicago Press.
Dewey, J. (1916). *Democracy and Education*. New York: The Free Press.
Dewey, J. (1926). Affective thought. *Journal of the Barnes Foundation, 2*(April), 3–9.
Dewey, J. (1929). *Experience and Nature* (2nd edn). Chicago, IL: Open Court Publishing Company.
Dewey, J. (1930). Qualitative thought. *Symposium, 1*(January), 5–32.
Dewey, J. (1931). *The Way Out of Educational Confusion*. Cambridge, MA: Harvard University Press.
Dewey, J. (1933). *How We Think: A Restatement of the Relation of Reflective Thinking to the Educative Process* (rev. edn). Boston, MA: D.C. Heath and Company.

Dewey, J. (1934). *Art as Experience*. New York: Capricorn Books.

Dewey, J. (1938). *Experience and Education*. New York: Collier Books

Dewey, J. (1981). Experience and nature: A re-introduction. In J. Ratner (Ed.) *John Dewey, the Later Works* (Vol. 1, pp. 330–361). Carbondale, IL: Southern Illinois University Press.

Fenwick, T. (2003). *Learning through Experience: Troubling Orthodoxies and Intersecting Questions*. Melbourne, FL: Krieger Publishing Company.

Heidegger, M. (1985/1925). *History of the Concept of Time: Prolegomena* (trans. T. Kisiel). Bloomington, IN: Indiana University Press.

Heidegger, M. (1994/1937–38). *Basic Questions of Philosophy: Selected 'Problems' of 'Logic'* (trans. R. Rocjewicz & A. Schuwer). Bloomington, IN: Indiana University Press.

Heidegger, M. (1996/1927). *Being and Time* (trans. J. Stambaugh). Albany, NY: State University of New York Press.

Joplin, L. (1981). On defining experiential education. *Journal of Experiential Education, 4*(1), 17–20.

Knapp, C.E. (1997). Environmental and outdoor education for the 21st century. *Taproot, 10*(4), 3–9.

Koschmann, T., Kuutti, K. & Hickman, L. (1998). The concept of breakdown in Heidegger, Leont'ev, and Dewey and its implications for education. *Mind, Culture, and Activity, 5*(1), 25–41.

Lave, J. (1988). *Cognition in Practice: Mind, Mathematics and Culture in Everyday Life*. Cambridge: Cambridge University Press.

Popkewitz, T.S. (2007). Alchemies and governing: Or, questions about the questions we ask. *Educational Philosophy and Theory, 39*(1), 64–83.

Priest, S. (1986). Redefining outdoor education: A matter of many relationships. *Journal of Environmental Education, 17*(3), 13–15.

Roberts, J. (2011). *Beyond Learning by Doing: Theoretical Currents in Experiential Education*. New York: Routledge.

Quay, J. (2003). Experience and participation: Relating theories of learning. *Journal of Experiential Education, 26*(2), 105–116.

Quay, J. (2013a). More than relations between self, others and nature: Outdoor education and aesthetic experience. *Journal of Adventure Education and Outdoor Learning, 13*(2), 142–157.

Quay, J. (2013b). *Education, Experience and Existence: Engaging Dewey, Peirce and Heidegger*. Oxfordshire: Routledge.

Quay, J. (2015). Understanding Life in School: From Academic Classroom to Outdoor Education. New York: Palgrave Macmillan.

Quay, J. & Seaman, J. (2013). *John Dewey and Education Outdoors: Making Sense of the 'Educational Situation' Through More Than a Century of Progressive Reforms*. Rotterdam, NL: Sense Publishers.

Seaman, J. (2008). Experience, reflect, critique: The end of the 'learning cycles' era. *Journal of Experiential Education, 31*(1), 3–18.

Seaman, J. & Nelsen, P.J. (2011). An overburdened term: Dewey's concept of experience as curriculum theory. *Education & Culture: The Journal of the John Dewey Society for the Study of Education and Culture, 27*(1), 2–25.

Seaman, J. & Rheingold, A. (2013). Circle talks as situated experiential learning: Context, identity, and knowledgeability in 'learning from reflection'. *Journal of Experiential Education, 36*(2), 155–174.

5

Healing the split head of outdoor recreation and outdoor education

Revisiting Indigenous knowledge from multiple perspectives

Philip Mullins

UNIVERSITY OF NORTHERN BRITISH COLUMBIA

Gregory Lowan-Trudeau

UNIVERSITY OF CALGARY, UNIVERSITY OF NORTHERN BRITISH COLUMBIA

Karen Fox

UNIVERSITY OF ALBERTA

Worldwide, Indigenous peoples are increasingly revitalising, sustaining and sharing worldviews and practices grounded in intimate relationships with the natural world and specific spaces and places for the benefit of Indigenous and non-Indigenous peoples alike (Cajete, 1994; Battiste, 1998). Cajete (2001) has called for healing the 'split head' of North American society, working to heal the physical and existential fissures between Indigenous and Western communities, and between humanity and ecology. Our chapter explores outdoor recreation and education in this spirit from a North American perspective grounded in understandings of European colonialism worldwide.

As Euro-Canadian (Phil and Karen) and Métis (Greg) scholars and educators, we aim to explore the problematic historical relationships that outdoor recreation and education have with Indigenous peoples, and to encourage possibilities for alternative ways of thinking and doing outdoor recreation and education informed by Indigenous ways of knowing and being. Specifically, we explore relational issues of power and colonialism that haunt outdoor recreation and education programming, the implications of foundational paradigms that situate humans within or outside the natural world, and ethical issues related to working with or using Indigenous scholarship or knowledges. Throughout, we attempt to disrupt dichotomous thinking and create rhythms around producing spaces for reimagining human–environment relations through outdoor recreation and education.

We start by offering one among many possible narratives to describe the colonialism that, in part, contextualises the relationships Indigenous perspectives have within outdoor recreation and education internationally. Beginning in the 15th century European imperial powers set about exploring the globe and establishing colonies to enrich themselves and exercise global influence (Smith, 1999). European explorers and settlers encountered Indigenous civilisations that had come to know their environments and establish societies long before European arrival (Dunlap, 1999).

Although European imperial powers often claimed to be a 'civilising' force, colonialism was and is insidious, brutal, oppressive and sometimes enslaving to Indigenous populations (Smith, 1999). Moreover, it depended on and promoted ethnocentric notions and values of civilisation, culture and nature. Colonialism corrupted autochthonous ways of life, learning, language and identity (Battiste, 1998). Since European contact, Indigenous communities have contended with settlers' social, economic and educational systems, which have come to dominate, but not always eliminate, Indigenous traditions. These meetings brought together many different worldviews, and their interrelation produced wholly new nations, such as the Métis in Canada, peoples of mixed Indigenous and European ancestry most often, but not exclusively, associated historically with the fur trade (Lowan-Trudeau, 2013). These unique histories and contexts continue to shape realities for all those involved.

The colonial haunting of Western outdoor recreation and outdoor education

Dominant Western outdoor recreation and education are haunted by various forms and impulses related to Western colonial understandings of Indigenous people and the environment (Lowan-Trudeau), 2009; Loynes, 2010). Historically, Baden-Powell's international Scouting Movement, and Seton's related Woodcraft Indians, were inspired by heroic interpretations of British military scouts and stereotypes of Indigenous peoples as stoic warriors on the colonial frontier; supposed Zulu and '"Red" Indian' rites of passage were appropriated as models for masculine character development (MacDonald, 1993). These forms of outdoor education pur- portedly allowed predominantly European youth to escape to nature, 'go native' and become disciplined citizens in response to popular fears of the softening effects of urbanisation and industrialisation (MacDonald, 1993). In Canada these same fears and appropriations influenced the development of recreational canoe tripping (Haun-Moss, 2002) and summer camps (Wall, 2005). Supposed Indigenous traditions were invented, appropriated, and represented in ways that reflected the prejudices, stereotypes, imaginations and purposes of the dominant settler society through outdoor recreation and education (Wall, 2005).

The appropriation of Indigenous practices by more contemporary outdoor educators has been done largely (but not exclusively) without permission, often lacked cultural and/or spir- itual context, and has tended to portray Indigenous peoples in warm and romantic terms devoid of the historical and persistent impacts of colonisation (Oles, 1995; Friedel, 2011), and the con- temporary resilience and adaptability of Indigenous peoples (Battiste, 1998).

Colonialism also haunts through the uncritical emulation and celebration of European explorers and their adventures abroad and in the wilderness; examples include British youth expeditions (Loynes, 2010), mountaineering conquests (Bayers, 2003) and canoe tripping as naturalising Canadian nationalism (Dean, 2012). Moreover, persistent appeals to character build- ing within rationales and theories of outdoor education remain, despite being largely unfounded and disproven by social psychologists (Brookes, 2003; Lowan-Trudeau), 2009). Within outdoor education, Western and Indigenous worldviews support distinctly different understandings and relationships with land that are not easily reconciled (Raffan, 1993).

Western conceptualisation of land as space to be conquered, occupied and visited, but not inhabited, and culture as place-independent have been essential to European colonialism (Ingold, 2000), and reinforced popularly, symbolically, legally and on the ground through concepts such as wilderness, *terra nullius*, Doctrine of Discovery, and Manifest Destiny (Bordo, 1997; Miller, Ruru, Behrendt & Lindberg, 2010). In North America, Indigenous populations were systematically decimated and stripped of their lands through opaque political tactics, disease, school systems and violence (Brody, 1998). Ironically, landscapes and wilderness have, over the years, been interpreted by settler societies as essential to the development of national characters distinct from colonial parent countries (Cronon, 1996; Dunlap, 1999). The reported demise of the Frontier combined with a Romantic back-to-nature movement that celebrated sublime wilderness led to the creation of national parks first in the USA and then in Canada; such wilderness protection has been central to Western forms of environmentalism in North America as a critique of contemporary Western industrial society (Cronon, 1996). Nevertheless, parks have tended to promote particular experiences of nature as unpeopled wilderness – still reflecting a Eurocentric nature–culture dichotomy – at the expense of Indigenous and other inhabitants' livelihoods and ways of being and knowing the land through, for example, ceremonial activity as well as cultivating and gathering traditional foods, which run counter to 'no impact' policies (Guha, 1998; Binnema & Niemi, 2006; Reti, 2012).

Imperial and Romantic interpretations of wilderness, frontier and Indigenous inhabitants provided rich mythic fodder and purpose around which to conceptualise the outdoors as providing liminal experiences of nature, wilderness and the colonial Other as distinct from civilisation. Doing so supposedly allowed youth of European descent to escape the city, explore wilderness frontiers, build character, understand dominant national identity, conquer mountains and/or 'go native' (if only for a short time) in service of the nation.

Many Western explorers and adventures were inspired by, and the willing instruments of, larger imperial forces and acts. They also lived personal, interpersonal and cross-cultural realities in particular places. In some cases their experiences opened receptivity to Indigenous ways of life, care for regions and adapted identities (see Horne, 2005). Indigenous people also resisted and transcended imperialism through their involvement with expeditions (Bayers, 2003). Such instances of resistance and the revival of Indigenous knowledge provide important insights into possible ways forward as we seek to heal the split head of our respective societies.

Indigenous knowledge

Shared interests in education through experience, as well as environmental learning, and knowledge of place suggest outdoor recreation and education potentially provide collaborative ground for Indigenous and non-Indigenous scholars, managers and educators. In the past, Indigenous voices were largely absent from critical discussions and considerations in the Western-dominated Academy. Indigenous peoples have increasingly found and fought for space to express 'First Voice' (Graveline, 1998). As such, any critical consideration of the relationship between Indigenous peoples and outdoor recreation and education warrants serious consideration of these contributions.

Indigenous scholars have explained clearly the characteristics of Indigenous knowledge. These characteristics may be unfamiliar to non-Indigenous scholars and practitioners of outdoor education, people who have added responsibility to change self-referential systems of thought and practice that reinforce their own dominance, and who are in privileged positions to do so (Ryan & Fox, 2001; Cordova, 2004). Understanding these characteristics may better inform creative and collaborative efforts, and benefit both Indigenous and non-Indigenous peoples and practitioners of outdoor recreation and education.

Practical

Practical application or embodiment is a highly valued element of Indigenous knowledge. Burkhart (2004) described that 'for American Indians, knowledge is knowledge in experience or, if knowledge does not simply amount to this, it is at least the most important knowledge' (p. 20). The experiential nature of Indigenous knowledge allows for empirical understanding through continued close attention to, and dialogue with, particular phenomena within one's life world. Such knowledge arises from experience in a particular context, approached in a particular way, and exists in embodied performance; it is evident in the way people act, the products they make (e.g. art, ceremonies, educational experiences), and the ways in which they shape their world (Kenny, 2002). Thus, Indigenous knowledge is related to questions of ontology: knowledge is displayed in *being,* how a person, animal or thing *is* or is brought into being (Waters, 2004). For example, Paariaqtuqtut, a land-based education programme led by Inuit Elders in Igloolik, Canada, revives traditional land skills and, perhaps more importantly, an understanding of what it means to be Inuit (Takano, 2005). Outdoor craft and travel have also been used by the Coastal First Nations in BC, Canada, as well as the Maori in Aotearoa New Zealand for protest and resistance as well as cultural revitalisation and expression (Dean, 2012; Reti, 2012).

Being is related to identity and so identity is in part connected to practice in Indigenous worldviews. According to Burkhart (2004), how people behave shapes meaning in the world because performance alters a world that is already meaningful, and expresses a person's and community's knowledge of that world. Waters (2004) explained that, for many Indigenous groups, personhood and gender *become* through the learning and performance of particular tasks that express identity. Waters used Kehoe's description of the Blackfeet to explain that personal tasks, competency and skill are essential for establishing autonomy and shaping identity. People are distinguished from one another and related to community, according to Burkhart, through their actions and specific relations. Such an approach allows for personal agency while demanding individual and collective responsibility. The performative aspect of Indigenous knowledge further implicates ecological relations. As Cajete (2004) explained, humans pragmatically engage with their world in '*creative participation*' (p. 49), and 'as co-creators with nature . . . how we act in the world impacts . . . everything' (p. 52).

Relational

Indigenous knowledge is relational because it develops through and exists within experiences that are always-already social, spiritual and ecological: a communal approach very different from Western individually centred understanding of intelligence and creativity (Marker, 2006). Burkhart (2004) described Indigenous knowledge as primarily communal understandings of the world, and experiences of it, shared across generations through story and ceremony: 'If it is "We" that is first and not "I", then what counts as the data of experience is quite different' (p. 26). As Lightning (1992) described, the compassionate mind – a humble orientation towards one's world and understanding of it – is embodied in processes of collaboration that require participants to think together, share meaning and attempt explanation. Jojola (2004) described Pueblo journeys alone and with others as contributing to knowledge of community, self and place because the surroundings are understood to be rich and storied with much to reveal if travellers are helped to look, listen, feel and think with care. Burkhart explained that relatedness means being attentive and responsive to the persons and things around one's self and one's relations with them, and is a core principle of Indigenous philosophy understood as essential to maintaining social and ecological wellbeing.

Burkhart (2004) and Deloria (2004) described Indigenous knowledges as contextual, with truth or reality dependent on a person's understanding of the situation. Each situation comprises a set of relationships ecologically rooted in the earth itself (Cajete, 2004). The process of life establishes relationships between things, persons and places, which become meaningfully understood. Lowan-Trudeau) (2011) observed that, through rural livelihoods (farming, logging, fishing), people are 'often more keenly aware of and deeply connected to the Land around them than the urban environmentalists who so often criticize and dismiss them with scorn' (p. 27). According to Jojola and Deloria (2004), biography situates Indigenous identity within a social and ecological context. Self, in this sense, is understood through one's history and practices in relation to persons (human and non-human) and places (Cajete, 1994). Raffan (1993) and Reti (2012) have described the land as teacher, and dependence on nature as fostering deep connections to place. Reciprocity, therefore, is particularly important to Indigenous social and person–place relations: it recognises that others and the earth provide, and should in return be shown thanks, respect and care. Whitt (2004) described reciprocal gift giving as central to enacting and understanding Indigenous relationships that bind people and the non-human world together while acknowledging and building community (cross-cutting Western distinctions between nature and culture/society). According to Whitt, reciprocity helps to moderate behaviour, position individuals as within a relational world, and avoids the commodification of knowledge and nature by keeping them in community.

Ethical

The applied and relational nature of Indigenous knowledge gives it an ethical quality (Whitt, 2004). Indigenous worldviews give high priority to processes and trust that practices and behaviours established and judged by one's community to be 'balanced' lead to acceptable results and understandings for individuals (Ingold, 2000; DuFour, 2004). DuFour described that, in addition to content, the processes used for acquiring wisdom and knowledge show degrees of wisdom and knowledge themselves. Therefore, specific customs, instructions and norms are followed and established by experienced practitioners as socially acceptable processes for learning. Burkhart (2004) explained that, in Indigenous philosophy, the universe is a moral one in which 'all investigation is moral investigation' centred on the question 'what is the right road for humans to walk?' (p. 17). There are, then, ethical and unethical, acceptable and unacceptable, paths to knowing because, DuFour argued 'proper care of and concern for one's beliefs ought to be of great significance, not only to the believer but to the community the person belongs to' (p. 38) because all are related within a shared community of life.

Not only do discovery and application of knowledge have ethical consequences, but so too the knowledge itself. Knowledge can be more or less morally good or bad, appropriate or dangerous for certain people, communities and situations, depending on the specific context and how it is learned (DuFour, 2004). This has the effect of making some knowledge off limits to certain people, in certain places and at certain times: an important concern when dealing with culturally significant and politically contested social and environmental issues and landscapes.

Holistic

Indigenous knowledge is holistic in that it incorporates the intellectual, physical, emotional and spiritual expressions of personhood. These four aspects are not understood to be separate, but rather as interconnected and interdependent (Cajete, 2004). Indeed, Sunchild (Lightning, 1992) considered a balanced body, mind, emotion and spirit to be crucial for compassionate mind, and the essence of humanity. While a holistic approach may seem overwhelming, Sunchild suggested that inquiring individuals are better off approaching a situation of interest 'in a humble state of knowing nothing which really and truly benefits [is useful to] a person . . .' (Lightning, 1992, p. 226). Perhaps holism can also be embraced through pedagogical processes that follow Urion's (1999) suggestion for holistic research embodying and cultivating inclusiveness, care and compassion.

In consideration of such growing understandings of Indigenous knowledges and philosophies, how might people find mutually beneficial common ground in outdoor recreation and education?

Healing the split head: what next?

In order to survive and prosper as individuals, communities and Nations, most Indigenous people have had to learn and live within multiple worlds, often referred to as 'walking in two worlds'. Henze and Vanett (1993) described this metaphor, common in Indigenous education, as problematic because it promotes a dichotomy that values either a traditional Indigenous world that is largely no longer available, or a Western world to which many Indigenous people do not have full access. Moreover, the metaphor fails to acknowledge the pain and difficulty of such living, as well as present-day forms of Indigenous life as legitimate cultures in which to ground identity. As such, several Indigenous scholars have suggested Western and Indigenous communities reconcile our common colonial pasts and find ways to move forward collectively for the benefit of all. However, as this field has grown, differing views have emerged regarding how this might be achieved.

Some Indigenous scholars, such as Kimmerer (2013), believe that Western and Indigenous knowledge should co-exist in mutual respectful and beneficial, but distinctly separate, harmony. Others advocate for more complete mixing or blending. In the area of ecological science and philosophy education, a collective of Mi'kmaq and Euro-Canadian scholars developed 'Two-Eyed Seeing', in which students learn to approach the natural world through Western and Indigenous eyes to form a fused and balanced whole (Hatcher, Bartlett, Marshall & Marshall, 2009). For Cajete (2001), healing the split head would involve Indigenous and Western peoples together addressing social and ecological irresponsibility and injustice, and developing shared societies and communities of life that flourish. For example, Lowan-Trudeau) (2011, 2013) developed ecological métissage as an approach to outdoor and environmental education at the existential and epistemological intersection of Western bioregionalism and deep ecology with traditional Indigenous knowledge.

Marker (2006) cautioned that Indigenous ways of life present deeper challenges to Western worldviews than do other forms of 'cross-cultural' education. First, they bring out long-held stereotypes and hostilities concerning understandings, claims and identities related to land and natural resources. These are potentially explosive in Western urban-centric outdoor education that identifies strongly with romantic and colonial notions of wilderness (Cronon, 1996). Second, they involve an 'epistemic collision' (p. 488) between Western knowledge that is disembodied and secularised; and Indigenous knowledge that is mythic, sacred and locally ecological. Marker suggested that working across this divide requires teachers to help students interpret their surroundings as constructed out of contested ideological and ecological histories, to 'focus a mirror rather than a magnifying glass at native people' (p. 499). Cordova (2004), however, reminded readers that the metaphor of the mirror should not be used to mistake the Other for one's self, or to subsume other ways of thinking into one's own, but to learn by contrasting one's own ways of thinking with the diversity of human thought.

In practice, outdoor and environmental education programmes, such as Outward Bound Canada's Giwaykiwin have tried with limited success to integrate Indigenous perspectives into Western models (Lowan-Trudeau), 2009); others like Rediscovery, a firmly established international family of programmes, begin with locally grounded Indigenous ways of knowing and work alongside allies to expressly overcome challenges from colonialism that face youth and their communities (Lertzman, 2002). Swayze (2009) also acknowledged the inherent politics of curricula when redeveloping as place-based Bridging the Gap, an environmental education programme for urban Indigenous youth that had relied on a provincial science curriculum.

In Aotearoa New Zealand, Legge (2012) reflected on significant personal challenges, limits and benefits of developing cross-cultural competence as an outsider Pākehā (New Zealander of European descent) trying to cultivate understanding of Māori among her students. Root (2010) also provided a strong example of a Euro-Canadian scholar examining reflexively her outdoor educational praxis through a lens of decolonisation. Mullins and Maher (2007) and Mullins (2009) used Ingold's (2000) theory of inhabitation – which draws together Indigenous and Western human experience – for critical self-reflection on the nature of wilderness canoe travel; and Mullins (2014) proposed a participatory ecological approach to outdoor recreation and education using this ecological ontology. These approaches begin with recognition of diverse ways of knowing and being, extend through difficult individual and communal self-reflection and challenge regarding realities shaped by colonial forces, and strive to honour and move beyond such dynamics in outdoor recreation and educational praxis.

Summary

Outdoor recreation and education is haunted by colonial histories. Western approaches have had problematic relationships with Indigenous peoples and perspectives that still inform its theory and practice in ways that go deeper than stereotypes, misappropriated and invented cultural practices. The colonial legacy persists in conceptions of land as frontier wilderness; environmental ethics that cleave human ways of life from their complex ecologies; romantic myths of exploration that drive practice; imperial approaches to outdoor activities and claims to nationalism; as well as ignorance regarding the Indigenous people on whose territories outdoor activities occur.

Contemporary Indigenous approaches to outdoor recreation and education have drawn on Indigenous knowledge to rebuild and reclaim culture, identity and relationships to place damaged by colonialism, and to work powerfully towards safeguarding traditional rights and ecological wellbeing. Western approaches to outdoor education might learn something about engaging politics and socio-environmental issues from Indigenous practices. Hopefully it is now clear that colonialism is not an 'Indigenous' issue: it permeates and implicates scholars, practitioners and students whether or not they are Indigenous, but does so in very different ways.

We introduced and contextualised works describing Indigenous knowledge by philosophers who are Indigenous. We also highlighted Indigenous, Western and Métis scholars of outdoor recreation and education who have made a start at self-reflective practice variously informed by Indigenous perspectives that challenge the Western nature–culture dichotomy, which structures much outdoor recreation and education theory and practice. We have tried to encourage the healing of the 'split head' by honouring colonial histories while encouraging critical self-reflection and creativity. However, engaging and respecting deeply different epistemologies and ontologies presents serious limits but also exciting opportunities for researchers, educators and students to learn, reflect and create new approaches to, and understandings of, outdoor recreation and education. We hope this chapter fosters careful self-reflection within Western outdoor studies and practice through further reading and decolonising practice, and ultimately enables more effective collaboration among Indigenous peoples and Western allies.

Without misappropriating Indigenous traditions and content, what characteristics might outdoor recreation and education have when informed by the description we provided of Indigenous knowledge? Indigenous people and/or their works would be more directly involved whenever and however possible. Outdoor activities and travel would help participants understand and express how oneself, community and others have lived, are living and desire to live in relation to places and environments. That is, they would facilitate learning right ways to live by closely engaging and observing human and non-human surroundings over time, learning across generations, and through critique and self-reflection. Programmes, practitioners and participants would recognise, anticipate and learn to practice social and ecological reciprocity and responsibility. Programmes, teachers and leaders would mentor expertise, skills and abilities that enable participants' continued involvement and action towards a changed world (and self). More broadly, outdoor educators and programmes might assess critically the social and ecological acceptability of their practices, curricula (explicit and implicit), knowledge and activities. Learning would be guided by humility, inclusivity, care and compassion. Activities and programmes – and the stories told about them – would respect the specific histories, environments, places, landscapes and inhabitants implicated, and support the desired change. Programmes, whether Indigenous or Western, would at a minimum work towards decolonisation through critical self-reflection and creative action to address and redress their own imperial and colonial hauntings.

References

Battiste, M. (1998). Enabling the autumn seed: Toward a decolonized approach to Aboriginal knowledge, language, and education. *Canadian Journal of Native Education, 22*(1), 16–27.

Bayers, P.L. (2003). *Imperial Ascent: Mountaineering, Masculinity, and Empire*. Boulder, CO: University Press of Colorado.

Binnema, T. & Niemi, M. (2006). 'Let the line be drawn now': Wilderness, conservation, and the exclusion of aboriginal people from Banff National Park in Canada. *Environmental History, 11*(4), 724–750.

Bordo, J. (1997). The terra Nullius of wilderness. Colonialist landscape art (Canada & Australia) and the so-called claim to American exception. *International Journal of Canadian studies/Revue Internationale D'études Canadiennes*, (15), 5–12.

Brody, H. (1998). *Maps & Dreams*. Long Grove, IL: Waveland Press.

Brookes, A. (2003). A critique of neo-Hahnian outdoor education theory. Part one: Challenges to the concept of 'character building'. *Journal of Adventure Education & Outdoor Learning, 3*(1), 49–62.

Burkhart, B.Y. (2004). What Coyote and Thales can teach us: An outline of American Indian epistemology. In A. Waters (Ed.) *American Indian Thought* (pp. 15–26). Malden, MA: Blackwell.

Cajete, G. (1994). *Look to the Mountain: An Ecology of Indigenous Education*. Skyland, NC: Kivaki Press.

Cajete, G. (2001). Indigenous education and ecology: Perspectives of an American Indian educator. In J.A. Grim (Ed.) *Indigenous Traditions and Ecology: The Interbeing of Cosmology and Community*. Cambridge, MA: Harvard University Press.

Cajete, G. (2004). Philosophy of Native science. In A. Waters (Ed.) *American Indian Thought* (pp. 45–57). Malden, MA: Blackwell.

Cordova, V.F. (2004). Approaches to Native American philosophy. In A. Waters (Ed.) *American Indian Thought* (pp. 27–33). Malden, MA: Blackwell.

Cronon, W. (1996). The trouble with wilderness: Or, getting back to the wrong nature. *Environmental History, 1*(1), 7–55.

Dean, M. (2012). *Inheriting a Canoe Paddle: The Canoe in Discourses of English–Canadian Nationalism*. Toronto, ON: University of Toronto Press.

Deloria, V.J. (2004). Philosophy and the tribal peoples. In A. Waters (Ed.) *American Indian Thought* (pp. 3–12). Malden, MA: Blackwell.

DuFour, J. (2004). Ethics and understanding. In A. Waters (Ed.) *American Indian Thought* (pp. 34–41). Malden, MA: Blackwell.

Dunlap, T.R. (1999). *Nature and the English Diaspora: Environment and History in the United States, Canada, Australia, and New Zealand*. Cambridge, UK, and New York, NY: Cambridge University Press.

Friedel, T. (2011). Looking for learning in all the wrong places: Urban Native youths' cultured response to Western-oriented place-based learning. *International Journal of Qualitative Studies in Education, 24*(5), 531–546.

Graveline, F.J. (1998). *Circle Works: Transforming Eurocentric Consciousness*. Halifax, NS: Fernwood.

Guha, R. (1998). Radical American environmentalism and wilderness preservation: A third world critique. In D. Van DeVeer & C. Pierce (Eds.) *The Environmental Ethics and Policy Book* (2nd edn) (pp. 515–522). Toronto, Ontario, Canada: Wadsworth.

Hatcher, A., Bartlett, C., Marshall, M. & Marshall, A. (2009). Two-eyed seeing: A cross-cultural science journey. *Green Teacher, 86*, 3–6.

Haun-Moss, B. (2002). Layered hegemonies: The origins of recreational canoeing desire in the Province of Ontario. *TOPIA: Canadian Journal of Cultural Studies, 7*, 39–55.

Henze, R.C. & Vanett, L. (1993). To walk in two worlds: Or more? Challenging a common metaphor of Native education. *Anthropology & Education Quarterly, 24*(2), 116–134.

Horne, W.C. (2005). The phenomenology of Samuel Hearne's journey to the Coppermine River (1795): Learning the Arctic. *Ethics, Place & Environment, 8*(1), 39–59.

Ingold, T. (2000). *The Perception of the Environment: Essays on Livelihood, Dwelling and Skill*. New York, NY: Routledge.

Jojola, T. (2004). Notes on identity, time, space, and place. In A. Waters (Ed.) *American Indian Thought* (pp. 87–96). Malden, MA: Blackwell.

Kenny, C. (2002). Blue Wolf says goodbye for the last time. *American Behavioral Scientist, 45*(8), 1214–1222.

Kimmerer, R.W. (2013). The fortress, the river and the garden. In A. Kulnieks, D.R. Longboat & K. Young (Eds.) *Contemporary Studies in Environmental and Indigenous Pedagogies* (pp. 49–76). Rotterdam: Sense Publishers.

Legge, M. (2012). Bicultural perspectives of education outdoors part 1: A Pākehā perspective on biculturalism in education outdoors. In D. Irwin, J. Straker & A.M. Hill (Eds) *Outdoor Education in Aotearoa New Zealand: A New Vision for the Twenty-first Century* (pp. 138–145). Christchurch, NZ: CPIT.

Lertzman, D. (2002). Rediscovering rites of passage: Education, transformation, and the transition to sustainability. *Ecology and Society, 5*(2), Article 30.

Lightning, W.C. (1992). Compassionate mind: Implications of a text written by Elder Louis Sunchild. *Canadian Journal of Native Education, 19*(1), 215–253.

Lowan(-Trudeau), G. (2009). Exploring place from an Aboriginal perspective: Considerations for outdoor and environmental education. *Canadian Journal of Environmental Education, 14*, 42–58.

Lowan(-Trudeau), G. (2011). Ecological métissage: Exploring the third space in outdoor and environmental education. *Pathways: The Ontario Journal of Outdoor Education, 23*(2), 10–15.

Lowan-Trudeau, G. (2013). Considering ecological métissage: To blend or not to blend? *Journal of Experiential Education, 37*(4), 351–366.

Loynes, C. (2010). The British youth expedition: Cultural and historical perspectives. In S.K. Beames (Ed.) *Understanding Educational Expeditions* (pp. 1–15). Rotterdam: Sense.

MacDonald, R.H. (1993). *Sons of the Empire: The Frontier and the Boy Scout movement, 1890–1918*. Toronto and Buffalo: University of Toronto Press.

Marker, M. (2006). After the Makah whale hunt: Indigenous knowledge and limits to multicultural discourse. *Urban Education, 41*(5), 482–505.

Miller, R.J., Ruru, J., Behrendt, L. & Lindberg, T. (2010). *Discovering Indigenous Lands: The Doctrine of Discovery in the English Colonies*. New York: Oxford University Press.

Mullins, P.M. (2009). Living stories of the landscape: Perception of place through canoeing in Canada's north. *Tourism Geographies, 11*(2), 233–255.

Mullins, P.M. (2014). Conceptualizing skill within a participatory ecological approach to outdoor adventure. *Journal of Experiential Education, 37*(4), 320–334.

Mullins, P.M. & Maher, P.T. (2007). Paddling the Big Sky: Reflections on place-based education and experience. Retrieved from www.fs.fed.us/rm/pubs/rmrs_p049/rmrs_p049_402_410.pdf.

Oles, G.W.A. (1995). 'Borrowing' activities from another culture: A Native American's perspective. In K. Warren, M. Sakofs & J.S.J. Hunt (Eds) *The Theory of Experiential Education* (pp. 195–200). Dubuque, IA: Kendall Hunt.

Raffan, J. (1993). The experience of place: Exploring land as teacher. *Journal of Experiential Education, 16*(1), 39–45.

Reti, H. (2012). Bicultural perspectives of education outdoors part 2: E Tohu: A direction for Māori in the outdoors. In D. Irwin, J. Straker & A.M. Hill (Eds) *Outdoor Education in Aotearoa New Zealand: A New Vision for the Twenty-first Century* (pp. 146–147). Christchurch, NZ: CPIT.

Root, E. (2010). This land is our land: This land is your land? The decolonizing journeys of white outdoor environmental educators. *Canadian Journal of Environmental Education, 15*, 103–119.

Ryan, S. & Fox, K.M. (2001). Working to honour difference. *Leisure/Loisir, 26*(1–2), 61–84.

Smith, L.T. (1999). *Decolonizing Methodologies: Research and Indigenous Peoples.* New York, NY: Zed Books.

Swayze, N. (2009). Engaging Indigenous urban youth in environmental learning: The importance of place revisited. *Canadian Journal of Environmental Education, 14*, 59–72.

Takano, T. (2005). Connections with the land: Land-skills courses in Igloolik, Nunavut. *Ethnography, 6*(4), 463–486.

Urion, C.A. (1999). Hope and healing: Implications for research design. Keynote Address, Canadian Association of Psychological Oncology (CAPO), Edmonton, AB, May.

Wall, S. (2005). Totem poles, teepees, and token traditions: 'Playing Indian' at Ontario summer camps, 1920–1955. *Canadian Historical Review, 86*(3), 513–544.

Waters, A. (2004). Language matters: Nondiscrete nonbinary dualism. In A. Waters (Ed.) *American Indian Thought* (pp. 97–115). Malden, MA: Blackwell.

Whitt, L.A. (2004). Biocolonialism and the commodification of knowledge. In A. Waters (Ed.) *American Indian Thought* (pp. 188–213). Malden, MA: Blackwell.

6

Health and wellbeing benefits of activities in the outdoors

Cathryn Carpenter

VICTORIA UNIVERSITY, AUSTRALIA

Nevin Harper

OUTWARD BOUND CANADA

As the world grows ever more complex a fundamental truth becomes increasingly evident: human health and wellbeing is enhanced through meaningful connections between people and places. Unfortunately, our predominantly urban lifestyles have distanced individuals and communities from rural and natural environments. Just as houses become larger and gardens evolve into concrete entertaining areas, the health and wellbeing benefits of being active outdoors are gaining credibility as a valid and effective approach to improving health.

The World Health Organization's declaration that health is the 'complete state of physical, mental and social wellbeing, and not merely the absence of disease or infirmity' (WHO, 1946, p. 1) enabled the development of multi-layered approaches to, and interpretations and visions of, what comprises 'health and wellbeing'. The biomedical model of health that treats illness or disease in isolation from person and place is no longer accepted (Marmot & Wilkinson, 1999; Murphy, 2004; Baum, 2008) indicating that models incorporating the social and environmental context are increasingly relevant.

Research suggests that outdoor activities enable people to engage physically, intellectually, emotionally and spiritually with other people within outdoor environments. This chapter utilises a socio-ecological model to frame an exploration of literature clarifying how human health and wellbeing is enhanced through engagement in outdoor experiences. After introducing the origins of the socio-ecological model we will discuss health and wellbeing for the individual, followed by an examination of social and 'significant other' relationship benefits. Primarily focusing on the human or anthropocentric perspective, the next section explores ways in which the natural environment contributes to our health and wellbeing. The final section challenges us to consider if 'doses of being active outdoors' can assist us to reconnect with the health benefits a life more closely entwined in nature could provide.

Cathryn Carpenter and Nevin Harper

Socio-ecological health and wellbeing

The development of a socio-ecological understanding of health and wellbeing, considering the context and history of the individual, enables a fuller depiction of his or her health needs. As Murphy (2004) suggests:

> Socio-ecology refers to the complexity of interactions between people, and their social and physical environments. The socio-ecological approach to health acknowledges the influence that infrastructure and systems can exert on these interactions, particularly with respect to social and health outcomes. (p. 165)

Health can broadly be described as 'the capacity of people to adapt to, respond to, or control life's challenges and changes' (Frankish, Green, Ratner, Chomik & Larson, 2001, p. 406). Furnass (1995) suggests wellbeing includes 'satisfactory human relationships, a meaningful occupation, opportunities for contact with the natural environment, creative expression, and making a positive contribution to human society' (p. 6). To be 'healthy', then, implies empowerment of individuals to manage their lives. These definitions align with the objectives of many outdoor activity programmes that aspire to enhance personal development, social engagement and community responsibilities. The challenge is to design programmes that facilitate individual growth, positive social dynamics, and develop interdependent relationships with both their community and outdoor environments. In short, to promote health through a multi-dimensional (i.e. socio-ecological) approach.

One of the early ecological models connecting human experiences to their environmental context was developed by Bronfenbrenner (1986). It was a complex illustration of consequential links that shape the behaviour of the individual located within a context that includes their family, school, peer group, local neighbourhood and community. Concerned by Bronfenbrenner's perceived hierarchical layering of systems, Fraser (2004) simplified the behavioural influences into three system-related domains: 'the individual psychosocial and biological characteristics, family factors, and environmental conditions' (p. 6). The development of this adapted socio-ecological model combines aspects of Bronfenbrenner and Fraser's models to emphasise key protective factors of outdoor activities for holistic health.

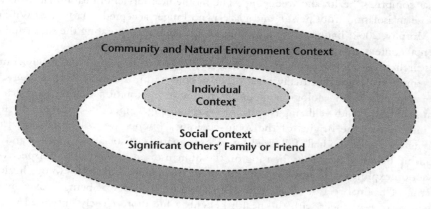

Figure 6.1 Socio-ecological health and wellbeing domains
Source: Adapted from Fraser (2004)

60

Conceptually, the individual is depicted as being nested within their community and environment. The social context in which they operate includes significant others; be they family or friends. The permeated boundaries also indicate that each domain influences the other domains. This model illustrates contextual influences – self, others and environment – that need to be positively developed for optimal health and wellbeing.

Individual context for health and wellbeing

Participants in outdoor programmes generally eat healthy diets, complete daily physical activity, have lowered distractions or stress from their usual daily living, and subsequently provide their bodies with an opportunity to cleanse and heal. Detoxification from alcohol, drugs, tobacco and even processed foods occurs during outdoor programmes. Outdoor living and travel conditions demand individuals and groups maintain vigilance over their own, and others' health and wellbeing.

Dubbert's review of health-related literature concluded more than twenty years ago that insufficient exercise reduces life expectancy and is a major contributing factor to many chronic illnesses (1992). While not difficult to find supportive literature for the physical benefits of exercise, it is only recently that research has emerged that looks explicitly at the benefits of exercising in outdoor 'green' environments, and subsequently linking the physical benefits to overall health and wellbeing (see Barton & Pretty, 2010).

Simply being active outdoors demands physical effort (e.g. walking on uneven surfaces or carrying a pack). The constant physical demands of the environment requires a moderate level of physical activity, which has been suggested as the most effective approach to reaching and maintaining physical health (Dubbert, 1992; Hansen, Stevens & Coast, 2001). Taking moderate levels of activity throughout the day has been suggested to be more effective than single doses of vigorous activity for general health and wellbeing, although not as effective in developing cardiovascular fitness (Hansen, Stevens & Coast, 2001). Physical activity, however, is only one aspect.

Research in outdoor programmes has consistently demonstrated improvements in adolescent wellbeing as measured by mental health standards (Hattie, Marsh, Neill & Richards, 1997; Russell, 2003; Bowen & Neil, 2013). Measures of physical health and psychological wellbeing from participation in outdoor programmes form a growing area of research and are bringing promising results (e.g. Beil, Hanes & Zwicky, 2014). Increasing rates of disease and mental health issues all emphasise that people do not generally have the willpower or desire to pursue health and wellbeing objectives over their lifestyle choices (Ackland & Catford, 2004). Outdoor programmes can assist through ensuring that individuals' goals for change are more consistently discussed and implemented, especially since 'having and progressing towards valued goals is central to major theoretical approaches to wellbeing' (MacLeod, Coates & Hetherton, 2008, p. 186).

Ryff and Singer (2008) also recognise the broader context within which dimensions of wellbeing exist: 'wellbeing . . . is profoundly influenced by the surrounding contexts of people's lives, and as such the opportunities for self-realisation are not equally distributed' (p. 24), which is why the authors emphasise the need for understanding the individual within their socioecological context. Table 6.1 incorporates these key characteristics or ways in which psychological health and wellbeing can be enhanced (Ryff & Singer, 2008, pp. 20–23) alongside narratives of experience typical of outdoor activity programmes.

Life circumstances can and do shape our health and wellbeing. The role of individuals in being able to have some authority over their lives in order to achieve a sense of wellbeing is one key element that completion of outdoor activities can achieve.

Table 6.1 Six dimensions of psychological wellbeing

Self-acceptance	Long-term self-evaluation that demonstrates awareness and acceptance of both personal strengths and weaknesses	• Beth lacked confidence in herself and would not contribute to group discussions. Conversations she had on the journey gained her a reputation in the group as a clear thinker and thoughtful person. Her opinion in group debates was sought and she started to believe in herself.
Positive relationships	Ability to love, empathise and care for others	• Participants quickly realised that to reach the summit meant they had to support one another, including redistributing the weight of their packs based on their strength and abilities.
Personal growth	Realisation of personal potential along with a focus on self-development, growth and becoming	• Sarah repeatedly caught herself saying 'I can't do this' until someone pointed out that she repeatedly proved herself wrong. She then was heard saying with conviction, 'I can do this'.
Purpose in life	Finding meaning and direction in life that can accommodate different stages in life	• Positive memories of Scouts drove Bob's decision to bushwalk as an adult. He soon realised that the adventure that motivated and inspired his involvement as a child was not important now. The forest environment and meaningful conversations met his current needs.
Environmental mastery	Capacity to create or control and engage in a surrounding context that suits personal needs	• Once Luc realised he could adjust his clothing and sleeping systems to the fluctuating temperatures, he no longer complained but, rather, began positively influencing his peers to do the same.
Autonomy	Sense of independence, self-determination and freedom that is not governed by outside influences	• When Katarina finished her outdoor expedition and returned home, she was surprised when her mother congratulated her on completing her chores without fuss.

Source: Adapted from Ryff and Singer (2008)

Social context: relationships

The traditional socio-ecological model needed to be more inclusive of the changing social dynamic. From our experience, primarily in programmes working with marginalised young people, it is clear that the 'significant other' in their lives is often not a 'traditionally' defined family member. These relationships with trusted, valued and loved 'significant others' are key indicators of health and wellbeing, as well as being important protective health factors (Fraser, 2004).

The group context is an important part of the experiential learning processes since the social dimensions of the group enable members to think beyond their own individual needs. Individuals come to acknowledge the interrelatedness of experience as well as their autonomy within the wider social system (Brah & Hoy, 1989; Warner Weil & McGill, 1989; Taylor, Segal & Harper, 2010). The social context of the individual within a group becomes significant when the physical remoteness of the programme's location elicits the need for human interaction for the progress, comfort and, potentially, the survival of the group. This dynamic and unpredicatable environment provides the basis of the challenges and problems with which the individual and the group

62

will be confronted. This encourages the group members to communicate and work together to achieve personal as well as group goals (Gibson, 1979; Gilsdorf, 2000; Schoel & Maizell, 2002), as well as developing healthy relationships and connections with others.

Marmarosh, Holtz and Schottenbauer (2005) provide support for the hypothesis that collective self-esteem and hope for self and psychological wellbeing develops from group cohesiveness. Forsyth (2001) suggests therapeutic groups as 'appropriate treatments for a variety of problems including addiction, thought disorders, depression, eating disorders and personality disorders' (p. 629), once again outlining how outdoor experiences can be valuable health solutions.

One intentional feature of outdoor activity programmes is the use of risk, challenge and group initiatives to generate new understandings of what is possible. This facilitated stress intentionally increases perceptions of risk and difficulty, and increases the likelihood that individuals will have the opportunity to work through and overcome difficult situations. Walsh and Golins (1976) described *adaptive dissonance* as the state created by these stress-related activities. The dissonance, or disconnect, occurs when an experience does not match an individual's perception, belief or knowledge of the given situation. The cognitive dissonance experienced in groups allows for restorative processes to return order or balance to the group (Matz & Wood, 2005; Taylor et al., 2010). The strength of cohesion within the group or the individual attachment the members have for the group in turn, will moderate the effects of cognitive dissonance.

Community and natural environment context

For many practitioners the socio-ecological approach to understanding health has appeared to ignore the human relationships with the natural world, focusing instead on the built environment or human-centric places. However, the model in Figure 6.1 emphasises that contact with surrounding environments, inclusive of gardens, parks and reserves, is equally important.

Dewey (1958) suggests that the very attempts by humans to define and describe their subjective experience of life emphasises the need for this separation since an 'unanalysed world does not lend itself to control' (p. 13). Humans can and do consciously separate themselves from the natural world in which they have evolved, as well as from the ways in which they connect with that natural world, and this shapes the ways in which they define their relationship with nature (Taylor et al., 2010).

Kellert (1997) suggests that one's degree of connection with nature is more than an expression of the need for material goods: 'our inclination to connect with nature also addresses other needs: intellectual capacity, emotional bonding, aesthetic attractions, creativity and imagination, even the recognition of a just and purposeful existence' (p. 6). He also suggests that these types of experience were 'frequently cited as an antidote to the pressures and relative unattractiveness of the modern world' (Kellert, 2004, p. 64).

Research is confirming the necessity for connections to nature for our health and wellness. Building on the foundations of biophilia (Wilson, 1978), recent studies have found that life stress can be buffered or reduced in children simply through living in proximity to nature (Wells, 2003), and that exposure to forest environments reduces cortisol levels, pulse rate, blood pressure and sympathetic nerve activity (Park, Tsunetsugu, Kasetani, Kagawa & Miyazaki, 2010).

Attention restoration theory stemming from the early work of psychologist William James depicted types of attention as being less taxing on the individual's cognitive and emotional faculties and even to possess restorative properties. These restorative properties were attributed to interesting or unique situations in which the individual is engaged but does not require concerted effort (i.e. directed attention) and experiences a reduction in mental fatigue (Kaplan, 1995; Kaplan & Kaplan, 2003). Kaplan integrates theoretical understandings of stress with the restorative properties of natural environments, and suggests that stress can be prevented or reduced through the restoration of directed attention. This 'healing power of nature' is reiterated throughout the literature as vitality enriching and capable of restoring mental health (Logan & Selhub, 2012).

If relationships with the natural world can be seen as an essential part of health and wellbeing, then adventures and journeys in remote locations – implemented with intention – can be utilised as effective ways in which to facilitate an enhanced relationship with both the natural environment and social communities (Harper, Carpenter & Segal, 2012). The need to access remote natural locations can be understood through an appreciation of the uniqueness of the experience. Kimball and Bacon (1993) allude to the potential for the wilderness environment to be unconsciously equated with Jungian 'Sacred Space', which Tacey (1995) describes as being the 'heart of humanity' (p. 1), and vital for our individual and collective health. Kimball and Bacon observe that 'most people who have participated in wilderness therapy programmes agree that there is an aesthetic, or archetypal, or even spiritual/transcendent aspect to the environment' (p. 27). The perception of sacred space by young people is recognition that something important is happening to them that may be meaningful in their lives.

Otto (1958) identified how most religious or spiritual experiences – he referred to as 'numinous' – comprise three components: mystery, terror and fascination. Combined, these elements are easily achieved in the majesty of nature and we find them in outdoor activities such as climbing or trekking in the mountains, and while paddling oceans and rivers. The combined beauty, overwhelming power and evolutionary attraction to nature is not only an ideal venue for spiritual experience, it may be an unavoidable benefit to those who participate.

As a society we are waking up to the need to re-experience 'numinous dimensions of nature [and this] is a primary challenge for us as individuals and for our educational and religious institutions as well' (Tucker, 2002, p. 68). An argument of spirituality for health is by no means a difficult one to make.

Nature and the numinous

Spirituality is one dimension of human existence, and often left out of the modern 'health and wellbeing' equation. Outdoor activities, intentionally facilitated or not, carry with them inherent significant prospects for numinous experience. Harper *et al.* (2012) argued for outdoor programmes to recognise potential such as spirituality in their design and delivery. Hay (2000) and Berry (1999) both posited that we as humans – in our modern Western world – are trapped by highly individualised thinking, and have lost our 'spiritual selves'. They also propose that our innate desire to connect with the more-than-human world may be central to our re-engagement with spirituality, leading towards increased maturity and spiritual health and wellbeing.

Classic and contemporary literature on nature has repeatedly described our connectedness to nature as a journey or expression of soul (e.g. Thoreau's transcendence). If outdoor activities and intentionally facilitated outdoor programmes might assist in transformational experiences that take us beyond our usual human experiences and open us to the numinous, and assuming our propositions, and those of most spiritual traditions, that spirituality is a meaningful contribution to one's health, then why would we not propose outdoor studies to include this as an important, if not core, element of the outdoor experience?

The uniqueness of outdoor programmes – small groups of people in natural surroundings while undergoing personal challenges and adventures; provides an important socio-ecological approach to increasing people's holistic health and wellbeing (Pryor, Carpenter & Townsend, 2005). The accumulated evidence emphasises that health and wellbeing are enhanced through activities in the outdoors, with some researchers calling for increased sophistication in the 'prescription' of outdoor activity (Berman *et al.*, 2012). We then responsibly must ask the questions of what type and how much is enough, or, conversely, is it possible to have too much?

The right dose: how much is enough?

Promoting a 'dose of nature' clarifies the minimum exposure people should have to their natural world and seeks to highlight what amazing benefits this natural and free product can provide. Current thinking internationally on physical activity levels, for example, is that we should each engage in at least thirty minutes of moderate to vigorous levels exercise daily. This approach has the full support of family doctors through to exercise physiologists – both products of the dominant allopathic medical system. Could it not be appropriate, then, to suggest a duration and intensity of outdoor activity or exposure for ideal human health?

Contact with nature can be significant in numerous ways (Maller *et al.*, 2008; Harper, 2012). It would be simplistic but acceptable to suggest simply adding nature to the current 30-minute dose of daily exercise. Emerging research has begun to support this notion. Pasanen, Tyrvainen and Korpela's (2014) recent investigation with more than 2000 Finnish people confirms this, concluding that 'Nature provides an added value to the known benefits of physical activity. Repeated exercise in nature is in particular, connected to better emotional wellbeing' (p. 1); the research is once again emphasising that it is being outside that brings additional health benefits.

Barton and Pretty's (2010) meta-analysis of ten 'green exercise' studies explored the question 'What is the best dose of nature in exercise?' Findings from their study suggest there are both short- and long-term benefits. Self-esteem and mood were most improved with short durations of green exercise (e.g. five minutes) regardless of age, gender, intensity or other variables assessed. Both factors diminished but remained positive over longer periods of outdoor exercise, but declined with growing intensity of activity (i.e. best results for light and continuous outdoor exercise).

Other notable results were that all types of green space produced positive results, water seemed to increase benefits, and the greatest impact seemed to be with the younger participants and to diminish with age. Barton and Pretty (2010) concluded that exercise in nature is a 'readily available therapy with no obvious side effects' (p. 3951). However, we must always acknowledge that nature can be harmful to human health (bites, stings, allergies, etc.) and that there may always be some people for whom the experience of nature creates anxiety and fear rather than being a restorative environment.

There is a call to address the growing epidemic in the Western world of chronic health issues such as obesity, cardio-pulmonary disease and diabetes. Nature-based activities have been identified as well positioned to promote health, family connectedness and psycho-spiritual growth (Flett, Moore, Pfeiffer, Belonga & Navarre, 2010). However, the authors also concluded that health and wellbeing will be improved when programmes have specific objectives, build participant confidence, and are challenging and, above all, fun. 'Ideal[ly] programs should offer both physical activity and ecologically meaningful nature experiences' (p. 292). Fortunately, these criteria are also key descriptors of many outdoor programmes. With a growing body of health-related evidence, the argument for increased time and activity outdoors gains strength (Thompson Coon *et al.*, 2011; Ward Thompson & Aspinall, 2011; Hartig, Mitchell, de Vries & Frumkin, 2014), and strategies to make it happen become clearer.

Prescribing a 'dose of nature' is in many ways almost the antithesis of our personal beliefs, philosophies and lifestyles. However the current path our global society is following demands a packaged approach that measures inputs and outputs. Promoting a 'dose of nature' clarifies the minimum time exposure people should be outdoors, and seeks to highlight the socio-ecological benefits this natural and free product can have for everyone. The current literature strongly supports spending time in natural environments for increased and significant health and wellbeing outcomes. Our recommendation, then, is for individuals to adopt lifestyle patterns that include a 'daily dose' of thirty minutes of moderate physical activity in parks, reserves or outdoor environments.

References

Ackland, M. & Catford J. (2004). Measuring population health status in Australia. In H. Keleher & B. Murphy (Eds.) *Understanding Health: A Determinants Approach* (pp. 70–96). Melbourne, Australia: Oxford University Press.

Barton, J. & Pretty, J. (2010). What is the best dose of nature and green exercise for improving mental health? A multi-study analysis. *Environmental Science & Technology, 44*(10), 3947–3955.

Baum, F. (2008). *The New Public Health* (3rd edn). Oxford: Oxford University Press.

Beil, K., Hanes, D. & Zwicky, H. (2014). Environmental influence on holistic health measures. *Explore (10)*2, 115–117.

Berman, M.G., Kross, E., Krpan, K.M., Askren, M.K., Burson, A., Deldin, P.J. *et al.* (2012). Interacting with nature improves cognition and affect for individuals with depression. *Journal of Affective Disorders, 140*, 300–305.

Berry, W. (1999). *The Great Work*. New York, NY: Bell Tower.

Bowen, D.J. & Neill, J.T. (2013). A meta-analysis of adventure therapy outcomes and moderators. *Open Psychology Journal, 6*, 28–53.

Brah, A. & Hoy, J. (1989). Experiential learning: A new orthodoxy? In S. Warner Weil & I. McGill (Eds.) *Making Sense of Experiential Learning: Diversity in Theory and Practice* (pp. 70–77). Philadelphia, PA: Open University Press.

Bronfenbrenner, U. (1986). Ecology of the family as a context to human development: Research perspectives. *Development Psychology, 22*, 723–742.

Dewey, J. (1958). *Experience and Nature*. USA: Dover Publications, Inc.

Dubbert, P.M. (1992). Exercise in behavioral medicine. *Journal of Consulting and Clinical Psychology, 60*(4), 613–618.

Flett, M.R., Moore, R.W., Pfeiffer, K.A., Belonga, J. & Navarre, J. (2010). Connecting children and family with nature-based physical activity. American Journal of *Health Education, 41*(5), 292–300.

Forsyth, D.R. (2001). Therapeutic groups. In M.A. Hogg & R.S. Tindale (Eds.) *Blackwell Handbook of Social Psychology: Group Process* (pp. 628–659). Oxford, UK: Blackwell.

Frankish, C.J., Green, L.W., Ratner, P.A., Chomik, T. & Larson, C. (2001). *Health Impact Assessment as a Tool for Population Health Promotion and Public Policy*. Vancouver, Canada: Institute of Health Promotions Research, University of British Columbia, 405–437.

Fraser, M. (Ed.) (2004). *Risk and Resilience in Childhood: An Ecological Perspective* (2nd edn). Washington, DC: NASW Press.

Furnass, B. (1995). Survival health and wellbeing into the twenty first century. *Proceedings of Nature and Society Forum Conference*, Australian National University, 30 November–1 December. Canberra, Australia: Nature and Society, Inc.

Gibson, P.M. (1979). Therapeutic aspects of wilderness programs: a comprehensive literature review. *Therapeutic Recreation Journal*, Second Quarter, 21–31.

Gilsdorf, R. (2000). Experience – adventure – therapy: An inquiry into professional identity. In K. Richards & B. Smith (Eds.) *Therapy Within Adventure* (pp. 57–76). Augsburg, Germany: Ziel.

Hansen, C.J., Stevens, L.C. & Coast, J.R. (2001). Exercise duration and mood state: How much is enough to feel better? *Health Psychology, 20*(4), 267–275.

Harper, N.J. (2012). Contact with nature as a research variable in wilderness therapy. In A. Pryor, C. Carpenter, C.L. Norton & J. Kirchner (Eds.) *Emerging Insights in Adventure Therapy: Proceedings of the 5th International Adventure Therapy Conference* (pp. 300–311). European Arts & Science Publishing.

Harper, N.J., Carpenter, C. & Segal, D. (2012). Self and place: Journeys in the land. *Ecopsychology, 4*(4), 1–7.

Hartig, T., Mitchell, R., de Vries, S. & Frumkin, H. (2014). Nature and health. *Annual Review of Public Health, 35*(1), 207–228.

Hattie, J.A., Marsh, H.W., Neill, J.T. & Richards, G.E. (1997). Adventure education and Outward Bound: Out-of-class experiences that make a lasting difference. *Review of Educational Research, 67*, 43–87.

Hay, D. (2000). Spirituality versus individualism: Why we should nurture relational consciousness. *International Journal of Children's Spirituality, 5*(1), 37–48.

Kaplan, S. (1995). The restorative benefits of nature: Toward an integrative framework. *Journal of Environmental Psychology, 15*, 169–182.

Kaplan, S. & Kaplan, R. (2003). Health, supportive environments, and the reasonable person model. *American Journal of Public Health, 93*(9), 1484–1489.

Kellert, S. (1997). *Kinship to Mastery: Biophilia in Human Evolution and Development*. Washington, DC: Island Press.

Kellert, S. (2004). Ordinary nature: the value of exploring and restoring nature in everyday life. In W.W. Shaw, L.K. Harris & L. Vandruff (Eds.) *Proceedings of the 4th International Symposium on Urban Wildlife Conservation*, 1–5 May, Tucson, AZ.

Kimball, R.O. & Bacon, S.B. (1993). The wilderness challenge model. In M. Gass (Ed.) *Adventure Therapy: Therapeutic Applications of Adventure Programming* (pp. 11–41). Iowa: Kendall/Hunt.

Logan, A.C. & Selhub, E.M. (2012). *Vis Medicatrix naturae*: Does nature 'minister to the mind'? *Biopsychosocial Medicine, 6*(11), 1751–1759.

MacLeod, A.K., Coates, E. & Hetherton, J. (2008). Increasing wellbeing through teaching goal setting and planning skills: results of a brief intervention. *Journal of Happiness Studies, 9*, 185–196.

Maller, C., Townsend, M., St Ledger, L., Henderson-Wilson, C., Pryor, A., Prosser, L. & Moore, M. (2008). Healthy parks healthy people: The health benefits of contact with nature in a park context: A review of current literature (2nd edn). *Social and Mental Health Priority Area, Occasional Paper Series*. Melbourne, Australia: Faculty of Health and Behavioural Sciences.

Marmarosh, C., Holtz, A. & Schottenbauer, M. (2005). Group cohesiveness, group-derived collective self-esteem, group-derived hope, and the well-being of group therapy members. *Group Dynamics: Theory, Research, and Practice, 9*(1), 32–44.

Marmot, M. & Wilkinson, R. (Eds.) (1999). *Social Determinants of Health*. Oxford, UK: Oxford University Press.

Matz, D.C. & Wood, W. (2005). Cognitive dissonance in groups: The consequences of disagreement. *Journal of Personality and Social Psychology, 88*(1), 22–37.

Murphy, B. (2004). Health education and communication strategies. In H. Keleher & B. Murphy (Eds.) *Understanding Health: A Determinants Approach* (pp. 152–169). Melbourne, Australia: Oxford University Press.

Otto, R. (1958). *The Idea of the Holy*. New York, NY: Oxford University Press.

Park, B.J., Tsunetsugu, Y., Kasetani, T., Kagawa, T. & Miyazaki, Y. (2010). The physiological effects of Shinrin-yoku (taking in the forest atmosphere or forest bathing): Evidence from field experiments in 24 forests across Japan. *Environmental Health & Prevention Medicine, 15*, 18–26.

Pasanen, T., Tyrvainen, L. & Korpela, K. (2014). The relationship between perceived health and physical activity indoors, outdoors in built environments, and outdoors in nature. *Applied Psychology: Health and Wellbeing, 6*(3), 324–346.

Pryor, A., Carpenter, C. & Townsend, M. (2005). Outdoor education and bush adventure therapy: A socio-ecological approach to health and wellbeing. *Australian Journal of Outdoor Education 9*(1), 3–13.

Russell, K.C. (2003). An assessment of outcomes in outdoor behavioral healthcare treatment. *Child and Youth Care Forum, 32*(6), 355–381.

Ryff, C.D. & Singer, B.H. (2008). Know thyself and become what you are: A eudemonic approach to psychological wellbeing. *Journal of Happiness Studies, 9*, 13–39.

Schoel, J. & Maizell, R. (2002). *Exploring Islands of Healing: New Perspectives on Adventure Based Counselling*. Beverly, MA: J. Weston Walsh Publishers.

Tacey, D.J. (1995). *Edge of the Sacred: Transformation in Australia*. Sydney, Australia: HarperCollins Publishers.

Taylor, D.M., Segal, D. & Harper, N.J. (2010). The ecology of adventure therapy. *Ecopsychology, 2*(2), 77–83.

Thompson Coon, J., Boddy, K., Stein, K., Whear, R., Barton, J. & Depledge, M.H. (2011). Does participating in physical activity in outdoor natural environments have a greater effect on physical and mental wellbeing than physical activity indoors? A systematic review. *Environmental Science & Technology, 45*(5), 1761–1772.

Tucker, M.E. (2002). Religion and ecology: The interaction of cosmology and cultivation. In S.R. Kellert & T.J. Farnham (Eds.) *The Good in Nature and Humanity* (pp. 65–90). Washington: Island Press.

Walsh, V. & Golins, G. (1976). *An Exploration of the Outward Bound Process*. Denver, CO: Outward Bound Publications.

Ward Thompson, C. & Aspinall, P.A. (2011). Natural environments and their impact on activity, health, and quality of life. *Applied Psychology: Health and Well-Being, 3*(3), 230–260.

Warner Weil, S. & McGill, I. (Eds.) (1989). *Making Sense of Experiential Learning: Diversity in Theory and Practice*. Philadelphia, PA: Open University Press.

Wells, N.M. (2003). Nearby nature: A buffer of life stress among rural children. *Environment and Behaviour, 35*(3), 311–330.

WHO (1946). *Preamble to the Constitution of the World Health Organization as Adopted by the International Health Conference*. New York: World Health Organization, 19–22 June.

Wilson, O.E. (1978). *On Human Nature*. Cambridge, MA: Harvard University Press.

7

Shifting perspectives on research in the outdoors

Emily Coates, Alan Hockley, Barbara Humberstone and Ina Stan

BUCKINGHAMSHIRE NEW UNIVERSITY

What is cutting edge in research methodologies in one discipline may be either unacceptable or thought of as ordinary in others. Approaches to understanding and making sense of material and social phenomena are changing continuously through critical reflection and practice. In outdoor studies, there is a variety of methodological approaches influenced by various schools of thought. We are not concerned here with research from positivistic perspectives using quantitative methodologies. There is insufficient space here. Certainly, as Sparkes and Smith (2014, p. 1) point out, there is considerable growth in qualitative forms of research across 'psychology . . . and social and health sciences', disciplines from which outdoor studies draws and that, reciprocally, can be informed by credible research from outdoor studies' fields.

Coates (2010), through her 'confessional tale' of journeying through her doctorate, highlights seven 'moments' that Denzin and Lincoln (2005) propose as historical developments of qualitative research. Suffice it to say that approaches adopted are based upon particular paradigmatic notions underpinning epistemological and ontological assumptions (Denzin & Lincoln, 2005, p. 22). If the outdoors and its considerable wealth of knowledge is to gain greater credibility outwith then it is important that outdoor research reflects critically upon, and engages with, theory and practice from its sister disciplines' literature. Due to limited space, we are unable to include all references we wish.

The following are examples of interpretative research in outdoor studies that exemplify later 'moments' (cf. Denzin & Lincoln, 2005) and draw upon perspectives often outside traditional outdoor studies. Ina Stan is concerned with the interaction between various participants: teachers, pupils, instructors and providers during residential outdoor learning experiences. Alan Hockley argues that auto-ethnography is a credible methodology for researching landscape and place through the practice of walking, drawing upon cultural geography theory. Emily Coates engages with social theory, and describes how interpretative research can be made available and accessible through fictional writing narratives of parents who climb. Each of these examples draws upon methodologies and theoretical perspectives currently employed in diverse social science fields. They are largely narrated in the first person as they are reflective accounts of their research.

Classroom interaction – Ina Stan

My doctoral research was concerned with the educational process within one residential outdoor centre involving groups of primary school children, their teachers, and outdoor facilitators and providers (Stan, 2008). It took broadly an ethnographic 'case study' approach to study group interaction between the participants in a natural setting by taking a holistic approach, giving an account of the pupils' outdoor learning experience in the context of a group (Stan, 2009). The rationale for this study was that, on reading literature about research in outdoor education, I noticed that most of research looked at how outdoor activity programmes were aimed at bettering the individual, at providing support for the individual, at educating the individual. However, the vast majority of outdoor activity programmes involve groups: groups of children, teenagers, adults, families, teams and so on.

Most programmes, although largely involving groups, rarely took account of the group factor. I considered that looking at what actually goes on within a group, how the relations within the group affect the learning process, and how group interaction influences the members within the group involved in the activity, were significant and interesting subjects of research. Focusing on group interaction meant focusing on all the participants involved in the outdoor programme, including centre managers and visiting teachers. This gives a holistic view of pupil experience and an understanding of the complexity of the outdoor education process.

Groups have been studied extensively in psychology, sociology and social psychology. However, most of this research has been undertaken from positivistic perspectives, within a controlled environment, limiting the spectrum of research (cf. Maykut & Morehouse, 1994; Hammersley & Atkinson, 1995). Furthermore, theories on small groups developed by psychologists and socio-psychologists tend to predominate in much outdoor education (Horizons, 2014). Groups have not received the attention that they deserve in outdoor education research from socio-cultural perspectives. Arguably, research within the field of outdoor education has paid little attention to the educational process itself, focusing mostly on outcomes rather than process. Rickinson *et al.* (2004, p. 56) maintain that research should be aimed more at process and social interactions between the participants, as these represent some of the 'blank spots' within research in outdoor education (see Beames, 2004; Seaman, 2007). My study attempted to fill in some of these blank spots by gaining an insight into the outdoor learning experience and by moving away from the traditional focus on the individual and recognising the importance of group interaction within the context of outdoor classrooms.

Educational research on classroom interaction has examined the intricacies of how pupils and teachers communicate with one another and act, shedding light on the complex interactions within such groups, while considering the perspectives of both the teachers and the pupils as significant (Pollard, 1985). I drew upon classroom interaction methodology and theory, as interaction generally should form the basis of teaching and learning in non-formal and formal learning contexts. Many of the studies on classroom interaction take an interpretative/qualitative approach, which arguably allows for an in-depth understanding of particular social phenomena. My ethnographic study was interpretative and qualitatively informed, using participant observation and semi-structured interviews to collect a variety of data. Ethnography was adopted as it enabled understanding of the perceptions and cultures of the people and organisations to be uncovered (see Humberstone, 1986; Walford, 2002; Stan & Humberstone, 2011). Ethnographic approaches are sensitive to the individual, and to social, group and cultural processes (Willis, 1977; Davies, 1984; Griffin, 1985).

Qualitative analyses of ethnography were used as a means to understand the experience of individuals in a group context (Griffin, 1985). This entailed identifying cultural domains, constructing taxonomies and carrying out a componential analysis of the cultural domains, which led to identifying the components of meaning assigned to the cultural categories. These procedures allowed me to identify recurrent themes within the data, which helped towards understanding the patterns within the outdoor classroom. Ethnography was considered the most suitable research perspective because it is sensitive enough to allow the capturing of the process in its wholeness (Fetterman, 1989), and it facilitates an insight into other people's experiences.

I looked outwith traditional outdoor education research drawing upon educational research on classroom interaction utilising ethnographic approaches. Applying ethnography to outdoor classrooms facilitates exploration of both the perspectives of teachers and pupils, and how their interplay impacts on the learning experiences in the natural context (Delamont, 1983). This provided for an understanding of what is going on when facilitators, teachers and pupils interact in the outdoors (Humberstone & Stan, 2011a). However, such research and the theory that underpins it, although it explained some of the phenomena within the outdoor classroom, did not fully elucidate how learning was constructed by the participants and what governed their relationships during group interaction. My research uncovered social aspects of learning at the heart of the outdoor centre. Therefore, I turned to social constructionism and socio-cultural learning theory to better understand some of these processes (Rogoff, 1990), and to explore classroom interaction in the outdoors. I integrated the findings from this research within theoretical frameworks that more fully explained these uncovered phenomena. Arguably, this could not have been possible if only one perspective had been used.

I continued to pursue research through the 'wellbeing and outdoor pedagogies' project. These ethnographic studies further uncovered the importance of considering the various participant perspectives in order to gain greater insight into the outdoor learning experience, while challenging some taken for granted assumptions (Humberstone & Stan, 2011b, 2012).

Wayfaring – Alan Hockley

This section discusses how my research developed from considering contemporary discourses surrounding landscape and place in the fields of anthropology and cultural geography. Additionally, methodologies of narrative and auto-ethnography are discussed. My interest started in wanting to discover how landscape and place might be interpreted through the act of walking. I was surprised that interpretations of landscape and the significance of walking had rarely been examined critically in much of leisure research or outdoor pedagogic practice. This is despite the fact that the (long distance) walk is central to many outdoor learning and recreational programmes. While there is emphasis on teaching navigation, safety, nutrition, equipment, teamwork and organisation, how the walk is experienced and meanings are made of landscape travelled through is rarely explored.

Furthermore, the landscape seemed often to be presented as a resource, a backdrop that provides the necessary components of hills, valleys and streams, and where there are few people, or as an example of a particular geology or natural environment while on a field trip. The walk appeared to be an incidental aspect. My interests regarding specific qualities of different landscapes, how all are repositories of particular histories, myths, stories and mysteries, and how these culturally influenced phenomena are perceived, felt and imagined by the walker have only recently been researched from pedagogic perspectives (Stewart, 2008; Wattchow & Brown, 2011). However, within other academic fields such as anthropology and cultural geography, such considerations of landscape and place have received serious enquiry. I discovered evolving discourses from these fields, with a recognition that exploring various landscapes through walking provides opportunities to engage with each kinaesthetically and in depth (Edensor, 2000; Wylie, 2005; Lorimer, 2011). Such deep engagements take landscape from being just a backdrop, appreciated only for its aesthetic qualities, to something that is alive, dynamic and evolving, a milieu of cultural and social engagements (Ingold, 2000), a space of memory, mystery and imagination. This form of engagement provides for the investigation of the relationships between the landscape or place and the individual (Tilley, 1994; Ingold, 2004; Ingold & Vergunst, 2008). In this way, the meanings and stories that may be drawn from landscape are explored through the feelings and emotions it provokes, and the affect it has upon the imagination. Furthermore, walking is an embodied practice that is at dialogue with the world; each is shaped by the other. As Ingold (2004, p. 333) observes, 'Through walking . . . landscapes are woven into life, and lives are woven into the landscape, in a process that is continuous and never-ending.'

Any experience, interpretation or understanding of landscape is problematical in that it defies a singular perspective because it is reliant on complex multi-faceted relationships between the individual, the cultural and the social. In exploring the disparate interpretations surrounding landscape, the concept of place and its specificity comes to the fore, as does the importance of the relationship between walking and how we make sense of place.

My research, therefore, sought to explore how a variety of landscapes are perceived, how cultural and social interpretations influence this perception, and whether these interpretations may be re-envisioned by wayfaring, or long distance walking as an alternate way of making understandings and meanings with landscape. Due to the storied nature of landscape, the role of narrative is central in exploring and unravelling these relationships. While writers describing their walking journeys in the commercial media often use narratives about their experiences, narrative is less commonly used by academics in the consideration of aspects of landscape, apart from some notable exceptions (Adams, 2001; Wylie, 2005; Lee & Ingold, 2006). Wylie (2005, p. 234) uses narrative and descriptive writing as a 'creative and critical means to discussing the varied affinities and distanciations of self and landscape emergent within the affective and performative milieu of coastal walking', from a single day's walking along the South West Coast Path.

Wylie's (2005) paper exemplifies how it is possible to use the narrative form of auto-ethnography to explore landscape from the walker's perspective, and provided an informative basis for my research. In the writing of an auto-ethnography it is the telling of a story using self-reflection that requires the reader not to sit back as a spectator, but to engage with it. It is through reading an auto-ethnography that 'we are taken into the intimate, embodied world of the other in a way that stimulates us to reflect on our own lives in relation to theirs' (Sparkes, 2002, p. 100). Furthermore, it can be a way of making communion between self and others, of time and space being interrelated, and also as a witness offering 'testimony to a truth generally unrecognized or suppressed' (Frank, 1995, p. 137). This approach is a relatively new developing field of inquiry, particularly in regards to how one relates to landscapes and making meanings from them. While this methodology has been utilised in the areas of contested identities including gender, sexual orientation, ethnicity and disability, its use is less common where the self-subject is not the 'other' at the borders of society speaking from a marginalised position and challenging established hegemonies. However, it is not necessary to be at these marginalised borders to use auto-ethnography as a methodological practice (see Nicol, 2014). If the research is about the subjective experience of walking and landscape, then writing about those experiences in the subjective way that auto-ethnography affords can be particularly applicable. My narratives, while employing many of the characteristics championed by Ellis and Bochner (2003), reflected rather an analytic auto-ethnography approach (Anderson, 2006). Such an approach allows for the researcher to be part of the research group or setting, for the discourse to include other voices, and for interpretation to be made by the researcher in developing theoretical understandings of broader social phenomena. My auto-ethnographical narratives were not meant to be an emotional journey for the reader of my subjective and personal experience, but rather to be creative and evocative accounts of my walking journeys that attempt to adhere to an 'accurate' portrayal of what I encountered and felt (Hockley, 2011).

Climbing families – Emily Coates

This section is concerned with research I undertook into the experience of parents who rock climb. I was interested in how they managed (if they did) to maintain their serious leisure practice when they became parents, and if the experience of managing climbing and parenting identities was gendered. This research was concerned to contextualise and understand the lives of the parents I interviewed and with whom I spent time. As Parry and Johnson (2014) have stated, to understand the complexity of lived experience one must contextualise; this is because identities are fluid and subject to a multiplicity of discourses (Foucault, 1980, 1983). Indeed Helstein (2007) recognises that Foucault sees subjects as positioned within often two or more subject positions, which can contradict. Thus the parents I interviewed held fluid identities as parents, climbers, workers and partners.

My doctoral supervisors enabled me to delve in and out of various research fields as they advised me to read widely and deeply in my first year, allowing me to develop both a research focus and an appropriate methodology. I was initially looking at masculinity and rock climbing and this led me to Robinson's (2004, 2008) work and then to the Kendal Mountain Film Festival in the Lake District, UK. At a symposium on women climbing, the issue of mothering was prominent and some of the points of this discussion were in relation to the media response to the death of Alison Hargreaves (Palmer, 2004; Gilchrist, 2007). I found that motherhood and adventure were not only under-researched but that there was little research on both parents in heterosexual couples and their leisure lives. This is particularly significant at a time when there is a culture of intensive parenting that seems in contradiction with an activity that requires a lot of commitment (both in terms of time and risk). Furthermore, it was by immersing myself in research into parenting, mothering, fathering and adventure sports that my methodological understanding began to emerge.

Methodological research approaches into the outdoors has tended to remain somewhat insular, and a positivistic approach to research has until recently tended to dominate both sports and outdoor activity research (Sparkes, 2002; Humberstone, 2009). Furthermore, it is this 'evidence-based' research that is more widely funded today (Dixon, Chapman & Hill, 2005).

In searching for alternative forms of research, it is not to deny that the 'traditional' positivistic research in the outdoors has been useful. Indeed it has allowed thoughts to develop and has fitted in with goals of standardised, generalisable results that can be applied to wider populations. However, the assumption that a single valid account that depicts social realities exists, is problematic and challenged (Schwandt, 2000). Instead, what we recognise in this chapter is that these conclusions cannot easily fit lives that are complex. Indeed, as Parry and Johnson (2014) find in leisure research, there is frustration 'with such limited goals for research and concern about their capacity to address social problems in the way leisure is lived' (p. 120). Both Sparkes and Humberstone point to the importance of not just conducting qualitative research but engaging with methodological issues, and they look to interpretivism as an alternative form of research.

Denzin and Lincoln (2005) suggest that interpretivism recognises the subjective nature of research; it sees knowledge as partial and contextual, and thus rejects the notion of a single generalisable truth. This does not mean research is pointless but instead allows for a greater understanding of the complexity of lived experience and an awareness of the researcher's role in this process (Wai Man, 2001; Smith, 2009; Parry & Jonson, 2014). Reflecting on one's position within the research implies examining one's own subjectivity in relation to the complex lives of those studied (see Coates, 2010, 2012).

An interpretive approach involves not just recognising the difficulties in understanding lived experience but also in representing these experiences, how to write about ourselves and others (Richardson, 2000). Creative forms of representation is what Denzin and Lincoln (2005) refer to as the '7th moment' in qualitative research, and it is one that has become more prominent in leisure and sport research (see Dennison & Rinehart, 2000; Sparkes, 2002) and is in the early stages of research into some aspects of the outdoors. The benefit of using what has become known as creative analytic practice (CAP) is that both the micro-personal and the macro-social experiences are represented. Furthermore, when written in the form of stories, it allows the identities of participants to remain hidden. For me, writing up my research as short stories allowed the participants' experiences to be represented ethically without losing the diverse, vivid, extraordinary and mundane parts of their lives.

Creating the 'stories' was not a simple task; the idea is that the stories provide the analysis and the presentation of the data. I was assisted in this process by the work of Goodley (2004) and Markula and Denison (2003, 2005), who make explicit how the data are used within their stories. First, in the analysis, I narrowed the research down using broad, overarching themes that came up in all of the interviews. I then re-read the data to look for commonalities and differences, particularly looking for rich detail. It is important to recognise that my interpretation was influenced by my use of Foucault as a theoretical approach. The stories thus sought to show how the discourses on parenting, gender, risk, childhood and climbing were drawn upon. This was not just to show how the identities were shaped by these but also to demonstrate how participants resisted constraints by enabling new ways of being (Foucault, 1981).

As to how these themes and details were represented, I created five short stories based around the broad themes that participants had in common (pregnancy and climbing, fathers climbing, mothers climbing, a family day out, and children climbing). The data were primarily from the interviews but also from observation, previous literature, theory and interviews that were used for a climbing magazine article (see Stirling, 2009, 2010), somewhat torn apart (through the process above) then put together using fictional writing techniques such as the creation of characters, phrases, dialogue and monologue. It is beyond the scope of this paper to provide examples, but see Coates (2010, 2012).

By looking outside of the outdoor studies field, I was able to engage in further research and to move into a new moment with qualitative inquiry. If scholars engage with interpretive approaches and alternative forms of representing the data then outdoor studies research could benefit. Not only is the research analytical and narrated in a way that provides rich description, details and context, but the field can move closer to other social studies research, allowing in future greater collaboration and interdisciplinary opportunities.

Discussion and conclusion

A number of strands come together in phenomenological research in outdoor studies where situation, context, elements and the body are brought together to understand and explore what it means to experience outdoor engagements through outdoor pedagogy and/or practising nature-based physical and environmental activities. The examples above highlight some current methodological approaches in practice, which draw on ethnography, auto-ethnography constructionism/interpretivism and how research might be 'more-than-representational' (see Carolan, 2008) through various forms, exemplified by ethnographic fiction writing. These explored engagements with landscape, outdoor pedagogies and families that climb.

Interaction with the world is with all our senses, not only sight, particularly so in the outdoor environment, yet there are few outdoor studies that 'seek the senses' to uncover meanings and feelings. Sparkes (2009, p. 27) argues through a wealth of literature for embodied, corporeal and sensuous research, where alternative ways of understanding are 'thoroughly embodied and connected to people's senses and sensualities. It is tied to specific locations, highlights the fusion that exists between experience and awareness, and reminds us of the mind's location within a fleshy body which is itself affected by material conditions and social relationships' (Mellor & Shilling, 1997, p. 56; Sparkes, 2009, p. 27).

Outdoor experiences embrace the sensorial. The outdoor sensorium affords more than the five Western dominant senses that can shape who we are and our relations with material and human-beings. Humberstone (2011a, 2011b) explores more senses, including balance when windsurfing, using in part 'poetic' form to elicit the experience, while authors in Brown and Humberstone's (2015) collection draw upon the their embodied and sensorial (auto)ethnographic tales to narrate/research seascapes. Auto-ethnographic narratives are far from self-indulgent. They not only provide the reader with insight into experiences, but also through critical analysis and dialogue with wider literature provide a broader understanding, and perhaps provoke social and environmental awareness.

While this chapter is concerned with phenomenological research paradigms, attention in outdoor studies might also be paid to other research models. Sparkes and Smith (2014, p. 244) talk of the significance of 'multi- and inter-disciplinary' research that draws upon qualitative and quantitative research from diverse traditions. This follows Denzin (2010, p. 40), who suggests that, 'there needs to be greater openness to alternative paradigms critique'. Through collaboration with diverse disciplines, valuable research from the outdoor fields may find greater reach than only within the outdoor field.

References

Adams, P.C. (2001). Peripatetic imagery and peripatetic sense of place. In P.C. Adams, S. Hoelscher & K.E. Till (Eds.) *Textures of Place: Exploring Humanist Geographies* (pp. 186–206). London: University of Minnesota Press.

Anderson, L. (2006). Analytic autoethnography. *Journal of Contemporary Ethnography, 35*(4), 373–395.

Beames, S. (2004). Critical elements of an expedition experience. *Journal of Adventure Education and Outdoor Learning, 4*(2), 145–157.

Brown, M. & Humberstone, B. (Eds.) (2015). *Shaped by the Sea: Embodied Narratives and Fluid Geographies.* Farnham, Surrey: Ashgate Publishing.

Carolan, M.S. (2008). More-than-representational. Knowledge/s of the countryside: how we think as bodies. *Sociologia Ruralis, 48*(4), 409–421.

Coates, E. (2010). A personal journey through 'moments': doctoral research into parents who rock climb. *Journal of Adventure Education & Outdoor Learning,* 10(2), 147–160.

Coates, E. (2012). A fine balance: Stories of parents who climb. Unpublished PhD thesis. Bucks New University, Brunel University.

Davies, L. (1984). *Pupil Power: Deviance and Gender in School.* London: Falmer Press.

Delamont, S. (1983). *Interaction in the Classroom: Contemporary Sociology of the School* (2nd edn). London: Methuen.

Denzin, N. (2010). *The Qualitative Manifesto: A Call to Arms.* Walnut Creek, CA: Left Coast Press.

Denzin, N. & Lincoln, Y. (Eds.) (2005). *The Sage Handbook of Qualitative Research.* California: Sage.

Dennison, J.M. & Rinehart, R. (Eds.) (2000). Imagining sociological narratives. *Sociology of Sport Journal,* 17(10), 1–5.

Dixon, A.D., Chapman, T.K. & Hill, D. (2005). Research as an aesthetic process: Extending the portraiture methodology. *Qualitative Inquiry, 11*(1), 16–26.

Edensor, T. (2000). Walking in the British countryside: Reflexivity, embodied practices and ways to escape. *Body & Society, 6* (3–4), 81–106.

Ellis, C. & Bochner, A. (2003). Autoethnography, personal narrative, reflexivity. researcher as subject. In N. Denzin & Y. Lincoln (Eds.) *Collecting and Interpreting Qualitative Materials* (pp. 199–258). London: Sage.

Fetterman, D.M. (1989). *Ethnography – Step by Step.* London: Sage Publications.

Foucault, M. (1980). Body/power. In C. Gordon (Ed.) *Power/Knowledge: Selected Interviews and Other Writings 1972–1977* (pp. 55–62). Harlow, England: Harvester.

Foucault, M. (1981). *The Will to Knowledge: The History of Sexuality Volume 1*. London: Penguin Books.

Foucault, M. (1983). The subject and power. In H.L. Dreyfus & P. Rabinow (Eds.) *Michel Foucault: Beyond Structuralism and Hermeneutics*. Chicago, IL: University of Chicago Press.

Frank, A. (1995). *The Wounded Storyteller*. Chicago, IL: University of Chicago Press.

Gilchrist, P. (2007). 'Motherhood, ambition and risk': mediating the sporting hero/ine in conservative Britain. *Media, Culture & Society, 29*(3), 395–414.

Goodley, D. (2004). Approaching: Methodology in the life story: A non-participatory approach. In D. Goodley, R. Lawthom, P. Clough & M. Moore (Eds.) *Researching Life Stories: Method, Theory, and Analysis in a Biographical Age* (pp. 56–60). London: Routledge and Falmer Press.

Griffin, C. (1985). *Typical Girls? Young Women from School to the Job Market*. London: Routledge & Kegan Paul.

Hammersley, M. & Atkinson, P. (1995). *Ethnography: Principles in Practice*. London: Routledge.

Helstein, M.T. (2007). Seeing your sporting body: Identity, subjectivity, and misrecognition. *Sociology of Sport Journal, 24*, 78–103.

Hockley, A. (2011). Wayfaring: Making lines in landscape. Unpublished PhD thesis. Bucks New University/Brunel University.

Horizons (2014). *Belbin Team Role Workshops (online). Horizons Corporate Development*. Retrieved from: www.horizons.co.nz/corporate_training_team_building.html.

Humberstone, B. (1986). Outdoor education – the quality of the learning experience. An application of ethnographic research method trends and developments in PE. *Proceedings of the V111 Commonwealth and International Conference on PE, Dance, Recreation and Health* (pp. 438–445). London: E&FN Spon.

Humberstone, B. (2009). In splendid isolation – is the field missing something? Research in outdoor sports and outdoor education: Principles in practice. In I. Turcová & A. Martin (Eds.) *Outdoor Activities in Educational and Recreational Programmes* (pp. 40–65). Prague: Charles University.

Humberstone, B. (2011a). Engagements with nature: Ageing and windsurfing. In B. Watson & J. Harpin (Eds.) *Identities, Cultures and Voices in Leisure and Sport* (pp. 159–169). LSA Publication No. 116. Eastbourne: Leisure Studies Association.

Humberstone, B. (2011b). Embodiment and social and environmental action in nature-based sport: Spiritual spaces. Special Issue: Leisure and the politics of the environment. *Journal of Leisure Studies, 30*(4), 495–512.

Humberstone, B. & Stan, I. (2011a). Outdoor learning: Pupils' experiences and teachers' interaction in one outdoor residential centre. *Education 3–13, International Journal of Primary, Elementary and Early Years Education, 39*(5), 529–540.

Humberstone, B. & Stan, I. (2011b). Health, (body) image and primary schooling or 'Why do they have to be a certain weight'? *Sport, Education and Society, 16*(4), 431–449.

Humberstone, B. & Stan, I. (2012). Nature in outdoor learning – authenticity or performativity: Well-being, nature and Outdoor Pedagogies project. *Journal of Adventure Education & Outdoor Learning, 12*(3), 183–197.

Ingold, T. (2000). *The Perception of the Environment. Essays in Livelihood, Dwelling and Skill*. Abingdon, Oxon: Routledge.

Ingold, T. (2004). Culture on the ground. *Journal of Material Culture, 9*(3), 315–340.

Ingold, T. & Vergunst, J.L. (Eds.) (2008). *Ways of Walking: Ethnography and Practice on Foot*. Aldershot, Hampshire: Ashgate Publishing Ltd.

Lee, J. & Ingold, T. (2006). Fieldwork on foot: Perceiving, routing, socializing. In S. Coleman & P. Collins (Eds.) *Locating the Field: Space, Place and Context in Anthropology* (pp. 67–86). Oxford: Berg.

Lorimer, H. (2011). Walking: New forms and spaces for studies of pedestrianism. In T. Cresswell & P. Merriman (Eds.) *Geographies of Mobilities: Practices, Spaces, Subjects* (pp. 19–34). Farnham: Ashgate Publishing Ltd.

Markula, P. & Denison, J. (Eds.) (2003). *Moving Writing: Crafting Movement in Sport Research*. New York: Peter Lang.

Markula, P. & Denison, J. (2005). Sport and the personal narrative. In D. Andrews, D. Mason & M. Silk (Eds.) *Qualitative Methods in Sports Studies* (p. 184). Oxford: Berg.

Maykut, P. & Morehouse, R. (1994). *Beginning Qualitative Research: A Philosophic and Practical Guide*. London: The Falmer Press.

Mellor, P. & Shilling, C. (1997). *Re-forming the Body*. London: Sage.

Nicol, R. (2014). In the name of the whale. In M. Brown and B. Humberstone (Eds.) *Seascapes: Shaped by the Sea. Embodied Narratives and Fluid Geographies*. Farnham, Surrey: Ashgate Publications.

Palmer, C. (2004). Death, danger and the selling of risk in adventure sports. In B. Wheaton (Ed.) *Understanding Lifestyle Sports: Consumption, Identity and Difference* (pp. 55–69). London: Routledge.

Parry, D.C. & Johnson, C.W. (2014). Contextualising leisure research to encompass complexity in lived experience: The need for creative analytic practice. *Leisure Sciences: An Interdisciplinary Journal, 29*(2), 119–130.

Pollard, A. (1985). *The Social World of the Primary School*. London: Holt, Rinehart & Winston.

Richardson, L. (2000). New writing practices in qualitative research. *Sociology of Sport Journal, 17*(2), 5–20.

Rickinson, M., Dillon, J., Teamey, K., Morris, M., Young Choi, M., Sanders, D. & Benefield, P. (2004). *A Review of Research on Outdoor Learning*. London: National Foundation for Educational Research and King's College London.

Robinson, V. (2004). Taking risks: Identity, masculinity and rock climbing. In B. Wheaton (Ed.), *Understanding Lifestyle Sports: Consumption, Identity and Difference* (pp. 113–130). Oxon: Routledge.

Robinson, V. (2008). *Everyday Masculinities and Extreme Sport: Male Identity and Rock Climbing*. Oxford: Berg.

Rogoff, B. (1990). *Apprenticeship in Thinking: Cognitive Development in Social Context*. New York: Oxford University Press.

Schwandt, T.A. (2000). Three epistemological stances for qualitative inquiry: Interpretivism, hermeneutics, and social constructionism. In N. Denzin & Y. Lincoln (Eds.) *The Sage Handbook of Qualitative Research* (pp. 189–208). California: Sage.

Seaman, J. (2007). Taking things into account: Learning as kinaesthetically mediated collaboration. *Journal of Adventure Education and Outdoor Learning, 7(1)*, 3–20.

Smith, J. (2009). Judging research quality: From certainty to contingency. *Qualitative Research in Sport and Exercise, 1*(2), 91–100.

Sparkes, A.C. (2002). *Telling Tales in Sport and Physical Activity: A Qualitative Journey*. Champaign, IL: Human Kinetics.

Sparkes, A.C. (2009). Ethnography and the senses: challenges and possibilities. *Qualitative Research in Sport and Exercise, 1*(1), 21–35.

Sparkes, A.C. & Smith, B. (2014). *Qualitative Research Methods in Sport, Exercise and Health. From Process to Product*. Abingdon: Routledge.

Stan, I. (2008). Group interaction in the 'outdoor classroom': The process of learning in outdoor education. Unpublished PhD thesis. Bucks New University/Brunel University.

Stan, I. (2009). Recontextualising the role of the facilitator in group interaction in the outdoor classroom. *Journal of Adventure Education and Outdoor Learning, 9*(1), 23–43.

Stan, I. & Humberstone, B. (2011) An ethnography of the outdoor classroom – how teachers manage risk in the outdoors. *Education and Ethnography, 6*(2), 213–228.

Stewart, A. (2008) Whose place, whose history? Outdoor environmental education pedagogy as 'reading' the landscape. *Journal of Adventure Education and Outdoor Learning, 8*(2), 79–88.

Stirling, S. (2009). Mountaineering mums. *UK Climbing*, March (online). Retrieved from: www.ukclimbing.com/articles/page.php?id=1739.

Stirling, S. (2010). Mountaineering and climbing dads. *UK Climbing*, June (online). Retrieved from: www.ukclimbing.com/articles/page.php?id=2710.

Tierney, W.G. (1998). Life history's history: Subjects foretold. *Qualitative Enquiry, 4*, 49–70.

Tilley, C. (1994). *A Phenomenology of Landscape. Places, Paths and Monuments*. Oxford: Berg Publishers.

Wai Man, K. (2001). Constructing social work: Stories of the developing social worker. Doctoral thesis, University of Bristol.

Walford, G. (Ed.) (2002). *Doing a Doctorate in Educational Ethnography, Vol. 7*. Oxford: Elsevier.

Wattchow, B. & Brown, M. (2011). *A Pedagogy of Place*. Clayton, Victoria: Monash University Publishing.

Willis, P. (1977). *Learning to Labour: How Working Class Kids Get Working Class Jobs*. Farnborough: Saxon House.

Wylie, J. (2005). A single day's walking: Narrating self and landscape on the South West Coast Path. *Transactions of the Institute of British Geographers, 30*(2), 234–247.

Part 2

Formal education in outdoor studies

Introduction

Heather Prince

University of Cumbria

Regional cultural perspectives involve outdoor studies in different ways in formal curricula. This section focuses on Western Europe, particularly the UK and Scandinavia, although also has a more international reach in Backman's consideration of the training of teachers and in place-responsive teaching as described by Mannion and Lynch. 'Outdoor studies' is not seen in curricula per se but under various more specialised aspects such as outdoor play, outdoor learning, environmental education, outdoor education, and outdoor and adventurous activities within or outwith the physical education curriculum in schools. In higher education, a range of nomenclature is described, with some programmes including the terms adventure and outdoor studies, sometimes accompanied by 'leadership' or 'management' and teacher training through physical education focused on adventure, skills and risk.

If cultures frame formal curricula, it may be questioned as to where and how the boundaries in our sections have been drawn. We acknowledge that they could be seen as diffuse in so far as some aspects of formal curricula are described in 'international voices and cultural interpretations', but strong historical and cultural perspectives are provided there in frameworks that provide a wide interpretation of the position of outdoor studies in a range of countries. The outcomes in the formal curricula here relate in the main to learning, education and pedagogy, whereas the broader international voice can speak for a wider influence and audience. Similarly, later in this Handbook, Cooper (Chapter 39) touches on formal curricula related to outdoor education, environment and sustainability following a more thematic approach. The authors in this section present outdoor studies in the formal curricula across their countries in the given context, rather than only through any particular project or initiative.

In successful school and pre-school outdoor curricula, there seems to be a clear emphasis on key values (or 'elements', 'capacities', 'habits') either at an institutional or on a personal level or both, and Christie, Higgins and Nicol demonstrate that in some curricula these are supported by policy. Teaching and learning outdoors provides many challenges as well as opportunities, which are discussed in all the chapters and pervade all age phases, from early years, as illustrated by Waite, and early childhood and care (ECEC), by Sandseter and Hagen, to higher education including teacher training, which are the focus of the chapters by Stott and Backman respectively. In school curricula in the UK, Prince and Exeter, Waite, and Christie *et al.*, all concur that measures of performativity and outcomes are at the forefront of considerations in the delivery of outdoor programmes. These can be supported through a whole-school approach, outstanding teaching and facilitation, and holistic approaches, as explained by Sandseter and Hagen. In delivering outdoor learning, there is an emphasis on a student- or child-centred pedagogy, involving affective and interpersonal domains as well as cognitive learning, with environment issues or environmental education and place considered by Mannion and Lynch to be important components, differentiating it from sport-oriented curricula.

The chapters in this section emphasise the unique teaching and learning in outdoor studies emanating from direct contact with the natural environment. In many settings, learning in the outdoors is the only way to achieve desired outcomes, child development or cognitive understanding, such as through Sandseter and Hagen, and Waite's approaches to outdoor play in the early years, and in fieldwork as advocated by Stott, even when virtual technologies can assist in bringing learning indoors. Pedagogical opportunities are enhanced in the outdoors, and curiosity, investigative and enquiry-based approaches are optimised. Prince and Exeter show that research into outstanding outdoor learning indicates that an emphasis on creativity and ownership for children through a progression of experiences and activities is important. Mannion and Lynch, however, suggest that there has been an overemphasis on cognitive and reflective processes, and advocate a place-responsive manifesto that privileges in-depth knowledge of places, place distinctiveness and sustainable responses to advance environmental and social justice. It could be that these writings emphasise different stages of outcomes that need to be scaffolded through process and cognition before a holistic and reciprocal model is achieved.

The richness and diversity of different regional cultural foundations is evident in the way that formal curricula have developed and are operating. The Scandinavian traditions of *friluftsliv*, 'law of common access' and direct contact with nature pervade the teaching and learning in these schools and pre-schools, but local culture is also important in Scotland and Australia. The UK perhaps has more of a tradition influenced by key educators such as Kurt Hahn reflected in the emphasis on young people becoming active and creative citizens; Waite introduces the term *cultural density* to provide a platform from which to discuss the competing and interrelated elements in the systems that influence outdoor learning in the early years.

Outdoor studies has an important part to play in environmental education, not least in the teaching of sustainability and sustainable development. Christie *et al.*, in Scotland, propose that the strategy of introducing 'Learning for Sustainability' into the curriculum is one of the most important recent developments for outdoor learning. Backman outlines how environmental education is usually positioned in a number of countries within general teacher education rather than within physical education teacher education (PETE), which emphasises physical activities. However, environmental education is found in many higher education programmes in 'outdoor studies', which can necessarily be more autonomous and broader in their provision. Stott examines the important place of fieldwork and expeditions in providing the interface of direct experience with the environment, real and virtual (see also Maher, Chapter 46 in this Handbook).

The position of outdoor studies in formal curricula seems to be at different stages of development and acceptance in the wider pedagogy of learning, education and consequent scrutiny both in age phases and in different cultures. The Scandinavian culture, with its direct contact with nature through family activities as well as formal teaching and learning, is long established with supporting research to evidence its efficacy (Henderson & Vikander, 2007). Outdoor studies including all its sub-sets, seems to be more developed and accepted in pre-school and early years education through outdoor play, easier to implement in primary education than secondary education, and influenced by developing technologies and traditional teacher training in higher education. It is interesting to note the change in higher education 'outdoor' programme provision in the UK even within the last ten years as institutions have changed names, merged, associated with other subjects to offer joint degrees, or withdrawn from the market (Humberstone & Brown, 2006). This may be largely as a result of the high level of resource needed in its widest sense, as Stott describes, and government drivers. However, whatever the stage of development, all the authors here are solution-focused, progressive and take a developmental stance in their assessment of the potential of outdoor studies in formal curricula.

There are challenges, issues and opportunities in, and associated with, outdoor learning in all cultural contexts. Some are operational in terms of teacher experience, confidence, qualifications, student–teacher ratios, and health and safety, with more mention of risk as a management challenge in the UK than elsewhere. Some are more driven by policy and institutional constraints, which include economic considerations.

Ogilvie (2013) gives a detailed and extensive history of outdoor education and outdoor learning in the UK, and voices concerns about its development in the 1990s after the introduction of the Education Reform Act in 1988, construed in outdoor pedagogical terms as the 'death of fun' (p. 507). While a prescribed curriculum that does not overtly include outdoor studies might be more limiting than the perceived freedom of previous curricula, most proponents of outdoor curricula would agree that teachers are curriculum creators rather than dispensers of a curriculum developed by others (Smith, 2002). Teachers and educators will enable learning in the outdoors through their passion and enthusiasm, and will interpret formal curricula to optimise learning as they believe it to be, as can be seen by the authors in this section and throughout this Handbook.

Learning outdoors, although grounded in outdoor studies and its constituent subjects and approaches, benefits from reciprocal support from other disciplines. Advances in fieldwork technology and teaching approaches in geography and the environmental sciences will enhance fieldwork in outdoor-related subjects. Synergistic benefits of introducing an outdoor context are evidenced by research, and organisations in Scotland use this to justify outdoor learning in their engagement with communities. In the early years, facilitating the health and wellbeing of children as a key part of child development is an important part of the outdoor curriculum. Place-responsive teaching should be a reciprocal ecosocial process with the aim of improving human–environment relations.

Authors in this section also draw on theoretical frameworks outwith the discipline to provide a greater understanding of practice. In early years education, outdoor play can draw on a Gibsonian approach (Gibson, 1988), which examines 'affordances' – the potential of a physical environment that will support direct engagement by children in it. Bronfenbrenner's (1979) ecological framework illustrates the complexity and interrelatedness of different elements within a system that are applied to early years education in the UK, and part of this may be teacher influence and reservations about the power relationship between teacher and student in outdoor contexts. There are concerns about uncritical and general statements that assume outdoor experiences to be inherently positive. Bowdridge and Blenkinsop (2011) call for a post-structuralist examination of such in a Foucauldian way to understand why some outdoor educators may not deliver from a reflexive position. If individual experiences and personal development are privileged through outdoor learning, then there are criticisms about the knowledge base of its discipline. Thus, there is the need to understand the relationship between teacher and child (and therefore the emphasis of teacher education) especially where freedom and unstructured individual expression are favoured.

It is important also to be conscious of the significant and diverse implications that neoliberalism has had on the direction of policy and practice of education in general, and outdoor learning in particular. Evans and Davies (2015, p. 10) explore how the narrative of 'freedom' has been used to validate 'changes to the structure and content of formal education in UK'.

Outdoor learning in formal and non-formal curricula is similarly affected by neo-liberal policies and practices. For the most part the chapters herein do not explicitly focus on the mechanisms of these influences, yet they represent and report current research and practice. We argue for further research that more explicitly explores the processes and implications of privatisation and commercialisation on outdoor learning globally following key papers discussing outdoor adventure as 'recreational capitalism' (for example, Loynes, 1998).

Although some of the pedagogical approaches have meanings and applications across the wider understanding of outdoor studies, the consideration of these within formal curricula is important as most children throughout the world receive an education through the structure of schools and schooling. Many of these school environments are not privileged in location, teacher expertise in outdoor learning or through financial support for outdoor activities and experiences, which are often seen as 'added value' or luxuries in curricula competing for resource. This part of the Handbook provides a cross-section of positive practice, with each author positing operational models for sustainable outdoor learning and for its future growth and development.

References

Bowdridge, M. & Blenkinsop, S. (2011). Michel Foucault goes outside: discipline and control in the practice of outdoor education. *Journal of Experiential Education*, *34*(2), 149–163.

Bronfenbrenner, U. (1979). *The Ecology of Human Development*. Cambridge, MA: Harvard University Press.

Evans, J. & Davies, B. (2015). Neoliberal freedoms, privatisation and the future of physical education. *Sport, Education and Society, 20*(1), 10–26.

Gibson, E.J. (1988). Exploratory behavior in the development of perceiving, acting, and the acquiring of knowledge. *Annual Review of Psychology*, 1–41.

Henderson, B. & Vikander, N. (2007). *Nature First. Outdoor Life the Friluftsliv Way*. Toronto: Natural Heritage Books.

Humberstone, B. & Brown, H. (2006). *Shaping the Outdoor Profession Through Higher Education. Creative Diversity in Outdoor Studies Courses in Higher Education in the UK*. Penrith: Institute for Outdoor Learning.

Loynes, C. (1998). Adventure in a bun. *Journal of Experiential Education, 21*(1), 35–39.

Ogilvie, K. (2013). *Roots and Wings: A History of Outdoor Education and Outdoor Learning in the UK*. Lyme Regis: Russell House Publishing Ltd.

Smith, G. (2002). Learning to be where we are. *Phi Delta Kappan, 83*(8), 584–594.

8

The primacy of place in education in outdoor settings

Greg Mannion

UNIVERSITY OF STIRLING

Jonathan Lynch

UNIVERSITY OF CUMBRIA

In this chapter, we explore and support the call for greater attention to be paid to place in outdoor education. We consider this call to have particular relevance since education in the outdoors can work as an antidote to what some have described as a sense of de-placement (Orr, 1994) as inhabitants of local places that are globally connected. Casey, analyst and interpreter of the deep history of philosophical perspectives on place, provides a starting point for our understanding of how, as educators, we might usefully take more account of place as an event that is always 'newly emergent' and radically heterogeneous (Casey, 1998).

Our main argument is that place has begun to, and needs to further '(re-)appear' as a primary eventful feature of our understanding of our life in the world, but that we need to push further to theorise and understand how in education in outdoor settings. We seek to theorise and suggest ways for how we might more sensitively plan and enact place-responsive outdoor education. We hope our contributions will have relevance for the fields of outdoor education (in formal or non-formal curricula) in outdoor experiential learning, adventure education, fieldwork and other forms of provision in education settings (such as outdoor play in early years) or in local areas (for example, in forest, beach or urban settings).

The reappearance of place in outdoor education

Across all disciplines and across theory and practice, place has emerged in recent years as a core concern, but it remains curiously less well connected to the literature on outdoor education. In the long tradition of outdoor education (Ogilvie, 2013), there have, of course, been varied commentaries on place through few comprehensive theoretical treatments. Historical and socio-cultural readings (Humberstone, Brown & Richards, 2003) encourage us to notice the way outdoor education's purposes have changed within its wider socio-political landscape.

Over time, as purposes have changed, 'place' has been colonised, harnessed, reinvented and renamed (as, for example, the 'outdoor gym', 'threatened environment' or the 'great outdoors'). Purposes such as 'fitness for war', 'character building', 'social education', 'recuperative holiday for socially disadvantaged young people' and 'progressive education' are all identifiable (Nicol, 2002) within a sustained emphasis on psycho-social outcomes.

In the past fifty years, with the rise in concern for environmental issues, experience in nature has gained renewed significance. For example, Mortlock (1989) posited that outdoor education could be conceptualised as contributing to the development of 'an awareness of, respect for, and love of self . . . others . . . and the environment' (1989, p. 18). Links across the 'character building', pursuits/adventure and environmental traditions became more explicit in the 1990s (Higgins & Loynes, 1997). Higgins (2002) comments that there are three emphases in the field of outdoor education: (i) environmental education; (ii) personal and social development; and (iii) outdoor activities. While any education in outdoor settings could be concerned at any one time with all three of these aspects, at times in practice many provisions appear to ignore the more person–place, relational outcomes of the environmental education emphasis. Reasons given for this failure to take account of place come, we suggest, from overemphasis on the other two dimensions. The first overemphasis (on personal and social development) can be built on the use of humanistic, experiential approaches that privilege the cognitive reflective process (wherein outdoor education is a 'method'); the other overemphasis comes when the activity is all embracing (where this is outdoor education's 'content') (see Quay & Seaman, 2013). Quay and Seaman (p. 38) overcome this dyadic emphasis – which we suggest may each ignore place – through their revisiting of an older definition of outdoor education being 'education *in, about* and *for* the outdoors' (Donaldson & Donaldson, 1958). Quay and Seaman (p. 93), using Dewey, see these three aspects ('in', 'for' and 'about') as having equal importance, working together connecting people, place and activity. Quay and Seaman call for outdoor educators to ask: 'what ways of being a person centrally involves the outdoors, and what does it take to knowledgably participate in these activities?' (p. 78).

There are many now longstanding arguments about how some approaches to outdoor adventure and personal development have been privileged at the expense of nature and people's relationship with community and place (Loynes, 1998; Brookes, 2003a, 2003b; Beames, 2006; Brown, 2012). There is some empirical work in this area that provides sustained support for a more relational position both in theory and practice concerning place. In Mannion, Sankey, Doyle, Mattu and Wilson's (2006) study, which looked at the narratives of young people's accounts of valued outdoor experiences, the categories of 'place', 'activity' and 'interpersonal' were found to be always intimately connected in any person's account of a valued outdoor event, pointing to the need to make curricula with place in mind, in ways that too carry these three interdependencies into experiences and learning. In recent years, a number of commentators do indeed appear to be 'getting back into place', as Casey might put it (see Brookes, 2002; Stewart, 2008; Brown, 2012; Quay & Seaman, 2013) and we turn to look at some of these next.

Theoretical orientations to place in outdoor education

Roberts (2011) identifies five 'currents' in experiential education (which is closely allied to outdoor education). These are Romanticism, Pragmatism, Critical Theory, a 'Normative' current driven by Market Rationality, and a fifth Hopeful Current directed towards democratic freedom. Extending, and at the same time converging, some of the analysis of Robert's here, we describe how place gets treated in the following three traditions: socio-historical and critical, (post-)phenomenological and pragmatic, and socio-ecological.

The socio-historical and critical traditions

Some researchers take an explicitly socio-cultural reading of outdoor education. Waite and Pratt (2011), for example, explore how learning opportunities emerge through relations between child, others and place, making a relational reading of person–place interaction the core concern. In the critical tradition, place-based education has brought a significant set of resources for outdoor education to draw upon. As a field, place-based education is concerned with facilitating meaningful relationships with places; noteworthy discourses include those that focus on anti-globalisation, and a desire to rebalance the importance of relationships in education through attention to community and place (Gruenewald, 2003, 2008; Gruenewald & Smith, 2008). Importantly, for our developing argument, Gruenewald (2008) differentiates place from community, but argues that place-based education is non-anthropocentric and includes the non-human world. Finally, we note that Tuck, McKenzie and McCoy (2014) show land education as emerging as a response to the concerns of political neutrality in place-based education in terms of land history and colonisation. They place indigenous epistemologies and ontologies at the centre and challenge colonial influences in education.

The (post-)phenomenological and pragmatic traditions

Another strand of writing in this renewed attention to place comes through employing phenomenology and pragmatism as a linked lens (Stewart, 2004, 2008; Wattchow & Brown, 2011; Quay, 2013). Quay (2013) provides a more nuanced view of how pragmatism (after Dewey) and phenomenology (after Heidegger) suggest in subtly different ways that self, other and nature need to be understood as connected via aesthetic activity (or 'occupation', after Dewey). Stewart employs a phenomenology of travel through place (with his tertiary education students). Wattchow and Brown's (2011) work on pedagogy and place in outdoor education takes a look at the experiences and dispositions of experienced expert outdoor educators *viz* place in their work to make a similar set of arguments.

What is of note, too, is how many authors seek to bring together more than one perspective in the shift towards place-sensitivity. Stewart (2008) takes the cultural, ecological and historical reading of landscape as a linked but core task. Brookes (2003b) sees the development of relationships between individuals, groups and places in particular 'situations' outdoors. Somerville, takes a more post-structural approach. She sees places as co-created through teachers' and learners' subjectivity: for her, place is relationally pedagogical (Somerville, 2008; Somerville, Power & de Cartaret, 2009). These contributions in quite different ways can be seen as responses to a shared goal: a desire to move the field towards a recognition of the importance of place as changing, as relational, as cultural and social, as human and more-than-human, as aesthetic, and focus for reflection, as experienced through embodiment, yet arising with its own agencies.

Taken together, we see possibilities for a post-phenomenological (see Payne, 2003) orientation to outdoor education as viable. We believe taking outdoor education as occurring in a place-based event in ways that take the physical location as more than container can help us frame and understand the ongoing convergence of inner and outer worlds. Post-phenomenological approaches would address place as a primary frame for an outdoor education that seeks to enhance person–place relations: 'it is, indeed, in and through place that the world presents itself' (Malpas, 2008, p. 15). The result of this kind of framing is a renewed attention to embodied and aesthetic experience of place as well as reflective practice. Doing both seems necessary for place-responsive teaching outdoors – but it may not be sufficient for a fully place-responsive approach linking social and ecological aspects which we outline below.

Socio-ecological approaches

Emerging theorising on place and place-based education is also helpful in recognising the onto-logical significance of the more-than-human, and the importance of a relational view of the social and the ecological (Wattchow et al., 2014). We identify Somerville, too, as an example of a place-based educator with a strong socio-ecological sensitivity. Her work is based on an understanding that place is co-created and relationally emergent. She posits that our relationship to place is con-stituted in stories and other representations: place learning is embodied and local, and it is a contact zone of cultural contestation (2009, p. 8). Somerville developed a 'place pedagogies' approach (Somerville, 2008), which emerged from the ways we learn about place and from community. Place pedagogies include a focus on Story, Body and Contact Zone; noting that our relationship to place and community is constituted in our stories, place learning is embodied and local, and learning place and forming community is a contact zone of contested stories.

Place and place-responsiveness both feature within the socio-ecological approach advocated by Hill (2012), which he sees as a framework that embraces diverse approaches to educa-tion which can meet the needs of individuals, communities, ecosystems and environments. McKenzie and colleagues (2013) noted that a socio-ecological pedagogy sees learning occurring relationally and involves being in places, being reflective, being creative, and engaging with communities. Taking a socio-ecological approach strongly reasserts the lived, embodied, eve-ryday aspects of pedagogy with and in place, such that we can generate viable responses. But there is a risk of overly resting on phenomenological hermeneutics or humanistic post-struc-tural socio-critical traditions, which may bring too much of a commitment to decontextualised anthropocentric perspectives or ends focused on the human. In response, we ask, in what ways can place-responsiveness be a reciprocal ecosocial process involving humans and other entities?

Place-responsiveness and outdoor educational provisions

Casey's (1998) general thesis is that the term and idea of 'place' fell from discussions in theology and physics over time to be replaced by the idea of abstract, absolute, homogeneous, Euclidean and infinite space or container (for example, with the use of the term 'universe' as against 'cos-mos'). Only later did the idea of place-as-event emerge with considerations of how time and embodied experience were taken on board as relevant to our understandings of life in the world. For our purposes, then, we take learning in the outdoors as always emplaced. Here, any given place is at once local, regional and global, intimate and infinite, limited and delimited for 'place itself is everywhere' (Casey, 1998, p. 305). Starting with Casey's ideas, we set out below some of the features of a place-responsive outdoor education.

Cameron (2003) offers the useful term 'place-responsiveness', now being picked up in the outdoor studies field. He notes:

> Place is not the mere passive recipient of whatever humans decide they wish to do upon the face of it. The land is an active participant in a very physical sense . . . it [sense of place] includes a growing sense of what the place demands of us in our attitudes and actions. (Cameron, 2003, p. 176)

For Cameron, place includes the more-than-human and we need to respond both to others, to the place via other stories of place (2003, p. 194). Wattchow and Brown (2011) take up the term place-responsive pedagogy (after Cameron, 2003) as challenging the trend of placeless curriculum making within globalisation. They seek ways to operationalise place-responsiveness in outdoor education, suggesting four signposts, as follows.

1   Being present in and with a place.
2   The power of place based stories and narratives.
3   Apprenticing ourselves to outdoor places.
4   The Representation of place experiences. (Wattchow & Brown, 2011, p. 182).

Wattchow and Brown (2011) and Somerville (2008) put forth appealing and strong arguments that move us towards a place-responsive pedagogy based in part on the work on story. But, if by 'stories' we mean human meaning making and solely representations of human lived experience, then we worry that concerns with place may get lost in a solely subjective story situated in the human life-world. We feel we should seek other framings of meaning making that are less reliant on humanist registers to open up pedagogical considerations of place that allow a broadening of the ontological significance of what is found outdoors.

Mannion, Fenwick and Lynch (2013) incorporate some of the influences of the emerging writing in place and post-structuralism to nuance what they mean by responding to place. They base a place-responsive approach on the view that people and places are relationally emergent. They suggest responding to place involves reciprocity, and involves explicitly teaching by-means-of-an-environment with the aim of understanding and improving human–environment relations. Their approach is more focused on linking purposes with an emergent ontology of place wherein stories reside. Here, learners, places, stories and all kinds of entities are intermingling and educationally relevant: all the material aspects of a place (stones, water, air) and the more-than-human (grass, trees, animals, etc.) can have a 'say'. Their approach seeks to move beyond the binary of person and place, indoor vs outdoors, to eke out the pedagogical potential of place from a view that understands the world is in formation. For Mannion and colleagues (2013) this is a question of accepting a relational ontology of place-as-event as always given – we are always inside place events.

Similarly, Mannion and Gilbert (2014) posit that people and places are relationally emergent through the activities of both people and many other entities and processes that allow life to unfold (including the weather, the activities of animals as much as humans). After Ingold (2011) agency no longer 'resides' in one location or in the human; it proceeds dynamically along connective tissue, which allows for the enactment of a relationship; within these interpenetrating socio-material relations, people and place co-emerge. In the project, Stories in the Land, Mannion and Gilbert (2014) used narrative approaches to explore the role of story for children and their local communities in ways that were connected to local landscapes. This contextualised approach counters a view of literacy as a decontextualised and portable skill that cuts across any context and can be learned in a formulaic way. Instead, we suggest we take seriously Somerville's idea that narratives, identities and experience are deeply connected and shaped by practices in particular places. We encouraged story making as a practice alongside the lived experiences of journey and place: these are the necessary co-ingredients in outdoor education (see Anderson, 2004).

Working with similar ideas but applying them to curriculum making, Ross and Mannion (2012) foreground the entanglement of people-place relations that are re-made through relationships between them. Importantly, they deny that solely cognitive representations of these experiences are either possible or necessary: 'The curriculum making here is not the manipulation of symbols or representations of environment. It is the manipulation of the constant, active engagement with the environment in which teachers and learners are both entangled and which both produce' (2012, p. 14). We are immersed in the world, not separate from it and hence, learning need not be overly reliant on decontextualised representations or symbols. They suggest the world becomes meaningful for its inhabitants through active socio-material inhabitation and involves something other than cognitive representation. We become in an entangled or interlaced manner in relation to other species and the environment as 'points of growth'.

To summarise, then, we argue that place-responsive outdoor education involves three interlinked aspects: (i) attending to the subjective, personal development and 'inner world' of experience of place (see for example, Higgins & Wattchow, 2013); (ii) without losing sight of the need to learn an activity itself – we need to attend to the aesthetic practice-oriented ways of being (or Dewey's 'occupations') (see Quay, 2013); yet (iii) all the while attending to the need to attune to the place-based, more-than-human, living and inanimate materials that are also active as agencies in curriculum making (see Rautio, 2013), whether these be local or further flung.

We warrant that place responsiveness as an idea in outdoor education now has significant implications for its planning and enactment. Our following guidelines for practice seek to provide some possible ways of taking these implications on board.

Planning with place: a typology

Mannion *et al.* (2011) draw on analysis of empirical examples to derive a heuristic tool for addressing place in the planning of outdoor education. Their analysis of teachers' lived experiences of teaching in outdoor settings generated a typology of dispositions to planning for outdoor learning. These 'types' are best considered as not completely distinct from one another but as existing on a continuum of place-responsiveness, as follows.

- **Place-ambivalent** teaching strategies do not actively plan to take much account of the place as a contributing factor in teaching and learning.
- **Place-sensitive** teaching strategies do plan to take some active account of the role the place will play in teaching and learning.
- **Place-essential** teaching strategies are planned so that they cannot be enacted if some specific location is not available for teaching and learning.

For Mannion *et al.* (2011), planning in a 'place-ambivalent' way means setting out to do a lesson that is almost completely transportable to any setting regardless of place-based contingencies such as time of day, season, weather, terrain, presence of other species, possibilities for encounters with local people, and so on. We have all seen times when teachers literally seek to bring a given lesson they would normally have done indoors to an outdoor place – perhaps because it is a warm day – bringing tables and chairs with them on occasion. In place-ambivalent planning, educators seek to reproduce or 'export' a teaching strategy from one place (perhaps indoors) into a new outdoor setting without actively taking much account of the affordances the place has on offer.

A further example of its use might help us explore what we mean here. In place-ambivalent planning, an educator might set out to educate about the ecological significance of light as a source of energy; to do the lesson, s/he may decide to take a lab experiment on plants in pots outdoors into the school grounds. Here, materials from indoors are brought outdoors as part of a replication of teaching approaches enacted in another indoor place.

In place-sensitive planning, an educator may indicate to the learners that the nearby woodland is a place with mixed-species woodland where there are various canopy densities (and various light intensities) and thus various levels of plant growth. Here, many alternative outdoor places with trees might therefore afford opportunities for such a lesson.

Planning education in outdoor settings as place-essential would mean that a specific place be relevant through what it can pedagogically offer – in other words, what will relationally emerge there. In a 'place-essential' approach, planning starts with the emerging place-as-event, and considers how and what forms of curriculum making might be possible within and through that set of processes. Hence, to consider our case example again, in a particular woodland, the educator, mindful that meaning will relationally emerge, might notice that the learners are noticing varying light intensity and that that could be part of the learning experience on a given sunny day in a given part of the woodland. In addition, they might consider the new understandings around light and plant growth as part of a wider framing of place relations: whose land it is, what species were planted there/were native/invasive, and what ongoing local practices of woodland management were ongoing or perhaps needing to be engaged in as a result. This is a departure from the established rational-linear models of planning where all learning objectives are set beforehand, and drive the planning process and where place is not factored as important in the planning other than as an container.

As Mannion *et al.* (2013) have found, taking a place-essential approach will mean educators are likely to benefit from knowing well the places where the teaching and learning experiences are to be enacted or knowing in some depth the kinds of things that are likely to happen in the place visited. Aside from planning in a place-responsive way, teachers also need to take a responsive attitude to the educational encounter in an ongoing manner, which may involve a degree of contingency. Indeed, in practice, as Mannion *et al's* (2013) research showed, whether we plan for it or not, places and people are reprocally responsive in a variety of ways.

In seeking to advance these kinds of adaptations to enacting teaching as much as in the planning, we have devised the following manifesto for place-responsive practice based on our arguments and discussions above. We have found this to be a useful text for prompting teachers (in-service and pre-service) to consider when and how place is harnessed explicitly into their teaching. We note the manifesto calls for a greater coming together of ethics and experience, ontology and epistemology, and the insertion of clearer place-related purposes into are pedagogies.

A Manifesto for Place-Responsive Teaching

In my teaching . . .

1   I strive to gain an *in-depth knowledge of places* to inform what I do as an educator.
2   I strive to help learners respond with, in and through place-based experiences:
    a   Before, during and after educational excursions to places, I strive to help learners gain an understanding and appreciation of places and what is distinctive about them.
    b   When appropriate, I bring learners back to the same or similar place to enable a greater depth of response to place.
    c   I strive to get learners to make responses that are embodied, cognitive, emotional, aesthetic and ethical.
    d   I actively invite learners to respond to selected happenstance, contingent, and unforeseen events encountered in places.
3   I strive to harness the *distinctiveness* of places in my teaching . . .
    a   Whether indoors or outside, I facilitate learning in ways that could not be easily replicated in a different place.
    b   When teaching outdoors, I facilitate learning in ways that could not be easily replicated in a different outdoor location.

4   I invite learners to make their own efforts to *create viable and more sustainable responses* to place in ways that advances environmental and social justice and equity in their own lives and the lives of others.

The manifesto is suggestive of the need for openness to encounters with place-differences that take us beyond ourselves. Happenstance encounters and experiences – for example, with a woodland owner, the sounds, smells and feelings emerging for participants when the sun shines on the leaves and on their cheeks – these might all need to be harnessed into the learning. Much of this will be unknown and unplanned at the outset. In place-responsive outdoor education, meanings will come about through the acceptance of knowledge emerging through the ongoing entanglement of people/place/the-more-than-human. And these entanglements are present whether we are experiencing a place, reflecting on it or transforming it on our own or with others.

Conclusion

We might have expected that place would never have needed to *re*-appear as a central concern since the location of such learning one would expect has always been clearly consequential. But critiques of the field of practice have noted that place has often been ignored in outdoor education, and its role has not only been unclear but has been under-theorised and quite contested. We have shown when and how 'place' is being reasserted as a key unifying concern that makes outdoor pedagogy viable, meaningful and worthwhile. This has taken many forms especially in outdoor education and outdoor learning since places themselves are so diverse as are our relations with them. This interest in place, although not new, seems now to be reasserted in response to dominant approaches that have overly privileged cognitive and reflective processes. The reassertion of place asks us to take greater account of the ecosocial, material place, to consider the purposes of programmes in these places, and the links between local and global places. We have also presented sources that help us understand how people, place and the more-than-human are relationally emergent in curriculum planning, and the enactment and transformation of outdoor curriculum making.

The contribution we hope to make with this chapter is to help open out and reposition a concern with place as part of a wider agenda within education as attending in material and embodied ways to differences that arise . . . noticing that these differences are always in a place. These can be more easily understood as necessary once (or if) educators take on board the significance of an ontology where people and place are always entangled in ongoing events that are reciprocal in nature. Within a reciprocal ontology of becoming, learning is always situated and is an ongoing happening and, therefore, could be said to always be locally 'performed' as a result of the responses people make within a particular person–place assemblage or enmeshment (see Ingold, 2011). Learning is influenced by what people do in and to a place and how places act back on them over time. Educationally, there is a need to plan for place-responsiveness and in the moment notice these person–place experiences harnessing them into the pedagogy in more responsive ways. Working more proactively to make curriculum making more place-responsive takes us back to the keynote idea by Casey in the introduction: place is pedagogically emergent and more than a cultural or historical 'container'. At a time when the planet faces diverse ecological and social challenges, given that place and meaning emerge in our co-extensive encounters with it, we think that the provision of education in outdoor settings can be planned and enacted more effectively when it does so with place in mind.

References

Anderson, J. (2004). Talking whilst walking: a geographical archeology of knowledge. *Area, 36*(3): 254–261.

Beames, S. (2006). Losing my religion: The struggle to find applicable theory. *Pathways: The Ontario Journal of Outdoor Education, 19*(1), 4–11.

Brookes, A. (2002). Lost in the Australian bush: Outdoor education as curriculum. *Journal of Curriculum Studies, 34*(4), 405–425.

Brookes, A. (2003a). A critique of neo-Hahnian outdoor education theory. Part one: challenges to the concept of 'character building'. *Journal of Adventure Education and Outdoor Learning, 3*(1), 49–62.

Brookes, A. (2003b). A critique of neo-Hahnian outdoor education theory. Part two: 'The fundamental attribution error' in contemporary outdoor education discourse. *Journal of Adventure Education and Outdoor Learning, 3*(2), 119–132.

Brown, M. (2012). Student perspectives of a place-responsive outdoor education programme. *New Zealand Journal of Outdoor Education, 3*(1), 64–88.

Brown, T., Jeanes, R. & Cutter-Mackenzie, A. (2014). Social ecology as education. In B. Wattchow, R. Jeanes, L. Alfrey, T. Brown, A. Cutter-Mackenzie & J. O'Conner (Eds.) *The Socioecological Educator* (pp. 23–46). London: Springer.

Cameron, J. (2003). Responding to place in a post-colonial era: An Australian perspective. In W. Adams & M. Mulligan (Eds.) *Decolonising Nature: Strategies for Conservation in a Post-colonial Era* (pp. 172–197). London: Earthscan.

Casey, E. (1998). *The Fate of Place: A Philosophical History.* London: University of California Press.

Donaldson, G. & Donaldson, L. (1958). Outdoor education: A definition. *Journal of Physical Education, Recreation & Dance, 29*(17), 17, 63.

Gruenewald, D. (2003). The best of both worlds: A critical pedagogy of place. *Educational Researcher, 32*(4), 3–12.

Gruenewald, D. (2008). Place-based education: Grounding culturally responsive teaching in geographical diversity. In D. Gruenewald & G. Smith (Eds.) *Place-based Education in the Global Age* (pp. 137–154). Abingdon: Taylor & Francis.

Gruenewald, D. & Smith, G. (2008). *Place-based Education in the Global Age.* Abingdon: Taylor & Francis.

Higgins, P. (2002). Outdoor education in Scotland. *Journal of Adventure and Outdoor Learning, 2*(2), 149–168.

Higgins, P. & Loynes, C. (1997). Towards consensus on the nature of outdoor education. *Journal of Adventure Education and Outdoor Leadership, 15*(1), 5–9.

Higgins, P. & Wattchow, B. (2013). The water of life: creative non-fiction and lived experience on an interdisciplinary canoe journey on Scotland's River Spey. *Journal of Adventure Education & Outdoor Learning, 13*, 13–18.

Hill, A. (2012). Introducing a critical socio-ecological approach for educating outdoors. In D. Irwin, J. Stracker & A. Hill (Eds.) *Outdoor Education in Aotearoa New Zealand: A Vision for the 21st Century* (pp. 46–64). Christchurch, New Zealand: CIPT.

Humberstone, B., Brown, H. & Richards, K. (2003). *Whose Journeys? The Outdoors and Adventure as Social and Cultural Phenomena.* Barrow-in-Furness: Fingerprints.

Ingold, T. (2011). *Being Alive: Essays on Movement, Knowledge and Description.* Oxon: Routledge.

Loynes, C. (1998). Adventure in a bun. *Journal of Experiential Education, 21*(May/June), 35–39.

Malpas, J. (2008). Disclosing the depths of Heidegger's Topology: A response to Relph. *Environmental and Architectural Phenomenology, 19*(1), 9–12.

Mannion, G., Sankey, K., Doyle, L., Mattu, L. & Wilson, M. (2006). *Young People's Interaction with Natural Heritage through Outdoor Learning.* Scottish Natural Heritage Commissioned Report No. 225. University of Stirling. Retrieved from: www.snh.gov.uk/publications-data-and-research/publications/search-the-catalogue/publication-detail/?id=877.

Mannion, G., Fenwick, A., Nugent, C. & I'Anson, J. (2011). *Teaching in Nature.* Report contracted to University of Stirling, commissioned by Scottish Natural Heritage.

Mannion, G., Fenwick, A. & Lynch, J. (2013). Place-responsive pedagogy: learning from teachers' experiences of excursions in nature. *Environmental Education Research, 19*(6), 792–809.

Mannion, G. & Gilbert, J. (2014). Place-responsive intergenerational education. In R. Vanderbeck & N. Worth (Eds.) *Intergenerational Space.* Abingdon: Routledge.

McKenzie, M., Butcher, K., Fruson, D., Knorr, M., Stone, J., Allen, S., Hill, T., Murphy, J., McLean, S., Kayira, J. & Anderson, V. (2013). Suited: Relational learning and socioecological pedagogies. In R. Stevenson, M. Brody, J. Dillon & A. Wals (Eds.) *International Handbook of Research on Environmental Education* (pp. 487–498). Abingdon: Routledge.

Mortlock, C. (1989). *The Adventure Alternative*. Milnthorpe: Cicerone Press.

Nicol, R. (2002). Outdoor education: Research topic or universal value? Part one. *Journal of Adventure Education & Outdoor Learning, 2*(1), 29–41.

Ogilvie, K. (2013). *Roots and Wings: A History of Outdoor Education and Outdoor Learning in the UK*. Dorset: Russell House Publishing.

Orr, D. (1994). *Earth in Mind: On Education, Environment, and the Human Prospect*. Washington, DC: Island Press.

Payne, P. (2003). Post-phenomenological enquiry and living the environmental condition. *Canadian Journal of Environmental Education, 8*, 169–190.

Plumwood, V. (2000). Belonging, naming and decolonization. *Ecopolitics: Thought and Action, 1*(1), 90–106.

Quay, J. (2013). More than relations between self, others and nature: Outdoor education and aesthetic experience. *Journal of Adventure Education & Outdoor Learning, 13*(2), 142–157.

Quay, J. & Seaman, J. (2013). *John Dewey and Education Outdoors: Making Sense of the 'Educational Situation' through more than a Century of Progressive Reforms*. Rotterdam: Sense Publishers.

Rautio, P. (2013). Being nature: Interspecies articulation as a species-specific practice of relating to environment. *Environmental Education Research, 19*(4), 445–457.

Roberts, J. (2011). *Beyond Learning By Doing: Theoretical Currents in Experiential Education*. New York: Routledge.

Ross, H. & Mannion, G. (2012). Curriculum making as the enactment of dwelling in places. *Studies in Philosophy and Education, 31*(3), 303–313.

Somerville, M. (2008). A place pedagogy for 'global contemporaneity'. *Educational Philosophy and Theory, 42*(3), 326–344.

Somerville, M., Power, K. & de Cartaret, P. (2009). *Landscapes and Learning – Place Studies for a Global World*. Monash University Australia: Sense Publishers.

Stewart, A. (2004). Canoeing the Murray River (Australia) as environmental education: A tale of two rivers. *Canadian Journal of Environmental Education, 9*, 136–148.

Stewart, A. (2008). Whose place, whose history? Outdoor environmental education pedagogy as 'reading' the landscape. *Journal of Adventure Education and Outdoor Learning, 8*(2), 79–98.

Tuck, E., McKenzie, M. & McCoy, M. (2014). Land education: Indigenous, post-colonial, and decolonizing perspectives on place and environmental education research. *Environmental Education Research, 20*(1), 1–23.

Waite, S. & Pratt, N. (2011). Theoretical perspectives on learning outside the classroom: Relationships between learning and place. In S. Waite (Ed.) *Children Learning Outside the Classroom: From Birth to Eleven* (pp. 1–18). London: Sage.

Wattchow, B. & Brown, M. (2011). *A Pedagogy of Place*. Clayton: Monash University Publishing.

Wattchow, B., Brown, T., Jeanes, R., O'Conner, J., Cutter-Mackenzie, A. & Alfrey, L. (2014) Conclusions and future directions: A socio-ecological renewal. In B. Wattchow, R. Jeanes, L. Alfrey, T. Brown & A. Cutter-Mackenzie (Eds.) *The Socioecological Educator* (pp. 205–228). London: Springer.

9

Scandinavian early childhood education

Spending time in the outdoors

Ellen Beate Hansen Sandseter and
Trond Løge Hagen

QUEEN MAUD UNIVERSITY COLLEGE OF EARLY CHILDHOOD EDUCATION

Background

Scandinavia comprises three countries: Denmark, Sweden and Norway. These three countries lie in the northern part of Europe and share a relatively cold climate, although there is great variation among the different seasons of the year. The winters are quite cold and snowy in the northern parts of Scandinavia, while the climate is milder in the southern parts, where winters are more wet than snowy. The coastal regions usually have milder winters than the inland areas. The summer climate also varies a great deal, and while Denmark and the southern parts of Sweden and Norway have quite warm and stable temperatures during summer, the northern regions are colder.

The terrain in the Scandinavian countries includes many mountains in the northern parts, especially on the western coast of Norway, and more flat landscape in the southern parts and especially in Denmark. Still, all three Scandinavian countries have a large proportion of forested land and wild, natural environments with easy access for most of their inhabitants. In addition, all three countries have a 'law of common access' that gives citizens free access to uncultivated land and the right to walk and stay in natural areas, such as woodlands, mountain areas, by the seashore, by rivers, etc., even though the land may be in private ownership.

Early childhood education and care (ECEC) policies in Scandinavia

In all three Scandinavian countries, early childhood education and care (ECEC) is placed within the wider educational system as a part of lifelong learning. ECEC is not mandatory for children in Scandinavia, but all three countries have laws that secure the right of all children to be offered a place in an ECEC setting in the years before they reach school age (up to 6 years of age in Norway and Denmark, and up to 7 years in Sweden). Because of this right, most children in these countries attend ECEC: 84 per cent of all 1–5 year olds in Sweden, 97 per cent of all 3–5 year olds and 67 per cent of all children 0–2 years old in Denmark, and 97 per cent of all 3–5 year olds and 80 per cent of all 1–2 year olds in Norway.

Scandinavian nations emphasise the holistic development of children as the focus for work in ECEC institutions. All three countries have a law regarding ECEC stating that the primary aim of the provision is to facilitate the wellbeing, health, development and learning of children (Swedish Ministry of Education and Science (SMES), 1985; Norwegian Ministry of Education and Research (NMER), 2005; Danish Ministry of Social Affairs and Integration (DMSI), 2011). According to each country's ECEC curriculum, ECEC work is commonly based on values such as child participation, democracy, human rights, play, social relationships, respect for nature, sustainability and individual needs (Danish Parliament (DP), 2004; NMER, 2006/2011; SMES, 2010). Children's wellbeing in Scandinavian ECEC is closely related to their right to participate and is based on democratic values (Borge, Nordhagen & Lie, 2003; Nilsen, 2008; Aasen, Grindheim & Waters, 2009; Sandberg & Ärlemalm-Hagsér, 2011). In practice, children should be viewed as active meaning makers with regard to their own lives. Therefore, children in Scandinavian ECEC institutions have the right to express their views concerning their everyday activities and have a significant degree of freedom with regard to choosing their activities and where they spend their time.

Although Scandinavian ECEC has a child-centred pedagogy and strongly emphasises children's freedom, a plan exists for their development and learning. The three curricula all include several knowledge areas or norms that are used to guide the pedagogical work of ECEC institutions, such as language and text; body, movement and health; nature and natural phenomena; mathematics; aesthetic art, etc. Nevertheless, the professional approach to children's learning in ECEC should be through play (Aasen *et al.*, 2009; Sandberg & Ärlemalm-Hagsér, 2011). As such, play is regarded as a phenomenon with instrumental value and a way of learning in different knowledge areas.

Outdoor play

One of the important values in Scandinavian ECEC is the acknowledgement of outdoor play and outdoor life as an important part of children's lives. In Scandinavian societies, the concept of *friluftsliv* (which is similar to the concept of 'outdoor life' but with stronger connotations of values and lifestyle) is an important part of the regional cultural heritage. The traditions of visiting nature areas, hiking in mountainous or forested areas, sleeping out in the wild, fishing, hunting and exploring have been maintained over generations as part of daily life (Borge *et al.*, 2003; Ärlemalm-Hagsér, 2008; Aasen *et al.*, 2009; Ejbye-Ernst, 2012). Furthermore, many Scandinavians habitually travel to parks, playgrounds and nature areas for hiking and recreation with family and friends in their spare time (Borge *et al.*, 2003; Nilsen, 2008).

The Norwegian white paper regarding outdoor life (*friluftsliv*; NME, 2000–2001) places a great responsibility upon all ECEC providers and schools to use outdoor life as an important part of rearing Norwegian children. Nilsen (2008) suggested that this responsibility might be a way in which policy is used to ensure that Norwegian traditions are continued among the younger generations during a time when there is concern that these traditions will decline due to the new activities and sports available for young people. Another discussion in Norway concerns the idea that nature and outdoor ECEC are just modern forms of Fröbel's original concept of kindergarten: gardens *for* children in which children learn and develop by being in the centre of things and acting in the physical world (Borge *et al.*, 2003). Nevertheless, Scandinavian outdoor ECEC programmes are solidly rooted in the beliefs of politicians, practitioners and parents that children are happy when playing outside (Borge *et al.*, 2003; Ärlemalm-Hagsér, 2008; Ejbye-Ernst, 2012).

The Scandinavian ECEC curricula all emphasise outdoor play and experiences in natural environments as vital for children's wellbeing, development and learning. In the Norwegian curriculum (NMER, 2006/2011, p. 16), outdoor play is particularly emphasised: 'Outdoor play and activities are an important part of child culture that must be retained, regardless of the geographic and climatic conditions.' Similarly, the Swedish curriculum states that 'outdoor life should give [children] opportunities for play and activities both in designed environments and in natural environments ... [and that] ECEC institutions shall have a strong emphasis on environmental questions and sustainability of nature' (SMES, 2010, p. 7). The Danish curriculum handbook (Kjær & Olesen, 2005, p. 12) also strongly emphasises the same theme through statements such as, 'Children in ECEC institutions shall have the opportunity to experience the joy of spending time in nature in different seasons, and they shall develop a respect for nature and the environment.'

The fundamental approach of Scandinavian ECEC settings is that children are naturally curious, and they explore their world and capabilities using their whole bodies. In this sense, the physical environment is important during this phase of life to ensure that children have a wide range of experiences across formal and informal learning situations. Scandinavian ECEC in general, and Norwegian ECEC in particular, expect learning and development to change within an individual's resource system as a result of encountering and mastering challenges and not due only to the increasing maturity associated with age (Hendry & Kloep, 2002). In addition, the Gibsonian (Gibson, 1988) approach (later revised by Heft, 1988, and Kyttä, 2006) has a strong standing in Norwegian ECEC. The idea of *affordances*, features of the environment that allow an individual to perform particular actions, is central to Gibsonian theory; however, the individual must have opportunities to explore to learn about the many affordances in their environments (Gibson, 1988). Therefore, Gibsonian theory emphasises direct engagement with the environment in order to learn about what the environment offers. Transmission of information through other methods (e.g. verbal or pictorial) is not adequate. Opportunities for exploration will be central to the pedagogy of practitioners working directly from a foundation of Gibsonian theory or extensions of Gibsonian theory (e.g. Heft, 1988; Kyttä 2006). This method will lead to a greater emphasis of the physical environment and a direct relationship between the environment and learning (Sandseter, Wyver & Little, 2012).

To give practitioners sufficient tools, both theoretical and practical, to fulfil the goals in the national framework plans, the Gibsonian view is prevalent in the different educational systems' practical training through direct contact with materials, elements and environments. Scandinavian early childhood teacher-education programmes vary in length from three years in Norway (180 in the European Credits Transfer System (ECTS)) to three and a half years in Sweden and Denmark (210 ECTS). The content is regulated through national framework plans (Swedish Code of Statutes (SFS), 1993; NMER, 2012; DME, 2014). Even though practical informal learning in different environments has been put at stake in favour of more formal theoretical learning through governmental regulations in the national framework plans, Scandinavian educational programmes for early childhood teachers remain focused on activities in relation to different materials and/or environments. The educational programmes are organised in themes, and students training to become teachers are given practical experiences working with the elements or outdoor environments (e.g. how to use natural materials such as leaves, sticks, moss and snow to make art) in order to gain knowledge about the natural world through excursions to different nature environments. Similarly, they acquire skills about how different outdoor environments can be used for different types of play in all seasons. The students must be able to demonstrate how they can facilitate theoretical learning through practical activities involving exploration and free play, with great emphasis on the environment. Practical training in pre-schools is also an important part of teacher education and is emphasised with approximately six months of practical training in Norway and Sweden and one year in Denmark. In Denmark, practical training is, in addition, partly paid, and the students function as employees with regular facilitation. The concept of how to become an adequate pre-school teacher involves a need for practical skills in an adapted learning environment as well as theoretical knowledge. The integration of these competences is of vital importance in order to adopt a holistic view when working with children.

Outdoor pre-schools

Although Scandinavian ECEC commonly focuses on outdoor education, an increasing trend is also seen for outdoor ECEC provision, so-called outdoor pre-schools, with a particularly strong focus on outdoor play and learning (Lysklett, 2013). Even though both Norway and Denmark had ECEC institutions focusing especially on outdoor life and hiking as early as around 1950, the outdoor ECEC institutions as we know them today were developed during the 1980s in all three countries. Today these ECEC settings are continuing to grow in number.

Thus, approximately 5 to 10 per cent of all Scandinavian ECEC settings are outdoor pre-schools (Änggård, 2012; Ejbye-Ernst, 2012). Still, even more might exist due to the difficulties of defining this type of ECEC and the fact that these settings, although compliant with governmental ECEC law, are autonomous with regard to their pedagogical profile and what they choose to call themselves. The Scandinavian cultural tradition of having a close relationship with nature and outdoor life associating the idea that children's wellbeing, development and desire for knowledge, physical activity and social relationships are both better addressed in natural rather than indoor environments (Borge *et al.*, 2003; Änggård, 2012).

Outdoor preschools typically emphasise natural environments as spaces for their pedagogical practice and work. Furthermore, they focus on actively using the diverse and changing features of nature, across seasons and climates throughout the year, as their way of working with the curriculum content (Lysklett, Emilsen & Hagen, 2003; Drougge, 2007; Ejbye-Ernst, 2012). Children in outdoor preschools in Scandinavia could spend up to seven hours outdoors daily in diverse environments (Borge *et al.*, 2003). The pedagogical arguments for such provision are that children gain knowledge and understanding from their close contact with nature and their activities in diverse natural environments, and that knowledge about the local natural and cultural environment is an important factor in order to preserve one's cultural heritage. In addition, research shows that children develop motor and physical skills by encountering challenges in natural environments (Grahn, Mårtensson, Lindblad, Nilsson & Ekman, 1997; Fjørtoft, 2000; Fiskum, 2004).

Although Scandinavia has a relatively large proportion of outdoor pre-schools, children in all types of ECEC setting spend between 30 and 70 per cent of their time in the setting outdoors (Mårtensson, 2004; Moser & Martinsen, 2010; Ejbye-Ernst, 2012). This means on average two hours per day in wintertime and five hours per day in summertime. From an international perspective, then, all Scandinavian ECEC settings might be regarded as outdoor preschools.

Research on outdoor play and learning in Norwegian ECEC

In Norwegian ECEC, time spent outdoors is closely related to non-organised play and physical activity (Moser & Martinsen, 2010). The children are given an outlet for their individual needs for movement and free play. All children are more physically active outdoors than indoors

(Giske, Tjensvoll & Dyrstad, 2010), but for those children who have a naturally high level of activity, the hours spent outdoors are particularly important. In the outdoors they can satisfy their bodily needs for movement in full measure. The qualities of the outdoor areas, the activities taking place there, and how these are facilitated by staff through policies, rules, and the balance between non-organised and organised activity, will also have an impact on children's choices of activities. The physical environment is very important in this phase of life to ensure that children have a wide range of bodily experiences through movement. To acquire and develop basic movements using a Gibsonian approach, children need space and challenges in the environment around them that inspire them to play.

Research shows that there are large variations in physical activity levels between children engaging in non-organised play outdoors (Storli & Hagen, 2010). Children who are more active in general are also more active outdoors and vice versa. These differences are evened at when the activity is organized by the staff, and the average level of physical activity increases for the whole group. This helps to substantiate the need for documentation of the intrinsic content of outdoor play and the routines the staff have to ensure documentation of the learning goals for the individual child.

Hagen (2012) conducted a study that mapped children's outdoor play in three ECEC settings in Norway. In this study, four children in each of the settings were used as informants, using elements from the 'mosaic approach' method (Clark, 2010). The method consisted of observing play in the playground, guided tours with the children in the playground, where children were explaining how they used the playground and what they liked about outdoor play, children's drawings about their favourite outdoor play, and interviews with staff and children. The aim of this multiple approach was to obtain a broad understanding of the use of the outdoor areas, with an emphasis on the perspectives of children. The results showed that fixed installations were of little interest, especially for the oldest children. The actual use of fixed installations also tended to focus on different play situations than those for which the installations had been created. The climbing frame, for example, was used mainly for role play; the swings were used for different conversations or singing games. These findings supported other studies (Norèn-Bjørn, 1977; Mårtensson, 2004; Refshauge, 2012) criticising the design of traditional playgrounds for being too static and uniform, due to often mono-functional equipment that promotes only functional play and exercise. When children were asked to draw their favourite outdoor activities, the drawings showed clearly that they preferred to incorporate natural elements (trees, loose material) in their play, and that they preferred social and dramatic play or play with a more dynamic character, such as bicycling, football or playing in the sandpit. These findings were also supported by interviews with the staff confirming that the fixed installations had interest for children mainly for a short period when they found challenges that corresponded with their abilities. Because of the mono-functionality of many of the installations, the children lost interest when they had explored and mastered the challenges such installations could offer them.

This study emphasises the value of the environment as an important educator in cooperation with the pedagogical role. The visible environment is one aspect; a survey of the invisible environment is also important to create awareness among staff about their fundamental educational principles in practice. Children prefer environments that provide varied and unpredictable opportunities for play and social interaction, and play that children themselves have taken the initiative to invent and that they perceive as relatively autonomous. The Norwegian ECEC curriculum has a strong emphasis on providing free play for all children, regardless of their functional level or cultural background (Hagen, 2012).

Children's wellbeing and participation outdoors in ECEC

A study that aimed to capture children's perspectives on their everyday lives (both indoors and outdoors) in ECEC settings, and their experiences of wellbeing and the opportunity for participation, was conducted in Norway (Bratterud, Sandseter & Seland, 2012). In this study, 171 children ages 4–6 years old were randomly selected from seventeen different ECEC settings in the middle part of Norway (Sør-Trøndelag county), 51.5 per cent were girls and 48.5 per cent boys. The children participated in structured interviews/conversations with the researchers, and their answers were recorded as quantitative data in an electronic questionnaire ('Questback') in pre-coded categories according to the content of their answers. During the conversation, the researchers focused on different themes and questions about the children's experiences of wellbeing and participation. In addition, in nine of the seventeen settings, two children were also drawn to participate in qualitative interviews. These interviews were conducted as a supplement to the structured and quantitative registered interviews with the 171 children, with an aim to gain more in-depth insight into the children's experiences of what influenced their wellbeing and participation in ECEC.

The results of the study showed that most of the children like their outdoor environment (87 per cent) and the toys and equipment outdoors (93.5 per cent) very much. The in-depth interviews showed that children preferred physical activities and physical play such as swinging, sliding/gliding, bicycling, jumping, rolling, climbing, rough-and-tumble/chaotic play, and playing with different textures such as sand and water. What they did not like about playing outdoors was bad weather such as rain and cold temperatures.

When asked about going on hikes with their ECEC group, most children reported that they liked to do this often (50 per cent) or sometimes (35.5 per cent), while about 14 per cent did not like this activity much. In the in-depth interviews, the children said that what they liked about going on hikes was the opportunity for free play in diverse environments, while, on the other hand, they did not like long walks or hikes where there was not enough time for free play.

Comparing children's opportunities for participation in their indoor and outdoor everyday lives in ECEC, the results showed that there is a significantly (p <.001) higher level of opportunity for being able to take part in deciding what to do outdoors than indoors. In addition, there are also significantly (p <.001) more opportunities to say 'no' to what the staff decide the children should do outdoors compared to indoors where the staff do not, to the same degree, accept children not wanting to participate in the activities that the staff have decided for them. When talking to the children about going on hikes, the results showed that there was a low degree of participation in planning the hikes, and most of the children (72 per cent) experienced that they were never allowed to say 'no' to participate on hikes. It seems that hikes as an activity in Norwegian ECEC are planned in a less child-democratic way than other parts of the outdoor life in the ECEC settings.

Overall, the correlation analysis showed that there was a positive relation between children's wellbeing and liking the outdoor environment in kindergarten (p <.01), and the toys and equipment outdoors (p <.05), as well as having the opportunity to decide what to do when outdoors (p <.05). There was also a significant positive correlation between children's wellbeing and liking the hikes in kindergarten (p <.01) and feeling there was enough time for free play on hikes (p <.05).

The results of this study indicate that children to a larger degree get to influence their everyday life in ECEC outdoors compared to indoors, while on the other hand, there is very little participation in planning and preparing hikes outside the kindergarten area, and the children do not have the option to say 'no' to going on hikes.

Summary

The aim of this chapter was to give an insight into how outdoor play and activities are central parts of formal Scandinavian early childhood education. Outdoor life forms an important part of Scandinavian ECEC content and practices, and is partly based in the region's strong cultural heritage and tradition for outdoor life. Values such as children's participation, democracy, human (and children's) rights, play, social relations, respect for nature, sustainability and children's individual needs are emphasised in the Scandinavian ECEC policy, and outdoor play and activity is looked upon as a means to work with these values in practice. In line with this, early childhood teacher education in the Scandinavian countries focuses on giving the students practical experiences with different outdoor environments and how to utilise this in their pedagogical work in ECEC. The students are encouraged to develop a holistic view of children's development and learning where the environment plays a central part, and the becoming pre-school teachers should have theoretical knowledge and practical skills to provide children in early childhood centres with opportunities for outdoor play and learning. Research from Norway shows that children prefer playing in natural environments over playgrounds with fixed installations, and that they like to engage in different kinds of physical play and exploration involving natural materials and textures. The research also shows that the level of children's participation in their everyday life in ECEC is significantly higher in outdoor activities than indoors. These results indicate that outdoor life and outdoor activities are a good way to meet children's individual needs and wishes, and to ensure participation and influence on their daily life and activities in ECEC.

References

Aasen, W., Grindheim, L.T. & Waters, J. (2009). The outdoor environment as a site for children's participation, meaning-making and democratic learning: Examples from Norwegian kindergartens. *Education 3–13, 37,* 5–13.

Änggård, E. (2012). Att skapa platser i naturmiljöer. Om hur vardagliga praktiker i en I Ur och Skurförskola bidrar till at ge platser identitet. *Nordic Early Childhood Education Research, 5,* 1–16.

Ärlemalm-Hagsér, E. (2008). Skogen som pedagogisk praktik ur et genusperspektiv. In A. Sandberg (Ed.) *Miljöer för lek, lärande och samspel* (pp. 107–135). Lund: Studentlitteratur.

Borge, A.I.H., Nordhagen, R. & Lie, K.K. (2003). Children in the environment: Forest day-care centers: Modern day care with historical antecedents. *The History of the Family, 8,* 605–618.

Bratterud, Å., Sandseter, E.B.H. & Seland, M. (2012). Barns trivsel og medvirkning i barnehagen – Barn, foreldre og ansattes perspektiver. Rapport 21/2012 Skriftserien fra Barnevernets utviklingssenter i Midt-Norge. Trondheim: NTNU Samfunnsforskning.

Clark, A. (2010). *Transforming Children's Spaces: Children's and Adults' Participation in Designing Learning Environments.* London: Routledge.

DME (2014) Bekendtgørelse om uddannelsen til professionsbachelor som pædagog. BEK nr 211 af 06/03/2014 Copenhagen: Danish Ministry of Education.

DMSI (2011). *Act of Pre-primary Education: LBK nr 668 af 17/06/2011.* Copenhagen: Danish Ministry of Social Affairs and Integration.

DP (2004). *Lov om ændring af lov om social service (Pædagogiske læreplaner i dagtilbud til børn).* Copenhagen: Danish Parliament.

Drougge, S. (2007). *I ur och skur i skolan: en handledning från Friluftsfrämjandet.* (Rev. edn). Stockholm: Friluftsfrämjandet.

Ejbye-Ernst, N. (2012). Pædagogers naturformidling i naturbørnehaver. PhD thesis, VIA University College.

Fiskum, T. (2004). Effekt av barnehagemiljø på motorisk og spatial kompetanse hos barn. En tverrsnittstudie av den motoriske og spatiale kompetansen hos barn i en friluftsbarnehage og barn i en tradisjonell barnehage. Master's thesis, Nord-Trøndelag University College, Levanger.

Fjørtoft, I. (2000). Landscape and playscape. Learning effects from playing in a natural environment on motor development in children. PhD Thesis, Norwegian School of Sport Science, Oslo.

Gibson, E.J. (1988). Exploratory behavior in the development of perceiving, acting, and the acquiring of knowledge. *Annual Review of Psychology, 39,* 1–41.

Giske, R., Tjensvoll, M. & Dyrstad, S.M. (2010). Fysisk aktivitet i barnehagen. *Nordic Early Childhood Education Research, 3*(2), 53–62.

Grahn, P., Mårtensson, F., Lindblad, B., Nilsson, P. & Ekman, A. (1997). *Ute på dagis.* Alnarp: University of Agriculture in Sweden.

Hagen, T.L. (2012). Qualitative data from a study of children's utilization of the child care centres' outdoor environment. Unpublished raw data.

Heft, H. (1988). Affordances of children's environments: A functional approach to environmental description. *Children's Environments Quarterly, 5,* 29–37.

Hendry, L.B. & Kloep, M. (2002). *Lifespan Development: Resources, Challenges and Risks.* London: Thomson Learning.

Kjær, B. & Olesen, J. (2005). *Informationshåndbog om pædagogiske læreplaner i dagtilbud.* Copenhagen: Danish National Board of Social Services.

Kyttä, M. (2006). Environmental child-friendliness in the light of the Bullerby Model. In C. Spencer & M. Blades (Eds.) *Children and their Environments: Learning, Using and Designing Spaces* (pp. 141–158). Cambridge: Cambridge University Press.

Lysklett, O.B. (2013). *Ute hele uka. Natur- og friluftsbarnehagen.* Oslo: Universitetsforlaget.

Lysklett, O.B., Emilsen, K. & Hagen, T.L. (2003). Hva kjennetegner natur- og friluftsbarnehager? *Barnehagefolk, Pedagogisk Forum,* 78–85.

Mårtensson, F. (2004). Landskapet i leken. En studie av utomhusleken på förskolegården. Doctoral thesis. Alnarp: Sveriges lantbruksuniversitet.

Moser, T. & Martinsen, M. (2010). The outdoor environment in Norwegian kindergartens as pedagogical space for toddlers' play, learning and development. *European Early Childhood Education Research Journal, 18,* 457–471.

Nilsen, R.D. (2008). Children in nature: Cultural ideas and social practices in Norway. In A. James & A.L. James (Eds.) *European Childhoods: Cultures, Politics and Childhoods in Europe* (pp. 38–60). Basingstoke: Palgrave Macmillan.

NME (2000–2001). *St.meld. nr. 39: Friluftsliv – Ein veg til høgare livskvalitet.* Oslo: Norwegian Ministry of the Environment.

NMER (2005). *Act no. 64 of June 2005 relating to Kindergartens (the Kindergarten Act).* Oslo: Norwegian Ministry of Education and Research.

NMER (2006/2011). *Framework Plan for the Content and Tasks of Kindergartens,* issued 1 March. Oslo: Norwegian Ministry of Education and Research.

NMER (2012). *Nasjonale retningslinjer for barnehagelærerutdanning.* Oslo: Norwegian Ministry of Education and Research.

Norèn-Bjørn, E. (1977). *Lek, lekplatser, lekredskap: en utvecklingspsykologisk studie av barns lek på lekplatser.* Stockholm: Lekmiljörådet/LiberFörlag.

Refshauge, A.D. (2012). PlayLab Cph. Design and use of public playgrounds in urban green spaces. *Forest & Landscape Research, 53.* Frederiksberg: Forest & Landscape.

Sandberg, A. & Ärlemalm-Hagsér, E. (2011). The Swedish National Curriculum: Play and learning with fundamental values in focus. *Australasian Journal of Early Childhood, 36,* 44–50.

Sandseter, E.B.H., Wyver, S. & Little, H. (2012). Does theory and pedagogy have an impact on provisions for outdoor learning? A comparison of approaches in Australia and Norway. *Journal of Adventure Education and Outdoor Learning, 12,* 167–182.

SFS (1993). No: 1993:100 Ministry of Education and Research, Sweden, issued 4 February.

SMES (1985). *Education Act (1985:1100).* Stockholm: Swedish Ministry of Education and Science.

SMES (2010). *Curriculum for the Preschool: Lpfö 98.* Stockholm: Swedish Ministry of Education and Science, Skoleverket.

Storli, R. & Hagen, T.L. (2010) Affordances in outdoor environments and children's physically active play in pre-school. *European Early Childhood Education Research Journal, 18*(4), 445–457.

10

Supporting early learning outdoors in the UK

Culture clash and concord

Sue Waite

PLYMOUTH UNIVERSITY

In this chapter, I consider how cultural perspectives can support provision of outdoor learning for the early years, using an ecological framework (Bronfenbrenner, 1979) to structure the different levels at which cultural influence can be perceived. I begin by briefly considering the educational climate in the UK, focusing specifically on England, and its implications for early years policy and provision. I then illustrate, through case studies of outdoor learning provision from early years settings, ways in which culture permeates available educational opportunities, highlighting mismatches and tensions between cultural perspectives. I propose cultural density (Waite, 2013) as a new conceptual tool to consider how clashes and concord between cultural perspectives might be handled productively, and might work towards rather than against greater social justice and opportunities for all through outdoor learning. Finally, I suggest some future directions for research enquiry and curriculum development.

An ecological framework

In Waite, Rogers and Evans's (2013) Economic and Social Research Council-funded study of the transition between Foundation Stage and Year 1 (primary education, 4–7 years), we employed a conceptual framework derived from Bronfenbrenner (1979) to support our thinking about the different influences operating on children's learning outside the classroom. The ecological model acknowledges the complexity and interrelatedness of different elements in a system for limiting or supporting actions within it.

I have adapted our original model in Figure 10.1 to show how policies and national cultural levels at the macro level frame what it is possible for schools and other institutions to offer. The values and ethos of the individual setting exert a further steer on the sorts of activities and curriculum planned for children at a meso level. At the micro level at which that study focused, we conceived interactive influences shaping the teaching and learning possibilities and that these included not only the social context of people involved, but also the place of learning as an active contributor to, rather than passive context for, enactment of practice. The macro- and meso-level influences are mediated by variable resistance and affordances at the micro-level, leading to a set of pedagogical possibilities.

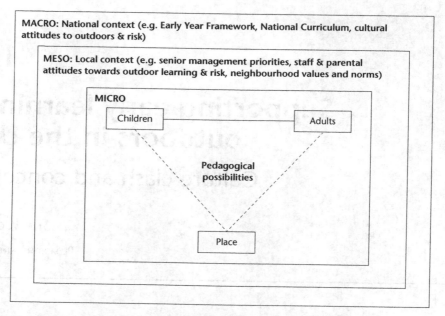

Figure 10.1 An ecological model of cultural influences

We found that the range of pedagogical possibilities adopted increased when the 'place' was outside the classroom. In the next two sections, I briefly describe why this might be so from a macro perspective.

Performativity pressures

Early years education in the UK has long been regarded as an apparent haven for outdoor learning during a period of education when many mainstream opportunities have been under pressure from performativity expectations. Although the 1944 Education Act made it a duty for Local Education Authorities to provide 'adequate facilities for recreation and social and physical training' (Cook, 1999, p. 161), there has subsequently been a marked shift from holistic development to educational attainment for children from the age of 5 upwards. This has resulted in narrowing aims and restricted opportunities for outdoor learning (McNess, Broadfoot & Osborn, 2003; Waite, 2010) and has been exacerbated by an increasing public concern with health and safety and minimisation of the risk of physical harm (Gill, 2009; Waite, Huggins & Wickett, 2014). The decline in holistic approaches to education since the 1980s has been traced to a secularisation of education away from its endeavour to create character, strength and moral fibre in the working classes (Freeman, 2011), but might also be attributed to increased individualism generated during the conservative Thatcher government (Keay, 1987). Performance of the individual became a more dominant discourse than the public good. At the same time, measurement of that performance in terms of educational attainment through standardised tests (and a consequent devaluation of alternative ways of learning that are less easily captured by pen and paper) became the norm (Gorard, Selwyn & Rees, 2002).

Research showing that early years experiences were fundamental to future success (e.g. Sylva, 1994) has meant that performativity has also become an issue for the early years sector.

While this recognition of its importance was welcomed in many respects, some commentators were concerned that an emphasis on children's educational and economic futures might fail to acknowledge the importance of childhood itself and could undermine play (Rogers & Rose, 2007). Large-scale studies such as Effective Practice in Pre-school Education (Sylva, Melhuish, Sammons, Siraj-Blatchford & Taggart, 2004) shaped the sorts of educational offer for very young children as the quality of early years provision became a key policy driver. Successive early years frameworks (Faulkner & Coates, 2013) have emphasised the importance of good learning environments and highly trained staff for effective early years practice, but recent government consultation suggests that both these may be in jeopardy as more private market-led provision and shorter training have been suggested (DfE, 2013). Although the revised framework does acknowledge the importance of foundational social and emotional aspects of learning and outdoor learning (DfE, 2012), there is also, increasingly, top-down pressure regarding preparation for formal learning or 'school readiness' (Whitebread & Bingham, 2011).

School readiness is a concept that has been variously defined (Whitebread & Bingham, 2011), and has become increasingly prominent in policy documents and reports over recent years (Ofsted, 2014). For example, the Field Report (2010) emphasised the importance of pre-school, focusing particularly on how home background affects children's school readiness; while Allen (2011) encouraged early intervention programmes to prepare all children to be 'school ready' at 5. Its relevance for learning outside the classroom is that this represents an arena in which community and school values often coalesce (Wickett & Huggins, 2011), thus supporting transitions (Waite et al., 2013). However, positioning learning outdoors as a means of preparation for school could be construed as presenting a threat to the free-flow role play that often characterises outdoor spaces by foregrounding the school's rather than the child's agenda (Rose & Rogers, 2012). Tickell (2011), in her report, rephrases the idea as school 'unreadiness', making the point that it is the school that should make itself ready to receive children at different developmental points. The expectation then becomes that pedagogical practice will respond to each individual child's needs rather than hurry every child towards conformity with schooling norms. This cultural shift is significantly supported by alternative pedagogies (Malone, 2008) that are co-constructed with 'ecological, emotional and social sensitivities to place' (Power & Green, 2014, p. 106). Arguably, appropriateness of pedagogy is the critical factor in considering 'readiness' and makes it vital that outdoor learning does not simply replicate indoor teaching if it is to successfully support children in transition (Waite et al., 2013).

Risk and the outdoors

In combination with performativity pressure, risk aversion presents an additional culturally based barrier to outdoor learning being fully embraced (Ernst, 2013). Over the past fifty years, children's freedom to play has steadily reduced as many parents in the UK have viewed traffic and dangerous strangers as increasing threats (Selwyn, 2000). A perceived growth in possible litigation in the past two decades and a few high-profile accidents have led to increased health and safety regulations intended to prevent harm (Gill, 2009). Yet, while discourse around outdoor education often focuses on the individual's risk of harm or need to develop independence and resilience (Bialostok & Kamberelis, 2010), early outdoor play has been demonstrated as fundamental to developing more socially sensitive and reducing risky behaviour because it is less closely determined by the adult agenda and allows young children to try out different ways of behaving and interacting (Stephenson, 2003; Little & Wyver, 2010; Waite et al., 2013; Jarvis, Newman & Swiniarski, 2014). Outdoor play's important contribution to the development of children's socially aware risk assessment should be acknowledged (Waite et al., 2014).

Thus we see that, although outdoor learning may be supported at a macro level in policies regarding young children for its contribution to their overall health and wellbeing (Bell, Wilson & Liu, 2008; HM Government, 2014), performative pressure around school readiness and attitudes towards risk and the outdoors exert influences over pedagogical possibilities at a meso level.

In the following section, we see how this can manifest itself at an intermediary institutional level through examples drawn from case studies of outdoor learning in five early years contexts – childminder, private nursery, playgroup, Foundation Stage and primary school – representing different meso-level cultures. Three visits were made to each setting, generating data through observations, interviews and focus groups. (For further details of this study, see Waite, Davis & Brown, 2006.)

Five cultural clips

Childminders in the UK look after children in their own homes, often alongside their own children, and are regulated and inspected as other early years settings. Although the limited outdoor space at her home was fully utilised, the childminder in our study also regularly made use of the local woods to take the children to experience a bigger and wilder outdoors, visiting them whenever and as often as she wanted. The use of this resource was principally up to her and her own values regarding the outdoors. She considered that it is 'important for the children to be able to access the freedom that outdoors provides that indoors doesn't provide, especially if you are in a confined space as we are here'.

Similarly, staff at the playgroup noted additional freedom in outdoor spaces, commenting:

> For the individual it benefits children with behaviour problems as it offers an open environment and children behave differently because they are so much freer. The benefits are that everybody is free more, being explorative and creating balance using the curriculum. Outdoor learning allows the curriculum to be seen through a different view.

However, in practice, their sessions were more structured both in their timing and resources. They were curtailed if the weather was poor and sometimes the same activities were available inside and outside so that being out in the fresh air became the only distinction between children's experiences in the two contexts. Playgroups in England are generally led by trained staff with parent helpers. Many activities were adult led and the resources that staff provided dictated available play opportunities. Although there was support for outdoor learning, its implications for pedagogy were not accepted or understood by all adults, perhaps due to a lack of effective leadership and/or fewer higher-level trained staff supporting the children's play in this setting. While adults sometimes capitalised on learning opportunities and contingently extended children's thinking, at other times adult intervention closed down their exploratory play.

In the private nursery, there was an area immediately outside the building and also a path to woodland. The teacher-in-charge/owner believed the wood offered 'freedom to explore a native environment [and] develop[ed] affinity for the natural world'. Her personal values about the benefits of the natural world for children's development were strongly influential on other staff and children in their attitudes and use of outdoor environment. When a child showed some reluctance, the nursery nurse encouraged her by slowing to the child's pace and praising her as she managed the steep slope to the woodland independently. Furthermore, it was considered that: 'attitudes and practices engendered at the nursery may also inspire parents to take children outdoors more often' (Waite *et al.*, 2006). Thus the nursery culture interacted with the wider community of parents. Clear and shared values and cultural expectations of staff and children created a strong basis for outdoor learning.

In the Foundation Stage context, the school was located in a deprived area and the Foundation Stage coordinator, following her master's-level study, was a keen advocate of outdoor learning, fundraising for, and designing, a rich learning environment within the school grounds. Another teacher commented:

> Most parents are really grateful that they've got the opportunity to [play outdoors at school] because quite a few of our children have not got access to a garden at home.

Through extensive consultation, involving Year 6 (upper primary school, 10–11 years) children in designing an appealing environment for the youngest children and a working party of parents, interaction between the wider community and the school became an important facet of the outdoor provision here. National frameworks influenced the production of a document, 'Opportunities for Effective Teaching and Learning in the Foundation Stage when using the Outdoor Learning Environment' (Byrne, Partington & Webb, 2003), to help identify specific and effective teaching and learning practices for outdoor teaching, such as linking curriculum guidance on mathematical development with the use of positional language when using the climbing frames. However, the headteacher talked of this document as merely a 'guide on the side' that was lightly used so as not to disrupt the children's own imaginative use of the space.

Finally, in a primary school noted for its support of outdoor learning, an emphasis on standards in schools (Ball, 2010) influenced the availability of outdoor learning for all children:

> Unfortunately having been a Year 6 teacher for the last several years, it is just revision of all those things, we don't actually get time to go out and do that, not until after SATs (compulsory national tests termed 'Standard Assessment Tasks'). (Lead on outdoor provision)

Yet the headteacher in this school also expressed values that resisted the pressure to let these opportunities become squeezed out, and was looking for ways to embed outdoor learning:

> where we can actually plan those within the curriculum rather than leave it to what normally happens, which is it is planned if it's OK, if it is good weather or it happens to fall in the right place . . . make it explicit in our documents rather than have it as a whim.

Cultural aspects of practice

In all five contexts freedom was mentioned as a key aspect of outdoor learning environments. Yet the availability of that freedom was experienced differently because cultural pressures at the macro and meso level interact with personal values (Waite, 2011). We see that the sole practitioner is free to interpret the regulations and guidance to provide as much outdoor learning as she wishes. Her interactions with the children capitalise on resources of a wider place and the children's own confidence and experience. In fact, she is operating at the micro level, having cut out the 'middleman' of an institution filtering macro cultural influences. In the playgroup, however, a lack of strong leadership for outdoor learning results in variable practice and opportunities, with some adults interrupting children's flow of play and learning as they closely managed the outdoor spaces. The personal enthusiasm of the owner and teacher-in-charge at the private nursery, however, creates a culture where outdoor learning and independence is the norm. As owner, she is perhaps in a stronger position to mediate macro-level influences on practice and policy than staff and parent volunteers at the playgroup (see also Maynard, 2007, for a discussion on a Foucauldian analysis of the flow of power between Forest School practitioners and early years teachers). In both the Foundation Stage and primary school located within mainstream schooling, the tensions between the macro, meso and micro levels are more evident. In the Foundation Stage, the personal enthusiasm of one individual created an environment rich in possibilities and, by conscious involvement of others, the culture had spread to her fellow teachers and community, and permeated the micro-level exchanges between adult, child and place. In the primary school, there were more ambivalent views expressed by children and staff about how outdoor learning can be supported within national standards policy, reflecting how performativity pressures tend to increase as children get older (Waite, 2010). However, a culture of sharing values and ownership throughout the school seemed to create opportunities for outdoor learning's further development. For example, the children themselves chose what markings would go on the playground through their family groups, where mixed ages met weekly with a staff member to discuss issues. The co-construction of pedagogical possibilities at the micro level was supported at a structural institutional level with senior management and governor support. In all the contexts, a national culture of risk aversion was resisted by cost–benefit analyses derived from clear locally held values which concluded that potential gains outweighed the risks involved (Waite et al., 2014).

Changing cultures

In the preceding discussion I suggest that resistance to macro-level discourse is observed and perceived as more or less possible in different contexts. The theoretical construct of cultural density (Waite, 2013) may support our understanding of how cultural influences impact differently within the overarching ecological framework. Cultural density is the idea that places are imbued with certain expectations, and that ways of being and doing things are established through cultural practice over time. Schools are prime examples of this and the term institutional habitus has been coined for how practices spread among participants in an institutional context (Thomas, 2002). Bourdieu's concept of habitus refers to how a context, or 'social field', shapes the norms of behaviour within that context (Bourdieu, 2002). However, the extent to which this occurs seems to depend on the strength or 'density' of cultural norms of habitus operating at the meso level. Reflecting on the examples discussed in the five cultural clips, we can see how different densities of habitus appear to influence interactions in specific places and pedagogical encounters. Alternative cultural densities developed through personal values, strong leadership and co-construction of learning environments appear to resist the impact of macro-level forces. Thus, as McInerney, Smyth and Down (2011) suggest, supporting learning effectively requires critical engagement with local cultural influences of community, environment and institution in relation to their impact on pedagogy.

Figure 10.2 illustrates how the meso and micro may interact and co-construction of respectful critical pedagogies occur. Where the three ellipses overlap, pedagogical possibilities engendered are rich as cultural practices are congruent, and build on existing knowledge and practices between actors (Somerville, Davie, Power, Ganville & de Carteret, 2011; Ofsted, 2014). Such cultural continuity may assist learners in relating new learning to their existing funds of knowledge. Failure to consider clash or concord in cultures is likely to contribute to persistent social inequalities within education as institutional habitus may dominate with demands that do not take account of the fit of the learning environment with prior socialisation of children (Reay, 2001). Successful early years environments take such mismatches into account and find ways to

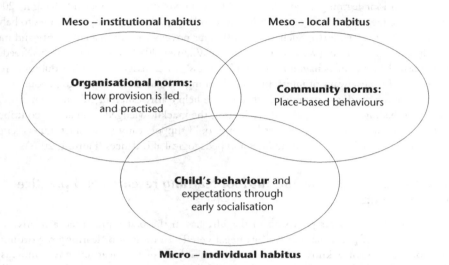

Macro – national policies, cultural attitudes

Meso – institutional habitus   **Meso – local habitus**

Organisational norms:
How provision is led
and practised

Community norms:
Place-based behaviours

Child's behaviour and
expectations through
early socialisation

Micro – individual habitus

Figure 10.2 Illustrating pedagogical possibilities: micro-level interactions in the context of different cultural densities

Source: Adapted from Waite (2013)

make links for children to extend the range of 'ways of being' that are open to them (Wickett & Huggins, 2011).

The necessary skill for the early years teacher is to extend the child's learning by contingent support – for example, following children's schema through sustained shared thinking (Sylva, Melhuish, Sammons, Siraj-Blatchford & Taggart, 2012, p. 5), or by acknowledging home interests and places that have meaning for children (Fantuzzo & McWayne, 2002; Wickett & Huggins, 2011). A lack of congruence also helps to explain why some children find it hard to engage in the expected behaviours of the setting if these are very alien to what they have thus far experienced. Authentic inclusion of diversity and special educational needs looks to how the setting can change to meet the needs of the child (Booth & Ainscow, 2002). Yet it is often assumed that the child should accommodate the cultural milieu of the setting; indeed, in some outdoor learning contexts, a culture shock is sometimes used purposefully as a pedagogical tool (Fabrizio & Neill, 2005). Where cultural clashes are extreme, using the visual imagery of our model in Figure 10.2, the ellipses representing different cultural milieu may not touch each other, leaving learning gaps that may appear insuperable to the child and alienate them from schooling. Conversely, a 'gap' may stimulate re-evaluation of perspectives by both pupil and teacher, and this might account for the value of novel situations discussed further below. However, even if there is an expectation that young children will become more adept at learning in formal contexts over time, transition from informal modes of learning requires sensitivity to continuing needs and respect for other ways of knowing that may be highly valued in other cultural communities beyond the setting. Outdoor contexts seem to offer a variety of opportunities to smooth that change, and honour children's other knowledge and habitus (Waite *et al.*, 2013).

The particularities of specific places should be taken into account in considering cultural influences (Waite, 2013). Non-didactic kinds of teaching and learning, such as exploratory and discovery learning, appear supported where meso and macro influences are less apparent; this may be the 'freedom' that the five settings referred to regarding their outdoor places and that is often claimed for outdoor learning, especially in wilder contexts such as woodland (Knight, 2009). Where there are few associations or established ways of acting, this creates opportunities to behave in new ways (Waite et al., 2013; Sucharita, 2014). This novelty can stimulate curiosity and motivate children to ask questions (Waite & Davis, 2007; Wilenski, 2014). I have termed this 'freedom' from established norms of behaviour 'cultural lightness', to envisage how some outdoor spaces are more open for new ways of interacting and learning (Waite, 2013). Thinking about cultural density in planning outdoor learning might therefore help clarify different cultural influences and their force in shaping learning spaces. Place itself is, then, acknowledged as an active contributor in micro enactment of pedagogy, and reflection would support early years practitioners' critical engagement with its educational possibilities and pedagogical affordances (Fjørtoft, 2001).

Defining future directions for outdoor learning research and practice in the early years

As we have seen, early years provision in the UK has in the past represented a relative oasis from the pressures of performativity and its negative effect on outdoor learning opportunities. Learning outdoors is still acknowledged as an important facet of early learning environments for health and wellbeing that is foundational for later learning. Yet, an increasingly strong call for school readiness, and a persistent and pervasive culture of fear, exert an opposite pull. To understand why and how this tension exists, we need to look across all levels of the system to unpick how rhetoric becomes enacted. Theorising the processes involved as suggested will unpick dynamic interactions between and within levels. It may also serve to highlight how policy might be supported in practice, but equally how local enactment might wish to redirect its broad intentions to include situated contextual factors. Further research is needed to focus on how and why outdoor learning is important for specific outcomes. Much existing research makes claims for relatively global benefits (Dillon & Dickie, 2012), but drilling down to associations between certain features of learning environments and specific outcomes will help us to create more nuanced understandings of what sorts of outdoor places and pedagogy will support what kinds of outcomes, and help us to construct well balanced curricula, environments and pedagogy for young children. In order to achieve such insight, we need to adopt mixed methodologies that, while acknowledging the impossibility of a clinical approach to educational interventions that are far more complex than a pill, combine control of some factors with detailed conceptually robust qualitative studies that can look beneath associations to theorise why and how. By theorising from empirical evidence using socio-cultural and psychological frames to explore associations, we may begin to employ or avoid culture clashes and concord critically and purposefully to create a more socially just distribution of these established public goods, education and our natural environment.

References

Allen, G. (2011). *Early Intervention: The Next Steps*. Report of the Independent Review of Early Intervention. London: Cabinet Office. Retrieved from: www.gov.uk/government/publications/early-intervention-the-next-steps--2.

Ball, S. (2010). New voices, new knowledges and the new politics of education research: The gathering of a perfect storm? *European Educational Research Journal, 9*(2), 124–137.

Bell, J.F., Wilson, J.S. & Liu, G.C. (2008). Neighbourhood greenness and 2 year changes in body mass index of children and youth. *American Journal of Preventative Medicine, 35*(6), 547–553.

Bialostok, S. & Kamberelis, G. (2010). New capitalism, risk and subjectification in an early childhood classroom. *Contemporary Issues in Early Childhood, 11*(3), 299–312.

Booth, T. & Ainscow, M. (2002). *Index for Inclusion: Developing Learning and Participation in Schools*. Bristol: Centre for Studies on Inclusive Education.

Bourdieu, P. (2002). Habitus. In J. Hillier & E. Rooksby (Eds.) *Habitus: A Sense of Place* (pp. 27–34). Aldershot: Ashgate.

Bronfenbrenner, U. (1979). *The Ecology of Human Development*. Cambridge, MA: Harvard University Press.

Byrne, S., Partington, Y. & Webb, S (2003). Opportunities for effective teaching and learning in the foundation stage when using the outdoor learning environment. Personal communication.

Cook, L. (1999). The 1944 Education Act and outdoor education: from policy to practice. *History of Education, 28*(2), 157–172.

DfE (2012). Statutory Framework for the Early Years Foundation Stage. Retrieved from: www.foundationyears.org.uk/wp-content/uploads/2012/07/EYFS-Statutory-Framework-2012.pdf.

DfE (2013). *More Great Childcare – Raising Quality and Giving Parents more Choice*. Retrieved from: www.gov.uk/government/publications/more-great-childcare-raising-quality-and-giving-parents-more-choice.

Dillon, J. & Dickie, I. (2012). *Learning in the Natural Environment: Review of Social and Economic Benefits and Barriers*. Natural England Commissioned Reports, No. 092:

Ernst, J. (2013). Early childhood educators' use of natural outdoor settings as learning environments: An exploratory study of beliefs, practices, and barriers. *Environmental Education Research, 20*(6), 735–752.

Fabrizio, S.M. & Neill, J.T. (2005). Cultural adaptation in outdoor programming. *Australian Journal of Outdoor Education, 9*(2), 44–56.

Fantuzzo, J. & McWayne, C. (2002). The relationship between peer play interactions and family context and dimensions of school readiness for low-income preschool children. *Journal of Educational Psychology, 94*, 79–87.

Faulkner, D. & Coates, E.A. (2013). Early childhood policy and practice in England: Twenty years of change. *International Journal of Early Years Education, 21*(2–3), 244–263.

Field, F. (2010). *The Foundation Years: Preventing Poor Children Becoming Poor Adults*. Report of the Independent Review on Poverty and Life Chances. London: Cabinet Office. Retrieved from: www.creativitycultureeducation.org/the-foundation-years-preventing-poor-children-becoming-poor-adults.

Fjørtoft, I. (2001). The natural environment as a playground for children: The impact of outdoor play activities in pre-primary school children. *Early Childhood Education Journal, 29*(2), 111–117.

Freeman, M. (2011). From 'character-training' to 'personal growth': The early history of Outward Bound 1941–1965. *History of Education, 40*(1), 21–43.

Gill, T. (2009). *No Fear: Growing Up in a Risk-averse Society*. London: Calouste Gulbenkian Foundation.

Gorard, S., Selwyn, N. & Rees, G. (2002). Privileging the visible: A critique of the National Learning Targets. *British Educational Research Journal, 28*(3), 309–325.

HM Government (2014). *Moving More, Living More: The Physical Activity Olympic and Paralympic Legacy for the Nation*. Retrieved from: https://www.gov.uk/government/publications/moving-more-living-more-olympic-and-paralympic-games-legacy.

Jarvis, P., Newman, S. & Swiniarski, L. (2014). On 'becoming social': The importance of collaborative free play in childhood. *International Journal of Play, 3*(1), 53–68.

Keay, D. (1987). Interview with Margaret Thatcher. *Woman's Own*. Retrieved from: www.margaretthatcher.org/speeches/displaydocument.asp?docid=106689.

Knight, S. (2009). *Forest Schools and Outdoor Play in the Early Years*. London: Sage.

Little, H. & Wyver, S. (2010). Individual differences in children's risk perception and appraisals in outdoor play environments. *International Journal of Early Years Education, 18*(4), 297–313.

Malone, K. (2008) Every Experience Matters: An evidence based research report on the role of learning outside the classroom for children's whole development from birth to eighteen years. Report commissioned by Farming and Countryside Education for UK Department of Children, School and Families: Wollongong, Australia. Retrieved from: www.face-online.org.uk/face-news/every-experience-matters.

Maynard, T. (2007). Encounters with Forest School and Foucault: A risky business? *Education 3–13, 35*(4), 379–391.

McInerney, P., Smyth, J. & Down, B. (2011) 'Coming to a place near you?' The politics and possibilities of a critical pedagogy of place-based education. *Asia-Pacific Journal of Teacher Education, 39*(1), 3–16.

McNess, E., Broadfoot, P. & Osborn, M. (2003). Is the effective compromising the affective? *British Education Research Journal, 29*(2), 243–257.

Ofsted (2014). *Are you Ready? Good Practice in School Readiness.* Retrieved from: www.ofsted.gov.uk/resources/140074.

Power, K. & Green, M. (2014). Reframing primary curriculum through concepts of place. *Asia-Pacific Journal of Teacher Education, 42*(2), 105–118.

Reay, D. (2001). Finding or losing yourself? Working class relationships to education. *Journal of Educational Policy, 13*, 519–529.

Rogers, S. & Rose, J. (2007). Ready for reception? The advantages and disadvantages of single point entry to school. *Early Years, 27*(1), 47–63.

Rose, J. & Rogers, S. (2012). *The Role of the Adult in Early Years Settings.* Maidenhead: Open University Press.

Selwyn, J. (2000). Technologies and environments: new freedoms, new constraints. In M. Boushel, M. Fawcett & J. Selwyn (Eds.) *Focus on Childhood Principles and Realities* (Chapter 10). Oxford: Blackwell Science.

Somerville, M., Davie, B., Power, K., Gannon, S. & de Carteret, P. (2011). *Place Pedagogy Change.* The Netherlands: Sense.

Stephenson, A. (2003). Physical risk taking: Dangerous or endangered? *Early Years, 23*(10), 35–43.

Sucharita, V. (2014). Negotiating between family, peers and school: Understanding the world of government and private school students. *Compare: A Journal of Comparative and International Education, 44*(3), 379–393.

Sylva, K. (1994). The impact of early learning on children's later development. In C. Ball (Ed.) *Start Right: The Importance of Early Learning* (Appendix C). London: RSA.

Sylva, K., Melhuish, E., Sammons, P., Siraj-Blatchford, I. & Taggart, B. (2004). The Effective Provision of Preschool Education Project: Findings from the preschool period. *Research Brief RBX13-03.* London: Institute of Education.

Sylva, K., Melhuish, E., Sammons, P., Siraj-Blatchford, I. & Taggart, B. (2012). *The Effective Provision of Pre-school Education (EPPE) Project: Findings from Pre-school to End of Key Stage 1.* Retrieved from: http://eppe.ioe.ac.uk/eppe/eppepdfs/RBTec1223sept0412.pdf.

Thomas, L. (2002). Student retention in higher education: The role of institutional habitus. *Journal of Education Policy, 17*, 423–442.

Tickell, C. (2011). *The Early Years: Foundations for Life, Health and Learning* (DFE-00177-2011). Report of the Independent Review on the Early Years Foundation Stage. London: Department for Education. Retrieved from: www.gov.uk/government/publications/the-early-years-foundations-for-life-health-and-learning-an-independent-report-on-the-early-years-foundation-stage-to-her-majestys-government.

Waite, S. (2010). Losing our way? Declining outdoor opportunities for learning for children aged between 2 and 11. *Journal of Adventure Education and Outdoor Learning, 10*(2), 111–126.

Waite, S. (2011). Teaching and learning outside the classroom: Personal values, alternative pedagogies and standards. *Education 3–13, 39*(1), 65–82.

Waite, S. (2013). Knowing your place in the world: How place and culture support and obstruct educational aims. *Cambridge Journal of Education, 43*(4), 413–434.

Waite, S. & Davis, B. (2007). The contribution of free play and structured activities in Forest School to learning beyond cognition: An English case. In B. Ravn & N. Kryger (Eds.) *Learning Beyond Cognition* (pp. 257–274). Copenhagen: Danish University of Education.

Waite, S., Davis, B. & Brown, K. (2006). *Five Stories of Outdoor Learning from Settings for 2–11 Year Olds in Devon.* Plymouth: Plymouth University.

Waite, S., Huggins, V. & Wickett, K. (2014). Risky outdoor play: Embracing uncertainty in pursuit of learning. In T. Maynard & J. Waters (Eds.) *Exploring Outdoor Play in the Early Years.* Maidenhead: McGraw-Hill Education/Open University Press.

Waite, S., Rogers, S. & Evans, J. (2013). Freedom, flow and fairness: Exploring how children develop socially at school through outdoor play. *Journal of Adventure Education and Outdoor Learning, 13*(3), 255–276.

Whitebread, D. & Bingham, S. (2011). *School Readiness: A Critical Review of Perspectives and Evidence.* TACTYC Occasional Paper No. 2.

Wickett, K. & Huggins, V. (2011). Using the local community as part of the early years environment. In S. Waite (Ed.) *Children Learning Outside the Classroom: From Birth to Eleven* (pp. 35–49). London: Sage.

Wilenski, D. (2014). We're a little bit lost aren't we? Outdoor exploration, real and fantastical lands and the educational possibilities of disorientations. *FORUM, 56*(1), 9–17. Retrieved from: www.wwwords.co.uk/Forum.

11

Curricular outdoor learning in Scotland

From practice to policy

Beth Christie, Pete Higgins and Robbie Nicol

UNIVERSITY OF EDINBURGH

... it is hardly possible to overrate the benefits that arise from this co-operation of teacher and taught in the open air ... directing their eyes to the outer world and leading them to take reverent heed of what may there be seen.

Archibald Geike, Scottish geologist, 1887

Taken together, indoor and outdoor experiences delivering outcomes across the evolving curriculum will meet national aspirations for every young person: the knowledge and understanding, skills, capabilities and attributes they will develop to embrace the challenges of their future.

Learning and Teaching Scotland, 2007

The Scottish context

More than a century has passed since Geike directed our eyes outwards to the landscapes of Scotland, little knowing the manner in which his guiding principle would be enshrined within a document prepared in 2007 by Learning and Teaching Scotland (LTS).[1] Geike recognised Scotland's rich and varied landscape: wild coastlines, glens, forests, lochs, moors and farmland alongside urban areas, cities, towns, and smaller rural and fishing villages. Similarly, LTS acknowledges that this blend of inspiring geophysical environments, layered with centuries of social and cultural history, combines with a changeable climate to provide fertile ground for a range of educational experiences. Collectively, this rich resource has been valued and acknowledged both historically and currently, and at local, national and international levels for its range of authentic outdoor contexts for teaching and learning; as such, Scotland is legitimately recognised as one of the first countries in the world to offer formalised outdoor education (Higgins, 2002).

Historically, milestones such as the 1944 Education Act and 1945 Education (Scotland) Act encouraged the use of the outdoors and the development of appropriate 'camps' (Higgins & Nicol, 2013), and aided the widespread development of outdoor education across Scotland

113

in the 1960s and 1970s. During that period of growth most local authorities converted old mansion houses and other stately homes into residential centres and teachers were prepared to deliver formalised physical outdoor activities by attending newly developed specialist courses at teacher training colleges. Scotland's structured approach to the development of outdoor education training and resources during that time drew international attention and, in particular, provision in the 1970s in the Lothian and Borders region was unrivalled (Cheesmond, 1979). However, the disaggregation of local authorities in the 1980s, and the associated economic impact, led to a decline in school-based and local residential provision, and many residential centres closed due to financial pressure.

Yet, following this decline and most notably over the past decade, research interest rather than provision per se, in outdoor education has begun to grow (for example, see reviews and work over different geographical locations of the UK by the Department for Education and Science, 2006; Mannion, Doyle, Sankey, Mattu & Wilson, 2007; Waite, 2010). Most notably in Scotland, this interest has risen sharply over the past five years and aspects have included a clear Learning for Sustainability agenda (for recent examples, see Britton, 2014; Christie, Beames, Higgins, Nicol & Ross, 2014; Mannion, Mattu & Wilson, 2015). Such interest has been fuelled by broader, yet significant, educational developments in Scotland such as the national educational framework – Curriculum for Excellence (CfE) (Scottish Government, 2004) – the Learning for Sustainability (LfS) agenda (Scottish Government, 2012a, 2013a; Higgins & Lavery, 2013) and the General Teaching Council for Scotland's[2] (GTCS) professional standards revision and update (GTCS, 2013).

Scotland is not alone here; rather its development reflects an increase in political and educational support for learning outside the classroom germane to other countries – for example, see publications such as Education Outside the Classroom guidelines (New Zealand Ministry of Education, 2008), the UK Manifesto for Learning Outside the Classroom (Council for Learning Outside the Classroom, 2006) and guidelines produced by Outdoor Education Australia (Outdoor Education Australia, 2015). Additionally, there are an increasing number of international peer-reviewed journals[3] that share, support and progress knowledge within the field.

The significance of Scotland's contribution to the international agenda stems from the position that outdoor learning and learning for sustainability hold within and across the country's educational and political systems. Such unified support lends legitimacy to the process of moving from the rhetoric and policies to enable the transformation that is required within schools, communities and the general population. In turn, Scotland has much to learn from other successful education systems in countries such as New Zealand, Australia and within the Nordic nations. Therefore the Scottish-centric view presented here should be considered in relation to this wider global context.

In summary the recent growth and renewed interest in outdoor learning in Scotland has been prompted, in part, by the clear policy coherence between recent educational developments, related aspects of professional registration and increased opportunity for the provision of interdisciplinary and experiential learning both within and beyond the classroom for 3–18 year olds. These strategic developments combine with recent research that highlights the need for strategic pre- and in-service teacher support in outdoor learning and learning for sustainability to enable the educational profession to implement and embed these approaches through research informed practice (see Thorburn & Allison, 2010; Christie *et al.*, 2014).

Additionally, further empirical and theoretical support for outdoor learning can be found within the wider, and growing, research community whose interests span health and wellbeing, urban and rural design, environmental and community development, and education for sustainable development (for example, see Sustainable Development Commission, 2008;[4] Burns, 2011; Ward Thompson, 2013;[5] Pearce, 2013;[6] Astell-Burt, Mitchell & Hartig, 2014). Also, many of the agencies and organisations that manage, protect and conserve the landscape and natural and cultural heritage of Scotland have produced guidance and educational resources[7] to support those wishing to teach and learn within the places they safeguard (see Archaeology Scotland, 2014; Historic Scotland, 2014; National Trust for Scotland, 2014). For example, the National Parks[8] continue to work closely with secondary and primary schools to showcase new projects being led by teachers, to other teachers and other sectors. This demonstrates what has been achieved and what is possible; practically exemplifying how the educational, environmental, cultural and heritage sectors can combine to deliver some of the broader educational, community and environmental agendas being highlighted by the Scottish Government. Education Scotland (2013) recognises the benefits of such an integrated approach to teaching and learning, and clearly state that 'the place in which people learn also helps them to make connections between their experiences and the world around them in a meaningful context' (p. 6). Further, they acknowledge the synergistic benefits afforded by introducing an outdoor context that provides a diversity of resources and spaces that is hard to replicate in an indoor environment (p. 6).

Towards a definition

While there has been a shift from using the term 'outdoor education' towards 'outdoor learning', both terms will be used interchangeably as we see no significant difference between them. Outdoor learning is commonly used within Scotland as it reflects the way in which it is seen as an approach to learning and embedded within mainstream schooling (Learning and Teaching Scotland, 2010a). This reflects the concentric-circles model of outdoor learning (Nicol, 2001; Higgins & Nicol, 2002) that places schools at the core and radiates to encompass local areas beyond the school grounds, day excursions or field trips, and residential or longer overnight stays. A final zone (not noted on the model) is Planet Earth, and considering it is important as it reflects the increasing significance of developing our understanding of sustainability and a need for outdoor learning experiences that can encourage those involved to care for the communities they engage with – communities of the natural and human worlds.

In the main we refer to 'outdoor learning', and in doing so we build upon our previous work, which positions experiential and adventurous approaches to learning as a central theme whatever the focus or context (Higgins & Nicol, 2013). Further, the emphasis remains on quality educational experiences whether these take place in an indoor or outdoor context.

Policy developments and coherence

Curriculum for Excellence

Curriculum for Excellence (CfE) was introduced to schools in Scotland in 2004. It promotes a coherent educational framework for all young people aged 3 to 18 (Scottish Government, 2004) and offers an increased opportunity for a more student-centred and holistic approach to teaching and learning through a flexible, and inter-disciplinary curriculum. It is delivered across the Broad General Educational Phase (early years to about 14 years of age) and the Senior Phase (about 14 years of age and beyond).

The development of the 'four capacities' (successful learners, confident individuals, responsible citizens and effective contributors) is core to CfE (Scottish Government, 2004). Further, as reinforced by Christie et al. (2014, p. 48), 'outdoor learning is explicitly positioned to deliver 'experience and outcomes' from all eight curricular areas'[9] and clear policy and practical guidance exists to support teachers to embed CfE through outdoor learning and make these curricular connections. There is, for example, Curriculum for Excellence through Outdoor Learning (Learning and Teaching Scotland, 2010a), Outdoor Learning 3–18 Self-evaluation Resource (Learning and Teaching Scotland, 2010b), Outdoor Learning: Practical Guidance, Ideas and Support for Teachers and Practitioners in Scotland (Education Scotland, 2011a), Building your Curriculum: Outside & In (Education Scotland, 2011b) and Going Out There: Scottish Framework for Safe Practice in Off-site Visits (Scottish Government, 2013b). Of this literature Curriculum for Excellence through Outdoor Learning (Learning and Teaching Scotland, 2010a) is the core document, and we suggest that it could be considered as offering some of the strongest outdoor learning policy language, arguably anywhere in the world (Christie *et al.*, 2014).

This clear policy guidance is underpinned by strong support from a recent Scottish Government Cabinet Secretary, who stated that 'outdoor learning is a key component' of CfE and it should be 'an integral part of a sustained approach throughout the school year' (Russell, 2014, pp. 1–2). However, policy and governmental support can only theorise and propose change. The practical implementation must come from the professionals who work within and around the educational system. Therefore, the challenge and opportunity for professional practice is to ensure that outdoor learning is embedded within a whole-school approach, both within and across curriculum areas and at planning and developmental stages. In some cases this may require a cultural and philosophical shift from outdoor learning being commonly positioned as a standalone 'week' in the Scottish school calendar to a fully integrated legitimate pedagogical approach that is woven in to the fabric of the school year (Christie & Higgins, 2012).

This 'shift' has important implications for the identity of the teaching profession and for the provision of outdoor learning. In the case of the standalone week it is likely to be residential (involving at least one or more overnight stays) and geographically remote from pupils' schools where the teacher/instructor provides outdoor adventurous activities in which they themselves are required to be suitably qualified or skilled. In such cases their expertise as pedagogues is built around the need to be technically proficient and safe while delivering these activities. However, from a whole-school perspective, the sort of expertise that is required from the classroom teacher is built around being willing and able to take the curriculum outdoors to local places. Of course these two approaches are not mutually exclusive, but they are presented in this way to highlight the support required for those teachers who may traditionally have thought of outdoor learning as solely the former and therefore a barrier to the latter. Clearly, this is the comprehensive professional identity that we are working towards.

Envisaged this way, a coherent approach to whole school or local authority planning and development can encompass and reflect a full spectrum of progressive outdoor learning experiences and support the transition of experience gained in primary into the secondary education system. The question of how this transition can be encouraged and maintained requires further consideration and investigation.

Historically, the secondary education sector has been hard to reach in terms of outdoor learning development (see Mannion *et al.*, 2015), yet recent research (Christie *et al.*, 2014) indicates that this sector appears keen to develop provision and needs support to do so. This 'shift' may be attributable to the structure of CfE and its Broad General Educational phase that spans from ages 3 to 14 years and a Senior phase (ages 14 to 18 years). According to the Scottish Government (2012b, p. 1) the Broad General Educational phase, core to CfE, offers increased flexibility for cross-curricular work, and affords greater scope for teachers to apply their professional expertise, creativity and knowledge in rich and rewarding ways. Education Scotland describes how this structural approach positions learners at 'the centre of curriculum planning rather than "fitted into" curriculum structures' (2012b, p. 1).

In terms of the context for outdoor learning, LTS (2010a) cautions against interpreting 'the promotion of the use of school grounds and local areas as an alternative to outdoor residential experiences' rather they advise a cohesive approach where experiences, both indoor and outdoor, local and distant, day and overnight, should complement and inform one another (p. 6). There is a need for a comprehensive understanding of the range of experiences that includes residential outdoor learning; this has been highlighted previously (see Christie & Higgins, 2012; Christie, Higgins & McLaughlin, 2013) and proposed as an area for future practical professional development work via Education Scotland's current Outdoor Learning Development programme.

Learning for Sustainability

The Scottish Government is developing a national approach to 'Learning for Sustainability'[10] and has established an implementation group which is charged with finding a way forward to ensure 'learning relating to sustainable development, global citizenship and outdoor learning is experienced in a transformative way by every learner in every school across Scotland' (Scottish Government, 2012a, p. 11). Bringing these three concepts together in Learning for Sustainability is an innovative if not unique strategy, regarded as one of the most important recent developments for outdoor learning in Scotland (Russell, 2014, p. 1).

This national agenda seeks to develop a whole-school approach that will 'enable the school, and its wider community to build the values, attitudes, knowledge, skills and confidence to develop practices and take decisions which are compatible with a sustainable and equitable society' (Scottish Government, 2012a, p. 9). Such an approach embedded within CfE through a combination of indoor and outdoor teaching and learning is intended to stimulate experiences that integrate concepts of global citizenship, sustainable development and ecological connectedness, which can help learners face issues such as climate change, global financial and social inequality, renewable energy sources and sound ethical and sustainable development, in positive ways. The Scottish Government supports this integrated approach and believes that CfE provides an opportunity 'to engage young people in sustainable development education in a meaningful and transformative way' and outdoor learning can provide the pedagogical ignition for such engagement (Scottish Government, 2010, unnumbered).

Professional standards: General Teaching Council Scotland

The General Teaching Council Scotland (GTCS), which is the independent professional body promoting and regulating the teaching profession in Scotland, strongly supports the Learning for Sustainability agenda. A recent revision of the professional standards introduced a requirement for all teachers in Scotland to incorporate learning for sustainability (defined as above) into their practice (GTCS, 2013). Responses to this have included the development at the University of Edinburgh of an MSc in Learning for Sustainability aimed at teachers, educational professionals and policy makers and the intended development of a bank of GTCS accredited Career Long Professional Learning (CLPL) opportunities for outdoor learning and learning for sustainability that relate to the GTCS updated professional standards, and enable teachers and whole-school clusters to translate the policy developments and professional update requirements into everyday practice. These developments add to an existing framework which includes a dedicated post for Outdoor Learning within Education Scotland, a series of teacher-led showcase events to highlight existing good practice, ongoing national networks and the "Going Out there" (Scottish Government, 2013b) guidance published to support those organising and leading off-site visits.

In short, the policy coherence between the Scottish Government, GTCS and Education Scotland is striking and, remarkably, is also congruent with research in the field. It is clear that learning for sustainability will be a central feature of Scottish education and as part of this the educational journey for all children in Scotland must include outdoor learning as a core and common practice (Higgins & Lavery, 2013; Russell, 2014). The clear ambition is to help both teachers and learners understand fundamental global sustainability issues and to develop personal perspectives and values that will help them to address them.

Future directions: current provision and quality assurance

Despite the interest in outdoor learning and the complementary policy support, evidenced through statements such as 'the journey through education for any child in Scotland must include a series of planned, quality outdoor learning experiences' (Learning and Teaching Scotland, 2010a, p. 6), the practical reality of this combined passion and commitment is variable (Mannion *et al.*, 2015). A recent submission of evidence to the Scottish Parliament Education and Culture Committee on the current state of outdoor learning implementation in schools describes the situation as 'some pupils receiving regular experiences and others a few days (paid for by their families) at an outdoor centre and others none at all' (Higgins, Nicol, Beames, Christie & Scrutton, 2013, p. 3). Additionally, recent research, conducted by the University of Edinburgh, which builds on previous research in 2006 by the same team, highlights that there has been progression within primary schools but there remains much room for improvement, especially at the secondary school level (Christie *et al.*, 2014).

Notwithstanding the political support and the patchy provision there remains no 'national policy, statutory requirements, regulatory mechanisms, formal teaching qualification nor quality assurance to encourage, establish and maintain standards of outdoor learning' (Higgins *et al.*, 2013, p. 5). In Scotland the HMIE[11] schools inspection process stimulates, regulates and assures quality standards for teaching and learning, however it is very rare for outdoor learning to be included in an HMIE schools schedule (HMIE, 2006). Curriculum design and delivery principles apply across all pedagogical approaches and formal educational practice. Therefore outdoor learning needs to become part of the comprehensive inspection process both within schools and outdoor centres in order to assure pedagogical rigour. Such formal regulation would motivate provision and regulate quality across Scotland.

We are witnessing support and growth within the field of outdoor learning and, despite variable provision and the lack of formal quality assurance across Scotland, much policy support does exist and, essentially, aligns to create a cohesive legitimacy and platform for increased strategic development. In short, Scotland's empathy with this pedagogical approach has been stirred.

Notes

1 Learning and Teaching Scotland is the Scottish Government's education support agency. In 2010 structural changes were made and its name changed to 'Education Scotland' (see www.educationscotland.gov. uk/). All references to the documents published etc. are attributed to the name appropriate to the time.

2 The General Teaching Council for Scotland is the independent professional body that promotes and regulates the teaching profession in Scotland (www.gtcs.org.uk).

3 See, for example, the *Australian Journal of Outdoor Learning*, the *Canadian Journal of Environmental Education*, the *New Zealand Journal of Outdoor Education* and the *Journal of Adventure Education and Outdoor Learning*.

4 The Sustainable Development Commission closed in March 2011 (www.sd-commission.org.uk/pages/ links.html). However, there are a number of organisations and networks that continue to work in this area; for example, see Learning for Sustainability Scotland, Scotland's United Nations Regional Centre for Expertise on Education for Sustainable Development (http://learningforsustainabilityscotland.org/).

5 See OpenSpace (www.openspace.eca.ac.uk/index.php) for further research into inclusive access to outdoor environments.

6 See Centre for Research on Environment Society and Health (http://cresh.org.uk) for further research focused on exploring how physical and social environments can influence population health, for better and for worse.

7 See Education Scotland for a list of relevant organisations and their resources (www.educationscotland.gov.uk/learningteachingandassessment/approaches/outdoorlearning/supportmaterials/resources/organisations.asp).

8 See the Cairngorms National Park website for further information (http://cairngorms.co.uk/learn/).

9 See Education Scotland (2013) for curriculum-specific experience and outcomes guides for outdoor learning.

10 See Scottish Government (2012a) for the full report that emerged from the One Planet Schools Ministerial working group. They were tasked with developing key recommendations to enable the development of the Learning for Sustainability agenda. Also, see Scottish Government (2013a) for the government's response to those recommendations.

11 In 2011 Education Scotland, as the Scottish Government's new integrated national development and improvement agency for education, brought together the resources and functions of Her Majesty's Inspectorate of Education (HMIE) (see www.educationscotland.gov.uk/inspectionandreview/).

References

Archaeology Scotland (2014). *Archaeology Scotland and Curriculum for Excellence*. Retrieved from: www.archaeologyscotland.org.uk/learning/for-teachers.

Astell-Burt, T., Mitchell, R. & Hartig, T. (2014). The association between green space and mental health varies across the lifecourse. *Journal of Epidemiology and Community Health, 68*(6), 578–583.

Britton, A. (2014). Education for global citizenship and sustainable development. In M. Carol & M. McCulloch (Eds.) *Understanding Teaching and Learning in Primary Education*. London: Sage.

Burns, H. (2011). How supportive environments generate good health. In S.J. Marr, S. Foster, C. Hendrie, E.C. Mackey & D.B.A. Thompson (Eds.) *The Changing Nature of Scotland* (pp.125–132). Edinburgh: TSO Scotland.

Cheesmond, J. (1979). *A Research Report of the Outdoor Education Programme in Lothian Region Secondary Schools 1978/1979*. Edinburgh: Lothian Region and Dunfermline College of Education.

Christie, B. & Higgins, P. (2012). Residential outdoor learning experiences and Scotland's school curriculum an empirical and philosophical consideration of progress, connection and relevance. *Scottish Educational Review, 44*(2), 45–59.

Christie, B., Higgins, P. & McLaughlin, P. (2013). 'Did you enjoy your holiday?' Can residential outdoor learning benefit mainstream schooling? *Journal of Adventure Education and Outdoor Learning, 14*(1), 1–23.

Christie, B., Beames, S., Higgins, P., Nicol, R. & Ross, H. (2014). Outdoor learning provision in Scotland. *Scottish Educational Review, 46*(1), 48–64.

Council for Learning Outside the Classroom (2006). Manifesto for learning outside the classroom. Retrieved from: www.lotc.org.uk.

Department for Education and Science (DfES). (2006). *Learning Outside the Classroom*. Nottingham: DfES.

Education Scotland (2011a). *Outdoor Learning Practical Guidance, Ideas and Support for Teachers and Practitioners in Scotland*. Retrieved from: www.educationscotland.gov.uk/resources/o/outdoorlearningpracticalguidanceideasandsupportforteachersandpractitionersinscotland.asp.

Education Scotland (2011b). *Building your Curriculum: Outside and In*. Glasgow: Education Scotland.

Education Scotland (2013). *Experience and Outcome Guides for Outdoor Learning*. Glasgow: Education Scotland.

Geike, A. (1887). *The Scenery of Scotland Viewed in Connexion with its Physical Geology*. London: Macmillan & Co.

General Teaching Council Scotland (GTCS) (2013). Revised professional standards. Retrieved from: www.gtcs.org.uk/about-gtcs/Consultations/consultation-revision-professional-standards.aspx.

Higgins, P. (2002). Outdoor education in Scotland. *Journal of Adventure Education and Outdoor Learning, 2*(2), 149–168.

Higgins, P. & Lavery, A. (2013). Sustainable development education. In T. Bryce, W. Humes, D. Gillies & A. Kennedy (Eds.) *Scottish Education* (4th edn) (pp. 337–342). Edinburgh: Edinburgh University Press.

Higgins, P. & Nicol, R. (Eds.) (2002). *Outdoor Education: Authentic Learning through Landscapes Volume 2*. An international collaboration project supported by the European Union Comenius Action 2. European In-Service Training Courses.

Higgins, P. & Nicol, R. (2013). Outdoor education. In T. Bryce, W. Humes, D. Gillies & A. Kennedy (Eds.) *Scottish Education* (4th edn) (pp. 620–670). Edinburgh: Edinburgh University Press.

Higgins, P., Nicol, R., Beames, S., Christie, B. & Scrutton, R. (2013). Education and Culture Committee, Outdoor Learning. Submission from Peter Higgins. University of Edinburgh. Retrieved from: www.scottish.parliament.uk/S4_EducationandCultureCommittee/Inquiries/Prof_Higgins_submission.pdf.

Historic Scotland (2014). Learning and resources. Retrieved from: www.historic-scotland.gov.uk/index/learning.htm.

HMIE (2006). Outdoor learning provision made by schools 2005–6. Retrieved from: www.educationscotland.gov.uk/resources/h/genericresource_tcm4616576.asp.

Learning and Teaching Scotland (2007). *Taking Learning Outdoors – Partnerships for Excellence*. Glasgow: Learning and Teaching Scotland.

Learning and Teaching Scotland (2010a). *Curriculum for Excellence through Outdoor Learning*. Glasgow: Learning and Teaching Scotland.

Learning and Teaching Scotland (2010b). *Practical Guidance Ideas and Support for Teachers and Practitioners in Scotland*. Glasgow: Learning and Teaching Scotland.

Mannion, G., Doyle, L., Sankey, K., Mattu., L. & Wilson, M. (2007). *Young People's Interaction with Natural Heritage through Outdoor Learning*. Perth: Scottish Natural Heritage.

Mannion, G., Mattu, L. & Wilson, L.M. (2015). *Teaching, Learning and Play in the Outdoors: A Survey of School and Pre-school Provision in Scotland*. Scottish Natural Heritage Commissioned Report No. 779.

National Trust for Scotland (2014). Curriculum links to NTS places. Retrieved from: www.nts.org.uk/Learn/schools_curriculumlinks.php.

New Zealand Ministry of Education (2008). Education outside the classroom guidelines. Retrieved from: http://eotc.tki.org.nz/EOTC-home/EOTC-Guidelines.

Nicol, R. (2001). Outdoor education for sustainable living?: An investigation into the potential of Scottish local authority residential outdoor centres to deliver programmes relating to sustainable living. Unpublished PhD thesis, University of Educational.

Outdoor Education Australia (2015). Teacher guidelines: Curriculum guidelines. Retrieved from: www.outdooreducationaustralia.org.au.

Pearce, J. (2013). An environmental justice framework for understanding neighbourhood inequalities in health and well-being. In M. Van Ham, D. Manley, D. Maclennan, N. Bailey & L. Simpson (Eds.) *Neighbourhood Effects or Neighbourhood Based Problems? A Policy Context* (pp. 89–111). Dordrecht: Springer Press.

Russell, M. (2014). Response from the Cabinet Secretary for Education and Lifelong Learning. Retrieved from: www.scottish.parliament.uk/S4_EducationandCultureCommittee/Inquiries/Learning_for_Sustainability_-_outdoor_learning_-_Response_to_Committee_-_21_March_2014.pdf.

Scottish Government (2004). *A Curriculum for Excellence*. Retrieved from: www.scotland.gov.uk/Publications/2004/11/20178/45862.

Scottish Government (2010). *Learning for Change: Scotland's Action Plan for the Second Half of the UN Decade of Education for Sustainable Development*, Action 10, p. 16. Retrieved from: www.scotland.gov.uk/Publications/2010/05/20152453/0.

Scottish Government (2012a). Learning for sustainability. Report of the One Planet Schools' Ministerial Advisory Group. Edinburgh: Scottish Government. Retrieved from: www.gov.scot/Topics/Education/Schools/curriculum/ACE/OnePlanetSchools/LearningforSustainabilitReport.

Scottish Government (2012b). Broad general education in the secondary school. Edinburgh: Scottish Government.

Scottish Government (2013a). Response to *Learning for Sustainability*. Retrieved from: www.gov.scot/Resource/0041/00416172.docx.

Scottish Government (2013b). Going out there: Scottish framework for safe practice in off-site visits. Edinburgh: Scottish Government. Retrieved from: www.goingoutthere.co.uk/download-going-out-there.

Sustainable Development Commission (2008). Sustainable development in government 2008. Retrieved from: www.sd-commission.org.uk/data/files/publications/SDiG_REPORT_08.pdf.

Thorburn, M. & Allison, P. (2010). Are we ready to go outdoors now? The prospects for outdoor education during a period of curriculum renewal in Scotland. *Curriculum Journal*, 21(1), 97–108.

Waite, S. (2010). Losing our way? The downward path for outdoor learning for children aged 2–11 years. *Journal of Adventure Education and Outdoor Learning*, 10(2), 111–126.

Ward Thompson, C. (2013). Activity, exercise and the planning and design of outdoor spaces. *Journal of Environmental Psychology*, 34, 79–96.

12

Teaching trainee teachers about outdoor education

Erik Backman

THE SWEDISH SCHOOL OF SPORT AND HEALTH SCIENCES

This chapter aims to illuminate how outdoor education (OE) and its equivalents – for example, adventure education, environmental education and Scandinavian *friluftsliv* – are expressed in the literature about teacher education, particularly physical education teacher education (PETE). The intention is also to point to some educational challenges for OE in teacher education. There is a significant amount of literature on outdoor leadership and outdoor learning in higher education (see e.g. Ogilvie, 1993; Miles & Priest, 1999; Priest & Gass, 2005) but in order to identify the work on OE that specifically concerns the preparation of teachers, I have used the keywords 'outdoor education', 'adventure education', 'physical education teacher education' and 'teacher education' in different combinations when searching through the database EBSCO. The work on OE in teacher education found through this search has revealed historical shifts and dominating as well as marginalised educational discourses. Some of the literature is somewhat outdated, which can be seen as a sign of a need for more attention to be paid to this field. Although not claiming to be a complete worldwide review, this chapter is a contribution to the discussion of OE in teacher education.

The early works

A large part of the work from the 1960s, 1970s and 1980s found in this review originates from North America and Canada. Several examples of guides and handbooks for teachers on how to implement OE in their teaching can be found. There are suggestions of learning objectives within OE, potential interdisciplinary areas of study, daily and weekly activities, equipment lists and forms and letters to parents (see e.g. Fox, 1966; Unknown, 1970; Gilfillan & Burgess, 1982). An unpublished paper from the early 1970s describes how teacher students at Northern Illinois University were also enrolled in an excursion to Austria and Germany (Hammerman, 1973). The paper involves a comparative analysis of OE between the USA and Europe. Hammerman emphasises that America places greater emphasis on training programmes while the European countries rely more on self-preparation and self study on the part of the teacher.

The position of outdoor education in educational settings

Education of teachers in the 'outdoors' occurs in different educational contexts. Today, there are opportunities to became a certified OE teacher (Zaurs, 2012). There are also several educational outdoor practices taking place within general teacher education. In some countries, OE is a part of teacher education – for example, in subjects like geography (Skavhaug & Andersen, 2013) and science (Sindel, 2010). For young children, a majority of the school day can take place outside, as Education Outside the Classroom (EOtC) is becoming more and more widespread among teacher education institutions (Lamorey, 2013). However, the most common and widespread position for OE is within the subject physical education (PE). OE is part of the PE curriculum in countries such as the UK (Cooper, 2000), Australia (Brooks, 2002), Canada (Cousineau, 1989), New Zealand (Boyes, 2012), Sweden (Backman, 2011), parts of the USA (Timken & McNamee, 2012) and Singapore (Ho, 2014). As a part of the PE curriculum, it also follows that OE generally has a prominent position within PE teacher education (PETE) in the aforementioned countries. In this chapter, OE will be discussed mainly from a PETE perspective.

The impact of teacher education

Some research in general teacher education has proven that educational content and methods have limited impact on students' future teaching compared to their personal experiences (Marton & Booth, 1997). The lack of learned pedagogy also seems to be the case for PETE students, whose orientation to sports practices when entering PETE is, to a large extent, decisive for their future teaching (Green, 2000; Larsson, 2009). There are also indications that there are difficulties in using educational knowledge and perspectives when entering the teaching profession in OE as for other content knowledge in PETE. For example, Preston (2011a) has discovered that what is commonly described as a 'wash-out-effect' of teacher education when entering the teaching profession also pervades students' perspectives and strategies in OE.

However, there is work that highlights the potential for teacher education to make an impact. In a study on how participation in a short outdoor course can strengthen teachers' self-efficacy on how to teach OE, Mosely, Reinke and Bookout (2002) found that the course had a short-term effect on teachers' self-efficacy. Further, Chróinín and Coulter (2012) showed that, by participating in an initial PETE course, students' perceptions of PE changed from being dominated by sport and health discourses into more educational discourses. In a study by Curtner-Smith (1997), first-year PE teachers, who had a coaching background when entering PETE, struggled to implement educational ideas they had learned during PETE. To the studies reporting on a positive impact of higher education for teachers we may also add the work of Xiang, Lowy and McBride (2002), who claim that participation in a PE methods course strengthened pre-service teachers' beliefs about the values and purposes of PE. The research on the impact of teacher education clearly points in different directions. Perhaps some of the themes discovered in this review can shed light on the reasons why the potential for OE in teacher education sometimes seems to be limited.

Themes in outdoor education within (physical education) teacher education

Adventure and risk

Expressions of adventure and risk have always had acknowledged positions within OE and within PE (Brown, 2006). While in some work, OE appears to have been replaced by adventure education (Zmudy, Curtner-Smith & Steffen, 2009), others point to adventure education as subordinate to the more comprehensive concept of OE (Brown, 2006). The underpinning ideas behind adventure education can be traced back to the German philosopher Kurt Hahn, the founder of the Outward Bound movement (Zmudy *et al.* 2009; Boyes, 2012). Established in the UK in the 1930s and 1940s, Outward Bound expanded to the rest of the world in the 1950s and 1960s, and has since then come to influence much of adventure education in school settings. Project Adventure, which was started in the 1970s, has served as inspiration for much of the adventure education in the USA (Dyson & O'Sullivan, 1998; Clocksin, 2006). In searching for reasons as to why some schools succeed in implementing adventure education, Dyson and O'Sullivan (1998) found five factors that emerged as supportive: a shared vision, external support for the schools' programmes, curricular integration, centrality of physical education, and shared decision making. Brown (2006) suggests that a student-centred pedagogy, and an innovative and holistic approach to movement, values often claimed to be a causal effect of adventure education, are in many cases based on pre-assumptions rather than empirical research. He also argues that the setting associated with adventure education can involve educational implications from a perspective of equity, equality, diversity and inclusion.

Among the few studies found on adventure education in PETE, Carlson and McKenna (2000) have examined Australian PETE students' perceptions of taking part in an adventure course. Their findings suggest that the students' experiences of being placed outside their own comfort zone resulted in exposure to personal feelings of self-doubt. According to the authors, adventure courses can serve to 'enlighten participants as to the intense feelings their students might experience during physical education classes' (2000, p. 24). Risk is also an element in Boniface and Bunyan's (1999) description of the 'Outdoor and Adventurous Activities Programme' (OAA) at Chichester Institute of Higher Education in the UK (now the University of Chichester). The philosophy underpinning this programme 'challenges the traditional view that exposure to the adventure environment per se manifests itself in personal growth, and that such growth is seen as desirable by society in general' (1999, p. 16). The PETE students all took an OAA course in their second year, including both theoretical work and practical outdoor activities such as sailing, climbing and walking. In their third year all PETE students followed a course focusing on teaching adventure education in schools. The students were also asked to examine critically the images that they held of adventure and the romantic notions of adventure that have formed part of our heritage. During the time since this was published, the described course has changed. However, these two rare and somewhat outdated examples of publications on how adventure education may be implemented and perceived in a PETE context may serve as a sign of the knowledge status of the field and as a point of departure for other research themes in this chapter. Closely related to adventure is, for example, also work focusing on technical skills in OE.

The meaning of skills

The significance of technical skills when teaching OE has been illuminated from different perspectives. Uhlendorf and Gass (1992) stressed the popularity of adventure activities in PE within US schools and its potential implications for PETE. In the guidelines for PETE educators in the USA in 1987 it is stated that graduate professionals must be able to demonstrate skill and knowledge to a point where they can 'plan, implement and evaluate physical activity in area of outdoor leisure pursuits' (1992, p. 33). These recommendations correspond to contemporary the findings of Larsson (2013) in an evaluation of PETE in Norway, where successful PE student teachers 'should be able to practice simple *friluftsliv* [OE] which includes moving in different environments during different seasons, be able to give CPR, rescue a friend in need and to choose appropriate outdoor equipment' (2013, p. 92, my translation). Despite the early guidelines for OE within PETE in the USA, Uhlendorf and Gass (1992) have stressed the fact that many PETE students 'experience difficulty in achieving competence in the area of outdoor leisure pursuits' (1992, p. 33). In order to ensure appropriate OE training of future PE teachers, they have argued that the original content of adventurous activities should not be replaced by more urban and sport-oriented activities as this may result in a loss of effectiveness.

Similar to the findings of Carlson and McKenna (2000), Timken and McNamee (2012) found that pre-service PE teachers struggled with the notion of their perceived skills when taking part in an OE course. Some of the participating teachers lacking success in kayaking and mountain biking experienced a decrease in motivation, a phenomenon that the authors believe could help the participants understand the similar experiences of their students. Furthermore, they suggest that exposure to feelings of being physically less skilled, through participation in unfamiliar OE practices, might help to understand the complexity underlying some pupils' unwillingness to participate in OE and PE, and also to reveal PE teachers' and PETE students' bias towards these pupils. There are also examples of a more critical approach to the notion of skills for future OE teachers. Thomas (2005) suggests that, although technical and movement skills such as kayaking, skiing and orienteering should be basic competences among outdoor teachers, this ability is not enough as an aim in itself. A critical approach to OE movement skills for their own sake is also provided by Backman (2008). Together with Backman and Larsson (2014), he argues that, in order for PETE students to view movement skills as part of their future teaching competence, the assessment of these skills must be closely linked to the practice of PE teaching, rather than separated and decontextualised.

With regard to skill acquisition among teacher students in OE and PE, Smith (2011) claims that our conceptual frameworks draw mainly from behavioural and cognitive psychology learning theories. As a reflection of this, Thomas (2007) discusses the direct instruction model, DEDICT (often also described as the EDICT model in, for example, the UK), which he describes as the dominant learning model for skill acquisition in OE, a fact that can be linked to the popularity of this approach in PE as well as in the military. In higher education in OE in Australia and in the UK, (D)EDICT has been particularly widespread in the teaching of canoeing. The (D)EDICT model includes six (or five) steps: demonstration, explanation, demonstration, imitation, coaching/corrections and trials, and it is described as a teacher-centred approach. Thomas (ibid.) describes some risks connected to the DEDICT model:

> . . . excessive teacher talk, students spending more time receiving information and waiting than practising motor skills, and the failure to provide appropriate levels of performance feedback to students . . . Direct instruction approaches can also create a competitive learning environment with little positive interaction between students. (Thomas, 2007, p. 15)

In relation to the instructional model, both Smith (2011) and Thomas (2007) ask for more alternative views on skill acquisition. Smith (2011) argues that skill should be viewed as a social construct, and emphasises the intentional actions of the individual. Skill, he suggests, should be seen as 'the outcome of the relational properties that give meaning to the actions of a socialized individual and a corresponding field of practice' (2011, p. 272). In relation to the DEDICT model, Thomas (2007) proposes FERAL, a model including five steps: frame the problem, explore for solutions, report back with solutions, adjust or thinking and motor plans, and by testing new solutions. In this model, characterised by student-centred and discovery learning, teachers' main function is to stimulate students' thinking through guidance and carefully thought out questions and to encourage experimentation when learning movements. When introducing this model, outdoor teachers may experience resistance as the students may need time to adjust to a teacher's new role of facilitating a learning process rather than being the owner of all the answers. However, Thomas (2007) claims that the FERAL model can strengthen students' learning as it 'does not encourage outdoor leaders to shepherd students towards a single solution to the movement challenge' (2007, p. 16).

Environmental education

The position of environmental education within OE, mainly to be found in general teacher education, can be seen to counterbalance the focus on the meaning of skills within OE in PETE. Thomas and Thomas (2000) exemplify critical OE through canoe paddling, characterised by a 'deliberate focus on educating participants for environmentally sustainable living' (2000, p. 47). By exploring the Australian landscape through canoe paddling on rivers, with great opportunities for the study of geology, flora, fauna and cultural imprints, they argue that human–nature relationships can be developed with almost no human impact. The works of Preston (2011a, 2011b) are other examples of working with a critical pedagogy in OE within Australian teacher education. She highlights the challenges for teacher education following the priority given to sustainability education in the Australian curriculum. Furthermore, she argues for an alternative way to think of environmental ethics in relation to the common moral codes and norms. The view of environmental ethics that she proposes encourages individuals to actively and self-consciously question their own ethical existence in relation to the environment. One of her papers (2011b) builds on a reflexive self-critique of her own role as an OE educator:

> Instead of preparing students to evaluate knowledge – and to recognise (my) 'authoritative' knowledge as incomplete and uncertain – I inadvertently provided students with guidelines and moral prescriptions which thwarted opportunity for doubt, uncertainty or new thought. (Preston, 2011b, p. 368)

A challenge for teacher educators in OE, she argues, lies in resisting the temptation to provide environmental models and remedies to teacher students. The issue of sustainability in teacher education has also been highlighted in Scotland by Higgins and Kirk (2006). They examined how the UNESCO declaration to reorient teacher education towards sustainable futures has been given attention at teacher institutions in Scotland. Their findings then pointed to a lack of attention to sustainability issues in teacher education in Scotland, partly due to a teacher education curriculum that was full, and partly due to weak political support. However, following curriculum reform in Scotland and the influence of a number of key individuals as agents for change, the government is developing a national approach to 'Learning for Sustainability'. This is a response both to a need for greater understanding of the cultural landscape and to the increasing promotion of sustainability in national and international education agenda. Drawing on women's conceptions of nature during an OE course in New Zealand, Cosgriff (2011) claims nature connectedness and care to be key elements for teacher education in OE if sustainability is to be implemented. In order to develop these elements among teacher students, she highlights three pedagogical principles of importance: repeated immersion in local nature environments, the decentralising of traditional performance discourses, and critical reflection. Besides the critical research focusing on issues of sustainability and environment there are also other perspectives represented in the critical approach to OE within teacher education.

Perspectives of power

During the last decade, several scholars have devoted attention to how power operates in and through OE in teacher education. The (re)production of claims and 'truths' about (positive) causal effects of outdoor education and its inherent values has been questioned, and there has been a call for more post-structural perspectives, in this case particularly the one provided by Michel Foucault, in order to understand how power operates in outdoor education (Zink & Burrows, 2006; Preston, 2011a, 2011b). The reason why this type of perspective is of particular interest in OE is emphasised by Bowdridge and Blenkinsop (2011):

> . . . hierarchical observation, normalizing judgments, and examination have demonstrated how each occurs in OEE, and how this might pose a problem for those who see themselves as proponents of freedom and self-determination. (pp. 157–158)

According to the aforementioned scholars, viewing OE as a discipline where power relations operate might help educators understand that their pedagogic messages are not delivered from a neutral position. Besides the work inspired by Foucault, there are also OE scholars drawing on the French sociologist Pierre Bourdieu. Boyes (2012) draws on the concept of 'field' to illustrate the tension in OE between adventure and learning. In a study of OE in Swedish PETE viewed as a field, Backman (2008) identified different positions. Analysing OE teacher educators' value preferences, he suggests practical skills, traditional OE activities and an exclusive conception of nature constitute symbolic capital within this field. Furthermore, he claims that the maintenance of this exclusive and physical OE discourse within PETE is made possible due to the fact that there are profits to be made by the OE teacher educators. Among these profits are: securing of the position as the expert, the students' appreciation when consuming outdoor experiences, and the satisfaction of personal taste for extreme nature experiences. Backman (2009) and Larsson (2009) also suggest that OE in PETE promotes ideas of personal development as a main purpose rather than viewing OE as professionally relevant for the teaching profession:

> . . . the respondents' [i.e. students'] expressions of OE do not include knowledge useful for the exercise of a future profession. Instead emphasis is put on the individual experience, to try something new and exciting, a kind of personal development. (Larsson, 2009, p. 225, my translation)

The position of an exclusive variant of OE in PETE, often legitimised as being an investment in the students as individuals, is also confirmed by Kårhus (2012) concerning how PETE institutions in Norway have to adapt to logic valid in the economic market. By using concepts such as 'customers', 'survivalism', 'outlets' and 'managerialism', the Deans of the PETE institutions who are interviewed by Kårhus express a pedagogic discourse in which economic values are privileged above knowledge relevant for the future teacher profession. By using Bernstein's regulative and instructional discourse he claims that the educational market shapes pedagogic discourses in PETE, and that OE is one of these discourses.

When summarising the principles and logic in OE within teacher education, my impression is that adventure, skills, a teacher-centered pedagogy and remote nature conceptions are privileged in OE educational practices within PETE. Critical pedagogy, student-centred pedagogy and environmental issues appear to be dominating principles within OE in general teacher education, i.e. the teacher education that takes place outside PETE. Naturally there are exceptions, and some of these have been provided in this review. I will now analyse this further and discuss the general impression of these trends in relation to Tinning's (2006) work of epistemological orientations within PETE.

Conclusions and educational challenges

From the previous review it appears that certain aspects of OE knowledge are privileged over others in teacher education in general as well as in PETE in particular. How are we to understand this? Inspired by the work of Tinning (2006) on theoretical orientations within PETE (Table 12.1), which builds on knowledge traditions in general teacher education (Doyle, 1990; Feiman-Nemser, 1990), I have tried to analyse the expressions of different educational practices in OE for future teachers.

Drawing on the model below (Table 12.1) as well as other research, the expression of skills in OE originates from a behaviouristic knowledge tradition, a tradition holding a strong position within PETE (Smith, 2011). Further, the marketisation of PETE as well as motives of personal development can be regarded as a reflection of the 'personalistic' (Tinning, 2006) orientation in OE (Kårhus, 2012). The expressions of adventure and remote wilderness settings emphasised in the review thus make sense when seen in relation to the personalistic orientation. The review also reflects that a teacher-centred pedagogy is closely connected to skills taught through direct instruction (Thomas, 2007). An educational discourse in which the teacher is seen as an instructor in possession of all the right skills and answers will risk maintaining and reproducing a certain distribution of power. Recent attention has been given to a post-structural and critical perspectives viewpoint concerning the importance for OE educators to be aware of their possession of power (Zink & Burrows, 2006; Bowdridge & Blenkinsop, 2011).

This review also shows few examples of environmental education taught through OE in PETE, but more within general teacher education (Thomas & Thomas, 2000; Cosgriff, 2011; Preston 2011a, 2011b). This can be seen as a reflection that knowledge traditions underpinning critical inquiry are not widespread among teacher educators in OE within PETE, but more so in general teacher education. When addressing non-frequently occurring content and perspectives in OE within PETE, we can also note a lack of examples of interdisciplinary approaches (for an example, see Rhead, 1967). This is perhaps a result of strongly classified subject traditions in universities (Macdonald, Kirk & Braiuka, 1999). Further, perspectives of cultural diversity and

Table 12.1 A model of theoretical orientations within PETE

Orientation	Worldview	Purpose of teacher education	Human interests	Research paradigm
Behaviouristic	Objective reality. Science for a better world	Prepare skilled technicians of teaching.	Technical. Prediction. Control.	Empirical-analytical. Natural science.
Personalistic	Multiple realities. Subjectivity meaning	To develop the individual teacher as a person.	Practical. Interpretive understanding.	Hermeneutic. Interpretive. Phenomenological.
Traditional/ craft	Reality exists in 'the field', not in theory, Practice is best.	Prepare teachers for the current system.	Practical. Technical mastery.	Simple descriptive modelling.
Critical inquiry	Reality is socially constructed. Social inequities, power and oppression.	Challenge the school system where necessary.	Critical. Liberation. Emancipation. Critical theory.	Action research. Case study. Feminist. Post-structuralist.

Source: Tinning (2006, p. 376)

social justice occur seldomly in OE within teacher education (for examples, see Goulet, 1998; Frazer, 2009). The fact that a large part of OE for future teachers occurs in PETE has consequences for what type of content and knowledge perspectives students encounter. The major conclusion that can be drawn from this analysis is that OE, as any educational content, is not neutral or free from values. Its expression and educational message to future teacher education students depends on in what context it is taught and by whom. Challenging current teaching in OE within teacher education in general and PETE in particular will also mean challenging dominating knowledge traditions and views of the purpose within teacher education.

References

Backman, E. (2008). What is valued in *friluftsliv* within PE teacher education? Swedish PE teacher educators' thoughts about *friluftsliv* analysed through the perspective of Pierre Bourdieu. *Sport, Education and Society, 13*(1), 61–76.

Backman, E. (2009). To acquire a taste for *friluftsliv* – a part of becoming a PE teacher? Swedish physical education teacher educators' thoughts about their students' preferences for *friluftsliv*. *Moving Bodies, 7*(1), 9–26.

Backman, E. (2011). What controls teaching of *friluftsliv*? Analysing a pedagogic discourse in Swedish PE. *Journal of Adventure Education and Outdoor Learning, 11*(1), 51–65.

Backman, E. & Larsson, H. (2014). What should a physical education teacher know? An analysis of learning outcomes for future physical education teachers in Sweden. *Physical Education and Sport Pedagogy*. Epub ahead of print. doi:10.1080/17408989.2014.946007

Boniface, M. & Bunyan, P. (1999). Outdoor and adventurous activities in undergraduate physical education teacher education at Chichester Institute. In P. Higgins & B. Humberstone (Eds.) *Outdoor Education and Experiential Learning in the UK* (pp. 16–23). Cumbria: Institute for Outdoor Learning.

Bowdridge, M. & Blenkinsop, S. (2011). Michel Foucault goes outside: Discipline and control in the practice of outdoor education. *Journal of Experiential Education, 34*(2), 149–163.

Boyes, M. (2012). Historical and contemporary trends in outdoor education. In D. Irwin, J. Straker & A. Hill (Eds.) *Outdoor Education in Aotearoa New Zealand* (pp. 18–37). Christchurch: CPIT.

Brooks, A. (2002). Lost in the Australian bush: outdoor education as curriculum. *Journal of Curriculum Studies, 34*(4), 405–425.

Brown, M. (2006). Adventure education in physical education. In D. Kirk, D. Macdonald & M. O'Sullivan (Eds.) *The Handbook of Physical Education* (pp. 685–703). London: Sage Publications.

Carlson, T.B. & McKenna, P. (2000). A reflective adventure for student teachers. *Journal of Experiential Education, 23*(1), 17–25.

Chróinín, D.N. & Coulter, M. (2012). The impact of initial teacher education on understandings of physical education: Asking the right question. *European Physical Education Review, 18*(2), 220–239.

Clocksin, B.D. (2006). Sequencing low adventure activities in elementary physical education. *Teaching Elementary Physical Education*, May, 16–22.

Cooper, G. (2000). Opportunities for outdoor education in the new national curriculum. *Horizons, 9*, 26–29.

Cosgriff, M. (2011). Learning from leisure: Developing nature connectedness in outdoor education. *Asia-Pacific Journal of Health, Sport and Physical Education, 2*(1), 51–65.

Cousineau, C. (1989). Increasing outdoor recreation participation through the schools perspective. *World Leisure & Recreation, 31*(2), 38–43.

Curtner-Smith, M.D. (1997). The impact of biography, teacher education, and organizational socialization on the perspectives and practices of first-year physical education teachers: Case studies of recruits with coaching orientations. *Sport, Education and Society, 2*(1), 73–94.

Doyle, W. (1990). Themes in teacher education research. In W.R. Houston (Ed.) *Handbook of Research on Teacher Education* (pp. 3–24). New York: Macmillan.

Dyson, B. & O'Sullivan, M. (1998). Innovation in two alternative elementary school programs: Why it works. *Research Quarterly for Exercise and Sport, 69*(3), 242–253.

Feiman-Nemser, S. (1990). Teacher preparation: Structural and conceptual alternatives. In W.R. Houston (Ed.) *Handbook of Research on Teacher Education* (pp. 212–233). New York: Macmillan.

Fox, D.C. (1966). *Teachers' Guide to Outdoor Education*. San Diego, CA: San Diego City Schools.

Frazer, R.L. (2009). Toward a theory of critical teaching for social justice in outdoor education studies: A grounded theory study of philosophical perspectives and teaching practices. Dissertation. Madison: University of Wisconsin.

Gilfillan, W.C. & Burgess, R.A. (1982). *The Teacher's Handbook for the Outdoor School.* Portland, OR: Multnomah Outdoor Education.

Goulet, L. (1998). Culturally relevant teacher education: A Saskatchewan First Nations case. Paper presented at the Annual Meeting of the American Educational Research Association, San Diego, CA.

Green, K. (2000). Extra-curricular physical education in England and Wales: A sociological perspective on a sporting bias. *European Journal of Physical Education, 5*(2), 179–207.

Hammerman, D.R. (Ed.) (1973). *Outdoor Education in Germany, Austria and Switzerland.* Oregon: Northern Illinois University.

Higgins, P. & Kirk, G. (2006). Sustainability education in Scotland: The impact of national and international initiatives on teacher education and outdoor education. *Journal of Geography in Higher Education, 30*(2), 313–326.

Ho, S. (2014). The purposes outdoor education does, could and should serve in Singapore. *Journal of Adventure Education and Outdoor Learning, 14*(2), 153–171.

Kårhus, S. (2012). Providers, consumers and the horizons of the possible: A case study of marketization and physical education teacher education pedagogical discourse. *Sport, Education and Society, 17*(2), 245–259.

Lamorey, S. (2013). Making sense of a day in the woods: Outdoor adventure experiences and early childhood teacher education students. *Journal of Early Childhood Teacher Education, 34*(4), 320–334.

Larsson, H. (2013). Utvärdera lärarutbildning i idrott och hälsa – utifrån vilka normer? [To evaluate physical education teacher education – based on what norms?] In E. Backman & L. Larsson (Eds.) *I takt med tiden? Perspektiv på idrottslärarutbildning i Skandinavien* (pp. 81–95). Lund: Studentlitteratur AB.

Larsson, L. (2009). *Idrott och helst lite mer idrott.* Dissertation. Stockholm: Stockholms Universitet.

Macdonald, D., Kirk, D. & Braiuka, S. (1999). The social construction of the physical activity field at the school/university interface. *European Physical Education Review, 5*(1), 31–51.

Marton, F. & Booth, S. (1997). *Learning and Awareness.* Mahwah, NJ: Erlbaum.

Miles, J.C. & Priest, S. (Eds.) (1999). *Adventure Programming.* Pennsylvania: Venture Publishing.

Moseley, C., Reinke, K. & Bookout, V. (2002). The effect of teaching outdoor environmental education on pre-service teachers' attitudes towards self-efficacy and outcome expectancy. *Journal of Environmental Education, 34*(1), 9–16.

Ogilvie, K.C. (1993). *Leading and Managing Groups in the Outdoors.* Cumbria: Institute for Outdoor Learning.

Preston L. (2011a). Sustaining an environmental ethic: Outdoor and environmental education graduates' negotiation of school spaces. *Australian Journal of Environmental Education, 27*(2), 199–208.

Preston, L. (2011b). Green pedagogy – guidance and doubt in teaching outdoor and environmental education. *Asia-Pacific Journal of Teacher Education, 39*(4), 367–380.

Priest, S. & Gass, M.A. (2005). *Effective Leadership in Adventure Programming.* Champaign, IL: Human Kinetics.

Rhead, R.E. (1967). A proposed interdisciplinary approach to an outdoor education program in the professional teacher preparation curriculum at Weber State College. Dissertation. Salt Lake City, UT: University of Utah.

Sindel, K.D. (2010). Can experiential education strategies improve elementary science teachers' perceptions of and practices in science teaching? Dissertation. St Charles, MO: Lindenwood University.

Skavhaug, T.W. & Andersen, H.P. (2013). Urban fieldwork in geographical education in Levanger, Norway. *Norwegian Journal of Geography, 67*(3), 179–183.

Smith, W.W. (2011). Skill acquisition in physical education: A speculative perspective. *Quest, 63*(3), 265–274.

Thomas, G. (2005). Traditional adventure activities in outdoor environmental education. *Australian Journal of Outdoor Education, 9*(1), 31–40.

Thomas, G. (2007). Skill instruction in outdoor leadership: A comparison of a direct instruction model and a discovery-learning model. *Australian Journal of Outdoor Education, 11*(2), 10–18.

Thomas, G. & Thomas, J. (2000). Moving water paddling as critical outdoor education. *Australian Journal of Outdoor Education, 5*(1), 47–54.

Timken, G.L. & McNamee, J. (2012). New perspectives for teaching physical education: preservice teachers' reflections on outdoor and adventure education. *Journal of Teaching in Physical Education, 31*, 21–38.

Tinning, R. (2006). Theoretical orientations in physical education teacher education. In D. Kirk, D. Macdonald & M. O'Sullivan (Eds.) *The Handbook of Physical Education* (pp. 369–386). London: Sage Publications.

Uhlendorf, K.J. & Gass, M.A. (1992). The preparation of physical education majors in adventure activities. *Physical Educator, 49*(1), 33–39.

Unknown (1970). *Outdoor Education Manual*. Toronto: Ontario Teachers' Federation.

Xiang, P., Lowy, S. & McBride, R. (2002). The impact of a field-based elementary physical education methods course on preservice classroom teachers' beliefs. *Journal of Teaching Physical Education, 21*, 145–161.

Zaurs, J. (2012). Outdoor education: Teachers qualifications, perceived knowledge and a developing course of study in Western Australia. *Horizons, 59*, 22–26.

Zink, R. & Burrows, L. (2006). Foucault on camp: What does his work offer outdoor education? *Journal of Adventure Education and Outdoor Learning, 6*(1), 39–50.

Zmudy, M.H., Curtner-Smith, M.D. & Steffen, J. (2009). Student participation styles in adventure education. *Sport, Education and Society, 14*(4), 465–480.

13

Pedagogic practice in higher education in the UK

Tim Stott

LIVERPOOL JOHN MOORES UNIVERSITY

Outdoor education in UK higher education (HE) first appeared in the late 1960s (Hardy & Stott, 2006), some of the earliest writings followed in the 1970s (e.g. Drasdo, 1972) and 1980s (e.g. Mortlock, 1984), with research interest growing through the 1980s and 1990s, with the *Journal of Adventure Education and Outdoor Leadership* established in the early 1990s and the *Journal of Adventure Education and Outdoor Learning* in 2000. Much of the research in outdoor education is of a pedagogical nature, and thus informs pedagogical practice. However, to date there appear to have been no formal or systematic attempts to share pedagogic practice in UK higher education, despite its growth in popularity since the 1960s, to a position today where the University and Colleges Admission System (UCAS) shows twenty-seven providers of programmes with the words Outdoor or Adventure in the title (Table 13.1).

While the UCAS search focused on the terms 'outdoor' and 'adventure', programme titles found suggest that subject areas covered also include or combine with: sport/sport development; physical education and coaching; recreation; management; leadership; tourism (and eco-tourism); some combine with other subjects or departments that include business, youth and community, environmental science, abuse studies and media. Given this diversity, pedagogic practice will surely vary enormously. This chapter will draw from the author's own experience gained over twenty years in teaching on one outdoor education programme at one institution, plus external examining for outdoor programmes at nine other UK institutions in Table 13.1.

HE programmes will contain a balance between indoor/classroom/lecture room teaching and outdoor teaching. At LJMU (Liverpool John Moores University) we strive to maintain a 50:50 balance of contact time between indoor and outdoor (off-campus) delivery over the three-year programme, although this inevitably varies week by week. This chapter will therefore be organised to cover teaching indoors then to cover fieldwork out-of-doors and to conclude with the practical teaching of outdoor skills.

Changes in outdoor education pedagogic practice indoors

The author's first few years in HE teaching in the early 1990s were about using overhead projectors, slide projectors (with carousels containing rows of slide transparencies, which you dare not drop!), sometimes blackboards and chalk, then whiteboards with coloured markers began

Table 13.1 UK higher education undergraduate programmes with the words Outdoor or Adventure in their title

Provider	Programmes offered in 2014
Bangor University	Sport Science (Outdoor Activities); Sport Science (Outdoor Recreation)
Bridgwater College	Public Services with Outdoor Education
Cornwall College	Public Services with Adventurous Activity Leadership
University of Central Lancashire	Outdoor Leadership; Outdoor Leadership (Top-Up); Adventure Sports Coaching
University of Chichester	Adventure Education; Education & Outdoor Learning
University of Cumbria	Outdoor Education; Outdoor Education (Top-up); Outdoor Studies; Outdoor Leadership; Adventure Media
University of Derby	Outdoor Activities; Outdoor Activity Leadership and Coaching; Outdoor Recreation and Adventure Tourism; Outdoor Recreation and Countryside Management; Countryside Management and Adventure Tourism; Ecotourism and Adventure Tourism; Outdoor Recreation and Adventure Tourism
Exeter College	Applied Outdoor Adventure; Outdoor Adventure Education; Adventure Tourism Management
Gloucestershire College	Outdoor Activities
Leeds Metropolitan University	Physical Education with Outdoor Education
Liverpool John Moores University	Outdoor Education
The Manchester Metropolitan University	Outdoor Studies; Outdoor Studies (Foundation); Abuse Studies/ Outdoor Studies; Business/Outdoor Studies; Childhood & Youth Studies/Outdoor Studies
New College Durham	FdA Outdoor Leadership
Newcastle College	Coaching (Outdoor Activities)
Plumpton College	Outdoor Adventure Facilitation; Outdoor Adventurous Activities
Plymouth University (Bicton College)	Outdoor Adventure Leadership and Management
Reaseheath College	Adventure Sports and Management
South Devon College	Outdoor Education
Southampton Solent University	Adventure and Extreme Sports Management (International only); Adventure and Extreme Sports Management (Sport, Event and Tourism Foundation only); Adventure and Extreme Sports Management.
SRUC (formerly Scottish Agricultural College)	Outdoor Pursuits Management
University of St Mark &St John	Sport Development (Outdoor Adventure Education); Business, Management & Outdoor Adventure; Outdoor Adventure Education
University of Stirling	Environmental Science and Outdoor Education
Teesside University	Outdoor Leadership
Truro and Penwith College	Outdoor Education

University of Wales Trinity Saint David	Outdoor Education
University of Worcester	Outdoor Adventure Leadership and Management; Physical Education & Outdoor Education
UHI	Adventure Tourism Management

Source: UCAS (2014)

to arrive. Staff used photocopiers to provide worksheets, learning resources or resource packs, which students took away after teaching sessions. At some point in the mid-1990s PowerPoint arrived, and staff began using data projectors and laptops to project text and images on to the large screens with animation! Gradually, acetates and slide transparencies became redundant as confidence in the new computer technologies grew. Staff development events on 'Open Learning' and 'Teaching Large Numbers' encouraged staff to move away from didactic teaching approaches, where the teacher was supposed to 'have all the knowledge', to becoming 'facilitators of learning'. The Open University was spreading and terms like 'blended learning' (Stott & Huddart, 2005) were starting to be used.

The internet became widely available in the late 1990s and university libraries were renamed learning resource centres (LRCs) when they started to host networked computers, and learning through information and communications technology (ICT) began (Stott, Hall & Bell, 1999). Student feedback surveys reported 'not enough computers' in the new LRCs. My own institution formed an e-Learning Group, of which I was a member, charged with evaluating the best virtual learning environment (VLE) for the institution and Blackboard was installed in 2001 (and is still in use today). Other HE institutions went with WebCT, Moodle, Learning Space and others. Then wi-fi hotspots began to be installed, first in LRCs and later all over campuses. Laptop computers were made available for loan in LRCs, the cost of laptop computers dropped and more students bought their own. Mobile learning was born. HE institutions began to rethink the design of learning spaces to create social learning spaces or meeting places with wi-fi, comfortable seating and tables for group working providing a relaxed atmosphere for learning. Most students today have internet-enabled smartphones, laptops and/or tablet PCs or iPads. My faculty now has a bank of sixty iPads, which are booked out by staff as class sets. Waterproof cases allow iPads to be used for fieldwork. Learning technologists now support academic staff and provide staff development as well as supporting students' independent learning.

So what has changed in the classroom? Today's students turn up with laptops and mobile devices. Many will have already visited the VLE and downloaded learning resources for the lecture (e.g. PowerPoint slides, PDF or Word files), which they may view before, during or after the teaching session. A proportion of outdoor education students (~15–20% annually) are diagnosed with having special learning needs so central university learning support services develop individual student learning plans (ISLPs) for them. HE pedagogy is moving away from the didactic 'giving of knowledge' to a problem-based approach where students are set assessed tasks for which they may be given guidance during the contact hours for their module. Typically, a module might be designed to require students to undertake 240 hours of learning activity over an academic year with five modules studied per year (typically 5 x 24 or 6 x 20 credits), but only fifty hours or less of this 240 is actual contact time with university staff. Therefore, module leaders and module teams design learning activities or assessment tasks to challenge students and motivate them to undertake around 190 hours of independent learning activity per module. This basic notion of independent learning at university has not changed, but is arguably the single biggest challenge facing students in their transition from school or college (Vinson *et al.*, 2010).

Outdoor educationalists believe in the power of the outdoors and the natural world to motivate learning. At LJMU, over the past decade, we have been developing virtual field guides (VFGs) to bring the outdoors inside (or at least online). Collaborating with staff in geosciences, we first developed the Ingleton Waterfalls Trail VFG (Stott, Clark, Milson, McCloskey & Crompton, 2009) followed by VirtualAlps[1] (Stott, Nuttall & McCloskey, 2009; Stott & Nuttall, 2010). Then with the Ensemble project at LJMU (Semantic Technologies for the Enhancement of Case Based Learning)[2] we developed VirtualAlps2[3] (Litherland & Stott, 2012; Stott, Litherland, Carmichael & Nuttall, 2013), which assesses our students in a different way. Students are set a problem, which is to assess the environmental impact of a proposed (hypothetical) hydro-electric power dam at our field site in the Morteratsch Valley, SE Switzerland. Analysis of students' work on this task, compared with the previously assessed tasks, showed that students used a wider set of real-life decision-making skills and handled a wider range of sources of evidence, which, as well as journal papers, included datasets in Excel collected by staff during research, videos, panorama movies, photos, online glossaries of terms and Google Earth as a tool for aerial/spatial analysis.

The Blackboard VLE has been used for evaluating the use of diagrams and video clips as alternatives to textual questions to support students' learning (Stott, 2007a), and the development and use of online revision quizzes (Stott, 2013), and we have investigated the relationships between students' attendance, performance and online engagement (Stott & Stewart, 2008; Stewart, Stott & Nuttall, 2010) and concluded that attendance is correlated better with performance than online engagement. To date, there appears to be no real substitute for students attending teaching sessions. It has been known for some time that students are strategic learners, being motivated and driven by assessment (Gibbs, 1999). Stott (2010a) has experimented with changing assessment in a geographical module within the outdoor programme over a ten-year period and examined the effect of doubling the number of assessment items on student performance. Students ranked 1 in the top quartile performed better in the so-called 'deep learning' assessments (field reports, weather analysis), whereas students in the lowest quartile performed better in 'shallow learning' assessments (online multiple-choice tests and written examinations).

Outdoor education fieldwork and expeditions

Fieldwork has long been recognised as playing a central role in geography, earth and environmental science (GEES) subjects (Kent, Gilbertson & Hunt, 1997; Boyle *et al.*, 2003; Fuller, Gaskin & Scott, 2003). Many GEES UK HE programmes offer field courses abroad, and interviews with staff (Andrews, Kneale, Sougnez, Stewart & Stott, 2003) make clear that these play an important role in the marketing, recruitment and retention of students. A number of UK outdoor education programmes recognise the importance of landscape interpretation, and the ability to make meaningful observations and measurements in the natural environment, as key skills for graduates to possess and fieldwork offers this. Research shows that outdoor graduates often find employment in field centres, environmental centres or even with organisations such as the Environment Agency or the National Trust (Prince, 2005; Stott, Zaitseva & Cui, 2014), where transferable field skills traditionally taught in GEES subjects can be important. The ability to design and lead safe and educationally worthwhile field courses is an attribute that outdoor programmes can offer our graduates (Couper & Stott, 2006).

Field teaching has moved away from the traditional 'walk and talk' or even 'coach tours' where 'expert' staff took students to key locations and pointed out features of interest that students then noted down, photographed or sketched. This approach has been largely replaced by 'investigative', 'problem-based' or 'enquiry-based' fieldwork, where students are set tasks, questions or problems that they investigate by collecting data in the field (Stokes, Magnier &

Weaver, 2011). For example, students may measure clasts on a scree slope to investigate the relationship between size and position on the slope. Examples of typical fieldwork investigations used in one of the LJMU outdoor programmes are shown in Table 13.2.

Increasingly, new technology is impacting fieldwork (Welsh, Mauchline, Park, Whalley & France, 2013). Stott (2007b) evaluated the use of low-cost personal digital assistants for field data collection by students. Personal hand-held computers (today's smartphones) can be used to take databases into the field. For example, photographs and video of a river in flood were shown to students at a field site, to enhance their understanding of river flow extremes. Waterproof digital cameras allow students to capture images in the field to incorporate into reports, and today students use smartphones (Welsh & France, 2012) or cameras during fieldwork, sharing the images with one another via social media. With wi-fi connections, real-time data can be used in the field. iPads and iPad Minis with waterproof cases are offering a huge number of useful apps for fieldwork investigations. In 2013 Apple announced it had one million apps. It is estimated that approximately 37 per cent of apps available through iTunes are free to download, with the average app costing around £2.30 (US$3.34) (Elmer De-Witt, 2011). Some examples of apps the author finds useful in outdoor teaching include: ViewRanger (OS mapping); GridPoint UK; Met Office/Mountain Weather Information Service; tide apps; iGeology; iFirstAid Lite; Night Sky; and various plant, animal and bird ID apps.

One student recently used a GoPro Hero camera to carry out a footpath condition survey on the Yorkshire Three Peaks footpath for a dissertation project. The time-lapse feature has great potential for monitoring short-term environmental changes. When staff undertake field trips abroad to collect data for their own research (e.g. Stott & Mount, 2007; Stott, Nuttall, Eden, Smith & Maxwell, 2008), students opt to join them to undertake fieldwork for dissertations.

Table 13.2 Examples of typical fieldwork investigations used in one UK HE outdoor programme

Location	Level	Task
Ainsdale, Formby	4	Transect to investigate the relationships between vegetation, soil properties and age of sand dunes
Moel Famau, Clywd	4	Changes in weather (air temperature, wind speed, direction, humidity) with altitude
University campus	4	Microclimate around buildings and different surfaces on a university campus
North Wirral Coast	5	10 km walk examining coastal defences; students research and give short talks in the role of park rangers leading a public walk
Delamere Forest	5	Soil development processes in a managed forest ecosystem
Langden Brook, Trough of Bowland, Lancashire	5	Valley evolution by measurements of glacial and fluvial deposits, and contemporary fluvial processes
Yorkshire Dales	6	Karst landscapes and cave evolution; limestone pavement development with cave hydrology measurements and cave survey
Morteratsch Valley, Switzerland	6	Glacial ablation processes and proglacial river discharge and sediment transport processes; individual student-designed field projects
Storeton Woods, Wirral and Bickerton Hill, Cheshire	6	Footpath erosion and management techniques
Thurstaston, West Wirral Coast	6	Glacial deposition models

Note: level 4 = university year 1; level 5 = year 2; level 6 = year 3

Specialist equipment is available, which includes flow meters, pressure transducers, turbidity sensors, automatic water samplers, sediment filtration equipment, waders, etc. TinyTag water-proof temperature data loggers[4] have proved to be very robust and popular with students for field projects and dissertations. A Vantage Pro automatic weather station is set up on the roof of the teaching block and students are set a level 4 assessment task to use data from this and another identical weather station located 35 km away to examine local differences in micro-climate.

Enhancing Fieldwork Learning[5] is a cross-disciplinary Higher Education Academy-funded project in which 'Pedagogy rather than technology drives our objectives.' The focus is on using affordable, ubiquitous technologies such as iPads, digital cameras and social networks to enhance fieldwork learning. There are currently huge opportunities for HE outdoor education providers to benefit from cross-discipline collaborations such as this Enhancing Fieldwork Learning project, which could enhance outdoor education students' HE experiences.

Another important area addressed by many UK HE outdoor/adventure programmes is that of expeditions. Many HE providers offer an expedition module, or options within modules or the programme for students to develop an expedition plan or to undertake an expedition, either independently in small groups, or led by university staff. Expeditions have been identified as important for personal development (e.g. Stott & Hall, 2003; Stott, Felter, Allison & Beames, 2013), as means for collecting scientific data (Stott, 2010b); the author and colleagues have collaborated on carrying out research in this area (see Forrester & Stott, 2009; Allison, Stott, Felter & Beames, 2011; Stott, Allison & Von Wald 2013)[6] and firmly believe that their inclusion in outdoor/adventure programmes at HE level is a valuable and important pedagogical approach. Short expeditions (such as one- or two-night overnight camps) are part of the Mountain Leader Award syllabus, while longer ones can challenge students, develop a range of useful skills, and can sometimes be a means to completing the data-collection phase for a dissertation project. Students often gain employment with expedition providers such as World Challenge, Outlook Expeditions or the British Exploring Society.

Teaching practical skills in outdoor education

Preparations and planning prior to departing for outdoor pursuits fieldwork

All preparations for outdoor pursuits fieldwork proceed with safety in mind. HE providers will work with the university's health and safety staff to write and update their health and safety policy documents. These will normally contain risk assessments for all activities and locations used, and from these the procedures for managing risk arise. These are likely to include the types and quality of safety equipment, the qualifications needed by staff to deliver activities, and appraisals of the locations used. A programme Health & Safety Committee will normally meet regularly (e.g. two or three times per year) to discuss issues arising, and to record all incidents and near misses. Students are represented on the programme Health & Safety Committee, which forms part of the Student Council. At the start of the academic year all new students are briefed on the health and safety policy, and sign to agree to the guidelines and codes of conduct. Thus, students start to take ownership of the guidelines and equipment used. Safety briefs for individual activities are ongoing.

Another important issue is that of transporting students to and from outdoor teaching locations. Professionally driven coaches can be used, but can be expensive and may not be able to access sites served by narrow roads or lanes. Minibuses have been the preferred transport mode for many years, but these days few students have the required endorsement on their driving licence to be able to drive them, so this usually falls to staff who passed their driving test before 1997 or who have passed a minibus driving test. This also applies to towing canoe trailers. In some cases, it is possible to use local locations served by public transport and to meet students at a railway station (as in the case of the Wirral Coast field day and the Swiss Field Course listed in Table 13.2). More recently, nine-seater vehicles, which students can drive with a car licence (and are covered under university insurance), have been used. Driving experience is an important employability skill, which students should be encouraged to gain.

Pedagogical approaches to outdoor pursuits in the field

At LJMU most outdoor pursuits teaching is delivered by programme staff who are qualified by holding national governing body (NGB) awards in the activities being delivered. These NGB awards include Mountain Leader (ML) (summer and winter), Single Pitch Award (SPA) and Mountain Instructor's Award (MIA) for hill walking, summer mountain leadership training, and assessment and winter skills training. For rock climbing, staff hold the MIA, and are approved providers of ML and SPA training and assessment courses. For paddlesports, staff hold British Canoe Union (BCU) level 3–5 coaching awards and UKCC paddlesport coaching awards. For skiing, staff hold Scottish Snowsports Alpine Ski Leader (ASL) and British Association of Ski Instructor (BASI) awards. HE providers must decide how much emphasis to place on students gaining NGB awards within/outside the programme. Most NGB awards require candidates to gain a minimum amount of experience (e.g. twenty quality mountain days for ML summer), then to attend a training course, complete a further period of gaining experience, then to present for an assessment course. How much should be within the contact hours delivered, and how much should be left to the student to complete in their own time? Most students understand the need to gain NGB awards if they wish to secure employment in the outdoors (Stott et al., 2014). Some students enrol on the programme already holding one or more NGB award. How can the programme be designed to encourage and reward students to engage in gaining NGB awards? What effect will the pursuit of NGB awards have on students' academic performance? Some of these questions are discussed by Stott (2007c). Where non-university staff are employed, appropriate checks must be made to ensure the validity of their qualifications and experience, and outside staff must be appropriately briefed about students' background, the module aims and learning outcomes, stage of learning and any medical issues.

Staff–student ratios will be different for outdoor teaching. These typically average 1:15 or 20 in UK universities normally, but clearly have to be reduced for outdoor pursuits in order to meet NGB guidelines, which are more likely to be 1:6 or 1:8 depending on the activity and location. Another consideration is how to address the diversity of experience in a group of six or eight students, when potentially one or more students might already hold an NGB award in the activity, while others in the group could be total novices. Sometimes it is appropriate for the students holding NGB awards to work alongside staff as assistant instructors (under supervision), to gain experience of instructing at this level. They develop coaching skills rather than becoming proficient in the activity. Examples of pedagogical projects that have been completed at LJMU include designing, developing and testing online learning resources to improve students' theoretical understanding of mountain navigation (Stott, Boorman & Hardy, 2004) and using handheld global positioning systems (GPSs) to teach navigation in the mountains (Hardy & Boorman, 2003; Boorman, Hardy & Stott, 2004). Another project (Boorman, Hardy, Stott & Martin, 2007) aimed at developing leadership skills in mountain leader trainees by using peer assessment.

In outdoor pursuits modules, considerable thought is given to how best to motivate, monitor and assess students' use of non-contact time to develop their practical skills. Students need to practise what they have been taught in a wide variety of situations in order to gain confidence and experience to present themselves for NGB training and assessment. Strategies to encourage wise use of non-contact time may include: requiring students to maintain a log of their activities; offering opportunities for students to volunteer to work with local schools/Duke of Edinburgh Award groups; allowing students to borrow university equipment (with conditions) to practise in their own time; offering evening swimming pool sessions to practice kayaking skills; making canoes and kayaks available for students' use any time at a local watersports centre; making local opportunities for students to assist coaching school groups who use the watersports centre; encouraging students to gain relevant employment during vacations (e.g. Camp America, local outdoor centres); appointing students to positions such as rock store, canoe store and ski store technician. These are just some strategies that HE outdoor education providers may use to develop students' skills outside of the formal module delivery.

Conclusion

This chapter examines outdoor education pedagogical practice in UK HE. With twenty-seven HE providers of outdoor or adventure undergraduate programmes in the UK, there is likely to be a diverse range of pedagogical approaches. Fieldwork, the use of mobile technologies and virtual field guides are discussed, along with smartphones and tablet PCs/iPads in outdoor learning. The final section of the chapter examines outdoor pursuits fieldwork in HE, and addresses issues such as health and safety policies, transport, staff qualifications, staff–student ratios and strategies for differentiating teaching.

Notes

1 www.virtualalps.co.uk
2 www.ensemble.ac.uk/wp/
3 www.ensemble.ac.uk/wp/archives/portfolio/environmental-education
4 www.geminidataloggers.com/data-loggers/tinytag-plus-2
5 www.enhancingfieldwork.org.uk/ A Higher Education Academy-funded project that aims to promote ways to enhance student learning during fieldwork through the use of technology.
6 www.expeditionresearch.co.uk Expeditions Research. A web resource developed by P. Allison, T. Stott and J. Felter to bring together expedition research for non-academics and providers of expeditions.

References

Allison, P., Stott, T.A., Felter, J. & Beames, S. (2011). Overseas youth expeditions. In M. Berry & C. Hodgson (Eds.) *Adventure Education* (pp. 187–205). London: Routledge.

Andrews, J., Kneale, P., Sougnez, Y., Stewart, M. & Stott, T.A. (2003). Carrying out pedagogic research into the constructive alignment of fieldwork. *Planet Special Edition 5: Linking Teaching and Research and undertaking Pedagogic Research in Geography, Earth and Environmental Sciences, December*, 51–52.

Boorman, A., Hardy, D.P. & Stott, T.A. (2004). Developing mountain navigation skills in outdoor education: Part 2, self and peer assessment. *JMU Learning & Teaching Press* 4(1), 35–38.

Boorman, A.B., Hardy, D.P., Stott, T.A. & Martin, D.J. (2007). Developing leadership in mountain leader trainees: Design and evaluation of a scheme developed in the JMU Outdoor and Environmental Education Programme. *JMU Learning & Teaching Press*, Mar-06.

Boyle, A., Conchie, S., Maguire, S., Martin, A., Milsom, C., Nash, R., Rawlinson, S., Turner, A. & Wurthman, S. (2003). Fieldwork is good? The student experience of field courses. *Planet Special Edition 5: Linking Teaching and Research and Undertaking Pedagogic Research in Geography, Earth and Environmental Sciences, December*, 48–51.

Couper, P. & Stott, T.A. (2006). Field safety training for staff in geography, earth and environmental sciences in HE: Establishing a framework. *Planet, 16*, 4–9. Publication of the Higher Education Academy Subject Centre for Geography, Earth and Environmental Sciences, Learning & Teaching Support Network.

Drasdo, H. (1972). *Education and the Mountain Centres*. Tyddyn Gabriel, Denbighshire: Frank Davies.

Elmer De-Witt (2011). Apple iTunes store 500,000 IOS apps and counting. Retrieved from: http://tech.fortune.cnn.com/2011/05/24/apples-itunes-store-500000-ios-apps-and-counting.

Forrester, B.J. & Stott, T.A. (2009). Monitoring changes in driver behaviour during a three week wilderness experience in Cariboo Mountains, British Columbia. *Innovations in Practice, 3*, 28–40.

Fuller, I., Gaskin, S. & Scott, I. (2003). Perceptions of geography and environmental science fieldwork in the light of foot and mouth disease, UK, 2001: What do students really think? *Planet Special Edition 5: Linking Teaching and Research and Undertaking Pedagogic Research in Geography, Earth and Environmental Sciences, December*, 55–57.

Gibbs, G. (1999). Using assessment strategically to change the way students learn. *Assessment Matters in Higher Education*, 41–53.

Hardy, D. & Boorman, A. (2003). Teaching, learning and developing navigation. *Association of Mountaineering Instructors Newsletter, 46*, July.

Hardy, D.P. & Stott, T.A. (2006). Taking stock, reviewing the journey and the route ahead: Outdoor and environmental education at I.M. Marsh, Liverpool John Moores University. In B. Humberstone & H. Brown (Eds.) *Shaping the Outdoor Profession through Higher Education: Creative Diversity in Outdoor Studies Courses in Higher Education in the UK* (pp. 93–102). Penrith: Institute for Outdoor Learning.

Kent, M., Gilbertson, D.D. & Hunt, C.O. (1997). Fieldwork in geography teaching: A critical review of the literature and approaches. *Journal of Geography in Higher Education, 23*(3), 313–332.

Litherland, K. & Stott, T.A. (2012). Virtual field sites: Losses and gains in authenticity with semantic technologies. *Technology, Pedagogy and Education, 21*(2), 213–230.

Mortlock, C. (1984). *The Adventure Alternative*. Milnthorpe: Cicerone Press Limited.

Prince, H. (2005). Graduate pathways: A longitudinal study of graduates in outdoor studies in the UK. *Journal of Adventure Education and Outdoor Learning, 5*(1), 21–33.

Stewart, M., Stott, T.A. & Nuttall, A. (2010). Student engagement patterns over the duration of level 1 and level 3 geography modules: Influences on student attendance, performance and use of online resource. *Journal of Geography in Higher Education, 35*(1), 47–65.

Stokes, A., Magnier, K. & Weaver, R. (2011). What is the use of fieldwork? Conceptions of students and staff in geography and geology. *Journal of Geography in Higher Education 35*(1), 121–141.

Stott, T.A. (2007a). Evaluation of the use of diagrams and video clips in Blackboard's on-line assessment. *JMU Learning & Teaching Press, 6*, 25–29. Liverpool John Moores University.

Stott, T.A. (2007b). Evaluation of low-cost personal digital assistants for field data collection and fieldwork leadership by students and staff. *Planet 18*, 12–17. Publication of the Higher Education Academy Subject Centre for Geography, Earth and Environmental Sciences, Learning & Teaching Support Network.

Stott, T.A. (2007c). Adding value to students in higher education: A 5-year analysis of student attainment of National Governing Body Awards in a UK Outdoor Education Degree Programme. *Journal of Adventure Education and Outdoor Learning, 7*(2), 141–160.

Stott, T.A. (2010a). Diversity in level 1 GEES assessment: Moving from less of more to more of less. GEES *Planet 23, Special Edition: Assessment for Learning in the GEES Disciplines*, 25–32.

Stott, T.A. (2010b). Science on expeditions. In S. Beames (Ed.) *Understanding Educational Expeditions* (pp. 45–53). Rotterdam: Sense Publishing.

Stott, T.A. (2013). Development and analysis of students' use of on-line revision quizzes in GEES teaching. *Planet 26*, 66–74.

Stott, T.A. & Hall, N.E. (2003). Changes in aspects of students' self-reported personal, social and technical skills during a six-week wilderness expedition in Arctic Greenland. *Journal of Adventure Education and Outdoor Learning, 3*(2), 159–169.

Stott, T.A. & Huddart, D. (2005). Blended learning? Design and evaluation of a level 3 undergraduate fluvial geomorphology course. *Planet 15*, 20–25. Publication of the Higher Education Academy Subject Centre for Geography, Earth and Environmental Sciences, Learning & Teaching Support Network.

Stott, T.A. & Mount, N.J. (2007). Alpine proglacial suspended sediment dynamics in warm and cool ablation seasons: Implications for global warming? *Journal of Hydrology, 332*(3–4), 259–270.

Stott, T.A. & Nuttall, A.M. (2010). Design, development and student evaluation of interactive virtual field guides for teaching geosciences at Liverpool John Moores University, UK. *Proceedings of the Tunku Abdul Rahman TAR) College Second International Conference on Learning and Teaching (TIC2010), Emerging Trends in Higher education Learning and Teaching*, 18–19 October, Kuala Lumpur, B4-2, 274–281.

Stott, T.A. & Stewart, M. (2008). Patterns of student attendance and online engagement with Blackboard in two outdoor education modules. *Innovations in Practice, 1*, 21–27.

Stott, T.A., Allison, P. & Von Wald, K. (2013). Learning outcomes of young people on a Greenland expedition: Assessing the educational value of adventure tourism. In S. Taylor, P. Varley & T. Johnston (Eds.) *Adventure Tourism: Meanings, Experience and Learning* (pp. 148–160). London: Routledge.

Stott, T.A., Boorman, A. & Hardy, D.P. (2004). Developing mountain navigation skills in outdoor education: Part 1, an evaluation of Questionmark Perception. *JMU Learning & Teaching Press*, *4*(1), 17–19.

Stott, T.A., Hall, N.E. & Bell, S. (1999). Enhancing teaching through information and communications technology, Liverpool John Moores University. *Internal Teaching Fellowship Report to the Learning Methods Unit*, 25pp.

Stott, T.A., Nuttall, A.M. & McCloskey, J. (2009). Design, development and student evaluation of a VirtualAlps field guide: www.virtualalps.co.uk. *Planet 22*, 64–71. Publication of the Higher Education Academy Subject Centre for Geography, Earth and Environmental Sciences, Learning & Teaching Support Network.

Stott, T.A., Zaitseva, E. & Cui, V. (2014). A longitudinal study of employability in a UK outdoor education degree programme using fresher and graduate identities. *Studies in Higher Education, 39*(5), 711–733.

Stott, T.A., Nuttall, A., Eden, N., Smith, K. & Maxwell, D. (2008). Suspended sediment dynamics in the Morteratsch proglacial zone, Bernina Alps, Switzerland. *Geografiska Annaler Series A: Physical Geography*, *90*(4), 299–313.

Stott, T.A, Clark, H., Milson, C., McCloskey, J. & Crompton, K. (2009). The Ingleton Waterfalls Virtual Field Trip: Design, development and preliminary evaluation. *Teaching Earth Sciences*, *34*(1), 13–19. Magazine of the Earth Science Teachers Association.

Stott, T.A., Litherland, K., Carmichael, P. & Nuttall A.M. (2013). Design, development and evolution of interactive virtual field guides for teaching geosciences. In V. Tong (Ed.) *Geoscience Research and Education: Teaching at Universities. Innovations in Science Education and Technology* Vol. 20 (pp. 163–188). London: Springer Dordrecht.

Stott, T.A., Felter, J., Allison, P. & Beames, S. (2013). Personal development on youth expeditions: A literature review and thematic analysis. *Leisure Studies*. DOI: 10.1080/02614367.2013.841744.

University and Colleges Admissions Service (UCAS) (2014). *Courses search tool*. Retrieved from: http://search.ucas.com/.

Vinson, D., Nixon, S., Walsh, B., Walker, C., Mitchell, E. & Zaitseva, E. (2010). Investigating the relationship between student engagement and transition. *Active Learning in Higher Education*, *11*(2), 131–143.

Welsh, K.E. & France, D. (2012). Smartphones and fieldwork. *Geography, 97*(1), 47–51.

Welsh, K.E., Mauchline, A.L., Park, J.R., Whalley, W.B. & France, D. (2013). Enhancing fieldwork learning with technology: Practitioners' perspectives. *Journal of Geography in Higher Education*, *37*(3), 399–415.

14

Formal curricular initiatives and evaluation in the UK

Heather Prince

University of Cumbria

David Exeter

Macmillan Academy

The formal education system in the UK, as in many educational systems, is outcome driven. There is a strong and substantial research base for the impacts of outdoor adventure programmes on young people's development in the affective and interpersonal domains but less evidence for the cognitive benefits (Rickinson *et al.*, 2004). Many schools would dream about being presented with a simple model in which the introduction of an outdoor curriculum impacts directly on higher pupil achievement, resulting in an upward trending profile in key performance indicators. The reality is that, even if such a relationship could be presented, the intangibility of variables would be such that the cause and effect could not be differentiated securely from factors such as further pedagogical initiatives, step–change, baseline data on student performance, and other intrinsic and extraneous influences. However, it is clear that an outdoor curriculum can pervade young people's attitudes, beliefs and self-perceptions, and enhance interpersonal and social skills (ibid.). The inter-relationship between the interpersonal, activity and locational dimensions of outdoor experiences has been shown to be valued by young people (Mannion, Sankey, Doyle & Mattu, 2007), and research has suggested that, 'it seems that adventure programs have a major impact on the lives of participants, and that this impact is lasting' (Hattie, Marsh, Neill & Richards, 1997, p. 43).

The range of provision for outdoor learning in the formal curriculum

In the UK, the launch of the Manifesto for Education outside the Classroom by the government in 2006 was a vision shared by a range of stakeholders including schools, youth groups and parents, in which direct experience was seen as paramount through an organised and powerful approach to learning (DfES, 2006). It signalled a shift to a broader interpretation of out-of-school experiences (which could include educational visits such as to the theatre or museums), but also helped to justify experiential and outdoor learning outwith the classroom. Critics commented on the relative paucity of funding against other initiatives. The Council for Learning Outside the Classroom (CLOtC)[1] was formed in 2009, and now takes on leadership and responsibility for the areas defined in the Manifesto, providing resources and guidance to teachers and leaders in the UK.

Many outdoor providers, particularly those involved with multi-agencies, aligned their work with a previous UK government agenda, 'Every Child Matters' (DfES, 2003), which was an initiative aimed at protecting children at risk of harm or neglect following several high-profile cases. The policies also set out to improve children's lives as a whole, to maximise their potential, and sought to give them support to be healthy, stay safe, enjoy and achieve, contribute to society positively and achieve economic wellbeing. The former coalition government chose not to continue with this child-centred initiative, which provided a useful framework of simple, yet well-articulated outcomes for outdoor curricula.

In England, outdoor and adventurous activities (OAA) has been part of the national curriculum within physical education (PE) since its inception in 1989, although after several iterations of the curriculum, has become optional at all key stages to 2013 (DfE, 2014). A new national curriculum implemented from September 2014 raises the profile of OAA in Key Stages 2 (7–11 years) and 3 (11–14 years). However, OAA in a PE curriculum is too often about teaching a skill – for example, rock climbing at GCSE (14–16 years) or A-level (16–18 years) – or a replicated use of a local area for orienteering rather than a whole-school approach to outdoor learning. Outdoor educators have been disappointed that this more holistic and cross-curricular approach cannot be adopted.

Adventurous activities are also part of the physical education curriculum at Key Stages 2 and 3 in the Curriculum for Wales, with an emphasis on increasing confidence and a progression towards leadership at Key Stage 4 (14–16 years). It strives to create an effective, coordinated holistic curriculum by promoting positive relationships and self-esteem, and by encouraging the inclusion of appropriate visits and visitors and extra-curricular experiences. Key values in terms of outdoor provision are teaching and learning in the natural environment and through residentials (Curriculum for Wales, 2014).

In contrast, the Northern Ireland physical education curriculum does not contain outdoor activities under any guise, although there is an emphasis on learning outdoors through play in the early years, and on personal development and mutual understanding at Key Stages 1 and 2.

In Scotland, however, the Curriculum for Excellence (CfE) draws away from subject orientation, placing more emphasis on young people developing as 'successful learners', 'confident individuals', 'responsible citizens' and 'effective contributors' – the four 'capacities' (Learning and Teaching Scotland, 2010a). Furthermore, the Scottish Government emphasises that children should have positive learning experiences in a variety of settings and thus is promoting experiences in the outdoors, legitimising and encouraging outdoor learning (Beames, Atencio & Ross, 2009). It has also invested in the production and promotion of guidance to support opportunities for teaching and learning in the outdoors (Learning and Teaching Scotland, 2010b).

Cognitive benefits of outdoor curricula

Schools rarely have evaluated out-of-classroom learning experiences and their impact on cognitive attainment or on other subjects in the curriculum (CUREE, 2009) and the 'evaluation of learning is not conducted systematically, not triangulated with other evidence and not evaluated or assessed externally' (Nicol, Higgins & Ross, 2006, p. 3).

However, more recently, there has been some emerging evidence of the link between the provision of outdoor experiences in the formal curriculum, be it outdoor 'learning' or outdoor 'education', to higher academic achievement among pupils. Generally, because of the time framework of the input factors, these examples have emerged from residential experiences.

The Paul Hamlyn Foundation (PHF), in the work on 'Learning Away' a funding and research opportunity of £2.25 million to thirteen clusters of sixty schools in the UK, has been available through a six-year period from 2008. This initiative provided an opportunity for some new thinking on a key aspect of outdoor learning: residential provision. CUREE (2009) provides evidence for the underlying rationale for its establishment and formative evaluation through a literature review of previous research.

> Learning Away is a . . . special initiative that aims to support schools in significantly enhancing young people's learning, achievement and well-being by using innovative residential experiences as an integral part of the broader adventure learning curriculum . . . [It] was founded on the belief that high quality residential experiences can provide extremely powerful learning opportunities for children and young people . . . the opportunity to engage young people with the much more intensive, rich and deep learning experiences that residential can offer is compelling.

> For some children a week's residential experience is worth more than a term of school. We know we want it for our own children – we need to make sure other people's children experience it too. (Tim Brighouse, former London Schools Commissioner and Advisor to the Paul Hamlyn Foundation Educational Programme (PHF, 2014))

In its interim report (PHF, 2013), evidence is provided for the influence of the programme on raising educational attainment, particularly in mathematics at the borderline mark (pp. iv, 16). In one cluster, 39 per cent of residential students improved their test score in mathematics, compared to only 14 per cent of the 'comparator group', who did not attend the residential. More than two-thirds (69%) of the residential group achieved a C grade at GCSE[2] compared to none of the comparator group (all students were C/D borderline). In addition to progress and attainment, the report also notes the increase in knowledge, skills and understanding and a greater engagement with learning, which have positive effects throughout the curriculum. Christie, Higgins and McLaughlin (2014) also provide evidence for the power of residential experiences in providing authentic contextualisation for oral and written work, and the consequential improvement of grades in French and English, although it might be that the impact of an improving self-construct, particularly self-confidence, cannot be a disaggregated effect.

In a wider context of learning outside the classroom and educational visits, there is evidence from museum education showing that 60 per cent of pupils' assessed work achieved a higher mark after a museum visit than the three previous pieces of work. Accelerated achievement was most evident for the lower achievers (Watson, Dodd & Jones, 2007).

Monitoring and reporting on outcomes

The accountability framework that impacts on curricula in the UK is complex, driven by ever changing policy decisions from government, including the national curriculum, examinations, Ofsted (the Office for Standards in Education, Children's Services and Skills in England) and school league tables. Ofsted is the inspection and regulation service reporting directly to Parliament, necessarily independent and impartial but the regulator of all organisations that care for children and young people and those providing education and skills for learners of all ages (but not higher education institutions, which are regulated by the Quality Assurance Agency (QAA)).

In the context of schools, it has proved to be open minded about the range of provision of outdoor learning, including OAA, field studies, residential provision and in-school outdoor learning. Reports in 2004 and 2008 (Ofsted, 2004, 2008) were widely received and respected by outdoor practitioners. Her Majesty's Inspector (HMI) Robin Hammerton, the author of the 2008 report, created a challenging title – 'How far should we go?' – and noted that, 'when planned and implemented well, learning outside the classroom contributed significantly to raising standards and improving pupils' personal, social and emotional development' (Ofsted, 2008).

There is considerable research evidence to suggest that outdoor adventure programmes can impact positively on young people's attitudes, beliefs and quality of learning. According to Ofsted:

- learning outside the classroom improved young people's development in all five of the Every Child Matters outcomes, especially in two areas: enjoy and achieve, and achieving economic well-being;
- well organised activities outside the classroom contribute much to the quality and depth of learning;
- learners of all ages say they enjoy working away from the classroom. They find it 'exciting', 'practical', 'motivating', 'refreshing' and 'fun'. They make such comments as: 'You see rather than listen', 'We learn in a fun way', 'We like learning by doing.' (Ofsted, 2008)

Learning Outside the Classroom was part of the Ofsted inspection criteria from 2007 to 2012. Schools are judged as 'Outstanding', 'Good', 'Requires improvement' (previously 'Satisfactory') or 'Inadequate' in terms of overall effectiveness. However, outdoor centres are not organisations that are subject to these inspections in their own right although case studies have been used in reports (Ofsted, 2004).

A recent project in a group of outdoor centres in England has been applying Ofsted criteria to the evaluation of every outdoor session (Graham, 2014). While many would make a self-judgement of a success for most outdoor sessions due to the positive feedback, body language and experiential nature of delivery, a more rigorous and quantified examination showed room for improvement. The initiative was designed to develop a model away from just experiential learning to a teaching methodology including an appropriate level of challenge for all pupils, good facilitation, pace and adaptability of the leader, and meaningful, personalised learning that results in interdependence of outcomes and the transfer of learning across activities and back into school. Using the Ofsted inspection criteria, the key attributes for outstanding learning were progression, ownership and creativity. The tree of outstanding learning (Figure 14.1) illustrates the thinking through the roots (teacher input), through the trunk (assessment of learning) to the branches (pupil outcomes).

A simple model of outdoor curriculum evaluation beyond setting objectives and monitoring whether or not these have been achieved is through a framework of 'safety, fun and learning'. Debate has centred around whether or not an activity should take place if it is deemed that safety is questionable, but it is argued that it is sometimes difficult to anticipate the boundaries of psychological comfort with an unknown group. Furthermore, dynamic risk assessments and on-site vigilance can and should highlight unforeseen safety concerns, which can be mitigated in the field. In an attempt to make a judgement about the quality of outdoor education, the Outdoor Education Advisers' Panel (OEAP, 2005) presented ten possible outcomes and concomitant key indicators around self and group constructs. This publication now updated by the English Outdoor Council (2015) as 'High Quality Outdoor Learning' provides a useful document for schools and outdoor centres to evaluate their practices.

Legislation and accreditation

As the result of a canoeing tragedy at Lyme Regis in 1993, when four teenagers drowned, an Act of Parliament, the Activity Centres (Young Persons' Safety) Act 1995, was passed with the establishment of an independent licensing authority (originally AALA, the Adventure Activities Licensing Authority) to inspect and license 'in scope' hazardous activities for young people under eighteen years. Although the provision of adventure activities by schools to their own pupils was exempt from the scheme, safety rightly became paramount on the agenda but, with it, a demand for extensive documentation and justification. External providers were subject to inspection and

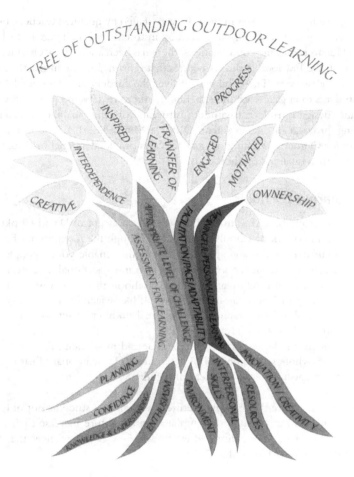

Figure 14.1 Tree of outstanding outdoor learning

Source: Graham (2014)

the AALA licence was the badge by which schools usually chose provision. Safety in this respect remains of prime importance to any school or participant undertaking adventurous activities, but there has been an increasing recognition of the importance of the pedagogy, facilitation and quality of teaching in the outdoors beyond that overseen by the Adventure Activity Licensing Scheme that is now in operation. Kitemarks have emerged to respond to 'out of scope' providers ('Adventuremark') and to the wider learning framework in the outdoors.

The Learning Outside the Classroom Quality Badge is designed as a national award that is a recognisable accreditation for all types of LOtC providers in the UK, and combines the essential elements of provision, learning and safety for teachers and children. The scheme is managed and developed by the Council for Learning Outside the Classroom in an attempt to facilitate the incorporation of learning outdoors by schools and teachers, and to shift the focus from process to outcomes. It is not clear if the efficacy and effectiveness of a kitemark scheme has been researched or comparator data examined.

The single largest factor in education is the quality of teaching and the impact on student learning and achievement (Nye, Konstantopoulos & Hedges, 2004; Ofsted, 2008). Historically, local authority outdoor education centres in the UK were staffed by qualified teachers, but a significant amount of other provision was being delivered by instructors with a range of technical outdoor qualifications. Due to economic considerations, there has been a shift in that balance of teachers to instructors now in the few local authority centres that remain. But the instructor matters, as does the teacher in the classroom. Their ability to deliver the curriculum, at a suitable pace, in a style that enables students to engage with the experience, and to review and process the experience, is key. Curriculum design is irrelevant without instructors with the capability to make an impact to student learning, progress and achievement (O'Boyle-Mitchell, 2013). The accreditation scheme of the Institute for Outdoor Learning[3] for practitioners provided a benchmark of staffing quality in the field other than qualified teacher status.

Adventure Learning Schools

Adventure Learning Schools (ALS) in the UK were the concept of David Hopkins. His intention was to create a network of schools that would, through the integration of adventure education into their curricula, ethos and approach to learning, enable young people to reach their potential, and to achieve excellence in their academic and vocational, and personal and social development. A number of primary and secondary schools in north-west England, Cumbria, UK, were part of the initial pilot, along with schools like Macmillan Academy (see exemplar below). The network developed rapidly from a small number of schools to more than forty across the UK within a few years (Hopkins, 2012).

ALS has its roots in the legacy of the Outward Bound movement, the work of Kurt Hahn and the concepts of 'whole school design' by reference to Expeditionary Learning in the USA. The vision in the prospectus for an ALS school stated:

> Imagine a school where the learning culture is so rich that students not only achieve high academic standards, but through the emphasis on adventure increase their competence as learners, develop their personality and enjoy a variety of experiences that broaden their view of and place in society. (ALS, 2014)[4]

Adventure was to be at the heart of the curriculum, in every subject. In essence, it was to be hoped that it would possible to take the 'tenacity of pursuit' and adventurous spirit and apply it to a science or mathematics lesson. Schools were redesigning curricula, timetables, content and pedagogy to meet the ALS accreditation criteria.

The curriculum was summarised in the ALS Handbook as follows:

> These will be schools where learning is not just enjoyable, but leads to genuine accomplishments, an appreciation of oneself, others and society, and where the skills, knowledge and dispositions acquired enable the student to become an active and creative citizen. In addition these schools will have a global outlook promoting greater understanding of the wilderness environment throughout their curriculum. These are schools where the great traditions of education often previously the privilege of a few, are now open to all. (Hopkins, 2012)

Towards a wider interpretation of the positive effects of outdoor curricula

Macmillan Academy, as an inner-city state school directly funded by the government, has been providing life chances for young people in the catchment of Middlesbrough, north-east

England, for more than twenty years. It provides a valuable case study of innovative curricular initiatives that draw upon outdoor learning. It is an organisation that rejects complacency and always strives for improvement, and as such has built up a reputation nationally and internationally not only for outstanding results but also for forward thinking. Staff at the school designed and delivered a new model for outdoor learning provision within the school, with curriculum, facilities and Academy Funding. The outdoor learning programme is unique, judged outstanding by Ofsted in 2007 and noted for its exemplary provision in 2013 with the core of its provision available to all as an integral part of the curriculum.

Outdoor Learning at Macmillan Academy had been a SSAT (Specialist Schools and Academies Trust) specialism from 2006 to 2012. Changes in government brought an end to the funding and the status, fuelled by the neo-liberal ideology of the coalition government, although the provision at the academy remains. Since the starting point in 2006 Macmillan had strived to give students an inclusive and progressive adventure learning curriculum. The Director of Outdoor Learning is on record as stating that:

> Outdoor learning works, adventure and challenges inspires, it's a deep learning experience that is memorable, meaningful and motivational. It's learning that lasts a life time. (Macmillan Academy, 2014)

At the end of the five-year journey in 2011 and completion of the initial vision there was time to review and think about the future development of outdoor learning. The staff re-examined their mission, values and range of programmes available to students. Above all, staff reinforced how they could continue providing outstanding provision and explore creative new ways of working.

Ofsted (in May 2013) stated that Macmillan Academy seeks to provide an education that is motivational, meaningful and memorable, and it is successful in doing so. Its motto, 'inspiring every student to succeed', is at the heart of everything the academy does. Ofsted confirmed that 'the academy uses outdoor learning exceptionally well to develop students' skills'.

> The mission of Outdoor Learning at Macmillan Academy is 'inspirational and memorable learning through adventure and challenge.' The core of our provision will be available to all and an integral part of the Macmillan Academy curriculum. We will maximise the use of existing resources for the benefit of our students. We will continually improve and develop our programmes and teaching practice. We value risk, real and perceived, as a powerful learning opportunity for our students. Fundamentally, we truly believe in the magic and power of outdoor learning as a catalyst for change. (Macmillan Academy, 2014)

The Centre for Outdoor Learning is the umbrella for the extensive range of outdoor learning facilities at Macmillan Academy. The low and high ropes course provides a range of individual and team challenges. Regarded as one of the fastest routes to improving a range of self-constructs (Attarian & Holden, 2005; Gillis & Speelman, 2008), this unique facility contributes to the ethos of 'I can'. The Climbing Centre contains twenty-four route corridors and more than one-hundred graded climbing routes across a range of feature walls, and is the largest and most extensive climbing wall within any school in the UK. The Expedition Unit has the ability to provide all the clothing and equipment (including a fleet of mountain bikes) for a range of educational visits and expeditions. Such facilities are a fundamental resource for on-site delivery of high-quality outdoor and adventure learning. The core staff come from the outdoor learning sector, bringing the technical skills and qualifications to lead their students in the outdoors. They are outdoor leaders, who balance the skills of teaching, facilitation and coaching to maximise the learning opportunities for students. The centre holds the LOtC Quality Badge, Adventure Mark and LOtC Mark Gold for its provision.

Outdoor learning is not just part of one department as it is in some schools in the UK (usually physical education). Instead, every department, year group and member of staff has the ability to contribute. In simple terms, outdoor learning is being led from the top, and is a whole-school approach and design.

At the core of the curriculum in Key Stage 3 (11–14 years), every student is timetabled to take part in a two-day intensive programme each year, balanced with three weeks of intensive provision, on residential and during a challenge week programme. In Key Stages 4 and 5, pathways exist for students within physical education for specific sport-based development.

Unique alternative timetabling can create opportunities for immersion-type experiences. For example, in Years 7, 8 and 9 (Key Stage 3) at Macmillan Academy every student takes part in a two-day course, part of the adventure learning school curriculum. In Year 7 this programme is called 'Kick Start'. In Year 8 the programme, with an element of service (for example, working for the North York Moors National Park), is linked to a Baccalaureate qualification, and in Year 9 the programme is based on a model of student co-creation where students design their learning outcomes and adventure experience to match. All programmes have at their core the Academies range of learning capacities or habits, based on the work of Guy Claxton (see Claxton, 2002).

These programmes benefit from the facility to work with small groups of students (maximum of twelve) off timetable for two days with the specialist outdoor learning instructors. The model is transferable to any school, with an approach that is experiential and personal. In two days a student would focus in detail on two learning habits, exploring in depth meaning and understanding, and demonstrating these habits.

Tasks in outdoor learning are only vehicles to students learning, but they are designed as dynamic, exciting and different activities to stimulate engagement, interaction and the learning of the habits. The process and the facilitated experience are also critical. One approach is how practitioners facilitate the learning by asking key questions to students during the course. Students are often asked to reflect on 'What went well?', 'What improvements could we make?' and, fundamentally, 'What was the real learning from that experience?' A powerful moment is when a student reaches a realisation that s/he can achieve.

Systematic evaluation of the outdoor learning programmes at Macmillan has been in place since its inauguration, through student written evaluations, student focus groups and parent/carer surveys balanced by external quality assurance agencies for kitemarks such as the LOtC quality badge and Adventure Learning Schools status (as well as Ofsted). The student evaluations 2006–2014 showed that the outdoor programme enhanced students' enjoyment of learning, and encouraged them to be more active, more confident and capable of dealing with new situations, and students believed that this learning would help them in the future.

> Macmillan Academy has a deep commitment to learning outside the classroom . . . mak[ing] a significant contribution to the development of students. Experiential learning is widely in evidence and outdoor education is totally embedded into the curriculum and valued by teachers, students and parents . . . a fine example of how outdoor education can become an inspirational way of life for a wide range of students. (LOtC Quality Badge Inspection, 2009)

Under the previous UK coalition government, and felt acutely in the financial years from 2011 onwards, there has been a systematic change and 'raising of the bar' in the education system, to compete with others internationally with higher PISA scores.[5] Financially many schools including Macmillan Academy were managing reducing budgets. Macmillan had to find ways of protecting and maintaining their provision for outdoor learning. It is hoped that the early strategy at conception of investing in buildings and facilities on the school site will be sustainable model for outdoor learning. Other more traditional models of resource intensive residential provision budgets are becoming less tenable with more local authority out-of-county residential provision being subject to closure. Strong initiatives also weather economically challenging times. Interestingly, the Paul Hamlyn Foundation 'Learning Away' programme came during the financial crisis that led to large-scale challenges in the UK and global economies. From a school perspective having some new thinking, research and creative ideas on how to deliver residential provision protected some provision for young people by providing new more affordable options.

Conclusions

The emphasis on measureable benefits in outdoor curricula follows thinking that the most important aspects of educational experiences are the processes of memory and knowledge (Kirschner, Sweller & Clark, 2006) but deviates from a Deweyan perspective that is child-centred and teacher influenced (Quay & Seaman, 2013). Algorithmic teaching and learning focused towards specific learning outcomes diminishes pupil responsibility and individuality (Loynes, 1998; Allison & Pomeroy, 2000), which now contradicts two key attributes of outstanding outdoor learning, creativity and ownership (Graham, 2014). Examples of successful outdoor curricula within formal education in the UK illustrate learning across the affective, interpersonal and cognitive domains, although the latter may be by inference through increased motivation, behaviour and contextualisation. Strong leadership, teaching and facilitation, together with a well-defined mission are contributors to a high-quality outdoor learning curriculum that, through monitoring and evaluation, is held accountable to scrutiny at a national level.

Notes

1 CLOtC (Council for Learning Outside the Classroom): www.lotc.org.uk
2 GCSE (General Certificate of Secondary Education) is a public examination taken in England and Wales generally at 15–16 years. It is graded A*–G with grades of C and above taken to be pass equivalent.
3 Institute for Outdoor Learning: www.outdoor-learning.org
4 Adventure Learning Schools: www.adventurelearningschools.org
5 PISA (Programme for International Student Assessment) is a study measuring the performance of 15 year olds worldwide in mathematics, science and reading. It is undertaken by OECD (Organisation of Economic Co-operation and Development), which started ranking countries in 2000 and from thence on a triennial basis.

References

Adventure Learning Schools (ALS) (2014). Resources. Retrieved from: www.adventurelearningschools.org/resources/.
Allison, P. & Pomeroy, E. (2000). How shall we 'know'? Epistemological concerns in research in experiential education. *Journal of Experiential Education, 23*(2), 91–98.
Attarian, A. & Holden, G.T. (2005). *The Literature and Research on Challenge Courses: An Annotated Bibliography* (2nd edn). Raleigh, NC: North Carolina State University and Alpine Towers International.
Beames, S., Atencio, M. & Ross, H. (2009). Taking excellence outdoors. *Scottish Educational Review, 41*(2), 32–45.
Christie, B., Higgins, P. & McLauglin, P. (2014). 'Did you enjoy your holiday?' Can residential outdoor learning benefit mainstream schooling? *Journal of Adventure Education and Outdoor Learning, 14*(1), 1–23.
Claxton, G. (2002). *Building Learning Power: Helping Young People Become Better Learners*. Bristol: TLO.
CUREE (Centre for the Use of Research and Evidence in Education) (2009). *Learning Away: A Small Scale Literature Review*. Retrieved from: www.phf.org.uk/page.asp?id=894.

Curriculum for Wales (2014). Retrieved from: www.wales.gov.uk/topics/educationandskills/schoolshome/curriculumwales/revisedcurriculumwales/.

Department for Education (DfE) (2014). *National Curriculum*. Retrieved from: https://www.gov.uk/government/collections/national-curriculum.

Department for Education and Skills (DfES) (2003) *Every Child Matters*. Retrieved from: https://www.education.gov.uk/consultations/downloadableDocs/EveryChildMatters.pdf.

Department for Education and Skills (DfES) (2006). *Learning Outside the Classroom Manifesto*. Nottingham: DfES Publications.

English Outdoor Council (2015). High Quality Outdoor Learning. London: English Outdoor Council.

Gillis, H.L. & Speelman, E. (2008). Are challenge (ropes) courses an effective tool? A meta-analysis. *Journal of Experiential Education, 31*(2), 111–135.

Graham, S. (2014). *Outstanding outdoor teaching and learning*. Presentation given at the Association of Heads of Outdoor Education Centres (AHOEC) Lake District Regional Meeting, 17 January.

Hattie, J., Marsh, H.W., Neill, J. & Richards, G.E. (1997). Adventure education and Outward Bound: Out-of-class experiences that make a lasting difference. *Review of Educational Research, 67*(1), 43–87.

Hopkins, D. (2012). *The Adventure Learning Schools Handbook*. Carlisle: Adventure Learning Schools.

Kirschner, P., Sweller, J. & Clark, R. (2006). Why minimal guidance during instruction does not work: an analysis of the failure of constructivist, discovery, problem-based, experiential and inquiry-based teaching. *Educational Psychology, 41*(2), 75–86.

Learning and Teaching Scotland (2010a). *Curriculum for Excellence*. Glasgow: Learning and Teaching Scotland.

Learning and Teaching Scotland (2010b). *Curriculum for Excellence through Outdoor Learning*. Glasgow: Learning and Teaching Scotland.

Learning Outside the Classroom (LOtC) Quality Badge Inspection (2009) *Inspection Report, Macmillan Academy*. Shrewsbury: Council for Learning Outside the Classroom. Unpublished.

Loynes, C. (1998). Adventure in a bun. *Journal of Experiential Education, 21*(1), 35–39.

Macmillan Academy (2014) HRH Duke of Kent visits the Academy. Retrieved from: www.macmillan-academy.org.uk/news_item.php?id=538.

Mannion, G., Sankey, K., Doyle, L. & Mattu, L. (2007). *Young People's Interaction with Natural Heritage through Outdoor Learning*. Perth: Scottish Natural Heritage.

Nicol, R., Higgins, P. & Ross, H. (2006). *Outdoor Education: The Views of Providers from Different Contexts in Scotland*. Dundee: Learning and Teaching Scotland.

Nicol, R., Higgins, P., Ross, H. & Mannion, G. (2007). *Outdoor Education in Scotland: A Summary of Recent Research*. Perth: Scottish Natural Heritage.

Nye, B., Konstantopoulos, S. & Hedges, J. (2004). How large are teachers effects? *Education, Evaluation and Policy Analysis, 26*(3), 237–257.

O'Boyle-Mitchell, L. (2013). Expectations of outdoor educators in the UK: A gap between educator competency requirements and promised programme outcomes. Unpublished MSc thesis, University of Edinburgh.

OEAP (2005). *High Quality Outdoor Education*. London: OEAP.

Ofsted (2004). *Outdoor Education: Aspects of Good Practice*. Retrieved from: http://webarchive.national archives.gov.uk/20140723032007/http://www.ofsted.gov.uk/resources/outdoor-education-aspects-of-good-practice.

Ofsted (2008). *Learning Outside the Classroom. How Far Should You Go?* Retrieved from: www.lotc.org.uk/wp-content/uploads/2010/12/Ofsted-Report-Oct-2008.pdf.

Paul Hamlyn Foundation (2013). *Evaluation of Learning Away: Interim Report 1.1, June 2013*. Leeds: York Consulting LLP.

Paul Hamlyn Foundation (2014). *About Learning Away*. Retrieved from: www.phf.org.uk/page.asp?id=894.

Quay, J. & Seaman, J. (2013). *John Dewey and Education Outdoors: Making Sense of the 'Educational Situation' through More Than a Century of Progressive Reforms*. Rotterdam: Sense Publishers.

Rickinson, M., Dillon, J., Teamey, K., Morris, M., Choi, M.Y., Sanders, D. & Benefield, P. (2004). *A Review of Research on Outdoor Learning*. Shrewsbury: Field Studies Council.

Watson, S., Dodd, J. & Jones, C. (2007). *Engage, Learn, Achieve: The Impact of Museum Visits on the Attainment of Secondary School Pupils in the East of England, 2006–2007*. University of Leicester, Research Centre for Museums and Galleries: Museums, Libraries, Archives East of England & Renaissance East of England.

Part 3

Non-formal education and training in/for/about outdoor studies

Introduction

Karla A. Henderson

<small>North Carolina State University</small>

A fine line exists between what might be defined as formal and non-formal education and training. They are more like two ends of a continuum than one or the other. Similarly, the relationship between formal and non-formal may be akin to yin and yang. They may appear as opposite or contrary forces, but they are actually complementary. Therefore, while we have chosen to structure this book in separate sections, education and training in outdoor studies have a good deal of overlap.

UNESCO (2014) suggested more than forty years ago that lifelong learning should be a master concept to shape educational systems. Formal schooling can address this concept but so can informal daily opportunities and non-formal organised educational activities. This distinction may be largely administrative but is important. We have chosen to use the term non-formal rather than informal to describe the structured education and training opportunities described in this section.

Formal education usually occurs in schools or further/higher education institutions and refers to classroom-based education provided by trained teachers or lecturers. Common synonyms for formal include official, proper, prescribed, recognised, strict and/or correct. Synonyms for informal can be relaxed, casual, familiar, easy, unceremonious, comfortable, easy-going, natural, unofficial, unauthorised, unsanctioned and/or unconfirmed. Therefore, we believe that the type of education that occurs outside the traditional school, college or university setting cannot adequately be described as informal.

Non-formal education includes structured out-of-school outdoor settings with designated leadership, such as after-school programmes, community-based organisations and summer learning environments. This outdoor learning can occur through public entities, non-governmental organisations and in the private sector. These non-formal locations also provide a means to combine education and leisure/outdoor recreation in highly complementary ways.

Non-formal organised outdoor projects and programmes are diverse in scope, as this Handbook shows. This educational activity usually provides different types of learning to diverse populations including both children and adults. Although the lines can be quite blurred between formal and non-formal learning, non-formal education is generally different from the prescribed nature of formal education. For example, although both schools and after-school programmes serve students, some children who may feel disenfranchised at school can blossom in out-of-school settings. Learning can happen in settings where young people, as well as adults, feel less intimidated or more comfortable than they do in formal classrooms.

Many non-formal organisations are non-governmental in nature and do not receive government funding as is the case with most formal school institutions. Therefore, they can operate within their own guidelines. Nonetheless, governments may require regulations that would apply regardless of the source of funding. In addition, more private organisations are getting involved in the non-formal outdoor arena, as discussed later in this introduction.

These non-formal education and training opportunities occur in structured organisations. They all have specific purposes and use trained, and sometimes credentialed, leaders similar to teachers in formal education. Issues related to careers, professionalism, ethics, justice and inclusion, and outcomes apply to all types of formal and non-formal outdoor studies.

This section of the book describes the organisation and practice of non-formal groups as well as how research is used to understand these approaches and settings. The chapters in the first part of this section identify some of the broad issues related to non-formal education and training – careers, just leadership, professionalisation through accreditation and certification, and ethical considerations. The majority of the chapters address specific ways that non-formal education occurs in the outdoors, including adventure education, challenge courses, organised camps, sail training, Forest Schools and adventure therapy. The final chapter describes the importance of connecting people to the diversity of experiences they have in the outdoors through review and reflection.

The authors of these chapters identify issues that require greater examination into the future, including connecting people and the outdoors, leadership and programme quality, outdoors for all, role of government and privatisation, research, and sustainability. Some of these issues are not unique compared to formal education but they offer additional considerations for the future of outdoor studies.

People and the outdoors

Richard Louv's popular book, *Last Child in the Woods* (2005), highlighted the problem regarding children's disconnect from nature, which he termed *nature deficit disorder*. Although concerns have existed about where nature fits into people's lives in today's technological world, the relationship of children to nature has received renewed concern in the 21st century.

Growing quantities of research suggest that frequent experience with the natural world produces positive physical, mental and emotional benefits in adults and children. For example, the outdoors can promote healthy behaviours by providing opportunities for exercise and stress release, can support cognitive experiences by increasing attention and memory, and can foster psycho-social benefits such as providing opportunities to interact with others and reducing depression.

Although research shows the benefits of the outdoors to children's health, their access to nature and outdoor play has diminished. Children spend less than half the amount of time playing outdoors than their parents did. Many people no longer have opportunities for experiencing nature. Further, concerns have been expressed that children who do not have experiences that promote pro-environmental behaviour will not learn to care about their environments (Chawla & Cushing, 2007).

The purpose of many of the non-formal outdoor programmes described in this book are aimed at bringing the outdoors into people's lives, especially since often formal organisations such as schools have not addressed these concerns. The chapters about adventure education, camps, sail training and Forest Schools provide examples of how the purpose of these types of opportunity emphasise using the outdoors and nature to address educational, developmental and recreational outcomes.

Leadership and programme quality

Leadership is a key issue in non-formal education and training. This leadership has implications for the non-formal outdoor opportunities offered as well as the physical and emotional safety of participants, and programme quality. Professional leadership careers in the outdoors are surveyed by Allin and West. They give examples of the possibilities and also describe the need to elevate the value of these outdoor professions. Brown, Harris and Porter emphasise the qualifications needed by professionals if the profile of practice is to be elevated.

The issues of certification and accreditation have been important in establishing the quality of outdoor experiences. These terms are sometimes conflated, as can be seen in the chapters by Attarian and Brown *et al.* The differences in definitions may be a result of cultural interpretations. Attarian argues that certification relates to the competencies of individuals and accreditation refers to programme quality. Brown *et al.* describe accreditation in the UK, which combines both the proficiencies of leaders as well as the excellence of programmes. Separating the two is difficult since competent individuals are needed to assure that programme quality is high regardless of how the terms are defined. Wagstaff raises the question of who should determine the standards of practice for particular activities like challenge courses. These chapters indicate that developing standards for accreditation or certification is difficult because outdoor studies is so broad. Whether certification and accreditation should be left to individuals and their reflective practice contrasted to the role of organisations and commercial entities remains an open question.

A common thread in discussing programme quality is the need for self-regulation and self-reflection relative to leadership competencies and programmes. Greenaway and Knapp make a strong case for how review and reflection are necessary when working with students. Attarian and Brown *et al.*, as well as Breunig and Rylander, call for reflective leaders aware of the competencies needed.

Outdoors for all

Most non-formal organisations concern themselves with assuring that outdoor opportunities exist for many different individuals, with a trend towards focusing on populations previously unserved or underserved. The central theme of Breunig and Rylander's chapter is the imperative for organisations to provide just leadership to assure that groups are not left out or experience unconscious discrimination. They emphasise that professionals in the field must go beyond tolerance to self-education. Therefore, leaders should possess cultural competency as well as social justice competence to assure that outdoor studies reinforces positive social relationships for all. Just as the notion of sports for all is embodied in many countries, the emphasis on the outdoors for all is evident in this section on non-formal education.

Some outdoor programmes address particularly populations such as the young children targeted in Forest Schools, or have therapeutic goals as described by Richards. These specialised groups, as well as many others that are not described in this Handbook, offer a means to assure that the outdoors is used to its maximum potential for all children and adults.

Role of government and privatisation

As Allin and West emphasise, outdoor studies is not a coherent industry and has many employment opportunities. However, since many of the providers of non-formal outdoor opportunities are not government sponsored, the role of government must be considered, especially in light of the growing commercialising and privatisation of outdoor studies programmes and opportunities. Attarian laments that governments will push regulations if the outdoor industry does not set standards that go beyond past traditions.

A growing concern among some people in the outdoors is the commercialisation or privatisation of the outdoors and what implications those changes have. The historical reasons for facilitating non-formal education and profit making are not always compatible. Wagstaff provides an example of how some challenge courses are changing from their initial purpose of building personal confidence and social interaction towards strictly recreational goals. Although safety remains important, the use of debriefing and other means to emphasise the outcomes has been abandoned by commercial providers who want primarily to provide excitement and thrills for participants. Self-reflection may not be emphasised as the providers of particular outdoor experience change.

Research

Research is often used to justify the various outdoor programmes available. This research, however, must be scrutinised to assure that it is both theoretically valid and methodologically reliable. More sophisticated research is evident, especially in the documentation of outcomes and programme quality as suggested by Sibthorp and Richmond, and Bialeschki, Fine and Bennett.

One important issue regarding research is what is measured. Wolfe and Samdahl (2005) provided a compelling critique of the research related to adventure education, which has implications for all areas of outdoor studies. They identified two central assumptions that have driven outdoor research, including the belief that risk, either real or perceived, leads to positive benefits, and that benefits are transferable to other aspects of life. Samdahl and Wolfe contended that much of the research has *assumed* that these positive benefits will occur, without being critical of the negative possibilities. They concluded that, by openly examining the assumptions that shape research as practice, researchers will be able to design better studies that produce insight into the benefits as well as the limitations of outdoor participation. Bialeschki *et al.*, Sibthorp and Richmond, and Wagstaff all raise questions about needing further research to question the assumptions about benefits. McCulloch also comments on research about sail training and advocates for the application of critical theory. He noted how positivist research has focused mainly on benefits while interpretive approaches might better address the broad spectrum of the experiences people have in the outdoors. Wagstaff also suggests that, while the educational and developmental aspects of the outdoors have been examined, the recreational benefits have scarcely been addressed.

Another research consideration that requires further examination is to acknowledge the role that that fidelity plays when researching outdoor programmes. Fidelity of implementation occurs when leaders use the strategies and deliver the content of a programme in the same way that they were designed to be used. Fidelity is necessary to achieve the same outcomes across particular programmes. In other words, non-formal outdoor education is not inherently good without examining how the programmes are conducted. Not all programmes should be operated in the same manner, but understanding the implications of programme quality is necessary to understand the value of research. All outdoor programmes are not the same, so they may not result in the same outcomes. Therefore, research in outdoor studies should include an evaluation of implementation fidelity if the true effect of the outdoor programmes is to be discerned. This idea is implicit in several of the chapters in this section.

The ethics of research in outdoor studies is interrogated by Ashworth, Maynard and Stuart. They provide an overview of how ethics has been assured based primarily on a biomedical model. Ashworth *et al.* argue that outdoor studies is different, and advocate for what they term aspirational ethics, based on good judgement. This philosophy complements what Attarian and Brown *et al.* suggested about assuring the competence of leaders. Bialeschki *et al.* also articulated the ethical problems of doing research in camps when it is considered intrusive. Richards provides useful observations about ethical frameworks for doing adventure therapy as well as researching it.

In addition to these issues, new opportunities associated with research are discussed. McCulloch noted that the research about the impact of sail training is just now emerging since research was rarely undertaken until the 21st century. Forest Schools also are a relatively new phenomenon but offer opportunities for research that might examine issues related to sense of place in the outdoors, as well as brain development.

Sustainability

The actual terminology of sustainability seldom occurs in the chapters in this section. It seems to us, however, that sustainability is central to the future of outdoor studies. We are defining sustainability to include environmental, social and economic aspects. Sustainability is frequently associated with the physical environment and certainly if abundant nature no longer exists, outdoor studies would not be possible. However, the social sustainability as well as the economic sustainability of outdoor studies have implications for non-formal education. For example, one aspect of outdoor studies discussed relative to research relates to the transferability of experiences described by Sibthorp and Richmond. This notion complements the idea of social sustainability. Doing research ethically is also about social sustainability. Regardless of how non-formal education might be privatised or not, economic sustainability is inherent in all these organisations.

Chick (2013) described sustainability in various contexts, which can include outdoor studies, and advocated that sustainability 'refers to the maintenance over time of the joy of living and hope for the future' (p. 211). This maintenance, or sustainability, is implicit in all the chapters in this non-formal section.

Summary

This part of the Handbook, about non-formal outdoor studies, provides an overview of common issues and the delivery systems that are being used. Many more examples of non-formal organisations could have been included. One example could have been how organisations like Outward Bound have provided the catalyst for many of the programmes that grew in the latter half of the 20th century. Some of these organisations emulated Outward Bound while others used their non-formal programmes for other clear alternatives.

The six themes reflected by the chapters in this section provide some coherence for the concerns that authors have highlighted. The themes are not mutually exclusive but do provide a framework to guide the reader through this broader topic of non-formal education and training. As noted earlier, overlap exists with other chapters in this Handbook since isolating non-formal education is not possible. Nevertheless, these opportunities have provided numerous experiences for many children and adults, and offer great prospects for the future.

Karla A. Henderson

References

Chawla, L. & Cushing, D. (2007). Education for strategic environmental behavior. *Environmental Education Research, 13*, 437–452.

Chick, G. (2013). Leisure in culture. In T. Blackshaw (Ed.) *Routledge Handbook of Leisure Studies* (pp. 202–215). London: Routledge.

Louv, R. (2005). *Last Child in the Woods: Saving Our Children from Nature-deficit Disorder*. Chapel Hill, NC: Algonquin.

UNESCO (2014). *Non-formal Education*. Retrieved from: www.unesco.org/iiep/PDF/pubs/K16.pdf.

Wolfe, B.D. & Samdahl, D.M. (2005). Challenging assumptions: Examining fundamental beliefs that shape challenge course programming and research. *Journal of Experiential Education, 28*(1), 25–43.

15

Careers in the outdoors

Linda Allin

NORTHUMBRIA UNIVERSITY

Amanda West

UNIVERSITY OF SUNDERLAND

The notion of career has become increasingly prominent in the outdoor literature, along with references to the outdoor profession (Humberstone & Brown, 2006) and the outdoor industry (Barnes, 1999; Humberstone, 2000). Yet outdoor careers are complex and hard to define. In this chapter we recognise the common association of career with work and working lives (Arthur, Hall & Lawrence, 1989). We also highlight that while popular views of working in the outdoors focus on the provision of adventure activities, the field of outdoor employment is broader and not easily harnessed into a coherent sector. An exhibition on outdoor careers in the UK (www.careersinthe-outdoors.co.uk/exhibitors.html) included representatives from adventure travel companies, outdoor activity centres, youth development charities, expedition organisers, field study centres and outdoor equipment manufacturers. To provide a delimitation and to exclude areas of the outdoors such as agriculture or fishing, we have drawn on Martin's (2001) mapping of the outdoor field and Humberstone's (2000) definition of the outdoor industry, which includes working in the outdoors to deliver adventure recreation, education, leisure, youth work, management training or therapy.

The literature on careers in the outdoor industry is fragmented and lacks a coherent theoretical underpinning. There are small pockets of research on outdoor practitioners or outdoor graduate careers (e.g. Barnes, 1999; Prince, 2005; Stott, Zaitseva & Cui, 2014), including a body of outdoor research that has explored women's outdoor leadership and outdoor education careers, and highlighted how such careers are gendered (e.g. Loeffler, 1995; Allin, 2003; Jones, 2012). However, relatively little is known about careers in the outdoor industry for either women or men. To find a way forward, we bring together the literature that exists and situate some of the key issues within contemporary career theories. We critically examine the extent to which the notion of the *boundaryless career*, prominent in the career literature, can be used as a preliminary framework to examine careers in the outdoor industry, and provide areas for the industry to consider regarding policy and practice.

Careers and the outdoor industry

A broad perspective of career is that it involves the unfolding sequence of a person's work experiences over time (Arthur *et al.*, 1989). The dimension of time is important to the concept of

159

career, and distinguishes it from the notion of a job or occupation. Careers also have objective and subjective dimensions. The objective face is about defined routes or career paths, whereas the subjective face of career refers to how an individual sees his/her career, or makes career choices or actions. The objective and subjective aspects of careers intertwine since personal decisions may influence or be influenced by career structures, or vice versa. This inseparability of objective and subjective career is highlighted in the work of Everett Hughes and the Chicago school of sociologists, who adopted a life histories approach to understanding careers in different life arenas (cited in Barley, 1989). This approach has been taken by authors such as Allin (2003) and, more recently, by Lorimer and Holland-Smith (2012), and can illuminate the complex lives of people working in the outdoor industry. For analytical purposes, however, we begin by critically examining the outdoor industry in terms of the traditional, objective notion of career.

The traditional understanding of a career is that of linear progressive steps and advancement through a series of jobs (Arthur et al., 1989), where success is marked by increasing pay, rank and/ or seniority, and development usually within a single organisation. This career model is most clearly seen in development paths through outdoor leadership, where leadership awards (in the UK) progress from levels 1–5, or in outdoor centres where an instructor may move to senior instructor and then to a senior management role. Traditional organisational careers can also be evident for outdoor workers in a university or school-based structure. Outside of these contexts, linear career pathways in the outdoors are not easy to see. Even within outdoor centres or leadership careers, opportunities are often limited and outdoor careers are characterised by periods of voluntary or part-time working, limited ongoing professional development and low levels of pay (Barnes, 1999; Skills Active, 2010). Prince (2005) also showed that, although two-thirds of graduates sampled from an outdoor studies degree were employed in careers related to outdoor studies, there was no trend towards graduate employment over time. Skills Active in the UK indicated that, despite the unstructured nature of careers in the outdoor industry, employment opportunities are numerous. They estimated that between 26,400 and 50,000 people are self-employed, freelance or in permanent positions as outdoor activities instructors in the UK, and that instructors typically work for small businesses, with more than half of all organisations having fewer than twenty employees. Research about therapeutic wilderness instructors in the USA found a high turnover of staff, with the mean length of employment just 11.85 months (Marchand, Russell & Cross, 2009). A similar finding was supported regarding outdoor staff in the UK by Barnes (2003). While there are some opportunities for hierarchical development, the typical outdoor career does not seem to fit the traditional career model.

The boundaryless career and the outdoor industry

The boundaryless career arose as a way to understand careers in a changing society. Increasing uncertainty and unpredictability has left employees facing involuntary job loss, career interruptions, and lateral job movements both across and within sectors. The boundaryless career is not restricted by development within an organisation, but is characterised by a series of employment opportunities across jobs and organisations (Goffee & Jones, 2000; Peiperl, Arthur & Anand, 2002). Less significance is attached to organisational structures and more to an individual's perceived marketability. A further feature is a focus on individual goals and psychological measures of success rather than organisational goals. Individuals navigate their careers against their personal priorities. The boundaryless career reflects a break not only with traditional assumptions about careers but also about career success.

DeFillippi and Arthur (1996) contended that boundaryless careers involve developing career competencies that can be applied by individuals in relation to shifting job opportunities.

DeFillippi and Arthur argued that these career competencies reflect three different ways of knowing: knowing why (i.e. an individual's motivations and identity); knowing how (i.e. a person's skills and expertise); and knowing whom (i.e. relationships and reputation). These ideas seem intuitively appealing in understanding careers in the outdoor industry, and provide fresh opportunities for researching the type of careers that arguably have existed in the outdoors for many years. In the following sections, we use the three elements of knowing why, knowing how and knowing whom to critically examine what is already known in outdoor career research, and suggest further avenues that can both aid theoretical development and afford practical implications for the outdoor industry.

Knowing why: personal goals and motives in outdoor careers

The career competency of knowing why focuses on personal 'motivational energy to understand oneself' (Eby, Butts & Lockwood, 2003, p. 691), consideration of alternatives, and a separation of the individual's identity from her/his employer. Personal values and motives become more salient than organisational goals, such as when individuals may decide against a new job or promotion because of different personal values compared to the organisation, or because of their personal lives (Arthur & Rousseau, 1996). Career success is not necessarily viewed in terms of salary or occupational seniority.

This aspect of the boundaryless career resonates with outdoor careers because of claims by authors such as Barnes (1999), who argued that working in the outdoors is more akin to a lifestyle or identity choice than a career. Barnes' (2003) article proposed that outdoor practitioners were not necessarily motivated by traditional career success. This finding was supported by Prince (2005) since those individuals in her study rated personal motives, values and satisfaction above salary and as key elements of importance in their careers. Stott et al. (2014) also explored the career identities of students undertaking an outdoor education degree in the UK. They found that outdoor education students had a strong sense of identity and remained committed to working in outdoor education with money a less important factor.

Research also suggests that outdoor practitioners take steps to adapt their careers to help maintain personal and social relationships. These steps include changing the activity instructed (Lorimer & Holland-Smith, 2012), securing teaching or lecturing positions (McDermott & Munir, 2012), or making changes to work patterns to accommodate family commitments (Lorimer & Holland-Smith, 2012). Boundaries between home and work are also crossed in outdoor careers. Lorimer and Holland-Smith's case study analysis of a male adventure coach revealed a melding of personal interest and career aspirations. Instructing facilitated the adventure coach's personal involvement in outdoor activities even if his achievement goals had to be subsumed to those of his clients. McDermott and Munir (2012) also found through interviews with twenty mountain guides that, when not working, they reported that rather than rest they chose to participate in outdoor activities for personal enjoyment.

The boundaryless career, however, pays insufficient attention to the role of gender. Enache, Sallan, Simo and Fernandez (2011) and Valcour and Tolbert (2003) suggested that, while women follow a boundaryless career path, men's careers reflect a more traditional career trajectory. The reason is that women are more likely to embrace a boundaryless career through taking flexible or part-time work. While Sullivan and Mainiero (2007) supported this conclusion, they suggested women actually experienced less physical mobility across organisations due to family or relationship commitments, but more psychological mobility by being able to base their self-identity on multiple roles and not just work. While the extent to which this explanation applies in the outdoors has not been explored, women leaders have highlighted how childcare responsibilities influenced their career pathways as outdoor instructors. Motherhood was a key transition point in their careers (Allin, 2003; Jones 2012). Women also cited how these career decisions were made in response to lack of facilities or support from outdoor organisations.

Although knowing why offers the opportunity for individuals to redefine success in personal or family terms, the extent to which this redefinition is freely done as a way to maintain self-identity is unclear. Allin (2003), for example, found that while some women outdoor educators were able to find career success in multiple roles, women who retained traditional notions of career success felt they had a *failed outdoor career*. Knowing why provides a way to legitimise different career choices as lifestyle choice, but more research into how both women and men in the outdoor industry define and value career success is needed, particularly as their identities shift and change across the lifespan.

The boundaryless outdoor career also ignores potential negative and disruptive elements associated with outdoor careers. The overlap of participation and employment in outdoor activities has consequences for instructors' physical and emotional wellbeing alongside their personal and social relationships (Thomas, 2001). McDermott and Munir (2012) noted from their research that some instructors' intense commitment to an outdoor life and career led to injuries, which as self-employed or freelance workers forced them to remain at work for their financial security and to create a good impression for potential employers. Older instructors in particular reported chronic overuse injuries to their joints. Instructors' commitment to their careers also meant that some reported spending long periods of time away from home on expeditions, which posed difficulties in both developing and maintaining relationships (Marchand *et al.*, 2009; Lorimer & Holland-Smith, 2012).

Taken together, the physical, emotional and social challenges of working may lead to premature disengagement from an outdoor career. A boundaryless career might offer the prospect of a self-identity that melds personal and professional, but Lorimer and Holland-Smith (2012) suggested that an outdoor life that is all-encompassing could lead to a narrower sense of both social and self-identity. The home–work boundary in outdoor careers is an area for outdoor industry leaders to consider in terms of their policies and practices (Warren & Loeffler, 2006).

Knowing how: competencies and marketability

For knowing how, the questions about the core skills and competencies of an outdoor practitioner and how these are developed remain important to understanding careers in the outdoor industry. Priest and Gass (1997) identified twelve competencies of an outdoor leader: technical skills, safety skills, environmental skills, organisational skills, instructional skills, facilitation skills, flexible leadership style, experience based judgement, problem solving, decision making, communication skills and professional ethics. However, Swiderski (1987) suggested that outdoor leadership training programmes have paid insufficient attention to human relations skills, problem solving, decision making, judgement and critical thinking. An emphasis on health and safety in outdoor adventure certainly has meant a focus on technical qualifications (Barnes, 1999). Some evidence within the outdoor literature has suggested that researchers are highlighting the importance of outdoor practitioners developing interpersonal skills and generic transferable skills, particularly within higher education outdoor study degrees (Prince, 2005). Shooter, Paisley and Sibthorp (2012) have also highlighted how interpersonal ability, benevolence and integrity, as well as technical skills, are related to the development of participant trust in outdoor leaders. However, research indicates that technical skills remain valued most highly both by outdoor employers and graduates, at least in the UK. Prince (2005) showed that 41 per cent of graduates in her study highlighted a lack of national governing body qualifications and experience as a problem in obtaining relevant outdoor employment.

Research examining skills and competencies required for outdoor careers has been divided into what has been termed *hard* (i.e. technical) skills and *soft* (i.e. interpersonal and related) skills. This distinction has become imbued with binary notions of gender and gender-related skills, with women being aligned with interpersonal skills and men with physical and technical skills on the basis of hegemonic forms of notions of masculinity and femininity (Humberstone, 2000). Warren and Loeffler (2006) suggested that privileging technical skills in outdoor programmes is detrimental to women's career development as they typically have fewer opportunities to develop such skills due to gender socialisation, or had less confidence in their abilities. Other evidence in the outdoor career research has supported this claim. Sharp (2001), for example, observed that male outdoor instructors reported higher levels of confidence about their technical ability than female instructors and attached greater value to technical ability than more interpersonal skills. Many female outdoor researchers have similarly focused on the area of women's physicality and physical competence as a key issue for women working in a traditionally male outdoor culture (Allin, 2000; Lugg, 2003; Jones, 2012). All of these researchers found that women often felt they needed to *prove* their physical and technical competence to be accepted in the outdoor field.

Warren and Loeffler (2006) suggested that the gender division in skills competency is misrepresentative. Rather, a mix-match exists between actual and perceived competency for both men and women. They proposed that men overestimate, while women tend to underestimate, their technical skill competency. They noted that women may need help to reclaim competency and to develop their potential. Moreover, as Warren and Loeffler (2006) and Dalla-Longa (2013) have highlighted, interpersonal skills should not be seen as the domain of women alone, just as physical competency and technical skills are not the domain of men. A growing body of research on women's physicalities (e.g. McDermott, 1996; Dilley, 2007) highlights how women can find empowerment through adventurous and physical activities. These researchers articulated how the multidimensional nature of physicality allows for other forms beyond that of physical competence.

We propose that the binary distinction between physical/technical and interpersonal skills needs to continue to be challenged in the workplace, with recognition of the equal value of different skills and skill sets in the outdoors. While not easy to achieve, Humberstone (2000) noted alternative cultures in outdoor education fields, which may provide scope for challenging existing hegemonies. We suggest researchers need to go beyond outdoor leadership adventure or education contexts, and seek to explore wilderness therapy and environmental contexts, which may value different competencies more highly. More research is also needed to examine both what are recognised as outdoor career competencies across different cultural contexts of the outdoor industry, and how such competencies are developed and experienced across gender, social class and ethnicity. More practical work is needed by organisations and outdoor practitioners to challenge gender stereotypes associated with physicality and technical competence.

Knowing whom: reputation

The development of professional networks and relationships is viewed as important in the boundaryless career to facilitate individuals' movement across or through job opportunities. Such networks operate as *social capital* (Bourdieu, 2003), which can facilitate further career opportunities. Professional networks include both internal communities and networks outside of the organisation. However, the ability to forge professional networks is also influenced by structures such as gender and ethnicity. Loeffler (1995), for example, found that female leaders in North America reported difficulties accessing the informal networks that can be helpful in securing employment.

Mentoring is particularly valuable in the boundaryless career for providing support, development and visibility. The full value and extent of mentoring in outdoor careers is unknown, but appears significant. Berns (2008) indicated that, without effective mentorship, many outdoor workers in their early career may develop low career self-efficacy and seek employment elsewhere. The women in Loeffler's (1995) study also identified the value of social support, as well as professional and mentoring networks, as ways to help facilitate the career development of women outdoors. Some of these networks were established with other women and were used to identify career options and opportunities for professional development. Allin and Humberstone (2006) noted that some women outdoor educators applied for jobs because they were encouraged by significant others (often male). However, feminist researchers such as McKeen and Burke (1989) have criticised the formal male mentor–female protégé relationship in organisations for potentially reinforcing patriarchal structure.

Networks in the boundaryless career do not refer only to formal mentors, bosses or senior staff who can facilitate job opportunities. Arthur, Khapova and Wilderom (2005) highlighted the significance of peer and community relationships based on mutual or overlapping interests (i.e. communities of practice; Lave & Wenger, 1991), which can also help individuals develop a sense of meaning in their careers or career success. Parker, Arthur and Inkson (2004) called these *career communities* and proposed that they arise from both within and outside the workplace and from attachments developed through involvement in such activities as voluntary societies, leisure groups, occupation, industries or projects. They may also arise through shared family, ethnic, gender or social identities, and can be a resource for learning as well as career enhancement. This notion of career communities also seems pertinent to boundaryless careers in the outdoor industry given the emphasis in the outdoors of a *like-minded community* (Barnes, 2000). It also resonates with outdoor careers where individuals may be involved with outdoor activities in their personal lives, and are likely to socialise and develop relationships with other outdoor enthusiasts. The extent to which outdoor practitioners develop or affirm their career identities and directions through these communities is worthy of further research. The nature and values of these communities are also worth investigation, as are the types of career identities they support. Researchers need to pay attention to the way in which communities and organisational cultures are supportive and inclusive regarding different gender, ethnic and sexual identities (Barnfield & Humberstone, 2008).

Theoretical developments and further thoughts

In this chapter we have used the concept of the boundaryless career as a preliminary framework to critically reflect on and examine current knowledge of careers in the outdoor industry. We have sought to identify where research is limited and where approaches are flawed, to provide some direction for the future. We have suggested that the notion of career competencies resonates with areas we intuitively consider pertinent about careers in the outdoor industry, including: the focus on personal motives and career success, the centrality of skills and competence, the value of social networks and the existence of communities of practice. In a review of the boundaryless career, Brocklehurst (2003) added *knowing where* – a sense of place – as an additional career competency that individuals may apply in considering job opportunities. This idea echoes the stories of outdoor educators' careers, where some of the women interviewed by Allin (2003) indicated that they remained in a particular job due to their love of the natural environment where they were able to live and work. This finding remains largely unexplored in outdoor career research.

We also recognise that the concept of the boundaryless career has been criticised as needing greater clarity, conceptualisation and measurement (Sullivan & Baruch, 2009). The concept is often presented as gender neutral with a lack of attention to power relations within different organisations and organisational cultures. We have highlighted these areas in each section and there may be avenues where critical perspectives may be applied in the future. We also are aware that even the notion of boundarylessness needs to be treated with care, as it gives a false sense of the individual as having freedom to negotiate their career free from cultural or structural dimensions. We feel that research that draws on the interdependence of objective and subjective careers, the intertwining of structure and action, and the recognition of how individual identities are structured and negotiated within different outdoor industry cultural contexts that involve power relations will give the greatest understanding of outdoor careers. We also reiterate Humberstone's (2009) proposal that outdoor career research needs to draw from broader career theory and sociological perspectives to engage more critically and theoretically with the key concepts and issues raised.

References

Allin, L. (2000). Women into outdoor education: Negotiating a male-gendered space – issues of physicality. In B. Humberstone (Ed.) *Her Outdoors: Risk, Challenge and Adventure in Gendered Open Spaces* (pp. 51–68). Eastbourne, UK: Leisure Studies Association.

Allin, L. (2003). Challenging careers for women? Developing career identities in outdoor education. Unpublished PhD thesis, Brunel University

Allin, L. & Humberstone, B. (2006). Exploring careership in outdoor education and the lives of women outdoor educators. *Journal of Sport, Education and Society, 11,* 135–153.

Arthur, M.B., Hall, D.T. & Lawrence, B.S. (1989). *Handbook of Career Theory*. Cambridge, UK: Cambridge University Press.

Arthur, M.B. & Rousseau, D.M. (1996). *The Boundaryless Career: A New Employment Principle for a New Organisational Era*. Oxford, UK: Oxford University Press.

Arthur, M.B., Khapova, S.N. & Wilderom, C.P.M. (2005). Career success in a boundaryless career world. *Journal of Organizational Behavior, 26,* 177–202.

Barley, R. (1989). Careers, identities, and institutions: The legacy of the Chicago School of Sociology. In M. B. Arthur, D.T. Hall & B.S. Lawrence (Eds.) *Handbook of Career Theory* (pp. 41–65). Cambridge, UK: Cambridge University Press.

Barnes, P. (1999). Motivations of staff in the outdoor industry. Unpublished PhD thesis, University of Strathclyde, Glasgow, UK.

Barnes, P. (2003). Outdoor leaders as cultural phenomena. In B. Humberstone, H. Brown & K. Richards (Eds.) *Whose Journeys: The Outdoors and Adventure as Social and Cultural Phenomena. Critical Exploration of Relations Between Individuals, 'Others' and the Environment* (pp. 241–252). Penrith, Cumbria, UK: Institute for Outdoor Learning.

Barnfield, D. & Humberstone, B. (2008). Speaking out: Perspectives of gay and lesbian practitioners in outdoor education in the UK. *Journal of Adventure Education and Outdoor Leadership, 8,* 31–42.

Berns, G.N. (2008). Perception is reality? Examining the effect of mentorship of career self-efficacy in outdoor recreation. *Journal of the Wilderness Education Association, 20,* 17–20.

Bourdieu, P. (2003). *Distinction: A Social Critique of the Judgement of Taste* (original work published 1984). London: Routledge.

Brocklehurst, M. (2003). Self and place: A critique of the boundaryless career. Paper presented to the Critical Management Studies Conference, University of Lancaster, UK, July.

Dalla-Longa, A. (2013). Women's engagement with outdoor education: A site of cultural struggle. *The Student Researcher, 2,* 39–48.

DeFillippi, R.J. & Arthur, M.B. (1996). Boundaryless contexts and careers: A competency-based perspective. In M.B. Arthur & D.M. Rousseau (Eds.) *The Boundaryless Career. A New Employment Principle for a New Organizational Era* (pp. 116–131). New York: Oxford University Press.

Dilley, R. (2007). Women's climbing physicalities: Bodies, experience and representation. *Special Issue of Sheffield Online Papers in Social Research, Gender and Extreme Sports: The Case of Climbing, August*(10). Retrieved from www.sheffield.ac.uk/socstudies/shop/10.

Eby, L.T., Butts, M. & Lockwood, A. (2003). Predictors of success in the era of the boundaryless career. *Journal of Organizational Behavior, 24,* 689–708.

Enache, M., Sallan, J.M., Simo, P. & Fernandez, V. (2011). Career attitudes and subjective career success: Tackling gender differences. *Gender in Management: An International Journal, 26,* 196–199.

Goffee, R. & Jones, G. (2000). Career, community and social architecture: An exploration of concepts. In M.A. Periperl, M.B. Arthur, R. Goffee & T. Morris (Eds.) *Career Frontiers: New Conceptions of Working Lives* (pp. 24–53). Oxford, UK: Oxford University Press.

Humberstone, B. (2000). The 'outdoor industry' as social and educational phenomena: Gender and outdoor adventure/education. *Journal of Adventure Education and Outdoor Learning, 1,* 21–35.

Humberstone, B. (2009). In splendid isolation – is the field missing something? Research in outdoor sports and outdoor education: Principles into practice. In I. Turcova & A. Martin (Eds.) *Outdoor Activities in Educational and Recreational Programmes* (pp. 40–49). Prague, Czech Republic: Charles University.

Humberstone, B. & Brown, H. (2006). *Shaping the Outdoor Profession Through Higher Education: Creative Diversity in Outdoor Studies Courses in Higher Education in the UK.* Penrith, Cumbria, UK: Institute for Outdoor Learning.

Jones, A. (2012). Women's experiences of the gendered environment of outdoor education in Aoteara, New Zealand – 'I felt a need to prove my right to be there'. Unpublished MA thesis, Massey University, New Zealand.

Lave, J. & Wenger, E. (1991). *Situated Learning: Legitimate Peripheral Participation.* Cambridge, UK: Cambridge University Press.

Loeffler, T.A. (1995). Factors influencing women's career development in outdoor leadership. Unpublished doctoral dissertation, University of Minnesota, Minneapolis, USA.

Lorimer, R. & Holland-Smith, D. (2012). Why coach? A case study of the prominent influences on a top-level UK outdoor adventure coach. *The Sport Psychologist, 26,* 571–583.

Lugg, A. (2003). Women's experience of outdoor education: Still trying to be 'one of the boys'? In B. Humberstone, H. Brown & K. Richards (Eds.) *Whose Journeys: The Outdoors and Adventure as Social and Cultural Phenomena. Critical Exploration of Relations Between Individuals, 'Others' and the Environment* (pp. 33–48). Penrith, Cumbria, UK: Institute for Outdoor Learning.

Marchand, G., Russell, K.C. & Cross, R. (2009). An empirical examination of outdoor behavioral health-care field instructor job-related stress and retention. *Journal of Experiential Education, 31,* 359–375.

Martin, P. (2001). Key issues in the industry: towards the summit. Paper presented at the 12th National Outdoor Education Conference (Education Outdoors: Our Sense of Place) Bendigo, Victoria, Australia, January.

McDermott, H. & Munir, F. (2012). Work-related injury and ill-health among mountain instructors in the UK. *Safety Science, 50,* 1104–1111.

McDermott, L. (1996). Toward a feminist understanding of physicality within the context of women's physically active and sporting lives. *Sociology of Sport Journal, 13,* 12–30.

McKeen, C.A. & Burke, R.J. (1989). Mentor relationships in organisations: Issues, strategies and prospects for women. *Journal of Management Development, 8* (6), 33–42.

Parker, P., Arthur, M.B. & Inkson, K. (2004). Career communities: A preliminary exploration of member-defined career support structures. *Journal of Organisational Behaviour, 25,* 489–514

Peiperl, M.A., Arthur, M.B. & Anand, N. (2002). *Career Creativity: Explorations in the Remaking of Work.* Oxford, UK: Oxford University Press.

Priest, S. & Gass, M. (1997). *Effective Leadership in Adventure Programming.* Champaign, IL: Human Kinetics.

Prince, H. (2005). Graduate pathways: a longitudinal study of graduate in outdoor studies in the UK. *Journal of Adventure Education and Outdoor Learning, 5*(1), 21–34.

Sharp, B. (2001). Take me to your (male) leader. *Gender and Education, 13,* 75–86.

Shooter, W., Paisley, K. & Sibthorp, J. (2012). Fostering trust in outdoor leaders: The role of personal attributes. *Journal of Experiential Education, 35,* 222–237.

Skills Active (2010). *The Outdoors Survey 2009.* London: Skills Active.

Stott, T., Zaitseva, E. & Cui, V. (2014). Stepping back to move forward? Exploring outdoor education students' fresher and graduate identities and their impact on employment destinations. *Studies in Higher Education, 39,* 711–733.

Sullivan, S.E. & Baruch, Y. (2009). Advances in career theory and research: A critical review and agenda for future exploration. *Journal of Management, 3,* 1542–1571.

Sullivan, S.E. & Mainiero, L. (2007). The changing nature of gender roles, alpha/beta careers and work–life issues: Theory-driven implications for human resource management. *Career Development International, 12,* 238–263.

Swiderski, M. (1987). Soft and conceptual skills: The often overlooked components of outdoor leadership. *The Bradford Papers Annual, 2,* 29–36. Bradford Woods Outdoor Education Center: Indiana University.

Thomas, G. (2001). Thriving in the outdoor education profession: learning from Australian practitioners. *Australian Journal of Outdoor Education, 6,* 13–24.

Valcour, P.M. & Tolbert, P.S. (2003). Gender, family and career in the era of boundarylessness: Determinants and effects of intra- and inter-organizational mobility. *International Journal of Human Resource Management, 14,* 768–787.

Warren, K. & Loeffler, T.A. (2006). Factors influencing women's technical skill development in outdoor adventure. *Journal of Adventure Education and Outdoor Learning, 6,* 107–120.

16

Beyond training for tolerance in outdoor experiential education

More than just leadership

Mary Breunig

BROCK UNIVERSITY

Elyse Rylander

PRESCOTT COLLEGE

I (Mary) recently attended a Wilderness First Responder Recertification course set in a winter environment replete with participants heavily clad in winter gear, ranging in age from their early twenties to late fifties. These courses provide one venue for acquiring and updating wilderness medical knowledge, and train wilderness guides and instructors in managing risk and medical issues in a backcountry setting. The courses are theory and scenario-based, including numerous simulations. During the debrief of one first aid scenario, the instructor asked for help in recalling if the patient was a woman and a male student responded, 'Well, that's debatable!' While everyone except a few of us laughed, the instructor meekly whispered 'Hey now' in response. Further into the course, I found myself *treating* a female patient who reluctantly announced 'birth control' when I inquired about any medications that she was assigned to say she was taking. I later asked this woman, who was a lesbian and in her mid-twenties, about how she felt about being assigned a birth control medication by the course instructor. I was curious about her response to the first scenario and she simply shrugged her shoulders, stating, 'I guess I am just used to it.' Later that day, I heard a student advise another course participant who was complaining about the cold, 'Geez, buddy, man up!' I left the course wondering if these comments occurred because of the less formal environment. I imagined that in a formal school, such instances would not go unaddressed.

In light of these and other similar experiences in non-formal outdoor educational environments and our own philosophical leanings, which centre on the belief that all outdoor experiential education should be *just* and non-oppressive, we explore learning and leadership in non-formal educational environments with a focus on outdoor experiential education (OEE) and social justice competency, encouraging outdoor leaders to go beyond educating for tolerance, engaging in more than just leadership.

Background

More than twenty years ago, Freire (1987) proposed that the purpose of any educational system is to make bold possibilities happen for students, and that public education has a duty to end oppression. Alongside that bold claim and during that same era, Goodale (1991) suggested, however, that traditional classroom-based education is limited in its ability to impact youth to become socially responsible. With traditional models of education often focused on knowledge transmission, non-formal educational settings such as OEE provide alternative models of education. Non-formal education embeds learning content in activities across an array of settings, providing wide latitude for self-direction and interpretation on the part of learners (Seaman, Beightol, Shirilla & Crawford, 2009).

Also more than twenty years ago, Ewert and Hollenhorst (1989) asserted that one specific non-formal educational setting, the wilderness, provides a site for young people to crystallise selfhood through personal testing, allows for exploration of life meaning and perspective, confers awareness of one's own mortality, and improves fear-coping mechanisms. During that same era, masculine subtexts of wilderness unproblematically invoked liberal notions of adventure that tended to encourage rugged individualism and efface difference (Warren, 1985; Beale, 1988; James, 1988). Historically, Outward Bound (OB), the National Outdoor Leadership School (NOLS) and other wilderness programmes were seen as programmes that would make men out of boys (Marsh & Richards, 1989; Petzoldt, 2000).

Considering the present-day assessment of socially just practices in traditional, classroom-based educational environments compared with non-formal OEE organisations and activities (e.g. Sierra Club trips, OB, service-learning experiences) is important. The advances, deficits and increased focus on social justice competency are worthy of examination.

Although social justice has numerous definitions, we define it as the process of striving for equity for oppressed groups and individuals. Greene's (1998) definition of social justice pedagogy resonates as she asserts that teaching it arouses 'vivid, reflective, experiential responses' that move students to seriously engage questions of justice and to take ameliorative action in the world around them (p. xxix). We believe in approaching social justice with an acknowledgement of inequities and oppression, and then with a provocation to query, 'What now shall I do?' Formal educational settings provide some justification for this approach.

Social justice in formal educational settings

Much of the social justice literature related to traditional, classroom-based settings maintains a focus on democratic citizenship (Hytten, 2013; Ladson-Billings, 2013), resonant with Dewey's (1938) progressive ideals emphasising education as the means to a just citizenry. Hytten maintains that one of the most important roles of education is to teach the habits, dispositions, attitudes and behaviours necessary for democratic citizenship, emphasising that openness, tolerance, respect, humility, moral commitment, concern for the common good and other social justice goals are automatically intertwined with democracy. One non-formal OEE organisation, the National Outdoor Leadership School (NOLS, 2014), aims to be the leading source of wilderness skills and leadership, and explores social justice ideals through a continuum of social relationships (see Figure 16.1).

Tolerance and respect lie in the middle of this continuum, identified as neutral dispositions and behaviours. However, these attitudes alone do not represent pro-social goals. Tolerance may be requisite but is also insufficient to any democratic or justice-oriented endeavour, which draws into question Hytten's (2013) claim that tolerance and respect are core pro-democratic behaviours. Increasingly, some school educators are critical of directly aligning social justice

Mary Breunig and Elyse Rylander

A Continuum Of Social Relationships Among Human Groups

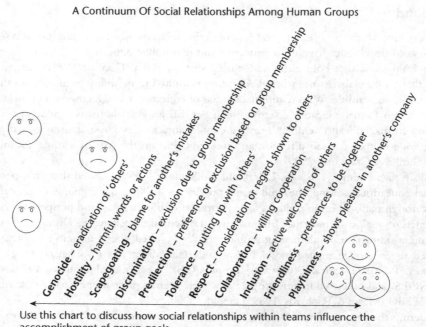

Use this chart to discuss how social relationships within teams influence the accomplishment of group goals.

Prejudice is an attitude based on group membership: where does that begin on this chart? Where does the chart begin to describe prosocial behavior, or what we call *good expedition behavior*?

Figure 16.1 A continuum of social relationships among human groups

Source: Reprinted with permission from Aparna Rajagopal-Durbin, NOLS

with democracy, suggesting that it is too strongly tied with Eurocentric assumptions and dominant culture and ruling class imperatives (Richardson & Villenas, 2000). Thus, the focus on education as preparation for democratic citizenry needs to be problematised.

Ladson-Billings (2013), a pedagogical theorist and teacher educator, impels educators to consider social justice pedagogy for new century children. These new century students have a deep connection to hip-hop culture, receive their news from the *Daily Show*, and tweet and instant message, viewing email as antiquated. They are 'shape-shifters' (p. 108), according to Ladson-Billings. They do not fit neatly into the rigid categories of race, class, gender, sexuality or national origin that have been used to make distinctions and create hierarchy, and as comparators (i.e. more privileged/less privileged). Today's youth are invested in social justice in a manner that previous generations have not been. Thus, social justice curricula must be culturally relevant and embedded in a living/emerging curriculum (Ladson-Billings, 2013; Tilley & Taylor, 2013).

Curricula that mirror students' lives are essential (Chubbuck, 2010). They may begin with ensuring that books portray racial, gender and economic diversity similar to the characteristics of the students in the classroom. When the classroom materials hold relevance to learners' lives, reading comprehension, writing quality and vocabulary all improve, particularly with students deemed 'at risk' (Schaedel & Lazarowitz, 2005/2006). Select texts, posters and other classroom materials provide platforms to stimulate dialogue among students, leading to classroom

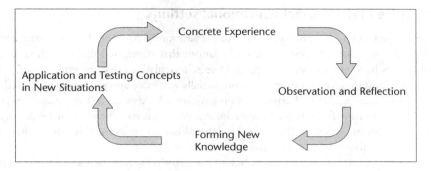

Figure 16.2 The experiential learning cycle

Source: Reprinted with permission from Lee, Williams, Shaw and Jie (2014)

conversations about issues of diversity, while promoting increased awareness among classroom participants.

Using a variety of pedagogical approaches can also lead to increased diversity awareness. Teachers who employ culturally relevant approaches to pedagogy experience increases in students' language skill development and see improvement in students' ability to critically analyse social power relations and enhance their cross-cultural awareness (Lopez, 2011). One study exploring students' experiences with a project-based human rights curriculum from two urban high schools identified that culturally relevant course content was directly linked to their lives. Students reported that the course provided 'meaningful opportunities to learn English while developing skills to articulate their struggles with racism, discrimination, gender issues, and immigration' (Schiller, 2013, p. ii). 'The ultimate outcome was an increase in critical consciousness, an awareness of systemic cultural issues, and a deeper connection to the individual and collective experience' (2013, p. 87).

Well-selected and well-facilitated participative exercises, case studies, guest lectures, games, role plays or simulations, poetry or creative writing, films and texts featuring various cultures, connections with others via social media sites or other online tools, and other experiential activities, can provide opportunities for students to increase awareness about themselves and people who are different from them (Bedini & Stone, 2008; Barrett, Byram, Lázár, Mompoint-Gaillard & Philippou, 2013). Lee, Williams, Shaw and Jie (2014) suggested that structuring classroom-based experiential activities using Kolb's (1984) model of experiential learning (see Figure 16.2) is an effective means to develop cultural competency. Reflective writing exercises, role plays, case studies and providing platforms for critical discourse that combine the four aspects of the cycle (i.e. experience, reflection, abstract conceptualisation and active experimentation) can purposefully lead students to further develop cultural awareness and competency.

Purposeful interactions that provide students with opportunities to confront previously held knowledge with complicating human realities is effective for what Lee *et al.* (2014) referred to as intercultural learning. Service-learning is one example. Over the course of the past decade, community service-learning and international field courses, as either elective or requisite components of a degree, have proliferated (Richards *et al.*, 2013). These experiences involve students working in a community-based organisation (i.e. homeless shelter or soup kitchen), a national organisation (i.e. Habitat for Humanity) or serving internationally (i.e. student abroad experiences). As a form of experiential education, demonstrated benefits to these programmes exist, including increases in civic engagement, student achievement, motivation, political attentiveness and activism, and cultural competency (Billig, 2000).

Social justice in non-formal educational settings

Classroom-based environments have integrated community-based and experiential activities and, ironically, non-formal educational organisations that developed many of these activities and approaches have not always kept apace. Despite articulations that the end goal of outdoor experiential education is the creation of a more socially equitable and just world (Association for Experiential Education, 2014; Warren, Roberts, Breunig & Alvarez, 2014), outdoor experiential leaders seem to have fallen behind their educator counterparts. There is equal representation of diverse peoples in schools as there is in society. What accounts for this lack of diversity in many OEE programmes and OEE organisations?

Warren *et al.* (2014) questioned why a lack of participation among people of colour in North America has led to the contested nature of outdoor places for oppressed groups. Johnson and Bowker (2004) identified that the social and collective memory of black people in the USA in relation to the outdoors (e.g. slavery, share cropping, lynching) does not resonate with the predominantly white hegemonic notion that the natural environment serves as a place of refuge. Latinos, likewise, have reported feeling unwelcomed or discriminated against despite many outdoor areas in the USA 'reminding them of their homelands' (Chavez, 2005, p. 32). Native Canadian author Lowan-Trudeau (2013) brought attention to the misappropriation of cultural and spiritual practices (e.g. sweat lodges) in OEE programmes leading to First Nations people feeling demeaned and opting out of participation (Hamilton, 2003). Work remains to create dialogues on how culture impacts people's perception of nature.

The gap, however, is not simply in representation. A curricular gap exists regarding what a culturally responsive OEE curriculum is and what an outdoor leadership training curriculum would include if the OEE profession sought to educate leaders for social justice competency and to have those leadership characteristics be outwardly demonstrated to programme participants and the external world.

Beyond training for diversity and inclusion

From its naissance and into middle age, the field of OEE referred to cross-cultural leadership training as instruction for diversity and inclusion. Many of these training models were structured around a deficit mentality with the base assumption centred around differences between the privileged *haves* compared to those who *have not*, people were more or less advantaged based on such factors as sexuality, skin colour, race, gender, age and ability. The proposed ideal was to train outdoor educators for increased understanding, recognition and tolerance of differences. Going beyond tolerance, however, is needed. Training for diversity/inclusion lacks relevancy in today's society given the constant flux of lived realities that call for a less bifurcated and less reductionist mode of training. Yet, too few programmes have 'moved beyond a basic recognition of the need to be culturally inclusive' (Roberts & Rodriguez, 1999, p. 2) to a critical examination of social justice (Frazer, 2009). Social justice and culture are thus intimately intertwined.

Cultural competency

Culture refers to integrated patterns of human behaviour that include the language, thoughts, communications, actions, customs, beliefs, values and institutions of racial, ethnic, religious or social groups (Kroeber & Kluckhohn, 1952). Competence implies having the capacity to function effectively as an individual or organisation within the context of the cultural beliefs, behaviours and needs presented by people and their communities. Competency-based education

(CBE) is a model that guides the educational process towards acquisition of the knowledge, skills and attitudes needed for effective professional practice (Hatcher *et al.*, 2013). Taken together, culture and competence represent a set of congruent behaviours, attitudes and policies that come together in a system, agency or among professionals, enabling effective work in cross-cultural situations. The term cultural competency originated in the field of health care and has expanded into the realm of education (Diallo & McGrath, 2013). The term cultural competency training is used increasingly with/in the field of adventure and wilderness education (Warren *et al.*, 2014).

As Goodman (2011) asserted, most cultural competency initiatives focus on developing the interpersonal skills needed to understand, work with and serve people from marginalised racial and ethnic groups. There is increasing interest in developing cultural competences related to other marginalised groups (e.g. based on socio-economic class, sexual orientation, gender identity, ability, religion, national origin) to address issues of social inequality. We believe social justice competency provides a more expansive view than cultural competency and this term will be employed in exploring its application in non-formal educational settings.

Social justice competency in non-formal educational settings

Non-formal educational settings and activities are complex, varied and require consideration of: mission/vision, goals, structures, leadership, physical environment, norms establishment, group equipment and individual equipment, as well as physical and emotional risk management. Additionally, many non-formal educational settings are indeterminate ones, involving high levels of uncertainty and unpredictability, which are inherent aspects to any experiential learning endeavour (Andresen, Boud & Cohen, 2000). Developing social justice competency is thus complex because of the unpredictable nature of the indeterminate settings where social justice competency gets enacted (e.g. the wilderness). However, similar to learning how to rock climb and belay (i.e. secure a climber with a rope and braking device), a burgeoning leader does not merely get thrown into a setting without specific technical skill training. Further, this leader should not be cast into that setting without training for social justice competency. The development of social justice competency, however, is not as elemental or as instrumental as learning to belay and checking off acquisition of that skill. It is nuanced, subtle and foundational to the definition of good leadership. We believe all leadership in non-formal environments should be socially just and anti-oppressive.

As is true of the acquisition of any new skill, the first step in developing social justice competency is to critically examine positionality in relation to the concept. Establishing positionality involves developing perspective about ideology, value systems and biases, and how these impact the worldview, leading to greater self-awareness. Goodman (2011) identified several competences relevant to developing self-awareness:

- awareness of social identities and their cultural influences and how they intersect;
- awareness of prejudices, stereotypes and biases; and
- awareness of internalised superiority and internalised inferiority – how people have internalised, often unconsciously, notions of the superiority of dominant/privileged social identity groups (i.e. internalised dominance) and the inferiority of subordinated/marginalised social identity groups (i.e. internalised oppression).

Developing self-awareness competences involves the recognition of privilege. Privilege is a special right, advantage or immunity granted or available to a particular person or group of people. Talking about privilege and oppression is never easy. Newberry (2000) concluded that privilege sometimes has the feeling of pointing fingers, and deflecting a finger coming one's way as a means to negate the discomfort of feelings of privilege is instinctive. The trick, Newberry said, is not to get tangled up in pointing and deflecting, resulting in emotional roadblocks, but for people to move towards taking responsibility for their places in the world. In her article, 'White privilege: Unpacking the invisible knapsack', McIntosh (1990) concluded that privilege is an invisible package of unearned assets that can be used each day – the carrier may be oblivious to some of these assets. Privilege is like an invisible weightless knapsack of special provisions, maps, passports, codebooks, visas, clothes, tools and blank cheques.

As a reader of this book, you may be carrying privileges of which you are unaware. You should not feel guilty about or faulted for this probability, but your consideration about unpacking your own knapsack may be one step towards developing your self-awareness competency.

Developing self-awareness also involves understanding prejudices and biases, and that process often begins with identifying beliefs and values, and how upbringing and current context inform worldviews. Epistemology is the branch of philosophy that studies the nature, sources and validity of knowledge. Epistemology means *ways of knowing*. It seeks to answer such questions as 'What is true?' and 'How do we know?' Epistemology is, therefore, rooted in an understanding of the sources of truth alongside an understanding of the particular lens used for viewing the world and interpreting sources of *truth*.

One sample activity that can assist people in exploring their epistemology is to deliberately engage in a relevant awareness activity (Breunig & Dear, 2013; see Figure 16.3). Draw a circle on a piece of paper. This circle represents an individual's epistemological lens. Then consider as many socially identifying factors as you can (e.g. home environment, family composition, education, religious belief, sexuality, gender expression, peer group, ableism and socio-economic class). Working from the inside of the circle outwards, write personal and specific early influencing factors into the inner lenses (e.g. lower class, farming family) and write present-day life context factors in the outer rings of the circle (e.g. university professor). In other words, write historically from the most inner circle to the outer rim, with recognition that some historically co-occurring events can be bundled into one concentric circle. Consider how this lens informs your view of the world while also considering how unique each individual's lens and worldview is.

This understanding also contributes to *naming* one's bias and privilege. A comprehension of privilege and bias leads to enhanced self-awareness and contributes to understanding the influence of individual positionality on the world stage to exploring broader OEE organisational queries (e.g. 'How can programme participation for economically disadvantaged persons or people with disabilities be improved upon?' or 'How do communities of colour find meaningful and relevant engagement in our programming?').

One common organisational approach to inclusion has been to provide scholarships to underprivileged programme participants. While this monetary support may help with aspects of programme access, it neglects the deeper underlying issues of inaccessibility (e.g. programmes that cater to white able bodies). Simply reducing cost barriers for access to the wilderness is insufficient. Roberts (2013) argued for more systemic organisational change, including: (i) creating and sustaining policies that foster respect and value for all differences; (ii) developing programmes that work to allay exclusion and racially and classist-based isolation; and (iii) enhancing communication between practitioners and academics to better inform policy and programme creation.

Chavez (2008) further specified that programme success relies on practical aspects of service such as: (i) written publications in multiple languages; (ii) examples of diverse clientele in programme brochures; (iii) avoiding assumptions about cultural background based on skin colour;

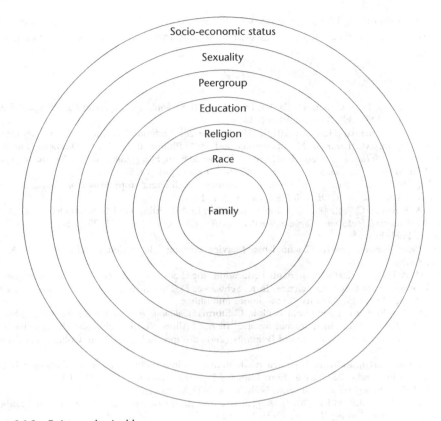

Figure 16.3 Epistemological lens

Source: Reprinted with permission from Breunig and Dear (2013)

(iv) employing people who speak more than one language; and (v) expanding service offerings. These conclusions suggest that the development of organisational cultural competency is equally important to individual cultural competency in OEE.

Increased awareness and direct action are warranted as outdoor experiential educators continue to develop social justice competency. The acquisition of the same skills that the OEE discipline is lauded for (e.g. ethical and professional dispositions, communication skills, relationship orientation and conflict-resolution skills) are also skills needed to promote pluralistic OEE organisations and programmes. These pluralistic organisations and programmes not only provide access to individuals from non-dominant groups but promote the social benefits from full participation and overtly demonstrate a commitment to change. This work needs to happen individually but also on an organisational level by advocating for practices, policies and organisational structures that are responsive to all individuals.

As feminist activist Lorde (2007) asserted, black and 'third world' people are expected to educate white people about difference and being the other. Women are expected to educate men. Lesbians and gay men are expected to educate the heterosexual world. All people need to self-educate and more fully engage in justice-oriented behaviours to effect change. In reflecting on Greene's (1998) claim that social justice arouses vivid, reflective and experiential responses that move students to seriously engage questions of justice and to take ameliorative action in the world around them, we like to imagine what the world could be, or ought to be, were social justice competency woven into OEE as well as in daily interactions and ways of being across all settings.

References

Andresen, L., Boud, D. & Cohen, R. (2000). In G. Foley (Ed.) *Understanding Adult Education and Training* (2nd edn) (pp. 225–239). Sydney: Allen & Unwin.

Association for Experiential Education (2014). *What is Experiential Education?* Retrieved from: www.aee.org.

Barrett, M., Byram, M., Lázár, I., Mompoint-Gaillard, P. & Philippou, S. (2013). *Developing Intercultural Competence through Education* (Council of Europe). Retrieved from: http://hub.coe.int/c/document_library/get_file?uuid=9396761c-aea8-43f3-86a6-c105b45ef756&groupId=10227.

Beale, V. (1988). Men's journeys and women's journeys: A different stop? *Journal of Canadian Outward Bound Wilderness School (COBWS) Education, 4*(1), 7–13.

Bedini, L.A. & Stone, C.F. (2008). Training for diversity. In A.T. Allison & I.E. Schneider (Eds.) *Diversity and the Recreation Profession: Organizational Perspective* (2nd edn) (pp. 261–290). State College, PA: Venture Publishing.

Billig, S. (2000). Research on K–12 school-based service-learning: The evidence builds. *Phi Delta Kappan, 81*, 658–664.

Breunig, M. & Dear, S. (2013). Experiential education, social and environmental justice pedagogies, and globalization: From theory to practice. In K. Schwab & D. Dustin (Eds.) *Just Leisure: Things That We Believe In* (pp. 117–125). Urbana, IL: Sagamore Publishing.

Chavez, D.J. (2005). Latinos and public lands in California. *California Recreation & Parks, 61*(2), 32–35.

Chavez, D.J. (2008). Invite, include, and involve! In A.T. Allison & I.E. Schneider (Eds.) *Diversity and the Recreation Profession: Organizational Perspective* (2nd edn) (pp. 223–232). State College, PA: Venture Publishing.

Chubbuck, S.M. (2010). Individual and structural orientations in socially just teaching: Conceptualization, implementation, and collaborative effort. *Journal of Teacher Education, 61*(3), 197–210.

Dewey, J. (1938). *Experience and Education*. New York, NY: Macmillan.

Diallo, A.F. & McGrath, M.M. (2013). A glance at the future of cultural competency in healthcare. *Newborn and Infant Nursing Reviews, 13*(3), 121–123.

Ewert, A.W. & Hollenhorst, S.J. (1989). Testing the adventure model: Empirical support for a model of risk recreation participation. *Journal of Leisure Research, 20*(3), 124–139.

Frazer, R. (2009). Toward a theory of critical teaching for social justice in outdoor education studies: A grounded theory study of philosophical perspectives and teaching practices. Unpublished doctoral dissertation, University of Wisconsin, Madison.

Freire, P. (1987). *A Pedagogy for Liberation*. New York: Bergin and Garvey.

Goodale, T. (1991). Educating for social responsibility: Aspirations and obstacles. *Schole: A Journal of Leisure Studies and Recreation Education, 7*, 81–91.

Goodman, D.J. (2011). *Promoting Diversity and Social Justice: Educating People From Privileged Groups* (2nd edn). London: Routledge.

Greene, M. (1998). Teaching for social justice. In W. Ayers, J.A. Hunt & T. Quinn (Eds.) *Teaching for Social Justice* (pp. xxvii–xlvi). New York, NY: New Press.

Hamilton, T. (2003). The representation and appropriation of Indigenous cultures at Ontario summer camps. *Pathways: The Ontario Journal of Outdoor Education, 15*(1), 9–16.

Hatcher, R.L., Fouad, N.A., Campbell, L.F., McCutcheon, S.R. Grus, C.L. & Leahy, K.L. (2013). Competency-based education for professional psychology: Moving from concept to practice. *Training and Education in Professional Psychology, 7*(4), 225–234.

Hytten, K. (2013). Philosophy and the art of teaching social justice. In W. Hare & J.P. Portelli (Eds.) *Philosophy of Education: Introductory Readings* (4th edn) (pp. 170–181). Edmonton, Alberta: Brush Education

James, B. (1988). Canoeing and gender issues. *Journal of Canadian Outward Bound Wilderness School (COBWS) Education, 4*(1), pp. 14–30.

Johnson, C.Y. & Bowker, J.M. (2004). African-American wildland memories. *Environmental Ethics, 26*(1), pp. 57–75.

Kolb, D.A. (1984). *Experiential Learning*. Englewood Cliffs, NJ: Prentice Hall.

Kroeber, A.L. & Kluckhohn, C. (1952). *Culture: A Critical Review of Concepts and Definitions*. New York, NY: Vintage Books.

Ladson-Billings, G. (2013). 'Stakes is high': Educating new century students. *Journal of Negro Education, 82*(2), 105–110.

Lee, A., Williams, R.D., Shaw, M.A. & Jie, Y. (2014). First-year students' perspectives on intercultural learning. *Teaching in Higher Education, 19*(5), 543–554.

Lopez, A.E. (2011). Culturally relevant pedagogy and critical literacy in diverse English classrooms: A case study of a secondary English teacher's activism and agency. *English Teaching, 10*(4), 75–93.

Lorde, A. (2007). Age, race, class and sex: Women redefining difference. In A. Lorde & C. Clarke (Eds.) *Sister Outsider: Essays and Speeches* (pp. 114–123). Berkeley, CA: Crossing Press.

Lowan-Trudeau, G. (2013). Considering ecological métissage: To blend or not to blend? *Journal of Experiential Education, 37*(4), 351–366.

Marsh, H.W. & Richards, G. (1989). A test of bipolar and androgyny perspectives of masculinity and femininity: The effect of participation in an Outward Bound program. *Journal of Personality, 57*(1), 115–138.

McIntosh, P. (1990). White privilege: Unpacking the invisible knapsack. *Independent School, 49*, 31–35.

National Outdoor Leadership School (2014). *Our Mission.* Retrieved from: www.nols.ca/about/values.shtml.

Newberry, L. (2000). 'My life as a boy-girl' and other stories: A feminist exploration of identity and outdoor pedagogy. Unpublished MA thesis, Ontario Institute for Studies in Education, University of Toronto.

Petzoldt, P. (2000). *On Belay: The Life of Legendary Mountaineer Paul Petzoldt.* Seattle, WA: The Mountaineers Books.

Richards, M.H., Sanderson, R.C., Celio, C.I., Grant, J.E., Choi, I., George, C.C. & Deane, K. (2013). Service-learning in early adolescence: Results of a school-based curriculum. *Journal of Experiential Education, 36*(5), 5–21.

Richardson, T. & Villenas, S. (2000). 'Other' encounters: Dances with whiteness in multicultural education. *Educational Theory, 50*, 255–273.

Roberts, N.S. (2013). Meeting at the crossroads: Progress for multiracial people or delicate balance amid old divides? In D. Dustin & K. Schwab (Eds.) *Just Leisure: Things That We Believe In* (pp. 27–34). Urbana, IL: Sagamore.

Roberts, N.S. & Rodriguez, D.R. (1999). Multicultural issues in outdoor education (ERIC Digest No. 8). Retrieved from: ERIC database (ED438151).

Schaedel, B. & Lazarowitz, R.H. (2005/2006). Literacy development in a multicultural city. *International Journal of Learning, 12*, 7.

Schiller, J. (2013). 'These rights go beyond borders and pieces of paper': Urban high school teachers and newcomer immigrant youth engaging in human rights education. Unpublished doctoral dissertation, University of San Francisco, San Francisco.

Seaman, J., Beightol, J., Shirilla, P. & Crawford, B. (2009). Contact theory as a framework for experiential activities as diversity education: An exploratory study. *Journal of Experiential Education, 32*(3), 207–225.

Tilley, S. & Taylor, L. (2013). Understanding curriculum as lived: teaching for social justice and equity goals. *Race, Ethnicity and Education, 16*(3), 406–429.

Warren, K. (1985). Women's outdoor adventures: Myth and reality. *Journal of Experiential Education, 5*(2), 10–14.

Warren, K., Roberts, N., Breunig, M. & Alvarez, A. (2014). Social justice in experiential education: Past, present, and future. *Journal of Experiential Education, 37*(1), 89–103.

17

Professional accreditation in the UK outdoor sector

Heather Brown

INSTITUTE FOR OUTDOOR LEARNING

Ian Harris

SOUTHAMPTON SOLENT UNIVERSITY

Su Porter

UNIVERSITY OF ST MARK AND ST JOHN

This chapter analyses the development of individual professional practice including its recognition and accreditation within the outdoor sector in the UK over the past twenty-five years. We consider the key influences affecting the sector and the future direction for outdoor professional accreditation. We emphasise that, in the UK, the word *qualification* is used to describe a training process that is assessed and quality assured (by an awarding organisation). This process may lead to or form part of an accreditation, which is awarded by a professional institute or other body that upholds and develops professional standards.

What is a profession?

We begin by considering what is meant by the term profession or professional in relation to employment, and then consider the context in the outdoor sector. Recognised ancient professions include the priesthood, law, medicine and university-level teaching, with the addition of surgery, dentistry and architecture in the medieval period, and engineering in the industrial era. Further professional groups arrived in the 20th century including teachers, social workers, accountants and personnel managers (Hoyle & John, 1995; Carr, 2000; Lester, 2010).

Professions are the result of a social construct developed over time, and each profession has its own history, culture and trends. The classical emphasis was on broad-based learning and education followed by specialising in a specific area of practice. The medieval emphasis was on practical training and experience, with an emphasis on time-serving. The industrial period brought the age of scientific reason and the idea of problem solving. Over the past thirty years a reflective or creative-interpretive model has emerged. 'It emphasises learning through action and reflection, making judgements in uncertain contexts and working with problematic situations rather than clearly defined problems' (Lester, 2010, p. 3).

As new interpretations of professions have been overlaid on old ones, descriptions of professional practice have evolved from using education and training as a way to denote professional standing to the 1990s functional analysis approach where a profession is defined more by roles and functions. Carr (2000) reflected the functional approach in the criteria of professionalism, as follows:

(i)   professions provide an important public service;
(ii) professions involve a theoretically as well as practically grounded expertise;
(iii) professions have a distinctive ethical dimension calling for expression in a code of practice;
(iv) professions require organisation and regulation for purposes of recruitment and discipline; and
(v)   professional practitioners require a high degree of individual autonomy – independence of judgement – for effective practice. (p. 23)

More recently, capability rather than functionality is used to describe a profession's practice where the capable practitioner is 'able to apply a repertoire of abilities in roles and situations that cannot all be envisaged in advance' (Lester, 2010, p. 6). The reference to core capability includes what practitioners are equipped to do, and provides a more flexible description that relates to the reflective–interpretive approach to professionalism (Schön, 1983).

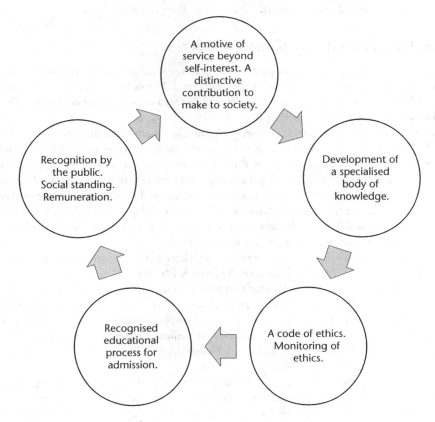

Figure 17.1   Signposts to a profession

Source: Martin (2001, p. 12)

A model of professionalism, shown in Figure 17.1, was put forward by Martin in 2001 based on a review of literature in the sectors of teaching and nursing (Martin, 2001; Humberstone, 2004).

Martin (2001) saw the first two signposts as motive and knowledge where the outdoor sector needs to collectively clarify its contributions and motives of service. The sector needs to recognise its connections and disconnections in the broad sector of outdoor learning. The next signpost is the code of ethics. 'A code of ethics [can be] seen as the cumulative wisdom and virtue of local codes of practice' (Sockett, cited in Goodland, Soder & Sirotnik, 1990, p. 243), and may cover areas such as professional integrity, professional responsibilities and relationships, and professional standards and environmental as well as cultural responsibilities. Joining the profession is the next signpost as a recognised educational pathway; members of the profession have an identified motive of service, and understand the body of knowledge and codes of ethics that apply. The final signpost is public recognition. No enterprise or sector can decide for itself that it is a profession. This status must be granted by society (Cruess & Cruess, 1997; Herzog, cited in Leigh, 2006).

Eraut (1994) reflected that, 'the ideology of professionalism embodies appealing values and in this case, service, trustworthiness, integrity, autonomy, reliable standards' (1994, p. viii). Hoyle and John (1995) also noted that professionality refers to a 'set of knowledge, skills, values and behaviours which is exercised on behalf of clients' (p. 16) that indicated more than technical competence. According to Schmidt and Adams (cited in Leigh, 2006), professionals are willing to put the welfare of the client and society as a whole above their own rights. They will behave in a totally moral and ethical manner (Kultgen, 1988; Porter, 2012).

Factors influencing the UK outdoor sector

Any interpretation of a profession or professional practice is influenced by internal and external factors that combine and impact on the sector concerned. In this section we discuss how recent events and trends in the UK outdoor sector have influenced its developing definition of professionalism and professional accreditation.

The outdoor sector in the UK is diverse, with providers including a mixture of organisations and individuals aiming to meet user needs. Specialisms range from people seeking educational benefits to recreation, from focusing on therapeutic outcomes to elite sporting performance (Skills Active, 2011; Ogilvie, 2013). Organisations from both the supply and demand side of the sector can come from the public sector in the form of national or primarily local government, the voluntary sector in the form of charities and member clubs, or the commercial for-profit sector. Each sector is influenced by its own unique factors along with economic, political and social issues, which have wider impact (Torkildsen, 2010).

In the late 1980s and early 1990s the details of the school national curriculum were developed following the passing of the 1988 Education Reform Act by the UK government (Department for Education and Science, 1991). Outdoor education unsuccessfully sought a place at the core of the curriculum either as a subject, a cross-curricular theme or as a compulsory residential experience for all pupils. However, outdoor and adventurous activities were identified as one of the potential activity areas within the statutory curriculum for physical education. This decision raised questions about the place and societal value of outdoor education, and of those who worked in the sector (Mitchell, 1992).

In 1993, the tragedy of four teenagers losing their lives during a canoeing trip as part of a multi-activity residential experience from school changed the focus of all individuals and organisations associated with the outdoor sector in the UK (Sharp, 2004). The tragedy, which was the result of criminal negligence, saw the company's managing director convicted and jailed for manslaughter, and the company found guilty of corporate manslaughter. This single incident resulted in a public outcry for the safety of all participants (Goodhead & Johnson, 1996; Harris, 2011a). The public pressure led to the introduction of the Adventure Activities (Young Persons' Safety) Act 1995 and the introduction of licensing of centres delivering selected activities to youth under 18 years (Barton, 2007).

The focus of the outdoor sector from this point forward was on safety, with little attention paid to enhancing the assumed benefits of pupil learning and development. The culture of fear in outdoor centres was also fuelled by a wider societal focus on promoting safety and minimising risk (Furedi, 2001; Gill, 2010), described by many as a *cotton wool culture*. The reaction within the outdoor sector was to increase paperwork in the form of detailed risk assessments and operating procedures, and to end activities where the risk could not be tightly controlled (Harris, 2011b). Because of the statutory requirement of licensing placed on centres undertaking forms of caving, climbing, trekking and watersports in challenging environments with youth, the importance of non-statutory accreditation through trade bodies and national governing bodies (NGBs) of sport also grew for providers outside the scope of licensing (Harris, 2011b). The effect on individual practitioners was to require them to gain qualifications in technical or *hard* skills, which had been developed by the NGBs of sports over many years. The training and assessment processes placed more weight on assessing technical skills than interpersonal skills or professional competence in enabling learning and development. During the late 1990s, the professional standing of individuals was judged to a greater extent on the range and level of short course qualifications held than on their value as educators or youth workers holding a degree and professional qualifications.

One attempt to develop a more unified approach to practitioner training was the creation of a single recognised coaching qualification structure for all sports. This approach aimed to provide a base for improving the consistency and quality of coaching practice through regular continuous professional development (CPD) and appropriate safety checks (Townend, 2009). Within the outdoor sector the British Canoe Union (now British Canoeing) and British Orienteering were the first NGBs to participate, but this structure has not been universally adopted across the sector.

In addition to developments in coaching, a debate around the balance between risk and benefit in outdoor practice began (Gill, 2010). A small backlash to the cotton wool culture developed with recognition that adventure education could not be delivered effectively within a totally controlled environment. This debate resulted in the start of a change of focus within some areas of the UK outdoor sector. While the importance of core activity skills did not go away, the importance of other aspects, including facilitation skills and reflective practice, started to be recognised. In the context of professional practice, the building blocks of hard skill national governing body coaching and leadership qualifications were seen by many as not creating the full package of an effective outdoor practitioner (Barnes, 2004).

The value of reflective practice and focusing on learning opportunities gained a place in the evaluation of outdoor experiences alongside the continuing expectation of not harming participants. This change was seen in the growth in the number of universities offering outdoor degree courses (Humberstone & Brown, 2006) and the introduction of professional accreditation by the Institute for Outdoor Learning (IOL) as the first sector-driven professional accreditation for outdoor practitioners.

Reflective practice in an outdoor context

The reflective process involves the exploration of self and challenges practitioners to reflect upon their outdoor and other life experiences. Reflective practitioners use their reflection to steer and guide how they carry out their work. They may reflect alone, with colleagues or with clients, but they think about how they have performed and seek to actively improve their practice (Schön, 1983; Wallace, 2005; Brown, 2006). The reflection process helps participants develop the judgement and wisdom necessary when working in situations and environments that are stimulating, challenging, rewarding and unforgiving.

Reflective practice is seen as a journey. Mortlock (2001) wrote about both the outward and the inward journey:

> There is another journey, however, that we all may take, which not only has uncertainty, but is also infinitely more mysterious. This is the journey into ourselves – the inner journey. Every experience we have of the external world has an effect, consciously or unconsciously, on our inner self. (p. 55)

The inward journey allows people to unlock, to evaluate and make sense of outward journeys where experiences with others and the environment are shared (Mortlock, 2001). The inward journey requires meta-cognitive awareness as learners are required to reflect on their own habits of mind, and to become aware of them and how they affect their practice. A growing body of research suggests that the physical and cultural environment in which outdoor leaders work has an effect not only on their approach to the physical environment but also on their cultural and sociological identity. This environment reflects their approach not only to their work professionalism and personal development, but also to their lifestyles and relationships to a broader society (Barnes, 1999). South (1986), Humberstone (1987), Mitten (1999) and Barnes (1999, 2001) uncovered some common elements including similarities in personal and ethical values and a morality that is grounded in relationships. Most outdoor staff share a set of values with a strong sense of community reflecting a shared purpose.

Developing professional accreditation for the UK outdoor sector

A need was perceived to raise the profile of outdoor learning practice, and to demonstrate the professionalism required and the professional status the sector demands. The nature, range, detail, balance and focus of the hard skills, and the additional soft skills areas needed, were debated to identify and recognise the core competencies and professional competence of an effective practitioner (Barnes, 2004).

In addition, people recognised that many outdoor practitioners did not build a traditional career in the outdoors, but moved in through non-standard routes (e.g. apprenticeships and work experience with few formal qualifications such as the military and after travelling rather than through graduation from college) and also often moved out into other sectors after a few years. Figure 17.2 gives some examples of routes into, through and out of the profession.

According to the Institute for Outdoor Learning (2014):

> Types of practitioners (include) youth workers, teachers, teaching assistants, therapists, development trainers, instructors etc. working within any branch of outdoor learning including adventure, environmental studies, forest schools, bushcraft, expedition work, recreation, drama, art or any other area of outdoor learning with a developmental aim.

Developing a language and system of qualifications or accreditation that were understandable across the sectors was crucial. Initial research indicated that practitioners wanted:

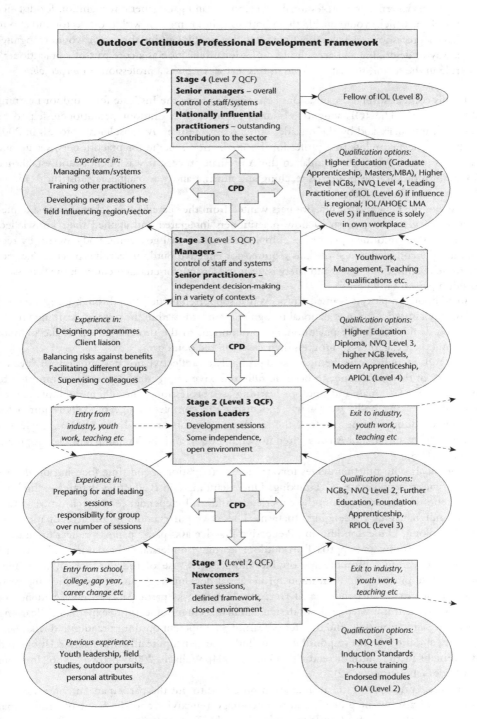

Figure 17.2 Outdoor continuous professional development framework

- a process to reflect on professional development and gain generic recognition for distance travelled, which would enable them both to gain promotion within the sector and also to have a professional development currency that people outside the sector would recognise;
- a way of describing and accrediting professional reflection as a core part of a practitioner's role in the sector, so that working in this sector is seen as a profession – a *proper job*.

In this context several organisations converged to form the Institute for Outdoor Learning (IOL) in 2001. The IOL sought to address the need that outdoor practitioners felt to be seen both internally and by the outside world as a profession. A consultative process in 2002 resulted in the first pilots of a professional accreditation scheme for practitioners, set up and quality assured by the IOL. Similar to the Australian process, it was built around established models of professionalism such as teaching and nursing and was mapped against the National Qualifications Framework.

Some of the benefits that practitioners wanted from the accreditation scheme were a framework for development to show how practitioners integrated and applied their knowledge, values and skills into their practice; a complement to national governing body awards by recognising the complete range of skills required for effective outdoor learning practice (i.e. not just those relating to technical and safety issues); and a route for engagement with the profession outside a person's own practice.

In addition, employers wanted a process that supported participants through using a trained and quality assured team, met national recognised standards within the outdoor learning profession, and demonstrated the practitioner's commitment to the professionalism of the outdoor sector and their eagerness to progress their career in the outdoors.

The IOL accreditation scheme is based primarily on reflective practice and aims to develop the ability of the practitioner to become fully reflexive in practice – a person committed to developing professionals and outdoor learning as a profession. The scheme complemented national governing body awards by recognising the complete range of skills required for effective outdoor learning practice, the ideologies put forward by Eraut (1994), Hoyle and John (1995), Schmidt and Adams (cited in Leigh, 2006), and the Training and Development Agency (2008).

Individuals who put themselves forward for accreditation spend time focusing on *the two pillars of professional practice*: (i) Thinking, Understanding and Reflective Practice – thinking about actions and learning from the experience; and (ii) Independence of Decision Making – leading and managing challenging situations. These two pillars underpin the accreditation criteria. Thinking, Understanding and Reflective Practice asks participants to reflect upon their personal philosophy and approach to outdoor learning, understand the nature and potential of outdoor learning, promote responsible and sensitive use of the outdoor environment, use reflective practice and continuous professional development, and apply values and professional integrity. Independence of Decision Making asks participants to give evidence to demonstrate their knowledge about design and management of learning experiences, learning processes, facilitation skills and transfer of learning, competent outdoor practice and risk management, and professional responsibilities including leadership, teamwork, client relations and involvement in the outdoor sector (Williams, 2004; Wallace, 2005; Brown, 2006; Institute for Outdoor Learning, 2012).

The basic principle of the accreditation process is to put the participant in control of the learning and assessment process, and to encourage reflexivity and the habit of professional development (Institute for Outdoor Learning, 2005). The accreditation process is completed with the support of a coach and constitutes transformative learning assisted by the coach and others. The participant can critically reflect on the assumptions upon which 'interpretations, beliefs, and habits of mind or points of view are based' (Mezirow, 1997, p. 7). This self-reflection can lead to significant personal transformations. This process also has echoes of the work of Freire (2001), who questioned participants about their practices to facilitate a move from *naive* to *critical consciousness*. The knowledge created is relevant to the learners, based on their experience and not externally prescribed. According to Freire, this new knowledge can be instrumental in enabling change at different levels – the personal, the community and the societal level (Bowie, 2011; Porter, 2012).

The IOL (2012) now offers a range of professional accreditation awards to suit outdoor practitioners at various stages of their career. Comments made in response to a research exercise (Mason, 2005) indicated that employers are recognising the benefits of the scheme: 'We have been able to make some direct comparisons between the APIOL [Accredited Practitioner of the Institute for Outdoor Learning] benchmarks and our own requirements; APIOL is an entirely relevant award for experienced practitioners' (p. 28).

The future of professionalism and accreditation

A view of what constitutes appropriate professional accreditation for the future outdoor sector needs to be developed using at least three viewpoints:

1   how the sector is developing, what outdoor learning will look like in the future and what needs this generates regarding practitioner development;
2   what practitioners say they need to develop their competence and professionalism; and
3   whether society considers outdoor learning as a profession. (Martin, 2001)

The IOL Strategic Forum in 2011 addressed visions of the future world that both practitioners and participants will be operating in. Jones and Dewing (2010) identified key future trends across society, as follows.

- Developments in the use of social media – people having multiple identities.
- Knowledge creation and sharing – intellectual property is no longer protectable.
- The search for the ordinary – the need for solitude and stopping – maintaining privacy, spending time with friends and family without technology, the popularity of organic gardening, the resurgence in the popularity of camping.
- The importance of *live* experience – the need to gather together to experience something as it is actually happening (i.e. an antidote to spending so much time in front of a virtual screen).
- Urbanisation and the importance of community living.
- Pressure on natural resources.

To respond to these changes, the definition of outdoor learning is now much wider than it was 25 years ago. The benefits of experiential outdoor learning – learning *through* outdoor activity and not just *doing* the activity – are widely recognised, including formal and informal education, management, leadership and therapy. The Council for Learning Outside the Classroom (2014) demonstrated the beneficial effects of the outdoor experience on maths and literacy results, in addition to wider personal and social development. This recognition not only applies in school and to young people, but also to the health and wellbeing agenda, to managers, leaders, starting life and ageing well.

In the past twenty-five years in the UK there has also been a drive to remove risk from outdoor practice, and to use qualifications and accreditations as one of the main indicators of good professional practice in the desire to offer certainty and a method to quantify and measure a professional's practice. The UK outdoor sector has changed from times when decisions about professional competence were left to the individual, and each practitioner had a personal definition not only of good professional practice, but also of ethics and environmental practice. The world of professional development and outdoor practitioners has become a world where practitioners look to a set of rules developed by others to describe good practice, rather than developing their own code of ethics.

A paradox is evident between the ambiguity of the future and society's desire for certainty in outdoor learning. Taylor (2010) suggested that, to survive and thrive in this new world, people would need:

- self-awareness and social focus (i.e. moving beyond possessive individualism);
- opportunities for discussion and disagreement in company, to make better decisions; and
- debate about the nature of progress – challenging the 20th-century assumption that pursuing progress is the same as improving human wellbeing.

These ideas suggest that it is even more important for outdoor learning providers to consider giving priority to positivity, flexibility, social focus and compassion. The more uncertainty there is in the world, the more reflective skills and skills of facilitation will continue to be crucial for practitioners alongside the technical skills that aim to ensure that adventures can be undertaken without misadventure. NGB skills awards alone will not, therefore, be enough to recognise the full competence of outdoor practitioners. Whether the IOL Accreditation Scheme grows and is taken up by many or not, reflective practice needs to be at the core of professional development. At the very least, the IOL criteria provide a starting point for a discussion about what constitutes good professional practice.

Therefore, we think that practitioners will need to continue to develop reflective practice skills and encourage reflexivity in participants. If reflective practice is at the heart of outdoor professional practice, not only will participants reflect and learn about themselves while working, but also they will learn skills that will enable them to continue reflecting and building their own ethical framework to flourish in the uncertain and exciting world of the future. Because outdoor learning is experiential, and engages heart and body as well as head, it is centrally placed to add value into the future.

References

Barnes, P. (1999). The motivation of staff in the outdoor education sector. Unpublished PhD thesis, University of Strathclyde, Glasgow, UK.

Barnes, P. (2001). Why do centre staff do the things they do? The multi-layered motivation model. *Horizons, 15*, 30–31.

Barnes, P. (2004). Outdoor leadership: Art or science? In Barnes, P. and Sharp, B. (Eds.) *The RHP Companion to Outdoor Education* (pp. 84–90). Lyme Regis, England: Russell House Publishing.

Barton, B. (2007). *Safety, Risk and Adventure in Outdoor Activities*. London: Paul Chapman Publishing.

Bowie, Z.J. (2011). Accredited practitioner with the Institute for Outdoor Learning: Self accreditation as a transformative process. Unpublished master's dissertation, School of Education, University of the West of England, Bristol, UK.

Brown, H. (2006). Ballparks and benchmarks. *Horizons, 35*, 28–31.

Carr, D. (2000). *Professionalism and Ethics in Teaching*. London: Routledge.

Council for Learning Outside the Classroom (2014). Learning outside the classroom changes live. Retrieved from: www.lotc.org.uk/.

Cruess, S.R. & Cruess, R.L. (1997). Professionalism must be taught. *British Medical Journal*, *315*, 1674–1677.

Department for Education and Science (1991). *Physical Education for Ages 5 to 16: Proposals of the Secretary for State for Education and Science*. London: Her Majesty's Stationery Office.

Eraut, M. (1994). *Developing Professional Knowledge and Competence*. London: Falmer Press.

Freire, P. (2001). *Pedagogy of the Oppressed* (30th edn). London: Continuum International Publishing Group Ltd.

Furedi, F. (2001). *Paranoid Parenting*. London: The Penguin Press.

Gill, T. (2010). *Nothing Ventured . . . Balancing Risks and Benefits in the Outdoors*. English Outdoor Council. Retrieved from: www.englishoutdoorcouncil.org/publications.

Goodhead, T. & Johnson, D. (1996). *Coastal Recreation Management*. London: E&FN Spon.

Goodland, J., Soder, R. & Sirotnik, K. (Eds.) (1990). *The Moral Dimensions of Teaching*. San Francisco, CA: Jossey-Bass.

Harris, I. (2011a). The inspector is coming. *Horizons, 56*, 6–8.

Harris, I. (2011b). From license holders to cowboys. *Horizons, 54*, 13–17.

Hoyle, E. & John, P. (1995). *Professional Knowledge and Professional Practice*. London: Cassell.

Humberstone, B. (1987). Organisational factors, teachers approach and pupil commitment in outdoor activities. A case study of schooling and gender in outdoor education. Unpublished PhD thesis, University of Southampton, Southampton, UK.

Humberstone, B. (2004). Professional qualifications in outdoor education and outdoor sports education: Balancing theory and practice in the degree curriculum outdoor sports education. *Proceedings of the International Symposium Hrubá Skála*, Bohemian Paradise, Czech Republic. Published by Duha, Senovážné nám in cooperation with Charles University, Faculty of Physical Education, and Sport Editors: Assistant Prof. Jan Neuman, PhDr CSc, Mgr. Ivana Turčová Jackson.

Humberstone, B. & Brown, H. (Eds.) (2006). *Shaping the Outdoor Profession through Higher Education*. Cumbria, England: Institute for Outdoor Learning.

Institute for Outdoor Learning (2005) *Accredited Practitioner of the Institute for Outdoor Learning, Principles of Assessment*. Cumbria, England: Institute for Outdoor Learning.

Institute for Outdoor Learning (2012). Retrieved from: www.outdoor-learning.org/Default.aspx?tabid=72.

Institute for Outdoor Learning (2014). Retrieved from: www.outdoor-learning.org/Default.aspx?tabid=207.

Jones, T. & Dewing, C. (Eds.) (2010). *FutureAgenda: The World in 2020*. Oxford, England: Infinite Ideas.

Kultgen, J. (1988). *Ethics and Professionalism*. Philadelphia, PA: University of Pennsylvania Press.

Leigh, R.J. (2006) Workers in the outdoor adventure sector – should they be considered part of a wider professional body of people? *Horizons 49*, 28–31.

Lester, S. (2010). On professions and being professional. Retrieved from: www.sld.demon.co.uk/profnal.pdf.

Martin, P. (2001). *Key Issues in the Sector: Towards the Summit in Education Outdoors: Our Sense of Place*. 12th National Outdoor Education Conference, Conference Proceedings. Victoria, Australia.

Mason, E. (2005). APIOL out and about. *Horizons*, 30, 28–31.

Mezirow, J. (1997). Transformative learning: Theory to practice. *New Directions for Adult and Continuing Education*, *74*, 5–12.

Mitchell, S. (1992). A foot in the door. Outdoor and adventurous activities in the physical education national curriculum. *Journal of Adventure Education and Outdoor Leadership, 9*(3), 19–21.

Mitten, D. (1999). Leadership for community building. In Miles, J. & Priest, S. (Eds.) *Adventure Programming* (pp. 253–261). State College, PA: Venture Publishing Inc.

Mortlock, C. (2001). *Beyond Adventure: An Inner Journey*. Cumbria, England: Cicerone Press Ltd.

Ogilvie, P. (2013). *Roots and Wings. A History of Outdoor Education and Outdoor Learning in the UK*. Dorset, UK: Russell House Publishing.

Porter, S. (2012). Professionalisation of the sector of outdoor learning, An evaluation of the professional accreditation scheme with the Institute for Outdoor Learning. Unpublished master's dissertation, University of St Mark and St John, Plymouth, UK.

Schön, D.A. (1983). *The Reflective Practitioner: How Professionals Think in Action* (Vol. 5126). New York: Basic Books.

Sharp, B. (2004). Risk in outdoor education. In P. Barnes & B. Sharp (Eds.) *The RHP Companion to Outdoor Education* (pp. 91–96). Lyme Regis, UK: Russell House Publishing.

Skills Active (2011). The UK outdoor sector: A guide. Retrieved from: www.skillsactive.com.

South, G. (1986). Editorial. *Journal of Adventure Education and Outdoor Leadership*, 3(1), 15.

Taylor, M. (2010). *CEO RSA 21st Century Enlightenment*. RSA 2010. Retrieved from: http://comment. rsablogs.org.uk/videos/page/2/.

Torkildsen, G. (2010). *Leisure and Recreation Management* (5th edn). London: Routledge.

Townend, R. (2009). *UK Coaching Framework Consultation Report*. Leeds: Sports Coach UK.

Training and Development Agency for Schools (2008). *Guidance on The National Occupational Standards for Supporting Teaching and Learning in Schools*. Training and Development Agency for Schools, UK.

Wallace, R. (2005). Accredited practitioner of APIOL – more than a name. *Horizons*, *31*, 30–31.

Williams, R. (2004). Professionalism, quality and the market place. In P. Barnes & B. Sharp (Eds.) *The RHP Companion to Outdoor Education* (pp. 165–169). Lyme Regis, UK: Russell House Publishing.

18

Certification in outdoor programmes

Aram Attarian

North Carolina State University

Adventure programmes and activities in the outdoors have grown during recent decades, resulting in greater interest from park and protected area managers, government officials and the general public (Ewert, Attarian, Hollenhorst, Russell & Voight, 2006; Cordell, 2012). As a result, qualified outdoor leaders and guides are needed. Qualified outdoor leaders work in a variety of settings with different clientele using professional practices and training (Priest & Gass, 2005). As part of this role, leaders need to be qualified and possess a basic set of technical, interpersonal and judgement skills to fulfil their responsibilities to their participants and the industry (Kosseff, 2010).

Outdoor leaders receive their training through personal experiences, academic programmes, apprenticeships, internships, in-house training programmes or specialised training programmes. Many organisations in the USA have implemented successful training programmes or identified certification programmes as a way to ensure that leaders have a basic level of skill and knowledge. However, no consensus exists in the adventure industry regarding what core competencies should be defined and tested and who should make these decisions (Cockrell, 1990). Instead, each outdoor organisation identifies competencies that are the most important and determines how leaders should be evaluated. Therefore, the intent of this chapter is to explore the training and certification of outdoor leaders primarily in the USA by reviewing the history of certification, explicating the pros and cons that have been argued, and suggesting ways to move beyond traditional ideas of certification to focus on best practices and needed future research. In the USA, certification refers specifically to the qualifications of an individual. Accreditation refers to the educational programmes offered to develop skills, but certification focuses on the leader, instructor or educator.

Certification programmes

Certification is a process in which minimum standards of competency that have been met or exceeded by a professional are evaluated by a non-governmental organisation or association (Senosk, 1976). The purpose of certification is to ensure to the public that an individual has mastered a body of knowledge and has acquired skills in a specific area. A certified individual has the responsibility to know their limitations and to practice within those limits. Most certifying bodies have a renewal process that occurs every three to five years, which can create a financial challenge for adventure programmes and their staff.

Proliferations of certification programmes have been created in skill areas to document the training of outdoor leaders in the absence of definitive industry standards (see Table 18.1).

Some people have argued that it is unclear what outdoor leaders should be certified to do, while others agree that certification is useful for developing technical skills in the outdoors (Cockrell, 1990). Current certification programmes in the USA, as well as in other parts of the world, are created by, sponsored or affiliated with associations, trade organisations or private vendors interested in raising standards. Many of these certification programmes are independent from non-governmental membership organisations but benefit from association support and endorsement.

Currently no overall outdoor leadership certification programmes exist in the USA. Instead, certification tends to be primarily vendor driven. Vendor driven refers to a business that has expertise in a particular adventure activity, receives payment for certification training and provides consultation in the creation of industry standards. Certifications are usually earned directly from a vendor or a vendor contracted by an outdoor programme or educational institution. Vendors grant recognition to an individual who has met specific predetermined qualifications established by the vendor. For example, the American Mountain Guides Association offers climbing skills oriented certificates of competency. In almost all cases, certification is time limited, and requires renewal to remain current. In some areas a government agency (e.g. US Forest Service, National Park Service) can require a certification *by law* to perform a certain task or job.

Certification may sometimes be confused with licensure. Licensure in the USA is the process by which a *state government agency* grants permission to individuals to engage in the practice of that profession, and prohibits all others from legally doing so (Garner, 2009). The certification assessment process may be similar to licensure and may differ only in legal status. In other organisations certification may be different and more comprehensive than licensure.

Three primary types of certification are used in today's adventure programmes. The first, *in-house certifications*, are created by individual adventure organisations for internal purposes, are the easiest to develop, but have limited transferability to programmes in other organisations. The second, *activity-specific certifications* focus on a particular activity (e.g. first aid, rock climbing, canoeing, challenge course, environmental ethics) and are usually recognised in programmes across the industry. *Association supported certifications* are least common in the American outdoor

Table 18.1 Certification opportunities for outdoor leaders in the USA

Examples of certifying organisations	Activity
American Canoe Association	Flat water canoeing, Whitewater canoeing, Kayaking, Sea kayaking, Rafting, Rescue
American Mountain Guides Association, Professional Climbing Instructors Association	Rock climbing, Mountaineering, Ski mountaineering
Association for Challenge Course Technology	Ropes and challenge courses, Ziplines
American Avalanche Institute	Avalanche training and rescue
American Avalanche Institute for Avalanche, Research and Education	
Leave No Trace Center for Outdoor Ethics	Outdoor ethics
National Association for Search and Rescue	Search and rescue
Professional Ski Instructors of America	Skiing, Snowboarding
Wilderness Medical Associates, Wilderness Medical Institute, SOLO	Wilderness medicine

adventure industry. In this certification an association is formed by a group of professionals who join together to create or improve professional standards, increase the level of practice and protect the public (e.g. Association of Challenge Course Technology, American Mountain Guides Association). Certification through associations is conducted through vendor members and is intended to be transferable to all organisations where a certified outdoor professional might work.

A historical look at certification in the USA

The idea of certifying outdoor leaders in the USA can be traced back to an article that appeared in *American Forests* titled 'Certified outdoorsman' (Wagar, 1940). Wagar noted that more Americans were venturing outdoors to areas made more accessible by innovations in technology including 'broad highways (or roads)' (p. 490), travel trailers, airplanes, gasoline camp stoves, outboard motors, automatic fishing reels and air mattresses. Wagar argued that the influx of inexperienced visitors to the nation's parks and protected areas was creating both social and environmental impacts previously unseen. He noted 'the woods are filled with folk with no idea of woods sanitation, care with fire, or outdoor good manners', and suggested, 'We need, in short, a certification of outdoorsmen . . . something which will definitely mark and reward those with wisdom and experience in outdoor living, resourcefulness in outdoor emergencies and with acceptable standards for outdoor conduct' (p. 492).

Wagar also identified who should be able to certify outdoors people. He noted, 'Certification can best be done by agencies with fine reputations for integrity, with great knowledge and experience in outdoor living and working, and with widespread organisations having offices and officers in many parts of the country' (p. 524). Some of the agencies identified by Wagar included the US Forest Service, National Park Service, State Parks and Forests, and organisations like the American Forest Association, Izaak Walton League, Wilderness Society and the National Wildlife Federation. These observations have continued to be important parts of the debate about leader certification in the USA.

Paul Petzoldt, Chief Mountaineering Instructor for the Colorado Outward Bound School (ca. 1963), became the first proponent of a standardised training course for outdoor leaders in the USA (Backert, 1987). Much like Wagar (1940), Petzoldt presented arguments supporting the certification of outdoor leaders. He described an increasing interest by the American public to pursue outdoor activities containing the elements of challenge and risk, and the increasing number of accidents associated with these activities. His second argument for certifying outdoor leaders centred on the ecological impacts associated with growing backcountry use.

In 1965 Petzoldt founded the National Outdoor Leadership School (NOLS) to train leaders capable of conducting wilderness programmes in a safe and rewarding manner (Petzoldt, 1984). Later, Petzoldt and others created the Wilderness Education Association (ca. 1977) based on the premise that education and the development of outdoor leaders should play an important role in backcountry safety and the preservation of protected areas. To achieve this vision, a curriculum was developed to train and certify leaders with the necessary judgement and decision-making skills to safely lead and teach the public about the proper care and use of America's backcountry areas.

In the UK, Australia and New Zealand similar interests in outdoor adventure activities and concerns for participant safety created a need for training outdoor leaders. As a result the British Mountaineering Council (ca. 1964) established the Mountain Leadership Certificate (known today as the Mountain Leadership Award) with the intent of providing a prescribed programme of training along with a way to assess individuals who had the responsibility for leading in the outdoors. The primary emphasis of these certificate programmes was to train experienced participants in the skills required for safe and effective mountain leadership (Coghlan & Webb, 1990).

Australia followed suit (ca. 1973) by establishing the Bush and Mountain Walking Leadership Training Board. This organisation emerged because of the mounting concern among educators and the recreational walking community about the standard of bushwalking leadership in South Australia, especially among walking parties organised by schools and youth groups. Concerns were focused mainly on poorly trained or inexperienced leaders guiding youth groups into backcountry and experiencing misadventures. In some cases groups were damaging the environment through poor environmental practices, were too large, and were poorly trained and equipped with little consideration given to risk management procedures. The death of an Australian youth during a school outing, as well as an incident in the UK in which six students died, caused officials to establish training schemes to prevent future tragedies. In 1995 the Bush and Mountain Walking Leadership Training Board was renamed the Board for Bushwalking Leadership South Australia (Bushwalking Leadership-South Australia, 2013).

In New Zealand a provisional Outdoor Training Advisory Board (OTAB) was established (ca. 1977) and funded to develop an outdoor leadership preparation scheme. Like its counterparts in the UK and Australia, the aims of the board were to create a framework for coordinated leader training, advise on existing programmes and act as an information clearing-house (Toynbee, 1982). The OTAB also published a *Logbook* and an *Outdoor Training Guide*. The unique feature about the OTAB was that it acted as an advisory agency. Instead of offering an outdoor leadership programme of its own, it assisted other organisations with their own in-house training programmes. As an advisory board, OTAB was concerned with staffing courses, avoiding replication of training courses, and making recommendations on standards and course offerings.

The pros and cons of certification in the USA

Based on the approaches used in other countries, as well as the earlier work of Petzoldt, groups in the USA in the 1970s began discussing the possibilities of establishing guidelines and standards for outdoor leaders along with an organisation that would manage these issues (Cockrell, 1990). This idea, however, did not move forward quickly because of the pros and cons associated with certifying outdoor leaders in the USA.

In support of certifying outdoor leaders

The pros and cons of certification have been debated for more than forty years in the US with no consensus reached on how certification would be conducted, what and who would be certified, and who would conduct the certification. The early proponents of certification suggested that minimising environmental impacts and concerns over visitor safety were the central reasons for why outdoor leaders should be certified (Wagar, 1940; Petzoldt, 1984; Cockrell, 1987). These reasons were not trivial. Within the past four decades, more people and organisations participated in and conducted their adventure activities on public lands (Ewert *et al.*, 2006; Cordell, 2012). Given this growth and interest, many state and federal land management agencies viewed certification, and in some cases licensure, as one way to manage both social and ecological impacts associated with parks and protected areas in the USA. For example, the National Park Service currently requires guides to possess professional certifications to lead commercial climbing activities in some of America's National Parks (e.g. Mt Rainier, Joshua Tree, Devils Tower and Denali) (American Mountain Guides Association, 2013). Similar certifications are required by the US Forest Service to guide customers on some of the nation's most popular rivers (Nantahala National Forest, 2014). In addition, more than twenty states require that persons taking clients into the backcountry for payment be licensed (Welch, Clement & Berman, 2009).

Supporters have also noted certification can provide a recognised set of skills that can be aligned with an organisation's mission, enhance professional development and competence, and in some cases, reduce staff turnover. A certification programme can improve organisations by providing employees with increased skills, confidence and motivation. Proponents also assert that certification can establish professional standards and competence, and raise the benchmark for individual performance. Certification also has the potential for promoting customer satisfaction, encouraging networking, enhancing public perception and emphasising accountability (Black & Ham, 2005; Product Development and Management Association, 2013).

The Australian tourism industry embraced these potential outcomes and considered certifying guides to improve the quality of tour guiding. To begin this process, an examination of a tour guide certification programme was undertaken to identify the components of a model certification programme (Black & Ham, 2013). The authors identified ten programme elements crucial for a professional certification programme: (i) need for a programme sponsor; (ii) clear communication and delivery of real benefits; (iii) reasonable and appropriate range of fees; (iv) variety of assessment options; (v) network of qualified and experienced assessors; (vi) simple and accessible administrative structure; (vii) code of ethics; (viii) specified timeframe and set of criteria for eligibility to apply for certification and recertification; (ix) business plan, including market analysis, marketing and implementation plans; and (x) distinctive and marketable programme title and logo. This information has been useful to programme administrators and managers when considering the development of certification programmes.

Why certification won't work

McGowan (2012), however, argued that the reasons against the certification of outdoor leaders is based on 'outdated perspectives developed over thirty years ago that no longer constitute meaningful objection to certification when faced with the transformation of adventure education into a fully commercialized industry' (p. 49). Furthermore, the universal certification of outdoor leaders failed in the USA because of the inability to examine outdoor adventure programming in an all-encompassing manner due to the diversity of programmes, their geographic locations and differing environments, and other factors that made each adventure programme unique (Attarian, 2001). People against certification also argued that unlike technical skills, the subjective leadership qualities of judgement and decision making, facilitation and expedition behaviour were difficult to measure, and therefore not certifiable (March, 1987).

March (1987) questioned the assessment process and declared that a valid certification process should be one that required all persons conducting the certification be: (i) professionally trained in assessment techniques; (ii) reassessed annually; (iii) liable for their certification; (iv) evaluated by candidates; and (v) able to have access to an appeals process. March also maintained that certification had legal status, implying that the public would expect a higher standard of performance from certified individuals. For example, dependence on a certified outdoor leader can in some cases cause the organisation that granted the certification be held liable when a client suffers harm while under the supervision of the certified leader. In this case, the injured could claim that the certifying organisation was negligent in granting the leader the certification and should therefore be liable for the resulting injuries (Tenenbaum, 2002). Concerns were also expressed about the fear that a government agency would intervene and manage the certification process (Petzoldt, 1975). Most people wanted the programmes to be monitored by designated non-governmental organisations.

Others suggested that the idea that certification was the solution to participant safety or environmental protection was flawed, since no research supported this argument (Watters, 1983).

In addition, certification had the potential to: (i) exclude experienced but uncertified people; (ii) attract the wrong people for the wrong reasons (e.g. someone who had limited experience, who *collects* certifications for the sole purpose of working in an adventure programme); and (iii) provide opportunities for *empire building* (e.g. organisations that create the standards, receive 'buy in' or acknowledgement from the rest of the industry, then develop and deliver a certification scheme – for example, the current model for Wilderness First Responder (WFR) potentially fits in to this idea of empire building, because three vendors, including the Wilderness Medical Associates, Wilderness Medical Institute and SOLO, deliver most of the WFR programmes in the US; (iv) become a bureaucratic nightmare for some administrators; and (v) be unable to evaluate outdoor leader competency and judgement (Green, 1982; Watters, 1983; Cockrell & LaFollette, 1985; Wilkerson, 1987; Gass, 1998).

Rollins (1983) noted both positive and negative sides to certification. Certification can protect the consumer and the experience, motivate outdoor leaders to higher standards and provide some support in liability issues. On the negative side, certification can be costly and time consuming, might test only a specific skill and may duplicate other preparation efforts (e.g. in-house organisation trainings). He suggested that organisations should create their own standards and certify their own leaders.

Similarly, a review of 150 North American professional certification programmes by Samuels (2000), in the tourism, hospitality and related industries, found a lack of consistency and quality across certification programmes, with professionals having a difficult time choosing a certification programme. Inconsistent standards and duplication of programmes led to confusion and lack of credibility among professionals. Given these findings, Samuels recommended that programmes be independently monitored, and similar programmes be combined and certification criteria broadened to allow more professionals access to these programmes. Hobbs (2012) argued:

> If programmes are not requiring certification of employees, if the public is not demonstrating demand by preferring programmes that are staffed by certified outdoor leaders, if no incentive exists for current professionals to obtain or maintain the certification, and if no external pressure exists for self-regulation, then certification is unnecessary. (p. 56)

Recent developments in adventure education and adventure tourism

Regardless of the pros and cons, experts (e.g. Loynes, 1998; Hardy, 2001; McGowan, 2012) have commented that contemporary adventure programming has become more commercialised and certification can provide a viable way to 'counteract the negative consequences of the commodification and commercialization of adventure programming' (McGowan, 2012, p. 49). McGowan suggested that certification can prevent commercialisation by preserving adventure programming's emphasis on human growth and development, and its ability to address important educational and societal issues.

Commercialised adventure (e.g. interest in indoor rock climbing, challenge courses, ziplines, aerial and adventure parks) is beginning to dominate the adventure industry (Attarian, in review). Activities that were once the exclusive domain of adventure programmes designed to enhance human growth and development are becoming mainstream. The commercialisation of adventure has introduced new activities and created significant changes in how the general public perceives adventure and how outdoor leaders are trained to deliver these adventure experiences. Along with these new approaches comes a growing concern over liability and safety issues. To address these issues, certification is becoming a requirement for staff leading these programmes and in some cases is being initiated by state or federal agencies rather than by the profession or an association – for example, the West Virginia Zipline and Canopy Tour Responsibility Act (West Virginia Legislature, 2014) and the Massachusetts Amusement and Entertainment Laws and Regulations (2014).

The growth of commercialised adventure has resulted in the need for a new type of outdoor leader. Traditionally, the outdoor leader, or *practitioner*, was a highly skilled professional who received training through varied personal adventure experiences, academic programmes and by the organisations who employed them. They were offered the technical, people and organisational skills necessary to deliver programmes in a safe and efficient manner. Commercialised adventure experiences have introduced the *activity instructor*, who often staffs these growing adventure experiences. Many of these individuals may have relatively little adventure experience, limited training and may be motivated by a pay cheque and customer tips rather than love of the activity.

Adventure programmes like OB and NOLS hire and train professional staff or practitioners to deliver quality adventure experiences. Activity instructors, on the other hand, are often trained in-house for specific tasks that might include belaying or guiding customers through an adventure park experience or monitoring guests as they descend a zipline. Because of the demand placed on these commercial entities, many vendors are beginning to design and implement programmes to train activity instructors to meet the requirements mandated by state statutes or by the standards created by associations (e.g. the Association for Challenge Course Technology).

Future directions

As the adventure industry grows and changes, discussion of what role certification should play in the outdoor adventure industry will continue. Perhaps certifying professional outdoor leaders may not be appropriate. Instead the current approach of activity-specific certification may be suitable, since this system seems currently to be working, especially in the USA. However, what might be worth exploring is whether or not the current vendor-driven/activity-specific approach should be the standard, or if another model might be more appropriate, such as the creation of a national or international association overseeing certification.

A good starting point in considering future models may be to examine what other professions are doing regarding certification. Examples might be tour guiding (Black & Ham, 2005) and ecotourism (Font, Sanabria & Skinner, 2003). Monitoring commercial adventure activities (e.g. ziplining, climbing walls) and noting what impact government regulations will have on the industry and what the *trickle-down* effect will be on non-commercial or the more traditional adventure programmes and activities will be important.

Other areas for investigation could include what role experience and academic degrees in outdoor leadership play in certification. Currently, more than sixty colleges and universities in the USA offer undergraduate degrees in outdoor leadership. Degree requirements focus on technical skill development, a varied core curriculum, and leadership experiences and training (Attarian, Brezovec & Piraino, 2008). None of these programmes offers a comprehensive certification based on a comprehensive exam. However, students in the majority of these programmes have the opportunity to receive activity certifications in areas such as Wilderness First Responder, Leave No Trace Trainer and American Canoe Association Canoe Instructor.

Questions also arise when academic programmes are considered. For example, should academic programmes be a requirement for certification? Should one, two or three years of field experience be required, along with a degree in outdoor leadership? Most people agree that relevant field experience is where the knowledge base acquired in training takes shape, is tested and fine-tuned. What about those individuals that have years of significant field experiences, but do not possess a formal degree in outdoor leadership? These questions, along with others, will need to be explored before moving forward with a national certification scheme, especially if it is to incorporate academic degree programmes in outdoor leadership.

In summary, professional outdoor certification is not likely to become required for a variety of reasons (Hobbs, 2012). First, the industry does not support certification. Second, evaluation is subjective and a minimum standard of care cannot be identified. Third, rather than a national standardised certification programme, individual programmes have trained leaders successfully on in-house training schemes. In the future, outdoor professionals are likely to continue the discussion on and the development of new approaches or alternatives to certification that can raise the standards and expertise of outdoor leaders.

References

American Mountain Guides Association (2013). *Credentials Requirement for Guiding on State and Federal Lands*. Boulder, CO: Author.

Attarian, A. (2001). Trends in outdoor adventure education. *Journal of Experiential Education, 24*(3), 141–149.

Attarian, A. (in review). Artificial settings for adventure. In R. Black & K. Bricker (Eds.) *Adventure Programming and Travel for the 21st Century*. State College, PA: Venture.

Attarian, A., Brezovec, L. & Piraino, L. (2008). The status of outdoor leadership programs in US colleges and universities. Coalition for Education in the Outdoors Ninth Biennial Research Symposium. Bradford Woods, Martinsville, IN, January.

Backert, D.W. (1987). The NOLS experience: Experiential education in the wilderness. Unpublished doctoral dissertation, North Carolina State University.

Black, R. & Ham, S. (2005). Improving the quality of tour guiding: Towards a model for tour guide certification. *Journal of Ecotourism, 4*(3), 178–195.

Bushwalking Leadership-South Australia (2014). Who we are, our history. Retrieved from www.bushwalkingleadership.org.au/Home/about.htm.

Cockrell, D. (1990). Outdoor leadership certification. In J.C. Miles & S. Priest (Eds.) *Adventure Education* (pp. 251–262). State College, PA: Venture Publishing, Inc.

Cockrell, D. & LaFollette, J. (1985). A national standard for outdoor leadership certification. *Parks and Recreation, 20*(6), 40–43.

Coghlan, J.F. & Webb, I. (1990). *Sport and British Politics since 1960*. Bristol, PA: The Falmer Press, Taylor & Francis.

Cordell, H.K. (2012). *Outdoor Recreation Trends and Futures: A Technical Document Supporting the Forest Service 2010 RPA Assessment. Gen. Tech. Rep. SRS-150*. Asheville, NC: US Department of Agriculture Forest Service, Southern Research Station.

Ewert, A., Attarian, A., Hollenhorst, S., Russell, K. & Voight, A. (2006). Evolving adventure pursuits on public lands: Emerging challenges for management and public policy. *Journal of Park and Recreation Administration, 24*(2), 125–140.

Font, X., Sanabria, R. & Skinner, E. (2003). Sustainable tourism and ecotourism certification: Raising standards and benefits. *Journal of Ecotourism, 2*(3), 213–218.

Garner, B. (2009). *Black's Law Dictionary*. Eagan, MN: West Publishing.

Gass, M. A. (1998). The status of certification and accreditation of adventure and outdoor leaders in North America. *Proceedings: Journal of the Leading Outdoor Organizations National Conference* (pp. 200–213). Leura, NSW, Australia: The Outdoor Recreation Council of Australia, Inc.

Green, P. (1982). *The Outdoor Leadership Handbook*. Tacoma, WA: The Emergency Response Institute.

Hardy, D. (2001). The McDonaldization of rock climbing: Conflict and counter conflict between climbing culture and dominate value systems in society. In R.A. Poff, A.N. Blacketer & M.L. Nunnally (Eds.) *Digital Archive of the Association of Outdoor Recreation and Education Conference Proceedings and Research Symposium Abstracts: 1984–2007*. Whitmore Lake, MI: Association of Outdoor Recreation and Education.

Hobbs, W. (2012). Certification: A solution looking for a problem. In B. Martin & M. Wagstaff (Eds.) *Controversial Issues in Adventure Programming* (pp. 55–61). Champaign, IL: Human Kinetics.

Kosseff, A. (2010). *AMC Guide to Outdoor Leadership*. Guilford, CT: The Globe Pequot Press.

Loynes, C. (1998). Adventure in a bun. *Journal of Experiential Education, 21*(1), 35–39.

March, B. (1987). Wilderness leadership certification – Catch 22. In J. Meier, T. Morash & G. Welton (Eds.) *High Adventure Outdoor Pursuits: Organization and Leadership* (pp. 489–494). Columbus, OH: Publishing Horizons.

Massachusetts Amusement and Entertainment Laws & Regulations (2014). Public safety, amusement devices, challenge course, climbing wall. Retrieved from: www.mass.gov/eopss/consumer-prot-and-bus-lic/license-type/amusements/amusement-and-entertainment-laws-and-regulations.html.

McGowan, M.L. (2012). Certification: Ensuring that adventure education will be a force for human growth and development. In B. Martin & M. Wagstaff (Eds.) *Controversial Issues in Adventure Programming* (pp. 49–54). Champaign, IL: Human Kinetics.

Nantahala National Forest (2014). *Operating Plan for Commercial Recreation Use*. Asheville, NC: Author.

Petzoldt, P. (1975). Adventure education and the National Outdoor Leadership School. *Journal of Outdoor Education, 10*, 3–7.

Petzoldt, P. (1984). *The Wilderness Handbook*. New York: W.W. Norton & Company, Inc.

Priest, S. & Gass, M.A. (2005). *Effective Leadership in Adventure Programming*. Champaign, IL: Human Kinetics.

Product Development and Management Association (2013). Benefits of certification. Retrieved from: www.pdma.org/p/cm/ld/fid=21.

Rollins, R. (1983). Leadership certification revisited. *Canadian Association of Health Physical Education and Recreation Journal, 50*(1), 8–9.

Samuels, J.B. (2000). Certification: A continually perplexing issue facing hospitality, tourism, and related professions. *Journal of Hospitality and Tourism Education, 12*(1), 47–52.

Senosk, E.M. (1976). *An Examination of Outdoor Pursuit Leadership Certification and Licensing within the United States in 1976*. Unpublished master's thesis, University of Oregon.

Tenenbaum, J.S. (2002). Association certification and accreditation programs: Minimising the liability risks. Retrieved from: www.asaecenter.org/Resources/whitepaperdetail.cfm?ItemNumber=12198.

Toynbee, P. (1982). Improving leadership training. In *Proceedings of the National Outdoor Education Conference* (pp. 132–136). Wellington, New Zealand.

Wagar, J.V.K. (1940). Certified outdoorsmen. *American Forests, 46*(11), 490–491.

Watters, R. (1983). Should outdoor leaders be certified? Association of College Unions, *International Bulletin*, June, 4–7.

Welch, T.R., Clement, K. & Berman, D. (2009). Wilderness first aid: Is there an 'industry standard'? *Wilderness and Environmental Medicine, 20*, 113–117.

West Virginia Legislature (2014). West Virginia Code. Chapter 21. Labor. *Article 15. Zipline and Canopy Tour Responsibility Act*. §21-15-1. Legislative purpose. Retrieved from: www.legis.state.wv.us/WVCODe/Code.cfm?chap+21&art=15.

Wilkerson, K. (1987). Another look at outdoor leadership certification. In J. Meier, T. Morash & Welton, G. (Eds.) *High Adventure Outdoor Pursuits: Organization and Leadership* (pp. 495–497). Columbus, OH: Publishing Horizons.

19

Ethical considerations in outdoor studies research

Letty Ashworth

UNIVERSITY OF CUMBRIA

Lucy Maynard

BRATHAY TRUST

Karen Stuart

KAZ STUART LEADERSHIP

This chapter explores the ethical considerations needed when carrying out research in outdoor studies. Because of the diverse scope of this book, a range of people (e.g. outdoor studies students, researchers or practitioners) could be engaging with a variety of outdoor studies research areas. This chapter focuses on research that involves people and social conditions. It is split into two parts: first, we provide an introductory overview of ethical considerations from a critical perspective; second, we explore the implications of this critique and propose alternative lenses to help guide future research.

An overview of ethical considerations

The term ethics is taken from the Greek word *ethos*. It literally translates to the *customary or habitual way of behaving*, and is often interpreted as the study of good and bad conduct (Shephard, 2002). Ethics concerns the morality of human conduct. More specifically related to areas of social research, it refers to moral deliberation, choice and accountability on the part of researchers (Edwards & Mauthner, 2002). Ethics concerns what 'ought to be done and what ought not to be done' (Denscombe, 2010, p. 59), and makes a move from the practical and logical considerations of methodology to moral perspectives.

These definitions have formed the foundations for professional groups to establish codes and standards of behaviour to regulate the actions of their members (Shephard, 2002). Most notable was the Belmont Report, which became the primary ethical framework for protecting human subjects in the USA (Zimmerman, 1997).

The field of ethics is vast. However, we provide here an overview of key ethical considerations, which can be used as a foundation or framework for research in outdoor studies. Although these considerations can act as guidelines, ensuring that these are critical rather than taken for granted is necessary; the context of outdoor studies is both diverse and complex, and applications can unearth dilemmas in practice. The following key considerations will be discussed: informed consent, purpose of research, risk of harm, anonymity and confidentiality, and the role of ethics panels and committees.

Informed consent

Before conducting any research, consent should be gained from all stakeholders (Christian, 2005). In this act of consent, the participants are agreeing to participate in the research process. Denscombe (2010) noted that *informed* relates to participants being aware of what may occur and what might be expected from them. Furthermore, they must be able to comprehend this information. *Consent* relates to the participant being able to make a rational and mature judgement of whether to participate or not, and that participation should be voluntary and free from coercion. According to Emanuel, Wendler and Grady (2000), informed consent should typically include the following, as well as any other considerations specific to a particular project:

- purpose – including research questions and the intended use of the research;
- confidentiality and anonymity – including the use of pseudonyms (or code names);
- safeguarding and disclosure (of risk or criminality);
- security of the data – including who will have access to it, where it will be stored and for how long, and how it will be disposed of;
- participant's access to their own data at any time;
- participant opportunity to review their data (participant validation);
- participant's right to withdraw their information at any point;
- how the research will be written up and who will see it.

People should be made aware that they have the right to withdraw their consent at any point – beginning, middle and end – and up to a pre-agreed point, where the research report is written. It should be made clear that individuals do not have to participate in all activities or answer all questions. Squirrell (2012) also emphasised the importance of ensuring that people have no obligation to state why they are withdrawing.

Participants should also be aware of, and consent to, how the research report is disseminated. The report should be available to all stakeholders in an accessible format, including details of the ethical decisions made, demonstrating the researcher's accountability as a considerate professional as well as adding transparency to the research report.

Informed consent needs to be accessible to participants, and therefore needs to be explained in ways that they can comprehend. These explanations can be in both written and verbal forms. Participants should be able to ask questions and get answers. Researchers should also be considerate of language issues (e.g. avoiding jargon such as *J-strokes* and labels such as *girly activities*).

In working with young people, researchers need to ensure that informed consent is given and gained from young people themselves as well as from an appropriate adult (e.g. teacher, youth worker, parent). These adults also work as gatekeepers, which is a critical process since researchers should not be able directly to access young people for information. Equally, researchers should not assume that gatekeepers who prevent access to young people are actually representing the young people's wishes.

Researchers need to reflect on how they make any of these considerations a reality rather than simply a routine statement of permission for participants. Crow, Wiles, Heath and Charles (2006) suggested that careful consideration of the informed consent process leads to better research. It helps prepare the researcher and participant, and establishes a more equal relationship between the two. This relationship gives the participants the confidence to be open and frank about the aspects of their lives pertaining to the research.

In considering the area of informed consent, researchers should be aware that some people may feel coerced into consenting by, for example, peers, managers, parents or the researcher. People need to understand that they are not obliged to consent and will have no repercussions regarding their choices.

Coercion also links to incentives for participation, which is a contentious area for two main reasons. First, people may feel they have to participate because they are receiving something in return. Further, they may feel they have to say the *right thing* to receive the incentive. This possibility may lead to inaccurate data. Second, there is also debate regarding what type of incentive people should receive. Some argue, from an equitable perspective, that this incentive should be a monetary payment (Noaks & Wincup, 2004). Others argue that payment may not be appropriate when working with vulnerable people, for example, as they may use their money for drugs or alcohol (Seddon, 2005). Alternative incentives include food vouchers or cinema tickets. Incentives are context specific and should be negotiated within the research design phase.

Crow *et al.* (2006) also noted a negative aspect in the process of gaining informed consent. It can inhibit the development of rapport necessary for the collection of authentic data. Crow *et al.* argued that the paperwork and concept of research can put up a barrier to inclusion for certain groups. While researchers have a duty to inform people, both timing and a dynamic approach can help in obtaining consent.

In summary, the process of informed consent is complicated, more about striking balances than following a set of rules (Wiles, Crow, Charles & Heath, 2007), and one where the information presented to participants is manageable, meaningful and in a timeframe that suits participants (Crow *et al.*, 2006). Outdoor studies, with links to experiential learning, lends itself to experiences that are spontaneous and novel, which are co-created in the moment (Beames, 2012). Not only are researchers examining people's experiences of something that cannot be predicted, they regularly use open-ended approaches such as questionnaires, interviews or personal journals to collect data. Hadjistavropoulus and Smythe (2001) suggested that open-ended or emergent ways of gathering data cause issues with the traditional notion of informed consent as participants do not know from the outset how the research will unfold. This dilemma has been addressed by the concept of *process consent*, which we address further in the discussion of alternative approaches to ethical considerations. After securing the consent of participants, researchers next need to consider who will gain from the research and what its purpose is.

Purpose

From the outset, the purpose of the research and who will gain needs to be considered. Researchers must ask these important questions and explicitly state the answers within the design and report process. How all stakeholders (e.g. participants, practitioners, organisations, funders or policy makers) will directly gain, or not, from participation should be made clear. Researchers must question if it is ethical to *take* the knowledge and experience from one stakeholder for the gain of others, (e.g. using data from participants to later secure organisational funding, which participants may not have known and agreed to at the time). Consent needs to be sought. Transparency about purpose and gain may also surface potential power dynamics, which can open ethical issues.

If the purpose of the research does not match the needs of the participants then practice dilemmas may be created. In the example above, the researcher may consider whether to pursue the data to ensure organisational security, or whether to respect the wishes of the participants. Another common example of practice dilemmas can occur in interview or focus-group settings, which may lead to participants disclosing inappropriate personal information. This disclosure may be the case following a powerful and profound outdoor experience. Remaining vigilant to the needs of the participants (i.e. protection) related to the purpose of the research (i.e. proving that the experience was worthwhile) is important.

These examples also highlight the tensions that a practitioner researcher can experience in balancing dual roles. Similarly, working in a research capacity can also lead to situations that mirror therapeutic practice since the strategies of researcher and therapist are similar (e.g. building rapport, listening, use of pauses, reading between the lines). The researcher can be led into ethical difficulties (Duncombe & Jessop, 2002). Birch and Miller (2000) indicated that 'in practice even skilled interviewers may find it difficult to draw neat boundaries around "rapport", "friendship" and "intimacy" in order to avoid the depths of "counselling" and "therapy"' (p. 113). Kvale (1996) also highlighted the difficulty in distinguishing between a therapeutic and research interview. A distinction can be made from the perspective of purpose and gain. The purpose of research is often to address the researcher's immediate agenda (i.e. answering the research questions) and the participant is helping the researcher, whereas in a therapy session the therapist is helping the client (Hart & Crawford-Wright, 1999). Despite this distinction, the acts of verbalising as well as being listened to, can be therapeutic (Buckle, Corbin Dwyer & Jackson, 2010). The researcher cannot control the potential outcomes; they can only ensure they manage the boundaries of their role. They have the dilemma of finding a balance between building rapport and setting clear, ethical boundaries of practice. Therefore, enacting ethical guidelines relating to purpose and gain is not a straightforward task and is closely related to minimising the risk of harm.

Risk of harm

Researchers need to consider any potential risk of harm for participants. This harm should be viewed from the perspective of all stakeholders, as well as the research project's impact as a whole. Risk might include the project failing (e.g. due to insufficient data), risk of damaging information about the service provider (Squirrell, 2012), or the risk of distress to participants and adverse impact on stakeholders. Our discussion focuses on the risk to participants.

Researchers should question all eventualities, such as psychological, emotional or physical risk. First, the research process should not be emotionally distressing or psychologically damaging. However, most people will have negative experiences during their lives and talking about the negative experiences may evoke negative or distressing emotions within the research process. Researchers should not ignore negative experiences or emotions. Buckle et al. (2010) offered support for these situations and argued that pain was not being caused, but that researchers were bearing witness to the pain that was already present.

Researchers need to manage the research process if it becomes distressing for a participant. Information about how to offer support, cease the research interview and/or offer to follow up with significant others should be considered before the research commences so that the researcher has strategies to deal with any such scenarios – for example, with lists of contacts, 'time out' cards, a postcard withdrawal form.

Furthermore, research participants should not be put at any physical risk from others by taking part in a study. This risk could be related to the location of the data collection were it in a dangerous geographical area or if the location were too public in exposing a participant's engagement. For example, we have had experiences of carrying out post-course interviews with people to understand the extent to which an outdoor programme impacted on offending behaviour. We, as researchers, were mistaken for the police which was a barrier we had to overcome as being associated with the police was a risk for the participants.

When considering all stakeholders, researchers should also consider themselves as potentially at risk related to psychological, emotional and physical safety. Researchers should have appropriate background checks and be well trained. They should not work beyond their capabilities (Weiss, 1998). Researchers should ensure they have the appropriate supervisory support structures in place to manage emotional and psychological safety. Therefore, protecting identities also is a significant aspect related to anonymity and consent.

Anonymity and confidentiality

Anonymity and confidentiality are similar but have different implications for participants. Anonymity means that no one associated with the research will know the identity of the participants, while confidentiality means that the researcher will know identities, but will not disclose them. Participants should be assured of their protection and that their names, or any information that could identify them, will not be used in the dissemination of findings. This assurance also applies within the process of data collection. Weiss (1998) highlighted the importance of not telling 'one respondent what another has said . . . as they will be able to piece together their identities' (p. 94).

In considering anonymity, Weiss (1998) explained that anonymity should be ensured unless an individual gives specific permission to be identified. In conducting research, we have interviewed people who wished to be identified usually because they felt strongly about a matter and wanted to help others learn from their experiences. However, revealing identities should be cautiously considered, particularly when working with vulnerable or disadvantaged young people. Respondents could regret their choice in the future. They could also inadvertently identify other young people by association.

Assuring confidentiality is important, but can be problematic. Confidentiality can be assured for most areas of research, for example dislike of a particular activity, but cannot be assured for disclosures of harm. If someone discloses that they are at harm (e.g. from relationship abuse) or are harming other people (e.g. through criminal activities), then the researcher has a duty to protect those individuals by passing this information on to relevant authorities.

Dealing with confidentially and risk is important, particularly related to young people under 18 years and vulnerable people, due to their heightened need for protection. Confidentiality can be assured only up until there is a safeguarding issue. This exception should be made clear to interviewees from the beginning (i.e. within the informed consent process) and be reiterated if the researcher senses a young person is starting to disclose too much. This honesty can have an adverse impact on rapport building with participants, but is essential. Confidentiality related to illegal or immoral issues is blurred and disputed. For example, Williamson, Goodenough, Kent and Ashcroft (2005) suggested that any disclosure relating to harm to self, others or criminality should be reported to authorities. In practice this requirement may be impossible when working, for example, with young offenders. Others debate the area more generally from a participatory perspective, arguing that young people should have more control of anonymity (Lansdown, 2013). We found that some young people may ask to be identified in the research report as they are proud of participating. In this situation the researcher has to decide whether to retain anonymity for the future protection of the participant, or whether to uphold their wish to be identified, allowing them to control the decision. Alignment of research practice with stakeholder and organisational policies on safeguarding, identification and disclosure will support researchers facing such dilemmas.

Squirrell (2012) highlighted how photos, tapes and video add an extra complexity to the discussion of anonymity. A specific reference to this type of data and how it will be used must occur within the informed consent process. This issue has increasing relevance because of the growing popularity of digital mediums and social networks.

Ethics panels and committees

The prime areas of ethics – purpose and gain, informed consent, risk of harm, and anonymity and confidentiality – are often described as ethical checklists. When using a checklist, the complexity of each of these four areas should be noted, rather than just *ticking the box*. Further, most researchers need their studies cleared by a panel of experts within a university or academic structure, or for larger research organisations and departments, from an internal panel. Clearance may not always be possible for carrying out research in outdoor studies unless organisations make provision for their own internal ethical review panels. To not adhere to ethical procedures is unethical, but ethics goes beyond just getting past the ethics panel. Participants and stakeholders are the ultimate consideration.

Ethics panels and committees have faced increasing critique and, according to Simpson (2011), act as a 'uniform aperture through which to pass research of all different shapes and sizes' (p 378). Simpson states that these apertures can be constricting, and proposed a need for more flexible ethics. This concern may be exacerbated further by the dynamic situations that occur in outdoor studies (e.g. interactions on a wilderness expedition). The remainder of this chapter considers what some alternative approaches to addressing ethics might be.

Alternative approaches to ethical considerations

Denscombe (2010) emphasised that basic codes of ethics, such as those previously described, are guidelines and not *rules of conduct*. Each principle should not be followed minimally but considered as a starting point. Any departure from the guidelines needs to be noted and justified. However, many researchers review these guidelines as strict rules. In a world of ever increasing bureaucracy, there is support for ethical guidelines not to become regulatory (Crow et al., 2006; Wiles et al., 2007).

Sparkes and Smith (2014) offered some useful insight in the area of sport, exercise and health. They are sceptical of traditional ethics and defined people as 'bounded, autonomous self-contained subjects rather than as dialogical and relational . . . [ethics are] modernist, male orientated and imperialist' (p. 207). Furthermore, ethics have been based on positivist traditions of biomedical research and many people often 'lack the ability to understand the nature of ethics as an emergent process in the field' (p. 208) related to new methods and research questions. Further, Sparkes and Smith suggested traditional ethics are largely bureaucratic and are set up to protect institutions.

Sparkes and Smith (2014) reinforced that traditional ethics are minimalistic and offer only a basic starting point. This view is supported by Simpson (2011), who suggested research has a 'series of ethical moments which arise throughout the research . . . rather than a single moment at its outset' (p. 377). The ethics process is ongoing and, rather than passing through a single aperture, researchers should be in a *continuous shoot mode*, where they constantly check and re-check that ethical procedures are working effectively. This process is sometimes termed *running* or *process ethics* (Ramcharan & Cutcliffe, 2001). This approach appears to be meeting the needs of social science researchers in the field of outdoor studies.

Alderson and Morrow (2006) advised the use of multidisciplinary research ethics guidelines, and for separating health care ethics from social research ethics. Simpson (2011) developed this argument by suggesting that researchers separate 'ethics of the body (with a person attached) and ethics of the person (with a body attached) (p. 377). Ethics of the body relate to traditional human subject research models developed out of a medical background. Ethics of the person allows for a *social subject research* in which researchers engage with an *open subject* with whom a relationship is possible. While Simpson recognised that neither the body nor the person is entirely separate, he concluded that social science research should have a different genealogy of ethics.

Although Sparkes and Smith (2014) are fairly scathing about what they consider to be traditionalist minimalist ethics, they draw on the work of Lahman, Geist, Rodriguez, Graglia and DeRoche (2011), and offer some examples of emerging alternatives that they term *aspirational* ethics.

Aspirational ethics

Lahman *et al.* (2011) considered aspirational ethics to include *virtue, relational, feminist, narrative, caring and reflexive ethics*. All may offer alternative considerations. Virtue ethics, for example, suggest a move away from abstract rules and consider that ethics should be based on the contexts and practices in which research is conducted. These ethics are driven by the situational contexts as opposed to predetermined rules (Sparkes & Smith, 2014), and rely to some extent on the moral background and reflexivity of the researcher. However, Blee and Currier (2011) suggested that ethics should not just be left up to the researcher. According to Simpson (2011) scholars should develop the role of research supervisors and mentors acting as *ethical consultants* that provide ongoing support. If ethics can be seen as ongoing and situational, then a one-time panel review may no longer be enough.

Similarly, aspirational ethics such as reflexive ethics are situational and emerge from the interactions between the researcher and participant. Sparkes and Smith (2014) suggested that researchers:

> (a) be sensitive to the interactions of self, others and situations, (b) notice the reactions to a research situation and adapt in a responsive, ethical, moral way, where the participant's safety, privacy, dignity and autonomy are respected, (c) pay special attention to the possible power imbalances between the researcher and the participants . . . (p. 212)

Both virtue and reflexive ethics, as outlined above, detail approaches to ethics that are more aligned with outdoor studies practice, which is often experiential and collaborative in nature. This practice aims to tip the power balance in the favour of participants and develop relationships between the facilitator and the participant that are based on honesty, trust, respect and reciprocity (Young, 2009).

Stern (2011) proposed that, typically, research ethics consists of a set of *negatives*, which relate mostly to avoiding harm and deception, for example, *don't* harm participants and *don't* identify participants. These negatives can be limiting and, moreover, can result in less focus on positive gains. Stern's work is helpful because he suggests turning a set of negatives, things that should not be done, to positive and empowering processes that focus on what should be done. We have experienced through our own work as well as through others (e.g. Buckle *et al.*, 2010) that ethics panels may deem it inappropriate to engage in open-ended interviews with vulnerable participants, reasoning that the outcome is unknown and potentially harmful. If managed well and set in the right context, however, these interviews can be empowering for participants if they feel listened to, as well as if they feel helped in clarifying an experience and learning from it.

Due to the complex nature of research ethics, no simple solutions exist. However, if researchers align research ethics with practice, and focus on what could be gained from both the research and the ethics process, outdoor researchers will not only improve research findings, but also the wellbeing of the research participants and researchers. Stern (2011) concluded that researchers know they have been ethical and right if they are thanked by participants for letting them be involved with a research project.

Summary

This chapter has defined ethics, traced a brief history and presented four key ethical considerations: purpose and gain; informed consent; risk of harm; and anonymity and confidentiality. We have problematised an approach that treats these considerations superficially and that relies on checklists or external panels to validate methodological decisions. We encourage: (i) thinking of guidelines as starting points; (ii) using discipline-specific frameworks; and (iii) being vigilant researchers and supervisors who are alert to arising and changing ethical issues. We present ethics as an ongoing process. This nuanced understanding of ethics has evolved partly because of the complex nature of research with people, and partly due to the nature of outdoor studies and experiential learning. The value base of outdoor studies is human centred. It respects and values participants, and views them as capable. Research in such settings will seek to share power and to be conversational rather than an interrogational. Researchers may experience tensions in their role, in protecting participants and *doing* the research, in respecting confidentiality and keeping participants safe, in ticking the ethics boxes and in remaining responsive. As a result of these tensions, ethical issues should always be complex, changing, and based on best judgement rather than hard-and-fast rules.

References

Alderson, P. & Morrow, V. (2006). Multidisciplinary research ethics review: Is it feasible? *International Journal of Social Research Methodology, 9*(5), 405–417.

Beames, S. (2012). *Learning Outside the Classroom: Theory and Guidelines for Practice*. London: Routledge.

Birch, M. & Miller, T. (2000). Inviting intimacy: The interview as a therapeutic opportunity. *Social Research Methodology, Theory and Practice, 3*(3), 189–202.

Blee, K.M. & Currier, A. (2011). Ethics beyond the IRB: An introductory essay. *Qualitative Sociology, 34*(3), 401–413.

Buckle, J.L., Corbin Dwyer, S. & Jackson, M. (2010). Qualitative bereavement research: Incongruity between the perspectives of participants and research ethics boards. *International Journal of Social Research Methodology, 13*(2), 111–125.

Christian, C.G. (2005). Ethics and politics in qualitative research. In N.K. Denzin & Y.S. Lincoln (Eds.) *The Sage Handbook of Qualitative Research* (3rd edn) (pp. 139–164). London: Sage.

Crow, G., Wiles, R., Heath, S. & Charles, V. (2006). Research ethics and data quality: The implications of informed consent. *International Journal of Social Research Methodology, 9*(2), 83–95.

Denscombe, M. (2010). *Ground Rules for Social Research: Guidelines for Good Practice* (2nd edn). Maidenhead, UK: Open University Press/McGraw-Hill.

Duncombe, J. & Jessop, J. (2002). 'Doing rapport' and the ethics of 'faking friendship'. In M. Mauthner, M. Birch, J. Jessop & T. Miller (Eds.) *Ethics in Qualitative Research* (pp. 107–122). London: Sage.

Edwards, R. & Mauthner, M. (2002). Ethics and feminist research theory and practice. In M. Mauthner, M. Birch, J. Jesson & T. Miller (Eds.) *Ethics in Qualitative Research* (pp. 14–31). London: Sage.

Emanuel, E., Wendler, D. & Grady, C. (2000). What makes clinical research ethical? *Journal of the American Medical Association, 283*(20), 2701–2711.

Hadjistavropoulos, T. & Smythe, W.E. (2001). Elements of risk in qualitative research. *Ethics and Behaviour, 11*(2), 163–174.

Hart, N. & Crawford-Wright, A. (1999). Research as therapy, therapy as research: ethical dilemmas in new-paradigm research. *British Journal of Guidance and Counselling, 27*(2), 205–214.

Kvale, S. (1996). *Interviews: An Introduction to Qualitative Research Interviewing.* Thousand Oaks, CA: Sage.

Lahman, M., Geist, M., Rodriguez, K., Graglia, P. & DeRoche, K. (2011). Culturally responsive relational reflexive ethics in research: The three r's. *Quality & Quantity: International Journal of Methodology, 45*(6), 1397–1414.

Lansdown, G. (2013). *Protection through Participation: An International Perspective.* Child Studies Conferences: Participation into Practice. Kings College, London.

Noaks, L. & Wincup, E. (2004). *Criminological Research: Understanding Qualitative Methods.* London: Sage.

Ramcharan, P. & Cutcliffe, J.R. (2001). Judging the ethics of qualitative research: Considering the 'ethics as process' model. *Health and Social Care in the Community, 9*(6), 358–366.

Seddon, T. (2005). Paying drug users to take part in research: Justice, human rights and business perspectives on the use of incentive payments. *Addiction Research & Theory, 13*(2), 101–109.

Shephard, R.J. (2002). Ethics in exercise science research. *Sports Medicine, 32*(3), 169–183.

Simpson, B. (2011). Ethical moments: Future directions for ethical review and ethnography. *Journal of the Royal Anthropological Institute, 17,* 377–393.

Sparkes, A.C. & Smith, B. (2014). *Qualitative Research Methods in Sport, Exercise and Health.* London: Routledge.

Squirrell, G. (2012). *Evaluation in Action: Theory and Practice for Effective Evaluation.* Lyme Regis, UK: Russell House Publishing.

Stern, J. (2011). From negative ethics to positive virtues in research. Paper presented at Value and Virtues in Practice-Based Research Conference in York, UK.

Weiss, C.H. (1998). *Evaluation: Methods for Studying Programs and Policies* (2nd edn). Upper Saddle River, NJ: Prentice Hall.

Wiles, R., Crow, G., Charles, V. & Heath, S. (2007). Informed consent and the research process: Following the rules or striking balances. *Sociological Research Online, 12*(2), 83–95.

Williamson, E., Goodenough, T., Kent, J. & Ashcroft, R. (2005). Conducting research with children: The limits of confidentiality and child protection protocols. *Children & Society, 19,* 397–409.

Young, K. (2009). *The Art of Youth Work.* Lyme Regis, UK: Russell House Publishing.

Zimmerman, J.F. (1997). The Belmont report: An ethical framework for protecting research subjects. *The Monitor.* Alexandria, VA: Clinical Association of Research Professionals. Summer Volume, 1–4.

20

Adventure education
Crucible, catalyst and inexact

Jim Sibthorp and Dan Richmond

University of Utah

The lure of adventure. Exciting, novel, risky, fun and, ultimately, enticing. Adventure education (AE) is about harnessing the inherent motivation for these experiences in ways that reinforce positives and limit negatives. AE provides an acceptable outlet for sensation seeking, at times replacing illicit options. However, it can also afford experiences that are both catalysts and crucibles for individual and group growth. This chapter addresses three major topics: (i) defining AE; (ii) discussing the status and challenges of contemporary AE practice; and (iii) explicating the limits and challenges to AE research.

Defining adventure education

The terms AE and outdoor adventure education (OAE) are often used interchangeably, and most definitions of either term share common elements. One definition classifies AE as:

> A variety of teaching and learning activities and experiences usually involving a close interaction with an outdoor natural setting, and that contain elements of real or perceived danger and/or risk, in which the outcome, while uncertain, can be influenced by the actions of the participant and circumstance. (Ewert & Sibthorp, 2014, p. 5)

To break this definition down, teaching and learning speaks to the intentional educational nature of AE, which differentiates it from solely recreational pursuits that may be educational but are not intentionally structured with educational goals and objectives. AE is typically outdoors, which means the environment is usually dynamic and nature-centric. Programmes include elements of real or perceived risk, a hallmark of what makes AE adventurous and exciting. The outcomes are uncertain, yet are not beyond influence.

Outside academic circles, people tend to define AE through referencing common practices or schools. Outward Bound (OB), with its international scope, is a common exemplar. However, OB includes variety in programming, practices, participants, activities, operating areas and purposes, which is true for many AE programmes whether they are large organisations, university programmes, smaller non-profits or commercial companies. The field includes a range of curriculum designs, teaching methods and philosophies that differ across organisations and activities. Homing in on *the* central essence that makes AE distinct is difficult.

Qualities of the adventure education experience

Some common qualities of AE exist. Most AE programmes include small groups working towards a shared goal. This group is typically separated from everyday life, establishing a degree of remoteness. Some common technical outdoor skills are involved in the travel and desired objectives. Novelty and challenge are evident, leading to risk and uncertainty while fuelling interest and engagement. As programmes typically follow a pedagogical model of teaching and learning, there are educational goals as well as expedition and participant goals. Learning is typically experiential and active. In AE, as opposed to recreational trips, leaders or instructors guide and facilitate the AE process while also overseeing risk management, managing group dynamics and addressing learning topics.

Consider a typical AE programme. A small group of students under the guidance of instructors embarks on a remote expedition into a natural environment. Transportation might entail sailing, kayaking, rafting, hiking or biking. Educational objectives are present and the instructors determine how, what and when to deliver certain lessons, accommodating the needs and motives of the group, and accounting for competing expedition factors such as terrain, hazards, fatigue, weather or group conflicts. These expedition factors are often used to prioritise lessons most useful and necessary for the group. Thus, the expedition parameters (e.g. route, participants, activities, equipment) influence, but do not determine, the outcomes. The combination of new people in a new and unpredictable outdoor environment creates a sense of novelty, challenge and uncertainty. The nature of the trip, physically and socially separated from others, creates a sense of remoteness that necessitates participants functioning as a group. The instructors rely on their wits and experience with limited additional resources.

Therefore, AE programmes are dense and intense, fostering rich learning environments. The dynamic nature of AE is what makes it both powerful and amorphous. Visceral and engaging experiences are frequent during AE, affording more learning potential than other settings (Sibthorp et al., 2015). Powerful transformative learning due to novelty and disorientation has also been linked to AE (D'Amato & Krasny, 2011). Despite their holistic and unpredictable nature, certain qualities of AE stand out.

The group is central to the AE experience, serving as a key mechanism for desired personal and group-level outcomes (Ewert & McAvoy, 2000; Sibthorp, Furman, Paisley, Gookin & Schumann, 2011). Learning from and through other group members is necessary in a setting where physical proximity is coupled with social interdependence and remoteness from people not on the course. Disentangling social dynamics from the objectives and outcomes of AE is hard since the group acts as a source of support and community (Goldenberg & Soule, 2011), as well as the means to practise outdoor skills, leadership, communication and teamwork (Paisley, Furman, Sibthorp & Gookin, 2008). The social world of AE is like other group-oriented experiences, from team sports to work teams, where group chemistry and available skill sets – complementary or otherwise – relate fundamentally to success and failure.

Within the community of an AE experience, instructors serve as designated leaders. Effective instructors provide an overall vision for the experience, help create and support a positive learning environment, manage real and perceived risk, and guide participants towards desired outcomes (Schumann, Sibthorp, Paisley & Gookin, 2009). Instructors positively influence student learning through engaging and interactive instruction, one-to-one coaching, role modelling and interpersonal relationships with students (Schumann et al. 2009). Effective instruction in

AE parallels good teaching in traditional classrooms, where positive student–teacher relationships, clear expectations and goals, opportunities for practice and mastery, and feedback result in significant impacts on student learning (Hattie, 2009). Instructors embody the spirit of the AE programme they represent, and participants depend on these leaders for guidance and support. The programmes themselves rely on instructors to facilitate the experience while delivering the course curriculum and working towards desired participant outcomes.

Between the parameters of the programme, the students and the instructors, a variety of goals operate in AE. Some goals are tied to physically completing the trip and route, others originate from students – from simply having fun, being social in nature, to educational goals that may include acquiring specific technical skills or learning more about the natural environment. The programme also articulates its own goals. Many emphasise teaching leadership, outdoor skills or teamwork. Instructors are responsible for aligning these varied goals into a successful AE experience, and leveraging student interest and motivation to push participants through course-related challenges.

Harnessing the power of intrinsic interest for adventure is an essential piece of the AE experience. While AE is not needed to embark on an adventure, AE provides an intentional structure and sequence managed by leaders. These elements allow participants to realise their desire for adventure without unbridled risk. Most adventure activities do not legally require participants to have a guide or instructor. However, unsupervised novices and inexperienced adventurers are less likely to mitigate and manage the inherent dangers and risks accompanying these activities. Conversely, structure, direction and supervision place constraints on the benefits. Unsupervised adventure recreation, because of its individual nature and autonomy, affords higher potential for benefits, but is concomitant with greater likelihood of costs (see Figure 20.1). In balance, participants in quality AE programmes are often afforded a more favourable likelihood for benefits and a lower likelihood for detrimental experiences.

These qualities have prompted some to consider AE a microcosm, a smaller and more responsive system that parallels aspects of the larger dynamic systems that surround people daily. The remoteness and necessary interdependence facilitates system responsiveness while allowing for experimentation, success and failure. If participants fail to complete a summit attempt, are not shouldering their share of the work or are experiencing conflict with others,

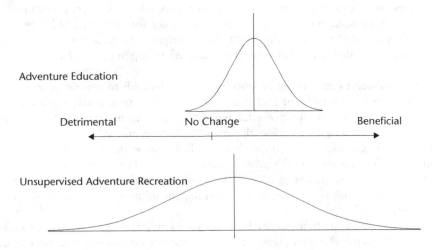

Figure 20.1 Likelihood of costs and benefits of adventure education and adventure recreation

they are often unable to avoid consequences or criticism. Feedback is inevitable, and leaving the AE microcosm is usually not an option. This feedback and the motivation to complete the programme's goals often necessitate reflection and learning. This small and responsive microcosm also provides positive feedback to reinforce desired behaviours in a similar way. The individual who successfully prepares a dinner or guides the group through a day of navigation is typically rewarded by a sense of accomplishment and unambiguous recognition of success. Ultimately, the combination of qualities inherent in AE creates distinctive opportunities for learning.

Outcomes of adventure education

Coming from the unique AE learning environment, participants have reported many outcomes. Hattie, Marsh, Neill and Richards (1997) found forty outcomes that they classified into six broad categories: academic, leadership, self-concept, personality, interpersonal and adventuresome. Others have broken outcomes into psychological, sociological, education and physical (Ewert, 1989), or cognitive, affective, social–interpersonal and physical-behavioural (Rickinson et al., 2004). More recently, Ewert and Sibthorp (2014) proposed two overarching categories of interpersonal and intrapersonal development. Interpersonal outcomes involve changes in how a person interacts with others, and include group-level outcomes such as group cohesion or sense of community. Intrapersonal outcomes are individual in nature and include self-constructs such as self-efficacy, skill building, values and mental states.

The main challenge for AE has been to articulate how outcomes are valuable after an AE course ends. Outcome utility has often been addressed through dialogue on the transfer of learning. Through facilitation participants may consider how they will apply lessons from AE in other contexts (e.g. Gass, 1999) or, through inherent reflection, participants may make connections between AE and other aspects of their lives. However, how transfer occurs and the level of transfer remains problematic (Furman & Sibthorp, 2012). Most of the studies on learning transfer in AE have shown that transfer of certain outcomes is probable, but often difficult to document. Brown (2010) reviewed years of research and found little empirical evidence of a clear connection between AE programmes and the transfer of knowledge and skills to future settings. However, qualitative findings tell a more favourable story for proponents of AE, indicating that programming has lasting impacts on outdoor skills, self-confidence, general leadership skills, teamwork, personal appreciation for nature, tolerance for adversity and life perspective (Sibthorp, Furman, Paisley & Gookin, 2008). AE participants do make connections between their experience and their lives, but researchers have yet to capture the full and lasting effect quantitatively.

Another approach to articulating benefits has been to link AE to generative outcomes, or outcomes that are known to foster further benefits. Outcomes such as self-regulation, persistence or coping skills are viewed as powerful, but they are general in nature and help individuals navigate a range of challenging situations that might be encountered at later times and in different contexts. Self-regulation, for example, has been linked to academic achievement, learning motivation and lifelong learning (Dignath & Buttner, 2008). Having to self-manage limited personal and group resources during AE can encourage learning about self-regulation and personal responsibility. Similarly, having to endure during an arduous travel day can illustrate the value of persistence.

An alternative way to understanding AE is to employ a holistic systems approach, taking into consideration the factors that contribute to post-experience trajectories of participants. In developmental psychology, the term *developmental cascades* describes the cumulative effects of social and cognitive adaptation tied to experience (Masten & Cicchetti, 2010). The critical difference in this approach is embracing the weak causal link between any one event or programme and a change in growth or development of an individual. Researchers in fields other than AE have used this framework to consider individual and contextual relations (e.g. out-of-school community involvement, neighbourhood factors, parenting) and to measure positive youth development, self-regulation and other outcomes (Lewin-Bizan, Bowers & Lerner, 2010). AE offers somewhat distinct qualities and often shakes participants from their current states. Shaking participants from their current beliefs or behaviour patterns may not lead to development, yet offers an opportunity for change. From a systems perspective, participants have a chance to change states. They may return with changed perspectives or behaviours. They may also return with the same mindset or behaviour pattern. Although this approach has not been studied widely in AE because it often requires complicated longitudinal studies, using developmental cascades as a conceptual framework may effectively capture the lasting relationship between AE participation and the personal development of participants.

Personal development through challenging and engaging outdoor experiences is at the heart of AE. The outcomes associated with participation reflect the original vision of Kurt Hahn, the founder of Outward Bound, who believed that outdoor experiences helped develop self-regulation, interpersonal competence, leadership and character (Miner & Boldt, 1981). Empirical research in AE supports that quality programmes can make a lasting impression (Hattie et al., 1997), as does anecdotal evidence available from enthusiastic alumni testimonials. The ongoing effort to capture and document outcomes continues to be a challenge, but the further examination of why and how particular programming works illustrates a widespread belief, especially in Western culture, in the developmental potential of AE.

Contemporary practice

Contemporary AE practice is increasingly fractured and disjointed. Programmes are becoming more diverse and international in scope. Changes within AE are inevitable due in part to demographic shifts and technological development as well as programme proliferation.

Internationalisation and diversity in AE

Although AE has a rich tradition in Western culture, its popularity is growing internationally and the field itself is becoming increasingly diverse. Outward Bound has schools now in at least thirty-three countries and caters courses to increasingly diverse populations (Outward Bound International, 2014). Likewise, as communication and transportation afford greater mobility and marketing, AE has continued to evolve in different ways. River tracing in Taiwan or *friluftsliv* in Norway embrace different models of AE. In short, AE uses activities with diverse populations for different purposes in a variety of contexts. This expansion is likely to continue as the interest in AE models and programmes expands around the world.

Even within Western countries, the historical populations and programmes are changing. In the United States, the demographics are shifting, with an increase in the proportion of older adults and racially and ethnically heterogeneous populations (US Census Bureau, 2012). While the audience for many AE programmes remains relatively homogeneous (i.e. young, male and Caucasian), programme administrators are examining ways to promote diversity and serve a wider range of participants (Bobilya, Holman, Lindley & McAvoy, 2010). Common initiatives include scholarship programmes, organisational partnerships, intentional staff recruitment, cultural competency training and directed marketing campaigns. Unfortunately, programmes continue to struggle to attract female participants and instructors in proportions comparable to males despite years of work to address underrepresentation via targeted recruiting, women-only experiences and staff development programmes (Warren, Roberts, Breunig & Alvarez, 2014). In addition, many AE providers are aiming at older adult participants who could benefit from tailored experiences (Bobilya *et al.*, 2010), and who may be interested in shorter and more accessible courses. For AE to remain vital and relevant, programmes must work to attract participants and employees that represent the broader population. To be sure, there are opportunities to create a more inclusive culture within AE that shares the benefits of participation with groups traditionally underrepresented in programming, particularly women and those with low socio-economic status. Moving forward, programmes will need to continually re-evaluate and retool programming and practices to address gaps in participation and changing demographics, and avoid the temptation of accepting the status quo.

The use of technology

Alongside shifting demographics, the emergence of new technology is reshaping AE. Global positioning systems, satellite telephones, personal locator beacons, tablets and e-readers are finding roles in contemporary AE practices. The activities that were once an *escape* from technology are becoming just another place where modern technology is present. How these new tools for communication, connection and learning will impact the inherent qualities of remoteness, outdoor skill development and hands-on learning remains unclear. Nevertheless, technology can provide useful tools, but modern gadgets may also distract from what makes AE powerful.

Programme proliferation

The changing environment surrounding AE has led to an increase in AE providers serving emerging niches within the field (Potter, Socha & Connell, 2011). In the past, there were mainly a few large, visible, players. The early formalised schools, such as OB or the National Outdoor Leadership School (NOLS), were the places to go for AE. The internet has provided wide exposure to adventure activities, leading to the diversification of programme offerings that go beyond traditional backpacking, rafting and climbing courses. Today, schools and colleges, public-sector programming departments and innumerable for-profit entities use AE as a means for education, training technical and interpersonal skills, and building community. While this diversification has expanded the field's reach and scope, it has also threatened the quality of the programmes and their survival.

An outside observer often has difficulty recognising the significant differences between a high-quality and a low-quality programme. Many aspects of higher-quality programmes occur behind the scenes. The planning, training, risk management and crisis response protocols essential for programme success are sometimes revealed only when the atypical occurs (e.g. an accident or evacuation). Organisations that have a culture of valuing feedback and continuous programme improvement are in a better position to offer high-quality AE programmes. However, a number of intangible and uncertain qualities also make a programme succeed or fail, which are often difficult to predict. Therefore, programmes with organisational expertise and familiarity with contingency options, such as alternate routes, conflict resolution strategies or evacuation resources, are often able to navigate the unanticipated problems more successfully. Recognising a need within the field, larger organisations are taking leadership roles in risk management education by sharing best practices with new and existing professionals through events like the Wilderness Risk Management Conference.

Research in Adventure Education

AE professionals are becoming enamoured with research and data, particularly outcome measures. A recent trend in AE has been a field-wide push for *evidence-based* curricula (Bobilya et al., 2010). Evaluation sessions are increasing in popularity as practitioners seek to measure and document the processes and outcomes of their programmes. Research and evaluation evidence can serve as a tool to improve programming, develop staff, support rationale in grant funding requests and make the case for participation to potential customers.

Data are often used to make decisions in everyday life. Online shopping, for example, gives immediate access to reviews, price and feature comparisons, and the power to make better-informed choices. Many popular sites condense reviews into summaries so that a consumer looking to make a purchase decision can quickly understand the reviews in a snapshot of a few main themes. Similarly, smartphones help avoid traffic congestion and allow for choosing among endless entertainment options on a given night. AE practitioners hope to use data in an analogous way, using evidence to help their organisations navigate towards larger strategic goals.

Programme evaluations are common in AE programmes, but programmes are expanding the evaluative process to gather more data to inform organisational decisions. Collection is facilitated through easily programmable survey software like SurveyMonkey, RedCap or Qualtrics. While evaluation is most often used for accountability or as a check on quality control, savvy organisations use evaluation as a particular form of research (Pinch, 2009). An example of the latter approach comes from NOLS, where end-of-course surveys are used both for programmatic assessment as well as for theoretically driven research studies.

Web-based surveys and survey applications for smartphones (i.e. apps) have made collecting and analysing data easier. Many of these tools require limited software programming experience, offer basic reporting and can easily export data to powerful analysis tools such as Excel, SPSS or NVivo software where extra analyses and data display options are available. In addition, less sophisticated but computationally powerful tools have aided time-consuming processes. Word cloud applications like Wordle are increasingly used for qualitative data crunching to graphically display the frequency of words, which reduces a labour-intensive process of data coding to a simplistic, yet accessible, enumerative process. Therefore, the accessibility of these data tools, paired with a need for measureable results, has resulted in increased expectations that AE can use data to inform processes.

Research challenges

Despite the need for good research and the availability of new data analysis tools, advancing research in AE is difficult. This issue is due to several interrelated reasons.

The lack of sizeable and obtainable research funding remains an obstacle. While AE professionals have attempted to intersect with contemporary societal issues, this research remains on the fringe. AE is, within the larger context of social science research, very specific and applied. Without more substantive ties to critical social issues, AE research will continue to struggle, fuelled mostly by local and individual initiatives and graduate student efforts.

Given the limited funding, graduate student research remains critical. A relatively small number of AE scholars are active worldwide. Upon a review of five journals with clear ties to AE research, we estimated the entire number of active AE researchers at fewer than fifty individuals. We defined active researchers as authors with more than five research publications over the past ten years. Even using these criteria, graduate students and advisees produce much of the published research in collaboration with established scholars, leading one to assume that some research is conducted at least partially for pedagogical purposes. This process is natural in most fields and not without benefits. Many students move into practice settings and continue to appreciate and use research. While this reliance on graduate students certainly has value, it has also led to a limited research base for AE, especially in comparison to other applied educational fields.

One of the main challenges in research is the holistic and dynamic nature that embodies AE. The ideas of equifinality and multifinality make measuring and using data in AE difficult. Equifinality means many paths to the same end, while multifinality refers to many ends to the same path (Cicchetti & Rogosch, 1996). Many programmes target amorphous and vague outcomes such as sense-of-self or global citizenship. Even programmes that have a clear mandate, such as outdoor skill building, have come to accept that other outcomes are also commonly reported by programme participants. Unless professionals acknowledge the many ways that AE can afford outcomes – and that AE can afford unintended outcomes to some individuals – researchers will remain challenged to document both the processes and the outcomes of AE.

Many larger AE organisations have embraced the challenges of research and evaluation in philosophy, but to a lesser extent in their budgets. Other service-based programmes – after-school programmes and other educational initiatives – have incorporated evaluation and feedback into their operating budgets because the charitable foundations and government organisations that fund these programmes require accountability. Conversely, no central oversight in AE exists, and a market-driven approach to business has relegated evaluation and research to the sidelines for most providers. Potential programme participants do not yet require the same level of data and outcome-based evidence that large funders often do. While there are certainly exceptions, the industry as a whole has yet to fully embrace research and evaluation.

Future directions for research

AE researchers have several paths that they can follow. First, topics may continue to change as individual interests wax and wane. Second, researchers could continue the quest for alignment with societal issues. For example, perhaps AE is especially well positioned to foster youth development, connect people with the natural environment or encourage physical activity. Third, large AE organisations and/or associations can provide funding and direction, helping the field as a whole to build a body of knowledge. Some combination of these paths is likely to drive the future of AE research.

Conclusions

Despite the research challenges and the ongoing evolution of practice, AE remains a powerful medium for growth and change. The active, hands-on and experiential nature of AE supports numerous opportunities for learning. Participants can learn about their strengths and weaknesses, discover new passions, re-evaluate personal values, gain new skills and make powerful connections with others. The distinctive qualities of AE – remoteness, a small community within a dynamic environment, opportunities for failure, success and mastery – often result in transformational experiences for participants, with benefits that are important. While universal access to AE may not be possible, or even desirable, AE clearly provides a valuable venue for optimal engagement and personal development distinct from other traditional learning environments. The future of AE is promising, especially as educators, policy makers and other leaders increasingly recognise the value of quality out-of-classroom (and non-work) experiences. Clearly, AE professionals face challenges similar to traditional education, ranging from demonstrating the efficacy of programmes and documenting desired outcomes to incorporating new ideas and balancing the role of technology. However, interest remains high in the potential of AE, and commitment and passion for the field are evidenced from practitioners and participants. Fuelled by this passion and promise, AE will remain a critical and visible part of outdoor studies.

References

Bobilya, A.J., Holman, T., Lindley, B. & McAvoy, L. (2010). Developing trends and issues in US outdoor and adventure-based programming. *Journal of Outdoor Recreation, Education, and Leadership, 2*(3), 301–321.

Brown, M. (2010). Transfer: Outdoor adventure education's Achilles heel? Changing participation as a viable option. *Australian Journal of Outdoor Education, 14*(1), 13–22.

Cicchetti, D. & Rogosch, F.A. (1996). Equifinality and multifinality in developmental psychopathology. *Development and Psychopathology, 8*, 597–600.

D'Amato, L.G. & Krasny, M.E. (2011). Outdoor adventure education: Applying transformative learning theory to understanding instrumental learning and personal growth in environmental education. *Journal of Environmental Education, 42*(4), 237–254.

Dignath, C. & Buttner, G. (2008). Components of fostering self-regulated learning among students. A meta-analysis on intervention studies at primary and secondary school level. *Metacognition and Learning, 3*, 231–264.

Ewert, A. (1989). *Outdoor Adventure Pursuits: Foundations, Models, and Theories.* Columbus, OH: Publishing Horizons.

Ewert, A. & McAvoy, L. (2000). The effects of wilderness settings on organized groups: A state-of-knowledge paper. *USDA Forest Service Proceedings, 3*, 13–26.

Ewert, A. & Sibthorp, J. (2014). *Outdoor Adventure Education.* Champaign, IL: Human Kinetics.

Furman, N. & Sibthorp, J. (2012). Adventure programs and learning transfer: An uneasy alliance. In B. Martin & M. Wagstaff (Eds.) *Controversial Issues in Adventure Programming* (pp. 39–45). Champaign, IL: Human Kinetics.

Gass, M.A. (1999). Transfer of learning in adventure education. In J. Miles & S. Priest (Eds.) *Adventure Education* (pp. 199–208). State College, PA: Venture.

Goldenberg, M. & Soule, K. (2011). How group experience affects outcomes from NOLS programs: A means–end investigation. *Journal of Experiential Education, 33*(4), 393–397.

Hattie, J. (2009). *Visible Learning: A Synthesis of Over 800 Meta-analyses Relating to Achievement.* London: Routledge.

Hattie, J., Marsh, H.W., Neill, J.T. & Richards, G.E. (1997). Adventure education and Outward Bound: Out-of-class experiences that make a lasting difference. *Review of Educational Research, 67*(1), 43–87.

Lewin-Bizan, S., Bowers, E.P. & Lerner, R.M. (2010). One good thing leads to another: Cascades of positive youth development among American adolescents. *Development and Psychopathology, 22*(4), 759–770.

Masten, A.S. & Cicchetti, D. (2010). Developmental cascades. *Development and Psychopathology, 22*(3), 491–495.

Miner, J.L. & Boldt, J. (1981). *Outward Bound USA: Learning Through Experience in Adventure-based Education.* New York, NY: William Morrow.

Outward Bound International (2014). Retrieved from: www.outwardbound.net.

Paisley, K., Furman, N., Sibthorp, J. & Gookin, J. (2008). Student learning in outdoor education: A case study from the National Outdoor Leadership School. *Journal of Experiential Education, 30*(3), 201–222.

Pinch, K.J. (2009). The importance of evaluation research. *Journal of Experiential Education, 31*(3), 390–394.

Potter, T.G., Socha, T.L. & Connell, T.S.O. (2011). Outdoor adventure education (OAE) in higher education: Characteristics of successful university degree programmes. *Journal of Adventure Education & Outdoor Learning, 12*(2), 99–119.

Rickinson, M., Dillon, J., Teamey, K., Morris, M., Choi, M.Y., Sanders, D. & Benefield, P. (2004). *A Review of Research on Outdoor Learning.* Preston Montford, Shropshire: Field Studies Council.

Schumann, S.A., Sibthorp, J., Paisley, K. & Gookin, J. (2009). Instructor influences on student learning at NOLS. *Journal of Outdoor Recreation, Education, and Leadership, 1*(1), 15–37.

Sibthorp, J., Collins, R., Rathunde, K., Paisley, K., Schumann, S., Pohja, M., Gookin, J. & Baynes, S. (2015). Fostering experiential self-regulation in college age students through outdoor adventure education. *Journal of Experiential Education.* DOI: 10.1177/1053825913516735, 38(1), 26–40.

Sibthorp, J., Furman, N., Paisley, K. & Gookin, J. (2008). Long-term impacts attributed to participation in adventure education: Preliminary findings from NOLS. *Research in Outdoor Education, 9*, 86–102.

Sibthorp, J., Furman, N., Paisley, K., Gookin, J. & Schumann, S. (2011). Mechanisms of learning transfer in adventure education: Qualitative results from the NOLS transfer survey. *Journal of Experiential Education, 34*(2), 109–126.

US Census Bureau (2012). *Statistical Abstract of the United States.* Washington, DC: US Census Bureau.

Warren, K., Roberts, N.S., Breunig, M. & Alvarez, M.A.G. (2014). Social justice in outdoor experiential education: A state of knowledge review. *Journal of Experiential Education, 37*(1), 89–103.

21

Challenge course programming

On the rise or in compromise?

Mark Wagstaff

RADFORD UNIVERSITY

Imagine yourself 12 metres (40 feet) off the ground traversing a metal cable that sways with each step. You are connected to a belayer who manages your safety line as you intently focus your attention to achieve the platform on the opposite side. You are oblivious to the boisterous cheers your supporters shout with each step. You are immersed in a classic ropes course experience!

Challenge course (also known as ropes course) programming makes up an important component of informal education and training within outdoor studies. The European Ropes Course Standards define ropes courses as:

> constructed facility consisting of one or more activity systems (i.e. elements, platforms, access), support systems (i.e. trees, poles, anchors, guy lines, belay systems), and if needed, belay and/or safety systems. A ropes course is distinct from a playground equipment in that it has restricted access and requires supervision. (Adventure Activities Industry Advisory Committee, 2011, p. 9)

This popular adventure-based activity holds international appeal among an array of entities such as non-profit organisations, educational institutions, commercial enterprises and therapeutic services. Although the inspiration for traditional challenge course activities evolved from military obstacle courses, current trends have elevated it to a thriving economic industry. Large-scale corporate team-building events, canopy tours, aerial adventure parks and mega ziplines in conjunction with the thousands of traditional challenge courses worldwide appear to make the challenge course industry one of the most successful stories in contemporary outdoor pursuits. Most outdoor educators cannot practise their profession without some involvement in challenge course programming.

The European Ropes Course Association 2010 conference report (ERCA, n.d.) provided an estimate that 4000-plus courses exist in Europe serving more than 25 million participants. The report also projected industry worth to be £400,000,000, or $654,000,000. Attarian (2001) indicated that 15,000 courses exist in the United States alone. These older statistics are only estimates and, in my opinion, gross underestimates of the industry's global reach in 2014.

This chapter provides a historical overview of the industry and defines the traditional challenge course experience. Basic definitions and terminology are presented, as well as common programming models to enhance an understanding of the industry. Challenge course related activities such as canopy tours and aerial adventure parks also are explored as the new non-traditional trend. This chapter will take a critical look at the purpose and outcomes of challenge course programming. The challenge course industry has evolved into big business and seems to be driven by the pervasive, neo-liberal value system that drives modern economics. Three primary goal orientations are related to the broad purposes of challenge course programming: (i) recreational; (ii) educational; (iii) therapeutic. A section of the chapter describes the growth of the profession through the advent of associations and international standards. Finally, an overview of challenge course industry research and development is presented, along with discussion concerning the future growth and direction of the industry.

Background

Traditional challenge courses

Traditional challenge experiences typically consist of obstacles (i.e. elements) constructed of cable, rope and wood, anywhere from .3 to 18 metres (i.e. 1 foot to 60 feet) off the ground. Participants typically belong to intact groups who navigate these challenging obstacles with the assistance of a trained facilitator. A day-long event includes a progression of activities starting with warm-ups, games and icebreakers. The group then progresses to a series of initiatives or problem-solving activities led by facilitators. Classic low elements such as the spider's web, the wall and trust fall are integrated into the progression before tackling the final series of activities, the high elements. High elements require a belay system to manage the safety issues off the ground. Throughout the day's progression, facilitators use experiential methods to achieve intended outcomes. Groups discuss, reflect, analyse and apply what they are learning throughout the day. Most experiences culminate in a final group activity to formally close the experience. For individuals reading this chapter with little or no traditional challenge course experience, numerous current and classic resources are available to provide further reference regarding terminology, facilitation practices and technical information (e.g. Rohnke & Butler, 1995; Rohnke, Wall, Tait & Rogers, 2003; Martin, Cashel, Wagstaff & Bruenig, 2006; Prouty, Panicucci & Collinson, 2007).

The intended outcomes for traditional experiences vary but tend to be educational or developmental in nature. Challenge course programmes used for educational purposes originated from the military obstacle course. Educators, most notably George Hébert and Kurt Hahn, were the first to integrate the military obstacle course into an educational context. In 1913, Hébert, a French naval officer in charge of physical training, addressed the French Physical Education Congress as an advocate for obstacle course training beyond military applications. He believed that students who engaged in obstacle course training outdoors would improve their physical conditioning and discover personal potential as well as personal limitations. Kurt Hahn and his teaching staff used the military obstacle course in their curriculum as Outward Bound (OB) schools developed in the 1930s and 1940s in the United Kingdom. Earnest 'Tap' Tapley recalled constructing and facilitating the first challenge course he built in 1961 in the United States at Marble Canyon, Colorado for Outward Bound USA. He received training at the Eskdale OB School in the UK and used his prior military experience to influence the design of this course. He trained US students to belay one another and then debriefed the process to enhance the experience (Wagstaff, 2003). Challenge course programming grew significantly in the USA, with growing numbers of OB instructors applying their skills and knowledge of ropes courses in traditional education settings. Project Adventure, for example, was one of the first US organisations with a mission to integrate adventure-based education into school systems in the 1970s. The challenge course served as a primary vehicle to transform traditional educational methods.

Growth of the industry

The USA experienced significant growth of challenge course programmes in the 1980s. In 1988, the first group of challenge course professionals met formally at the North Carolina Outward Bound School. This seminal meeting resulted in establishing the first professional association in 1993, the Association for Challenge Course Technology (ACCT). ACCT published the first edition of its construction standards in 1994.

In 1998, the German Ropes Course Association (GRCA) was founded. The initial eighteen members represented builders, ropes course operators and trainers, under the leadership of Mrs Silke Körner, the first president. The GRCA standards were published in 2000 and included chapters on ethics, operations and building. In 2001 and 2002 working groups were formed to develop training and inspection standards used today. The success achieved through standards development resulted in an increase in the number of German and international members. In 2003 other European countries joined to become the European Ropes Course Association (ERCA Main Office, personal communication, 9 February 2014).

In addition to ERCA and ACCT, other professional organisations added to the industry's vitality. The Professional Ropes Course Association (PRCA), also founded in the USA, was established in 2003. The primary goals of the PRCA are similar to those of the ACCT. The International Adventure Parcs Association (IAPA) is a German organisation of about 150 members. Other associations are the Syndicat National des Exploitants de Parcours Adventure (SNEPA) in France and the Parchi Avventura Italiani (PAI) in Italy.

From traditional to non-traditional

Traditional challenge course experiences are synonymous with experiential education techniques, with an emphasis on educational or developmental outcomes. While the traditional challenge course model originally developed by Hébert and Outward Bound is linked to modern-day adventure education activities, the challenge course industry evolves in other areas. Travel, tourism and leisure providers exert great influence on the industry. Ziplining, canopy tours and aerial adventure parks are thrilling adventurous alternatives with the purpose of providing leisure experiences.

Canopy tours, or zipline courses, were originated by scientists studying the jungle canopy. In 1974, Donald Perry, a biologist, developed a system for researchers to access jungle canopy using a crossbow, ropes and climbing techniques (ERCA Conference, n.d.). The most efficient way for botanists and biologists to study the lush jungles of Central and South America was to zip from treetop to treetop using Perry's systems. In 1995, Perry developed a commercial venture, Eco-Tram, to give tourists access to the jungle canopy of Costa Rica. Canadian Darren Hreniuk moved to Costa Rica in 1992 and created his business, the Original Canopy Tour, to provide tourists with a jungle adventure while raising environmental awareness. Since the inception of canopy tours in Costa Rica, this ropes course technology has spread around the world. Canopy tours, also known as zipline tours, are now found in most popular tourist destinations. Ski resorts, whitewater rafting companies, hotels, outdoor education centres and a host of other entities have embraced this activity option for guests.

In France, the first aerial adventure park was established in the French Alps in 1995 (PT. Awang Adventure, n.d.). Aerial adventure parks are similar to traditional challenge courses but with distinct differences. Adventure parks, or treetop adventures, are designed to provide a quality leisure experience with little to no emphasis on education and personal development. Customers are trained to navigate a series of obstacles independently with minimal assistance from guides or instructors. Aerial adventure parks are typically designed as circuits to include traditional challenge course high elements such as ziplines, swinging bridges and balance beams, with other challenging obstacles at least 2 to 20 metres (6 to 65 feet) above the ground. Designers typically build these parks with different levels of difficulty so people of all physical abilities can take advantage. As with canopy tours, aerial adventure parks are found in some of the most popular tourist destinations around the world. French aerial parks have had significant influence on the development of ropes course standards in Europe. This growth has exerted pressure on governing bodies to regulate these businesses.

The purpose of challenge course experiences

All challenge course related programmes tend to fall on a goal orientation continuum: (i) recreational; (ii) educational; and (iii) therapeutic. These orientations serve as overarching constructs for specific programme purposes, philosophies, leadership competences, and intended benefits and outcomes. They become the basis for research in explaining why people seek out challenge course experiences. Figure 21.1, showing the challenge course programme continuum, builds on the work of Ringer (1999) and Ringer and Gillis (1995) by applying the purposes of adventure in a challenge course programming context.

The goal orientations address diverse programme purposes, activities and outcomes. For example, a challenge course programme designed to be recreational may produce more than the outcomes of fun and excitement. The experience could include unintended therapeutic outcomes to improve the individual's wellbeing, such as increased self-confidence or social functioning. Further, clients involved in a psycho-educational support group may experience fun and social engagement typically associated with a recreational-oriented experience. Viewing challenge course programmes on a continuum alleviates stereotyping challenge course activities within a single focused context.

As depicted in Figure 21.1, differences among the goal orientations are based on programme structure. For example, therapy-based experiences tend to be more highly structured and require specialised facilitation skills to facilitate individual treatment plans. At the other end of the continuum, recreational experiences tend to be less structured and necessitate different facilitation skills and leadership styles. Professional practitioners, regardless of their orientation (i.e. recreational, educational or therapeutic) are responsible for facilitating the appropriate programme structure to produce intended outcomes.

A dichotomy unfolds

As challenge course history clearly depicts, educators were largely responsible for making challenge course experiences accessible to the public. With the proliferation of commercial entities such as aerial adventure parks, canopy tours and ropes course programmes for play, not all are pleased with industry commodification. Some people argue that the integrity of the traditional challenge course experience has been compromised by this trend. Many private businesses as well as educational institutions focus on volume by getting as many people through the experience as possible for financial gain. This mass participation violates the small-group experience where time

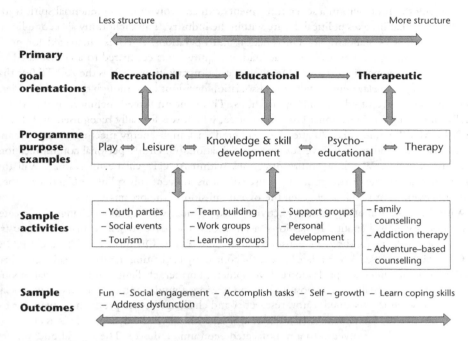

Figure 21.1 Challenge course programme continuum

is structured to process, reflect and learn experientially. For some outdoor professionals, this focus on commercialisation betrays sacred methodology developed to empower and improve the self and community.

Loynes (1998) warned outdoor educators of the 'McDonaldization', or recreational capitalism, that appeared to be infiltrating the social movement of adventure education. He argued that capitalism would impinge upon core values of outdoor adventure programming such as community building and connection to the natural environment. The use of terms such as *industry* and *service providers*, he argued, indicated the shift from a focus on the collective good to a neo-liberal orientation of self-centredness and entrepreneurial values. It appears that Loynes' warnings are now a reality. Throughout this chapter, the term industry has been used liberally and deliberately. Neo-liberalism is characterised by political and governmental entities moving from an administrative focus on human wellbeing to a transference of power to global industries that promote individualism through entrepreneurship (Davies & Bansel, 2007). This political philosophy falls between classic liberalism and collectivism.

The neo-liberal value system is firmly engrained in modern-day society and rewards people who pursue their self-interests. Challenge course builders and programme providers are experiencing unprecedented economic prosperity and are exploiting emerging growth potentials. However, people also are aware of what Loynes recognised in 1998. Many professionals continue to position themselves in the philosophical roots of adventure education. They are fiercely loyal to the notion that adventure education is part of a social movement focused on a collective good. These educators advocate for the wellbeing of all, including the disadvantaged and underserved groups of society. They serve their participants based on the experiential education components of community, experience and learning (Cassidy, 2008).

Balancing the roots within a social movement with an evolving entrepreneurial spirit is just one challenge that invokes political debate within the industry. This dichotomy also complicates the development of standards for construction and operations. A course managed for profit differs in design, equipment used and facilitation requirements compared to a course used for educational or therapeutic purposes. Members within organisations such as the ACCT fear that the growth of *pay to play* venues will drive association decisions even though their mission identifies the importance of educational applications. This concern forced members of the ACCT to rally and create an Educational Use Committee, which was formally recognised in 2013. At the 2014 ACCT conference, 70 attendees gathered for a high-energy meeting to support and explore issues around education versus commercialisation. (G. Grout, personal communication, 19 February 2014). Watching future directions within ACCT will be interesting. Will this movement fracture the organisation and cause educators to eventually splinter off and form their own organisation, or will it strengthen the overall mission of the organisation?

With the evolution of any outdoor activity, mass popularity brings about change that creates challenges as well as benefits. Professional associations that strive to self-regulate the industry play a major role in tackling these issues and are important. Organisations like the ERCA, ACCT, IAPA and PRCA formulate systems of control by facilitating standards, leader certifications, ethical guidelines and professional development. Further, challenge course associations are not immune to internal political positioning and tensions found among all professional associations in all disciplines. As an educator, researcher and challenge course programme manager for the past thirty years, I have witnessed and questioned with others the dynamic shifts as challenge course education has evolved into a multifaceted economic industry. The critical question for challenge course professionals to ask is: Can we preserve the social value of challenge course experiences while reaping the outcomes associated with a capitalistic industry?

State of the profession

Challenge course programming clearly is a dynamic outdoor pursuit with multiple benefits stemming from intentional programme design. The infrastructure ensures that a quality challenge course experience rests on the professionalisation of the industry and the issues that influence growth or stagnation. Primarily, the role of professional associations heavily influences industry direction and overall success related primarily to standards.

Advent of recognised standards

The initial development of standards in the 1990s by professional organisations marked a significant advancement for the industry. More recent activities have further enhanced the efforts of professionals to solidify industry practices. Around 2005, German, French and British challenge course professionals took steps to create ropes course standards to be recognised by the European Committee for Standardization, or Comité Européen de Normalisation (CEN). The CEN was founded in France in 1961 as a non-profit organisation that now serves thirty-one member countries. The CEN oversees numerous standards in a variety of industries. The European Norm (i.e. EN 15567) came into effect in 2008, and was developed to address construction and operation standards for all ropes courses (AAIAC, 2011).

During this major advancement in Europe, the PRCA and the ACCT underwent a similar process in 2005 and 2006, respectively, in the USA. The PRCA and the ACCT became accredited standards developers for the American National Standards Institute (ANSI). Similar to the CEN, ANSI accredits representatives from industries to develop industry-specific standards.

Challenge course standards developed by the PRCA and ACCT also cover aerial adventure parks, canopy tours, ziplines, team challenge courses and climbing structures.

The alignment of standards with those of organisations such as the CEN and ANSI is important. These standards are not laws, but are followed on a voluntary basis by challenge course builders and operators. However, they serve as the foundation for risk management practices and the prevention of litigation issues. These standards are viewed as the norm and considered best practices in the court of law. Any challenge course business that finds itself in court will be scrutinised against the recognised standards. More importantly, a larger benefit of creating internationally recognised standards revolves around the concept of self-regulation. During the evolution of most professionally based industries, there is fear of control from larger non-related bodies. The perception is that other governing bodies (e.g. national or regional governments) do not have the expertise and knowledge to adequately regulate the industry. Professions from the challenge course industry do not want rules and regulations imposed that might compromise the integrity of their product or service. Legitimate fears exist that the challenge course industry could be subjugated to regulations that control playground equipment use or amusement park rides due to legal cases around accidents and injuries. Therefore, obtaining CEN and ANSI recognition represents a proactive step in advancing the autonomy of an expanding industry.

Other countries in addition to the USA and European nations are experiencing growth within the industry. Australia, for example, has a thriving challenge course industry. However, minimal national standards exist that regulate the construction and operation of challenge course related activities. Many Australian challenge course professionals, therefore, adopt the standards developed by the ACCT or ERCA. The French are active in building aerial adventure parks in Asia, South America and North America. Leisure service businesses all over the world now have the option to contract builders who follow recognised international standards. This option provides a high level of quality assurance. However, some builders do not take advantage of these standards and may potentially compromise quality assurance. For example, some builders claim they follow international standards but do not belong to one of the recognised professional associations. Organisations such as ACCT and ERCA have systems in place to assess the credentials of members and hold them accountable as part of the accreditation and membership process.

Research and development

A growth trend that I discovered while compiling research for this chapter is the increased communication within the larger challenge course professional network. European nations, the USA, Canada, Australia, New Zealand and Asian nations are borrowing from, collaborating with and learning from one another. Professional associations have spurred this sharing of knowledge and resources. Research plays an important role as the industry experiences rapid growth.

Two important areas should be considered when using research to understand the impacts of the industry. The first revolves around the benefits and outcomes associated with challenge course experiences. At this point, the majority of the benefit and outcome research has been conducted in the USA. Three comprehensive studies have served as overviews and foundational resources for the challenge course industry.

The most recent contribution was a statistical review of the challenge course literature published by Gillis and Speelman (2008). They conducted a meta-analysis that included forty-four studies based on specific research design parameters examining the impact of participating in challenge course activities. Gillis and Speelman found that challenge course experiences served as an effective tool to influence psychological and educational constructs in diverse populations. They reported that challenge course experiences focused on therapeutic outcomes had the most impact, followed by developmental (i.e. behavioural changes) and then educational oriented outcomes. They also found that challenge course experiences increased group effectiveness, which affirmed the role of challenge course programming as a team-building tool.

Attarian (2005) developed the first and currently only annotated bibliography of challenge course research related publications. He cited and provided brief summaries of 174 publications that reflected both peer-reviewed and non-peer-reviewed sources since 1985. Journal articles, popular articles, manuals, books, newsletters, websites and other sources were documented. The purpose was to provide a comprehensive resource to better understand the challenge course experience.

Further, Wolfe and Samdahl (2005) questioned the typical assumptions that drive challenge course research. The central assumptions were that risk and challenge produce positive outcomes and these outcomes are transferable outside the challenge course context. The authors provided perspectives on how to improve the quality of challenge course research by questioning these well-established assumptions. They proposed that practitioners and researchers question current research methods and instruments, and critically examine and question challenge course benefits. Qualitative methods must be exercised that access the powerful stories told by participants to enable us to be 'better able see our own beliefs and assumptions that had been invisible to us' (Wolfe & Samdahl, 2005, p. 41). Taken together, the studies by Gillis and Speelman (2008), Attarian (2005), and Wolfe and Samdahl (2005) are helpful starting points when examining challenge course research.

Considering goal orientations, the majority of past and current research falls within the educational and therapeutic portion of the continuum. A deficit in the research is a focus on the leisure or recreational benefits of challenge courses. With the increased development of leisure-based offerings such as aerial adventure parks and zipline tours, many opportunities exist for needed research in this area. For example, many zipline or canopy tour based businesses claim to increase the customer's knowledge of the natural and cultural environment. Some commercially run challenge course businesses also claim to be socially and environmentally responsible. Because tourism based businesses are on the rise, analysing these claims from an objective viewpoint would be a worthy industry agenda.

Another needed area of research beyond the study of outcomes and benefits revolves around exploring the overall economic impact of the industry. For example, accurate information around basic industry statistics does not exist. How many ropes courses actually exist globally is not known. The implications of the challenge course industry for economic impact and job generation have not been examined in particular within a tourism or community development context.

The researchers who tend to be educational and therapeutic oriented have not been inclined to address larger industry questions. Therefore, the majority of research occurs within the human development realm. The challenge course industry, with its emerging neo-liberal value system, has matured to the point that new research could support a more socially conscious philosophy of providing leisure and tourism oriented services. Green businesses, ecotourism, socially conscious tourism, sustainable community development and other best practices should become part of challenge course technology. While traditional educational and therapeutic benefits seem to dominate the current interests of social researchers, the impact of challenge courses needs additional attention from leisure, recreation and tourism standpoints. An important question is whether challenge course businesses are being developed and operated for the good of the communities and natural environments they occupy. An understanding of this question might better provide for decisions and future directions within the challenge course industry.

Conclusion

The traditional challenge course/ropes course experience has significantly evolved since the efforts of early educators to adapt military obstacle courses. In 2005, Attarian defined the challenge course as 'a collection or series of events or obstacles suspended from trees, utility poles and other structures; and or activities that provide participants with unique problem solving opportunities for self-discovery, physical challenge, risk taking, and group support' (p. 5). Canopy tours, aerial adventure parks, and zipline businesses have significantly transformed this traditional experience into a diverse economic industry. While the first part of Attarian's definition applies, the second portion is often limited when current trends are considered. I propose a more inclusive definition:

> Challenge courses are a collection or series of activities, which can include obstacles suspended from trees, utility poles and other structures that provide adventure-based experiences designed to produce intended participant outcomes within the context of three possible programme goal orientations: recreational, educational or therapeutic.

The emergence of professional associations has established challenge programming as a profession that offers many experiences to individuals. In particular, establishing recognised building and operations standards as well as facilitator certification has accelerated the level of professionalism within the industry. Challenge course programming is now considered a popular outdoor pursuit made available to the masses through many avenues. Research exists that supports the efficacy of challenge course programming and new energy must be dedicated to understanding the effects of challenge course business on economies, communities and natural environments. The evolution of challenge course technology marks a success story within the context of economic success. However, scholars and practitioners must critically ask if the challenge course profession is 'selling out'. Are the roots within the social movement being replaced by a neo-liberal value system? The industry will continue to expand, yet I believe professionals must act consciously to preserve a tradition of social consciousness. Challenge course professionals must find a way to selflessly serve others for the betterment of society while maintaining economic prosperity.

References

AAIAC (2011). *The UK Ropes Course Guide* (3rd edn). Adventure Activities Industry Advisory Group.

Attarian, A. (2001). Trends in outdoor adventure education. *Journal of Experiential Education, 24*(3), 141–149.

Attarian, A. (2005). The literature and research on challenge courses: An annotated bibliography (2nd edn). Raleigh, NC: North Carolina State University and Alpine Towers International. Retrieved from: http://acct.affiniscape.com/displaycommon.cfm?an=1&subarticlenbr=34.

Cassidy, K.J. (2008). A contemporary model of experiential education. In K. Warren, D. Mitten & T.A. Loeffler (Eds.) *Theory & Practice of Experiential Education* (pp. 282–296). Boulder, CO: Association for Experiential Education.

Davies, B. & Bansel, P. (2007). Neoliberalism and education. *International Journal of Qualitative Studies in Education, 20*(3), 247–259.

ERCA Conference (n.d.). ERCA International Ropes Course Conference 2013. Retrieved from: www.etouches.com/ehome/uk2013conference/134471/.

ERCA (n.d.). ERCA UK Ropes Course Conference Report. Retrieved from: www.amiando.com/ERCA_International_Ropes_Course_Conference_UK2010.html.

Gillis, H.L. & Speelman, E. (2008). Are challenge (ropes) courses an effective tool? A meta-analysis. *Journal of Experiential Education, 31*(2), 111–135.

Loynes, C. (1998). Adventure in a bun. *Journal of Experiential Education, 21*(1), 35–39.

Martin, B., Cashel, C., Wagstaff, M. & Bruenig, M. (2006). *Outdoor Leadership: Theory and Practice*. Champaign, IL: Human Kinetics.

Moriarty, N. (2013). What is a ropes course? (PDF document). Retrieved from: www.google.com/url?sa=t &rct=j&q=&esrc=s&source=web&cd=2&ved=0CEIQFjAB&url=http%3A%2F%2Fwww.tollymore. com%2FNR%2Frdonlyres%2F5A40EE77-4908-4B3E-B698-559899241F53%2F0%2FRopesCourse.

Prouty, D., Panicucci, J. & Collinson, R. (Eds.) (2007). *Adventure Education: Theory and Applications*. Champaign, IL: Human Kinetics.

PT. Awang Adventure (n.d.). *Treetop Adventure Park: Construction and Maintenance of Treetop Adventure Parks*. Retrieved from: www.youblisher.com/p/96901-Construction-of-Treetop-Adventure-Parks/.

Ringer, M. (1999). The facile-itation of facilitation? Searching for competencies in group work leadership. *Scisco Conscientio, 2*(1), 1–19.

Ringer, M. & Gillis, H.L. (1995). Managing psychological depth in adventure programming. *Journal of Experiential Education, 18*(1), 41–51.

Rohnke, K. & Butler, S. (1995). *Quicksilver: Adventure Games, Initiative Problems, Trust Activities and a Guide to Effective Leadership*. Dubuque, IA: Kendall/Hunt Publishing.

Rohnke, K., Wall, J., Tait, C. & Rogers, D. (2003). *The Complete Ropes Course Manual* (3rd edn). Dubuque, IA: Kendall/Hunt Publishing.

Wagstaff, M. (2003). History and philosophy of challenge courses. In S. Wurdinger & J. Steffen (Eds.) *Developing Challenge Course Programs for Schools* (pp. 3–16). Dubuque, IA: Kendall/Hunt Publishing.

Wolfe, B.D. & Samdahl, D.M. (2005). Challenging assumptions: Examining fundamental beliefs that shape challenge course programming and research. *Journal of Experiential Education, 28*(1), 25–43.

22

The camp experience
Learning through the outdoors

M. Deborah Bialeschki
AMERICAN CAMP ASSOCIATION

Stephen M. Fine
CANADIAN CAMPING ASSOCIATION

Troy Bennett
UNIVERSITY OF UTAH

Since the earliest days of the organised camp movement more than 150 years ago, leaders have advocated that the outdoors is an influential site of learning for youth and that the camp experience is a valuable educational tool to promote nature-based learning. The evolution of camps was similar within the USA and Canada, while a great many camps were established within the former USSR in the years following the First World War. In the 21st century, camps have become a global phenomenon. At summer camp, children are motivated by the fun and camaraderie of peer and staff interaction, interesting settings and physically dynamic activities. Additionally, the pace of learning is accelerated through personal insights, social interaction, mentorship and skills development that overlap and can occur within a short span of time.

In this chapter, we provide a context for exploring the value of the camp experience, a broad overview and analysis of key research efforts that highlight camps' contributions to outdoor learning, as well as suggestions on directions and issues in the future. In this time of scrutinising educational institutions and systems, acknowledgement of the increasing disconnect between children and nature, and concern about the apparent loss of a legacy towards environmental stewardship in this generation of young people, the camp experience may offer a realistic solution for authentic learning that develops the whole child through outdoor experiences.

Background

Since its beginning, camp has been a context for learning and a site for outdoor education. Camp activities emphasise outdoor knowledge and skills through small-group living that offers opportunities to develop social, emotional and cognitive skills that contribute to the total development of campers regardless of age. From the late 19th century and into the early 20th, camps in the USA were focused primarily on getting young people out of cities and into healthier rural environments. Concerns were for the poor immigrant children who had fewer formal educational opportunities, were often in ill health and usually lived in urban environments cut off from the natural world. By the 1930s, the progressive reforms in education advocated by US educators such as John Dewey (1916, 1925) had taken hold, with visibility given to experiential education in general and outdoor education in particular. The pragmatic Canadian philosopher, William H. Kilpatrick, believed that camping and traditional schooling could be mutually beneficial. On the educational efficacy of camping, Kilpatrick (1931) stated: 'Not being counted educative, in the traditional sense, the camp is free – if it will – to be honestly and seriously educative in the true sense' (p. ix).

The camp experience, often offered as school camping, became the ideal context for experiential learning, with more emphasis on the educational values of camp and a particular focus on the natural sciences as integral to instructional camp activities. As camping education became popular and aligned with general progressive aims, a rapid rise 'in school camping, and the term *outdoor education* began to be applied more generally' (Eells, 1986, p. 129). This focus on learning through the outdoors in camps became highly valued for the total development of youth, as evidenced by Mason (1930) when he wrote that, if camp is worthy, it can be one of the greatest socialising, humanising and civilising factors in a child's life.

Over the next several decades, the progressive educational reform movement in the USA lost some prominence, but camps continued to expand into non-profit youth organisations like the Girl Scouts, Boy Scouts and the YMCA/YWCA, as well in many religious organisations (Carlson, 1957; Smith, 2006). These large organisations advocated their belief that camp was a valuable context for learning through the outdoors. Camps were set up in countries around the world where these youth organisations were located. Governments of various countries also explored using the camp experience for learning and youth development, which explains the current oversight of camps in many countries as resting with their governmental departments of education. Perhaps most clearly seen in Australia, camps were embraced as an integral part of school life, with a strong emphasis on outdoor education and as the application site for many forms of outdoor studies (Brookes, 2002).

The continued development of the camping movement from the mid-20th century to today had an ebb and flow in its prominence. Irwin (1950) saw great promise for school camping programmes in the future of education. Between the years of 1931 and 1947 the states of 'California, New York, Michigan, and Virginia enacted legislation which permits school districts to use public school funds for the establishment of public school camps' (Irwin, p. 15). By 1947, more than 500 school boards in the USA were operating camping programmes in outdoor education. The environmental movement of the 1970s and 1980s brought visibility to the camp experience, with research emerging that documented the value of these outdoor learning opportunities not only within environmental education, but also on the psycho-social, cognitive, physical and intellectual development of the children. Adventure and challenge programmes gained popularity in camps as the Outward Bound model developed in England spread to the USA and other countries. This model capitalised on learning that occurs while engaging in challenging activities in outdoor environments.

Throughout all of these historical periods, the camp experience maintained a close connection with its educational roots. Although the methods, organisational structures, staffing practices and the establishment of standards evolved over time, the mainstay of the camp experience continued to be the value placed on education in the outdoors. Learning through nature-based experiences and the authenticity of the relationships, particularly under the supervision of caring adults who themselves are committed to the outdoors, has helped bring camp experiences to youth and adults around the world.

Within the current discourse and critique of formal education, the value of informal learning environments in out-of-school-time (OST) settings has taken on new importance. OST opportunities have begun to be recognised as contributing to the total learning of children and as validating learning that occurs outside of traditional classroom walls. In light of recent advancements in brain research, experts recognise that learning occurs in ways that reflect developmental stages that are actually triggered by physiological changes (Madrazo & Motz, 2005; Worden, Hinton & Fischer, 2011). These findings provide evidence supporting what outdoor educators have touted for decades: *kids learn best by doing*. The research suggests that a *village* is needed to educate children to their full potential.

Research on the camp experience

A substantial body of work has evolved over the decades about the camp experience. The research often reflected the social issues of the time, as well as outdoor studies frameworks found in adventure education, environmental education and school camping. The early research on camp and the principles upon which many camps were founded highlighted common pedagogical influences associated with child-centred, communitarian and experiential approaches to educational philosophy (Dimock & Hendry, 1929; Sharp, 1930). The evidence supplied by this body of research lent credibility to camp experiences that aimed to promote physical activity, caring relationships, and emotional, social, cognitive and spiritual growth in campers and staff.

Contemporary camp-related research has focused on developmental characteristics of high-quality camp settings, camps designed for special medical needs, connecting children with nature and the environment, global cross-cultural experiences, and the relationship between camp and learning. The American Camp Association (ACA) described camp as an experience that:

> encourages children to value their uniqueness and to understand and appreciate their part in the larger community. [The Camp community] helps children develop self-esteem, character, courage, responsibility, resourcefulness and cooperation ... camp experiences help children develop the healthy emotional and social skills necessary to grow into strong, considerate, competent adults. (2014, p. 1)

In 2005, the ACA released *Directions*, its initial report on youth development outcomes and the first part of a three-phase national study to 'better understand children's experience at camp' (ACA, 2005, p. 2). Subsequently, *Inspirations* (ACA, 2006a), examined the efficacy of camp experience in relation to the extent of developmental processes. Together these studies provided the blueprint for *Innovations* (ACA, 2006b), which advanced a design for programme improvement and intentional programming to increase outcome achievement.

Further US studies have been informed by these ACA studies, and have been as diverse as developmental outcomes and programme innovations (Garst, Browne & Bialeschki, 2011), the benefits of intentional programming (Henderson *et al.*, 2006) and multidimensional growth through camp experience (Thurber, Scanlin, Scheuler & Henderson, 2007). Contemporary camp research has investigated the facilitation of increased independence, improved self-confidence, leadership development, friendship skills, interest in adventure and exploration, identity construction, global citizenship, the influence of the peer community at camp, and the supportive relationships formed between youth and adults (Bialeschki & Sibthorp, 2011; Fine, 2012). The positive influences of camp have extended beyond children and youth to include young adult staff. Camp counsellors have attributed developing marketable job skills, identity exploration, leadership skills and the ability to work as part of a team to their experience working at camp (Johnson, Goldman, Garey, Britner & Weaver, 2011).

Camp programmes achieve developmental outcomes by focusing on structural elements such as programme quality assessments, staff behaviours and formal outcome measurements. Programme quality assessments help camp administrators identify potential areas for programme improvements. Research-based quality assessments have been developed for use in the special settings and environments of camp. Some of the most important components to achieving high levels of quality, however, are related to the behaviours of camp staff. Creating a welcoming and inclusive environment, facilitating appropriate levels of challenge and encouraging self-reflection are staff behaviours that have been linked to outcome achievement (Larson, Rickman, Gibbons & Walker, 2009). These outcomes are increasingly measured through formal outcome measurements. Reliable and valid tools such as the ACA Youth Outcomes Battery (YOB) have been developed specifically for camp administrators interested in documenting the impact of their programme. The YOB includes age-appropriate camper self-assessment tools, as well as counsellor and parent perceptions of camper learning versions (Sibthorp, Bialeschki, Morgan & Browne, 2013).

Camp experiences have been found to be a positive influence for people with special medical needs, chronic illnesses, disabilities and psychological issues. Outdoor opportunities may offer a novel way for these participants to learn. Specially designed camps provide accessibility, treatment and support in a fun and caring environment. In addition to research on camps serving people with specific medical conditions or disabilities, an increasing number of camp programmes serving veterans as well as families of recently deployed soldiers have been established in the USA. The character of the camp setting and the potential learning through outdoor studies are intentionally used as a vehicle through which healing and understanding can be addressed (Ashurst *et al.*, 2014).

The value of nature-based settings is well documented. Benefits include the acquisition of a sense of wonder (Louv, 2005), cognitive development (Pyle, 2002), better concentration (Wells, 2000), and creative outdoor play that fosters language and collaborative skills as well as critical thinking and problem solving (Fjortoft, 2001). The outdoor education philosophy of learning by doing fits with current educational trends where project-based learning is touted for its connection to real-world situations and learners are encouraged to work together to creatively solve problems (English & Kitsantas, 2013). Researchers have explored the connection between educational experiences in outdoor settings and future attitudes related to the preservation of natural wild places (Ewert, Place & Sibthorp, 2005) and making environmentally responsible choices (Collado, Staats & Corraliza, 2013).

Challenges exist in conducting research on outdoor studies within the camp experience. These challenges include instrumentation, intrusiveness, units of measurement and sampling. The camp experience is such that standardised instruments adapted from other fields have potential reliability and validity issues. Intrusiveness issues include challenges around parental permission (and for research about camp programmes in schools, getting school approval) and perceptions by camp administrators that data collection will alter and detract from camper activities. As a result, evaluation and research processes are often missing from many camp programmes. The focus on individuals as the unit of measurement is common but may overlook the influence of peers, staff and/or programme structure on related outcomes. The variability of these factors is not easily controlled or measured. Lastly, sampling across camps is challenging because programme and staffing differences can affect fidelity. Trying to meet the experimental standard of intervention and control groups is almost impossible. Qualitative data offer some solutions to these challenges, but individual experiences may be difficult to generalise to larger populations.

Global and cross-cultural aspects of camp research present additional challenges. Researchers may feel ill equipped in international contexts due to deficiencies of language, cultural knowledge, social understanding, and an insufficient awareness of the research traditions and processes that are followed within different national contexts (Hantrais & Mangen, 1996). Consideration must also be given to methodologies designed in one culture that may not readily transfer to a cultural context different from the original. For example, an intervention focused on exploring differences between girls and boys on a particular outcome may need to be implemented differently in some instances where cultural mores prohibit girls and boys participating together in a programme. An assessment of the equivalence of specific constructs and curriculums across cultures is needed (Brookes, 2002; Chang, 2010). The challenge for global and cross-cultural researchers is to design theories and instruments that have the ability to remain sensitive to local contexts (Ho & Cheung, 2007).

Education, learning and outdoor studies

The role of camp as a context for learning has important implications in today's global economy. The camp experience has the capacity to foster interest and motivation that transfer to later life accomplishments (Fine, 2005; Garst et al., 2011). Skills such as problem solving, collaboration, leadership, communication, curiosity and imagination have been identified as being critical for the *new* world of work in the 21st century (Wagner, 2010). These 21st-century skills are closely aligned with non-cognitive measures for predicting academic achievement (Farrington et al., 2012). These skills are often found within components of outdoor studies in camps and have been associated with positive outcomes for young people. For example, perceptions of personal abilities and the extent to which an activity is valued may influence a young person's motivation and persistence, which can lead to improved academic outcomes and future workforce competency (Gutman & Schoon, 2012).

Throughout the world, camp programmes have been used to facilitate education. International studies have addressed camp as a context for informal learning and learning transfer (Fine, 2005; Dahl, Sethre-Hofstad & Salomon, 2013; Glover et al., 2013), and globally minded citizenship (Fine & Tuvshin, 2010). Gender issues at Girl and Boy Scout camps have been explored in Denmark, Portugal, Russia and Slovakia (Bjerrum Nielsen, 2004). Many thousands of Young Pioneer Camps that were established in the former USSR now continue within the Russian Republic and former satellites through government-sponsored, NGO and private camps. In addition to sports and other outdoor studies and activities, a new educational focus is now on economics, the promotion of business initiatives, and entrepreneurship (Comai, 2012). In Finland, outdoor education is concomitant with basic education and is provided through camp schools (National Core Curriculum for Basic Education, 2004). Student camper experiences in rural camp schools offer possibilities for learning and teaching both school subjects and sustainable living (Smeds, Jeronen, Kurppa & Vieraankivi, 2011). Outdoor camp programmes also have been used to combat summer learning loss, such as in Canada where combining the fun of summer camp with curriculum enhances the teaching of mathematics (Tichenor & Plavchan, 2010).

Camp-based environments are also being used to serve the science, technology, engineering and mathematics (STEM) communities. STEM camps, more commonly known as science camps, use constructivist approaches that interweave the social and experiential characteristics of camp settings. For example, camps can offer youth opportunities to work on science-related challenges in natural environments that encourage exploration, creativity, innovation and teamwork while having fun and gaining support from staff. Summer science programmes are offered throughout the world (Crombie, Walsh & Trinneer, 2003; Miliszewska & Moore, 2010; Chen,

Sheen, Yueh, Chiang & Chang, 2012; Brown, 2013), and encourage young women, marginalised youth and uninspired middle-schoolers, as well as gifted students, to consider STEM-related career choices.

The field of educational psychology offers insights into the camp experience as a catalyst to success in both academics and in later life. Stankov, Morony and Lee (2014) identified *confidence* as 'the best (known) non-cognitive predictor of achievement on cognitive tests' (p. 24). Although closely associated with self-efficacy, 'in assessing self-efficacy the participant is not required to work out a solution to a problem whereas in assessing confidence, the solution has to be recorded' (p. 25). Results from a Canadian national study on science camps concluded that 'presenting science in a hands-on, interactive way may be an important factor contributing to the increases in confidence and valuing of science and technology found in the present study' (Crombie *et al.*, 2003, p. 267). Confidence equals 'I can do it!' and camp programmes can offer opportunities for children and young people to experience these 'I can do it!' moments through experiential outdoor studies.

Although most camp-related research reported in scholarly journals is positive, negative experiences undoubtedly occur. However, few researchers have explored these potential negative aspects of camp. For example, under Hitler's reign, youth camps were used for political indoctrination, with the mass manipulation of impressionable youth – yet little examination of these types of camp experiences can be found. Negative experiences like bullying can occur at camp if staff supervision is not adequate; staff who are overworked and undertrained may not offer quality experiences to their campers; and not every camp is right for every participant. The right opportunities should be matched to the needs and developmental appropriateness of camp for participants. Although negative manipulation of camp experience is not ethical, more critically posed questions may offer other views about the camp experience, as well as a greater understanding of the personal and environmental vulnerabilities that could exist in camps.

The future

Outdoor learning in camps is important for youth development opportunities. The education sector defines outdoor learning in different ways (i.e. academic-based learning that occurs in the outdoor classroom vs learning about nature and outdoor skills through nature-based experiences). Regardless, outdoor learning within both contexts offers a range of outdoor activities within camps. Although research exists, numerous questions remain to be answered. A comprehensive discussion of the future research agenda for camps is beyond the scope of this chapter, but we would like to suggest several areas for potential study.

Conduct longitudinal projects. Few examples of longitudinal studies exist in the camp literature, which means little is known about the impact of the experience over time. While findings from aggregated one-shot data collection are important, tracking individuals for five to ten years would cast light on how youth as well as adults can grow through outdoor camp experiences.

Move from camper-specific outcomes to setting-level outcomes. Much has been learned about individual outcomes from varied outdoor learning experiences at camp. However, little is known about outcomes at the setting level. A more aggregated approach that moves to analyse setting variables (e.g. structure, policy, procedures) in addition to the individual could lead to a deeper understanding of considerations that may influence outcomes.

Assess practices behind successful programme models. The *black box* of the camp experience has opened somewhat as researchers try to determine best practices. If camps are to be most effective, identifying aspects such as best practices by staff in domains such as interaction patterns, emotional safety, building a sense of belonging, active learning, planning and reflection, enabling camper voice, and setting challenges are important to explore.

Explore the health and wellness benefits of camp (i.e. physical activity, mental wellness, and nutrition considerations). Findings suggest that outdoor learning in camps may offer intersections among varied components, including healthy lifestyle choices, stress reduction, learning readiness and other skills that emphasise the mind–body experience. With near epidemic rates of childhood and adult obesity in many countries, camp may be an intervention that helps address challenges of inactivity due to increased screen time, lack of access to outdoor spaces and a general disconnect with the natural world. However, a dearth of research leaves questions such as the necessary dose of physical activity, lasting impacts and the role of staff in modelling desired behaviours.

Investigate the role of camp experiences as turning points. Certain life experiences that awaken a latent interest/motive in a young person and subtly alter their life trajectory (Gotlib & Wheaton, 1997) may emerge from camp experiences. Given the concerns about developing environmental stewardship, career interests in STEM areas and healthy lifestyles, the concept of turning points attributed to camp is important to explore related to later career and life impact.

Explore developmental cascades found in the camp experience. These cascades are cumulative impacts of experiences of youth over the lifespan that are necessary for both attaining and maintaining positive life trajectories (Lewin-Bizan, Bowers & Lerner, 2010). Camp professionals usually believe that developmental cascades occur within the camp experience, but little evidence exists to support that belief.

The camp experience has been associated with learning and human development. This learning often takes place in enjoyable informal outdoor experiences that have a holistic human-centred approach. The outdoors becomes a *classroom* or *laboratory* where questioning, exploration and problem solving are encouraged by supportive adults and peers, and where opportunities are offered to build perseverance, resilience and coping skills. Camp is also a workforce development setting where young adult staff members have opportunities to learn and develop skills, behaviours and knowledge that help them perform their work at camp, and also continue their own personal and professional development. Experiential learning through the camp experience has a rich history of human development in nature-based settings. Camps in the future must continue to innovate around these traditional outdoor skills, behaviours and concepts.

References

American Camp Association (ACA) (2005). Directions: Youth development outcomes of the camp experience. Retrieved from: www.acacamps.org/research/enhance/directions.

American Camp Association (ACA) (2006a). Inspirations: development supports and opportunities of youths' experiences at camp. Retrieved from: www.acacamps.org/research/enhance/inspirations.

American Camp Association (ACA) (2006b). Innovations: Improving youth experiences in summer programmes. Retrieved from: www.acacamps.org/research/enhance/innovations.

American Camp Association (ACA) (2014). *ACA's vision, values, mission and ends.* Retrieved from: www.acacamps.org/about/vision-values-mission-ends.

Ashurst, K.L., Smith, L.W., Little, C.A., Frey, L.M., Werner-Wilson, T.A., Stephenson, L. & Werner-Wilson, R.J. (2014). Perceived outcomes of military-extension adventure camps for military personnel and their teenage children. *American Journal of Family Therapy, 42*(2), 175–189.

Bialeschki, M.D. & Sibthorp, J. (2011). Celebrating the camp experience through eighty years of camp research. *Taproot Journal, 20*(2), 13–24.

Bjerrum Nielsen, H. (2004). European gender lessons: Girls and boys at scout camps in Denmark, Portugal, Russia and Slovakia. *Childhood, 11*(2), 207–226.

Brookes, A. (2002). Lost in the Australian bush: Outdoor education as curriculum. *Journal of Curriculum Studies, 34*(4), 405–425.

Brown, S. (2013). Science teacher educator's partnership experience teaching urban middle school students in multiple informal settings. In M. Diaz, C. Eick & L. Brantley-Dias (Eds.) *Science Teacher Educators as K-12 Teachers: Practicing What We Teach* (pp. 149–168). New York: Springer.

Carlson, R.E. (1957). Organized camping. *Annals of the American Academy of Political and Social Science, 313,* 83–86.

Chang, C. (2010). Message framing and interpersonal orientation at cultural and individual levels. *International Journal of Advertising, 29*(5), 765–794.

Chen, T.-L., Sheen, H.-J., Yueh, H.-P., Chiang, F.-K. & Chang, P.-W. (2012). Designing nano-biotechnology summer camp with experiential learning theory. *International Journal of Engineering Education, 28*(5), 1078–1087.

Collado, S., Staats, H. & Corraliza, J.A. (2013). Experiencing nature in children's summer camps: Affective, cognitive and behavioural consequences. *Journal of Environmental Psychology, 33,* 37–44.

Comai, G. (2012). Youth camps in post-Soviet Russia and the Northern Caucasus: The cases of Seliger and Mashuk 2010. *The Anthropology of East Europe Review, 30*(1), 184–212.

Crombie, G., Walsh, J.P. & Trinneer, A. (2003). Positive effects of science and technology summer camps on confidence, values, and future intentions. *Canadian Journal of Counseling, 37*(4), 256–269.

Dahl, T.I., Sethre-Hofstad, L. & Salomon, G. (2013). Intentionally designed thinking and experience spaces: What we learned at summer camp. *Learning Environments Research, 16*(1), 91–112.

Dewey, J. (1916). *Democracy and Education.* New York: Macmillan.

Dewey, J. (1925). *Experience and Nature.* Chicago, London: Open Court Publishing Company.

Dimock, H.S. & Hendry, C.E. (1929). *Camping and Character: A Camp Experiment in Character Education.* New York: Association Press.

Eells, E. (1986). *Eleanor Eells' History of Organized Camping: The First 100 Years.* Martinsville, IN: American Camping Association.

English, M.C. & Kitsantas, A. (2013). Supporting student self-regulated learning in problem- and project-based learning. *Interdisciplinary Journal of Problem-based Learning, 7*(2), 127–150.

Ewert, A., Place, G. & Sibthorp, J. (2005). Early life outdoor experiences and an individual's environmental attitudes. *Leisure Sciences, 27,* 225–239.

Farrington, C.A., Roderick, M., Allensworth, E., Nagaoka, J., Keyes, T.S., Johnson, D.W. & Beechum, N.O. (2012). *Teaching Adolescents to Become Learners. The Role of Noncognitive Factors in Shaping School Performance: A Critical Literature Review.* Chicago, IL: University of Chicago Consortium on Chicago School Research. Retrieved from: http://ccsr.uchicago.edu/publications/teaching-adolescents-become-learners-role-noncognitive-factors-shaping-school.

Fine, S. (2005). Contextual learning within the residential outdoor experience: A case study of a summer camp community in Ontario. University of Toronto. Retrieved from: http://ccamping.org/resources/research-papers/.

Fine, S. (2012). A burgeoning world of camp research. *Camping Magazine, 85*(5), 40.

Fine, S. & Tuvshin, T. (2010). Cosmopolitan citizenship through the residential camp experience: Comparative research in North America and Central Asia. Paper presented at the 10th Biennial Coalition for Education in the Outdoors Research Symposium, Indiana University, Bradford Woods, January. Retrieved from: http://ccamping.org/resources/research-papers/.

Fjortoft, I. (2001). The natural environment as a playground for children: The impact of outdoor play activities in pre-primary school children. *Early Childhood Education Journal, 29*(2), 111–117.

Garst, B.A., Browne, L.P. & Bialeschki, M.D. (2011). Youth development and the camp experience. *New Directions for Youth Development, 130,* 73–87.

Glover, T., Graham, T., Mock, S., Mannell, R., Carruthers, A. & Chapeskie, A. (2013). Canadian summer camp research project, phase 3: Parent perception of changes in children after returning home from camp. Retrieved from: http://ccamping.org/resources/research-papers/.

Gotlib, I.H. & Wheaton, B. (1997). *Stress and Adversity Over the Life Course: Trajectories and Turning Points.* Cambridge, UK: Cambridge University Press.

Gutman, L.M. & Schoon, I. (2012). Correlates and consequences of uncertainty in career aspirations: Gender differences among adolescents in England. *Journal of Vocational Behavior, 80*(3), 608–618.

Hantrais, L. & Mangen, S. (1996). Cross-national research. *International Journal of Social Research Methodology, 2*(2), 91–92.

Henderson, K.A., Marsh, P.E., Bialeschki, M.D., Scanlin, M.M., Whitaker, L., Thurber, C. & Burkhardt, M. (2006). Intentional youth development through camp experiences. *Camping Magazine, 79*(5), 1–3.

Ho, S.M.Y. & Cheung, M.W.L. (2007). Using the combined etic–metic approach to develop a measurement of interpersonal subjective well-being in Chinese populations. In Ong, A.D. & van Dulmen, M.H.M. (Eds.) *Oxford Handbook of Methods in Positive Psychology* (pp. 139–152). New York: Oxford University Press.

Irwin, F.L. (1950). *The Theory of Camping: An Introduction to Camping in Education*. New York: Barnes.

Johnson, S.K., Goldman, J.A., Garey, A.I., Britner, P.A. & Weaver, S.E. (2011). Emerging adults' identity exploration: Illustrations from inside the 'camp bubble'. *Journal of Adolescent Research, 26*(2), 258–295.

Kilpatrick, W. (1931). Foreword. In Dimock, H.S. & Hendry, C.E. (Eds.) *Camping and Character: A Camp Experiment in Character Education* (pp. vii–xi). New York: Association Press.

Larson, R., Rickman, A.N., Gibbons, C.M. & Walker, K.C. (2009). Practitioner expertise: Creating quality within the daily tumble of events in youth settings. *New Directions for Youth Development, 121*, 71–88.

Lewin-Bizan, S., Bowers, E.P. & Lerner, R.M. (2010). One good thing leads to another: Cascades of positive youth development among American adolescents. *Development and Psychopathology, 22*(4), 759–770.

Louv, R. (2005). *Last Child in the Woods*. Chapel Hill, NC: Algonquin Books.

Madrazo, G.M. & Motz, L.L. (2005). Brain research: Implications to diverse learners. *Science Educator, 14*(1), 56–60.

Mason, B. (1930). *Camping and Education*. New York: The McCall Company.

Miliszewska, I. & Moore, A. (2010). Encouraging girls to consider a career in ICT: A review of strategies. *Journal of Information Technology Education, 9*, 143–166.

National Core Curriculum for Basic Education (2004). *Finnish National Board of Education, 12*, 39–40. Vammala, Finland: Vammalan kirjapaino.

Pyle, R. (2002). Eden in a vacant lot: Special places, species and kids in community of life. In Kahn, P.H. & Kellert, S.R. (Eds.) *Children and Nature: Psychological, Sociocultural and Evolutionary Investigations*. Cambridge: MIT Press

Sharp, L.B. (1930). *Education and the Summer Camp: An Experiment*. New York: Teachers College, Columbia University.

Sibthorp, J., Bialeschki, M.D., Morgan, C. & Browne, L. (2013). Validating, norming, and utility of a youth outcomes battery for recreation programmes and camps. *Journal of Leisure Research, 45*(4), 514–536.

Smeds, P., Jeronen, E., Kurppa, S. & Vieraankivi, M. (2011). Rural camp school eco learn – outdoor education in rural settings. *International Journal of Environmental & Science Education, 6*(3), 267–291.

Smith, M.B. (2006). 'The ego ideal of the good camper' and the nature of summer camp. *Environmental History, 11*(1), 70–101.

Stankov, L., Morony, S. & Lee, Y.P. (2014). Confidence: The best non-cognitive predictor of academic achievement? *Educational Psychology: An International Journal of Experimental Educational Psychology, 34*(1), 9–28.

Thurber, C.A., Scanlin, M.M., Scheuler, L. & Henderson, K.A. (2007). Development outcomes of the camp experience: Evidence for multidimensional growth. *Journal of Youth & Adolescence*, 36(3), 241–254.

Tichenor, M. & Plavchan, J. (2010). Summer camps: A fun way to reinforce math skills. *Journal of Instructional Psychology, 37*(1), 71–75.

Wagner, T. (2010). *The Global Achievement Gap: Why Even Our Best Schools Don't Teach the New Survival Skills Our Children Need and What We Can Do About It*. New York: Basic Books.

Wells, N.M. (2000). At home with nature, effects of 'greenness' on children's cognitive functioning. *Environment and Behavior, 32*(6), 775–795.

Worden, J.M., Hinton, C. & Fischer, K.W. (2011). What does the brain have to with learning? *Phi Delta Kappan, 92*(8), 8–13.

23

Sail training

Ken McCulloch

University of Edinburgh

Sail training as a term describes a variety of practices that are referred to by their advocates as youth sailing, youth work at sea, adventure sailing and sail training. It is a modern phenomenon with deep historical roots. Sail training incorporates traditions and practices with differing emphases on types of vessel, criteria for participation, voyage duration and expressed purpose. Theoretical and research perspectives have included psychological studies on the development of confidence and self-esteem (e.g. Grocott, 1999), and sociological analyses using concepts such as social capital formation (Finkelstein & Goodwin, 2005) as an outcome of participation, and the *total institution* concept (Goffman, 1961; McCulloch, 2002) as illuminating the nature of the experience for participants.

Most practitioners will tend to say that they are not principally concerned to train young people as sailors, although that may be a by-product of the work. The waters can also be muddied by the common usage of the phrase *sail training* in a more restricted technical sense as training in sailing skills. The essential features of sail training are the use of sailing vessels of a size that can accommodate a group of young people as trainees and one or more adult staff living aboard for a period, time spent at sea normally under sail power and motives that give priority to the trainees' development as people. The experience may have as one outcome the learning of sailing and seamanship skills. However, to qualify as sail training this outcome is not generally the primary purpose. The definitional boundary between *sailing schools*, which provide courses of instruction in sailing, and *sail training organisations* can be blurred, but these key features are sufficient as an opening definition.

The smallest sail training vessels are yachts of around 10m length carrying two crew or staff and four or five trainees. The largest are ships upwards of 40m carrying a dozen or more staff and, in some cases, more than a hundred trainees. Evidence from about 1998 (Hunter, Boyes, Maunsell & O'Hare, n.d.) suggests that the majority of sail training experiences use boats around 20m in size with ten to twelve trainees and four or five staff aboard.

Size is not the only dimension to be considered. The technologies by which sailing vessels operate range from traditional to modern, with many steps between. Alongside consideration of the variables that the vessels themselves embody, the significance of the particular waters sailed, length and duration of voyages, and weather conditions experienced, all contribute to the experiences available to participants.

The origins of sail training

The roots of modern sail training can be identified by examining the traditions and practices of professional seagoing in the age of sail and recreational sailing since the late 19th century, but the contemporary practice of sail training was brought into being deliberately during the decades following the Second World War. Both the characteristics of the experience offered, and the number and diversity of those who become participants are significant. The belief that the seafaring life had peculiar benefits is widespread and of long standing. Ships and the sea have a strong cultural significance, and compelling evidence suggests that sail training has qualities attributed to its associations with seafaring generally. Participants, practitioners and onlookers understand sail training as a maritime adventure strongly linked to a wider context of contemporary and historical seafaring. These associations provide evidence that at the beginning of the 21st century going to sea in wind-powered vessels still has important symbolic meaning. Seafaring is valorised both as an individual achievement and as an expression of national character. The importance of these associations is in the ways they shape understandings of the nature, purpose and meaning of sail training. The question about whether sail training provides 'different social and environmental contexts to those of offshore competitive sailing' (Humberstone, 2000, p. 32) helps to locate sail training in relation to racing and, by extension, to the broader context of leisure sailing.

One key strand in the development of sail training was the Outward Bound movement. In its earliest form, young merchant seamen were helped to acquire skills thought to increase their chances of survival in the event of a ship sinking (Miner, 1990). The emphasis was on both personal resourcefulness and on the psychological qualities or dispositions that were believed to improve chances of survival. Little was known at that time about the mechanisms of hypothermia, and survival was seen as an outcome of personal determination rather than of physiological mechanisms. After the end of the Second World War, the Outward Bound movement began to reframe its purposes. The emphasis began to shift towards social purposes, and particularly to notions of character building through physically demanding activities in the outdoors (Loynes, 1990).

Sail training may provide a context for learning, but sailing and seamanship skills form only one part of the content of that learning. Alfred Holt, co-founder of the first Outward Bound School at Aberdovey, Wales, is quoted as advocating 'less a training *for* the sea than *through* the sea' (Miner, 1990, p. 59; original italics). Within this general definition lie many differences arising from different conceptions of purpose. Differences also manifest in features such as the types of vessel used and in the culture and practices characteristic of particular approaches. For example, as Phillipson's (1996) account illustrated, elements of one sail training tradition can be traced almost in a straightforward line from the practices of the (British) Royal Navy at that time. More generally, the values of sail training may be related to ideas and practices concerned with the development and growth of individuals, citizenship and social order, and crime and punishment. The recognition that seafaring can have a powerful impact on participants is not novel, and the developments that culminated in what has been called the great age of sail from the 17th to the 19th centuries provide a historical backdrop. The notion that seagoing might also have a pleasurable recreational dimension as distinct from mercantile and military purposes emerged in the 19th century, when it became economically possible for the *leisure class* (Veblen, 1899) to operate yachts for pleasure.

A tradition of sail training aboard large square-rigged vessels as part of the professional training of seafarers is widespread. During the 19th century, the Royal Navy introduced dedicated training ships for boy seamen. HMS *Illustrious* was appointed by the Admiralty as the first training ship for boys in 1854. The experiment was judged successful in achieving the aim of inculcating in trainees a love of the sea and pride in the service (Phillipson, 1996). Despite the progressive replacement of sailing warships with steamships, other vessels were commissioned as training ships. The sinking of two of these square-rigged training ships, the *Euridice* in 1878 and the *Atalanta* two years later, and the associated loss of life, however, led to a public outcry and the beginning of the end for sail training in this traditional sense as part of Naval induction in the UK. During the late 19th century the last sailing warships were phased out as the transition to steam gathered pace. As Phillipson's account illustrated, many of the traditions of the 18th- and 19th century Navy were retained long after the technology that gave them their original significance had been superseded. Many other Northern European nations, however, retained this professional sail training tradition. Poland, Germany, Denmark, Norway and Russia all have more or less continuous histories of using large square-rigged vessels as a key part of their professional maritime training system (Hamilton, 1988). Beyond Europe, for example, the US Coast Guard employs the square-rigger USCGC *Eagle*[1] as part of its training programme, and since 1982 the Mexican Navy has operated *Cuauhtemoc* on a similar basis (Hamilton, 1988).

Alongside the tall ships tradition is a second tradition, which I have characterised as leisure yachting. The origins of this approach are British and European (McCulloch, 2002). The London Sailing Project is cited as both seminal in terms of the timing and impact of its emergence in 1960, and as archetypal in respect to specific practices. (Hamilton 1988). In parallel at the same time, Chris Ellis, an Eton schoolmaster, and his friend Rev. A.C. Courtauld, began using their own private yachts to take sailing both boys from public school and, through the public school settlement movement, from working-class areas of London. They were following an impulse that led to the beginnings of the Ocean Youth Club, which was formally constituted in 1960 (Ocean Youth Club, 1985) and was succeeded in 1999 by five autonomous regional trusts.

What distinguishes this leisure yachting tradition in its origins was the use of privately owned yachts to take small groups of young novice sailors to sea. This was undertaken in a spirit of what might be called patrician philanthropy. Beliefs in the benefits of sailing as recreation merged with a concern to, as it was and still is claimed, break down the barriers of social class. The means of pursuing these objectives are, however, profoundly different from those employed in the tall ship tradition. The use of vessels accommodating a dozen trainees and a handful of staff provided the setting for what one informant described as a *family atmosphere*. The pioneers of this approach were apparently seeking to provide for young people who often would not have had the opportunity, the same kind of experiences as they had valued in sailing with their own families. These men were from prosperous middle- or upper-middle-class families for whom recreational sailing was a normal part of their life and expectations. (See McCulloch (2002, 2006) for a fuller account.)

The seminal event in the emergence of the modern international sail training movement was the organisation of the first Tall Ships Race in 1956. A London solicitor, Bernard Morgan, is usually credited with the original idea, which was to be a celebratory farewell to the age of sail. Up until 1939 commercial sailing ships were successfully trading, mainly carrying non-perishable cargoes and taking advantage of the low running costs of sailing vessels. Morgan and his collaborators sought to create an event as a final gathering of vessels symbolising the end of an era. The races became an annual event and the idea of sail training took hold over the following decades, spreading across Northern Europe, and into in the USA and Canada with the formation of the American Sail Training Association in 1973. Similar patterns are evident in Australia, New Zealand, Japan and a growing number of smaller nations. The newest recruit to the movement is China. The China Sail Training Association was started in 2012 by expatriate Chinese to promote participation in sail training by the growing number of expatriates in the West, and to promote sail training to China.

Research and theory

Until the beginning of the 21st century, fewer than a dozen publications could be described as research on sail training. Of these, Hamilton's (1988) was the first comprehensive account. The author was a thoroughly experienced practitioner and offered a descriptive study of the state of the field in the late 1980s. The value and benefits of sail training were treated as unproblematic and implicit. Hamilton asserted that 'there are two types of youngsters who can benefit from sail training' (p. 12). One type was youth who were training as professional seamen, and a second type was trainees participating in a singular or occasional experience. Hamilton did not, however, explicitly describe the benefits.

Gordon *et al.* (1996) offered a study of one group of seven trainees who participated as Blue Watch in a sail training voyage on STS *Leeuwin* based in Western Australia. The analysis of benefits to participants focused on notions of self-confidence, self-esteem, motivation, tolerance and the opportunity to display talents. Purpose was construed in terms of these benefits, and the trainees were characterised as marginalised in terms of ethnicity or economic and social class statuses. A related approach was pursued by Grocott (1999) in a study of the effect of a ten-day voyage on self-concept, and more recently by Hayhurst, Hunter, Kafka and Boyes (2013), focusing on resilience. These studies reflect the mainstream of the research literature on outdoor education, and appear more concerned with the psychological concepts and their measurement than with the character of sail training or with exploration of the effects for participants.

A second strand of research is evident, with a focus on sail training in association with the justice system or crime prevention. Bottomley and James (1994) undertook a study of a project in which Humberside Probation Service clients were offered the opportunity to participate in STA voyages as part of a programme of individual rehabilitation. The findings of the study were equivocal regarding the benefits of participation. Although participants were positive in their assessment of the experience, and showed low rates of reoffending, it was also clear that those probation clients who accepted this experience were a self-selected group unlikely to reoffend.

Smith and Paylor (1997) presented an evaluation of several projects in Lancashire in the mid-1990s, which were funded specifically to work with young people aged 13–20 years who were *at risk* of offending. The main emphasis was on a case study that described in detail a group of young people going on a sailing trip with a vessel and organisation not explicitly identified. The paper described positively the response of the young people to the experience. While making no specific claims regarding changes in subsequent behaviour, a belief was expressed that the experience may have had important consequences for the young people. Karabinas, Monaghan and Sheptycki (1996) also presented an evaluation of a summer activity programme funded as a crime reduction strategy. Results showed that the programme was successful notwithstanding its relatively high cost.

Other common-sense practitioners' accounts are mostly straightforwardly descriptive. Scrope's (1987) article was typical, describing a North Sea crossing from Essex to Norway in a 45-foot yacht by a group of Essex schoolchildren who had just completed their 16+ examinations. Few details were given, and the account focused on skills and knowledge, working as a team, seasickness, cold weather and living in close quarters. Pride and self-respect were described as key outcomes, and the article included a claim that this trip was the most ambitious sailing expedition ever attempted by a single group of schoolchildren from Essex. The internal publications of sail training organisations offer many other similar descriptive accounts. Such material provides useful evidence of beliefs about the benefits of participation, but consistently lacks critical distance from the practices described.

Research on sail training since 2000 has developed significantly. Master's dissertations, such as those of Lyth (2012) and Pijoan (2013), have been produced in universities in Europe and elsewhere. Several doctoral projects that focus on sail training are in progress in the USA, UK, Poland and Australia. Only a few of these projects have achieved formal publication. One large-scale funded study was undertaken in a collaboration in 2006–2007 between the University of Edinburgh and Sail Training International. The main project publication (McCulloch, McLaughlin, Allison, Edwards & Tett, 2010) is significant as the first recognition in a mainstream education research journal of sail training as an *educational* practice. What all these studies have broadly in common is a view of sail training as a beneficial experience for young people, and confirmation with differing emphases on participants developing social and self-confidence, capacities such as cooperation with others, and attitudinal change in relation to, for example, tolerance of diversity.

Future directions for research

Both practitioners and sail training organisations as providers have a growing interest in developing understanding and analysis of what sail training does for participants, why and how it affects their life trajectories, and how the practices of sail training might respond and change in the light of these new understandings.

Theoretical starting points are significant because, whether acknowledged or not, all research proceeds from a set of beliefs and assumptions about the world, about the nature of knowledge, and about the kinds of questions possible or worthwhile to explore. Theories of research do not stand alone separate from other kinds of concerns, but are bound up with wider questions. The research undertaken and what is possible or desirable as objects of enquiry, is tied up with economic, social and political contexts.

In the contemporary world, the dominance of neo-liberal economic theory creates conditions required to understand the world as consisting, at least in part, of markets of various kinds. In this context researchers have a strong incentive to generate findings that enable market positions to be established or modified. Thus, research on sail training takes place in a context where *proving the value* of the experience is a key motive, thus establishing its position in a market where different activities and experiences compete for attention, funding and resources. Researchers, therefore, find themselves in a context where *proving* that sail training *works* in the sense of providing particular outcomes for participants, is seen as one of the more valuable roles that research can provide. Researchers using qualitative interpretivist approaches may also be pushed towards a search for truth and proof. However, if research on sail training does not support the field in this way, it might be argued, there may be no point in undertaking it.

In addition to this concern, other imperatives ought to be considered, and other theoretical starting points examined. Research should not be solely concerned as currency in a quasi-market but also can perform a reflexive role in the field. Research is about helping proponents of sail training to analyse and think about what they do and to provide persuasive evidence that individuals, institutions and governments should support and encourage the work. Research that asks why it works as it does, how the particular experiences of different programmes impact on participants, or research that attempts to describe, compare or understand the different cultures and traditions of sail training are all important.

Positivist theory is about proving truth or falsity. In this context it commonly leads to research that seeks to measure the benefits of participation in sail training, or to compare the merits of using different vessels. Why such research is important and why people want to do this work is easy to recognise. It is useful for the field, and I would not discourage anyone from supporting or undertaking this approach. Research and evaluation of this kind will always be necessary and important.

Interpretivist research is more concerned with questions like what and how. It is about trying to understand what sail training is, why it goes on, and how participants experience their involvement. For example, ethnographic and phenomenological accounts seek to describe and analyse the cultures of sail training, and to understand the nature of the subjective experience of participants (McCulloch, 2007). The usefulness of such research is evident both for providers as organisations striving to improve the quality of their clients' experience, and for practitioners who seek a fuller understanding of, for example, the experience of trainees arriving aboard for the first time and how they make sense of the new and unfamiliar context.

Critical theory might seem more controversial. Critical theorists start from a recognition that the world is unfair, unequal and sometimes unjust in various ways. Research that grows from this origin is about identifying and making clear the character, origins and limitations of social justice. Research on sail training from a critical theory perspective might focus on issues such as the ways power, authority and discipline are manifested aboard sail training vessels, how decisions are made and how trainees' voices are recognised in that context (McCulloch, 2005). At a more structural level, critical theorists might explore questions about the structures and governance of sail training organisations, their funding, and the outcomes that are sought or claimed. The key difference between critical and some other theoretical starting points is that critical theorists will not treat the social and economic context as an unproblematic given, but will have as one of the purposes of research to challenge and change that context in ways that promote values such as social justice and equality.

Different theories tend to lead to different kinds of questions, and moving back and forth between thinking about theory and about the questions research addresses is important. Some questions that are both intrinsically interesting and worth exploring in the current early 21st century context are as follows.

- What is the character of the sail training experience itself? What is it like to participate in particular programmes and why are they different, if they are?
- Does the kind of vessels used matter? The 2006–2007 STI/UoE study suggested that voyage outcomes are much the same from a large square-rigged ship or a modest-sized cutter or ketch (McCulloch et al., 2010). It has been speculated that whether the vessel uses sails or engines might not make much, if any, difference to the experience for participants.
- Most research has concentrated on trainees as participants. What is known about staff and volunteers, what motivates them, what benefits they experience and how careers in sail training, whether voluntary or paid, take shape?
- Who pays the bills, either for individuals' participation or by larger-scale investment in the commissioning of new vessels? What motivates funders and what do they think the benefits are? Understanding how sail training is seen in the wider world and asking questions about funders and funding is important.
- Operators use different types and sizes of vessel for a variety of reasons, including economic, cultural and traditional imperatives. Not all of these vessels have been designed for sail training. A trend in the UK recently has been to adapt vessels originally designed for long-distance passage racing for sail training purposes. Such vessels are different from those in use a decade or two earlier in terms of accommodation, character and sailing performance demands. What are the consequences of these newer vessel technologies?

Considering the wider context of sail training is important. The lives young people lead, wherever they are in the world, are different now in the second decade of the 21st century compared to the lives their parents or grandparents led when sail training was emerging and developing in the decades following the Second World War. Young people's experiences of sail training are embedded in their lived experience, of which researchers need to take account in understanding the interplay between the sail training experience and the social, economic and cultural influences that shape people's lives. What, for example, are the implications of technology and new media? Young people are more connected now than at any time in history. The isolation from outside influences traditionally associated with seafaring is no longer a given in the way it was even at the end of the 1990s. Trainees can find material, films, blogs and accounts of sail training prior to participation. They can also, if they choose, maintain contact with former crewmates across continents with a speed and ease that would have been inconceivable a decade ago.

These changes have consequences for the practice of sail training. Understanding the consequences is important. These changes also represent a new opportunity for researchers. If young people are more readily connected to one another, there are also opportunities for researchers to become more connected and to use those connections as opportunities to generate new data.

Finally, globalisation, however understood, is part of reality. As part of the shrinking and connected world, increasing interest exists in questions about citizenship and democracy. Sail training as an international, but not yet universal, movement or network is uniquely placed to build bridges between nations and cultures. Such connections were one key motive of the founders of the modern sail training movement. Sail training is also vulnerable in that it is predominantly a feature of the rich developed *global north* and might be seen with some justification as yet another manifestation of Western or Northern cultural imperialism. Research on the policy and politics of sail training might not be a comfortable or easy project, but it is important to scrutinise these aspects with a view to describing and understanding both positive possibilities and potential difficulties, and to identify opportunities and threats.

Finally, people should pay attention to the relationship of sail training to the environmental crisis. Climate change, pollution, overfishing, and destruction of habitat and wildlife are key aspects. Sail training is well placed to contribute to the promotion of environmental justice. Research could contribute to that objective by, for example, identifying models of practice, uncovering gaps in the knowledge and understanding of staff and volunteers, and identifying resources, networks and possible collaborators (Lyth, 2012).

Sail training is treated with some justification by practitioners and proponents as an end, as a good in itself. The fundamental test, however, has to be whether and to what extent sail training can contribute directly or indirectly to the development of solutions and constructive responses to pressing human problems.

Note

1　*Eagle* was built in 1936 as *Horst Wessel*, a sail training vessel of the *Hitlerjügend*, but was taken into US ownership as war reparation and commissioned into the USCG in 1946.

References

Bottomley, K. & James, A. (1994). *The Humberside Probation Service Sail Training Project: Final Evaluation Report for the Rank Foundation*. Hull, UK: The Centre for Criminology and Criminal Justice, University of Hull.

Finkelstein, J. & Goodwin, S. (2005) *Sailing into the Future: Final report on ARC Linkage Research Project*. Sydney, Australia: Department of Sociology and Social Policy, University of Sydney.

Goffman, E. (1961). *Asylums: Essays on the Social Situation of Mental Patients and Other Inmates*. Garden City, NY: Doubleday.

Gordon, S., Harcourt-Smith, K., Hay, K. & Priest, S. (1996). Case study of Blue Watch on STS Leeuwin. *Journal of Adventure Education and Outdoor Leadership, 13*(1), 4–7.

Grocott, A.C. (1999). Sailing and self-esteem: The effect of a ten day developmental voyage at sea on the multidimensional self-concept. Unpublished MSc dissertation, University of Otago.

Hamilton, J. (1988). *Sail Training: The Message of the Tall Ships*. Wellingborough, UK: Patrick Stephens Ltd.

Hayhurst, J., Hunter, J.A., Kafka, S. & Boyes, M. (2013). Enhancing resilience in youth through a 10-day developmental voyage. *Journal of Adventure Education & Outdoor Leadership*. Published online: DOI: 10.1080/14729679.2013.843143.

Humberstone, B. (2000). The 'outdoor industry' as social and educational phenomena. *Journal of Adventure Education & Outdoor Leadership*, *1*(1), 21–35.

Hunter, J., Boyes, M., Maunsell, S. & O'Hare, D. (n.d.) *Sail Training in the International Arena: The Value of Sail Training to Young People Today*. Dunedin, NZ: University of Otago.

Karabinas, A., Monaghan, B. & Sheptycki, J.W.E. (1996). An evaluation of the Craigmillar Youth Challenge. *Howard Journal of Criminal Justice*, *35*(2), 113–130.

Loynes, C. (1990). Development training in the United Kingdom. In J. Miles & S. Priest (Eds) *Adventure Education* (pp. 45–51). State College, PA: Venture Publishing, Inc.

Lyth, L.E. (2012). A critical evaluation of marine environmental education needs within the sail training industry. Unpublished MSc thesis, University of Portsmouth, UK.

McCulloch, K. (2002). Four days before the mast: A study of sail training in the UK. Unpublished PhD thesis, University of Edinburgh, UK.

McCulloch, K. (2005). Ideologies of adventure: Authority and decision making in sail training. *Journal of Adventure Education and Outdoor Learning*, *4*(2), 185–197.

McCulloch, K. (2006). Tall ships and gentlemen's yachts: Sail training in the UK. In Gilchrist, R., Jeffs, T. & Spence, J. (Eds.) *Drawing on the Past: Studies in the History of Community and Youth Work* (pp. 211–223). Leicester, UK: Youth and Policy/National Youth Agency.

McCulloch, K. (2007). Living at sea: Learning from communal life aboard sail training vessels. *Ethnography and Education*, *2*(3), 289–303.

McCulloch, K., McLaughlin, P., Allison, P., Edwards, V. & Tett, L. (2010). More than mere adventure: Sail training as education. *Oxford Review of Education*, *36*(6), 661–676.

Miner, J.L. (1990). The creation of Outward Bound. In J.C. Miles & S. Priest (Eds.) *Adventure Education* (pp. 59–70). State College, PA: Venture Publishing, Inc.

Ocean Youth Club (1985). *Silver Jubilee Spunyarns. Special Edition of the OYC House Journal – A Concise History 1960–1985*. Gosport, UK: The Ocean Youth Club.

Phillipson, D. (1996). *Band of Brothers: Boy Seamen in the Royal Navy 1800–1956*. Stroud, Gloucestershire, UK: Sutton Publishing Ltd.

Pijoan, M. (2013). A fantastic world: Sail training as a transforming experience for young people from different countries. Unpublished master's thesis, University of Barcelona, Spain.

Scrope, K. (1987). Letting fresh air into education. *Adventure Education*, *4*(3), 8–9.

Smith, D. & Paylor, I. (1997). Reluctant heroes: Youth workers and crime prevention. *Youth & Policy*, 57, 17–28.

Veblen, T. (1899). *The Theory of the Leisure Class*. Boston, MA: Houghton Mifflin.

24

Forest School in the United Kingdom

Sara Knight

Anglia Ruskin University

Forest School in the UK is a relatively new discipline in the pantheon of outdoor pedagogies and pursuits. It is a way of spending repeated and prolonged time in wilder spaces focusing on developing both emotional intelligence and a love of the natural environment through simple shared tasks chosen by the participants. It evolved from observed practice in Scandinavian kindergarten, but in the UK is used to great effect across all age groups.

A new idea tends to go through a developmental phase when it is natural for practitioners to spend much of their energies and time in establishing the ground rules and agreeing the general principles, which is the case with Forest School. By the middle of 2012, the Forest School Association was established to identify agreed guiding principles and a shared ethos, which have been published on the Association website (www.forestschoolassociation.org). A platform for discussion and debate was created, and four successful conferences held in different locations around the UK. Those activities have enabled the Forest School community to move to the next phase of growth. Practitioners have started researching more rigorously, and the Association has formed a research group working with Good for Woods, a lottery-funded research project led by the Silvanus Trust and the University of Plymouth in partnership with the Neroche Scheme, the Woodland Trust and Forest Research (www.silvanustrust.org.uk/index.php?page=good-from-woods). Reflecting on the origins of Forest School and the research conducted is the basis for this chapter.

Into the 21st century

In 1993 a team from the UK, from Bridgwater College, Somerset, visited Denmark on an exchange; the lecturers were inspired by the emphasis the Danish early years settings gave to facilitating children's wilder and adventurous outdoor play activities. On their return to Somerset, the team reflected on what they had seen, and related it to known theory and practice in the early years in the UK. They also debated the cultural differences and educational trends in England and Denmark, considering what approaches could be imported wholesale and which needed 'translating'. From these reflections they devised the first Forest School programme, initially for children aged 2 to 5 years attending the college day nursery, and later for other groups of students attending the college.

The model has now become widely accepted across the British Isles as a valuable model for being outside in wilder spaces with all ages and client groups, and for a variety of purposes. Working backwards through history from that point it is possible to explore those theoretical influences that led first to the development of the initial pedagogy, and later to the philosophical principles and ethos that underpins Forest School in the UK today.

The 20th century

One step backwards leads to another Danish link, which came from the adventure playground movement started in the 1930s by a retired Army major who was concerned about the effects of urban life on children, and particularly on their opportunities for creative play. The idea for adventure playgrounds was brought to the UK in 1948 and thrived until the 1980s, allowing the development and recognition of playwork as a separate and distinct way of working with children (Shier, 1984). Playwork continued and today is a discipline, influencing the ways holiday play schemes, after-school clubs and breakfast clubs in the UK are run. However, health and safety restrictions in the late 20th century almost brought those first urban adventure playgrounds to an end. Recent years have seen a revival in London (Learning and Teaching Scotland, 2010), and adventure playgrounds are once again available in urban settings.

Key links exist between playwork, adventure playgrounds and Forest School; they both encourage activities to be participant led, and allow for construction, destruction and change. This approach fits with the theoretical ideas of playworkers about the value of 'loose parts' as being vital to the free exploration of ideas and creativity (Hughes, 2012, p. 110). Loose parts are elements that might be described as *found objects* and are useful for creative activities of all kinds. Another shared element is the facilitation of risk taking, an otherwise endangered undertaking in modern risk-averse UK society (Gill, 2007). Else (2009) claimed that this risk taking is necessary, 'as it helps us fully experience life' (p. 83), and explains that risks can be both physical and mental. This risk taking is illustrated as an important, although sometimes potentially difficult, learning opportunity in Forest School for children and adults who have experienced adversity in their lives before experiencing Forest School (Wicks, 2011). Claiming this link with the pedagogy of playwork illuminates why Forest School practitioners see their work as important to children's healthy development at all ages.

The effects of the 19th century

Taking another step back in history, the concerns around urbanisation and the resultant disconnect from nature had begun in the UK as soon as urbanisation took place. Urbanisation was largely a result of industrialisation, which in the UK started in the mid-19th century. The socialist reformers Margaret and Rachel McMillan and others made the links between children's healthy development and learning, and to opportunities for them to spend time outside. The sisters opened the Open-Air Nursery School & Training Centre in Deptford in 1914, the first truly open-air early years facility in the UK, and aimed their programme at the children of families living in urban deprivation. However, after the 1940s the recognition of the importance of outdoor spaces for children in the early years tailed off in the UK until the early part of the 21st century (Selbie & Wickett, 2010). Nevertheless, training for workers at all levels in the early years sector in the UK included recognising the work of the McMillan sisters in the pantheon of pioneers, and their espousal of the outdoors as the healthiest place for young minds and bodies. This recognition is probably why Forest School has been adopted so readily by early years settings.

Early years professionals recognise in Forest School a way to provide for exploratory play outside, and, more importantly, they understand the benefits the outdoors brings. As a consequence, the advice in the English Early Years Foundation Stage Guidance (Department for Education, 2012) requiring the provision of outdoor play opportunities fell on receptive ears and improved the provision of outdoor experiences in early years settings. The spread of access to Forest School sessions provided very young children with opportunities to develop as healthy, independent and energetic learners engaged with their local environments (Knight, 2013).

Influences from the 17th century

Another strand in education that resonates with Forest School, and which can be traced back to the thinkers of the Enlightenment, emphasised *how* rather than *what* children learn. Claxton's approach, which he called Building Learning Power (BLP), intends 'helping them [children] build up the mental, emotional, and social resources to enjoy challenge and cope well with uncertainty and complexity' (Claxton *et al.*, 2011, p. 2). This goal resonates for most UK Forest School practitioners (Wellings, 2013). In conversation with teachers using BLP, Forest School practitioners have agreed that Forest School and BLP appear to complement each other perfectly, probably because the seeds of both pedagogies lie in the Enlightenment. At the time that Locke was expressing the importance of critical thinking and of treating children as rational beings, Hegel was propounding the rights of children to an education and Voltaire was espousing the freedom of all to engage in critical debate. When these ideas are filtered through the later educational practices of Pestalozzi, Steiner and Montessori, and the educational pragmatism of Dewey, the outcome is a Forest School pedagogy that is 'learner-centred . . . responsive to the needs and interests of the learners . . . [and] develop[s] emotional intelligence' (Knight, 2013, p. 19).

Forest School has also concerned itself with the environment, while BLP has remained focused on activities inside the classroom. These roots are reflected in traditional teacher training and practice. To see why Forest School is steadfastly set in the forests and woods of the UK requires the reader to further understand the Northern European traditions of contact with the outdoor world.

Viking influences

Understanding how and where Forest School trends and traditions have developed requires recognising that the importance of access to the outdoors has been preserved more easily in countries with fewer people, more space, less industry and stronger links to nature. For example, *Friluftsliv* is a term often linked to Forest School. It is a Norwegian word loosely translated as *open air life*, which was first used in print by the famous Norwegian writer, dramatist and poet Henrik Ibsen in 1859. Norway's law of allemannsrett encourages *Friluftsliv*. Literally translated, allemannsrett means *all man's right*. Norway honours the right of access to, and passage through, uncultivated land in the countryside, regardless of who owns it (Sandell, 2007, p. 90). It is also applied to cultivated land when it is frozen and snow covered. Allemannsrett can be traced back to the Viking period and is institutionalised in Norway through the Outdoor Recreation Act 1963. Similar rights of access extend across most of the Scandinavian countries as symbols of the importance of the outdoor environment to the cultural life of citizens.

Where this cultural expectation does not exist or has been eradicated, for example as in England, a need for a remediation movement such as Forest School is needed. Forest School allows settings and schools to encourage children to get outside and engage with their surroundings from an early age. Through Forest School experiences children can come to embrace outdoor activities as a normal part of their own cultural life, despite this element being missing from the lives of many in their parents and carers' generation. To see why Forest School practitioners might consider this fundamental aim for their practice, it is helpful to engage with the 20th century Norwegian philosopher Arne Næss, who proposes a need for this link that goes deep into the human psyche, and that has existed for a long time.

Links from an agrarian past

Næss proposed eight principles to underpin a worldwide deep ecology movement seeking solutions to global environmental problems (Drengson, 1999). The Green Parties in Europe have widely adopted these principles. This eco-philosophical framework emphasised the importance for people to have a love of nature as well as a love for other humans, embracing the concept of biophilia (Wilson, 1984), and the idea that people have an innate and subconscious need for a relationship with nature in all its forms.

The expression of environmental responsibility in the Forest School ethics document (Knight, 2013) is a reflection of the two-fold ecological stance of most UK Forest School practitioners. First, Wilson's ideas about biophilia are helpful in identifying why people feel healthier and happier outside (Cree, 2011). Second, if children do not develop a love for and a respect for nature at a young age they will fuel the environmental crises in the future: 'like a fire, humans tend to consume and consume until the fuel is gone' (Holland, 2012, p. 144).

Forest School practitioners believe that an important part of their work is to engage learners in developing a connection with their surroundings. In an agrarian past the human links to the landscape were clear. It directly provided benefits for people or it did not, as in the case of universal threats like flood, famine and fire, which suggests that the past should not be idealised (Heywood, 2001). However, there is no longer always an immediate link of observable consequences, so Forest School practice acknowledges that people need to recognise their agrarian roots and those links to the past that promote health and wellbeing, take the best of the past and acknowledge the benefits of the future. During their activities, practitioners make opportunities to point out seasonal and weather-related changes, and discuss consequences and expectations with participants.

Tribal places

People who live closer to nature respect its power. Tribal peoples from all parts of the globe and all periods of history, including the UK's own tribal cultures in pre-Roman and Roman times, found objects and places in nature to value and/or venerate. Forest School practitioners recognise that learners in Forest School sessions develop rituals, songs and stories that result in connections to self-identified objects and places. An early record came from Waller (2007), who observed such identifications by pre-school children in spaces that they used regularly for wilder outdoor play. He evidenced children developing their identity and social relations through a sense of place.

I have also observed this story-making engagement with spaces when working with young children, and have connected this experience to creative work done by older children and adults in Forest School. I have observed the impact a sense of place has for 'commitment, growth and learning' (Knight, 2013, p. 138). Creating this sense of place is possible by repeated access to identifying objects and places, and allowing time for the rituals to develop. An important feature of Forest School is repetition since sessions take place week after week, and are not a one-off event. The development of that sense of place through repetition is one of the consequences of this approach, which builds confidence 'to meet nature on her own turf' (Knight, p. 53).

Storytelling in tribal cultures is often the responsibility of a bardic or shamanistic figure, who maintains and perpetuates the transmission of important cultural ideas and beliefs. Many Forest School practitioners use opportunities for storytelling in their sessions, particularly starting them around a campfire at a time of meeting and reflection. The campfire as a central and focal point is another common link between Forest School and the tribal past. This storytelling is often the way in which positive attitudes to pro-environmental sustainability can be fostered in the participants (Cree & Gersie, 2014). It also develops emotional literacy as participants (i.e. children or adults) are led through allegorical tales and parables. Active listening and response tasks linked to the stories develop empathy as well as the participants' skills in recognising their own feelings and how to deal with them.

This multi-layered approach enables each person to take his or her own route through to a deep personal understanding of their place in their outdoor space. The Scottish Government's plans for Sustainable Education (Scottish Government, 2010) recognise the importance of natural heritage places for developing sustainability, acknowledge the role that traditional sites play, and use local outdoor places in developing a sense of community and learning (Learning and Teaching Scotland, 2010). I would argue that this recognition is timely regarding the importance of developing a sense of belonging to a particular natural environment through repeated usage of those places and spaces, something that Forest School has incorporated into its pedagogy from the start.

New biology, old brains

The benefits of repetition are evident when considering what is known about brain development, an area of research that has been fruitful as recording, imaging and scanning techniques have improved. Although the basic structure of the brain has not changed in evolutionary terms since prehistoric times, two aspects in recent years about how the brain develops have had an impact on increasing an understanding of children's learning. The first is that people have sensitive periods when it is easier to learn some things than others. This idea is related to the attention given to an experience and the number of times it is repeated (White et al., 2013). Therefore, early, repeated and engaging exposure to nature is likely to have a lasting effect on children's understanding and valuing of nature. It also helps to develop the vocabulary with which to communicate that knowledge and understanding if those experiences take place in those early years that are sensitive periods for language development.

The other aspect that develops the brain best is a rich environment providing opportunities to engage physically with that outdoor richness, rather than simply to watch (Farah et al., 2008). This argument supports bringing learners to the best learning environments and getting them out and dirty, which is more successful as an educational strategy than watching nature programmes on TV. As Sunderland (2013) said, 'We can be splendid or terrible . . . Our brains carry the potential for both.' Without environmental stimuli children are unlikely to become as splendid as they have the potential to be. Forest School is not the only way, but it does have the advantage of facilitating deep and time-rich engagement with those elements that individual learners find fascinating at a particular time.

For some time researchers have linked access to nature with healing (Kaplan, 1995) and with developing coping strategies to prevent mental health problems (Perry, 2002). The UK National Health Service (NHS) has become interested in the impact of outdoor experiences on health and wellbeing in recent years, to the extent of supporting access to green spaces on or near NHS land (Centre for Sustainable Healthcare, 2014). This access is not exclusive to Forest School, but specific to Forest School is that it can be started with very young children, that it is a repeated and lasting programme of engagement outside, and that it utilises the holistic nature of learning through experience. The level of scientific understanding is new, but human brains are old, and looking back to ways in which people evolved illuminates the needs of people today.

Evolutionary adaptations

To be healthy people need to feel more than just respect. They need love and, in this case, love of the outdoors. Theories of evolutionary psychology illuminate the importance of ancient links with nature to health and wellbeing, and also to the health and wellbeing of the planet. Kellert (2002) and Kahn (2002) both emphasised this duality. Humans are an adaptive species, and could not have survived and multiplied without being adaptive. However, people do not always make the healthiest choices as a result. Walter (2013) showed that adult learners benefit from being outside as a remediation of the effects of continued exposure to a screen-based society. Observations of young children show them as adept screen users, but concerns are being raised about their social and language development (Gifford, 2014), and recently about the development of their distance vision (Ernest *et al.*, 2014). Being both indoors and focused on screens restricts visual development opportunities. Associated with these restrictions is the recognition that most screen-based activity requires receptive language development but seldom expressive language development, and rarely in a face-to-face social engagement. Children who engage in Forest School sessions are inevitably going to be screen users, since screens are a part of their normal way of being. However, they will also be outside at regular intervals using their eyes to look at distant objects, socialising with their peers and learning new words to express the world about them. Nature will always survive in some way or another – known as the Gaia principle (Dyke & Weaver, 2013) – but restoring a link to that nature will help people to survive.

Conclusion

Forest School in the UK is analogous with one of its trees. It has its roots in the evolutionary past, prompting a love of nature. It has its trunk in tribal and agrarian societies, enabling people to develop bushcraft, social and language skills. The many branches of practice show how Forest School can happen in urban and rural settings, provided the ethos is maintained (Knight, 2011)

The leaves are the breathing links with the theorists who have shown how people learn and develop, and the research that continues today. With love, respect and care, Forest School practitioners can produce healthy and happy children who will be the fruits for tomorrow.

References

Centre for Sustainable Healthcare (2014). NHS forest: Growing forests for health. Retrieved from: http://nhsforest.org/.

Claxton, G., Chambers, M., Powell, G. & Lucas, B. (2011). *The Learning Powered School: Pioneering 21st Century Education*. Bristol, UK: TLO Ltd.

Cree, J. (2011). Maintaining the forest school ethos while working with 14 to 19 year old boys. In S. Knight (Ed.) *Forest School for All* (pp. 106–120). London: Sage.

Cree, J. & Gersie, A. (2014). Storytelling in the woods. In A. Gersie, A. Nanson & E. Schieffelin (Eds.) *Storytelling for a Greener World: Environment, Community and Story-based Learning* (pp. 54–73). Stroud, UK: Hawthorn Press.

Department for Education (2012). *Statutory Framework for the Early Years Foundation Stage*. Runcorn: Department for Education. Retrieved from: https://www.education.gov.uk/publications/standard/AllPublications/Page1/DFE-00023-2012.

Drengson, A. (1999). Ecophilosophy, ecosophy and the deep ecology movement: An overview. Retrieved from: www.ecospherics.net/pages/DrengEcophil.html.

Dyke, J.G. & Weaver, I.S. (2013). The emergence of environmental homeostasis in complex ecosystems. *PLoS Computational Biology, 9*(5), e1003050.

Else, P. (2009). *The Value of Play*. London: Continuum.

Ernest, J., Causey, C., Newton, A., Sharkins, K., Summerlin, J. & Albaiz, N. (2014). Extending the global dialogue about media, technology, screen time, and young children. *Childhood Education, 90*(3), 182–191.

Farah, M., Betancourt, L., Shera, D., Savage, J., Giannetta, J., Brodsky, N., Malmud, E. & Hurt, H. (2008). Environmental stimulation, parental nurturance and cognitive development in humans. *Developmental Science, 11*(5), 793–801.

Gifford, R. (2014). Environmental psychology matters. *Annual Review of Psychology, 65*, 541–579.

Gill, T. (2007). *No Fear: Growing Up in a Risk-averse Society*. London: Calouste Gulbenkian Foundation. Retrieved from: www.gulbenkian.org.uk/pdffiles/--item-1266-223-No-fear-19-12-07.pdf.

Heywood, C. (2001). *A History of Childhood*. Cambridge, UK: Polity Press.

Holland, C. (2012). *I Love My World*. Otterton, UK: Wholeland Press.

Hughes, B. (2012). *Evolutionary Playwork* (2nd edn). London: Routledge.

Kahn, P. Jr. (2002). Children's affiliations with nature: Structure, development, and the problem of environmental amnesia. In P. Kahn Jr. & S. Kellert (Eds.) *Children and Nature: Psychological, Sociological and Evolutionary Investigations* (pp. 93–116). London: The MIT Press.

Kaplan, S. (1995). The restorative benefits of nature: Toward an integrative framework. *Journal of Environmental Psychology, 15*, 169–182.

Kellert, S. (2002). Experiencing nature: Affective, cognitive, and evaluative development in children. In P. Kahn Jr. & S. Kellert (Eds.) *Children and Nature: Psychological, Sociological and Evolutionary Investigations* (pp. 117–152). London: The MIT Press.

Knight, S. (2011). *Forest School for All*. London: Sage.

Knight, S. (2013). *Forest School and Outdoor Learning in the Early Years* (2nd edn). London: Sage.

Learning and Teaching Scotland (2010). *Curriculum for Excellence through Outdoor Learning*. Glasgow, Scotland: LTS London Play. Retrieved from: www.londonplay.org.uk.

Perry, B. (2002). Childhood experience and the expression of genetic potential. *Brain and Mind, 3*(93), 79–100.

Sandell, K. (2007). The right of public access: The landscape of *friluftsliv*. In B. Henderson & N. Vikander (Eds.) *Nature First: Outdoor Life the Friluftsliv Way* (pp. 90–99). Toronto: Natural Heritage Books.

Scottish Government (2010). *Learning for Change: Scotland's Action Plan for the Second Half of the UN Decade of Education for Sustainable Development*. Edinburgh, Scotland: Scottish Executive.

Selbie, P. & Wickett, K. (2010). Providing an enabling environment. In R. Parker-Rees, C. Leeson, J. Willan & J. Savage (Eds.) *Early Childhood Studies* (3rd edn) (pp. 75–87). Exeter, UK: Learning Matters.

Shier, S. (1984). *Adventure Playgrounds: An Introduction*. Retrieved from: www.londonplay.org.uk/resources/0000/1190/1984_Intro_to_APs_Harry_Shier.pdf.

Sunderland, M. (2013). *Winning Hearts and Minds in Forest Schools*. Kendal, UK: Forest School Association Conference. Retrieved from: www.forestschoolassociation.org.

Waller, T. (2007). 'The trampoline tree and the swamp monster with 18 heads': Outdoor play in the foundation stage and foundation phase. *Education 3–13, 35*(4), 393–407.

Walter, P. (2013). Greening the net generation: Outdoor adult learning in the digital age. *Adult Learning, 24*(4), 151–158.

Wellings, E. (2013). Forest school ethos. In Knight, S. (Ed.) *International Perspectives on Forest School* (pp. 5–7). London: Sage.

White, E., Hutka, S., Williams, L. & Moreno, S. (2013). Learning, neural plasticity and sensitive periods: Implications for language acquisition, music training and transfer across the lifespan. *Frontiers in Systems in Neuroscience, 7*(90), 1–18.

Wicks, R. (2011). Forest school and looked after children. In S. Knight (Ed.) *Forest School for All* (pp. 153–161). London: Sage.

Wilson, E.O. (1984). *Biophilia – The Human Bond with Other Species*. Cambridge, MA, and London: Harvard University Press.

25

Developing therapeutic outdoor practice

Adventure therapy

Kaye Richards

LIVERPOOL JOHN MOORES UNIVERSITY

Outdoor education has a long tradition of addressing the personal and social development needs of individuals, which has been core to the value and rationale of its provision for decades. Not surprising in understanding these related developmental processes, questions of how outdoor provisions can address psychological issues has become a driver in understanding the potential application of outdoor practices. This agenda has been central to the emergence of what is commonly termed adventure therapy. The psychological dimensions of change and opportunities afforded by outdoor and adventure experiences for initiating psychological growth have led to working with mental health and psychological wellbeing agendas, as can be seen in interventions addressing psychological difficulties. Examples include emotional and behavioural disorders in young people (Tucker, Javorski, Tracy & Beale, 2013), post-traumatic stress disorder (Gelkopf, Hasson-Ohayon, Bikman & Kravetz, 2013), traumatic brain injury (Shanahan, McAllister & Curtin, 2009) and depression (Kyriakopoulos, 2011).

Wider appreciation and evidence exists of the value of being outdoors in supporting general psychological wellbeing and health (e.g. the restorative effects of natural environments; Kaplan & Kaplan, 1989). This growing recognition of the therapeutic benefits of going outdoors can also be seen with initiatives to improve mental health by doing activities outside (Mind, 2013) and the development of *healing gardens* for improving recovery from illnesses (Sherman *et al.*, 2005).

Given the benefits, adventure therapy is a recognised approach both across outdoor learning and, perhaps more importantly, in the counselling and psychotherapy arena. This more recent positive recognition of adventure therapy from mainstream psychological therapies represents a 'new horizon' in the field of counselling and psychotherapy (McLeod, 2009). It signals, therefore, a turning tide in the ways outdoor practices are viewed and implemented, and also brings wider psychotherapeutic challenges. Although adventure therapy has a platform from which to establish itself more fully, challenges remain in consolidating its position. Some of the complex professional agendas that underpin psychotherapeutic practice and relevance to adventure therapy are important, but too multifaceted to be fully addressed in this chapter. This chapter offers, instead, an introductory overview to considerations in this growing area, and briefly contextualises adventure therapy from a counselling and psychotherapy perspective. This perspective is often lacking for outdoor practitioners.

Psychological therapies: an overview

The provision of psychological therapies has developed over many years, and historical and theoretical influences have steered its development and applications of practice to date. Counselling and psychotherapy are key health agenda issues supported by governmental policies and funding. Research evidence is important in understanding associated ongoing debates and strategic issues (Wampold, 2001; Lambert, 2013), and is important in locating adventure therapy. Further, counselling and psychotherapy have well-developed training and professional monitoring systems to ensure ethical practice is maintained and practitioners are equipped to offer ongoing ethical professional psychological services. In comparison, this approach is something that is arguably lacking across the outdoor field, especially in certain geographical locations (e.g. the UK).

Given this backdrop to psychological therapies, a challenge to outdoor practitioners is how to integrate these professional frameworks. Adventure therapy clearly operates within professional frameworks of outdoor learning, yet it should not overlook and operate outside understandings and standards of a psychotherapeutic profession. A notable challenge is not to sacrifice adventure therapy's uniqueness as a therapeutic practice in a different environment to that of therapeutic practice indoors.

A key goal of someone seeking counselling or psychotherapy through adventure therapy may be to address problems causing distress or difficulty, or to change some aspect of self-limiting behaviour so individuals can move towards more effective functioning in everyday life. Often people find themselves experiencing psychological difficulties that do not necessarily fall into a diagnosable mental health issue, but nevertheless benefit from professional support to navigate through difficult times (e.g. bereavement, relationship breakdown, life crisis, stress). Therapeutic interventions to address these life transitions can act to prevent onset of more recognised mental health disorders. (e.g. depression, anxiety and eating disorders) that are also commonly treated by psychological therapies including adventure therapies.

Definitions are available for, and outcomes are associated with, counselling and psychotherapy. A general definition of counselling is, 'a principled relationship characterized by the application of one or more psychological theories and a recognized set of communication skills, modified by experience, intuition and other interpersonal factors, to clients' intimate concerns, problems or aspirations' (Feltham & Dryden, 1993, p. 6).

McLeod (2009) identified three broad potential outcomes of counselling, which can be considered from an adventure therapy context. The first is *resolution* of the original problem, enabling a client to achieve understanding, perspective and acceptance, and thus become more inclined to take growth-producing action. A second outcome is *learning* that develops the client's ability to tackle future situations and problems more effectively. Third, *social inclusion* can occur, whereby people can enhance their capacity of acting for social good and supporting others' wellbeing.

Although the terms counselling and psychotherapy are often used interchangeably, psychotherapy is most applied to clients who have longstanding historical issues to explore. Debate, however, continues regarding the relevance of a differentiation between counselling and psychotherapy, and many professional contexts do not make a formal distinction between the two (Palmer, 2000). Instead, they are often used collectively to represent a range of talking therapies, and adventure therapy falls under this broad banner. Appreciating foundations and developments in counselling and psychotherapy enables adventure therapy to form an identity that responds to the growing demands required of effective therapeutic interventions.

Definitions and principles of adventure therapy

Different terms are often used for therapeutic practice outdoors such as adventure therapy (Gass, 1993), wilderness therapy (Cole, Erdma & Rothblum, 1992; Davis-Berman & Berman, 1994), adventure-based counselling (Schoel & Maizell, 2002), nature therapy (Burns, 1998) and eco-therapy (Clinebell, 1996). As the field emerged, terms that were commonly used were adventure therapy and wilderness therapy, yet all these terms have developed concurrently over the past three decades and have often been used interchangeably across international practices (Itin, 1998; Richards & Smith, 2003; Bandoroff & Newes, 2005; Mitten & Itin, 2009; Pryor, Carpenter, Norton & Kirchner, 2012). Other terms reflect specific orientations of practice to different parts of the world, including North America's *Outdoor Behavioural Healthcare* (Russell, 2003), and Australia's *Bush Adventure Therapy* (Pryor, Carpenter & Mardie, 2005). Regardless, all terms work from a basis of using outdoor and/or adventure experiences in therapeutic applications.

Some general theoretical principles underpin adventure therapies. These include: (i) the role of risk taking, both real and perceived, through participating in outdoor adventure activities, and creating psychological disequilibrium to facilitate change; (ii) a strengthening of therapeutic metaphors that support client insight and behavioural change; (iii) novelty enabling thematic issues to manifest and, therefore, be more easily observed by the therapist; (iv) immediacy of feedback that enhances self-responsibility and self-awareness; (v) negotiating and overcoming challenges that foster self-belief and recognition; (vi) experiencing self in new environments over a prolonged period of time, creating a catalyst for change; and (vii) capitalising on the existential givens of nature (Gass, 1993; Greenway, 1995; Hartford, 2011). These principles are reflective for defining adventure therapy as 'the prescriptive use of adventure experiences provided by mental health professionals, often conducted in natural settings that kinaesthetically engage clients on cognitive, affective, and behavioural levels' (Gass, Gillis & Russell, 2012, p. 1).

In the past, dominant ideas across adventure therapy seemed to place focus on activity and the therapeutic relationship, rather than placing the relationship a person has with nature as a key facet to experience (Beringer, 2003). The human–nature relationship has always been considered an essential component of outdoor learning, especially in environmental education dimensions of outdoor learning practices. Because nature can be unforgiving and punishing, as well as inspiring and rewarding, this relationship provides profound learning. Furthermore, a key premise from a therapeutic perspective is that a relationship with nature not only offers healing benefits, but that detachment from the natural environment has negative consequences for physical and psychological wellbeing. For example, looking through a window upon nature has associated benefits (Ulrich, 1984). As Burns (1998) stated, 'we are part of our environment, and unless we are living in a state constant with that environment, we cannot expect neither health nor happiness' (p. 4).

The interrelationship between nature and psychological wellbeing has been extended by eco-psychology concepts partly born out of psychotherapists locating the environmental crisis and relationships with the natural world as a factor in human suffering. This agenda has been termed the *greening of psychotherapy* and has influenced terms such as eco-therapy and horticultural therapy (Simson & Straus, 1998; Buzzell & Chalquist, 2009). Sometimes these approaches can overlook longstanding traditions of nature connections that underpin outdoor learning, and thus the emergence of adventure and wilderness therapies. Yet, they all fall within the scope of outdoor therapies and inform areas of practice in many ways.

Regardless of the term used, identifying the basis of an approach and defining whether a managed psychotherapeutic process is present or not is needed since therapy can be interpreted in different ways. Distinguishing between what is personal development and what is a psychotherapeutic experience is difficult. For example, adventure therapy may infer therapeutic benefits without any psychotherapeutic knowledge or techniques used. This non-psychotherapeutic work outdoors is valuable, but a distinction is a key ethical requirement as clients may be misled into believing they are being offered psychotherapeutic practice when they are not. The model of intervention offered may be more in line with a developmental training model or even a recreational approach. Peeters (2003) highlighted this issue and suggested that 'all too often adventure activities are taken out of an educational, or even recreational framework, and presented and counselled in an almost identical and standardised way within an adventure therapy programme' (p. 127). The debates around similarities and differences in approaches continue across international perspectives.

Theoretical perspectives to therapeutic practice

An ongoing question and debate is whether adventure therapy is a therapeutic approach with a separate identity from other therapeutic modalities, an eclectic approach or, simply, 'a specialist application of adventure activities' (Ringer, 2003, p. 3). The debate about whether a single theoretical model exists continues, and ambiguity remains. As Gillis (1998) previously identified, 'writings on models of therapy that fit with adventure are one of the weakest areas available to our field at the moment' (p. 19). This weakness stands today.

An understanding of theoretical modalities in counselling and psychotherapy helps point to orientations that influence adventure therapy practice. A range of theoretical positions has been adopted in the process of engaging an individual in psychological change. These positions offer specific theories of personality and theories of change. The diversity of theories available indicates that psychotherapeutic practice is not a straightforward approach to understanding and working with people and enabling psychological change. However, some mainstream schools of counselling and psychotherapy are commonplace and have a growing evidence base associated with different client groups, including examples related to humanistic, psychoanalytic and cognitive behavioural therapy (Stiles *et al.*, 2006).

From each of these overarching approaches sub-theories have developed. For example, the humanistic traditions include the person-centred and the Gestalt approach, Freudian and Jungian psychodynamic approaches come from psychoanalytic traditions, and cognitive behavioural therapy and solution-focused approaches emerge from the cognitive and behavioural traditions. More recently, however, greater eclecticism across psychotherapeutic modalities has been advocated (Cooper & McLeod, 2011).

Given these approaches, tensions exist between competing approaches to therapeutic work in the outdoors whereby Gestalt, client-centred, psychodynamic and narrative orientations have all vied for influence (e.g. Gilbert, Gilsdorf & Ringer, 2004). Psychotherapeutic foundations of a trans-theoretical approach to adventure therapy have been argued by Gass *et al.* (2012). Pluralism in mainstream psychotherapies would suggest room for a variety of applied theoretical modalities in adventure therapy. Thus, the question of whether adventure therapy needs a single theoretical identity could be partly redundant in its ongoing development.

Irrespective of modality preference, any aspiring adventure therapist needs to recognise the scope of these approaches to appreciate the breadth of available perspectives. Practitioners can make informed decisions about a preferred philosophical approach to human development and recognise how these philosophies might inform the basis of therapeutic practice in the outdoors. For example, a person-centred approach used in facilitating a ropes course-based activity has a different emphasis in its process compared to a cognitive behavioural approach applied in this context. Furthermore, the extent to which any approach might be effective in an outdoor setting raises an important research question: what forms of psychological distress are most responsive to what methods of adventure therapy?

Knowing what works best for whom, as well as why and how, is a cornerstone of the development and delivery of psychotherapeutic interventions (Roth & Fonagy, 2005). In mainstream psychological therapies factors have been examined to understand what contributes to and determines therapeutic improvement and change. These factors include relational (e.g. therapeutic alliance and interpersonal skills), technique and practice (e.g. cognitive, contracting and boundaries), therapist (e.g. training, beliefs and values), and client (e.g. outcome and process expectations, motivation) (Cooper, 2009). In mainstream psychological therapies the therapeutic relationship is estimated to account for 30 per cent of the variance in therapeutic outcomes, and only 15 per cent of the variance is attributed to a therapist's specific techniques or models (Assay & Lambert, 1999). These findings pose critical questions for therapeutic work outdoors, including how these factors translate to an outdoor setting, and how outdoor and adventure processes influence them. For example, Harper (2009) examined the therapeutic alliance during wilderness therapy. These agendas highlight how a research agenda in adventure therapy needs to build upon and be informed by mainstream counselling and psychotherapy research and practice. This approach means not just knowing if adventure therapy works, but examining the processes at work. Comparing both outcomes and processes of adventure therapy with other therapeutic approaches that have an evidence base will help to ascertain value and benefit.

Developing outdoor and adventure therapy practices

Outdoor therapeutic practice delivery can be achieved by therapists and outdoor adventure professionals working together to provide adventure therapy. In such collaborative approaches, practice needs to be fully aligned and integrated with adherence to relevant ethical frameworks. The challenge of any approach is how the practitioner facilitates a deepening of psychotherapeutic processes in an outdoor setting and helps clients to identify and work on individual therapeutic objectives. A straightforward way is obviously individual psychotherapeutic work indoors, both before and after outdoor activities, which provide a focus on an individual's needs and enable psychological depth to be enhanced with a strengthening of a therapeutic alliance. Retaining relational perspective and psychotherapeutic depth throughout the outdoor activity also needs to be facilitated.

A range of techniques can be used to enhance therapeutic opportunities. Interpersonal Process Recall (IPR) is one technique that has proved helpful (Richards, 2008). IPR is frequently used in therapy research as a way of supporting individuals in the recall and analysis of the therapeutic process (Elliott, 1986; Elliott & Shapiro, 1992). The IPR process consists of video recording the therapeutic events, which are then played to the client, providing a cue for memory retrieval. The client watches the therapeutic events (e.g. ropes course activities) and then pauses the video at points that have personal meaning. Through dialogue, clients are supported by a therapist to uncover the meaning of significant moments. Once the event has been processed, the client continues the same procedure throughout the remainder of the video recording, continuing to bring aspects of the experience (e.g. feelings and thinking) into greater awareness.

To illustrate an adventure therapy process in action, which uses an IPR technique, a short account of one woman's experience of an intervention for the treatment of eating disorder is offered. Prior to an adventure therapy intervention Susanna reported how she used food as a way of dealing with emotions and how she felt continually troubled by her eating patterns. Feeling out of control and experiencing feelings of guilt and shame were common and linked to her *stuffing down* emotions with food:

> The past few weeks have been out of control as far as food is concerned. I have been eating loads of rubbish, not so much bingeing all at once, but just eating more than I really need – eating to stuff down the feelings of stress, anger, fear, hatred, anxiety etc., which doesn't work because then I feel stuffed fat, horrible, angry again and GUILTY! I keep telling myself that it doesn't matter what weight I am for the programme, but I would still love to shed some by April. It will make me feel better about myself, more comfortable. I suppose if I were really truthful, I would say that I am scared of being judged by the others, for the way I look – that's how it always is. I don't want to be that way anymore.

Taking Susanna's story forward a few weeks later, she recalled her experience as she prepared to take part in a ropes course activity as one aspect of an adventure therapy intervention. A person-centred focusing approach (Gendlin, 1996) was part of this therapeutic work. Her account described her experience of the therapeutic process prior to the outdoor activity itself:

> Before the rope work, we each had ½ hour with our individual therapists. This was extremely useful as quite a bit of stuff came up, particularly the knot in my stomach which I feel when I get angry. The therapist asked me to close my eyes and focus on the knot, and to go inside it and try to describe what it looked like and felt like. The image that came to mind was of a roaring furnace, which we linked to me feeding the furnace [anger] with food. The session ended with the therapist asking me to think about what it would take to start putting the furnace out. I was able to cry in the session with her. Part of me wanted to do this, for the release and possibly also to let her know how bad I had been feeling. But another part of me felt very foolish and silly and completely ashamed of myself, but hopefully I am beginning to overcome this part of me, realising it's just fine to have a good cry and let it all go.

Moving on to the outdoor activity itself, she felt a sense of achievement from taking part, which pointed towards therapeutic benefits often reported across outdoor activities more broadly:

> Today we went on the high ropes. I was anxious about it for most of last night and first thing this morning, I had agreed to go first, as yesterday I let [made] Jackie go first. This was doubly scary, as I could not see how anyone else coped with it. I just had to get on with it! [The fear of the unknown.] When I got up to the first obstacle I became frozen with fear and could not move. I was rooted to the spot unable to go forwards or backwards and I started to cry at this point. I felt quite silly at first, but then I just let them flow and I felt a bit better for the release. With support and encouragement from the others, I managed to move on and complete the course. It was really scary, but I DID IT! And what a sense of achievement at the end. I can conquer the world! And I was able to help the next member with the obstacles. It was worth going through the fear to feel GREAT!

Finally, Susanna recalled her experience of IPR immediately after the ropes course experience. The process led to meaningful insight and movements of change where she was able to acknowledge how she was becoming more self-accepting about aspects of herself that related to dynamics of her troubled eating:

> I then looked back over the two videos of the rope work with the therapist [IPR]. It was a strange experience, because I felt so much empathy as I watched Susanna go around the course. It was like I had stepped back and distanced myself from me. I have never felt this way before, I usually cringe at the sight (or even the thought) of myself on video, usually with much hatred and self-loathing – but today it was different: nice, comfortable.

Susanna's reflection suggested a deeper exploration of self, moving beyond the achievement of pushing through fear, and indicated experience of *osmotic* change. Suzanna's description of a 'strange' experience appeared to be a fundamental psychological shift in her relationship to herself and body image. She continues to gain insight into the dynamics of how her troubled eating manifested:

> I was also able to make some links between all my issues around fear. Feeling trapped etc. and my eating behaviour but some of them still need exploring deeper. The therapist mentioned about going into the woods and crying with the emotion of its beauty. Because she struck a chord in me, the tears flowed yet again. I feel like something is really beginning to happen, things are changing and for the better. And I feel I am finally making contact with the real me, my inner strength, my own healing forces. For me, this trip is proving to be really successful to now.

This account points to the nuances, yet significant aspects, of therapeutic movement for Susanna, highlighting how outdoor activities facilitated therapeutic metaphorical meanings. It illustrates how therapeutic practice combined with outdoor adventure enhanced insight for Susanna and, subsequently, psychological change.

Conclusion

The opportunities for extending recognition of outdoor adventure therapy's contribution alongside established mainstream approaches open new directions for people's wellbeing. However, these opportunities also bring a renewed responsibility in professional arenas that need be addressed to ensure adventure therapy's reputation and effectiveness (e.g. ethics, research, training, risk management and supervision). Managing the ongoing development of outdoor and adventure therapy across two different professional landscapes requires careful navigation. The phenomenal work undertaken in the great outdoors is well documented. Similarly, the potency of psychotherapeutic experience for healing people in distress is long established. The challenge is to recognise the alchemic potential of the coming together of outdoor learning and psychotherapy. In doing so, the opportunities are extended to individuals who could benefit from taking the therapy room outside.

References

Assay, T.P. & Lambert, M.J. (1999). The empirical case for the common factors in therapy: Quantitative findings. In M.A. Hubble, B.L. Duncan & S.D. Miller (Eds.) *The Heart and Soul of Change: What Works in Therapy* (pp. 33–56). Washington, DC: American Psychological Association.
Bandoroff, S. & Newes, S. (Eds.) (2005). Coming of age: The evolving field of adventure therapy. *Proceedings of the Third International Adventure Therapy Conference, Vancouver Island, Canada*. Boulder, CO: Association for Experiential Education.

Beringer, A. (2003). Being moved by nature: Adventure therapy and spinal cord injury rehabilitation. In K. Richards & B. Smith (Eds.) *Therapy within Adventure: Proceedings of the Second International Adventure Therapy Conference, University of Augsburg, 20–24 March, 2000* (pp. 197–212). Germany: Zeil Verlag.

Burns, G.W. (1998). *Nature-guided Therapy. Brief Integrative Strategies for Health and Well Being.* Philadelphia, PA: Bruner/Mazell, Taylor & Francis.

Buzzell, L. & Chalquist, C. (Eds.) (2009). *Ecotherapy: Healing with Nature in Mind.* San Francisco, CA: Sierra Club Books.

Clinebell, H. (1996). *Ecotherapy: Healing Ourselves.* Minneapolis, MN: Fortress Press.

Cole, E., Erdman, E. & Rothblum, E.D. (2003). *Wilderness Therapy for Women: The Power of Adventure.* New York: The Haworth Press, Inc.

Cooper, M. (2009). *Essential Research Findings in Counselling and Psychotherapy. The Facts are Friendly.* British Association for Counselling and Psychotherapy. London: Sage Publications.

Cooper, M. & McLeod, J. (2011). *Pluralistic Counselling and Psychotherapy.* London: Sage Publications Ltd.

Davis-Berman, J. & Berman, D.S. (1994). *Wilderness Therapy: Foundations, Theory and Research.* Dubuque, IA: Kendall/Hunt Publishing.

Elliott, R. (1986). Interpersonal process recall (IPR) as a psychotherapy process research method. In L.S. Greenberg & W.M. Pinsof (Eds.) *The Psychotherapeutic Process: A Research Handbook* (pp. 503–528). New York: Guildford Press.

Elliot, R. & Shapiro, D.A. (1992). Client and therapists as analysts of significant events. In S. Toukmanian & D. Rennie (Eds.) *Psychotherapy Process Research: Paradigmatic and Narrative Approaches* (pp. 163–186). London: Sage Publications.

Feltham, C. & Dryden, W. (1993). *Dictionary of Counselling.* London: Whurr.

Gass, M. (1993). *Adventure Therapy: Therapeutic Applications of Adventure Programming.* Dubuque, IA: Kendall/Hunt Publishing.

Gass, M., Gillis, L.M. & Russell, K.C. (2012). *Adventure Therapy: Theory, Research, and Practice.* New York: Routledge.

Gelkopf, M., Hasson-Ohayon, I., Bikman, M. & Kravetz, S. (2013). Nature adventure rehabilitation for combat-related posttraumatic chronic stress disorder: A randomized control trial. *Psychiatry Research, 209*(3), 485–493.

Gendlin, E.T. (1996). *Focusing-orientated Psychotherapy. A Manual of the Experiential Method.* London: The Guildford Press.

Gilbert, B., Gilsdorf, R. & Ringer, M. (2004). Playing with ideas about adventure therapy: Applying principles of gestalt, narrative and psychodynamic approaches to adventure therapy. In S. Bandroff & S. Newes, (Eds.) *Coming of Age: The Evolving Field of Adventure Therapy. Proceedings of the 3rd International Adventure Therapy Conference* (pp. 32–55). Boulder, CO: Association for Experiential Education.

Gillis, L. (1998). The journey in OZ. From activity based psychotherapy to adventure therapy. In C.M. Itin (Ed.) *Exploring the Boundaries of Adventure Therapy International Perspectives: Proceedings of the First International Adventure Therapy Conference: Perth, Australia* (pp. 9–20). Boulder, CO: Association for Experiential Education.

Greenway, R. (1995). The wilderness effect and ecopsychology. In T. Roszak, M.E. Gomes & A.D. Kanner (Eds.) *Ecopsychology: Restoring the Earth, Healing the Mind.* San Francisco, CA: Sierra Club Books.

Harper, N.J. (2009). The relationship of therapeutic alliance to outcome in wilderness treatment. *Journal of Adventure Education & Outdoor Learning, 9*(1), 45–59.

Hartford, G. (2011). Practical implications for the development of applied metaphors in adventure therapy. *Journal of Adventure Education and Outdoor Learning, 11*(2), 145–160.

Itin, C. (1998). *Exploring the Boundaries of Adventure Therapy: International Perspectives. Proceedings of the First International Adventure Therapy Conference, Perth, Australia.* Boulder, CO: Association for Experiential Education,

Kaplan, R. & Kaplan, S. (1989). *The Experience of Nature: A Psychological Perspective.* Cambridge, NY: Cambridge University Press,

Kyriakopoulos, A. (2011). How individuals with self-reported anxiety and depression experienced a combination of individual counselling with an adventurous outdoor experience: A qualitative evaluation. *Counselling and Psychotherapy Research, 11*(2), 120–128.

Lambert, M.J. (2013) *Bergin and Garfield's Handbook of Psychotherapy and Behavior Change* (6th edn). Hoboken, NJ: John Wiley & Sons, Inc.

McLeod, J. (2009). *An Introduction to Counselling* (4th edn). Berkshire, UK: Open University Press.

Mind (2013). *Feel Better Outside: Feel Better Inside. Ecotherapy for Mental Wellbeing, Resilience and Recovery.* London: Mind.

Mitten, D. & Itin, C. (2009). *Connecting with the Essence: Proceedings of the Fourth International Adventure Therapy Conference, New Zealand.* Boulder, CO: Association for Experiential Education.

Palmer, S. (Ed.) (2000). *Introduction to Counselling and Psychotherapy: The Essential Guide.* London: Sage Publications.

Peeters, L. (2003). From adventure to therapy. Some necessary conditions to enhance the therapeutic outcomes of adventure programming. In K. Richards & B. Smith (Eds.) *Therapy within Adventure: Proceedings of the Second International Adventure Therapy Conference, University of Augsburg, 20–24 March, 2000* (pp. 127–137). Germany: Zeil Verlag.

Pryor, A., Carpenter, C. & Mardie, T. (2005). Outdoor education and bush adventure therapy: A social-ecological approach to health and wellbeing. *Australian Journal of Outdoor Education, 9*(1), 3–13.

Pryor, A., Carpenter, C., Norton, C. & Kirchner, J. (Eds.) (2012). *International Adventure Therapy: Emerging Insights. Proceedings of the Fifth International Adventure Therapy Conference Edinburgh.* Czech Republic: European Science and Art Publishing.

Richards, K. (2008). A feminist analysis of developing an adventure therapy intervention for the treatment of women with eating disorders. Unpublished PhD dissertation, Liverpool John Moores University.

Richards, K. & Smith, B. (Eds.) (2003). *Therapy within Adventure. Proceedings of the Second International Adventure Therapy Conference.* Augsburg, Germany. Zeil: Augsburg.

Ringer, M. (2003). Tribal wisdom: Reflections on adventure therapy and its social context. In K. Richards & B. Smith (Eds.) *Therapy within Adventure: Proceedings of the Second International Adventure Therapy Conference, University of Augsburg, 20–24 March 2000.* Augsburg, Germany: Zeil Verlag.

Roth, A. & Fonagy, P. (2005). *What Works for Whom? A Critical Review of Psychotherapy Research* (2nd edn). New York: Guildford Press.

Russell, K.C. (2003). An assessment of outcomes in outdoor behavioural health-care treatment. *Child and Youth Care Forum, 32*(6), 355–381.

Schoel, J. & Maizell, R.S. (2002). *Exploring Islands of Healing: New Perspectives on Adventure Based Counselling.* Beverly, MA: Project Adventure/J. Weston Walch, Publisher.

Shanahan, L., McAllister, L. & Curtin, M. (2009). Wilderness adventure therapy and cognitive rehabilitation: Joining forces for youth with TBI. *Brain Injury, 23*(13–14), 1054–1064.

Sherman, S.A., Varni, J.W., Ulrich, V.L. & Malcarne (2005). Post-occupancy evaluation of healing gardens in paediatric cancer center. *Landscape and Urban Planning, 73,* 167–183.

Simson, S.P. & Straus, M.C. (Eds.) (1998). *Horticulture as Therapy: Principles and Practices.* New York: The Haworth Press.

Stiles, B., Barkham, M., Twigg, E., Mellor-Clark, J. & Cooper, M. (2006). Effectiveness of cognitive-behavioural, person-centred and psychodynamic therapies as practised in UK National Health Service settings. *Psychological Medicine, 36*(4), 555–566.

Tucker, R.A., Javorski, S., Tracy, J. & Beale, B. (2013). The use of adventure therapy in community-based mental health: Decreases in problem severity among youth clients. *Child Youth Care Forum, 42,* 155–179.

Ulrich, R.S. (1984). View through a window may influence recovery from surgery. *Science, 224*(4647), 420–421.

Wampold, B.E. (2001). *The Great Psychotherapy Debate: Models, Method and Findings.* Mahwah, NJ: L. Erlbaum Associates.

26

Reviewing and reflection

Connecting people to experiences

Roger Greenaway

REVIEWING SKILLS TRAINING

Clifford E. Knapp

WONDEREARTH.ORG

'How many things have to happen to you before something occurs to you?' asked poet Robert Frost.

We both have a strong interest in how reflecting and reviewing can lead to learning and personal development. We are intrigued by Frost's question. If events and experiences pass by without reflecting (i.e. looking back) or reviewing (i.e. looking again), much of the potential value and significance is likely to be missed: something *happens* but nothing *occurs*.

We start our chapter by trying to beat an Anglo-American pathway through the terminology jungle. We explain our own usage of key terms so we can communicate with an international audience about the benefits of reviewing and reflection, the books on this topic that we have found useful, relevant theoretical models and their limitations, and how to use questions and other methods to facilitate reflection. We consider that one of the most powerful outcomes that arises from effective reviewing is a greater sense of connection with self, others and environment – from which many other benefits can flow.

Some synonyms for reflecting or reviewing are: processing, active processing, bridging, teaching for transfer, debriefing, critiquing and critical thinking. Reflecting is a type of thinking that helps you to make sense and meaning from experiences. Reflecting can also increase your capacity to apply what you learn from experience to similar situations in the future. There will be times when you reflect on your own about life events and try to learn from them. For example, if you develop a leg cramp while hiking a mountain, you might stop and reflect, and try to figure out how to prevent this from recurring. However, the main focus of this chapter is on the kind of reflecting that is facilitated by a leader (e.g. a teacher or outdoor guide) who wants to help participants gain greater understanding from a shared activity. This reflection might happen, for example, during or after a wilderness experience when the leader gathers the group together and conducts a reviewing session in which participants reflect, share and analyse what happened. New insights during the reviewing session may lead to further exploration and action.

Terminology

Writing in an international context is difficult in a field with little consistency and agreement about terminology. In an article entitled 'Diversity in Language', Turčová, the compiler of an English–Czech outdoor dictionary, stated that even among UK academics there is a range of different views about how key terms in the outdoor education field relate to one another (Turčová, Martin & Neuman, 2005). Beyond the UK the diversity of usage multiplies, especially in the area of reviewing and reflection. We feel obliged to bring some clarity to our own use of the four terms below, especially regarding who does what.

1 *Reflecting* (or reflection) typically refers to what the learner is doing. This type of thinking helps to make sense of experiences. You can reflect alone or with others. You can reflect with or without the aid of a leader who is trying to facilitate your learning.
2 *Reviewing* can be used as a synonym for reflecting. Reviewing can also be used to refer to what a leader does when facilitating reflection in a group. Reviewing in this second sense refers to facilitation that supports experiential learning.
3 *Processing* generally refers to what the leader does. However, it can also refer to what the learner is doing. The range of potential meanings of processing as used in US English is much the same as reviewing, which is the more common term in British English.
4 *Debriefing* generally refers to what the leader is doing, but with some exceptions.

The four terms above are listed in a progression from learner activity to leader activity – with the middle two sometimes spanning the whole spectrum. Within this chapter we will mostly use *reflecting* (or reflection) for what the learner does and *reviewing* for what the leader does. Whatever your own preferred terminology, we hope this clarification helps you to decode our own usage.

Why review and reflect?

Every so often we encounter the *big* question about whether reviewing is necessary or advisable – especially in situations where direct experience appears to have had a significant and positive impact. This question was raised by James (1980) in his essay entitled: 'Can the mountains speak for themselves?'

We do acknowledge that some pleasurable experiences may not be enhanced by reviewing them. We feel sceptical enough to say that experiences might even be spoiled by reviewing them. Further, we are professional enough to be pleased with our habit of looking out for *learning opportunities* and *teachable moments*. We care enough to intervene whenever experiences seem to be overwhelming or underwhelming. We believe that most experiences can benefit from reviewing. We are thinking about the following kinds of benefits.

- When reviewing increases interaction in groups, participants are likely to get to know and like one another and themselves more.
- Reviewing demonstrates that leaders are genuinely interested in and care about participants' experiences and in what they have learned (and could learn) from their activities.
- Reviewing helps participants make sense of experience, learn from experience, retain more value, and be better able to apply what is learned to new situations.
- A reviewing session can broaden participants' perspectives on the topic as they listen to others communicating about the significance of their experiences.
- An imaginative and sensitive approach to reviewing can help participants find the medium, opportunity, symbol or question through which they can most readily express themselves.

- Reviewing can help participants find and enjoy success, understand how it happened and become accustomed to the idea that they can be successful.
- Reviewing can be a valuable safety net. The reassurance that support will be available in the event of failure encourages participants to take risks that will be supported.
- Reviewing provides a range of strategies for getting unstuck, for overcoming blocks to learning and for becoming more open to learning from experience.
- When leaders focus on improving group dynamics through reviewing, participants improve in their communication, empathic and cooperation skills.
- In a group reviewing session involving expression of feelings or the discussion of values and ideas, participants can learn from one another as well as from their leaders.
- A reviewing session can benefit leaders who ask for feedback from participants about how effective they were in helping them reach the intended objective.
- If the reviewing session engages participants' interests, they are more likely to enter into other sessions with positive attitudes and with a motivation to learn from them.
- Reviewing sessions allow participants to develop personal strategies for reflecting on their future experiences in different contexts – whether on their own or with others.

A timely, caring and balanced approach to reviewing can result in many benefits, whereas leaving potentially significant experiences alone can be wasteful and insensitive.

> Let mountains speak for themselves and students may only hear the echoes of their hopes and fears – or silence. Let facilitators talk too much and that is all that students will hear. Give students a chance to voice their experiences and you and they will find endless rewards in learning from experiences outdoors. (Greenaway, 2004)

Books about reviewing and reflection

Reflection is not a recent discovery. According to Houston (1988), the concept of reflection is ancient. In Greece, Socrates (as often quoted by Plato) stated, 'The unexamined life is not worth living' (http://en.wikiquote.org). In China, Confucius and Lao Tzu, in the Middle East, Solomon, and in India, Gautama the Buddha, all recognised the value of reflection. Despite its ancient roots, this tradition of reflecting on experience can appear to be new and revolutionary compared to the more recent educational tradition that is dominated by the expertise and knowledge of the teacher. Emerson (1837) claimed that knowledge did not come from schools and colleges but from curiosity, experiment and observation. A century later Dewey (1938) followed Emerson's lead and emphasised the value of students reflecting on their experiences. Freire (1972) asserted that action and reflection are necessary to bring about meaningful change. More recently, in the field of adventure education, Mortlock (2001) noted, 'Quality action and quality reflection on that action are of fundamental and equal importance' (p. 119). Caine, Caine, McClintic and Klimek (2005) stated that reviewing 'is probably the most overlooked and unappreciated aspect of powerful teaching' (p. 180).

In 1974 Pfeiffer and Jones began publishing their series of *Annual Handbooks of Structured Experiences for Human Relations Training*. These books included a model and advice for debriefing training exercises. Borton (1970), a classroom teacher, introduced the surprisingly popular trio of reviewing questions: *What? So what? Now what?* During the 1980s few books were available for helping leaders to develop their reviewing skills. Leaders depended mostly on journal articles and book chapters. For example, in the *Journal of Experiential Education*, Joplin

(1981) presented a five-stage model of experiential education that included debriefing as a form of feedback. Knapp (1984) provided a list of processing questions designed to meet specific objectives. Quinsland and Van Ginkel (1984) explained six steps in processing experience by using Bloom's taxonomy of cognitive processing. Further, Hammel (1986) wrote about how to design a debriefing session.

One of the early books written specifically about reviewing was by Bacon (1983), who was a clinical psychologist working with Outward Bound. His treatment of reviewing was limited to using metaphors to extend participants' meaning making beyond the outdoor experience. Boud, Keogh and Walker (1985) described different aspects of reflection. Hunt and Hitchin (1989) described the theory and practice of reviewing. Knapp (1992) produced a teachers' guide to reflecting on experience. Knapp's book offered guidance about asking questions and described twenty alternative activities for reflecting. That same year Nadler and Luckner (1992) merged state-of-the-art counselling theory with adventure-based programming. They selected the term *processing* and likened its use to a yellow highlighter that 'teases out the richness of experience' (1992, p. 3). Their second edition (1997) included strategies to generalise learning. Greenaway (1993) wrote a comprehensive guide to *active reviewing*. This guide described reflective tasks designed to engage participants in multiple ways other than in a traditional discussion circle.

The new century brought more books about reviewing and reflection into the marketplace. Priest, Gass and Gillis (2000) set out to help facilitators promote change in the workplace following workshop experiences. Sugerman, Doherty, Garvey and Gass (2000) dedicated a whole book to reflective learning. After three chapters of theory (including guidelines for ethical practices), they added thirty-eight activities categorised according to how they can be used pre and post-experience. In *12 Brain/Mind Learning Principles in Action*, Caine and colleagues (2005) aimed to help experiential educators make some of the needed connections of *active processing* to human brain research. Cain, Cummings and Stanchfield (2005) described 123 reviewing activities in *A Teachable Moment*. Simpson, Miller and Bocher (2006) included several features: reference notes, a facilitator's field guide, a processing quiz, and a model that gives the book its name, *The Processing Pinnacle*.

More recently, two cognitive scientists have joined with a storyteller to provide a rich resource on the science of successful learning (Brown, Roediger III & McDaniel, 2014). They cite several examples supporting the importance of reflection for reinforcing memory and learning. Examples include receiving corrective feedback, retrieving recent knowledge, practising techniques, doing difficult but achievable tasks, connecting learning to prior knowledge, and applying learning to life situations.

These books are useful for both novice and expert facilitators who want guidance in the art and science of reviewing and reflection. The progression since the 1970s shows a maturation of the topic as it is combined with related disciplines and venues in which these skills are applied.

In the past few decades there has been a steady growth of university courses, conferences, workshops, books, research reports and academic journals related to outdoor studies and experiential learning. An abundance of sources are available from which to find theoretical models that provide useful guidance for the reviewing of outdoor experiences.

Models: their uses and limitations

Models of experiential learning are about how learners learn. Theories about how to facilitate such learning are also relevant. Models about reflecting in an outdoor or group context also apply. Theories about growth, development, adventure and challenge should also inform reviewing practice, especially when programme goals are described in these terms.

Models are valuable because they simplify and illuminate key features. Models also are dangerous because they tend to hide more complex realities. They are dangerous when they are applied without reading or understanding the *small print* – the author's explanations and reservations. Further, models are often used well past their *use-by-date* by people who are not aware of subsequent research or critiques that have challenged, discredited or improved the model.

Experiential learning cycles present an orderly image of a one-step-at-a-time sequence that includes one or more reflective stages. Such cycles can provide a useful reference point to help leaders facilitate reflection. But, do the creators of such models actually believe that experiential learning is or should be so simple and tidy? Kolb's 1984 presentation of his theories of experiential learning and development combined dialectical tensions with a quadrant, a cycle and a three-dimensional cone. The model is complex. Researchers pull it apart and critique it, while practitioners may pick up a simplified form of the model and follow what they mistakenly believe to be a sound foundation for their facilitation of learning.

Seaman's (2008) critique of learning cycles is one example of new thinking that suggests caution about applying linear sequences, whether in the shape of funnels, cycles or spirals. These linear models may help to explain how learning sometimes happens. However, there are many different kinds and patterns of good learning conversations so attempting to steer a conversation or discussion along a fixed pathway is highly restrictive. A model of learning should not inadvertently become a model of facilitation.

There is a particular problem with experiential learning theory in outdoor studies concerning the abundance of data outdoors, especially when an activity is intensive, challenging or sustained. Pfeiffer and Jones (1983) expressed the view that facilitators should be careful that the activity does not generate excess data. However, people go outdoors because of the abundance of sensory data there, for the vastness of the natural surroundings and for the rich learning environment to be explored. The idea that practitioners expose students to just enough experience and no more seems to come from a controlled and limiting version of experiential learning.

The approach to reviewing and reflection, therefore, should be neither controlling nor limiting. Questions can alert people to their senses and become more observant and mindful. The more that people notice, the more they are able contribute to later stages of a review. But, increased awareness can itself have a profound impact without further reviewing. Sports psychologists, inner game coaches, teachers of meditation, narrative therapists and appreciative facilitators (Torres, 2001) know about this impact. All are guided by the principle that what people pay attention to becomes their reality. Mortlock (1981) encouraged students to pay respectful attention to self, others and the environment. Noticing readily leads to respecting and caring, which in turn leads to other benefits. The higher the quality of observation, the higher the quality of whatever follows. In *Sharing the Joys of Nature*, Cornell (1989) advocated a sequence that dwells on paying attention: awaken enthusiasm → focus attention → direct experience → share inspiration. This linear sequence is equivalent to just one stage of other learning sequences – sometimes one stage is enough.

Using questions to facilitate reflection

Paying attention to experience is a fundamental reflective process that can be of value in itself and can also lead in many directions. There may be a natural flow in the subsequent learning process, but we believe that asking the right questions at the right time is an important skill for generating meaningful learning. One of the skills of leading a reviewing session is knowing how to apply the art and science of questioning. Walker asked, 'Is there anything more painful than realizing you did not know the right questions to ask at the only time on earth you would have the opportunity?' (2007, p. 1).

Books about reviewing and reflection tend to focus on the importance of questioning. Psychologist Max Wertheimer (1945) explained, 'Often in great discovery the most important thing is that a certain question be found' (p. 123). To help leaders find the right questions, authors have organised questions in different ways.

Simpson *et al.* (2006) devoted a chapter to developing better questions and answers. They stated, 'The most common and arguably the most reliable method of processing is a question and answer session conducted immediately after the action portion of the learning experience' (p. 102). They defended this method of reviewing by explaining that questions and answers involve both the leaders and participants. They believe that leaders can control the direction of the discussion and also can step back to let the participants control the flow of conversation.

Many outdoor leaders know the three categories of questions posed by Borton (1970): *What? So what?* and *Now what?* These questions could suggest an order and sequence to a reviewing session. For example, the leader could start with a *what* fact-finding question such as: 'What words of encouragement did John offer to Sue as she was rappelling down the cliff?' This question could be followed by a *so what* interpretive question such as: 'Did John's words have any influence on how you felt or on what you did?' Finally, a *now what* transfer question could be asked, such as: 'At home how important is it to support your friends through words and non-verbal messages?' Borton encouraged teachers to use these question stems to generate both convergent and divergent questions.

Chapter 13, on debriefing, in Schoel and Maizell's (2002) book provides more detailed guidance on using these three question types. Some examples: 'If the *What?* is reflective ... then we are going back over the experience. It is a recapitulation' (p. 246); 'It is in making sense, in interpreting, that it is possible to connect to that other prong of sequencing, the deepening' (p. 247); and 'The *Now What?* is a time to talk about spiral goal setting, using the energy of the experience to stimulate the group to think about what they can do in other areas of their lives' (p. 253).

Paul and Binker (1990) described how Socrates developed a way of teaching that involved asking questions to draw out what was learned. They divided questions into three groups: spontaneous, exploratory and issue specific. Knapp (1992) divided a list of eighty-five questions into eleven groups according to programme goals and objectives such as communicating effectively, listening, cooperating, trusting, and leading and following others. Nadler and Luckner (1992) provided four pages of sample reviewing questions divided into four categories: Awareness, Responsibility, Experimentation, and Generalization and Transfer. These groupings correspond to their suggested sequential levels of processing. Greenaway (1993) divided a list of questions into four categories based on elements in his active reviewing cycle: Facts, Feelings, Findings and Futures. He also described several active and creative reviewing methods that can be used to explore each of the four elements.

Choosing the right method or question at the right time is never easy. The success of question asking depends largely upon the ability of the leader to make accurate observations and inferences concerning the individual and the group dynamics.

Other ways of facilitating reflection

While asking good questions is a key skill for any leader, when facilitating reflection on experience, there are also many other ways of engaging participants in reflecting. These other ways are often more inclusive and effective. These methods are designed to engage a wider range of intelligences and learning skills than is likely to happen in a question-and-answer session.

One useful way into this broader view of outdoor learning is to recognise that reflecting and reviewing are also *experiences*: we do not stop experiencing when reflection starts nor do we stop reflecting when involved in an outdoor activity. A reviewing process can even be more of an intellectual and emotional rollercoaster than the experiences being reflected upon. Both activities and reviews are capable of generating an enormous range of experiences such as boredom, loneliness, embarrassment, a sense of belonging, a sense of pride, frustration, discovery, excitement, adventure, empathy, anger, responsibility, empowerment and significance. Such experiences can be the source of even more intense feelings during a review.

If potentially valuable experiences can happen both in activities and reviews, then what might a more 'experiential' approach to reflection look like?

- More space and thinking time for individuals: solo time such as a few minutes in self-chosen *magic spots* in nature can serve to deepen reflection and increase self-awareness.
- More reflection work in pairs: each person is listened to five times more than the average individual time available in a group of ten people. This creates more *me time*.
- More use of visual communication aids: participants use pictures, diagrams or objects to help express and communicate their thoughts and feelings and so become more understood.
- More use of intelligences and learning skills: participants work together to make a map of a journey, prepare feedback gifts for individuals, or make a picture of a person who is needed in their group.
- More group activity: re-enactments of key events engage more senses, get closer to the truth, include everyone in an active process, and are often a source of fun and mutual support.
- More responsibility: participants are responsible for giving feedback to one another, for observing and supporting one another, and for interviewing and representing one another.
- More movement: walking and talking, miming, using physical scales and giant diagrams, moving through different perspectives – all use movement to assist and enable learning.

These examples of alternative approaches to reviewing do not replace the need for good questioning skills, partly because many active reviewing methods include questioning as an integral part of the process. These practices are inspired and informed by a broader view of reflection that looks beyond words and is focused on what the learner is doing and experiencing while reflecting. It is tempting to list the various theories underlying these broader practices, but if you are involved in outdoor studies you are already familiar with the benefits of movement, using multiple senses, whole-body engagement, stimulating places, group support, and the value of challenge and responsibility. We suggest that you draw on your own rationale for using the outdoors and apply as much of it as possible to the whole programme including reviewing and reflection.

Reviewing outdoor experiences

Outdoor experiences involve immersion in masses of sensory data. Reviewing brings only some of these data into the foreground. Without the background, however, the foreground loses its significance: you don't get a marathon experience by starting the race 100 metres from the finish. Learning from fleeting experiences is unreliable, whereas any learning from deeper or more extended experiences tends to be both more reliable and more significant. The value of any experience is enhanced by adopting a reviewing strategy that is in tune with participants, that engages each and every person, and that provides sufficient time for each participant to reflect in meaningful ways.

Perhaps the most important reason for reviewing outdoor experiences is *connection*. Connection is with self, others and the environment. Connection happens with the weaving of stories before, during and after experiences. We take stories of expectation into the outdoors, we generate new stories in the outdoors, and our stories change and develop as we listen to the stories of others. Without connection our experiences remain isolated and insignificant, and we feel disconnected from the world, one another and ourselves. Through experience, connection and the making of meaningful stories, participants can gain increasing joy and satisfaction in living and learning.

References

Bacon, S. (1983). *The Conscious Use of Metaphor in Outward Bound.* Denver, CO: Colorado Outward Bound School.

Borton, T. (1970). *Reach, Touch and Teach.* New York: McGraw-Hill.

Boud, D., Keogh, R. & Walker, D. (Eds.) (1985). *Reflection: Turning Experience into Learning.* London: Kogan Page Ltd.

Brown, P.C., Roediger III, H.L. & McDaniel, M.A. (2014). *Make it Stick: The Science of Successful Learning.* Cambridge, MA/London: The Belknap Press of Harvard University Press.

Cain, J., Cummings, M. & Stanchfield, J. (2005). *A Teachable Moment: A Facilitator's Guide to Activities for Processing, Debriefing, Reviewing and Reflection.* Dubuque, IA: Kendall/Hunt Publishing Company.

Caine, R.N., Caine, G., McClintic, C. & Klimek, K. (2005). *12 Brain/Mind Learning Principles in Action.* Thousand Oaks, CA: Corwin Press.

Cornell, J. (1989) *Sharing the Joy of Nature.* Nevada City, CA: Dawn Publications.

Dewey, J. (1938). *Experience and Education.* New York: Collier Books.

Emerson, R.W. (1837). The American scholar: An oration before the Phi Beta Kappa Society. *Works of Ralph Waldo Emerson.* London: Routledge.

Freire, P. (1972). *Pedagogy of the Oppressed.* Harmondsworth, England: Penguin.

Greenaway, R. (1993). *Playback: A Guide to Reviewing Activities.* London: The Duke of Edinburgh's Award.

Greenaway, R. (2004). Facilitation and reviewing in outdoor education. In Barnes, P. & Sharp, R. (Eds.) *The RHP Companion to Outdoor Education.* Lyme Regis, UK: Russell House Publishing. Chapter available at http://reviewing.co.uk/articles/facilitating-outdoor-education.htm.

Hammel, H. (1986). How to design a debriefing session. *Journal of Experiential Education, 9*(3), 20–25.

Houston, W.R. (1998). Reflecting on reflection. In H.C. Waxman, H.J. Freiberg, J.C. Vaughan & M. Weil (Eds.) *Images of Reflection in Teacher Education* (pp. 7–8). Reston, VA: Association of Teacher Education.

Hunt, J. & Hitchin, P. (1986, 1989). *Creative Reviewing.* Kendal, Cumbria: Groundwork Group Development.

James, T. (1980). Can the mountains speak for themselves? Retrieved from: www.wilderdom.com/facilitation/Mountains.html.

Joplin, L. (1981). On defining experiential education. *Journal of Experiential Education, 4*(1) 17–20.

Knapp, C.E. (1984). Idea notebook: Designing processing questions to meet specific objectives. *Journal of Experiential Education, 7*(2) 47–49.

Knapp, C.E. (1992). *Lasting Lessons: A Teacher's Guide to Reflecting on Experience.* Charleston, WV: ERIC Clearinghouse on Rural Education and Small Schools.

Kolb, D.A. (1984). *Experience as the Source of Learning and Development.* Englewood Cliffs, NJ: Prentice Hall, Inc.

Kraft, R.J. (n.d., c.1985). Towards a theory of experiential learning. In R. Kraft & M. Sakofs (Eds.) *The Theory of Experiential Education* (2nd edn) (pp. 7–38). Boulder, CO: Association for Experiential Education.

Mortlock, C. (2001). *Beyond Adventure.* Milnthorpe, Cumbria: Cicerone Press.

Nadler, R.S. & Luckner, J.L. (1992). *Processing the Adventure Experience.* Dubuque, IA: Kendall/Hunt Publishing Company.

Nadler, R.S. & Luckner, J.L. (1997). *Processing the Experience: Strategies to Enhance and Generalize Learning* (2nd edn). Dubuque, IA: Kendall/Hunt Publishing Company.

Paul, R. & Binker, A.J.A. (1990). Socratic questioning. In R. Paul (Ed.) *Critical Thinking* (pp. 269–298). Rohnert Park, CA: Center for Critical Thinking and Moral Critique.

Pfeiffer, J.W. & Jones, J.E. (1983). *Reference Guide to Handbooks and Annuals*. La Jolla, CA: University Associates, Inc.

Priest, S., Gass, M. & Gillis, L. (2000). *The Essential Elements of Facilitation*. Dubuque, IA: Kendall/Hunt Publishing Company.

Quinsland, L.K. & Van Ginkel, A. (1984). How to process experience. *Journal of Experiential Education*, 7(2), 8–13.

Schoel, J. & Maizell, R.S. (2002). *Exploring Islands of Healing: New Perspectives on Adventure Based Counseling*. Beverly, MA: Project Adventure, Inc.

Seaman, J. (2008). Experience, reflect, critique: The end of the 'learning cycles' era. *Journal of Experiential Education, 31*(1), 3–18.

Simpson, S., Miller, D. & Bocher, B. (2006). *The Processing Pinnacle: An Educator's Guide to Better Processing*. Oklahoma City, OK: Wood 'N' Barnes Publishing.

Sugerman, D.A., Doherty, K.L., Garvey, D.E. & Gass, M.A. (2000). *Reflective Learning: Theory and Practice*. Dubuque, IA: Kendall/Hunt Publishing Company.

Torres, C. (2001). *The Appreciative Facilitator*. Maryville, TN: Mobile Team Challenge.

Turčová, I., Martin, A.J. & Neuman, J. (2005). Diversity in language: Outdoor terminology in the Czech Republic and Britain. *Journal of Adventure Education and Outdoor Learning, 5*(2), 101–118.

Walker, A. (2007). *On Courage Newsletter*. Denver, CO: Loretto Women's Network, Spring, 1–4.

Wertheimer, M. (1945). *Productive Thinking*. New York: Harper & Row.

Part 4

International voices and cultural interpretations

Introduction

Karla A. Henderson

North Carolina State University

Many of the chapters in this Handbook provide a global perspective on various topics. Our intent is to be as inclusive as possible given that as co-editors we represent an Anglo-American viewpoint. We are limited because English is our first language, and we live in geographic areas that privilege us to the research and practice related to the outdoors from our ethnocentric perspectives. We are aware, however, that other standpoints exist and we highlight a few of them.

The chapters in this section on 'International voices and cultural interpretations' represent perspectives from Singapore, Norway, Czech Republic, Japan, Africa and Brazil. Many more countries probably could have been represented, but these offer an opportunity to uncover examples of outdoor studies that are evolving around the world. Further, outdoor studies might be experienced through formal school, such as Ho, Atencio, Michelle and Ching describe in Singapore, or may be asserted through governmental mandates such as in the case of friluftsliv in Norway, or through non-governmental agencies described in Africa, Japan and the Czech Republic. Camps in Brazil seem to be moving towards sponsorship by the private sector. These types of organisational structure are not unlike other organisations described previously in this Handbook.

We do not wish to *Other* these cultural interpretations by setting them into a separate section. However, we do present *voices* metaphorically as text and written language from particular cultural and historical backgrounds and perspectives. We highlight how outdoor studies are understood and perceived aside from the more dominant discourse of this book. By including this section of the book, we emphasise the multi-literacies (Cope & Kalantzis, 2000) that surround outdoor studies. These cultural assessments are important because they allow traditional as well as emerging ideas to come forward based on varying cultural interpretations of the outdoors.

Culture and globalisation

Culture represents learned and shared knowledge, values and beliefs. Culture can be embodied in language, art, religion, ritual, customs and, as these chapters show, nature and the outdoors. Culture is both instrumental (i.e. how individuals as members of a group go about their lives) and expressive (i.e. what gives meaning to people's lives). These areas are not separate but blend with one another (Chick, 2003).

Talking about cultures is sometimes difficult today given the way that cultures mix with one another, which is evident in the chapters in this section. Further, homogeneity and stability do not define most cultures. Chick (2003) noted that the value of culture as an explanatory variable should be replaced with the idea that culture is something that should be explained and explored. The examples in this section provide explanations of how culture and outdoors are understood from both perspectives in different countries.

One reason that distinct cultures may no longer exist is because of globalisation. Globalisation is a process of interaction and integration among the people, organisations and governments of different nations. Globalisation has both positive and negative implications for areas like leisure (Rowe, 2006), and we would add for outdoor studies. In outdoor studies as well as other areas, globalisation is greatly aided by information technology. A fine line may exist between cultural identity and growing globalisation – an idea Rowe calls the *local–global nexus*. Differences between and among countries are becoming blended. As discussed below, however, outdoor studies seems to be a venue where globalisation could result in a deeper cultural identity.

None of the chapters in this book talks extensively about cross-cultural studies. Some authors, such as Okamura, as well as Palhares and Carnicelli, allude to how other countries initially influenced their understanding of outdoor programmes, but each chapter in this section provides its own story, or voice, about the current status of outdoor studies. Perhaps more cross-cultural research is needed, but rather than emphasise differences, the future of outdoor studies from international and cultural perspectives may best be understood by identifying trends that appear to exist across cultures, as noted by the authors of these chapters.

Trends and challenges in international and cultural outdoor studies

In examining the chapters in this section on international voices and cultural interpretations, several challenges and trends emerge. The challenges relate to language, understanding the value of the outdoors within history and culture, and documenting the impact of outdoor studies in both cultural and globalisation terms. Salient trends emerging include identifying how outdoor studies contributes to national and cultural identity, and vice versa, and the importance of the instrumental and expressive components of the outdoors to address national and social problems.

Language

Language related to outdoor studies continues to be a challenge concerning both the literature that is available as well as the translations and meanings of language. More people speak Mandarin than any other language, even though more countries have English as their primary language. Although English is also the most common second language (UNESCO, 2014), we suspect a great deal of literature about outdoor studies exists in other languages. The authors of the chapters included in this book had strong English writing skills so we were able to include these chapters realising that many voices exist that were not translated for this book. We acknowledge that the use of English as the language of communication also is contextual within the social, cultural and political influences of the ideas presented (Cope & Kalantzis, 2000).

A second aspect of language is the translations and meanings that are associated with outdoor studies. Even in a single language like English, many interpretations might be offered, but additional challenges may exist in translations. For example, Cheung (2014) provided an examination of Eastern perspectives on outdoor adventure education. He used the description of the Chinese translation of adventure, which means taking risks at some costs. Yet this term is not accurate given that risk taking is usually not encouraged among Chinese people. Risk is taken only out of necessity so the meanings of the words are not the same; education should create a sense of security and safety, and never danger. Thus, adventure education is a difficult term to translate because of the culture.

The chapters in this section use culture as an explanatory variable as well as describe how culture can be explained. How the culture of *friluftsliv* in Norway, *turistika* in the Czech Republic and the outdoor curriculum in Singapore are portrayed is evidence of how culture is explanatory. Other authors in this section, writing about Japan and Africa, show the paradigms of culture as an explanatory variable in comparison somewhat to existing Anglo-American traditions. Regardless, challenges for the future include ensuring that cultural understanding is addressed in interpreting and promoting outdoor studies.

The value of the outdoors

Related to how language has meanings is the challenge in understanding the essence and value of the outdoors as it relates to historical and cultural interpretations from different countries. As is true of any element of culture, such as art, the way that the outdoors is embraced and perceived is a part of culture. There are multiple histories of connections with the outdoors in all countries, but these connections have not always been evident. For example, Okamura describes the significance of the mountains in Japan. Gurholt illustrates the evolution of the outdoor experience known as *friluftsliv*. These histories define the culture of the country, and the way that the outdoors is valued and studied. Culture also defines the essence of particular organised outdoor experiences, as Ooko and Muthomi suggest when describing the contributions outdoor programmes can make to peace.

Although implicit in these chapters, similarities exist across cultural perspectives related to the value of the outdoors for health. In different ways, the outdoors provides opportunities for individual physical, social and mental health, and also offers a means to address broader environmental issues that exist in particular countries and that affect everyone. Dustin, Bricker and Schwab (2010) have argued for a broader conception of health beyond human physical and mental health, to include familial, communal, national, international and global ecological health. They contend that the challenge is to embrace this ecological reality and reconnect with nature in ways that contribute to the individual and collective health of all living things. Ho *et al.*, in particular, highlight how relationships with the outdoors are essential for the wellbeing of individuals, society and the environment. All the chapters in this section point to these possibilities, regardless of geography.

Documenting the impact of outdoor studies

A third challenge highlighted in this international voices and cultural interpretations section is the need further to evaluate and assess the outcomes of outdoor programmes both in school-based as well as non-formal programmes. Emerging approaches and ways to evaluate and conduct research in, for and about outdoor programmes is a common dilemma described in each chapter.

Ho *et al.* portray how the government of Singapore deemed that outdoor education was important enough that it could not be left to after-school programmes. Although the Singapore curriculum is still in its developmental stages, the Ministry of Education has begun with evaluating teachers' views while striving to incorporate student voices into the future. Further, *friluftsliv* is a belief as well as an activity, and documenting the participation of all Norwegians is an important step. Outdoor educators in Japan have conducted studies related to activities as well as student involvement, which have not been translated beyond Japanese. However, Okamura advocates for more scales and methods for evaluation that cut across cultures. He also acknowledges, however, that evaluation in Japan may not be generalisable to other Asian countries since each country is distinct. Ooko and Muthomi evaluated their three-year outdoor programme, which was intentionally aimed at changing attitudes towards ethnic groups in the country and peace making. They ascertained that their programme had, indeed, made a difference. Palhares and Carnicelli noted that any camp programme was only as good as the staff involved. Therefore, they examined staff issues and how programmes could be improved through staff training and education.

The examples of evaluation and research from these countries provide guidance for the future. Around the world, however, continued documentation of the outcomes of outdoor studies in different sectors from various perspectives will be challenging, but imperative.

Globalisation's contribution to cultural outdoor identity

As noted, globalisation is a trend as well as a challenge that describes the connectedness that exists across the world. The distribution, range of information, people and services have helped to define globalisation. Therefore, what happens anywhere in the world affects everyone. Innovations in outdoor studies can inform practices around the world. For example, as indicated in the programme descriptions in Japan as well as Africa and Brazil, outdoor programmes were initially modelled after US programmes such as the Wilderness Education Association, National Outdoor Leadership School (NOLS) and American camps, respectively. However, although an American model provided a foundation, each of these countries interpreted the model so it would fit their cultural circumstances. For example, the mission of NOLS in the USA has not been to promote peace making but the outdoor strategies used in NOLS fit the needs in Kenya.

The chapters about *friluftsliv* and the Singapore Outdoor Education curriculum, on the other hand, show how their cultural outdoor identity is firmly rooted in their national perspectives. Martin, Turčová and Neuman also describe how *dramaturgy* as a method for outdoor curricula design presents a useful approach for the Czech Republic due to the merging of sports, *turistika* and creative activities. In all cases, the success of these specific national programmes may provide useful guidance for other countries into the future.

The conclusion from these chapters seems to be that countries today are looking to define themselves based on what is known about their cultures as well as what is known about others. One criticism of globalisation is that it tends to diminish national identity. Yet, in the case of outdoor studies, this globalisation is creating distinct ways that countries are using their unique, and not distinct histories and cultures to show how outdoor studies enhance the quality of life for their citizens.

The instrumental and expressive outcomes of the outdoors

An important trend that appeared in this section's chapters is the instrumental and expressive possibilities of the outdoors regardless of the cultural perspective. The outdoors has benefits that all of us know who have any interest in the outdoors, whether as scholars or as citizens. Both the recreational and educational benefits are part of the experience and a false dichotomy is evident if they are disentangled. The instrumental and expressive aspects of culture are two ends of a continuum and these international voices show that connection.

The chapters in this section point to how problems in society can be addressed through outdoor studies. In Singapore, the belief is that health can be enhanced through the lifelong pursuit of outdoor recreation, and this outcome has a wider agenda to build youth resilience, emotional bonding with the country, critical thinking and ecological literacy. Palhares and Carnicelli propose that the value of exposing children to nature and outdoor experiences can lead to social transformation in Brazil by developing critical and conscious citizens. In Norway, *friluftsliv* not only focuses on young people staying physically active and healthy, but also on how this involvement is a key cultural symbol. Further, the way that outdoor programmes have been used in Africa to address greater national issues leading to a more peaceful society elevates the potential of going beyond important outdoor skill building.

Summary

The chapters in this section offer broad views of how outdoor studies is interpreted and presented in countries around the world. These chapters give a voice to national approaches and how the outdoors makes sense in these cultural contexts. Along with the other chapters in this book, this section complements and supplements a global understanding of outdoor studies related to language, values, documentation, globalisation and identity, and broad outcomes. All of us can learn from one another in terms of how to advance the imperatives of outdoor studies globally.

References

Cheung, A. (2014). Outdoor adventure education: An Eastern perspective. In A.W. Ewert & J. Sibthorp (Eds.) *Outdoor Adventure Education: Foundations, Theory, and Research* (p. 19). Champaign, IL: Human Kinetics.

Chick, G. (2003). Culture. In J.M. Jenkins & J.J. Pilgrim (Eds.) *Encyclopedia of Leisure and Outdoor Recreation* (pp. 94–97). London: Routledge.

Cope, B. & Kalantzis, M. (2000). *Multiliteracies: Literacy Learning and the Design of Social Futures*. London: Routledge.

Dustin, D.L., Bricker, K.S. & Schwab, K.A. (2010). People and nature: Toward an ecological model of health promotion. *Leisure Sciences, 32*(1), 3–14.

Rowe, D. (2006) Coming to terms with leisure and globalization. *Leisure Studies, 25*, 423–436.

UNESCO (2014). Basic issues. Retrieved from: http://portal.unesco.org/ci/en/ev.php-URL_ID=16917&URL_DO=DO_TOPIC&URL_SECTION=201.html.

27

The inclusion of outdoor education in the formal school curriculum

Singapore's journey

Susanna Ho

MINISTRY OF EDUCATION, SINGAPORE

Matthew Atencio

CALIFORNIA STATE UNIVERSITY – EAST BAY, USA

Yuen Sze Michelle Tan

UNIVERSITY OF BRITISH COLUMBIA, CANADA

Chew Ting Ching

ASSUMPTION ENGLISH SCHOOL, SINGAPORE

Curriculum construction and change emerges as a politically as well as socially constructed process (Penny, 2006). It is, therefore, not surprising that much of the impetus for curriculum change has come from national governments such as in the United Kingdom, Australia and New Zealand, as well as Singapore. Particularly in Singapore, education has been regarded as potentially contributing to the realisation of political and economic agendas. The Singaporean education curriculum evolved from the late 1970s and was shaped by policies aimed at mass education where academic achievement was considered paramount to national survival. Later iterations of the education system increasingly focused on the notion of academic excellence and standardised efficiency through a hierarchical and centralised system led by the Ministry of Education (MOE).

Singapore's education policies have tended towards pragmatic considerations such as social and economic imperatives related to the future of a small and young nation-state without natural resources. We discuss some of the local and global imperatives that have been influential in shaping the outdoor education (OE) curriculum in Singapore as an introduction to this chapter. Following this discussion, empirical findings based on a study will shed light on the key challenges of the curricular reform.

With a relatively short history compared to the other parts of the world, such as Australia, New Zealand, the UK and North America, OE in Singapore has its roots embedded in Anglo-militaristic and Scouting origins, as well as North American adventure-based education. A majority of the schools provide camping for their students, which is seen as contributing towards the national agenda of building a 'rugged society' (*Straits Times*, 1990, p. 1) and resilient youths with 'ruggedness of mind' (Shanmugaratnam, 2004, p. 1). To support and guide schools in the implementation of their OE co-curricular programmes, often as outdoor pursuits or camping, an OE department was set up in MOE in the late 1990s.

In 2014, OE became formalised as part of the PE curriculum, as opposed to being a co-curricular activity that was conducted after formal school hours. This change was largely due to systemic review and (re)conceptualisation of the Singaporean PE curriculum aimed at fostering 21st Century Competencies[1] (21CC) deemed necessary for students to thrive in a globalised world. The subsequent sections of this chapter are dedicated to discussing the process and deliberations arising from this curricular reform in PE for the inclusion of OE in Singapore.

Situating outdoor education in the Singaporean PE curriculum

Underpinning curriculum reform is a debate over the content chosen, the processes undertaken, and by whom and for whom. Deliberate efforts were made by the Singapore MOE to seek and be inclusive in discussions on curricular reforms in PE. The dates of the meetings for such reviews were made known so that anyone who was interested was welcome to participate in the discussions. Administrators, curriculum specialists, teachers and lecturers from tertiary institutions were appointed as part of the review team so multiple and diverse interests in and for physical education could be heard. The result of this review led to the integration of two distinctive subjects, PE and health education with the inclusion of OE, to form the new PE curriculum implemented in 2014. The review also clarified the purpose of PE, which was 'to enable students to demonstrate individually and with others the physical skills, practices, and values to enjoy a lifetime of active, healthy living' (Ministry of Education, 2013, p. 3). Before this review, outdoor education had never been considered a learning area within the formal PE curriculum in Singapore. It had been positioned, if mentioned at all, as 'other physical activities' (Ministry of Education, 2006, p. 40).

To engender a case for OE to be included as part of the new PE curriculum, the potential contribution to the purpose of PE was examined in the review process. A scan of educational systems revealed that OE has been taught as adventure education, or as forms of outdoor pursuits in PE classes in the USA, the UK, New Zealand and Australia. In some of these countries, OE has been conceptualised as an approach to teaching knowledge, skills and attitudes to serve physical educational needs. For instance, OE in New Zealand is situated within the Health and Physical Education (HPE) curriculum aimed at providing students with opportunities to develop personal and social skills; to become active, safe and skilled in the outdoors; and to protect and care for the environment (Zink & Boyes, 2006). Australia, on the other hand, described OE as a sub-discipline of PE (ACHPER, 2009) similar to other components of PE such as aquatics, athletics, ball games and other physical activities. There has, however, been strong lobbying for OE to be considered as a subject distinctly separated from PE. This argument stems from the viewpoint that OE offers 'unique opportunities to develop positive relationships with the environment, others and ourselves through interaction with the natural world. These relationships are essential for the well-being and sustainability of individuals, society and our environment' (Martin, 2010, p. 5). Related to wellbeing, growing research also shows positive relationships between the time spent outdoors and the level of physical activity (Bird, 2004;

Pretty *et al.*, 2007; Muñoz, 2009). This increase in levels of physical activity is potentially beneficial to children's health, including tackling issues like obesity (Muñoz, 2009) and stress levels (Nielson & Hansen, 2007).

Previous local studies argued that OE in Singapore can be seen as having the potential to serve wider national agendas such as building resilience, emotional bonding with the country, critical thinking and ecological literacy (Martin & Ho, 2009; Ho, 2014). Therefore, OE could potentially fulfil larger national goals and purposes than those set out in PE. The inclusion of OE in the PE curriculum could enable more students to acquire the rudiments of outdoor living skills, knowledge and attitudes, which could facilitate their lifelong pursuit of outdoor physical recreation. OE could further provide opportunities for theoretical work traditionally taught in the classroom (e.g. health education and risk assessment topics) to be enacted and experienced in the outdoors.

Based on the global scan on HPE, and mounting evidence that linked nature to children's health and wellbeing within the Singaporean context, the review by the Singaporean MOE led to delineating three distinct but related strands for the learning outcomes of OE in the PE curriculum:

1   Physical health and well-being;
2   Risk assessment and management; and
3   Sense of place.

The syllabus document states OE as an integral component of PE that 'engages the students' sense of adventure through the exploration of both natural and urban environments' (Ministry of Education, 2013, p. 54). The OE in PE framework, depicted in Figure 27.1, serves to guide the teaching and learning of OE in PE.

Similar to other aspects of learning, the review indicated that skills taught in the PE lessons should be scaffolded and conducted in stages. Therefore, starting the students with the familiar and local before introducing them to the remote and unfamiliar will be necessary. The acquisition of outdoor living skills will enable students to become comfortable in the outdoors. While impossible to include camps and learning journeys within the PE curriculum time allotted, these experiences will be positioned as opportunities for application and demonstration of the skills and attitudes that students have acquired during OE in the PE lessons.

The following sections elaborate how each strand of the learning outcomes could be achieved through the teaching of OE.

Strand 1: Physical Health and Wellbeing

Available literature provides compelling evidence that contact with nature is fundamental to human health and wellbeing. In the PE curriculum, OE could deliberately seek to teach students how to recreate, explore, enjoy and learn from time with (and in) nature. In a highly urbanised city-state such as Singapore, many students are likely to experience their *firsts* with nature through OE in schools. In this regard, Louv (2005) argued for OE to provide for students' primary experiences of nature, where they can 'see, feel, taste, hear or smell' (p. 64) for themselves. This concept is premised on the notion that these sensory experiences link children's exterior world with their interior (i.e. affective) world. Since the natural environment is the principal source of sensory stimulation, freedom to explore and play in the outdoors through the senses is essential for healthy development of their affective life (Louv, 2005). Studies by Muñoz (2009) and Bird (2004) also found positive relationships between time spent outdoors

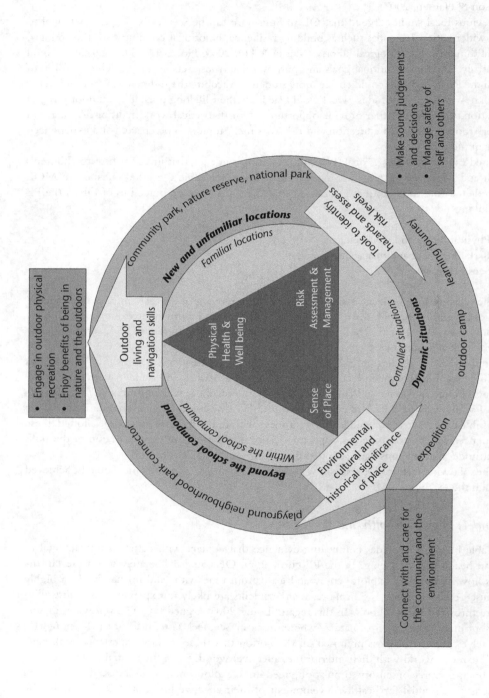

Figure 27.1 A framework to guide the teaching and learning of OE in PE

Source: Ministry of Education (2013, p. 58)

and the level of physical activity. Hence, children who spend time in the outdoors and are taught skills (e.g. navigation and outdoor living skills), knowledge (e.g. basic ecological literacy, sustainable living) and attitudes (e.g. personal choices, environmental stewardship) feel comfortable in the outdoors and engage in physical activity that is higher in level and quality.

Learning how to be comfortable in the outdoors could be the first step towards enjoyment and appreciating the natural environment. Enhanced knowledge, understanding and skills gained through outdoor experiences gradually could help students develop personal attitudes and intended behaviours that would be based on their understanding of the interdependencies between themselves and nature (Flowers, 2010). From their study on pre-service PE teachers' reflections on OE, Timken and McNamee (2012) found that teachers realised the importance of introducing students to activities such as mountain biking, in which they can participate for the rest of their lives. They realised that some of the traditional competitive team sport activities in PE failed to result in lifetime activity habits. This instance demonstrates how OE can expand beyond the traditional model of PE to promote lifelong physical activity through authentic and meaningful outdoor learning scenarios (Rovegno & Dolly, 2006).

Strand 2: Risk Assessment and Management

No other subject in the school can confront students with the assessment and management of risk in the way that outdoor education can. Although sports activities entail a certain amount of risk, students participate in a tight code of rules in which they have limited control. In these instances, students would not be required to assess risk and they could leave the issue of risk to the referees and those who designed the game. However, outdoor play as an approach where individuals could be placed in an unfamiliar environment has been used to develop children's understandings of risk (Muñoz, 2009). Fjørtoft (2001) posited that the natural environments represent dynamic and rough 'playscapes' (i.e. diverse natural environments; p. 112) that could potentially be beneficial to children's motor development specifically in strength, balance and coordination. The physical diversity of the natural environment could increase the opportunities for learning and development. For example, the topography (e.g. slopes and rocks) could afford natural obstacles that require children to cope. The vegetation could provide shelters and trees for climbing. The meadows are for running and tumbling. Fjørtoft verified that children using forests as a playscape performed better in motor skills than the children on traditional playgrounds.

Outdoor education in Singapore could, therefore, offer diverse opportunities for teaching students about risk assessment and management of risk. In an outdoor setting, 'communicating risk includes the identification of the benefits to be gained, the hazards to be encountered and likelihood of occurrences' (Martin, 2010, p. 7). Since risk assessment and management are an analysis of a given situation in a particular context, the actions and decisions taken would have direct consequences and could, therefore, facilitate effective learning. For instance, the *Outdoor Journeys* embarked on by 8- to 11-year-old primary school students in Scotland entailed identifying hazards and deciding as a group how the hazards could reasonably be managed (Beames & Ross, 2010). The advantage lies in that concepts of risks and hazards could be taught as a process in a safely monitored context, and learning could be transferable to other situations in and out of the school.

Strand 3: Sense of Place

One of the earliest experiential education philosophers, John Dewey (1915), advocated immersing students in the local environment. He believed that experience outside the school has geographical, artistic, and literary, scientific and historical sides (Louv, 2005). We previously discussed that outdoor education could reconnect children and youths to nature. Noting at this juncture that the nature and outdoors discussed should take into account human constructions of environments (McClaren, 2009), including cityscapes, local parks and park connectors in the Singaporean context is important. Given the prevalence of urban environments in Singaporean children's experience, as well as for teachers and outdoor educators, the sense of place and the local areas ought to be closely linked to its identity and heritage.

Singapore's predominantly urban landscape might be perceived as lacking in wildlife or natural habitat. Contrary to such public perception, many terrestrial and marine ecosystems exist within the city-state (National Parks Board, 2007; Tan, Chou, Yeo & Ng, 2010). Such national heritage could be part of the country's legacy, in which outdoor education could potentially help students learn and appreciate.

Outdoor education in Singapore could help develop a strong connection with Singapore, particularly with local places such as green spaces around the schools (e.g. park connectors, local parks). Outdoor education, with its emphasis on experiential learning in a particular environment could provide multi-layered opportunities for place-based education. However, attachment to place grows over time until 'mere words and thoughts give way to something deeper' (Orr, 2005, p. 102). A study by Beames and Ross (2010) with primary school students who underwent a place-based journey programme indicated that students exhibited a high degree of initiative and consciousness of local history and ecology. Their evidence also showed that some students were more likely to undertake their own adventures outside of their formal schooling than their peers. Outdoor education in the PE lessons could provide Singaporean students with the means to learn about the world in which they inhabit through repeated visits to nearby local parks. In doing so, the students would have sufficient time and space to be engaged in learning in (i.e. experiencing) and about (e.g. oral histories, topography) these places (see Atencio, Tan, Ho & Chew, 2014).

Curricular deliberations as a curriculum development process

After the curriculum was developed, a collaborative research team comprising local policy makers and university researchers was formed to consider challenges that PE teachers could face when required to teach OE beginning in 2014. The success of curriculum reform efforts relies on teachers as institutional actors who enact prescribed curriculum (Clandinin & Connelly, 1992) and who act as change agents (Fullan, 2007, 2011) has long been recognised. Reid (2006) acknowledged teachers as commonplace in curricular deliberations and critical sources of curriculum knowledge.

The aims of the research were multi-pronged and targeted at levels of curriculum development:

- To shape the curriculum development process by allowing the PE teachers' knowledge and understandings to influence the initial phases of curriculum design, and
- To challenge curriculum designers to explore and reflect on new approaches to the complexity of curriculum development.

With the conviction that the pursuit of the newly prescribed OE curriculum should take into account teacher knowledge as well as their dispositions, views and beliefs, the mixed-methods study aimed to ascertain the perceptions that pre- and in-service PE teachers at the secondary level had of OE. This study was framed within this context as a means of generating teachers' perspectives that could underpin contemporary curricular deliberations (Reid, 2006) surrounding the purpose and practice of OE. The survey and interview questions were formulated to probe for teachers': (i) understandings of outdoor education; (ii) attitudes and beliefs towards teaching outdoor education; (iii) aims of enacting an outdoor education curriculum; (iv) experiences in enacting outdoor education (if any); and (v) perspectives in enacting an OE curriculum (i.e. perceived readiness to teach outdoor education and support that was necessary).

Qualitative findings

The findings gleaned from the initial survey with 200 PE teachers included follow-up semi-structured interviews with thirty-five of the teachers, who provided rich insights into their perceptions and understandings of OE as the curriculum was being developed. A typical conception of OE was encapsulated by the following quote:

> Ok, first thing when we look at outdoor education is basically we are looking at camps, taking you out of comfort zone, you know, and it's basically just purely a camp, overnight stay in a camp. And then you have activities in the camp. It could be outdoor activities. It could be orienteering, could be field-cooking kind of thing. It is something that will take you out of your comfort zone, and you have some hands on where you get to experience outdoors. (Andy)

A common theme that evolved from the findings involved character building and instilling values through adventurous activities that could challenge students living in 'comfort zones', grounded in the belief that learning mostly occurs when an individual is placed in a stressful situation (Brown, 2008). Some of the teachers interviewed expressed that OE has a role to play in toughening up a perceived 'strawberry generation':

> Our students now are a little bit more protected? They don't go out as often, and even if they do, I think – for example now, I think we do still live – or rather, our camps are usually in bunks and not necessarily in tents. I would say it really builds their character and being resilient in a very uncomfortable environment for them, and I feel that it's important to transcend to any part of their lives. Even in studies and things like that, when things get uncomfortable, when things get difficult, it's something that they should overcome. And I think outdoor education plays a big role in that. Yeah, getting them to be in uncomfortable situations I guess. (Nora)

> They [students] are too pampered and if we [teachers] did not bring them out to the discomfort zone, they would really be spoilt. (Ming)

In a previous study by Martin and Ho (2009), educators and instructors ranked outcomes such as building resilience and personal and social development as most important to OE in Singapore. The perceptions and understandings of OE among Singaporeans seemed to mirror the government's concern about the increasingly affluent and sedentary lifestyles. This finding could be a result of a lack of understanding of what OE entails, resulting in the majority employing 'managerial speak' (Velayutham, 2007, p. 166), articulating national agendas, and/or official policies as impetus for curricular rationale. The lack of teachers' understanding of the OE curriculum was further substantiated by the interviews with them.

They gave us some idea of what the learning outcome was going to be like, for next year. So one of the- I mean values and life skills was not in there, which I find kind of strange, but there were things like learning about safety and taking risk? You know. That's one of the learning outcomes that they put up . . . (Anna)

Now if you look at the profile of PE teachers, they are more into sports and games. Probably that's what they were taught in NIE, especially the recent few batches. They are more into sports and games that kind of thing. So when they come into school context they talked about outdoor education, it's very lacking there . . . So when you come in to school now you want to push for that outdoor education. This is where I feel they need to know a bit about knowledge. (Nick)

Quantitative findings

Our quantitative data highlighted two areas of teachers' professional development needs: (i) knowledge of the OE curriculum; and (ii) the teaching of outdoor skills. These quantitative findings, as shown in Figure 27.2, complemented the qualitative data on teachers' readiness to teach OE.

The findings of this study provided insights into the PE teachers' understandings, beliefs and readiness to enact a curriculum that had not been featured in their pre-service teachers' training. Their understandings of OE were based largely on their own prior experiences or

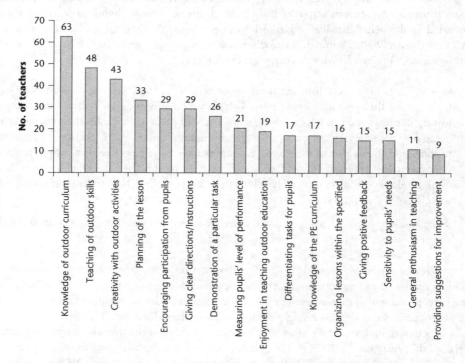

Figure 27.2 Findings on areas of professional development needs of teachers: key challenges of curricular reform

through in-service courses that focused on the training of instructors for adventure ropes courses, kayaking and rock climbing. In reality, such specialised courses focused on technical skills could limit teachers' knowledge and understanding of outdoor education's broader possibilities. Findings in our study made explicit the challenges associated with curriculum reform efforts. The challenges surfaced, and having a good grasp of teachers' readiness in light of the new curriculum, could serve as a guide to curriculum developers and advisers of its implementation.

Pre-service teacher training in OE has remained as one of the most pressing challenges in Singapore. The lack of understanding of OE and teachers' low levels of readiness to teach it could be attributed to the void in teacher training. The MOE could leverage multiple and varied platforms to engage PE teachers in the impending curricular changes, especially regarding the inclusion of OE in PE. Apart from the twice-yearly forums that heads and senior PE teachers attend, two nationwide curriculum implementation workshops were conducted for all PE teachers in 2013. More platforms could be mounted for teachers to voice their views, and provide inputs and suggestions to shape the curriculum that they would be enacting.

Future curriculum research and deliberations

> Curriculum is 'unfinished', 'always in the making'; in the process of (de- and re-) construction and furthermore, contested and contestable throughout what have traditionally been referred to as 'stages' of making (or construction) and implementation (or 'delivery'). (Penny, 2006, p. 567)

This quote is a reminder that curricular deliberations are iterative and ongoing. As the first phase of the PE curriculum is being implemented, the curriculum for the next phase of implementation in the following year is currently being written. Therefore, trials with schools on the enactment of the curriculum, workshops to prepare teachers, evaluation of the curriculum implementation, and curriculum review meetings are simultaneous and ongoing.

Curricular reforms premised themselves on the assumptions that they are self-evident and that teachers will find ways to implement them (Ng, 2008). Given the challenge of teachers' readiness in light of the new curriculum, the MOE will need to work with schools and teachers as co-constructors to trial the curriculum and lessons before system-level structural changes and provisions can be made. These schools and teachers could subsequently serve as models that other schools and teachers could consult. System-wide implementation would be effective if the deeper and subtler issues and needs could be understood and addressed prior to such implementation.

Penny (2006) highlighted the importance of research to explore curriculum from the perspective of both teachers and students, if they were to be regarded as *co-constructors* of the curriculum. Little research to date has been done to elucidate students' voices in shaping the pedagogical form and focus of the curriculum that they have experienced. Brown (2006) called for concerted research efforts on grounding the claims of the benefits of OE. He felt it timely and imperative that practitioners and researchers document both the outcomes and processes involved to improve the scholarly base of the field, and therefore, improve the educational experiences of students. As the next phase of curriculum implementation is planned, traction with the ground ought to be maintained, which should include the pulse for *what works* as well as those aspects that need refinement. Therefore, the scope for future research will be to focus on documenting teachers' and students' experiences and learning OE in the PE curriculum.

Note

1 These emerging competencies are Civic Literacy, Global Awareness and Cross-Cultural Skills; Critical and Inventive Thinking; and Communication, Collaboration and Information Skills (Ministry of Education, 2014).

References

ACHPER (2009). The ACHPER National Statement on the curriculum future of health and physical education in Australia. Retrieved from: www.achpersa.com.au/wb/pages/about-us/achper-media-releases.php.

Atencio, M., Tan, M., Ho, S. & Chew, T.C. (2014). The place and approach of outdoor learning within a holistic curricular agenda: Development of Singaporean OE practice. *Journal of Adventure and Outdoor Learning*. Published online. DOI: 10.1080/14729679.2014.949807

Beames, S. & Ross, H. (2010). Journeys outside the classroom. *Journal of Adventure Education and Outdoor Learning*, *10*(2), 95–109.

Bird, W. (2004). *Can Green Space and Biodiversity Increase Levels of Physical Activity?* Bedfordshire, UK: Royal Society for the Protection of Birds.

Brown, M. (2008). Comfort zone: Model or metaphor? *Australian Journal of Outdoor Education*, *12*(1), 3–12.

Clandinin, D.J. & Connelly, F.M. (1992). Teacher as curriculum maker. In P.W. Jackson (Ed.) *Handbook of Research on Curriculum* (pp. 363–401). New York: Macmillan.

Dewey, J. (1915). *The School and Society* (2nd edn). Chicago, IL: University of Chicago Press.

Fjørtoft, I. (2001). The natural environment as a playground for children: The impact of outdoor play activities in pre-primary school children. *Early Childhood Education Journal*, *29*(2), 111–117.

Flowers, A.B. (2010). Blazing an evaluation pathway: Lessons learned from applying utilization-focused evaluation to a conservation education program. *Evaluation and Program Planning*, *33*, 165–171.

Fullan, M. (2007). *The New Meaning of Educational Change* (4th edn). New York: Teachers College Press.

Fullan, M. (2011). *Change Leader. Learning to Do What Matters Most*. San Francisco, CA: Jossey-Bass.

Ho, S. (2014). The purposes outdoor education does, could and should serve in Singapore. *Journal of Adventure Education and Outdoor Learning*, *14*(2), 152–171.

Louv, R. (2005). *Last Child in the Woods: Saving Our Children from Nature-deficit Disorder*. Chapel Hill, NC: Algonquin.

Martin, P. (2010). Outdoor education and the national curriculum in Australia. *Australian Journal of Outdoor Education*, *14*(2), 3–31.

Martin, P. & Ho, S. (2009). Seeking sustainability and resilience: Outdoor education in Singapore. *Journal of Adventure Education and Outdoor Learning*, *9*(1), 79–92.

McClaren, M. (2009). The place of the city in environmental education. In M. McKenzie, P. Hart, H. Bai & B. Jickling (Eds.) *Fields of Green: Restorying Culture, Environment, and Education* (pp. 301–306). Cresskill, NJ: Hampton Press.

Ministry of Education (2006). *Physical Education Syllabus (Primary, Secondary, Pre-university Levels) 2006*. Singapore: MOE. Retrieved from: www.moe.gov.sg/education/syllabuses/aesthetics-health-and-moral-education/files/physical-education.pdf.

Ministry of Education (2013). *PE Teaching and Learning Syllabus 2014*. Singapore: MOE.

Ministry of Education (2014). *21st Century Competencies*. Singapore: MOE. Retrieved from: www.moe.gov.sg/education/21cc/.

Muñoz, S.-A. (2009). *Children in the Outdoors: A Literature Review*. Moray, Scotland: National Sustainable Development Centre.

National Parks Board (2007). *Singapore's Natural Heritage: Poster Series Teacher's Guide*. Singapore: National Parks Board.

Ng, P.T. (2008). Educational reform in Singapore: From quantity to quality. *Educational Research for Policy and Practice*, *7*(1), 5–15.

Nielson, T.S. & Hansen, K.B. (2007). Do green areas affect health? Results from a Danish survey on the use of green areas and health indicators. *Health and Place*, *13*, 839–850.

Orr, D. (2005). Recollection. In M.K. Stone & Z. Barlow (Eds.) *Ecological Literacy: Educating Our Children for a Sustainable World* (pp. 96–106). San Francisco, CA: Sierra Club Books.

Penny, D. (2006). Curriculum construction and change. In D. Kirk, D. Macdonald & M. O'Sullivan (Eds.) *Handbook of Physical Education* (pp. 565–579). London: Sage Publications.

Pretty, J., Peacock, J., Hine, R., Sellens, M., South, N. & Griffin, M. (2007). Green exercise in the UK countryside: Effects on health and psychological well-being, and implications for policy and planning. *Journal of Environmental Planning and Management, 50*(2), 211–231.

Reid, W.A. (2006). *The Pursuit of Curriculum: Schooling and the Public Interest.* (2nd edn). Greenwich, CT: Information Age Publishing.

Rovegno, I. & Dolly, J.P. (2006). Constructivist perspectives on learning. In D. Kirk, D. Macdonald & M. O'Sullivan (Eds.) *Handbook of Physical Education* (pp. 242–261). London: Sage Publications.

Shanmugaratnam, T. (2004). Speech by Acting Minister for Education at the Singapore Schools Sports Councils' 45th Anniversary Celebration on 1 June. Retrieved from: www.moe.gov.sg/speeches/2004/sp20040601.htm.

Straits Times (1990). Chok Tong calls for return to a rugged society. *Straits Times*, 11 March, 1.

Tan, H.T.W., Chou, L.M., Yeo, D.C.J. & Ng, P.K.L. (2010). *The Natural Heritage of Singapore.* Singapore: Pearson.

Timken, G.L. & McNamee, J. (2012). New perspectives for teaching physical education: Preservice teachers' reflections on outdoor and adventure education. *Journal of Teaching in Physical Education, 31,* 21–38.

Velayutham, S. (2007). *Responding to Globalization: Nation, Culture and Identity in Singapore.* Singapore: Institute of Southeast Asian Studies.

Zink, R. & Boyes, M. (2006). The nature and scope of outdoor education in New Zealand schools. *Australian Journal of Outdoor Education, 10*(1), 11–21.

Funding acknowledgement

This article refers to data from a grant (OER 43/12 MT), National Institute of Education, Singapore. The views expressed in this article are solely those of the authors.

28

Friluftsliv

Nature-friendly adventures for all

Kirsti Pedersen Gurholt

NORWEGIAN SCHOOL OF SPORT SCIENCES

In 2015, Norway held its third National Year of *friluftsliv* (literally *free-air-life* or *free-life-under-the-open-sky*), a year-long promotion of the role of outdoor life in society and support of the National Strategy for Active *Friluftsliv* 2014–2020 (Ministry of the Environment, 2013). Numerous events were launched by two national *friluftsliv* umbrella associations that since the late 1980s have played a key role in promoting the overall state policy of *Friluftsliv for all*, which was inaugurated in the early 1970s. At that time a first official definition was articulated: '*Friluftsliv* means dwelling/wayfaring, and physical activity in open spaces during leisure time to participate in a variety of environments and foster aesthetic experiences of nature [*naturopplevelser*]' (Ministry of the Environment, 2000, p. 9).

Previous year-long national tributes to *friluftsliv* were held in 1993 and 2005, to coincide with the 125th anniversary of the Norwegian Trekking Association (established in 1868), and the 100th anniversary of Norway's independence declared in 1905. The first of these praised national identity and a common culture as defined by closeness to nature. The second was dedicated to motivating young people to stay physically active, slim and healthy. The theme of the 2015 events was activating inactive groups and broadening popular awareness of the right to public access and joyful experiences of nature close to home (Ministry of the Environment, 2000, 2013).

The right to roam freely on uncultivated public and private land was officially recognised in the Friluftsliv Act of 1957. This legislation codified, with minor restrictions, ancient legal rights to hiking and temporary overnight stays, to pick berries and mushrooms, and to fish and hunt in Norway's vast sparsely populated areas of mountains, forests, lakes, rivers and long rugged coastline located on the north-west fringe of Europe. Moreover, the democratic right to roam is grounded on a cultural legacy of trust and mutual respect between landowners and visitors, which includes a recognised obligation to be considerate and leave no traces. Practical principles such as always being prepared to care for oneself by carrying everything needed for a safe hike are embedded in the ethos of *friluftsliv*.

In this chapter, I aim to examine *friluftsliv* as a dynamic and complex socio-cultural phenomenon and as a key cultural symbol with a spectrum of meanings. As noted, *friluftsliv* is a discursive field of politics and organised interests. It is also a social field of self-organised undertakings, a moulded substance in school and higher education, and an evolving field of research. The cultural-historical narrative that I present encircles five analytical themes: first, *friluftsliv* represents a broad range of 'close to nature' activities deriving from a dual legacy of Romantic and Pragmatic (urban and rural) ways of life; second, the two-fold nature of adventure in Norwegian/European cultural history emphasising risk versus curiosity as motivating forces; third, curiosity-driven adventure linked to experience and the building of nature literacy through *erfaringer/Erfahrungen* of nature; fourth, a cultural shift arising that highlights intense moments of subjective and aesthetic experience – the *opplevelse/Erlebis* of nature; fifth is an interconnectedness of adventure and nature-friendly perspectives.

A culture of closeness to nature?

The word *friluftsliv* can be traced back to the Norwegian playwright Henrik Ibsen (1828–1906). It appeared for the first time in his epic poem *Paa Vidderne* [*On the Heights*], published in 1859. The poem's sixty-four stanzas reflect a Romantic motif telling a story about a solitary hunter – a farmer's young son – who is torn between the lure of a free life roaming in the mountains and a desire to be with his beloved down in the valley. While hunting 'on the heights', his solitary encounters with the mountains release an edifying process that provides him with 'a deeper view of life' and '*friluftsliv* for my thoughts'. In the end it leaves him steeled, self-sufficient and firm in resolve; as 'man enough to fend for myself' (Ibsen, 1859/1991, pp. 479–483).

In a contextualised reading, I have analysed (Gurholt, 2008a) how the story reflects both the, at the time, gendered culture and the modern life's radical break from the subsistence society. Thus, the word *friluftsliv* was initially imbued by the new poetic attitude towards nature, the transformation of subsistence undertakings into leisure, while at the same engraved with a gendered division. Male identities were symbolised by mountains, freedom, breadth of vision and high-quality life in which character was formed through interaction with pristine nature. Femininity was represented as a fumbling, inferior and passive adaptation to daily routines of village life.

The further evolvement of *friluftsliv* as a concept that covers a variety of perceptions and practical ways of approaching nature for its own sake is complex. The concept was picked up by several authors and groups to describe their new aesthetic appreciation of nature. In particular the concept may have become more widely known through a famous speech directed to Norwegian students in 1921 by Fridtjof Nansen (1861–1930), the Norwegian polar explorer, scientist (and later humanist and Nobel Peace Prize winner), who was the first person to cross the Greenland ice cap on skis, in 1888 (Nansen, 1922). In the speech he defined *friluftsliv* as simple nature life and extolled the character-building benefits of exploring uncultivated nature. His thinking reflected a romanticised view of nature. It may also have been inspired by the ascetic pietistic Protestant ethic, which influenced Norwegian culture (Gåsdal, 2007).

When *friluftsliv* became subject to academic exploration and discourse in the 1970s, one interpretation widely considered it to have its origin in two cultural strains. One was the Romantic, aesthetic and adventurous ideal (mentioned above) popular in the urban upper and middle classes since the late 19th century. The other was a pragmatic approach that prevailed in the rural subsistence economy (Breivik, 1978). The two strands were seen to influence Norwegian culture well into the post-war era due to the country's relatively late urbanisation, in ways that seem to have much in common with what Tim Ingold (2011) calls dwelling and wayfaring. Notwithstanding, *friluftsliv* has widely been regarded as a socio-cultural field of undertakings, which reduces social inequalities.

Beginning in the 1970s, oil wealth created the economic foundation for today's welfare, leisure and knowledge-based society. A well-developed infrastructure ensures that all of the country's five million people – including every inhabitant of Oslo, the capital city – are within thirty minutes of uncultivated land, travelling either on foot or by public transport. According to a recent national survey, 97 per cent of parents reported that their children are within walking or biking distance of a green area (Skår *et al.*, 2014).

The influence of *friluftsliv* as a core belief in Norwegian everyday culture can be verified in life-history research (e.g. Svarstad, 2010; Gurholt, 2014) and national surveys. Since the 1960s, and most recently in 2010, the government agency Statistics Norway (2009, 2012) has generated data on participation in *friluftsliv*. These surveys confirm the continuing popularity of walking: four out of five Norwegians aged 16–79 report that they hike locally on foot and ski every year. Nearly half say that they have been hiking in more distant forests and mountains. The most popular activities are shorter walks, day trips on foot, and cross-country skiing in nearby natural environments. In summer, the favoured activities are swimming, sunbathing and day trips by bike. In contrast, fewer than one in ten Norwegians surveyed reported that they engaged in skill-oriented activities such as skating on a frozen lake, horseback riding or climbing, or had spent several days on a hunting, kite-skiing, rafting, canoeing or cycling trip. About one-third reported that they had foraged for berries, mushrooms or fish during the previous year.

The survey also revealed significant generational differences. Of the respondents aged 16–24, half said they had abandoned traditional hiking in favour of specialised adventurous activities such as Telemark skiing, snowboarding, kiting, cross-biking and various watersports, though they did not compete in them. Participation in outdoor activities also reflected socio-economic status. Individuals with high levels of education and income were most active. Children in low-income and immigrant families were less active than children growing up in high-income families and in families with second homes located somewhere in the countryside (Statistics Norway, 2009, 2012).

Participation by women has grown over the past four decades. They were significantly less active than men in the 1960s and 1970s, spending less time on outdoor activities, participating in fewer activities and rarely going on trips lasting several days. A major cultural shift took place in the 1990s, and today's young Norwegians grow up and are educated in an environment that puts a strong emphasis on equality. Currently, girls and women are more active than men in all age groups between 16 and 79 years when activities such as walking, ski-touring and hiking for pleasure, and just being in nature, are taken into account. The proportion of girls participating in challenging outdoor pursuits is increasing, even though boys spend more time and devote more regular attention to such activities (Statistics Norway, 2012). On the other hand, more girls than boys value courses related to *friluftsliv* in secondary school (Gurholt, 2014) and enrol in *friluftsliv* studies at the university level.

To summarise, in contemporary society, *friluftsliv* has become a dynamic and pluralistic cultural-political concept. It encompasses complex relations and practices ranging from daily walking in green areas, sustainable awareness and an aesthetic experience of nature (naturopplevelse) to skill-oriented and technology-based adventurous journeys into remote uncultivated environments. It extends from the most prosaic daily activities to the most sacred feelings of identity bonding with nature. What the diverse cultures of foraging, walking for pleasure and specialised high-tech adventurous lifestyles share is engagement in non-competitive and non-motorised ways of moving in/across natural landscapes (Pedersen, 2003). Within that broad conception, *friluftsliv* has undergone complex transformation in recent decades and participation varies considerably according to social class, gender, ethnicity and age. The formerly self-organised, self-cultivated, self-reliant and private initiatives are today guided by global markets and a raft of experts – politicians, leaders of volunteer associations, professional guides, teachers, youth social workers and researchers.

The dual nature of friluftsliv education: curiosity and risk

In the Norwegian culture, the concept of *friluftsliv* was from the beginning connected with the concepts of venturing at and of *eventyr*, which translates into adventure. According to Becker (2008), the concept of *adventure* begins in Greco-Roman mythology and the medieval (French) culture of chivalry. Its roots can be traced to the *advenire* Latin *res aventura/abventura*, meaning 'what is about to happen' and French associated predominantly with unforeseen, sudden and surprising events that require an immediate response and have an uncertain outcome. As the power of the merchant class grew in the 16th century, the word adventure became linked to the economic activities of the so-called merchant adventurers who undertook extraordinarily risky voyages in pursuit of profit – originally meaning sailing around a dangerous rocky outcrop. Thus, the willingness to accept risk became associated with expectations of comparably large rewards, and an increasing need for security. Ever since then, the concepts of adventure, risk and security have been closely linked. Over time, the word adventure was invoked in a range of contexts and meanings, including long-distance journeys, exploration and expansion of the known world, and development of new knowledge about the world.

The origin of ideas linking adventure to notions of personal development can also be traced to the medieval European belief that, by following their own curiosity – by seeing, asking, and listening – people could free themselves from a familiar world and transform themselves and their reality. The earliest known example of this modern attitude to life, and the torments associated with it, can be found in the Italian scholar and poet Francesco Petrarch's (1304–1374) account of his ascent of Mont Ventoux in southern France in 1336. From the top, he could see two seas – the Mediterranean and the Atlantic Ocean, in addition to the Alps – but gnawing at his conscience was a concern that he might have committed one of the great sins of his age – *curiosity*, a trait that, it was commonly believed, lured people away from God and traditional values.

Over the centuries, stories of people following their curiosity including departure, journeying, homecoming and personal change have become classics of European literature. They were originally written in a variety of languages, including Norwegian (Ibsen's male hunter and *Peer Gynt*). These stories share a common structure linking adventure to ideas of human growth achieved by individuals who abandon familiar ground and go travelling to explore unknown regions. These travellers, internally motivated by a desire to obtain first-hand knowledge of the world, are exposed to challenges, and summon the courage and intelligence to overcome them (Gustavsson, 2001).

When the word *œfvintŷr* (*eventyr*, in modern Norwegian) entered the Norwegian language in the Middle Ages it meant 'experience, occurrence, and narrative'. The idea of surrendering oneself to *eventyr* became a metaphor for journeys of discovery and encounters with surprising and remarkable events that generated human growth. However, over time the word *eventyr* became associated with folk tales about 'all that walks and breathes', as well as the journeys on which these phenomena were encountered. Likewise, concepts such as *fjelleventyr* and *vintereventyr*, meaning mountain or a winter adventure, were used as leitmotif and metaphors associated with *friluftsliv*. An example is Nansen, who already in the early 1880s compared himself with the popular Norwegian folk tale hero, *Askeladden* (the Ash Lad) when relating his polar adventures to children. In 1926, when he was appointed Lord Rector of St Andrew's University in Scotland, the title of his Rectorial Address was 'Adventure', a speech in which he claimed risk-taking European merchant adventurers as his predecessors (Gurholt, 2010).

Around 1970, polar explorers like Nansen came to inspire the introduction of *friluftsliv* as an academic discipline in higher education among other sources. This innovation helped

291

legitimise the role of explorative adventures *by simple means* in mitigating deleterious effects of modern industrialised culture, and as preparation for an emerging leisure society. The popularity of *friluftsliv* was also enhanced by the burgeoning environmental movement and deep ecology. This philosophy, motivated by the Norwegian climber and philosopher Arne Næss (1912–2009), explicitly linked 'richness in life with simple means', mountaineering and *friluftsliv* (Næss, 1976/1989, p. 178). Concurrently, an ethos of asceticism came to influence the approach to *friluftsliv* within higher education and public schools, and as a public policy issue under the aegis of the Ministry of Environmental Preservation (established in 1972). In contrast, the Ministry of Church, Culture, and Education was responsible for (nature-based) sports.

The discourse of and practical approaches to *friluftsliv* as an academic discipline were also influenced by *Askeladden* (Kvaløy, 2007) as a metaphor for the pedagogical principles of quest for self-enculturation through first-hand experiences. *Askeladden* is known for being endlessly curious and helpful, spontaneous, shrewd, quick-witted and always ready to venture into the unknown to try his luck. He is bursting with confidence in his own abilities and never at a loss for what to do. He finds solutions to every challenge that comes his way by transforming everything he finds, however broken or worn out, into something useful. In current usage, the word *eventyr* and the Norwegian concept of *eventyr*-pedagogy are closely associated with a folkloric storytelling tradition in a way that gives the compound a connotation that differs significantly from the English/German meaning of adventure education/*Abenteuer Pedagogik*. Nevertheless, the concept of *friluftsliv* includes the same association with human condition and growth by exposing oneself to unknown circumstances that is pervasive in the broader European tradition of adventure (Gurholt, 2010).

Experience as erfaringer and dannelse: becoming nature literate

The establishment of *friluftsliv* as an academic discipline was motivated from diverse sources. One issue was a widespread concern that Norwegians were losing their skills in hiking and survival in snow-covered mountains. Another premise was that professional guidance and formal education in *simple nature life* literacy, including dwelling and wayfaring, would promote environmental awareness and green lifestyles among young people. Despite its Romantic inspiration, the first attempt to develop deliberate pedagogical strategies focused on instruction, which was in the climate of 1970s' critical theory criticised for being authoritarian. In their place, education programmes introduced ideas inspired by sources such as *Askeladden*, Nansen and deep-ecology philosophy. This approach gave a deeper meaning to the concept of a rich life with simple means. It came to imply self-reliant and nature-friendly hiking and camping, in combination with enjoyment of nature and a search for adventure in uncultivated environments. The explicit premise was that people can acquire rich knowledge and mastery of nature by doing, trying and experiencing things through bodily sensation and vigorous immersion in what was frequently called uncultivated nature – high mountains, deep forests and rushing waters. Further, the aspiration to overcome *whatever might happen* while hiking in natural environments was implicitly connected to traditional ideals of daring and *manly* deeds (Gurholt, 2008a).

In this context, *Askeladden* was explicitly promoted as a role model of enculturation – what Germans refer to as *Bildung* and Norwegians as *dannelse* (Løvlie, 2002) – of upbringing and growth into a culture coupled with aspects of formal education/schooling (Gurholt, 2008b). In German/Norwegian Bildung literature, as well as in pragmatism (Dewey, 1938), phenomenology and hermeneutics (Gadamer, 1960/2004), the complex concept of *experience* is regarded as vital to understanding human interactive existence and growth in the world.

The Norwegian *verb å erfare* and the noun *erfaringer* (in German, *erfahren/Erfahrungen*) are rooted in the German word fahren, meaning to venture out and experience. The noun ending *ung/-ing* refers to processes and is associated with ideas of going somewhere and through something, exploring, and getting to know by getting out, and also with enduring, suffering and becoming well travelled/experienced. Hence, *erfare/erfaringer* is associated with the acquisition of knowledge, skills and insights through processes that entail engaging in asking, searching, probing and testing – all actions that may involve challenges and pain. Recognition and reflection are seen as fruits of experience.

Accordingly, *erfaringer* implies the kind of knowledge, skills and wisdom about individuals and their natural and cultural surroundings that can be gained only through participation in life situations and contexts. *Dannelse* may thus be understood as the embodied sum of our lifelong personal and immediate experiences of interacting with the world, even though we may no longer remember what we were struggling to learn or were initially affected by. A common characteristic of everything that has to be learned through intense cultural activity about hiking and survival in nature, about being too cold, about clothing and other aspects eventually comes to be seen as purely *natural*.

From its inception, the concept of *vegledning* (i.e. trip leadership or mentoring) means self-reliant dwelling and wayfaring in uncultivated nature over several days as part of a small heterogeneous team. This team respects democratic principles of dialogue and decision-making involving both students and a mentor/teacher. Among its obligations is to leave no traces. Although these groups are expected to encounter unforeseen challenges, including physical danger, they are expected to avoid unnecessary and fatal risks. The goal is to deepen each individual's understanding of and respect for nature through a combination of inquisitive exploration and first-hand experience/*erfaringer*. Fostering the participants' confidence in their ability to be safe – and feel at home – in nature was the explicit formulated goal, expressed as becoming a *kjentmann* – someone who is *Bewandert* (i.e. well-travelled/experienced) (Faarlund, 1974). These concepts refer to someone who has achieved a profound familiarity with nature, and thus is capable of finding solutions to whatever conditions and events she/he may encounter.

Experience as opplevelse: condensed moments of aesthetic appreciation of nature

The English word experience has a slightly different meaning than the German/Norwegian equivalents, as it further translates into *Erlebnis/opplevelse*, emphasising the individual subjective feelings. *Opplevelse*, which recently also translates into adventure, has become a catchphrase of our time. It is regularly introduced in new contexts that broadly refer to moments of intense feeling, e.g. for nature. In Norwegian contexts the concept of *opplevelse* is frequently replacing *efaring*, indicating a potential cultural shift from an emphasis on formative experiences of nature, and nature literacy, towards placing a premium on vivid moments when nature adventurers feel fully alive.

The German philosopher Hans-Georg Gadamer (1900–2002) provided a helpful exegesis of the word Erlebnis. He asserted that it first appeared as a noun in the 1870s to connote 'both the immediacy, which precedes all interpretation, reworking, and communication, and merely offers a starting point for interpretation' (Gadamer, 1960/2004, p. 53), and that *Erlebnis* became a common term in the early years of the 20th century. It represented a response to Romantic biographical writers' need for a new vocabulary that could express their deepest thoughts and feelings, and their antipathy to the cold rationalism of the Enlightenment, industrialisation and the rigidity of bourgeois lifestyles. In consequence, *Erlebnis/opplevelse* referred to something experienced in the first person.

The concepts of *Erlebnis* and adventure were also explicitly connected (Simmel, 2011). Thus, adventure was revealed as an aspect of life that must be sought out, and can be experienced in many ways, including in everyday life. Adventure, Simmel asserted, signifies a discontinuity, a form of experience that lifts the individual out of the ordinary course of life creating a sense of being present in a singular moment when time disappears. In fact, life itself is as a form of adventure. Lives are shaped by a random process of lucky and unlucky events in which the future is always uncertain.

Over time, the words *opplevelse* and adventure have begun to signify an individual's immediate impressions that resonate with profound and comprehensive meaning.

The European/Norwegian cultural perspective of educative adventures/*friluftsliv* seems broader than the Anglo-American concept of outdoor adventure education, which frequently links itself solely to potentially life-endangering physical risk (Mortlock, 1984; Miles & Priest, 1990; Wurdinger, 1994; Roberts, 2012).

Bridging adventurous and nature-friendly outlooks

The introduction of Nansen and *Askeladden* as metaphors for educational work with children and young people in the Norwegian context exemplifies the paradoxical, ambivalent and possibly irreconcilable contradictions and tensions that exist within adventurous and nature-friendly wayfaring and dwelling as they are currently conceived and practised. While educators emphasise seeking out and cultivating adventure in the sense of (physical) challenges and (life-threatening) risks as values or goals in themselves, they also accept calculated risk with a possible catastrophic outcome, which Mortlock (1984) calls misadventure. This effort is at odds with their belief that exploratory hikes into natural landscapes form an inseparable, existential and necessary part of what it means to live and be(come) conversant with the world. Seeking out situations that endanger one's life for the purpose of deepening the sense that one is alive and exists is quite different from developing an understanding that curiosity, unpredictability, and expectation of sudden events and challenges are necessary conditions of human life, growth and maturity.

Nansen exemplifies adventurers thinking of themselves as conquerors. He was well prepared by possessing the best know-how, equipment and skiing ability of his time. He tested his capacity to perform manly deeds by pitting his courage, strength, powers of endurance and character against the forces of nature. Nansen's venture to cross Greenland had more at stake than acquiring true wisdom, moral improvement, and expanding and maturing a human mind. It was a scientific expedition, and his entry into a worldwide race to be first to cross a boundary in a way that by definition could never be repeated. He was willing to risk his life. However, in achieving this goal he performed a unique heroic deed and won worldwide immortal fame.

Askeladden of traditional Norwegian folk tales represents another aspect of contemporary *friluftsliv*. He is a roaming vagabond and inquisitive adventurer, eternally on the move along the paths of life, ready to explore whatever comes his way and try his luck. *Askeladden* issues all kinds of challenges, and tests his courage, strength and endurance against unforeseen events, trolls and other forces of nature. He is someone who seeks out trials continuously, and cleverly overcomes all challenges that he encounters. In general, all goes well for him. By using his heart and brain, wisdom, creativity and good humour, he makes use of the forces of life and nature, never risking his life on purpose. On the contrary, he copes with danger again and again, while at the same time gaining new wisdom, happiness and appropriate rewards. Frequently he shouts out *I found it! I got it!* In sum, *Askeladden* is an adventurer who recognises the paradoxes and tensions in life, and relies on his strengths, but also on his luck. *Askeladden* can be seen as someone who accepts the existence of unknown uncertainties and also dangers, and lives his life as if these dangers are known, finite and surmountable.

As applied in *friluftsliv*-pedagogy, the ethos of richness in life with simple means expresses an attitude towards life and nature that combines ideas of environmental awareness, roaming in uncultivated areas, and openness to potential adventures that may occur around the next bend in the path or beyond the far blue distant hills.

The Norwegian *eventyr*/folk tale theme also suggests another perspective. All adventures have a beginning and an end. Each encounter with a different reality – which any adventure involves by definition – alters the adventurer's experience and narrative. Returning home, they can reflect on where they have been and what they have done; whom and what they have encountered, seen and heard; and how the wayfaring has affected them personally. After completing this process of self-reflection, they may plot a new course and seek out new adventures (Becker, 2008).

Closing remarks

The designation of national years that celebrate *Friluftsliv for all* involves paradoxes. While these popular campaigns may show the fertility of Norway's culture of closeness to nature, they also suggest that *friluftsliv* is under siege. Notwithstanding the power of its ideals of richness in life with simple means, the Act of Public Access, and that *friluftsliv* explicitly has been part of national school curriculum since the 1970s, one of its competitors, leisure consumption, is growing at an even faster rate than everyday consumption (Aall, Klepp, Engeset, Skuland & Støa, 2011).

In closing, this Norwegian-inspired comparative perspective, I would argue that instead of establishing dichotomies between concepts such as adventure and nature awareness, curiosity and risk, certainty and uncertainty, male and female, these should be considered as a series of dialectical relationships of *erfaringer–opplevelse*. Each one defines its partner. A nuanced style of understanding can reveal inconsistencies, complexities, and new understandings, and at the same time generate negotiations and compromises to handle the tensions inherent in human existence and development. Correspondingly, outdoor educators could seek practices allowing young people to become nature literate and care for nature, and at the same time feel fully alive.

References

Aall, C., Klepp, I.G., Engeset, A.G., Skuland, S.E. & Støa, E. (2011). Leisure and sustainable development in Norway: Part of the solution and the problem. *Leisure Studies, 30*(4), 453–476.

Becker, P. (2008). The curiosity of Ulysses and its consequences: In search of an educational myth of the adventure. In P. Becker & J. Schirp (Eds.) *Other Ways of Learning* (pp. 199–210). Marburg, Norway: BSJ.

Breivik, G. (1978). To tradisjoner i norsk *friluftsliv*. In G. Breivik & H. Løvmo (Eds.) *Friluftsliv fra Fridtjof Nansen til våre dager* (pp. 7–16). Oslo: Universitetsforlaget.

Dewey, J. (1938). *Experience and Education.* New York: Kappa Delta Phi.

Faarlund, N. (1974). *Hva-Hvordan-Hvorfor-Friluftsliv.* Oslo: Norges idrettshøgskole.

Gadamer, H.-G. (1960/2004). *Truth and Method.* London, New York: Connection.

Gåsdal, O. (2007). Norwegians and *Friluftsliv*: Are we unique? In B. Henderson & N. Vikander (Eds.) *Nature First. Outdoor Life the Friluftsliv Way* (pp. 75–82). Toronto: Natural Heritage Books.

Gurholt, K.P. (2008a). Norwegian *Friluftsliv* and ideals of becoming an 'educated man'. *Journal of Adventure Education and Outdoor Learning, 8*(1), 55–70.

Gurholt, K.P. (2008b). Norwegian *Friluftsliv* as *Bildung*: A critical review. In P. Becker & J. Schirp (Eds.) *Other Ways of Learning* (pp. 131–155). Marburg: BSJ.

Gurholt, K.P. (2010). Eventyrlig pedagogikk: *Friluftsliv* som dannelsesferd. In K. Steinsholt & K.P. Gurholt (Eds.) *Aktive liv* (pp. 175–204). Trondheim: Tapir Akademisk Forlag.

Gurholt, K.P. (2014). Joy of nature, *friluftsliv*-education and self: Combining narrative and cultural-ecological approaches to environmental sustainability. *Journal of Adventure Education and Outdoor Learning, 14*(3), 233–246.

Gustavsson, B. (2001). Dannelse som reise og eventyr. In T. Kvernbekk (Ed.) *Pedagogikk og laererprofesjonalitet* (pp. 31–48). Oslo: Universitetsforlaget.

Ibsen, H. (1859/1991). *Paa Vidderne*. In *Samlede verker 2* (pp. 479–483). Oslo: Den norske bokklubben.

Ingold, T. (2011). *Staying Alive. Essays on Movement, Knowledge, and Description*. New York: Routledge.

Kvaløy, S. (2007). The Ash-Lad: Classical figure of Norwegian ecophilosophy. In B. Henderson & N. Vikander (Eds.) *Nature First. Outdoor Life the Friluftsliv Way* (pp. 83–89). Toronto: Natural Heritage Books.

Løvlie, L. (2002). The promise of *Bildung*. *Journal of Philosophy of Education, 36*(3), 467–486.

Miles, J. & Priest, S. (Eds.) (1990). *Adventure Education*. State College, PA: Venture Publishing, Inc.

Ministry of the Environment (2000). *Friluftsliv: ein veg til høgare livskvalitet*. St.meld., *39* 2000–01. Oslo.

Ministry of the Environment (2013). *Nasjonal strategi for et aktivt friluftsliv 2014–2020*. Oslo.

Mortlock, C. (1984). *The Adventure Alternative*. Milnthorpe, Cumbria: Cicerone Press.

Næss, A. (1976/1989). *Økologi, samfunn og livsstil*. Oslo: Universitetsforlaget. Trans. D. Rothenberg, *Ecology, Community and Lifestyle*. Cambridge: Cambridge University Press.

Nansen, F. (1922). *Friluftsliv*. In *Den norske turistforenings årbok 1922* (pp. 3–5). Oslo: Den norske turistforening.

Pedersen, K. (2003). Discourses on nature and gender identities. In K. Pedersen & A. Viken (Eds.) *Nature and Identity* (pp. 121–150). Kristiansand: Høgskoleforlaget.

Roberts, J.W. (2012). *Beyond Learning by Doing: Theoretical Currents in Experiential Education*. New York: Routledge.

Simmel, G. (1911). *The Adventure*. Retrieved from: http://condor.depaul.edu/dweinste/theory/adventure.html.

Skår, M., Gundersen, V., Bischoff, A., Follo, G., Pareliussen, I., Stordahl, G. & Tordsson, B. (2014). *Barn og natur. Nasjonal spørreundersøkelse*. Lillehammer: Norsk Institutt for Naturforskning.

Statistics Norway (2009). *Mosjon, friluftsliv og kulturaktiviteter. Levekårsundersøkelsene fra 1997 til 2007*. Oslo: Statistisk Sentralbyrå.

Statistics Norway (2012). *Tidenes skifter: Tidsbruk 1971–2010*. Oslo: Statistisk Sentralbyrå.

Svarstad, H. (2010). Why hiking? Rationality and reflexivity within three categories of meaning construction. *Journal of Leisure Research, 42*(1), 91–110.

Wurdinger, S.D. (1994). *Philosophical Issues in Adventure Education*. Dubuque, IA: Kendall/Hunt Publishing Company.

Acknowledgements

I am grateful to Prof. Em. Dr Peter Becker, Marburg, and the Transcultural European Outdoor Studies joint master's degree programme.

29

Turistika activities and games, dramaturgy, and the Czech outdoor experience

Andrew J. Martin

MASSEY UNIVERSITY

Ivana Turčová

CHARLES UNIVERSITY

Jan Neuman

CHARLES UNIVERSITY

The Czech educator Comenius (Jan Amos Komenský, 1592–1670) wrote about outdoor experiences and games some 400 years ago. His work can be understood as a basis for the roots of experiential education (*výchova prožitkem*) and education in nature (Spinka, 1943). Comenius believed in educating the whole person and linking the ideals of the Greek holistic philosophy of education, *kalokagathia*, involving educating the mind, body and soul through experiences in nature using all the senses. He also believed in the use of games, play and travelling in achieving educational outcomes particularly for improving youth self-esteem and interpersonal relationships (Comenius, 1632/1907).

Eastern Europe and Scandinavia's (*frilufstliv*) education in nature traditions are strongly connected to a *journey* (Henderson & Vikander, 2007). While the English term outdoor education is accepted in Czech as *výchova v přírodě*, its translation as education in nature involves *turistika* activities defined as travelling for fun and playing games with the aim of learning about nature (Guth-Jarkovský, 1917/2003). The original form of *turistika* involved active movement on foot (i.e. walking, hiking), but now includes cycling, canoeing, skiing and mountaineering. *Turistika* also involves other outdoor and cultural activities (e.g. local history, art, music and entertainment, mushroom and berry picking). While some tourism definitions involve travelling away from local environments (Mason, 2003), *turistika* is culturally unique and specific to the Czech context and environment (Turčová, Martin & Neuman, 2005).

Scouting and *stays in nature* connected with camping can also be included as *turistika* (Guth-Jarkovský, 1917/2003). The tramping movement (Waic & Kössl, 1994), involving camping or hiking at weekends, is also a particular Czech historical and cultural phenomenon. Tramping was influenced by the German romantic youth movement *Wandervogel*, British Scouting, American Woodcraft and the American culture of the Wild West (Seton, 1917). It provided young people opportunities for freedom in nature and to protest against imposed society rules and restrictions. Tramping, as with scouting, developed its own culture, slang, songs, clothes, flag, anthem, rituals, magazines, literature, sports (especially canoeing and kayaking) and small settlements (i.e. cottage colonies). These special settlements, with wooden cabins and simple places for camping with a campfire, were built in beautiful natural environments especially near rivers around Prague and other bigger towns. Activities were adapted to the specific conditions of the country and are part of the creation of an indigenous Czech culture of *turistika* activities (Martin, Turčová & Neuman, 2007). Tramping traditions are still alive and popular including many unique tramping songs.

In this chapter, we discuss the historical development, cultural differences, educational applications and contexts of outdoor sports and activities within the Czech Republic. When studying these connections it is important to consider that Czech outdoor history has been externally influenced by the country's geographical position in the centre of Europe. The advantages of this location have been business, educational and cultural connections, but the disadvantages have been the wars and political fights that have taken place. The recent history is also linked to the Velvet Revolution led by Václav Havel.

The Turistický club and Sokol movement

Czechoslovakia was founded in 1918, and separate Czech and Slovak Republics were later formed in 1993. In the 19th century, however, the main influence on activities in nature in the Czech Lands (*Země koruny české*) was the rapid development of *Sokol* (the biggest physical education movement, founded in 1862) and the *Turistický* club (*Klub českých turistů* – the official title of the Club of Czech Tourists, founded in 1888 by Vojtěch Náprstek). *Sokol* founder Dr Miroslav Tyrš, professor of aesthetics at Charles University, advocated for not only physical activities, but organised trips outdoors to significant places representing Czech history and culture. These trips were motivated by patriotism following years of Austrian Habsburg rule (1740–1914) and German influence. Gradually, outdoor games and physical activity were included into the trip programmes along with walking and social pastimes (Martin, 2011).

British influence linked to the Scouting Movement of Baden-Powell spread across Western Europe and further influenced Czech outdoor activities at the beginning of the 20th century. Stays in nature in the Czech context are historically related to the *Sokol* movement, camping and outdoor activities. Going outdoors and undertaking physical activities was a framework for bringing together groups of Czech nationals. Initially the *Turistický* club was instrumental in developing a range of previously traditional *turistika* activities. By the end of the 19th century, due to British and German influence, there was also a rapid development of outdoor sports including rowing, water sports, skiing and cycling, which further influenced the separation of sports from *turistika* activities. Newer types of *turistika* activities started to be formed using bikes, canoes and skis.

In the 1930s, *Sokol* focused on the development of physical activities and stays in nature (e.g. walking trips, camping and camps on the move). Summer camps involving *turistika* activities usually moved from one campsite to another. These activities also led to building artificial obstacles (i.e. today's sport playgrounds and ropes courses). These developments occurred despite the increasing influence of German fascism prior to the Second World War. Criteria for awarding qualifications were established. Exams consisted of theory, professional knowledge (e.g. giving signals, orientation, knots, archery, grenade and boomerang throwing, camp works and constructions), learning about nature, camping, swimming, games, physical education and first aid. Other requirements were public service and practice in leading camps (Martin *et al.*, 2007).

Outdoor sports and games

The Czechs, under Austria-Habsburg rule, were active in outdoor sports inspired by France, the UK and North America. Jiří Rössler Ořovský, a businessman and diplomat, founded many sport clubs in the Czech lands, often earlier than in the West (e.g. cycling, yachting, canoeing, skiing and rowing), and also helped found the Czech Olympic Committee.

In the late 1800s, education in nature activities were also organised by teachers, and the Club for Games of Czech Youth (1892) was formed to create new games in nature for young people. In the 1920s and 1930s pedagogical reform introduced experiential education into schools. In 1934 professor F.H. Stuerm visited Czechoslovakia from the USA and praised the new approaches in pedagogy informed through discussion with John Dewey (Stuerm, 1938). *Wandervogel* and the countryside schools of H. Lietze also influenced the German part of Czechoslovakia. For example, pupils of the Metzner Free School in Litoměřice (1928–1938) made trips to nature and undertook outdoor activities encouraging a balance of physical and intellectual character development (Kasper, 2008).

Liga lesní moudrosti (Woodcraft Indians)

Woodcraft, inspired by American Indians, was founded and led by E.T. Seton, writer and illustrator of nature science books. The Czech promoter of Woodcraft was the secondary school teacher Miloš Seifert through the *League for Outdoor Education – Wisdom of the Forest* [*Liga pro výchovu v přírodě – Moudrost lesa*] (1924). He connected the movement with Slavic traditions, which are still popular and have deep roots in the Czech lands today.

Junák (Scouting)

The Czech Scouting organisation in the Czech lands, *Junák*, founded in 1914 by A.B. Svojsík, unsuccessfully tried to connect with *Sokol*'s stays in nature, and was formed independently. Svojsík found support from politicians, educators and doctors, who stressed the need for education in nature rather than the Baden-Powell origins of discipline connected with service to God and the King. Czech scouts also initiated a new type of tent with a wooden base, and many original games and competitions (Svojsík, 1912). Jaroslav Foglar (1907–1999), through his work as a long-term Scouting leader and writer, is recognised as having influenced through his stories of adventure at least three generations' relationship to nature, camping and Scouting (Jirásek, 2007). He led the development and chronicled the history of *Junák* in Czechoslovakia for more than sixty years, specifically summer camps from 1925–1985. Scouting summer camps (*tábory*) involved children and young adults spending two to three weeks living in nature, playing games and learning outdoor skills (i.e. *turistika,* physical/sport, creative arts and environment activities) (Neuman, Turčová & Martin, 2007). His book *Boys from the Beavers' River* [*Hoši od Bobří řeky*] (Foglar, 1937) was about friendship through exploring and having adventures in nature. In 1938, Foglar started his cartoon serial, 'Swift Arrows' [*Rychlé šípy*], which most Czech children and adults have read. His educational methods were progressive, but often clashed with traditional Scouting, which often got Foglar into trouble with other Scout leaders (Jirásek, Martin & Turčová, 2009).

Of note is the contribution of Eduard Štorch, who with the support of T.G. Masaryk, who was the first President of Czechoslovakia, rented a piece of land on the Prague Libeň Island in

1926, which was almost a wilderness at that time. He built an outdoor school for youth education with a focus on the concept of *eubiotics* (in Greek eu = good; bios = life), life in balance with nature. Štorch (1929) organised trips, encouraging learning by exploring local history, archaeological and work opportunities. Unfortunately, he had to leave Libeň in 1934 due to other interests.

Outdoor development since the Second World War

The development of outdoor sports and *turistika* activities was interrupted by both world wars, but was quickly restored upon their conclusion. During the Second World War, physical education, sport and scout organisations were dictated by German occupation, which resulted in many members of these organisations working for the resistance, and subsequently dying.

In 1945, organisations that had existed before the war started up again, including the *Turistický klub*, *Sokol* and *Junák*. However, when the Soviet/Czechoslovak communist regime took power in 1948, channels with the outside world were limited for the next forty years, and organisations such as the Scout Movement were banned (Martin *et al.*, 2007).

Nevertheless, outdoor sports and *turistika* activities were incorporated into the school curriculum. Schools in nature provided opportunities for children in cities to live in nature for a week or two studying normal lessons involving education about nature alongside outdoor activities. Many schools also incorporated ski trips and summer courses into their school-related activities.

The Soviet influence began to spread throughout all spheres of life, but tramping and Scouting were never completely restrained (Neuman, 2001a). 'Walls have ears, but trees, rivers and mountains do not!' (Martin *et al.*, 2007, p. 205). *Turistika* activities in nature throughout Czech history provided opportunities to continue nationalistic attachment to the Czech culture and language even when under the influence of oppressive outside regimes.

An increased focus on competitive outdoor sport (e.g. canoeing), performance levels and qualifications systems grew. A Department of *Turistika*, Outdoor Sports and Outdoor Education, was formed in the Faculty of Physical Education and Sport (FPES) at Charles University Prague in 1953 at the first Physical Education Institute of Higher Education, then from 1958 at FPES (Neuman, 2001b). Its programmes integrated sport and *turistika* activities with group experiences, games and learning about nature, and strongly influenced teaching in schools through new outdoor activities added to the curriculum.

Development of these concepts was influenced by the political regime since opinions that did not correspond with socialistic views were suppressed. In 1968, the year of the Prague Spring, there was a brief period when more democratic liberal activities resurfaced, but soon the country was occupied again by the Russian Army. However, from 1970 to 1976, within the Socialist Youth Union organisation, new experimental and creative forms of educational courses in nature emerged, called *Gymnasion*, despite the impact of the Communist regime.

The outdoors since 1989

Since the fall of communism and during the Velvet Revolution of November 1989, organisations have reconnected recent activities with Czech traditions that had flourished prior to 1948. Tramping and all forms of *turistika* (i.e. foot, bikes, canoes and skis) remain popular, and small informal groups spend weekends at campsites often working with forest administration on environmental projects. Family groups continue the traditions of log cabin sites, with people leaving the cities at weekends and during holiday periods to spend time in forest cottages.

Figure 29.1   Turistický club marked paths

Many people also continue traditions of mushroom and berry picking, along with playing games while walking in the many forests of the Czech Republic. Walking and cycling in the countryside are made easier by an extensive network of well-maintained and signed paths, which link forests, villages and towns. The system of signed paths is unique in the Czech Republic. The first path was signed by Vojtěch Náprstek (founder of the *Turistický* club). Signs have four colours: red, yellow, green and blue (see Figure 29.1), and each colour has meaning related to the type of path. The same system is used today and *Turistický* club trained volunteers look after the signed paths and sign new ones.

Other institutions are developing more formal education in nature programmes (e.g. schools, government, youth, environmental, commercial organisations). Among the most influential institutions in this field is the FPES at Charles University, Prague as well as FPC (Faculty of Physical Culture), Department of Recreology at Palacky University, and the Department of Outdoor Sports, Masaryk University in Brno. Participation in these outdoor and physical education programmes remains compulsory at all universities and schools today.

Dramaturgy

Vacation School Lipnice

Vacation School Lipnice (*Prázdninová Škola Lipnice*, VSL, founded in 1977) is a non-profit organisation formed as a result of long-term effort to establish educational value-based courses in nature. Initially it was funded by the Central Socialist Youth Organisation as a necessity dictated by the socialist regime. Dr Allan Gintel, a psychologist, established leadership of a team of about twenty instructors (Turčová, Neuman & Martin, 2003; Martin, Franc & Zounková, 2004).

Today VSL has about a hundred active members-volunteers coming from all over the Czech Republic, Slovakia and other countries. The aim of the VSL courses is to provide ways for personal growth, connection to nature and awareness of cultural heritage using the *dramaturgy* approach to course design (Martin, Leberman & Neill, 2002). The term dramaturgy comes from the sphere of theatre, film and TV, and means the art of theatrical production (Shantz, 1998). Instructors *choreograph* the course by planning, selecting and then ordering individual activities with the goal of maximising the pedagogical, educational, recreational and other course aims (Martin *et al.*, 2004). Courses bring together body-and-mind challenging adventure activities; the distinct elements of creative art, music and drama workshops; group discussions; and reflections.

Since 1991 VSL has been a member of Outward Bound. In 1993 VSL founded Outward Bound Czech Republic (*Česká cesta*), which offers corporate team-building courses using the dramaturgy methodology of VSL and traditional Outward Bound activities (VSL, 2013). International courses have also been developed using these methods (Martin, 2001a; Martin *et al.*, 2004; Kubala, 2007; Martin, 2011). Kudláček, Bocarro, Jirásek and Hanuš (2009) highlighted how these methods and courses have also been adapted to be inclusive for people who are physically or mentally challenged.

Krouwel (1994) suggested that the VSL dramaturgy methods and balance of creative games offered a different approach to facilitating outdoor and experiential education programmes. 'These days the outdoors is quite "old hat" to many people . . . other challenges, especially "real ones", can only help personal and team development' (pp. 141–142). Krouwel (2000) argued that the VSL courses presented a more holistic approach than traditional physical activity-based outdoor courses. This view was supported by Zapletal (quoted in Holec, 1994), a Czech educator, who had reviewed education literature from around the world and yet nowhere I found such a perfectly worked out educational system for young people, standing at the threshold of adulthood, as the one, which Vacation School Lipnice created over the last few years' (p. 145). Participant evaluations have highlighted the benefit of this holistic approach when applied successfully in international settings involving open enrolment (Martin, 2001a; Martin *et al.*, 2002) and management development courses (Leberman & Martin, 2005).

Dramaturgy methods

VSL and the FPES have their philosophical roots linked to *kalokagathia*, and balancing mind, body and soul experiences. The combination of sport, *turistika* and creative activities has been foremost in the development of Czech education in nature programmes over the past thirty years. Dramaturgy is characterised by the intertwining of a variety of social, physical, creative and reflective/emotional games and activities in nature, and is carefully sequenced using the *dramaturgy wave* (Martin, 2001b) with associated peaks and troughs (see Figure 29.2). A significant feature is the course intensity, with little free time for participants. The idea of integrating waves is both a diagnostic and planning tool. At each stage of the course instructors reflect upon the balance of the waves, so that one does not override another.

A metaphor for this process comes from waves crashing on a beach, with the bigger waves swamping the smaller ones. Similarly, the physical activity 'wave' in traditional outdoor courses tends to dominate. Faarlund (2009) characterised current outdoor activity trends by the tendency towards using nature as a sparring partner where environmental aims are often swamped by the outdoor sports or outdoor pursuits experiences (Kvasnička, 2009). Dramaturgy aims to balance and integrate the impact and intensity of each wave. The traditional adventure wave (Schoel, Prouty & Radcliffe, 1988) sequenced a series of mainly outdoor physical activities, which were first briefed and then debriefed. However, the dramaturgy wave offers not just a physical wave. Parts of the programme include activities previously not associated with outdoor adventure activities. For example, strategic, socio-psychological, and semi-structured games are integrated with musical, dramatic role play, and creative fine arts games, which are all an essential part of the course design (Martin *et al.*, 2004; Martin & Krouwel, 2006). The key elements of this experiential education process are a holistic approach to course design that integrates activities involving reflection; the learning environment, which is safe and creates a positive and supportive atmosphere that allows participants to play; the range of instructor facilitation methods; and a diverse group of participants (Martin, 2001a).

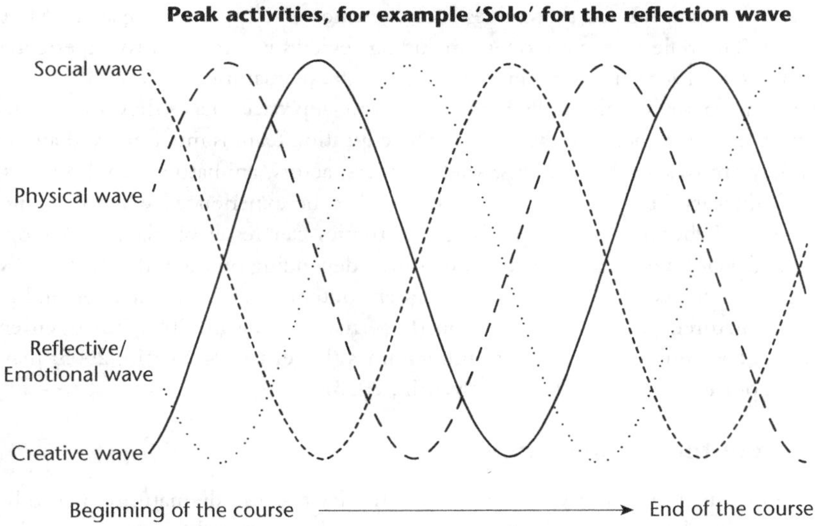

Peak activities, for example 'Solo' for the reflection wave

Social wave

Physical wave

Reflective/
Emotional wave

Creative wave

Beginning of the course ———————————————→ End of the course

Figure 29.2 The dramaturgy wave

Source: Martin, Franc and Zounková (2004, p. 25), Martin (2011, p. 73)

VSL has been an important organisation in the development of education in nature programmes alongside scouting, woodcraft, *Sokol* camps, YMCA camps, summer or winter youth camps, and obligatory courses at all types of school. VSL courses have also become well known in the Czech Republic thanks to books of these games in nature, *Zlatý Fond Her I & II* (Golden Fund of Games, 1990, 1998). The application of dramaturgy integrates challenges and provides opportunities for creative programming practice, the development of experiences involving all the senses, and a more holistic approach to experiential courses as advocated by the Czech educators, Comenius (Spinka, 1943) and Foglar (Jirásek, 2007).

Games and play

Games can be seen as a playground for acting out interactions and evaluating reactions in different outdoor natural or urban environments, and many games are designed specifically for indoor settings. This play stage, or exploration and experimentation stage of the adventure experience, is important in developing peak experiences (Maslow, 1962) and a state of flow (Csikszentmihalyi, 1991). Fun and play are also important in removing social barriers and stress, and increasing intrinsic motivation and relaxation. This importance is often reinforced during activities that involve psychological and/or perceived physical risk, and push participants to extend their comfort zone (Leberman & Martin, 2002). Leberman and Martin indicated that participants may not produce the most learning when pushed out of their comfort zones. The dramaturgy wave helps push comfort zones in an atmosphere of physical, social and emotional safety, as this pushing of comfort zones is related to the individual's perceived risk of any activity. Each individual's perception of risk is, however, different and may be physical, social, psychological or spiritual (Dickson, Chapman & Hurrell, 2000), an important factor that is acknowledged when considering programme design.

Framing games in fantasy and the use of play are important elements in these programmes in achieving educational outcomes (Martin, 2011). 'The wide range of powerful learning activities "let the mountains speak for themselves" for a greater variety of participants' (Martin *et al.*, 2004, p. 20). The reflection component including reviews is important to experiential education (Schoel *et al.*, 1988) and is integrated as part of the dramaturgy.

While some games are physically hard, the holistic approach means they are integrated with the *soft* and creative elements of the course. The education team is much more than instructors. At times they are task or drill masters, safety officers, actors, animators, play leaders, therapists or group facilitators. However, instructors do need to be experienced when pushing people's comfort zones (Leberman & Martin, 2002). Activities can result in play, recreation, adventure/drama, development or therapeutic outcomes, depending on the individual. Every participant brings his/her past experiences, so subsequent outcomes are individualised and cannot be predicted. Structured post-course reflection (Leberman & Martin, 2004) for open enrolment courses as well as outdoor management programmes (Leberman & Martin, 2005) may assist in reinforcing course outcomes (Rhodes & Martin, 2013).

The Czech outdoor experience

The indigenous nature of the Czech *turistika* activities and the dramaturgy methods of creative course design have attracted recent attention in international outdoor journals (Martin, 2011), particularly in the research based text *Outdoor and Experiential Learning* (Martin *et al.*, 2004), which describes the dramaturgy methods and activities in more detail. Historically, *turistika* activities have been developed through the *Turistický* club, *Sokol* movement and *Junák* (Scouting). Czech traditions of stays in nature, tramping and summer camps have added to the rich array of specific Czech cultural and educational activities in nature. These *turistika* activities have continued to develop during periods of oppression, and have provided opportunities to preserve the Czech culture and language.

The Czech outdoor methods and activities provide examples of the approaches and lessons that can be found in traditions that are currently under-represented in the English-language-dominated outdoor experiential education literature (Martin, 2011). The ever expanding field of adventure and outdoor experiential learning worldwide needs to increasingly embrace differing ideas of education in nature from other diverse geographical areas. The Czech methods go beyond traditional interpretations of outdoor adventure training allowing for the integration and balance of physical, social, creative, and reflective games and activities. The concepts provide opportunities for creative programming practice and applications to develop more holistic outdoor and experiential courses for youth and adults globally.

References

Comenius, J.E. (1632/1907). *The Great Didactic of John Amos Comenius/Translated into English and Edited with Biographical, Historical and Critical Introductions by M.W. Keatinge* (2nd edn). London: Black.
Csikszentmihalyi, M. (1991). *Flow: The Psychology of Optimal Experience*. New York: Harper Perennial.
Dickson, T.J., Chapman, J. & Hurrell, M. (2000). Risk in the outdoors: The perception, the appeal, the reality. *Australian Journal of Outdoor Education, 4*(2), 10–17.
Faarlund, N. (2009). Outdoor activities: Time for a paradigm change! In I. Turčová & A. Martin (Eds.) *Proceedings of the 4th International Mountain and Outdoor Sports Conference, 24–26 November 2008. Hrubá Skála, Czech Republic* (pp. 61–64). Prague: International Young Nature Friends.
Foglar, J. (1937). *Hoši od Bobří řeky*. Praha: Kobes.
Guth-Jarkovský, J. (1917/2003). *Turistika. Turistický katechismus*. Praha: Baset.
Henderson, R. & Vikander, N. (Eds.) *Nature First: Outdoor Life the Friluftsliv Way*. Toronto: Natural Heritage.
Holec, O. (1994). Dramaturgie. In *Outward Bound Czech Republic: Prázdninová Škola Lipnice, Instruktorský slabikář* (pp. 37–50). Prague: Nadace Rozvoje Občanské Společnosti.

Hrkal, J. & Hanuš, R. (Ed.) (1998). *Zlatý Fond Her II.* Prague: Portál.

Jirásek, I. (Ed.) (2007). *Fenomén Foglar.* Praha: Prázdninová škola Lipnice.

Jirásek, I., Martin, A.J. & Turcová, I. (2009). A symbol of games and play: Jaroslav Foglar's influence on Czech education in nature. *Horizons, 45*(Spring), 28–32.

Kasper, T. (2008). *Dějiny německého hnutí mládeže v českých zemích – analýza, prameny, interpretace.* Liberec: TUL.

Krouwel, W. (1994). The Czech way to personal development. *Training Officer, 30*(5), 140–142.

Krouwel, W. (2000). An investigation into the past, current and potential role of outdoor development (and particularly) outdoor management development practice in Britain in the light of practice at Vacation School Lipnice and Ceska Cesta in the Czech Republic. Unpublished master's thesis, University of Lancaster, UK.

Kubala, P. (2007). Intertouch. In I. Turčová, D. Bartůněk & A.J. Martin (Eds.) *Proceedings of the 3rd International Mountain and Outdoor Sports Conference 23–26 November. Hrubá Skála, Czech Republic.* Prague: International Young Nature Friends IYNF.

Kudláček, M., Bocarro, J., Jirásek, I. & Hanuš, R. (2009). The Czech way of inclusion through an experiential education framework. *Journal of Experiential Education, 32*(1), 14–27.

Kvasnička, T. (2009). Equipment and changing outdoor culture in the Czech Republic. *Anthropology of East Europe Review, 25*(1), 53–63.

Leberman, S.I. & Martin, A.J. (2002). Does pushing comfort zones produce the most learning? *Australian Journal of Outdoor Education, 7*(1), 71–81.

Leberman, S.I. & Martin, A.J. (2004). Enhancing transfer of learning through post-course reflection. *Journal of Adventure Education and Outdoor Learning, 4*(2), 173–184.

Leberman, S.I. & Martin, A.J. (2005). Applying dramaturgy to management course design. *Journal of Management Education, 29*(2), 319–332.

Martin, A.J. (2001a). Dramaturgy: An holistic approach to outdoor education. *Australian Journal of Outdoor Education, 5*(2), 34–41.

Martin, A.J. (2001b). The dramaturgy wave. *Horizons, 15,* 26–29.

Martin, A.J. (2011). The dramaturgy approach to education in nature. *Journal of Adventure Education and Outdoor Leadership, 11*(1), 67–82.

Martin, A.J. & Krouwel, W. (2006). Creative course design: Reflection on a workshop for trainers. *Horizons, 33,* 6–9.

Martin, A.J., Franc, D. & Zounková, D. (2004). *Outdoor and Experiential Learning.* Aldershot, UK: Gower.

Martin, A.J., Leberman, S.I. & Neill, J.T. (2002). Dramaturgy as a method for experiential program design. *Journal of Experiential Education, 25*(1), 196–206.

Martin, A.J., Turčová, I. & Neuman, J. (2007). The Czech outdoor experience: Turistika and connections to Friluftsliv. In R. Henderson & N. Vikender (Eds.) *Nature First: Outdoor Life the Friluftsliv Way* (pp. 197–208). Toronto: Natural Heritage.

Maslow, A.H. (1962). *Toward a Psychology of Being.* Princeton, NJ: Van Nostrand.

Mason, P. (2003). *Tourism Impacts: Planning and Management.* Oxford: Butterworth Heinemann.

Neuman, J. (2001a). Introduction to outdoor education in the Czech Republic. In A. Nilsson (Ed.) *Outdoor Education: Authentic Learning in the Context of Landscapes* (pp. 31–41). Kisa, Sweden: Kinda Education.

Neuman, J. (2001b). The Czech way of outdoor experiential education. In F.H. Paffrath & A. Ferstl (Eds.) *Hemingsles Erleben* (pp. 329–338). Augsberg: Ziel.

Neuman, J., Turčová, I. & Martin, A.J. (2007). Being in nature: Summer camp, but not as we know it. *Horizons, 40,* 25–30.

Prázdninová Škola Lipnice (1990). *Zlatý fond her.* Prague: Mladá Fronta.

Rhodes, H. & Martin, A.J. (2013). Professional development after adventure education courses. Do work colleagues notice? *Journal of Experiential Education, 37*(3), 265–284.

Schoel, J., Prouty, D. & Radcliffe, P. (1988). *Island of Healing: A Guide to Adventure Based Counselling.* Hamilton, MA: Project Adventure.

Seton, E.T. (1917). *Woodcraft Manual for Boys: The Sixteenth Birch Bark Roll (Woodcraft League of America).* Garden City, NY: Doubleday, Page & Co.

Shantz, C. (1998). *Dictionary of the Theatre: Terms, Concepts and Analysis.* Toronto: University of Toronto Press.

Spinka, M. (1943). *John Amos Comenius that Incomparable Moravian.* Chicago, IL: University of Chicago Press.

Štorch, E. (1929). *Dětská farma. Eubiotická forma školy.* Brno a Praha: Nákladem ústředního spolku jednot učitelských na Moravě a Dědictví Komenského v Praze.

Andrew Martin *et al.*

Stuerm, F.H. (1938). *Training in Democracy. The New Schools of Czechoslovakia.* New York: INOR Publishing Company.

Svojsík, A.B. (1912). *Základy junáctví: návod pro výchovu české mládeže na základě systému sira R. Baden-Powella 'Scouting' a za laskavého přispění četných odborníků.* Praha: České lidové knihkupectví a antikvariát.

Turčová, I., Martin, A.J. & Neuman, J. (2005). Diversity in language: Outdoor terminology in the Czech Republic and Britain. *Journal of Adventure Education and Outdoor Learning, 5*(1), 99–116.

Turčová, I., Neuman, J. & Martin, A.J. (2003). The outdoors from a Czech perspective. *Horizons, 24,* 26–29.

Vacation School Lipnice (2013). *Vacation School Lipnice.* Retrieved from: www.psl.cz/.

Waic, M. & Kössl, J. (1994). The origin and development of organized outdoor activities in the Czech countries. In J. Neuman, I. Mytting & J. Brink (Eds.) *Outdoor Activities: Proceedings of International Seminar Prague '94 Charles University* (pp. 18–22). Lunenburg: Vela Edition Erlebnispädagogik.

30

Outdoor studies in Japan

Taito Okamura

BACKCOUNTRY CLASSROOM, INC.

The Wilderness Education Association Japan (WEAJ) was established in 2013 in affiliation with the Wilderness Education Association (WEA) in the USA, which was established in 1977. This sequence may suggest that Japanese outdoor studies and practices are more than thirty years behind those of the USA. That conclusion, however, is not completely true, as I will demonstrate in this chapter. Japan has a long history of outdoor education, with about 550 public outdoor centres throughout the country. On the other hand, the lack of outdoor leadership training systems in higher education and the barrier of language (i.e. most outdoor materials are written in English) has delayed the growth of outdoor studies in Japan.

Outdoor studies and practice are strongly influenced by the philosophy and history as well as the educational systems of any country. In this chapter, the philosophy and history of Japanese outdoor education is reviewed, along with the current status of outdoor leadership training systems, practices, and research. Outdoor studies in Japan include the overlapping ideas of wilderness education, outdoor education, adventure education and organised camping.

Philosophy and history

The traditional view of nature in Japan is known as monism, which recognises the unity of all organisms including nature and human beings (Terada, 1948; Imanishi, 1966). Japanese ancient life was heavily dependent and deeply influenced by the natural environment including the four seasons and frequent disasters. People found God in nature and nature was exalted above humans. The sense of *awe* integrating emotional states of fear, respect and thanks explained the Japanese view of nature.

In the Nara Era (AD 710–794), a mountain religion called *Shugendo* was established by Enno Ozunu (Gojo, 1983, 2002). The followers meditated and disciplined themselves by connecting with nature in the mountains. This mountain religion spread throughout the country and Japanese mountains were valued by everyone. By the end of Edo Era (AD 1603–1868), religious hiking groups were born. Gojo stated that there were eight (i.e. the number *eight* is the symbol for countless in Japan) hundred and eight hiking groups and eighty thousand hikers on Mt Fuji during the Edo Era.

This religious hiking culture influenced the modern school system in the Meiji Era (AD 1868–1912). Miyashita (1982) described how outdoor activities such as hiking, swimming in the sea, skiing, skating, snow hiking and hunting were introduced into elementary school curricula by the end of Meji Era. These curricula were established as mountain schools and seaside schools in the next Taisho Era (AD 1912–1926). Ukai (1923) used the words *outdoor education* to describe these mountain schools, and the use of this term occurred twenty years before Sharp (1943) popularised it in the USA.

The first Western-style organised camping programme was founded by YMCA Osaka in 1911 and this group developed the roots for the later Boy Scout Movement in Japan. (Ebashi, 1987). The YMCA, YWCA, Boy Scouts and Girl Scouts developed residential camping areas throughout Japan and led Japanese camping education after the Second World War. In 1955, the Ministry of Education, Science and Culture (currently called the Ministry of Education, Culture, Sports, Science and Technology) started the Central Workshop for Educational Camp Leadership in response to the growing movement. The Ministry published the *Handbook of Educational Camps* in 1956. These private and public camp movements resulted in the establishment of the National Camping Association of Japan in 1966.

From the mid-1950s to the mid-1970s, the Japanese youth population and economy grew rapidly. The government constructed 27 National Outdoor Centres and more than 500 public outdoor centres to accommodate the post-war baby boom youth (Ministry of Education, Science and Culture, 1993). Ebashi (1987) named this active period as the *Outdoor Education Movement* in Japan.

Yoshida (1988), however, noted that conflicts were occurring in outdoor education because of the changing social system and the increasing numbers of school students. Yoshida described the interrelated problems of: environmental degradation, lack of safety management, and the limitations of the school teachers who usually led these outdoor programmes. Related to the limitations of school teachers, Hoshino (1988) noted particularly that outdoor education led by physical educators was problematic. The outdoor education system in the USA during the 1940s and 1950s, which strongly influenced Japanese outdoor education, focused on outdoor living skills and leisure education, but was part of the American Association of Health, Physical Education and Recreation (AAHPER). This US alignment shifted Japanese outdoor education into physical education. As a result, *outdoor activity* was defined in the Sports Promotion Act in 1961 as part of physical education. Hoshino regretted that Japanese outdoor education remained aligned with physical education while US outdoor educators began to specialise in adventure and environmental education during the 1970s. Nakamura (1995) also lamented that the *Handbook of Educational Camps* published by the Ministry of Education in 1956 stereotyped Japanese outdoor education as mostly activities such as outdoor cooking and hiking/orienteering. Those stereotypes seem to continue in Japan today.

In the 1990s, Japanese environmental education became active with the establishment of the Japan Environmental Education Forum. Shibata (1992), similar to Hoshino (1988), criticised how Japanese outdoor education tended towards physical education and away from nature study and environmental education. Yamaoka (1989) and Abe (1995) cited the environmental degradation resulting from the rapid development of youth camping and a changing philosophy that humans were more important than nature. Tsukuhara (1996) emphasised that outdoor educators must practise outdoor ethics as tacit rules to sustainability. During this movement towards environmental education, many school camps modified mountain hiking activity programmes to encompass environmental education to address the growing environmental issues.

The first outdoor pursuits and education laboratory established in higher education was at Tokyo University of Education in 1964. In 1969, Iida (1992) led the establishment of the

Yoshonen Camp Society, with its emphasis on outdoor studies, outdoor leadership and local community contributions through camp programmes for youth. After Iida completed his dissertation under Betty van der Smissen at Penn State University in 1976, he returned to the University of Tsukuba and resumed operating the Yoshonen Camp Society. He brought the latest American information about outdoor studies and practice, and experimented with them in this Japanese camp programme. Yoshonen Camp Society provided the earliest significant contributions to Japanese outdoor research.

Japanese outdoor education attracted attention again in the 1990s because of educational reform that emphasised alternative forms of education. In 1996 the government used the term outdoor education officially in the governmental report, *The Fulfillment of Outdoor Education for Youth*. Further, the National Outdoor Education Forum started in 1997 by gathering private agencies, university teachers and public administrators together. At that same time, the Japan Outdoor Education Society (JOES) was established as the first academic society for outdoor studies in Japan, with Iida as the first Chair of the Board. Iida named 1997 as the Japanese first year of outdoor education.

Outdoor practice

Outdoor education is strongly related to outdoor practices. In Japan, three types of setting for outdoor practices include school camps in public outdoor centres, youth agency organisations (e.g. YMCA, YWCA, Boy Scouts, Girl Scouts) and private outdoor agencies.

School camping is the largest component of Japanese outdoor practice. More than 500 public outdoor centres are available for school students. According to the Committee of Research for Promotion of Outdoor Education for Youth's report (1996), 70 per cent of these camping opportunities were for two-day periods, 22 per cent were three-day experiences, and the small remainder lasted longer than three days. The outdoor leaders at these centres are school teachers. Staff training quality and stereotypic programmes have been issues for some time, as noted earlier. In addition, the short-term nature has been a concern as have the uncertainty of the educational purpose and the lack of outcome evaluation.

On the other hand, these camps in public outdoor centres have frequently provided important research data because of the many students available as subjects and because some centres have good relationships with local universities. Collaborations between researchers and practitioners have resulted in obtaining governmental funding for outdoor studies projects. For example, Frontier Adventure Projects (1988–89) emphasised challenge-based programmes and ten-day experiences in eighty-four programmes over the course of two years (National Olympic Memorial Youth Centre, 1990). This project was significant in promoting the concept of adventure education in Japan. After this project, some centres started longer-term camp programmes with their own budgets, and new outdoor leaders were trained to administer these programmes. Funding for the Long-Term Outdoor Experience Project for Youth (1999–2000) also helped 120 camp programmes to offer fourteen-day or longer experiences (Ministry of Education, Culture, Sports, Science and Technology, 2001). Nakagawa, Okamur, Kurosawa, Araki and Yoneyama (2005) compared the outcomes of long-term camp programmes with typical three-day programmes through this project, and found that outcomes regarding self-development and nature awareness were increased in long-term camp programmes. However, they also concluded that more systematic and continuous research is needed.

Youth agencies such as YMCA, YWCA, Boy Scouts and Girl Scouts have their own historical background, traditional camp programmes and staff training systems. Rarely do these organisations conduct research projects. In my personal experience as a committee member for the camping programme of a YWCA from 2011 to 2012, recruiting participants was the biggest issue the organisation faced. The main goal of the committee was to increase the number of participants in summer camps. The camp programme could have been strengthened by more experienced and dedicated volunteer staff leaders and by having national and international networks to help them improve their organisation and outdoor programme.

In addition, outdoor practice has been undertaken by private agencies that differ greatly in character from schools or youth agencies. Some enterprises developed outdoor schools as a part of their corporate social responsibility. For example, Toyota is operating outdoor schools using a registered World Heritage Site. Some large companies have outdoor education divisions that manage outdoor schools. However, the organisations underpinning most Japanese private outdoor opportunities are small companies with few staff and small budgets. The Non-Profit Organization Promotion Act (NPO Act) of 1998 pushed to establish small businesses related to outdoor education.

Since 1993, these small businesses have formed the Japan Outdoor Network (JON), which currently includes sixty-five organisations. This network is active and sponsors some nationwide events for outdoor education. JON meets twice a year to share business information. JON Fest is a workshop for developing new skills and knowledge. JON Training School also is available for new staff in private businesses. Additionally, the Outdoor Leader Youth Meeting is supported by the government as a forum for young staff and university students to gain experience in the outdoor industry. The academic background of JON staff and employees is often from general disciplines since few training programmes exist in higher education for outdoor leadership. Nevertheless, JON has possibilities for offering rich research data because it provides high-quality outdoor programmes.

Thus, collaborations between JON and universities have the potential to further the evolution of outdoor studies in Japan for the future. Most Japanese higher education institutions compel undergraduates as well as graduate students to do theses. Therefore, universities can be the providers of outdoor research studies as well as outdoor leaders.

Outdoor leadership education

Professional training of outdoor leaders has historically occurred in physical education and sport programmes in universities. However, as noted earlier, the Japanese traditional discipline of physical education has focused on outdoor skills more than outdoor education.

The traditional Japanese view of physical education has three pillars: human and social science, natural science and coaching. Outdoor leadership is usually included in the human and social science pillar, emphasising education, psychology and sport management. However, when associated with coaching, the skills needed focus on outdoor pursuits. For example, when I taught in the University of Tsukuba, outdoor education classes were part of the sports management curriculum for undergraduates. Although some master's programmes are broader, doctoral degrees in outdoor education often included faculty in sport coaching who also focused on training top athletes. Many outdoor education degrees in sport colleges face similar patterns. The commingling with sport sometimes has hindered the development of systematic outdoor leadership education and outdoor research studies.

In 2003, Biwako Seikei Sport College was the first private sport college offering an outdoor education degree for undergraduates. It has two departments: Athletic Sport and Lifelong Sport. The outdoor education programme is one option along with school physical education and the community sport course that comprises the Department of Lifelong Sport. Faculty in this college were not constrained by the traditional disciplinary system, so they were able to create an ideal curriculum for outdoor education. They now have six outdoor faculty members and a number of outdoor students.

Another opportunity for outdoor leadership education is within teacher training in Japanese colleges. The government announced a policy of a 5,000 Teacher Reduction Plan at the beginning of 1990s because of the decreasing birth rate. National teacher colleges were forced to cut faculty in teacher training and transfer them to other general education units. Outdoor education was one area of emphasis within general education in teacher colleges such as Shinshu University, Kyoto University of Education, Nara University of Education and Hokkaido University of Education. However, because of the retirement of the first baby-boom teachers, the small-class policy of government, and the declining pool of teachers, a shortage of school teachers arose in large cities. The government stopped the teacher reduction policy and teacher colleges were forced to return to teacher training curricula. As a result, outdoor classes became optional and few programmes now offer outdoor leadership education.

Nara University of Education, my previous workplace, is typical example of this story. The Lifelong Sports Department including outdoor education has recruited students since 1999 in response to governmental plans. The faculty moving from teacher training to this new general education department including lifelong sports from interdisciplinary perspectives. The university established the Environmental and Outdoor Education Course in graduate school, which was the first graduate programme that used the term outdoor education in its name. However, the university administrators decided to return the faculty to teacher training curricula gradually, and the Lifelong Sports programme stopped admitting students in 2007. Faculty members were recalled to teacher training, and the new Environmental and Outdoor Education degree lasted only two years.

Similarly, Shinshu University and Kyoto University of Education abolished the Department of General Education after the policy change. Only Hokkaido University of Education has protected the outdoor education programme as part of teacher training. Unfortunately, outdoor leadership training in higher education has been at the mercy of governmental policies and university business decisions.

Therefore, outdoor leadership training in higher education in Japan seems to be lagging behind that of other countries largely because of the lack of opportunities to promote outdoor education, develop systematic curricula and provide professional education through graduate school. This situation has been a detriment to the growth of Japanese outdoor studies. Other training institutes for outdoor leaders include youth agencies, volunteer schools in national and public outdoor centres, and staff training in individual private agencies. Fortunately, these groups are more flexible than universities, so they can provide customised alternatives for professional training/education systems.

Outdoor studies

Outdoor studies in Japan is spread over multiple disciplines. Describing what constitutes outdoor study and what databases are available is sometimes difficult. However, most outdoor research projects in Japan have been registered into the database named Resources for Outdoor Pursuits (ROP) developed by the Outdoor Education and Pursuits Lab at the University of Tsukuba.

Several trends have occurred in the outdoor studies literature and resources. More than 7000 studies have been published since 1936 and are recorded in ROP. Imura and Tachibana (1997) reported that, seventeen years ago, more than 50 per cent of the studies focused on skiing. Skiing is one of the most common classes in university curricula, whether associated with outdoor education or not, and getting data about this activity has been relatively easy. The latest review of studies indicated that only 33 per cent of the ROP studies are about skiing. The trend appears to be towards broadening into other areas. Analyses of ROP also showed that, in camping studies, adventure education had increased from the 1980s to the 1990s, and environmental education also had grown since the beginning of the 1990s. The studies of adventure education had been led by the Yoshonen Camp Society from Camp Hanayama. Environmental education studies also have increased since the start of Japanese environmental education at the end of the 1980s (Sashima, 1999).

Okamura (2002) identified further issues when reviewing articles relating to outcome research published in the *Japan Outdoor Education Journal* from 1997 to 2002. He categorised the independent variables of outcome research into relationship with self, others, environment. The results showed that Japanese outdoor studies focused on self-development, and most of the studies were re-examinations of American studies. Examining independent variables had reached saturation. He appealed that the research paradigm for outdoor studies should shift independent variables from the whole camp outcomes to the elements of programme, environment, participants and leaders. He also noted the lack of qualitative research, and philosophical and historical research in Japanese outdoor studies.

In the 2000s, comprehensive camp outcome measurements became popular in Japan. Tanii and Fujii (2001) developed the Outcome Scale of Outdoor Experience for Early Adolescents, to be used for general-purpose outdoor outcomes. The scales were constructed around five factors: decision making, environmental awareness, leadership, interpersonal skills and self-development. Nishida, Hashimoto and Yanagi (2002) also developed an Inventory of Organized Camp Experiences for Children, to measure the typical outdoor experiences occurring in camps: challenge and achievement, collaboration, open-mindedness, intrapersonal and nature based. Using both scales, Yasunami, Okamura, Yamada and Ashida (2006) identified significant findings related to outdoor camp outcomes including the positive relationship between outdoor pursuits programmes and open-mindedness, intrapersonal and nature experiences.

Tachibana and Hirano (2001) developed the Zest for Living Scale. The government announced *zest for living* as a new educational goal for schools and social education (Central Education Council, 1998). Large budgets flowed to outdoor education under this policy. The scale was developed to evaluate the effect of camping on zest for living. Tachibana, Hirano and Sekine (2003) reported the significant effect of camping on zest for living by examining sixty-seven camp programmes. Although the Zest for Living Scale has been used by many camp programmes, Okamura *et al.* (2011) were concerned that using such a scale to evaluate general camp outcomes did not aid in improving programmes. They noted a lack of theoretical interpretation between camp programmes and zest for living, and limitations in explaining the relation between cause and effect. The American Camping Association (2005) also developed the Camper Outcome Scale for a national survey, and Okamura *et al.* (2011) translated this scale and tested fifty-five camp programmes run by camp directors certified by the National Camping Association of Japan. They reported that important aspects that influenced camp outcomes were primitive setting, proper size with around thirty campers, and a staff ratio of less than 1:3. Developing comprehensive camp outcome measurements helped to integrate the benefits of camps and explore questions about outcomes and their causes.

The newest trend is the *Experiential Education Evaluation Form* (3 E Form). The software was developed by Okamura (2012a, 2012b) based on means–ends theory to identify meanings and connections among activities, experiences and outcomes of camping. This software made evaluation easier for practitioners due to the ease of data gathering, inputting the data and understanding the results. At the 2013 Japan Outdoor Education Society conference, about 10 per cent of researchers reported using this software (e.g. Inagaki *et al.*, 2013; Kobayashi *et al.*, 2013; Nakagawa, Takayama, Ota & Okamura, 2013; Wagstaff & Okamura, 2013).

When new theories are born in psychology, outdoor researchers often have tried to apply them to the outdoor field. For many outdoor programmes, however, these theories do not apply directly. Outdoor programmes vary greatly and these theories are not always appropriate. As Ewert (1987) also concluded, traditional pre-post design is useful, but studies ascertaining cause and effects in camp phenomenon would be useful in the next decade.

New dimensions of Japanese outdoor studies

Japanese outdoor studies have several ongoing issues that need to be addressed: (i) environmental degradation; (ii) short-term stereotyped programmes; and (iii) professional outdoor leadership training. The initiation of WEAJ in 2013 is significant in addressing the future of outdoor studies in Japan with a focus on these three areas.

Leave No Trace (LNT) is a powerful programme to connect outdoor education with environmental education. Tokuda and Okamura (2014) identified that the main issue in promoting LNT in Japan was to raise consciousness towards the environment. Okamura et al. (2014) evaluated the effect of the LNT programmes in organised camping on environmental awareness, and concluded that camps should introduce programmes to emphasise LNT and improve environmental awareness. WEAJ began to train LNT trainers in 2013 under the affiliate of LNT Centre for Outdoor Ethics. More than thirty individuals had been trained by March 2014. This training will be one important means to address environmental concerns.

Most outdoor programmes are short term, stereotypic in their activities and place based. Introducing longer wilderness trips in Japanese outdoor practice has been difficult. However, many studies (e.g. Hattie, Marsh, Neill & Richards, 1997; Yasunami et al., 2006; Okamura et al., 2011) point to greater outcomes associated with longer-term wilderness settings and outdoor pursuits. Most of the more than 500 Japanese outdoor centre areas are located in places having natural environments like a mountainside, seaside, lakeside and/or riverside. Most have accessibility to wilderness areas. If a WEA instructor were associated with each outdoor centre, they could contribute to increasing positive outcomes, decreasing environmental degradation, promoting safety management and organising a variety of programmes using the wilderness.

The Japan Outdoor Education Society was started with the aim of linking researchers and practitioners. This aim, however, has not been realised because the immediate benefits of research are not always available to agencies and private businesses. Further, interpreting and applying research results is often difficult. One mission of WEAJ is to develop outdoor leadership through academic research. Practitioners can touch the research world and connect university researchers with their activities. Ideally practitioners should be able to understand research results as they evaluate and develop their own programmes. On the other hand, researchers can also benefit from connecting with practitioners to improve their outdoor leadership skills and increase the opportunities to collect research data.

Concluding remarks

Much of the world's outdoor education has been led by Western countries, with the influence of their culture, environment, social system and worldview. Western and Eastern outdoor studies, however, are frequently not connected. Western outdoor educators know little about the Eastern world because of language issues. An activity of WEAJ is to connect Japanese practitioners and researchers with American practitioners and researchers. WEAJ has some English speakers on the board and is making efforts to translate English information and send Japanese information translated into English. It is inviting American practitioners and researchers to the Japanese conference every year as small steps towards integrating world outdoor studies.

Asian countries do not have one view of outdoor studies because of different languages, cultures, religions and histories. However, Japan has a long history and culture that has connected to nature with lifestyles dependent on the environment. Unfortunately, setting national standards and systematic training for outdoor leaders has been delayed. Introducing the Western system, blending it with Japanese culture and nature values, and giving alternative paradigms for outdoor studies and education are necessary to develop Japanese outdoor studies in the future.

References

Abe, O. (1995). Environmental education and camping. *Modern Esprit, 334*, 51–58.

American Camping Association (2005). *Youth Development Outcomes of Camp Experience* (report). Martinsville, IN: American Camping Association.

Central Education Council (1998). *Developing the Mind to Open the Tomorrow's Era: The Crisis of Losing the Mind to Develop the New Generation* (governmental report). Tokyo: Central Education Council.

Committee of Research for Promotion of Outdoor Education for Youth (1996). *The Fulfillment of Outdoor Education for Youth* (governmental report). Tokyo: The Division of Life Long Learning in the Ministry of Education, Culture, Sports, Science and Technology.

Ebashi, S. (1987). *Theory and Practice of Outdoor Education.* Tokyo: Kyorinshoin.

Ewert, A. (1987). Research in experiential education: An overview. *Journal of Experiential Education, 10*(2), 4–7.

Gojo, J. (1983). *The Mind of Shugendo.* Osaka: Tokishobo.

Gojo, J. (2002). *The Learning from Shugendo.* Osaka: Tokishobo.

Hattie, J., Marsh, H., Neill, J. & Richards, G. (1997). Adventure education and Outward Bound: Out-of-class experiences that make a lasting difference. *Review of Educational Research, 67*(1), 43–87.

Hoshino, T. (1988). The study of modern educational camping: The trend and direction of American and Japanese educational camping. *Meiji Human and Social Science Journal, 35*, 82–96.

Iida, M. (1992). *The Outdoor Education Using Forest.* Tokyo: National Association of Forest Improvement and Development.

Iida, M. (1997). Toward the first year of outdoor education. *Education and Information, 473*, 2–7.

Imanishi, K. (1966). *My View of Nature.* Tokyo: Kodansha.

Imura, H. & Tachibana, N. (1997). The construction of the database of research on outdoor pursuits in Japan and its trends analysis. *Japan Outdoor Education Journal, 1*(1), 33–44.

Inagaki, T., Komatsu, A., Tanahashi, S., Yanaka, R., Ota, Y., Osugi, N., Karagias, M.K., Shiroishi, R. & Ihara, K. (2013) Can wilderness programs contribute professional sport team development. *Proceedings of the 16th Annual Conference of the Japan Outdoor Education Society 2013*, 54–55.

Kobayashi, D., Sunayama, S., Takayama, M., Shimazaki, S., Yoshida, Y., Terada, T., Osawa, M., Sato, H., Imamura, A., Nakagawa, Y., Shiroishi, R., Komatsu, A., Inagaki, T., Tokuda, M., Kurosawa, T. & Okamura, T. (2013). Using experiential education evaluation form to examine the effect of freshman training including wilderness program. *Proceedings of the 16th Annual Conference of the Japan Outdoor Education Society 2013*, 56–57.

Ministry of Education, Culture, Sports, Science and Technology (2001). *Long-term Outdoor Experience Project for Youth* (governmental report). Tokyo: Ministry of Education, Culture, Sports, Science and Technology.

Ministry of Education, Science and Culture (1993). *Social Education Survey.* Tokyo: Ministry of Education, Science and Culture.

Miyashita, K. (1982). The study of the history of outdoor education in Japan. *Juntendo University Bulletin of Health and Physical Education, 25*, 96–107.

Nakagawa, M., Okamura, T., Kurosawa, T., Araki, E. & Yoneyama, K. (2005). The effects of long-term and short-term camping on IKIRU CHIKARA (zest for living) of early adolescents. *Japan Outdoor Education Journal, 8*(2), 31–43.

Nakagawa, Y., Takayama, M., Ota, T. & Okamura, T. (2013). The effect of the difference of hiking program in freshman training camp on its outcome. *Proceedings of the 16th Annual Conference of the Japan Outdoor Education Society 2013*, pp. 60–61.

Nakamura, M. (1995). The trend of outdoor education in 1950s. *Journal of Leisure and Recreation Studies, 31*, 112–113.

National Olympic Memorial Youth Center (1990). *Frontier Adventure* (governmental report). Tokyo: National Olympic Memorial Youth Center.

Nishida, J., Hashimoto, K. & Yanagi, H. (2002). The construction of an inventory of organized camp experience for children and its reliability and validity. *Japan Outdoor Education Journal, 6*(1), 49–61.

Okamura, T. (2002). The beginning of adventurous research in adventure education. *Japan Outdoor Education Journal, 6*(1), 10–13.

Okamura, T. (2012a). The development of experiential education evaluation form: 3 E Form. *Proceedings of the 16th Camp Meeting in Japan 2012*, 10–11.

Okamura, T. (2012b). The development of experiential education evaluation form: 3 E Form. *Proceedings of the 15th Annual Conference of Japan Outdoor Education Society 2012*, 140–141.

Okamura, T., Hirano, Y., Takase, H., Tada, S., Kai, T., Tsukiyama, Y., Nagayoshi, H., Hayashi, A., Yamada, R. & Okada, M. (2011). The influence of camp components on youth developmental outcomes of camp experience. *Japan Outdoor Education Journal, 15*(1), 1–12.

Okamura, T., Matsumoto, C., Hayashi, A., Suizu, M. & Okada, M. (2014). The effect of leave no trace program in Japanese organized camping toward participants' environmental attitude. *Proceedings of the 2014 International Conference of Outdoor Leadership, 8*.

Sashima, T. (1999). The issue and direction of environmental education: The role of human development. In National Olympic Memorial Youth Center (Eds.) *Environmental Education for Youth in the 21st century*. Tokyo: National Olympic Memorial Youth Center.

Sharp, L.B. (1943). Outside the classroom. *The Education Form, 7*(4), 361–368.

Shibata, T. (1992). Environmental education and nature study. In Sashima T. (Ed.) *Environmental Issue and Environmental Education* (pp. 145–157). Tokyo: Kokudosha.

Tachibana, N. & Hirano, Y. (2001). The constituent characteristics of IKIRU CHIKARA (Zest for Living). *Japan Outdoor Education Journal, 4*(2), 11–16.

Tachibana, N., Hirano, Y. & Sekine, A. (2003). The effects of the long-term camping on IKIRU CHIKARA (Zest for Living) of early adolescents. *Japan Outdoor Education Journal, 6*(2), 1–12.

Tanii, J. & Fujii, E. (2001). Evaluation scale of nature experience program for elementary and lower secondary school children. *Japan Outdoor Education Journal, 5*(1), 39–47.

Terada, T. (1948). *The View of Nature of Japanese*. Tokyo: Iwanamishoten.

Tokuda, M. & Okamura, T. (2014). How to spread leave no trace in Japan: The necessity and obstacles. *Proceedings of the 2014 International Conference of Outdoor Leadership, 8*.

Tsukuhara, M. (1996). The athletic character and environmental issue of outdoor education. *Environmental Education, 5*(2), 13–12.

Ukai, E. (1923). *Japan Alps and Mountain School*. Tokyo: DOBUNKAN.

Wagstaff, M. & Okamura, T. (2013). Assessing the impact of a WEA Outdoor Leadership Course. *Proceedings of the 16th Annual Conference of Japan Outdoor Education Society 2013*, 112–113.

Yamaoka, H. (1989). How to integrate with nature. In H. Yamaoka (Ed.) *The Door for Neo Environmental Education* (p. 5). Tokyo: Japan Book Publishers Association.

Yasunami, Y., Okamura, T., Yamada, M. & Ashida, S. (2006). Influence of program type at Nyogo Nature School on social and emotional developments in the fifth grade. *Japan Outdoor Education Journal, 9*(2), 31–43.

Yoshida, A. (1988). Outdoor education in the future. *Social Education, 43*(505), 13–18.

31

Using outdoor adventure to contribute to peace

The case of Kenya

Shikuku W. Ooko

WILDERNESS EMERGENCY MEDICAL TECHNICIAN

Helen N. Muthomi

KENYATTA UNIVERSITY

Many communities across Africa have experienced war and conflict that left physical, psychological, emotional, mental and social devastation to those affected (Kaviti, 2009). Leaders often rush to military solutions to address conflicts and demonstrate national strength. Not surprisingly, violence often becomes an acceptable way for people to express frustration, domination and control (JustFaith Ministries, 2012). However, Reich and Pivovarov (1994) observed, 'Since wars begin in the minds of men [*sic.*], it is in the minds of men that the defences of peace must be constructed' (p. 11). Therefore, education can be an instrument of acculturation to peace.

Education has the potential to refine the sensitivities and perceptions of individuals, and lead to the development of desirable attitudes and the inculcation of positive values (Reich & Pivovarov, 1994). These possibilities warrant the creation of awareness among people, especially youth. Outdoor adventure education has the potential to move beyond just talking about peace building. Midura and Glover (2005) advocated that adventure education gives youth the chance to practise educational values like peace building.

Pathways to Peace was a project designed to examine peace building using adventure education in Kenya. It was modelled from other successful peace-building outdoor programmes such as Unity Programme, which is a youth programme that initiates compassionate social change (North Carolina Outward Bound School, 2012; Ooko, Oketch & Muthomi, 2013). Kaviti (2009) asserted that one of the major components of peace building is the enhancement of harmonious human relationships or restoration of relationships that have been broken due to offences previously committed. *Pathways to Peace* was undertaken in wilderness settings across Kenya from 2010–2012. It involved students from different tribes/regions in mixed-gender groups. Three-day courses were conducted regionally in Ndere Island National Park in Lake Victoria (for Western and Nyanza Region schools), Lake Nakuru National Park (for Rift Valley Schools), National Museums of Kenya IPR Ololua Forest in Karen, Nairobi (for

Central, Nairobi and Mt Kenya Region schools), and Mombasa Marine National Park (for North Eastern, Coast and Eastern Region schools). The ten-day Wilderness Expeditions were conducted in the Loita Hills of Narok County for the graduates from all three-day courses.

The project was led by the first author, Ooko Willy Shikuku, whose life and attitudes were expanded and changed when he did his first National Outdoor Leadership School (NOLS) outdoor leadership expedition in 1984 as a young adult. He witnessed others' metamorphosis as he led or supervised outdoor adventure expeditions for almost two decades with NOLS in East Africa and in the United States. When NOLS closed its operations in East Africa, his Luo family chose to remain in a predominantly Kikuyu settled rural area. The 2007–2008 Post Election Violence (PEV) crisis was a political, economic and humanitarian eruption. During this time, the friendships and connections that Shikuku had made on his outdoor expeditions helped to ensure that his family and home were safe. In gratitude, he founded a non-profit organisation, the Janam Peace Building (JPB) Foundation, in 2009. He believed that cross-cultural team building through an outdoor expeditionary framework could have profound and lasting positive effects on attitudes and behaviours.

Kenya, a country in the eastern part of Africa, has valuable outdoor opportunities and various destination centres for outdoor adventure. Weather conditions range from high altitude and cold weather to low altitude and warm or hot weather. Kenya has sites to explore caves, gorges, rivers, moorlands and cliffs, as well as national parks and game reserves. These natural resources afford diverse outdoor adventure activities like butterfly watching, game-viewing safari, white-water rafting, guided nature walk, bungee jumping, bird watching, kite surfing, hot air ballooning, mountain biking, scuba diving, rock climbing, mountain climbing and go-karting (Kenya Tourism Board, 2014).

Pre-Pathways to Peace project outdoor adventure education in Kenya

Outdoor adventure education has roots in peace building. The early Kenyan programmes were adapted from the Outward Bound (OB) model, which was set up during wartime to place young sailors in situations of real consequence to combat a perceived lack of inner resources in the young men (Outward Bound International, 1997). By the end of the Second World War, Britain's leaders were openly enthusiastic about the new OB programme and wanted to see its successful continuation during peacetime (Hopkins & Putnam, 1993). As a British Colony, Kenya was host to one of the earliest OB schools outside Britain. Tunstall-Behrens (cited in Freeman, 2011) noted that early OB overseas ventures took place in Kenya and Germany in the early 1950s. OB Kenya was established in 1951 (Muthomi, 2011), and was the first outdoor adventure institute outside Britain. The school was based at Oloitoktok on the eastern slopes of Mt Kilimanjaro.

While Government of Kenya (GOK) uniformed officials (both military and administrative) benefited from the OB programmes, the corporate sector also found OB outdoor adventure ideal for training young administrative personnel. The programmes were conducted mainly by Ministry of Education physical education teachers with secondment by the Teachers Service Commission (TSC) serving as OB instructors. In the early 1990s, however, due to strained diplomatic relations between Kenya and Tanzania, all OB Kenya participants were required to pay park fees as foreigners to hike Kilimanjaro National Park. The GOK decided to start its own outdoor institution (the Kenya School of Adventure and Leadership – KESAL). KESAL used Mt Kenya National Park as an outdoor classroom and, in the process, GOK transferred all TCS staff to its new base on the northern slopes of Mt Kenya. KESAL, therefore, gave Kenyans another option for outdoor adventure experiences as doors were opened to non-government staff participants.

The second international outdoor school that was established in Kenya in 1974 was the US-based, non-profit National Outdoor Leadership School (NOLS). The founders, Paul Petzoldt and 'Tap' Tapley, served as instructors in the inaugural semester course. Petzoldt had previously travelled to Kenya as a trip leader of USA Apollo 11 astronauts. He had admired the glaciated equatorial peaks of Mt Kenya while visiting Tree Tops hotel in Abardare National Park and wanted to bring the NOLS experience to Mt Kenya (personal communication, 16 March 1990). Petzoldt based the first NOLS course in Naro-Moru on the western slopes of Mt Kenya. Over the years the school had participants on its short (multi-week) and semester-long (multi-month) expeditions not only drawn from university students from the USA, but also from the Kenya conservation and outdoor education sector. The first author served as a NOLS field instructor and was the Deputy Director from 1989 to 2003.

The NOLS operation in Kenya closed in 2003 due to global security concerns after the school had expanded into an East African operation with courses conducted especially for Kenya Wildlife Service, Tanzania National Parks and Uganda Wildlife Authority. Like OB, NOLS was a household outdoor name and training was sought not only by government conservation agencies but also by private outdoor education institutions and individuals due to its dynamic and comprehensive Outdoor Leadership programme. NOLS used its US Kenya alumni to raise funds to ensure participation by deserving East African nationals was affordable through a scholarship programme, the National Outdoor Education Programme (NOEP).

Most of the champions of outdoor adventure education in Kenya are alumni of NOLS, KESAL or OB. The first and second authors are graduates and former staff of the first two institutions respectively. Most of the instructors who were involved in conducting the *Pathways to Peace* project were staff from NOLS Kenya. Some of them had worked as OB instructors in Kenya and South Africa before joining NOLS.

Outdoor adventure education for peace building

For a period of more than two years, JPB engaged 120 high-school students from Wildlife Clubs of Kenya (WCK) across the country in both short (three-day), and long (ten-day) wilderness-based courses. The programme used outdoor adventure activities as a mechanism through which the youth could develop self-efficacy, interpersonal relationships and peace advocacy skills. The programme was also designed to be an avenue for PEV psycho-social healing. Students first participated in a three-day programme that laid a foundation for the identification, appreciation and tolerance for diversity through class presentations and discussions. The topics for discussion included creating positive learning/non-discriminating environments, developing social and leadership styles, and understanding privilege and injustice. Participants also took part in team-building activities, which included ropes courses and group living in tents. At the end of every programme, participants reflected on their newly acquired skills and wrote up action plans to guide their implementation of skills for their WCK clubs, schools and communities. This approach related to the work of Bruce, Cashel, Wagstaff and Brenig (2006), who suggested that people learn so they can adapt to their surrounding world.

Action plans were undertaken prior to the next programme. These included: planting flowers and trees, organising talks with community members, contributing to support community activities, doing environmental cleaning and conservation, assisting with animal husbandry and bird keeping, participating in writing poems and singing, acting in plays, creating artwork for peace advocacy, competing in essay writing, debating about discrimination and inter-tribal peace, organising exhibitions from students to parents during parents day, being present and available for people in conflict, interacting with youth groups in formal and informal forums, distributing literature on peace building to students, organising a wildlife club rally dubbed 'Make Peace, NOT War', making workshop presentations/audio-visuals on peace building, sharing experiences with others, and celebrating environment days. This involvement of the participants resonated with what Edginton, Gassman and Gorsuch (2010) advocated for in promoting independence and self-directed learning, whereby young people draw from a programme as much as they put into it.

The ten-day wilderness expedition involved self-contained backpacking trips where participants learned outdoor living skills including camping, navigation skills, the natural and cultural history of the Loita Hills, Leave No Trace conservation ethics, wilderness first aid, leadership and teamwork. Participants were also given opportunities to share with one another about how they had implemented their action plans, as well as some of the challenges and opportunities realised. Peace building was woven in to all aspects of the outdoor adventure programmes. To ensure that the content was based on the principles of outdoor education, the programme used the context of the natural environment. This environment provided deliberate and purposeful planned opportunities to participate in compelling, intense, challenging and adventurous activities, which focused on the mind and body (Kolb, Boyatzis & Mainemelis, 1999; Priest & Gass, 2005).

The programme was carefully sequenced to address the aims of outdoor education programmes. The tasks required frequent and intense group problem solving and decision making. Each activity was followed by a debriefing session designed to create an avenue for reflection based on Kolb's experiential learning theory (Kolb & Kolb, 1995). An external evaluation of the programme was conducted to establish the progress of the JPB courses after two years. The results indicated that wilderness experiences had important effects on the youth, including positive change of attitude towards other ethnic groups and peace making (Ooko et al., 2013).

Education and peace initiatives

Peace means a way of living together when people give their fellow creatures the space and, if necessary, the mutual support to live their lives to the fullest (Service Civil International, 2009). Peace includes social justice, mutual respect and community spirit, freedom of opinion and speech, and a healthy environment and sustainable use of natural resources. It is not a static situation that can be created once and for all. Webel and Galtung (2007) pointed out that peace should be understood from the viewpoints of nature within and nature outside people. Peace-building programmes should ensure the following related to a major emphasis on outdoor adventure training;

1   Recognise whole systems, whether natural, social or technological, and understand the relationship between a system and the environment into which it fits;
2   Perceive oneself and all others as members of a single species, sharing the same biological origin, common individual needs, and similar community problems;
3   Respect, protect, and foster the diversity of people, their cultures, values, and ways of life, including domestic ethnic cultures, and the cultures of other nations; and
4   Respect and protect the living systems which make up the Earth's biosphere; recognising that there is no inherent contradiction in the possibility of humans, their technology, and nature living together harmoniously. (Reich & Pivovarov, 1994, p. 27)

Learning in the outdoors

Wilderness environments are restorative environments. They involve being away from typical surroundings. Natural is dominant, 'with opportunities for fascination and learning occurring in a set of regularities within the environment that lead to coherence' (Hattie, Marsh, Neill & Richards, 1997, p. 76). The natural settings require cooperation, clear thinking and planning, careful observation, resourcefulness, common sense, creativity, persistence and adaptability. The outdoor environment provides fascination (i.e. an involuntary form of attention requiring effortless interest, or curiosity), a sense of being away (i.e. temporary escape from one's usual setting or situation), and scope (i.e. a sense of being part of a larger whole) (Kaplan & Kaplan, 1989; Hartig, Evans, Jamner, Davis & Garling, 2003). These elements result in healthy psychological functioning as the individual interacts dynamically with the environment. As Gilmer (2010) indicated, lessons learned through time spent in the outdoors can have a profound effect on the development of a young person's worldview. Denton (cited in Gilmer, 2010) noted that being cold, wet, tired, hungry, thirsty, smelly and dirty helps young people to prioritise those things that are most important to their immediate survival. According to Kellert and Derr (1998), prolonged and challenging immersion in the outdoors, especially in relatively pristine settings, can exert a powerful emotional influence on youth. Experiencing the outdoors teaches youth that outcomes that have no saleable value, such as peace and quiet, clean air, clean water, wildlife, forests and others, are largely ignored, yet these things are what often make people contented in the long run.

The natural environment, combined with the lack of distractions found in the participant's normal home environment, provided a calming effect and opportunities for reflection. The lack of competing stimuli in the wilderness setting compared to the modern daily lifestyle enhanced a different perspective in the participants. Bunting (2006) indicated that reflection is necessary for learning. Guided reflection on peace using outdoor adventure experiences promoted peace education. The opportunities for reflection provided important moments for self-examination, which led to an evaluation of one's behaviour, and acknowledgement of a more independent and mature approach. The exploitation of the natural world and the misuse of its finite resources discloses a pattern of violence (Kimberly, 2011). Therefore, learning to relate to the natural environment can restore the right relationship between people and the world. Youth can learn to care for the Earth as their home in the future.

Future hopes

Peace relates to a relationship with others and with nature. We hope that in the future outdoor adventure opportunities can contribute to peace by developing a sense of identity that promotes self-efficacy, creates harmony within a person's inner self, creates harmony in inter-group relations, and fosters positive ethnic identities.

Peace and a sense of identity that promotes self-efficacy

Self-efficacy refers to a person's self-belief in his or her ability to successfully perform a task (Bandura, 1997). This cognitive belief has a strong relationship to actual performance. Enhancement of self-efficacy arises when skills are developed, and may also be useful in directly fostering a positive belief about personal capability. Bandura theorised that a core set of determinants underlies social cognitive theory that influences behaviour. These determinants include self-efficacy, outcome expectations, goals, facilitators and impediments. Self-efficacy influences choices of activities to pursue, goal setting, the degree of effort expended in the pursuit of the goals, and the level of persistence shown regarding feedback, setbacks, difficulties and failures. Despite the importance of success, failure may also play a role in achieving positive outcomes in outdoor adventure.

The unfamiliar environment in the outdoors enables participants to develop new perspectives about themselves and their normal environments (Kellert & Derr, 1998). The outdoor classroom provides a setting in contrast to the home environment. The unknown aspect of the environment requires an independent and self-reliant approach from the participants to solve problems. As a result, Stiehl and Parker (cited in Dickson, Gray & Mann, 2008), found that self-efficacy is one of the psychological benefits of outdoor and adventure activities. Knowing about peace and its value is not sufficient if individuals do not believe that they have the capabilities to bring about peace building in their lives and in their communities. Applied to outdoor adventure for peace building, youth can learn to apply choice, effort and persistence in peace building, and be able to evaluate their success.

Outdoor adventure education is a medium for enhancing personal development and personal awareness. The outdoor activities, wilderness environment, supportive group environment and intense personal interactions are intentionally selected and systematically introduced to increase self-awareness, which includes recognition of both strengths and weaknesses. This recognition leads to a more realistic self-image. This outcome is also reflected in the African philosophy of Ubuntu. As indicated by Kaviti (2009, p. xvi), in the words of Desmond Tutu, 'A person who is open and available to others, affirming others, does not feel threatened that others are able and good; for he or she has a proper self-assurance.'

Peace and harmony within a person's inner self

Tudge (2012) argued that human beings need to stay in touch with nature for their own sake. Nature has a healing effect on human beings. People are creatures of nature, and when they spend all their time in an artificial world, they are cut off from natural resources. Alienation then ensues. As noted by Rickinson et al. (2004), relating to the natural unspoiled wilderness brings people inner peace. The purpose of outdoor adventure training pursuits is to enable participants to relate to the natural world as an expression of life. This relationship strengthens and enhances quality of life and results in inner peace. The outdoors provides quietness, calmness, tranquillity, serenity and time for personal reflection. It offers quiet waters, still air, horizons, stars, the moon, sights, sounds, clear colours and interesting shapes – all contributing to peaceful qualities of discovering oneself and self-renewal.

The calmness during outdoor adventure can elicit feelings of safety and inner peace to participants (Townsend & Weerasuriya, 2010). Wysong (cited in Townsend & Weerasuriya, 2010) indicated that the peace, inspiration and pleasure brought by contact with nature is therapeutic. The reflective aspects of wilderness privacy are closely associated with the tranquillity and peacefulness offered by outdoor adventure. Connecting with nature relates closely to human emotional, cognitive, aesthetic and spiritual growth (Kellert & Derr, 1998).

Peace and harmony in inter-group relations

Outdoor adventure education can be used to help people maintain and enhance inter-group relationships. Such programmes can be used as areas of reform in peace building (GSDRC, 2013). Barret and Greenaway (1995) noted that the group dimension of outdoor education can be highly significant in bringing about the personal and social development of people. Neill, Marsh and Richards (1997) argued that social skills are core components of being effective in one's personal life. Priest and Gass (2005) also indicated that outdoor education allows the development of social attitudes through group cooperation, which seeks to encompass the ability of an individual to function effectively while working in a group setting. Outdoor adventure programming usually provides an intense interaction between participants since most tasks are tackled by the group as a team, enhancing their ability to work with and through other people to achieve both group and individual goals (Midura & Glover, 2005; Bunting, 2006).

Being in natural environments also can invoke a sense of oneness with nature and the universe (Rohde & Kendle 1994). As indicated by Service Civil International (2009), 'man's [*sic.*] heart, away from nature, becomes hard, and lack of respect from growing, living things soon lead to a lack of respect for humans, too' (p. 38). Few experiences in life exert as powerful and consistent an impact on people as the beauty and attractiveness of elements of the natural world. People discern unity and order in natural features, and these aesthetic impressions inspire and instruct their relationships with nature and with others.

Peace and positive ethnic identity

In Africa, ethnic identity is referred to as tribe. Kaviti (2009) emphasised that tribes include relationships between groups whose members consider themselves distinct. This distinction is in terms of kinship socialisation or social identity based on ethnic contrasts of people interacting with others who are from a different tribe. Many times in Africa, politics are based on ethnic pillars as a strategy to win elections. These politics were evident in Kenya and resulted in the 2007/2008 PEV. When promises are made to favour certain communities in resource allocation, mistrust among ethnic groups arises, with feelings of exclusion.

Outdoor adventure experiences can represent deep affection, fondness and attachment for people (Kellert & Derr, 1998). These sentiments can foster feelings of relationship and connection, and provide a means for expressing and developing capacities for intimacy, trust and kinship. With rare exceptions, people crave affection, relationship and connection in their lives (Kaviti, 2009). These qualities can be nurtured through emotional ties during the outdoor adventure programmes. Cultivating an emotional relation to the outdoors, especially in the company of others, can also promote cooperation and sociability. These experiences can enhance positive ethnic identity. The former South African President Thabo Mbeki (cited in Africa Development Bank, 2014) stressed that, although security forces could be deployed to enforce peace, this is not sustainable as long as the root causes of the conflict have not been addressed. One need for people in conflict is to be educated on the need to live together in harmony. Outdoor adventure education can be a tool to achieve this need in Africa.

Conclusion

Outdoor adventure has a long history in Kenya. The sectors that traditionally relied on outdoor adventure for leadership and team-building development include not only the corporate sector but also government officials. For the purpose of human resource development to support such ventures, universities and colleges have continued to develop their education courses both at diploma and degree levels to include physical education and recreation. As the demand for leadership and team building has grown, instructors from traditional outdoor programmes have offered experiences to meet this demand.

A trend is to use outdoor adventure as alternative rites-of-passage programmes both for girls and boys, especially when they finish their eighth year of primary school and before joining high school. In addition, we recommend that high schools offer outdoor adventure with a focus on peace building as a way to develop social cohesion among classmates, as well as school-wide, to avoid situations of social unrest that have occurred in some schools in Kenya. The same might be required of university or college students. For the purposes of national cohesion, the Chair of the Kenya National Cohesion and Integration Commission, K.N. Mzalendo (personal communication, 29 November 2012), upon receiving the *Pathways to Peace* project report, suggested that the model be adopted by the government and used for high-school graduates around the country. The greatest hindrance is securing the financial resources to support the programmes. When funds are inadequate, the experiences may be compromised, and the safety of participants might be an issue since well-trained staff and adequate equipment quality and inventory are necessary.

When problems arise in people's hearts, homes and local communities, and they close their eyes and ears on a daily basis, peace is impossible. Outdoor adventure education is a means to nurture the responsibility of being one another's keeper. The shared responsibility of adults, parents, government and educators is to infuse youth with hope so that they will be motivated to make positive life changes for themselves, regardless of previous life experiences. Kaviti (2009) asserted that humanity strives to achieve freedom, justice, peace and equality. Encounters with the outdoor environment have potential in creating awareness of inner peace and peace towards humanity (Neill *et al.*, 1997). Therefore, outdoor adventure programmes can be used as one of the methods to teach concepts and skills for peacefully resolving conflicts (Lavay, French & Henderson, 2006) in a country like Kenya as well as among other ethnic groups in other countries. People can achieve heightened feelings of meaning and purpose through enhanced connection with nature. Eleanor Roosevelt summed up what needs to be done: 'It isn't enough to talk about peace. One must believe in it. One must work at it.' Therefore, the work of peace building requires citizens and professionals to use different tools and designs. Outdoor adventure education is one such tool that can make a difference in creating peace in the world.

References

Africa Development Bank (2014). African leaders call for harmonized approach to conflict prevention, management. Retrieved from: www.afdb.org/en/news-and-events/article/african-leaders-call-for-harmonized-approach-to-conflict-prevention-management-13175/.

Bandura, A. (1997). *Self-efficacy: The Exercise of Control*. New York: Freeman.

Barret, J. & Greenaway, R. (1995). *Why Adventure? The Role and Value of Outdoor Adventure in Young People's Personal and Social Development: A Review of Research*. Coventry, England: Foundation for Outdoor Adventure.

Bruce, M., Cashel, C., Wagstaff, M. & Brenig, M. (2006). *Outdoor Leadership: Theory and Practice*. Champaign, IL: Human Kinetics.

Bunting, C.J. (2006). *Interdisciplinary Teaching through Outdoor Education*. Champaign, IL: Human Kinetics.

Dickson, T., Gray, T. & Mann, K. (2008). Australian outdoor adventure activity benefits catalogue. Retrieved from: http://outdoorcouncil.asn.au/doc/OutdoorActivityBenefitsCatalogueFinal270808.pdf.

Edginton, C.R., Gassman, J. & Gorsuch, A.J. (Eds.) (2010). *Managing for Excellence: Programs of Distinction for Children and Youth*. Urbana, IL: Sagamore Publishing.

Freeman, M. (2011). From 'character-training' to 'personal growth': The early history of Outward Bound 1941–1965. *Journal of the History of Education Society, 40*, 21–43.

Gilmer, D.G. (2010). A critical analysis of the theological aspects of outdoor and nature involvement in support of Liberty University's Adventure and Outdoor Leadership Program and associated communication plan. Retrieved from: https://scholar.vt.edu/access/content/group/5b95dc6f-a3ef-4ce5-8e1a-875819148663/MNR%20Capstone%20Projects/FINAL_Paper_Part_%20I_Gilmer.pdf.

GSDRC (2013). *State–Society Relations and Citizenship*. Retrieved from: www.gsdrc.org/.

Hartig, T., Evans, G.W., Jamner, D.L., Davis, S.D. & Garling, T. (2003). Tracking restoration in natural and urban field settings. Retrieved from: http://webcache.googleusercontent.com/search?q=cache:pHu_1wjMMRwJ:https://socialecology.uci.edu/depart/research/cihs/articles/2003_JEnvirPsy.pdf+&cd=1&hl=en&ct=clnk.

Hattie, J., Marsh, H.W., Neill, J.T. & Richards, G.E. (1997). Adventure education and Outward Bound: Out-of-class experiences that make a lasting difference. Retrieved from: www.wilderdom.com/abstracts/Hattieetal1997AdventureEducationMetaanalysis.htm.

Hopkins, D. & Putnam, R. (1993). *Personal Growth through Adventure*. London: David Fulton Publishers.

JustFaith Ministries (2012). Just Peacemaking initiative: The challenge and promise of nonviolence for our time. Participant packet 2012. Retrieved from: www.paxchristi.net/sites/default/files/documents/2012-0025-en-gl-pb.pdf.

Kaplan, R. & Kaplan, S. (1989). *The Experience of Nature: A Psychological Perspective.* New York: Cambridge University Press.

Kaviti, L. (Ed.) (2009). Seek peace: Enhancing peace building in church and community. A paper by Hope for Kenya forum for World Relief and Africa Leadership Reconciliation Ministries (ALARM). Nairobi, Kenya: Executive Printing Works.

Kellert, R.S. & Derr, V. (1998). A national study of outdoor wilderness experience. Retrieved from: www.zotero.org/groups/landcare_benefits/items/itemKey/NZ9TT5SB.

Kenya Tourism Board (2014). *The Kenya Travel Guide and Manual.* Retrieved from: www.magicalkenya.com.

Kimberly M. (2011) Building peace, building solidarity. Paper by JustFaith Ministries. Retrieved from: http://justfaith.org jf_voices-11q1.pdf.

Kolb, D., Boyatzis, R. & Mainemelis, C. (1999). *Experiential Learning Theory: Previous Research and New Directions.* Retrieved from: www.medizin1.uk-erlangen.de/e113/e191/e1223/e1228/e989/inhalt990/erfahrungslernen_2004_ger.pdf.

Kolb, Y. & Kolb, D. (1995). *Learning Styles and Learning Spaces: Enhancing Experiential Learning in Higher Education.* Retrieved from: www.jstor.org/stable/40214287?seq=1#page_scan_tab_contents.

Lavay, B.W., French, R. & Henderson, H.L. (2006). *Positive Management in Physical Activity Settings.* Champaign, IL: Human Kinetics.

Midura, W.D. & Glover, R.D. (2005). *Essentials of Team Building: Principles and Practices.* Champaign, IL: Human Kinetics.

Muthomi, N.H. (2011). Impact of a three-day outdoor education programme on the perception of life effectiveness qualities of staff trainees in Kenyan corporate settings. Unpublished doctoral dissertation, Kenyatta University, Nairobi.

Neill, J.T., Marsh, H.W. & Richards, G.E. (1997). The life effectiveness questionnaire: Development and psychometrics. Retrieved from: http://wilderdom.com/pdf/NeillinpreparationLEQPsychometricsDec2002.pdf.

North Carolina Outward Bound School (2012). Schools and groups: Unity program. Retrieved from: www.ncobs.org/programs/schools-groups#tab-unity-program.

Ooko, S.O., Oketch, G.O. & Muthomi, H.N. (2013) Impact of outdoor adventure education on Kenyan youth, in peace building. Paper presented at the 2nd Leisure and Recreation Association of South Africa (LARASA) International Congress in Durban, South Africa, September.

Outward Bound International (1997). Outward Bound International. *Retrieved from:* www.outwardbound.org/about-outward-bound/philosophy/.

Priest, S. & Gass, M. (2005). Effective Leadership in Adventure Programming. Champaign, IL: Human Kinetics.

Reich, B. & Pivovarov, V. (Eds.) (1994). *International Practical Guide on the Implementation of the Recommendation Concerning Education for International Understanding.* Paris: UNESCO. Retrieved from: www.unesco.org 34_64.pdf.

Rickinson, M., Dillon, J., Teamey, K., Morris, M., Young, C.M., Dawn, S.D. & Benefield, P. (2004). A Review of Research on Outdoor Learning. *London: National Foundation for Educational Research and King's College.* Retrieved from: https://www.field-studies-council.org/media/268859/2004_a_review_of_research_on_outdoor_learning.pdf.

Rohde, C. & Kendle, D. (1994). *Human Well-being, Natural Landscapes and Wildlife in Urban Areas: A Review.* Retrieved from: http://webcache.googleusercontent.com/search?q=cache:hwmgdyHrZWgJ:manual148.fortypdf.org/2b1fod_human-well-being-natural-landscapes-and-wildlife-in-urban-areas-english-.pdf+&cd=2&hl=en&ct=clnk.

Service Civil International (2009). *Peace Messengers Handbook.* Retrieved from: http://webcache.googleusercontent.com/search?q=cache:UEy__nK4XbYJ:cid.mk/new1/images/stories/download/peacemessengerhandbook.pdf+&cd=10&hl=en&ct=clnk.

Townsend, M. & Weerasuriya, R. (2010). Beyond Blue to Green: The Benefits of Contact with Nature for Mental Health and Well-being. Retrieved from: http://webcache.googleusercontent.com/search?q=cache:G61EaChNP_QJ:www.hphpcentral.com/wp-content/uploads/2010/09/beyondblue_togreen.pdf+&cd=1&hl=en&ct=clnk&client=ubuntu.

Tudge, C. (2012). It is dangerous how cut off children are. The *Guardian* debate on whether the National Trust is right to say losing touch with nature is damaging children. Retrieved from: www.theguardian.com/commentisfree/2012/mar/30/nature-deficit-disorder-children.

Webel, C. & Galtung, J. (2007). *Handbook of Peace and Conflict Studies.* Retrieved from: http://guessoumiss.files.wordpress.com handbook-of-peace-and-conefac82ict-studies.pdf.

32

Outdoor activities in Brazilian educational camps

Marcelo Fadori Soares Palhares

SÃO PAULO STATE UNIVERSITY

Sandro Carnicelli

UNIVERSITY OF THE WEST OF SCOTLAND

The Brazilian educational camp movement started in the 1940s and was strongly influenced by the camping culture of the American YMCA. The movement was organised by the Brazilian group ACM (*Associação Cristã de Moços*). Not until the 1990s, however, did these educational camps grow in popularity and became commercially managed. The Brazilian camping movement developed so rapidly during this period that an Association (*Associação Brasileira de Acampamentos Educacionais*) was created in 1999 to open dialogues among the different camp owners.

Initially the educational camps in Brazil had religious/Christian values guiding activities. More recently, the camps adopted a different approach, focusing on developing the physical, psychological, ethical and cognitive abilities and skills of children and teenagers through recreational and outdoor activities. This chapter explores the development of educational camps in Brazil, as well as the use of outdoor recreation in their programmes. Two points are important. The first is that we recognise the existence of many camps with different objectives in Brazil, such as leisure camps, religious camps and football camps. However, this chapter will focus on those camps with an educational philosophy and programme. Therefore, in this context, Brazilian educational camps address educational outdoor activities in the holiday seasons for children aged 6–17 years. The second point is that these educational camps are organisations aiming to contribute to the preparation of campers to live well in communities. In this context, social interaction and contact with nature are essential parts of educational camps.

Educational camps: the concept

Associação Brasileira de Acampamentos Educacionais (ABAE) is responsible for congregating and certifying the educational camps in Brazil. ABAE defines an educational camp as an establishment that prepares specific recreational, sporting, and cultural programmes aimed to act together with formal education in the development of human beings. The camp programmes are designed to address the social, cognitive, physical and emotional development of campers. To achieve the goal of a holistic education, the camps must have skilled professionals acting in an adequate and safe place (Associação Brasileira de Acampamentos Educacionais, 2014).

Vivolo-Filho (2003) further defined educational camps as places with a safe and organised physical structure that provides recreational activities and learning experiences, as well as using specialised staff to facilitate these experiences. As noted earlier, educational camps are establishments that aim to contribute to the preparation of campers to live well in communities when they become adults. Camps are present in many countries in Europe, South and North America, Asia and Africa (Eells, 1998). In Brazil these camps gained an elevated importance due to the deficits of formal public education and the many social problems in the country. Thus, Brazilian educational camps became an important tool to enhance formal education, as discussed further in this chapter.

Camp development in Brazil: a historical overview

Educational camps in Brazil started with the *Associação Cristã de Moços* (ACM), the Brazilian branch of the Youth Men's Christian Association (YMCA). According to Silva (2004) the first Brazilian educational camping experiences occurred in 1948 with Donald Kennedy, an American priest, who aimed to provide joyful experiences and teach accepted social values using outdoor activities. The 1948 camp season of *Paiol Grande* was exclusive for males but females were allowed to join in the following year. The 1949 season at *Paiol Grande* had seventy boys and seventeen girls between the ages of 10 and 16 years. Not until 1953, with the creation of the *Nosso Recanto* camp, did Brazil have its first camp supervised by a Brazilian educator – Affonso Maurício Vivolo. Through physical outdoor activities, Affonso provided a rich and significant way to learn positive social values (Vivolo-Filho, 2003). The camp period in Brazil at that time was organised during the summer and winter breaks, and the programmes offered continuous education using outdoor learning (Stoppa, 2004).

The 1970s was the period of great growth in educational camping in Brazil, with the opening of new camps mainly in the south-eastern part of the country. Subsequently, the 1980s was the period of increased participation by young children, and the 1990s found the educational camps moving mainly to commercial configurations (Vivolo-Filho, 2003).

Although originally designed to operate only during summer and winter breaks, the educational camps had to attract more business and stay open throughout the year. Camps began to host other groups, including adults from companies, church groups and families. These others initiatives are not discussed in this chapter as they simply reflect the renting of the camping space, but they are important to mention as part of the commercialisation of the camping environment.

Independently of the profile of participants, Silva (2004) pointed out that educational camps should not forget their philosophy and original educational aims. While some educational camping programmes focused more on moral and ethical values during their outdoor learning activities, other camps' programmes concentrated on areas such as sporting/physical abilities, and the natural environment and its morphology.

In this context, with the growth in the number of camps new approaches to outdoor learning gained emphasis (e.g. using outdoor activities to learn languages and gain knowledge about different cultures) (Silva, 2004; Chamlian, 2005). These developments and the escalation in the number of camps, as well as the increasing responsibility of organising educational camps required the creation of ABAE that could provide communication among the different stakeholders.

The Brazilian Association for Educational Camps (Associação Brasileira de Acampamentos Educacionais – ABAE)

In May 1999, ABAE was founded. The ABAE was created to facilitate the collaboration between camp owners and to provide opportunities for sharing experiences. A second goal of the Association is to clarify questions for clients and media about the activities performed in educational camps, as well as to offer marketing strategies and activities to boost the emerging camp industry.

ABAE also offers information for parents to help them with the decision-making process about sending their children to camp. The Association provides details about the different educational camps, their philosophies and educational approaches, and the outdoor activities that are offered in their programmes. Although ABAE has only nineteen members and does not include all Brazilian educational camps, the Association works as a reliable source for parents looking for educational holiday programmes.

To become a member of ABAE, a camp needs to be an established organisation with safe facilities and a trained group of professionals as staff. The camps also need to have been operating for at least three consecutive years, with evidence of educational components in their activities. An educational camp desiring to join the ABAE needs to provide a formal written request to the Executive Board, and is scrutinised and evaluated before being accepted in the Association. The ABAE members can then participate in all regular meetings and events that are organised to discuss programmes and developmental actions related to educational camps. A frequent concern for ABAE is the professional development and educational knowledge of staff in Brazilian educational camps.

The professional profile of camp counsellors

Lettieri (1999) illustrated the importance of outdoor activities in educational camps developed by staff prepared and skilled to achieve the educational goals. According to the ABAE, the ideal counsellor for an educational camp should have specific abilities and capacities such as understanding children's psychological and physical development, as well as leadership skills and good humour (ABAE, 2014). These characteristics could help counsellors in camps to promote and perform outdoor recreational activities that are entertaining, socially integrating and that benefit the personal development of the campers (Chamlian, 2005).

According to Camargo (1998), counsellors at educational camps must be able to interact with people from different cultures. However, interaction is not enough to be a good counsellor. Counsellors also need knowledge about the natural environment and the area of the camp to avoid problems and keep the campers safe during the activities. In addition, they must have good problem-solving skills.

This ability to manage and solve problems was evidenced by the counsellors themselves in research conducted by Palhares (2011). He investigated the perceptions of the counsellors in an educational camp regarding their educational roles. All thirty respondents in the study saw themselves effectively as educators with the ability to solve problems quickly in a respectful way.

Chamlian (2004) observed that the professional profile of educational camp counsellors included an educational commitment, the necessity to be creative and extroverted, knowing how to work in groups, and having the ability to emphasise ethical values. Isayama (2009) found that being extroverted and funny was important but should not be the main element in evaluating the performance and quality of educational camp staff. Counsellors, with their abilities to lead outdoor activities and present educational values, are instrumental for camps to achieve their main goals. However, Stoppa and Isayama (2001) noted that the misbehaviour of counsellors was a problem commonly faced by educational camps. Unfortunately, the development of outdoor activities and recreation is seen by Brazilian society as an amateur profession (i.e. something that can be done by anyone without training). This attitude devalues the job of camp counsellors and perpetuates the misleading idea that, in Brazil, outdoor recreation is an easy way to earn money during the college or university years.

People often consider the camp counsellor job 'easy' or 'delightful' because the counsellors have fun while receiving money. These people forget the political, cultural and social elements that are involved in working in any leisure industry (Isayama, 2009). Marcellino (1990) pointed out that, to work in the leisure industry (i.e. in this context the work with educational camps) without a serious and professional approach and attitude, can compromise professional performance and put the safety and wellbeing of customers (i.e. campers) in danger. He argued that leisure professionals should have alliances with other fields related to outdoor education, such as tourism, hospitality, physical education, education and biology. Silva (2004) concurred with Marcellino and showed that educational camp professionals have two primary responsibilities: to focus on the personal and social aspects of human beings; and to guide and develop awareness of people about the natural environment, to promote meaningful leisure experiences.

To address and overcome the notion that some fields, like camp counselling, are amateur in character, Brazilian educational camp administrators have emphasised the social-cultural characteristics of counsellors' work. This perspective aims to help people understand and be reflective about the ways that camps address social issues of Brazilian society and help people engage with nature (Carvalho, 1977; Isayama, 2009). The counsellor addressing socio-cultural issues has a broad responsibility not only in the operational plan of outdoor activities but also in the planning, elaboration, execution and evaluation of them. From a socio-cultural perspective, the outdoor activities in educational camps can be an opportunity to provide meaningful experiences and influence positive behaviours among campers. According to Schwartz (2004), the socio-cultural approach linked to outdoor activities in educational camps can enhance the construction of citizenship and help nurture responsible attitudes.

Thus, educational camps can assist in the development of social, emotional and ethical skills through outdoor experiences that encourage responsible citizenship. This citizenship can occur by focusing on the social and educational values present in Brazilian camps.

Values and educational camps

As noted, camps in Brazil during the 1990s shifted their values to adapt to a macro context characterised by the constant commercialisation and marketing of products and processes, including the open spaces that could be used for leisure experiences (Ziberman, 1990). The values of educational camps were reflected as they adjusted to capitalist principles such as supply and demand, competition and profit.

The change in educational camps due to a commercialised approach was a phenomenon not limited to Brazil or to the camping sector, but was global in scale, affecting other types of leisure activity (McKendrick, Bradford & Fielder, 2000). McKendrick et al. explained that leisure activities began to be explored in the 20th century through different markets. In this context fields began to supply the demand in areas such as tourism and hospitality.

Inside this new commercial logic, the educational camps adopted some strategies that could attract greater numbers of campers based on the new customers that were emerging in Brazilian society. These new customers believed the process of learning social values could not be the only benefit to sending children to educational camps. Therefore, educational camps adapted their style to satisfy these new customers. These changes created at least two new consequences: neutral religious approaches and the inclusion of adventure sports.

First, camps adopted a more neutral position in relation to religious values. With the growth of other religions in Brazil, the educational camps had to abandon their strict Christian values and search for non-religious positions to boost marketing opportunities.

The second consequence of incorporating adventure sports by educational camps went beyond outdoor recreation towards an adventure sport strategy. Adventure sports became popular among Brazilian citizens during the late 1990s. Urban citizens were looking to escape the city environment and reconnect with the natural environment (Carnicelli-Filho, Schwartz & Tahara, 2010). The camps with commercial views started to create more sources of income through merchandising and offering adventure sports, requiring additional charges.

The changes in the camp values were positive in being more appealing to an urban population with different beliefs and lifestyles. However, the changes did not contribute to the massification of the camping phenomenon as an informal educational process, but made the activities more exclusive for the economically privileged classes.

The commercialisation of educational camps is a social/economic barrier impeding lower classes from engaging with this experiential form of education. The impediments are mainly economic, with prices for a week of experiential learning being around US$700 (i.e. equivalent to about two months of salary for many Brazilian workers). Another hindrance is that, geographically, most of the camps are situated in the south-eastern part of Brazil, which is a region economically richer when compared to the north or north-east of the country.

The educational camps in Brazil and their outdoor activities programmes remain an important tool of informal education through addressing positive social values with the belief that participation in such activities stimulates youth to appreciate social harmony. Camp programmes provide activities and situations in which these values are embedded, including the importance of keeping living spaces clean, contributing to teamwork activities and showing concern about friends in disadvantaged situations.

Palhares (2011) noted that the main values stimulated by counsellors included a sense of justice, respect, ethics, responsibility, tolerance and patience. Guided by these social values, the counsellors emphasise to campers that they will need to deal with different people and a range of personalities during their life, and such values will help them to build new social relationships.

The construction of positive social values during the stay in an educational camp could also help directly in formal education. An improvement in school behaviour and grades as a result of education camps is emphasised in anecdotal reports, but this aspect still needs empirical data collected through future research.

Lynch and Dibben (2014) have argued that adventure recreational events can incorporate positive social values for both organisers and participants who are involved in facilitating these social values. In this context, adventure events within educational camps appear to be able to develop positive social values as well as promote recreational opportunities.

Camps and human development

According to Chamlian (2004), each educational camp has its own philosophy, which in turn is reflected in the programming of activities. The philosophy is what distinguishes camps as they create their identities, offer opportunities for different markets and expand their programme activities. In the past many camps restricted traditional activities to outdoor sport practices, recreational activities without competitive elements, and outdoor night games that stimulated rational thinking and overcoming of fearful situations.

However, because the social changes occurring at macro levels created the necessity to adapt to the new market, more adventure activities have been added to the programmes of educational camps. Some of these new activities are now provided inside camps, while others are outsourced and offered in partnership with adventure companies. Among the adventure activities offered today by Brazilian educational camps are whitewater rafting, canoeing/kayaking, rock climbing and abseiling, and high ropes circuits. These activities are planned to satisfy specific groups of clients and are adapted to the age of participants.

Almost all the activities in Brazilian educational camps are organised by age group. Each camp has a division of age groups, which influences the programming of outdoor recreation. The divisions of the programmes are based on the psycho-motor capacities and abilities of each age group. However, educational camps in Brazil usually divide young people into two age groups: children (6–10 years) and teenagers (10–17 years). Some educational camps accept children under 6 years old and others have a triple division of 4–8 years, 9–12 years and 13–17 years. We focus on the two divisions termed children and teenagers.

In the children's group, psycho-motor development includes physical, behavioural, social and emotional changes. Kraus and Scanlin (2003) wrote specifically about children attending educational camps and observed some of the main characteristics including:

- an increase in the difference between physical capacities of boys and girls with the boys being stronger generally (around 10 years old);
- improved motor coordination;
- an average capacity to pay attention;
- great physical energy (i.e. being eager, active, quick and enthusiastic);
- emotional instability;
- increasing awareness regarding the concepts of right and wrong, as well as moral and ethical values;
- becoming more independent and prepared to stay away from home and parents;
- preferring to play with children of the same sex, with sometimes hostility between the sexes.

Regarding teenagers and their characteristics Kraus and Scanlin (2003) asserted that this developmental stage is related to the beginning of puberty with the following observations:

- anthropometric changes in height and weight, especially at the beginning of adolescence;
- hormonal changes, especially in the reproductive system, which may cause anxieties and fears;
- greater autonomy and knowledge about sport and games;
- high capacity for concentration and willingness for rewards arising from long-term targets;
- self-affirmation, concern with popularity and aesthetic standards;
- interest in the opposite sex.

Based on the characteristics described by Kraus and Scanlin (2003), educational camps try to provide outdoor activities that will contribute to the social, psychological and physical development of children and teenagers. The recreational activities are usually performed in groups with the possibility to add competitive or cooperative elements. The role of the counsellor is also important as someone who manages the conflicts that can arise during the activities and group work.

According to Palhares (2011), some of the campers may not deal appropriately with the concept of defeat in competitions so counsellors, in their educational role, can help children and teenagers to overcome their feelings of frustration. In their creation of outdoor games and activities, counsellors can also try to stimulate social values of cooperation, including respect, fairness and equality. The work with teenagers, in terms of social values, can be made deeper by including tougher decision-making opportunities and more complex reflections. At this developmental stage, it is possible to have concrete and/or imaginary situations in which decision making can be crucial to the outcome of the experience and the success of the group. Teenagers' concrete and abstract thoughts and broad argumentation can lead to richer discussions regarding behavioural change and positive attitudes.

In educational camps the campers have responsibilities and rights, but they are supervised as necessary to contribute to the welfare of the group. All campers can participate in constructing the rules. Such rights are sometimes systematically denied in other areas, such as family and school. In an educational camp the rules are mutually agreed upon between campers and counsellors, and followed by both groups (Stoppa, 1998). Such responsibilities might include: being honest and fair during the activities, respecting their friends and colleagues, making their own bed, being responsible for their belongings, and cooperating in the housekeeping of shared bedrooms. On the other hand, campers have the right to participate in all the activities, have their own space and have their preferences respected. Brazilian educational camps aim to contribute to campers' preparation for adulthood through long-lasting memories of the camp experiences.

In research published by Silva (2004), many teenagers reported that the educational camp experience was a unique opportunity that would always be remembered. These memories were cherished because of positive and meaningful experiences in that camp environment. Unfortunately, educational camps have limited time to foster strong and positive social relationships. Nevertheless, camps are like a micro-society, where rights and responsibilities as well as norms and values are essential for successful community living. Silva's research emphasised that educational camps have contributed to the development of positive citizenship behaviours among former campers.

Final considerations

The Brazilian culture of educational camps increased in the 1990s by establishing their own values separate from North American camps. The initiative in Brazil aims to provide the development of campers in social, cognitive, physical and emotional growth. Even with a more commercial approach, the educational camp movement continues to focus on the informal educational process by providing significant learning experiences for campers.

The use of traditional outdoor recreation is now mixed with the new adventure sports such as rafting, mountain biking and rock climbing. The activities have gained a more contemporary perspective, incorporating issues of the post-modern society such as consumerism, disconnections from rural and natural areas, and environmental awareness. In terms of access, the changes in values were positive because these camps started to attract a wider audience. However, the changes have increased the fact that educational camping is an expensive activity directed to the economically richer social classes.

At the beginning of the educational camp movement in Brazil only boys had the opportunities, but girls were quickly included. Today, camps address a large public, including adults and elderly people, as well as children and teenagers. A consequence of this increased focus on the public is that the profile of children and teenagers attending the educational camps has changed and the increasing costs have limited participation to middle and upper social classes. Marcellino (1983) noted that some barriers related to leisure context, such as gender, age, level of education and stereotypes, are significantly associated with economic factors. This economic aspect often limits forms of leisure for some members of the population. The right to leisure should not be limited to those people who can pay for it, and this logic also applies to educational camps.

Leisure is a phenomenon linked to different segments of social life, and can maintain social order or question the social inequality in society (Marcellino, 1990). Leisure is determined by the position of the participants in such experiences, and the attitude of people about their choices and the level of knowledge prior to decision making. Thus, leisure as well as camp programmes can be possible spaces for questioning and transforming society, and not just a consequence of actions disconnected from global reality (Marcellino, 1983). This social transformation in educational camps is based on the recognition that campers should not be limited by an unequal and capitalist society.

The Brazilian educational camps can contribute to this context of social transformation through programmes that include a safe place, skilled staff, adequate activities, construction of values and living in small communities aiming for a holistic education for life. Through this work, the educational camps can contribute to the formation of critical and conscious citizens and people actively working for a more equal society. For all these reasons the educational camps continue to have great potential for developing more socially responsible citizens that will lead Brazil into the changes necessary for a more equitable society.

References

Associação Brasileira de Acampamentos Educativos (2014) *O que é um acampamento educativo?* Retrieved from: www.abae.org.br.

Camargo, L.O. de L. (1998). *Educação para o lazer.* São Paulo: Moderna.

Carnicelli-Filho, S., Schwartz, G.M. & Tahara, A.K. (2010). Fear and adventure tourism in Brazil. *Tourism Management, 31*(5), 953–956.

Carvalho, A.M. (1977). *Cultura física e desenvolvimento.* Lisboa, Brazil: Compendium.

Chamlian, L.A. (2005). *Políticas públicas de educação e a formação para o conviver: o acantonamento como uma boa saída da escola.* Master's dissertation, Universidade da Cidade de São Paulo.

Eells, E. (1998). *História do acampamento organizado: os primeiros 100 anos.* Campinas, Brazil: Associação Evangélica de Acampamentos.

Isayama, H.F. (2009). Atuação do profissional de educação física no âmbito do lazer: a perspectiva da animação sociocultural. *Motriz, 15*(2), 407–413.

Kraus, R.G. & Scanlin, M.M. (2003). *Monitor de acampamento: Privilégio e desafio.* São Paulo: AEA.

Lettieri, F. (1999). *Acampando com a Garotada.* São Paulo: Ícone.

Lynch, P. & Dibben, M. (2014). Maintaining leisure values in adventure recreation events: The role of trust. *Annals of Leisure Research, 17*(2), 180–199.

Marcellino, N.C. (1983). *Lazer e humanização.* Campinas, Brazil: Papirus.

Marcellino, N.C. (1990). *Lazer e educação.* Campinas, Brazil: Papirus.

McKendrick, J.H., Bradford, M.G. & Fielder, A.V. (2000) Time for a party! Making sense of the commercialization of leisure space for children. In S.L. Holloway & G. Valentine (Eds.) *Children's Geographies: Playing, Living, Learning* (pp. 86–100). New York: Routledge.

Palhares, M.F.S. (2011). *O papel do monitor de acampamentos como educador.* Honours dissertation, Universidade Estadual Paulista.

Schwartz, G.M. (2004). Aspectos Psicológicos do lazer. *Licere, 7*(1), 9–21.

Silva, R. (2004). Atividades recreativas em acampamentos de férias. In G.M. Schwartz (Ed.) *Atividades recreativas* (pp. 72–93). Rio de Janeiro: Guanabara Koogan.

Stoppa, E. (2004). Acampamento. In C.L. Gomes (Ed.) *Dicionário Crítico do Lazer* (pp. 9–11). Belo Horizonte, Brazil: Autêntica.

Stoppa, E.A. (1998). *Lazer nos acampamentos de férias: Uma análise da ação dos animadores sócio-culturais.* Master's dissertation, Universidade Estadual de Campinas.

Stoppa, E.A. & Isayama, H.F. (2001). Lazer, mercado de trabalho e atuação profissional. In C.L.G. Werneck, E.A. Stoppa & H.F. Isayama (Eds.) *Lazer e mercado* (pp. 71–100). Campinas: Papirus.

Vivolo-Filho, M.A. (2003). Acampamentos no Brasil: aspectos históricos e importância social. MBA dissertation, Universidade de São Paulo.

Ziberman, R. (1990). *A produção cultural para a criança.* Porto Alegre, Brazil: Mercado Aberto.

Part 5

Social and environmental justice and outdoor studies

Introduction

Barbara Humberstone

Buckinghamshire New University

Outdoor studies cannot be complete without consideration of social and environmental thought, and how outdoor studies might be located within these discourses. This introduction presents brief overviews of diverse frameworks that may inform outdoor studies, highlighting contradictions and complexities. We explore how the social, environmental and spiritual inter-relate and thus indicate webs of connection to which outdoor studies, nature-based sport and outdoor learning are integral.

For Nada-Rajah (2010), drawing on McLaren (2003), 'The basic premise of environmental justice is the notion that all people have an equal right to live in a healthy environment and, correspondingly, that environmental harms should be equitably distributed amongst all social groups.' Inherent in this position is the tension identified by Dobson (2003) that social justice and environmental sustainability, 'are not always compatible objectives' (p. 83). Nada-Rajah highlights the conflict between social justice perspectives, which are human centred, and deep green perspectives, which centre the non-human world.

Absent from this analysis and much recent environmental discourse is reference to feminist thought and, more particularly, ecofeminisms. In both theory and praxis, ecofeminism(s), since at least the 1970s until the late 1990s, has influenced thinking and action in relation to the significant *interconnections* between social and environmental oppressions and degradation. Identifying reasons for the apparent demise of ecofeminism, Gaard (2011) asked:

> As a community of radical scholars and eco-justice activists, what have we lost by jettisoning these earlier feminist and ecofeminist bodies of knowledge? Are there features of ecofeminism that can helpfully be retrieved, restoring an intellectual and activist history and enriching current theorizing and activisms? (p. 27)

Gaard's analysis provides a substantive historical overview, largely from the USA, of the theoretical and activist foundations of various forms of ecofeminism, identifying the 'antifeminist backlash' in the late 1990s to be based on diverse interpretations, from 'feminist and environmentalist resistance to ecofeminism's analyses of the connections among racism, sexism, classism, colonialism, speciesism, and the environment' (p. 26). Making connections between social injustices and the abuse of the non-human world at a theoretical and practical level is clearly complex, and fraught with contradictions and tensions. This is no less true for outdoor studies.

For the UK outdoor practitioner of the 1980s and 1990s, Mortlock's (1984) mantra, 'awareness, respect, love of self, for others and the environment', was well rehearsed and gave a sense of inspiration. Yet there may have been little awareness or understanding of sexism and racism, or even speciesism, among many practitioners or even academics researching outdoor education. Notable exceptions include those working from pro-feminist perspectives where there has been substantial research and writing on gender and the outdoors since 1980s, but with limited acknowledgement of environmental issues. Despite this proliferation of research on gender and increased female participation in the outdoors, Warren's chapter points to the continued male dominance in the field, the tendency towards heteronormativity and the little attention given to transgender. In this chapter she examines the development of women-only experiences and programmes, and the invisibility in the literature of women of colour. Roberts' chapter, concerned with race and ethnicity, takes a look at the unequal access to the outdoors for recreational pursuits. She argues that outdoor resources are managed predominantly for the white person. Her chapter considers access to the outdoors from a social justice perspective, examining ways in which race and ethnic participation can be considered and encouraged.

Reciprocally, there were few acknowledgements from outdoor scholars exploring outdoor learning or environmental issues to these social justice analyses. For example, Pedersen-Gurholt's pro-feminist critiques of Norwegian *friluftsliv* (Pedersen, 2003; Gurholt, 2008) were largely ignored by academics exploring *friluftsliv*. In the late 1990s, outdoor learning scholars tended to see feminist critiques of the outdoor professions and programmes as belonging to 'women's studies' and not outdoor learning. Many of these outdoor educators were concerned with environmental issues, but largely ignored social issues. We could equally argue that much gender research in outdoor studies tended to neglect the degradation/oppression of the non-human world. Nevertheless, at the same time, ecofeminist work attempted to analyse the complex interconnections of human oppression and the environment's demise (see Diamond & Orenstein, 1990; Mies & Shiva, 1993; Warren, 1997; Humberstone, 1998). Connell's (1996) research into masculinities and the green movement highlights the consequential challenge to hegemonic masculinity by men engaged in environmental movements, emphasising the significant connections between social and environmental issues of oppression and degradation.

For the most part, the chapters in this section focus on either social issues or the environment. However, Collins and Anantharaman's chapter explores equality and inclusion, and the complex human connections with nature, from largely Indian perspectives. This chapter points to the political influences surrounding poverty and exclusion, and highlights the undermining of traditional environmentally friendly agro knowledge, held and practised mainly by women, in the pursuance of large-scale agricultural practices that exploit the natural environment. Collins and Anantharaman's research seeks out the views of a selection of Indian interviewees to explore their relations with nature and the influences on them historically, and how this may shape future actions in relation to caring for nature. They draw attention to teachers (outdoor educators) and the ways in which education can/might foster such care through culturally specific learnings of and in nature. This chapter touches implicitly on the global reach of neo-liberalism influences, and the implications of class and caste. A significant gap in this section concerned with social and environmental justice is that of class, and we would argue for future research that examines aspects of outdoor studies and attendant pedagogies in the light of privatisation and commercialisation (see Evans, 2014, for a pertinent discussion in relation to physical education).

An emerging major social issue is the increase in the predicted number of older people. The 21st century has been daubed the 'silver century', the century of the older person (Magnus, 2008). Those over 60 years of age are set to become a significant proportion of industrialised Western society, and it is projected that those born now can expect to live for more than a hundred years. Boyes' chapter considers the potential benefits for older persons engaging in a variety of outdoor activities, and how these benefits are mediated and influenced by the older person's social positioning. Crosbie's chapter, concerned with disability, draws attention to a range of strategies for the inclusion of people with disabilities in various outdoor programmes. Informed by the social model of disability and recent research, Crosbie takes a pragmatic approach to enabling people with disability to take part in outdoor activities.

Spirituality is included in this particular section since arguably spirituality, however it may be understood, is a powerful energy that seems to connect human and non-human worlds, particularly within Eastern and native/lost/pagan cultures/religions. This is acknowledged in Collins and Anantharaman's chapter on Indian perspectives. In Heintzman's chapter, spirituality is identified as a positive force in nature and, in it, he synthesises recent empirical research that explores the relationship between outdoor activities and spirituality. A framework is offered that makes connections between preceding circumstances, contexts and the recreational activity and the growth of spirituality. That is not to say religious ideologies cannot have negative influences and may on occasions incite oppressive social actions and destructive practices. Although many traditional Eastern religions take for granted human-non-human interconnections, recognising webs of connections, by honouring all nature some forms may tend to miss/dismiss the inequalities of power locally and globally.

Drawing upon a number of writers, including Taylor (2007) and Thrift (2008), Humberstone (2011) pulled together theoretical and personal experiences in nature-based sport, through ethno and auto-ethnographic methodologies, to argue the significant connection between body, affects, emotions and the senses as the body engages with natural elements. She takes seriously Thrift's speculative notion of *kinetic empathy* embodied through various physical activity practices in nature. On occasions, some experiences might be interpreted as embodying a sense of spirituality or oneness with nature, and it is 'through this that one learn(ing)s to be in the body in nature' (Humberstone, 2015, p. 34). This body pedagogics (Mellor & Shilling, 2010) arguably may provide for environmental and social action locally, and perhaps globally, through connected practice in nature (see Olive, Chapter 49 in this Handbook). The thrust of Cooper's chapter draws attention to the dramatic impact that Western values associated with consumerism are having on environmental degradation and the challenges young people currently face (see Sandlin and Mclaren, 2010). Taking a pragmatic approach, Cooper calls for outdoor learning to move from a largely personal development approach to emphasis on community and environment, engaging with environmental education. He shows how outdoor education might encompass aspects of environmental education through educators' critical approaches.

Such critical approaches have potential to work, as Nicol (2015), also arguing from a pragmatist perspective, suggests:

> [i]f we are to pay more than just lip service to purposeful movement towards connecting mind with world, and world with mind, then significance and meaning must extend beyond the individual. More and more sea kayakers are joining the growing body of enthusiasts who look to seascapes for their recreation, health and well-being. This sector comprises individuals spanning all classes, all professions, all ages and genders. The point is that these people, through their familiarity with sea and landscapes, represent a mind/world link to many aspects of economic society where decisions are made about

the production, distribution and consumption of goods and services. Those who search for meaning through direct engagement in the outdoors are already part of a social web contained within the web of life itself. This is why it is so important that those who 'play' in seascapes remind themselves of the relationship between people and sea places because once motivated they are in a position to do something about it across a broad range of societal functions (for example local and central government, industry, commerce, consumer practices and so on). (p.152)

This argument can be made for all practitioners involved in forms of nature-based sports and outdoor learning, whether these take place on land or sea. Another pragmatist approach that focuses on social justice is highlighted by Aitchison and Henderson (2013). Their argument is in relation to leisure but is just as meaningful to outdoor studies:

> People's reality, and especially the reality of women, is not just individual experience or a social construction, but is created through community, organisational and cultural contributions . . . Although leisure can sometimes reproduce inequality, leisure projects, programmes and research are also powerful means of addressing and resisting inequality, and thus foster equality through social change and empowerment for individuals and communities. (p. 202)

This vision can be applied to nature-based sport/recreation and outdoor learning programmes and projects, and in relation to diverse individuals and groups. The significance is in the importance of recognising community, organisational and cultural contributions to social and, in the spirit of ecofeminism, environmental change. Mansfield's chapter emphasises the practical conflicts of interest among those who wish to use the outdoors as a resource, be it for recreational purposes or commercial purposes. She highlights the accidental unintended damage left behind by recreational users, and describes various management and other approaches used to reduce this conflict.

Outdoor studies can/should address these issues at pragmatic levels as well as theoretically. Indeed, outdoor education and nature-based sport are, as we see in the forthcoming chapters, crucially positioned in the arena of social and environment justice. The writers in this section identify and conceptualise issues and offer suggestions for practice for equality and social and environmental justice.

References

Aitchison, C. & Henderson, K. (2013). UNICEF and UN women's evidence gathering to address inequalities in the post-2015 global development agenda: Leisure as a site of inequality and a means of addressing inequality. *World Leisure Journal, 55*(2), 193–203.

Connell, R.W. (1996). *Masculinities*. Oxford, UK: Polity Press.

Diamond, I. & Orenstein, G.F. (Eds.) (1990) *Reweaving the World: The Emergence of Ecofeminism*. San Francisco, CA: Sierra Club Books.

Dobson, A. (2003). Social justice and environmental sustainability: Ne'er the twain shall meet? In J. Agyeman, R.D. Bullard & B. Evans (Eds.) *Just Sustainabilities: Development in an Unequal World* (pp. 83–98). London: Earthscan.

Evans, J. (2014). Equity and inclusion in physical education PLC. *European Physical Education Review, 20*(3), 319–334.

Gaard, G. (2011). Ecofeminism revisited: Rejecting essentialism and re-placing species in a material feminist environmentalism. *Feminist Formation, 23*(2), 26–53.

Gurholt, K.P. (2008) Norwegian friluftsliv and the ideals of becoming an 'educated man'. *Journal of Adventure Education and Outdoor Learning, 8*(1), 55–70.

Humberstone, B. (1998). Re-creation and connections in and with nature: Synthesizing ecological and feminist discourses and praxis? *International Review for the Sociology of Sport*, *33*(4), 381–392.

Humberstone, B. (2011). Embodiment and social and environmental action in nature-based sport: Spiritual spaces. *Leisure Studies*, *30*(4), 495–512.

Humberstone, B. (2015). Embodied narratives: Being with the sea. In M. Brown & B. Humberstone (Eds.) *Seascapes: Shaped by the Sea: Embodied Narratives and Fluid Geographies* (pp. 27–40). Surrey: Ashgate Publications.

King, A.S. (1996). Spirituality: Transformation and metamorphosis. *Religion, 26*, 343–351.

Magnus, G. (2008). *The Age of Ageing: How Demographics are Changing the Global Economy and Our World*. London: John Wiley & Sons.

McLaren, D. (2003). Environmental space, equity and the ecological debt. In J. Agyeman, R.D. Bullard & B. Evans (Eds.) *Just Sustainabilities: Development in an Unequal World*. UK: Earthscan.

Mellor, P.A. & Shilling, C. (2010). Body pedagogics and the religious habitus: A new direction for the sociological study of religion. *Religion, 40*, 27–38.

Mies, M. & Shiva, V. (1993). *Ecofeminism*. London: Zed Books.

Mortlock, C. (1984) *The Adventure Alternative*. Milnthorpe, Cumbria, UK: Cicerone Press.

Nada-Rajah, R. (2010). *Stories of Environmental Injustice. A Review of 'Environmental Justice' Research in the UK*. APE (Artist Project Earth). Retrieved from: http://environmental-justice.com/research/.

Nicol, R. (2015). In the name of the whale. In M. Brown & B. Humberstone (Eds.) *Seascapes: Shaped by the Sea: Embodied Narratives and Fluid Geographies* (pp. 141–154). Surrey: Ashgate Publications.

Pedersen, K. (2003). Discourses on nature and gender identities. In K. Pedersen & A. Viken (Eds.) *Nature and Identity. Essays on the Culture of Nature* (pp. 121–150). Kristiansand, Norway: Hogskoleforlaget.

Sandlin, J.A. & Mclaren, P. (Eds.) (2010) *Critical Pedagogies of Consumption. Living and Learning in the Shadow of the 'Shopocalypse'*. London: Routledge.

Taylor, B. (2007). Surfing into spirituality and a new, aquatic nature religion. *Journal of the American Academy of Religion*, *75*(4), 923–951.

Thrift, N. (2008). *Non-representational Theory: Space, Politics, Affect*. London: Routledge.

Warren, K.J. (Ed.) (1997). *Ecofeminism. Women, Culture and Nature*. Bloomington, IN: Indiana University Press.

33

Race, ethnicity and outdoor studies

Trends, challenges and forward momentum

Nina S. Roberts

SAN FRANCISCO STATE UNIVERSITY

The commitment of outdoor recreation professionals to embrace social justice efforts including race and ethnicity has grown with the worldwide dynamic shifts in society. Similarly, research efforts have increased exponentially. As parks and outdoor spaces become repository for multicultural enjoyment, park managers are faced with new challenges in blending environmental and social justice factors via new perspectives and forward thinking.

The multifaceted subject of outdoor recreation, parks and leisure studies has enabled exploration for more than fifty years across race relations and cultural diversity (see Gramann, 1996; Henderson, 1998; Rodriguez & Roberts, 2002; Sasidarhan, 2002; Chavez, Winter & Absher, 2008). Such studies are meant to be of benefit across international borders. We have come a long way yet continued progress requires innovation and development of new theoretical frameworks. A variety of sample studies based in different countries are thus included in this chapter to ensure balance of global perspectives and sample methodological approaches. Furthermore, the need to break down barriers to recreational enjoyment in parks and other natural spaces persists. In this chapter, I offer a taste of the following: exploring the landscape; sample theories, conceptual frameworks and methodological approaches; why geography matters; and an overview of barriers and constraints. I close with a few recommendations for future research.

Exploring the landscape and experiencing natural surroundings

From rugged individualism and conquering-the-mountain days of Roderick Nash and his seminal work on *Wilderness and the American Mind* (Nash, 1967) to the first ever *Black and Brown Faces in Americas Wild Places* (Edmonson, 2006), the United States has contributed to the advancement of popular literature as well as scholarly research agendas (see Chavez *et al.*, 2008); each mode has become an integral part of the other. Various annotated works and edited compilations have aided in our empirical understanding of attitudes and experiences (e.g., Gramann, 1996; Roberts & Rodriguez, 2002; Chavez *et al.*, 2008; Stodolska, Shinew, Floyd & Walker, 2013) with acknowledgement of how the popular literature has supported our scholarship. Crossing continents, Gentin (2011) also provides a review of outdoor recreation and ethnicity in Europe.

Focusing on the British minority experience, Rishbeth (2001) argues that, in previous studies, what transpired is that 'landscapes have a symbolic dimension, and aspects of landscapes can be recognized as familiar or alien, welcoming or excluding' (p. 351). She maintains that white British people experience nature differently from other minority ethnic groups, and consequently, 'to treat people equally, it is important to respond to their diversity' (p. 351). Rishbeth suggests that landscape architects and managers take this into consideration while implementing inclusive design of outdoor spaces. Every community has disparate needs based on community characteristics, the physical environment and context. Rishbeth's research into British studies concluded that the outdoor/green space experience can be enjoyed by everyone because a landscape is 'an honest reflection of contemporary society that embodies a dynamic and multifaceted culture' (p. 364).

It is my conviction that outdoor spaces can be even more effective when programmes are designed with diversity and respect for cross-cultural differences in mind. In modern society, we see variety in many sectors of life, including cuisine, art, music and fashion. Letting this openness to an inclusive cultural identity permeate into outdoor recreation and individual/collective experience of landscapes, I believe, would ultimately contribute to a richer human experience. Understanding how ethnic minorities explore the landscape, and how park and protected area managers engage all people to ensure positive experiences when immersed in the natural environment, continues to be strewn with both challenges and opportunities.

Sample theories, conceptual frameworks and methodological approaches

Many years ago, Gramann (1996) indicated that research on parks and leisure, and the outdoor recreation behaviour and mindset of various ethnic groups, had been sparsely carried out since the 1960s. Several practical issues related to policy and programme development, planning, and daily open space operations have been brought to light over the years. Gramann's suggestion was that further studies should use surveys and focus groups, and include education of managers and planners to shed light on the problems, and ultimately 'increase visitation and political support from traditionally underrepresented populations' (p. 58). Since then, other scholars have indeed built upon this research, many of whom profess more qualitative work is necessary (see Sasidharan, 2002; Chavez et al., 2008; Stodolska et al., 2013).

Byrne and Wolch (2009) focused their approach on geographic perspectives on park use, with a keen eye on political, cultural and environmental justice landscapes. Park spaces are shaped and undeniably function from both from the behaviours of visitors and various 'historical, socio-ecological, and political-economic processes' (p. 1) that lead to different uses of parks; often these are determined by geography, which reflects a certain class, age, gender and ethnicity of visitors. Citing many seminal papers and studies, Byrne and Wolch (2009) acknowledge the ethno-racial differences that mark visitation and use patterns in all parks, no matter their type or location. Therefore, in an ideal world, the processes recommended by outdoor recreation researchers and practitioners (e.g. park managers) must reflect the dynamics – and diversity – of park use. Yet, in reality, such considerations of how racial diversity elements factor into park visitation have a decided influence on use or non-use of park spaces are rarely made in both research and practice.

In her review of minority park use across Europe, Gentin (2011) indicates topics such as outdoor recreation patterns, access to green space and non-Western immigrants' perception of nature saturate the literature. Yet, Gentin notes the results are 'difficult to compare', because different methods have been used including differing categories to discern ethnic affiliation.

Among the implications for future research, not only do European scholars need to become more sensitive towards ethnic affiliation, it seems to me that anyone exploring this topic needs to understand that the within-group heterogeneity of ethnic minorities must be taken into consideration.

Stodolska *et al.* (2013) discuss how most leisure literature on ethnicity in the 1990s focused on cultural and structural assimilation. These are well-known constructs in the world of sociology and have been explored for decades in outdoor recreation. This assimilation framework, broadly, is relevant today not only in the United States and Canada, but also in European countries, where the heavy influx of Hispanic/Latino populations is evident, and where African and Asian immigrants crossing borders continues to take place. Hence, each situation has to be – ideally – evaluated on a case-by-case basis and according to geography.

One important conceptual framework in the analysis of race relations growing in the recreation field is Critical Race Theory (CRT). Roberts (2009), for instance, addresses CRT in relation to ethnic diversity and outdoor recreation in response to white privilege through combating racism. Hence, the importance of exploring these patterns, especially in regards to nature-based leisure and green space use, should be everyone's prerogative, not just that of a privileged few. More work is encouraged to explore this valuable theory.

Geography matters

The global literature on race and green space offers a broader perspective of the context of culture and belonging. Global shifts in the geographic and socio-economic landscapes are immense; characterised by increased mobility, integration and an increasingly complex 'melting pot', multicultural perspectives today are necessary to include in outdoor recreation research and to challenge dominant perspectives.

Public open spaces, landscapes, sense of place: a global perspective

Askins (2009) explored individuals from African, Caribbean and Asian descent regarding use of, and perceptions related to, the English countryside. Over time, the word 'rural' in the UK was construed as meaning a nature place outside the city. Askins also stressed the emotional connection of individuals with nature, offering insight into perceptions of green spaces across racial backgrounds. Consequently, Askins suggested a 'transrural' concept of rurality based on mobility and desire to break down 'dominant notions of rural England as only an exclusionary white space, and reposition it as a site within multicultural, multiethnic, transnational and mobile social imaginaries' (p. 366).

Challenging Anglo constructions of rurality beyond existing norms, it has been asserted throughout the literature how rurality as a concept in itself, including 'nature place', is more often perceived as 'a space of whiteness'. In England, as one of several examples, the very thought of the British countryside is associated with whiteness (CABE, 2010). By dubbing rural spaces as portals for racism and racist thinking, while conversely classifying the urban environment as open and welcoming of all races, one avoids owning the responsibility for racial narratives, which continue to be perpetuated over time. Thus, a sense of segregation persists as these perceptions of urban and rural imaginaries remain in place – when, in reality, there should be no ownership of public green spaces by any one dominant culture over another.

Yet what defines sense of place, and by whom, matters. Newell (1997) studied populations from Senegal, Ireland and the United States to find out their favourite place and reasons for such preference. Places allowing for social interaction and recreational activities, such as sports and entertainment, were favoured by the Senegalese, but far more similarities than differences were identified among other cultures and nationalities. Therefore, here we find common ground on which to build, while remaining sensitive to cultural differences and recreational desires. Study results show park and woodland users wish to work together with park managers to create an environment that all – regardless of background, age, physical ability or race – could enjoy unhindered. Also evident is that open space management involves central considerations for issues of safety, community enhancement and involvement, social interaction, inclusion and cooperation.

An interesting point posed by Byrne and Wolch (2009) references how parks have been, throughout history, places for 'social control', namely for 'disciplining working class and racialized bodies, and redirecting ethno-racial and class tensions' (p. 755). There is general acknowledgement that parks represent 'urban spaces with considerable potential to offset the social and environmental problems facing cities in the new millennium' (p. 755). Scholars have analysed and discussed park visitor perceptions, and what such individuals and groups expect to receive from their park experiences. Consequently, it is not only nature that shapes an individual or society; it is society itself – and the individuals within it – that shape the natural space.

Hence, geography matters as much as ecology, cultural ideology and political landscape, so it is my belief that what lies at the intersection generates particular experiences for visitors. It is imperative, therefore, that such experiences remain positive. Subsequently, nature–society relations, and a view of any cultural landscape, offer a unique perspective on environmental justice and the political dynamics that support or hinder it. There is no doubt that urban parks, for instance, have faced problems not only with respect to considerations such as public health, ecosystem damage or visitor discrimination, but also issues from a geographical perspective; that is, while some parts of a city provide green spaces, these are often lacking in other areas, which reflects an uneven distribution of green spaces in urban environments, broadly. These insights are important to note both from a theoretical and practical perspective, and thus merit further study.

The next logical step would be to move from consideration of public access to parks, to attitudes of discrimination and racial inequality that still surface based on use. Depending on the geography and/or political and cultural environment, not everyone has or feels they have the same quality of access to open green spaces as members of another race or culture. In essence, 'the cultural landscape perspective shows us how landscapes can become racialized, shifting the scale of environmental injustice from the home, the factory or the neighborhood to entire landscapes' (Byrne & Wolch, 2009, p. 756).

Challenges and seeking balance

Balancing biodiversity and the human dimension

International commitment to protecting biological diversity has drawn together different agencies, nature experts and professionals, which include, among others, leaders of Indigenous peoples, rural union leaders and advocates for the poor. I cannot emphasise enough that to preserve an outdoor space, appropriate for recreation opportunities, without hearing the voices of different stakeholders is neglectful. Protected natural areas around the world have life to give; no wonder the land can support a community's needs only when its managers are knowledgeable about those needs. As beautifully stated by Sexton et al. (2013), 'The more we know about our audiences, the more knowledge we have to contextualize the management issue . . . reaching beyond traditional networks of stakeholders is vital to effectively representing diverse public opinion' (p. 146).

Furthermore, according to Naughton-Treves, Holland and Brandon (2005), 'By global mandate, in addition to conserving biological diversity, protected areas are to provide economic benefits at multiple scales, alleviate poverty, protect threatened cultures, and promote peace' (p. 244). There is, however, a constant challenge to reach these goals despite population growth, political instability and mounting demands on the resources being protected. One positive outlook is that professionals and scholars are working diligently in outdoor recreation and parks, studying both the local people and ecosystems, and seeking effective governance for protected areas. Similarly, I believe that in multicultural environments, even in developed countries, park management – without awareness and knowledge of who is using parks and how – will fail.

In a realistic, contemporary world, multiple forms of management should be required to operate a park or outdoor space inclusive of multiple perspectives. Diversity, in itself, is not a subject that can be tackled with generalisations. Similarly, park managers need to be cognisant of differences, and adapt both management styles and policies accordingly. Beyond training, taking the pulse of the community would prove unavoidably beneficial. Still, the greatest park management challenge is striking a balance between conservation, development and visitor use. Active community involvement in management decisions is becoming commonplace to embrace in pursuit of this balance.

Community engagement including immigration

A growing topic of importance relating to immigration and immigrant wellbeing and achievement from a psychological perspective continues to expand (see Jay & Schraml, 2009). Immigration of people to highly developed countries (e.g. the USA, Russia, Germany, Canada) has caused a major shift in the global population in recent decades. Indisputably, immigration has social consequences. Citizens of the receiving countries will react in different ways to immigrants, who may or may not assimilate quickly into the dominant culture of the place or even outdoor space. Theories on prejudice and inter-group relations are therefore relevant in the context of engaging communities; the study of relations between immigrants and the society of the receiving country is, consequently, crucial in understanding related challenges from a multicultural and multi-ethnic perspective relating to the outdoors (see Lanfer & Taylor, 2005)

Different societies view nature, parks, and thus outdoor recreation, with different lenses. What constitutes enjoyment in one culture may not be shared by members of another culture. In Europe, the wilderness and enjoyment factors are given centre stage. For example, Sweden, whose first parks were established in the early 20th century, embraced its 'mountain lands, virgin forest, deciduous forest, swamps, archipelago, and old agricultural landscapes' (Curry, 2009, p. 231). National Parks in England and Wales were designed in the 1950s for purposes of 'access and amenity' (Curry, 2009). South Africa, on the other hand, gave precedence to game reserves preservation and eventually mixed in tourism development with its conservation efforts. According to Curry, all these examples indicate the assortment of primary motivations in park design, and this diversity ties in with the immigration argument. If a South African nature lover immigrates to Wales, for instance, a completely different scenario and different habits when it comes to parks and outdoor recreation will be faced. Imagine different races and beliefs converging together in one place; the differences could be loud and stark, yet unavoidable.

When people immigrate to a new land, they often retain links with their homeland as it is difficult to sever ties with one's country of origin. Is what they did in their home-country parks acceptable or considered 'appropriate' in their new homeland? The answer is often 'no', leaving them, and park managers alike, frustrated with fears and prejudices before being able to cross cultural boundaries of acceptance.

In parks and outdoor recreation settings, using the symbols of one culture rather than another may lead to one group feeling excluded, and vice versa. In places where multicultural tension and conflict prevail, use of cultural icons, accordingly, may provoke an undesirable emotional response. For example, in the USA the traditional National Park Service uniform is known affectionately by Americans as the prominent 'Green and Gray', yet to many Hispanic/Latino visitors this is representative of Mexican border patrol, evoking great fear and making community engagement, at times, more challenging (e.g. Roberts & Rodriguez, 2008; Roberts & Chitwere, 2011).

People of different cultures living in a foreign land generally live a dual life. With both feet on two sides of a fence, they experience the art of being both bicultural and binational. A policy of inclusion, therefore, cannot ignore one side of the fence in favour of another; rather, this complex reality must be acknowledged and discussed in depth.

Barriers and constraints to access

Constraints for racial minorities visiting parks and public lands have been explored for several decades. Social scientists have studied participation rates and experiences of ethnically diverse groups at different types of outdoor recreation areas, as well as barriers to visitation (see Gramann, 1996; Roberts & Rodriguez, 2002; Chavez et al., 2008; CABE, 2010). Over time, theories have been developed and best practices created for managing outdoor programmes and geographic areas as we know them today. Reaching out to and engaging a continuously changing population, as well as cultivating mutual respect and understanding, have led to great progress. So why do barriers persist? Whose stories are missing from the discourse?

Despite demographic shifts across the globe, racial and ethnic groups, and people from lower socio-economic backgrounds, remain underrepresented among visitors to public lands. How nature and the outdoors are appreciated, experienced, or even accessed, may differ across cultures. It is my conviction that we must therefore continue to understand what people care about and why, as well as how outdoor recreation resources are viewed, valued and are being used by our changing communities.

The case of Great Britain

A comprehensive British report (CABE, 2010) investigates various relationships among ethnicity, urban green areas, inequality, health and wellbeing. The report concludes that 'some of the most acute effects of deprivation are felt by black and minority ethnic communities living on a low income in urban areas' (p. 2). This is attributed to a poor standard of life due to an inadequate local environment with detrimental effects to health and wellbeing. Although people, including low-income minorities, appreciate the value of green spaces, they tend not to use them (at all or more perhaps infrequently) because of the quality and safety issues. A total of 50 per cent of study participants claimed they would use outdoor areas more if these issues were addressed; 60 per cent of participants believed they would see positive change in their health condition, while 48 per cent thought it would also be beneficial for their mental health. Interestingly, nearly half of all participants thought better, cleaner outdoor spaces would assist in improving their relationships with friends and family.

While the report found that African-Caribbean women, as well as Bangladeshi and Pakistani people (broadly), were more likely to report bad or very bad health in comparison to the general population, the CABE report concludes that improving urban green space contributes to improved health and enables positive local neighbourhood transformation. The greatest barriers to achieving this goal, though, remain the political and economic landscapes, which often are not conducive to progress due to many external considerations.

Economic and political landscape

I still find it fascinating that, historically, parks in the United States were originally conceived as spaces for exclusion (Byrne & Wolch, 2009). Indeed, urban park designers promoted a 'park's image as natural, sanctifying, wholesome, and white, counter-posing it against a city construed as artificial, profane, insalubrious, and colored' (Byrne & Wolch, 2009, p. 747). A drive for gentrification further displaced poor and vulnerable residents, the majority of whom were people of colour. For instance, Byrne and Wolch explain that, to build Central Park, African and Irish residents were evicted from Seneca Village and this area was unfortunately destroyed to make way for the park. With time, parks became more accessible and the issue of cultural diversity started to gain notice. Still, many park managers did not stop the imposition of rigid behavioural rules and dress codes 'to inculcate cultural norms of the elite within working-class and immigrant visitors' (p. 747).

Hence, the rules for park use constrained how such groups enjoyed these spaces (Taylor, 1999; Byrne & Wolch, 2009), thus creating a divide between rich and poor, haves and have-nots. Unfortunately, the economic and political divide persists, creating barriers to access to those most vulnerable and deprived when resources for beautification are pooled in affluent areas to the detriment of struggling neighbourhoods. In addition, Byrne and Wolch (2009) mention there are other factors to consider, aside from the economic and political landscape (e.g. addressing climate change).

Recommendations for future research

Many scholars propose recommendations that merit further study. Smith and Floyd (2013), for example, suggest that creating unique racialised patterns of access will give policy makers a picture as to the spatial consequences of growth. Such an instrument could prove useful in targeting groups that are marginalised. Therefore, to change, one must first understand, and it has been made clear throughout the literature that, due to the dynamic nature of racial and ethnic contexts, we have not yet arrived at a full understanding of this topic; this can vary considerably by geography.

For many youth, environmental education programmes with their schools are the gateway to eventually experiencing outdoor recreation. Two ingredients are needed for well-rounded programmes: multiracial audiences and racially diverse educators. Consequently, research on outdoor and environmental education could be strengthened and potentially better understood by means of a Critical Race Theory framework (see Roberts, 2009).

Another point of greater diversity in parks and outdoor recreation users also ties in to the need for a more ethnically diverse workforce in public land agencies and outdoor organisations. Research, for instance, should address how and why what Park (2007) refers to as equity, diversity and inclusion is something that should be the norm to create cultural synergy in the workplace; this, in turn, would lead to welcoming more diversity among park visitors.

From the perspective of park use, Byrne and Wolch (2009) suggest utilising the visitors/park users themselves as vehicles to gauge the direction of change. More geographic-centred research, globally, might also analyse activism in and around urban parks, particularly by marginalised populations. There are facets to park use that are under-explored in the literature. For example, 'What role . . . are people of color playing in reshaping their access to active recreation areas and urban nature?' (Byrne & Wolch, 2009, p. 755).

Jay and Schraml (2009) indicate an inadequate focus on immigrants when it comes to public policy and planning in relation to urban forests; consisting of prime natural surroundings to explore, studies lack investigation of the recreation habits and patterns of immigrant populations as influenced by their customs and perceptions. To analyse these patterns would go a long way towards enabling migrants' social integration into their new environments as the natural habitat offers 'a strong symbolic identification potential and also a public space for social interactions' (p. 283).

Additionally, Hibbler and Shinew (2002) discussed the matter of enhancing multiracial families' leisure experiences in the USA. Since then, very little research has explored the experiences of the multiracial family and related factors to enhance communications, engagement and/ or programming. Similarly, another untapped area in outdoor recreation research, in particular, is the lack of attention paid to biracial and multiracial people (Roberts, 2013). Hence, a global increase in interracial marriages denotes that more multiracial families are being formed, and these families may have unique leisure needs (see also Hibbler & Shinew, 2002) and may experience natural resources differently. As I have written before, 'it is also widely understood that access to parks and open space affords a type of leisure that can be extremely beneficial to individuals on many levels. Yet, barriers to participation for multiracial people continue to exist in the form of social isolation, inadequate facilities, and subtle discrimination' (Roberts, 2013, p. 33). Research is thus needed that provides a deeper understanding of the outdoor recreation patterns and preferences of mixed-race people; such knowledge is crucial for improving the systems of social and environmental justice, while encouraging a new demographic to be stewards of our parks and protected areas.

Although parks are places where people come in contact with nature, the diverse visions of what parks should be can trigger unrest and frustration that must be heeded and explored for a better understanding of community needs. Several ways exist to create dialogue with multicultural populations with respect to the provision of better-quality access to parks. A diverse workforce complemented by programmes that cater to the needs of these potentially underserved populations, are solid steps in the right direction.

Conclusions and discussion

General increased park visitation as well as environmental justice efforts have enhanced health trends and improved quality of life for racial minorities. This, in turn, has brought about increased awareness and support, as well as more frequent park use by minorities. Furthermore, it has been well established that parks and other green spaces can help to reduce the negative effects of deprivation, creating a stronger, sustainable community through its various health benefits (CABE, 2010). Longevity is enabled through a reduction in conditions such as lung disease and depression, and living in proximity to green space has also been found to reduce the large gap in life expectancy between the haves and the have-nots (CABE, 2010). Yet constraints continue to exist, and education and improvement involve a long process, globally, aimed at changing societal norms and challenging exclusions that still exist. Scholars, nature experts, outdoor educators, park managers and landscape designers have their work cut out for them in their effort to challenge the marginalisation of specific groups – from urban America and rural Britain, to the ethnic landscape of Sydney and rural India. For a racially and culturally diverse world to prosper, such diversity must first be acknowledged and respected. Acceptance guides problem solving and can lead to increased park access.

Breaking down racial homogeneity and related misperceptions can, therefore, assist in building a sustainable and just world where everyone has a voice and a story to tell. A diverse perspective is not only needed, it is crucial. In rural areas around the world, for instance, one may find different indigenous tribes with diverse customs living around a nature reserve – all these people are invested in the neighbouring lands and may draw their livelihood from these very spaces. On the other hand urban dwellers value city parks and whatever green space may exist for rejuvenation as well. So, to whom should we listen when proposals for development are presented to relevant authorities? Without voter support of parks and open space in perpetuity, public lands will diminish. Does it matter where people live or where racial minorities tend to concentrate? Whatever the case, the voice of the community across cultures should always be the one resounding voice that matters. Change is not possible any other way.

References

Askins, K. (2009). Crossing divides: Ethnicity and rurality. *Journal of Rural Studies, 25*(4), 365–375.

Byrne, J. & Wolch, J. (2009). Nature, race, and parks: Past research and future directions for geographic research. *Progress in Human Geography, 33*(6), 743–765.

Chavez, D.J., Winter, P.L. & Absher, J.D. (Eds.) (2008). Recreation visitor research: Studies of diversity. Gen. Tech. Rep. PSW-GTR-210. Albany, CA: US Department of Agriculture, Forest Service, Pacific Southwest Research Station, 216pp.

Commission for Architecture and the Built Environment (CABE) (2010). Community green: Using local spaces to tackle inequality and improve health. London, UK: CABE, 61pp.

Curry, N. (2009). National parks. In *International Encyclopedia of Human Geography*. Cheltenham, UK: Countryside and Community Research Institute.

Edmonson, D. (2006). *Black and Brown Faces in America's Wild Places*. Cambridge, MN: Adventure Publications.

Gentin, S. (2011). Outdoor recreation and ethnicity in Europe: A review. *Urban Forestry & Urban Greening, 10*(3), 153–161.

Gramann, J.H. (1996). Ethnicity, race, and outdoor recreation: A review of trends, policy, and research. Miscellaneous Paper R-96-1. Vicksburg, MO: US Army Corps of Engineers Waterways Experiment Station.

Henderson, K.A. (1998). Researching diverse populations. *Journal of Leisure Research, 30*(1), 157–170.

Hibbler, D.K. & Shinew, K.J. (2002). Interracial couples' experience of leisure: A social construction of a racialized other. *Journal of Leisure Research, 34*, 135–156.

Jay, M. & Schraml, U. (2009). Understanding the role of urban forests for migrants – uses, perception and integrative potential. *Urban Forestry & Urban Greening, 8*(4), 283–294.

Lanfer, A.G. & Taylor, M. (2005). *Immigrant Engagement in Public Open Space: Strategies for the New Boston*. Boston, MA: Barr Foundation.

Nash, R.F. (1967). *Wilderness and the American Mind*. New Haven, CT: Yale University

Naughton-Treves, L., Holland, M.B. & Brandon, K. (2005). The role of protected areas in conserving biodiversity and sustaining local livelihoods. *Annual Review of Environment and Resources, 30*, 219–252.

Newell, P.B. (1997). A cross-cultural examination of favorite places. *Environment and Behavior, 29*(4), 495–519.

Park, A. (2007). Mission critical: A new frame for diversity and environmental progress. In E. Enderle (Ed.) *Diversity and the Future of the Environmental Movement* (pp. 35–49). New Haven, CT: Yale School of Forestry and Environmental Studies.

Rishbeth, C. (2001) Ethnic minority groups and the design of public open space: An inclusive landscape? *Landscape Research, 26*(4), 351–366.

Roberts, N.S. (2009). Crossing the color line with a different perspective on whiteness and (anti)racism: A response to Mary McDonald. *Journal of Leisure Research, 41*(4), 495–509.

Roberts, N.S. (2013). Mixed race or mixed up? Making progress and breaking down barriers. In D. Dustin & K. Schwab (Eds.) *Just Leisure: Addressing Social and Environmental Justice in Parks, Recreation and Tourism* (pp. 27–34). Urbana, IL: Sagamore.

Roberts, N.S. & Chitewere, T. (2011). Speaking of justice: Exploring ethnic minority perspectives of the Golden Gate National Recreation Area. *Environmental Practice, 13*(4), 1–16.

Roberts, N.S. & Rodriguez, D.A. (2008). A mixed-method approach: Examining constraints effecting ethnic minority visitor use of national parks. *Ethnic Studies Review, 31*(2), 35–70.

Rodriguez, D.A. & Roberts, N.S. (2002). State of the knowledge report: The association of race/ethnicity, gender, and social class in outdoor recreation experiences. NPS Social Science Program, General Technical Report, Washington, DC: National Park Service.

Sasidharan, V. (2002). Special issue introduction: Understanding recreation and the environment within the context of culture. *Leisure Sciences, 24*(1), 1–11.

Sexton, N.R., Leong, K.M., Milley, B.J., Clarke, M.M., Teel, T.L., Chase, M.A. & Dietsch, A.M. (2013). The state of human dimensions capacity for natural resource management: Needs, knowledge, and resources. *George Wright Forum, 30*(2), 142–153.

Smith, J.W. & Floyd, M.F. (2013). The urban growth machine, central place theory and access to open space. *City, Culture and Society, 4*(2), 87–98.

Stodolska, M., Shinew, K., Floyd, M. & Walker, G. (2013). *Race, Ethnicity, and Leisure: Perspectives on Research, Theory, and Practice.* Champaign, IL: Human Kinetics.

Taylor, D.E. (1999). Central park as a model for social control: urban parks, social class and leisure behavior in nineteenth century America. *Journal of Leisure Research, 31*, 420–477.

34

Equality and inclusion
in the outdoors
Connecting with nature from
an Indian perspective

Di Collins

INSTITUTE FOR OUTDOOR LEARNING

Latha Anantharaman

FREELANCE WRITER, EDITOR AND TRANSLATOR

Introduction

This study developed through the shared interests of the authors. The enquiry evolved as we shared our perceptions of how the people we met, lived among and worked with related to nature and the outdoors. Latha Anantharaman is an environmentalist and writer. Rather than formal research, her investigations have taken the form of journalistic interviews. She will shortly publish a book, *Three Seasons* (in press), in which she recounts her observations of life in her rural community in South India. Di Collins is primarily an outdoor and community educator. Her research interests have been qualitative and interpretive. She has focused on issues related to equality, connecting with nature and developing a sense of belonging. She explored making connections with nature during a Churchill Fellowship to Australia, where cultural aspects of our connections became heightened. She has been visiting India for long periods over the past two decades and first met Latha eight years ago. Latha and Di share a love of being in nature. Both are concerned that it seems that, increasingly, people are becoming disconnected from nature. In this chapter, qualitative and interpretive research focuses on the characteristics of connections with nature. The interviewees represent a range of ages and a variety of educational backgrounds. After analysis, we then consider the implications for the practice of outdoor educators.

Defining our terms

As we commenced our collaborative work we identified a need to define the terms nature, outdoor education and equality. While we agreed that we had a shared understanding of the words that we were using in our conversations, we had to ensure that the participants in our research would also have that understanding. We use the word nature rather than outdoors deliberately. The outdoors has different understandings in India and the UK, perhaps partly because of the proportions of the populations living a lifestyle that is closer to the outdoors. In 2013, 68 per cent of India's population was living in a rural area, compared with 18 per cent of the UK's population (World Bank, 2015). In the UK, there is a clearer distinction between outdoor and indoor. Outdoor can be seen as more remote from everyday life. Being outdoors may demand a deliberate intention, perhaps involving additional clothing and addressing issues of access. However, in India, outdoors can simply mean not indoors. In particular, in South India, many people live a life that is predominantly not indoors. Latha explained that nature comes in to the house. As the climate is generally clement, life is conducted on verandas, balconies, roof terraces, on the streets and in gardens. Although nature is a contested word (Macnaghten & Urry, 1998), in this Indian context it has a greater clarity of definition and might be understood in a wider range of cultural settings than outdoors. Thus nature, rather than outdoor, has become our preferred word.

We also chose to avoid making reference to outdoor education, or outdoor learning, as the term outdoor education might be misconstrued by our interviewees. Outdoor education or learning might be seen as learning that does not take place under a roof. As we travel through South India, classes may be observed taking place under the shade of a large tree, although this is becoming far less common. Even when people do have a concept of outdoor education as a distinct learning process, Latey (2010) found that people new to the potential of outdoor learning perceive it in terms of activities containing a high level of structured, physical adventure, such as trekking and rafting. India's distinctive form of outdoor education is still developing. In addition, themes explored in the UK, such as bushcraft and spirituality, might be regarded as a general part of everyday life in India, particularly in rural areas. Here, we have both frequently observed activities such as the gathering of herbs for medicinal purposes and practices to mark the particular spiritual qualities of a place. Thus, because there is confusion over the term outdoor education, we decided to refer to 'learning about nature' in the interviews.

We also sought common ground when exploring terms and issues related to equality. There is a political aspect to equality and inclusion (Gadgil & Guha, 1995; Collins, Williams & di Leonardo, 2008). People who have equality of access can be said to be included. The antithesis is exclusion. Being socially excluded is defined in a United Nations (UN) publication as follows:

> involuntary exclusion of individuals and groups from society's political, economic and societal processes, which prevents their full participation in the society in which they live. (Atkinson & Marlier, 2010, p. 1)

However, exclusion is not always involuntary. People may choose not to be included for a variety of reasons, such as fear of repercussions, or apathy. In simple terms, the UN suggests that inclusion can be promoted by tackling issues related to poverty and exclusion.

In India, marginalised groups can be difficult to categorise. The interaction of a fast-growing economy, a rural population of 69 per cent, high levels of poverty and illiteracy, and a society in which women are generally awarded a lower status than men have proliferated inequalities. Arokiasamy (2002) has commented on the prevalence of a patriarchal society, in which women and children are of lower status. Latey describes India as 'a snake with its head in the 21st century and body dating back to the archaic times' (2010, p. 1). She describes an intricate social weave underpinned by a caste system. Initially we struggled to categorise our interviewees. Some inequalities are related to intellectual abilities and socio-economic impediments to accessing an education and gaining academic qualifications. More fundamental is a willingness to take action to be included and access opportunities.

Background to the research

With our interests in the possible negative consequences of a dislocation from nature, of particular relevance are Martin (2003) and Cooper's (2007) models. Martin (2003) writes of a formative process of moving from being alienated from nature, to travelling through nature, to caring for nature and, ultimately, to being integrated with nature. Cooper (2007) has defined a model for global citizenship, in which awareness and empowerment lead to a commitment to take action for the planet. However, applying these models in our research context is complicated. Gadgil and Guha (1995) describe events in India as contradictions and clashes between an environmentalism of the poor and an environmentalism born of affluence. They suggest that the rich and the poor have different perceptions of and relationships with nature. At one extreme is exploitation of the environment. At the other extreme is sustaining the environment. The rich, the state and large companies have the power and influence to take control of forests, agriculture and water supplies, and to exploit natural resources for financial gain or to maintain their power. In addition, Ananthapadmanabhan, Srinivas and Gopal (2007) point out that the rich create the carbon emissions and exploit the environment, while the poor suffer the consequences, in terms of pollution and poor yields. Gadgil and Guha (ibid.) argue that, on the other hand, in general terms, the poor have a more holistic and integrated relationship with nature. Wood lots and rain-fed water tanks may be used prudently and sustainably. There are sacred groves. Environmentally friendly agricultural practices are followed. Shiva (1988) argues that women are the holders of traditional knowledge of ecological processes. However, she warns that this knowledge is undermined and threatened by the pursuance of economic gain, using agricultural practices that exploit the natural environment and lead to long-term degradation. While these arguments may be generalisations, if people become alienated from the land, from nature, will they have the knowledge to argue for its protection? More importantly, will they have the power to take action, as described in Cooper's (2007) model?

Becoming global citizens (Cooper, 2007) may be reliant on the extent to which people understand issues related to the local and the global environment, and to their feelings of inclusion and belonging (Shiva, 2004; Leiserowitz & Thaker, 2012). This links back to the political dimensions associated with the UN's definition of inclusion (Atkinson & Marlier, 2010, p. 1). If people understand the issues related to the environment, do they feel adequately empowered to take action?

The research

Our research developed organically as we discussed issues relating to nature and learning. Our aim was to gain insights, which might have implications for the development of outdoor learning in both India and the UK. Our questions focused on the following: How did you learn about nature? How are you involved in or with nature? How do you promote it? What thoughts do you have about the future?

Our interviewees were selected through the process of snowballing (Maykut & Morehouse, 1994). Rather than drawing on random sampling, interviewees suggested other people to interview (Maykut and Morehouse, 1994, pp. 62–63). The number of interviewees was dictated by balancing saturation in identified categories of meaning against the ability to tolerate ambiguity. Notes were taken and the interviews were transcribed. Names have been changed to promote anonymity. Interviews were conducted mostly, but not exclusively, in English. In some cases,

Table 34.1 Characteristics of the people who participated in the interviews

Name	Current age group	Male/female	Education: standard/qualification
'Saheli'	15+	Female	12+
'Aolani'	15+	Female	11+
'Ratash'	20+	Male	Master's
'Ravi'	20+	Male	12+
'Sharang'	30+	Male	Master's
'Sachiv'	30+	Male	5
'Madhu'	30+	Male	10
'Sabal'	30+	Male	7
'Pahal'	30+	Male	0
'Ratnesh'	40+	Male	Bachelor
'Pallavi'	50+	Female	Bachelor
'Kishore'	50+	Male	Master's
'Jayanti'	50+	Female	Master's
'Sajan'	50+	Male	Bachelor
'Soumil'	50+	Male	PhD

an email interview was more relevant than a face-to-face interview. We also reflected on observations made during the course of our research.

In total, fifteen people were interviewed, eleven males and four females. It should be noted that it was difficult to identify women who were willing to be interviewed, but who had not completed their school education. Eight were graduates; two had completed their schooling; two had left school at the ages of 10 and 12 one at the age of 16 and one had not been to school; three intended to continue into higher education. The sample included people who had visited or spent significant time either in North America or in Europe. This included people who have not continued into higher education (see Table 34.1).

Formative experiences

Asked how they had learned about nature, the interviewees described a number of factors that were a part of their lifestyles. Growing up in a rural setting was significant for many. Saheli (15+) felt that she had grown up in nature. Other interviewees commented:

> I lived in nature . . . We were surrounded by lots of birds, foxes, trees . . . Sometimes we would sleep outside and watch the foxes. (Madhu, 30+)

> Yes! I grew up amidst the mountain, forests and the sea. However, my backyard interested me as well, and I would spend days playing around the trees and a series of small hills behind our house. I lived in the outdoors environment. (Sharang, 30+)

> As a child I was interested in the outdoors since our house had a huge garden and there was plenty of open space to play. We had quite a few pets at home . . . dogs, squirrels, parakeet. I even nursed a baby black kite that was being pecked at by crows for a while . . . we had a huge garden and good company was enough reason to be outdoors always. (Ratnesh, 40+)

> Thanks to a village life . . . I could enjoy nature with its diversity of flora & fauna. From our living room window, I could see the Western Ghats. (Jayanti, 50+)

> I loved admiring the sheer diversity of life in silence. (Sajan, 50+)

A number expressed the importance of mentors in their lives, as they learned about nature. Responses include:

> I learned from my mother and the neighbours about medicines and plants that are good for you and bad for you. (Sachiv, 30+)

> My *patti* [grandmother] used to walk with us in the evening . . . to the nearby fields to buy [vegetables]. I used to see the green, lush fields and the farmers [pumping water into] the fields, the contentment in their lives. (Jayanti, 50+)

Jayanti continued, commenting on the positive influences of the gardening skills of her mother and grandmother and her father's passion for photography.

The interviewees recalled everyday activities, such as calling out the names of the trees on the way to school (Kishore, 50+), which helped to foster a love of nature and being in the outdoors. Saheli (15+) described her long walk to school through the tea estate on paved roads, a bus ride along the highway and through a bit of forest, and then a long walk through forest. It was during that walk that she saw wildlife such as peacocks and other birds, and boar. Others commented:

> When I was little, I would play out rather than going to school. (Ravi (20+)

> Outdoors, I mostly looked for insects, caught them and left them later. I also walked and cycled a lot in my childhood. (Ratash, 20+)

> I looked after the cows, goats and [plant] nursery. (Sabal, 30+, farm labourer trainee)

> We swam in the rivers. (Sachiv, 30+)

> As a child, I would climb hills, hunt birds etc. As a teenager, I would go swimming into the open sea, snorkel etc. (Sharang, 30+)

> We walked and biked every day during my teens. (Pallavi, 50+)

> . . . swimming in the river, long walks and cycling. (Sajan, 50+)

> As a child I was interested in spending time outdoors, playing, traveling and exploring. (Soumil, 50+)

> I grew up in a tightly knit community, where the society was involved in promoting outdoor sports, viewing outdoor movies, hosting musical events, festival celebrations, and travel to parks and sites of historical importance near Hyderabad. This upbringing generated a lot of interest in the nature, outdoors, and working for the welfare of the community. (Soumil, 50+)

Visits into nature were also important enabling factors for a number of interviewees:

> My family would take me to frequent picnics, hop on a private boat, reach another island and have a great time with my friends and my parents' friends over bonfire and playing on the sand etc. My relationship with nature was built right in the initial days. (Sharang, 30+)

> We would visit the beach every week with the elders. (Ratnesh, 40+)

> As a child, my weekly outings were to Kolkata's Maidan [an open playing field with some trees at the periphery], local parks, Alipore Zoo, and the lake in south Kolkata. (Sajan, 50+)

355

For some this was an opportunity to experience the culture associated with place:

> I have visited many areas with family members [more often than] school trips. When I visited a place, first I will notice the peculiarities in that particular place and after that I will note down the importance of those places (the weather, temples, animals, trees, birds, traditional food, etc.) and take photos. (Aolani, 15+)

> The yearly outing to Thillai [their parents' ancestral village] was our exposure to a village with river, coconut grove and fields along with the monthly trip to see Marina beach [in Chennai]. (Pallavi, 50+)

Other everyday activities were described. Storytelling can be associated with beginning to identify with nature. Pallavi (50+) recalled her grandmother telling a story of a *rishi* (a Hindu sage) who had taken a vow of silence. He lived in the forest caring for abandoned cattle. Sharang (30+) described the ways in which folklore involving plants and animals had encouraged his learning. Others described ways of gathering information. Aolani (15+) spoke of Google and Wikipedia, Ratash (20+) recalled a television programme about a lion, and Pallavi (50+) talked of being inspired by the photographs in *National Geographic* magazines. Both Ratash (20+) and Sajan (50+) spoke of the importance of having access to books about nature.

There were also some constraining factors, which were noted by the younger interviewees. Ravi (20+) mentioned a school trip that involved rowing on a lake. However, such school trips were regarded as a reward for good behaviour and academic achievement. Thus, many less able pupils would be excluded. Girls and young women were also constrained from venturing into nature because of concerns for their personal safety and also their reputations. Sahelli (15+) explained that her grandparents did not allow her to go out unless her brother was available to act as a chaperone. She hinted at the unfairness of this as her brother had a greater freedom to go out.

Involvement with or in nature

As people have become older, many have struggled to find time to be in nature. However, Sachiv (30+) and Madhu (30+) work in tourism in a rural area. Madhu (30+) said, 'I work in nature. Sometimes we [the family] go walking. It's very important that they learn from it. The children want to see things.' Sachiv is enthusiastic to extend his own knowledge and understanding, and to increase that of his extended family:

> I hunt for healthy things in the wild. I teach the children things in nature . . . that's better than the TV and books, but I look up things in books. I also learn from the visitors. Things are more beautiful in the countryside. Traditional things in nature are tastier. In the garden things grow too quickly.

Meanwhile, others have made some efforts to continue their interests in nature. Sharang (30+) has 'undertaken trekking, whitewater rafting, a short course in rock climbing, have done parasailing, and went up on hot air balloon'. During a gap year he volunteered with a turtle conservation project. Ratnesh (40+) is a member of the Madras Naturalists' Society and used to organise bird-watching trips. He has visited many wildlife and bird sanctuaries. This interest has rubbed off on his family. Pallavi (50+) takes the family and often the children of neighbours on picnics and visits to countryside locations, including camping and following forest trails. Pallavi (50+) and Kishore (50+) encourage children to become involved in planting flowers, vegetables and saplings. Jayanti (50+) is a keen bird watcher, and shares her interest with family and friends. Soumil (50+) encourages his own children and their friends to engage in outdoor activities, such as visits to parks and hiking. He is also a keen astronomer.

While most people reported that they were able to continue their involvement in nature, if only in a small way, and also to promote it with others, Sharang (30+) has found that his enthusiasms have been blocked by parents' fears of perceived dangers. Both Latha and Di have observed people fearful of venturing into nature and the outdoors. People have expressed (occasionally justifiably) fear of insects and wild animals. People from urban areas have been fearful of going through a gate to take a circular walk around a lake, in case they could not find their way back. There were also some concerns about the right to access the countryside, as more plantations and farmland are being enclosed. Sabal (30+) commented, 'Before you could walk anywhere. There were no fences. At the old mango grove, you could hear the sound of water. Now everything is fenced off.'

Thoughts about nature and the future

When asked to consider issues related to connecting with nature and the future, the interviewees were less positive. When considering children and young people's connections with nature, a vicious circle was revealed. Ratash (20+), Sachiv (30+), Madhu (30+) and Sajan (50+) said that the current generation had fewer opportunities to connect with nature and the outdoors. However, while parents expressed a concern about high academic pressures leaving children little time for unstructured outdoor activity, they felt unable to challenge these priorities. Instead, children and young people who are under pressure to achieve academically spent long hours studying. In addition, parental fear can restrict children's freedom to roam (Sankaranarayanan, 2013). Moreover, rather than being outdoors, many young people favour using technology. Sachiv (30+) pointed out that knowledge about local vegetation and animals is being lost. At one time, mothers passed on much of this information, but their knowledge base is being reduced. This loss of knowledge is exacerbated by the fact that young teachers replace learning about the environment with academic rather than experiential learning processes. In addition, Saheli (15+) and Ravi (20+) said that they had learned about nature from going on a school visit, but that was a reward for their academic achievement. This suggests that the less academically able might miss out on these opportunities to have first-hand experience of learning about nature.

Urbanisation was identified as an issue. Some expressed concerns that, as more rural people move into cities, or as their semi-rural environments become more urbanised, they would become alienated from nature. Sabal (30+) believes that a failure to recognise what is happening to the environment at a local level will ultimately have an impact on global conditions. A major problem associated with this drift to urban areas is that fewer people are willing to work as farm labourers. This means that agricultural practices must become more mechanised, altering rural areas and rural life. In addition, harmful practices are employed. Sabal (30+) noted that monoculture is favoured. In the absence of effective agricultural policies, markets are flooded and prices drop, and people who earn their livelihood from the land are affected. He reflected:

> Education means that no one wants to do farm work. Farmers are not respected. Without farmers, there is no food . . . Once the goat people [a local tribal group] walked many kilometres, following the food. The children didn't go to school. Now they live in a village, in big houses and the children go to school . . . they won't want to look after goats . . . And now there is monoculture. All the birds and animals have gone.

Other concerns were expressed about a lack of commitment to sustainability and issues related to climate change. Ratash (20+) and Sharang (30+) noted an apparent lack of interest in or awareness of environmental issues, and a failure to react to visible changes. Sachiv (30+), Madhu (30+) and Sabal (30+), who are living in a rural area, endorsed this view. Ratnesh (40+) cited pollution and vehicle addiction as symptoms of this lack of interest or understanding. There was a feeling that many politicians were unwilling to act on issues related to the environment, water, deforestation and pollution. Pallavi (50+) stated:

> The weather is having its outbursts as tsunami, earthquakes, floods and storms. If we mistreat nature it will rebel and warn us in its own way. Still there is very little being done. We are heading in the wrong direction with this mass overproduction in one part of the world and famine in the other places.

Conclusions

Having flexible opportunities to be in nature, with the support of family, friends and mentors has been key in encouraging people of all ages to make connections with nature. These connections have been enhanced by understanding a little of the culture of the place. Access to resources or resource people have added to the strength of the connection. However, some people have not been offered such opportunities. In addition, it was found that young women were constrained in their abilities to explore nature. There were also fears for safety, the nature itself or other people in nature being perceived as dangerous. Children and young people are constrained more than their elders by the pressures to achieve academic qualifications. They also have the temptations of staying in doors to use technologies that were not available in their parents' time. With increasing urbanisation, there is a risk that accessing nature will become more problematic. There is also a fear that nature in agricultural and wild areas will be damaged by practices that exploit natural resources.

When defining our terms, we stated that marginalised groups could be difficult to categorise. Our analysis has confirmed our fears. When considering our findings in relation to equality, it seems that the marginalised can include children and young people, girls and women, people who do not have opportunities, whether for economic, geographical, academic or status reasons, and also people who lack the confidence or skills to access nature. When we defined our equality and inclusion, we suggested that it is bound up with having the confidence and will to take action. In reviewing the contents of these interviews, there is a general air of frustration and impotence. In general, people can identify what the issues are in relation to connecting with nature and taking action for the benefit of nature, but lack the confidence and skills to do so. While Gadgil and Guha's (1995) environmentalism of the poor and an environmentalism born of affluence may exist, it seems that more significant is the perceived power held by the super-rich, the state and large companies. This is far more influential than the power that the comparatively affluent in professional and middle classes may feel that they have. Thus, those who feel impotent to take action may also be marginalised.

Considering both Martin (2003) and Cooper's (2007) models, the ultimate goal is to be integrated with nature, with the ability to take action for the planet. Our interviewees appeared to care about the environment. Some seemed to express feelings of being integrated with the environment. They could identify the possible outcomes of weaknesses in connections with nature, but were struggling to make the huge actions needed for the benefit of the planet.

It is clear that our sample was not representative of the whole spectrum of Indian society. Our intention was not to conduct a meta-analysis, but to gain insights to inform the practice of outdoor educators. Our interviews indicate that having an outdoor habit was critical to people's desire to maintain connections with nature. Those who had memorable experiences in childhood, or even later in life, generally had a desire to continue their encounters with nature. Thus, outdoor educators have a responsibility to facilitate quality experiences for all age groups. However, the key area revealed by this research is the need for people to have the confidence to take action on behalf of nature, developing understanding, knowledge and skills that might include debating, decision making, discussing ethical issues and being assertive. This area for development is as pertinent to outdoor educators in the UK as to those working in India.

References

Ananthapadmanabhan, G., Srinivas, K. & Gopal, V. (2007). *Hiding Behind the Poor: A Report by Greenpeace on Climate Injustice*. Bangalore: Greenpeace India Society.

Anantharaman, L. (in press) *Three Seasons*. Kolkotta: Writers Workshop.

Arokiasamy, P. (2002). Gender preference, contraceptive use and fertility: Regional and development influence. *International Journal of Population Geography, 8*(1), 49–67.

Atkinson, A. & Marlier, E. (2010). *Analysing and Measuring Social Inclusion in a Global Context*. New York: United Nations.

Collins, J., Williams, B. & di Leonardo, M. (Eds.) (2008). *New Landscapes of Inequality: Neoliberalism and the Erosion of Democracy in America*. Santa Fe, NM: SAR Press.

Cooper, G. (2007) Going global in the outdoors: How outdoor leaders can encourage education for a fair and sustainable world. *Horizons, 40*, 4–7.

Gadgil, M. & Guha, R. (1995). *Ecology and Equity: The Use and Abuse of Nature in Contemporary India*. New Delhi: Penguin Books.

Latey, M. (2010). The significance and potential of 'outdoor pursuits' for women in India. Unpublished MA dissertation, Trinity College, Carmarthen.

Leiserowitz, A. & Thaker, J. (2012). *Climate Change in the Indian Mind*. Yale: Yale School of Forestry and Environmental Studies and Globespan, Inc. Retrieved from: http://environment.yale.edu/climate-communication/article/climate-change-indian-mind.

Macnaghten, P. & Urry, J. (1998). *Contested Natures*. London: Sage.

Martin, P. (2003) Outdoor education for human/nature relationships. *Australian Journal of Outdoor Education, 1*(3), 2–9.

Maykut, P. & Morehouse, R. (1994). *Beginning Qualitative Research. A Philosophical and Practical Guide*. London: Falmer Press.

Sankaranarayanan, A. (2013). Safety 101. *The Hindu*, 5 May, 6.

Shiva, V. (1988) *Staying Alive. Women. Ecology and Survival in India*. New Delhi: Kali for Women.

Shiva, V (2004) Biopiracy. Retrieved from: www.vshiva.net.

World Bank (2015) 3.1. World development indicators: Rural environment and land use. Retrieved from: www.wdi.worldbank.org/table/3.1.

35

Gender in outdoor studies

Karen Warren

HAMPSHIRE COLLEGE

Evidence of the male-dominated nature of the outdoor field persists despite advances by women and girls in outdoor participation. Gender role socialisation continues to be a factor in unequal power relationships in outdoor programmes and leadership positions for adult women, while feminist critiques of teaching and learning in the outdoors point out its gender-privileged nature. More recently, a movement towards studying girls' experience arose, with this literature suggesting effective strategies for girls' outdoor programming. This chapter will delve into these topics as well as questions about the continued emphasis on women-only experiences, gendered messages about the outdoor experience, intersectionality in the outdoors, and if new research can find ways to mitigate factors that continue to disadvantage women and girls in outdoor programming. Finally, gaps in the outdoor literature concerning gender, including the reluctance to explore masculinity in outdoor adventure, the invisibility of the experience of women/girls of colour, its heteronormative nature and nascent attention to transgendered issues, will be examined.

Scholars and practitioners have called for critical reflection of the gendering of outdoor adventure programming (Humberstone, 2000). Paramount to any critical discourse on gender in the outdoors is the question of whether the outdoor experience inculcates and reproduces static oppressive gender roles or is a site of social change with resistance to gender role conditioning. Some would say that the outdoors provides a respite from social conventions and is the great equaliser, however the egalitarian level playing field of the wilderness has been questioned as a myth and remains a complicated site of struggle for many female adventurers (Warren, 1985; Newbery, 2004). While individual agency allows many women to enjoy and enact lives of adventuring outdoors, social meanings and conditions continue to follow women into the wilderness (Little, 2002a). In a historical analysis of education outdoors in the United Kingdom, Cook (2001) concluded, 'it seems outdoor education generally reflected wider social assumptions about gender rather than challenged them' (p. 50). In contrast, Whittington (2006) found that girls' outdoor programmes 'challenged assumptions about their abilities and images of conventional notions of femininity' (p. 212).

In sum, hegemonic reproductions of gender in the outdoors demand an examination of the social meanings and constructs that continue to prevent outdoor education, recreation and adventure from being a location of progressive social justice.

Gender messages in the outdoors

Media and cultural messages of appropriate roles in the wilderness have mediated the outdoors as a site for participation of men and women. Gender socialisation has been revealed in these entrenched meanings of the outdoors, and continues to underlie proscribed ways men and woman might associate with the outdoors and be influenced by the wilderness experience (Warren & Loeffler, 2006). In studies of outdoor advertising, popular press and outdoor guidebooks, researchers have found that oppressive gender roles have been reified rather than disputed.

In one study analysing popular outdoor magazine advertising, conclusions showed that women were depicted as participating in less physically and time demanding engagements in outdoor pursuits, were shown as followers rather than leaders, and were seen as either escaping from motherhood or being the instigator of outdoor time with their families (McNiel, Harris & Fondren, 2012). Furthermore, women with exceptional outdoor skills and abilities were viewed as unique by possessing attributes beyond the outdoor abilities of the average woman (McNiel *et al.*, 2012), a phenomenon Warren (1985) calls the anomaly of the 'superwoman' who effectively vacates any role model status she might have due to her exemplary outdoor skills.

For men and boys, proscribed roles in the outdoors focus on rugged individualism and a conquering mentality that further make gender role socialisation concrete and influence the field of outdoor adventure in maintaining its male-dominated paradigms (Bell, 1997; Warren, 2012). In Denny's (2011) content analysis of the handbooks of Girl Scouts and Boy Scouts, messages for boys stressed self-oriented activity and heteronormative masculinity, while girls are influenced by gendered messages promoting other-oriented activity and femininity, and at the same time are exposed to messages promoting more progressive feminist identities, thus adding ambiguity to gender role identity negotiations in the outdoors for young women.

The literature of socialisation in the outdoors extends to guidebooks as well, where the required femininity of women in the outdoors is problematised. In comparing unisex outdoor guidebooks to those written for and about women, Glotfelty (1996) noted,

> Perhaps the most significant difference between the two sets of books is that all the women's guides contain a lengthy discussion of femininity. While unisex guides focus on '**how to**' skills, women's guides teach readers '**who to**' be. (p. 442)

While outdoor programmes have been employed to challenge constructs of femininity based on white, middle-class, heterosexual models of beauty (Whittington, 2006), the notion remains a source of gender role incongruity in the outdoors (Wittmer, 2001) where exemplary outdoor women require feminisation (McNiel *et al.*, 2012) and women participants in outdoor programmes face an untenable dilemma of trying to resist oppressive stereotypes of femininity while at the same time having to conform to these traditional notions to gain acceptance (Lugg, 2003).

The preponderance of gender message for both men and women in outdoor advertising and literature creates a climate where the cycle of socialisation flourishes, and continues to reinforce 'acting out' one's gender in the outdoors to find success or resist being ostracised.

Gender-sensitive outdoor leadership and pedagogy

Leadership in outdoor education and adventure has been called in to question with Bell's (1996) assertion of 'the gendered, race-based organisation of the subjectivity of the leaders, such that it is European, able-bodied, autonomous, objective and rational men who are predisposed to make sound decisions and be natural leaders' (p. 144). Others have noted gender-mediated issues in outdoor leadership, such as women who demonstrate traditional masculine leadership being devalued by participants and supervisors (Wittmer, 2001).

Feminist outdoor leadership and practice has been advanced in the outdoor field with inter-rogations of power relations playing an important role in the discussion of leading in the out-doors (Warren & Rheingold, 1993; Henderson, 1996; Haluza-DeLay & Dyment, 2003). While contemporary feminism is complex, situated and multifaceted, aspects of feminist outdoor lead-ership include validation of personal experience, democratic or consensus decision-making pro-cesses, attention to power dynamics in group processes, shared leadership, collective problem solving and communication, and honouring participant choice.

In outdoor learning environments, researchers have suggested that females may learn techni-cal outdoor skills differently than male participants and thus benefit from a gender-sensitive ped-agogy that accounts for these unique needs (Dingle & Kiewa, 2006; Warren & Loeffler, 2006). Others have found a hidden curriculum of adventure education that disadvantages women (Lugg, 2003; Mitten, Warren, Lotz & d'Amore, 2012). Additionally, women may seek differ-ent types of outdoor programmes than men or interact with activities differently. For example, activities based on trust and relationships were favoured by women, while men valued power and challenge (Lugg, 2003).

Gender-sensitive outdoor pedagogy involves reflection on the part of the educator about the personal bias and position they bring to their teaching (Wittmer, 2001). In technical outdoor skill teaching, providing non-competitive learning situations that minimise performance anxiety (Loeffler, 2000), offering repetitive practice of skills to account for lack of childhood techni-cal conditioning (Warren, 1985), addressing linguistic and territorial sexism in teaching envi-ronments (Warren & Loeffler, 2006), avoiding discriminatory programming techniques (Irish, 2006) and labelling traditional feminine strengths as positive (Haluza-DeLay & Dyment, 2003) have all been suggested as ways to enhance the learning experience of females.

Initially, feminist outdoor leadership and pedagogy was seen as effective for women and girls without an attempt to infuse a feminist consciousness into all outdoor programming (Jordan, 1992; Bell, 1996). More recently, the tenets of feminist outdoor leadership have begun to show up in more mainstream examinations of leading in the outdoors (Martin, Cashel, Wagstaff & Breunig, 2006), with the key question of whether what works well for females in the outdoors can be applied across the gender spectrum.

How women navigate professional positions of outdoor leadership is another factor to be addressed. Inequities and 'glass ceilings' that make the journey perilous at times influence women seeking a career in outdoor education. Allin (2003) questions the idea of an outdoor career for woman as a planned trajectory, and suggests that women's outdoor careers may lack a clear long-term career ladder and could be viewed more accurately through the lens of lifestyle and self-identity. Women leaders often feel inclined to overcompensate or outdo male leaders in order to be accepted, and this can lead to burnout and exit from the profession (Wright & Gray, 2013). Trip participants of both genders may also exhibit a lack of confidence in the ability of female leaders to facilitate a group or perform technical outdoor skills (Frauman & Washam, 2013).

Loeffler's (1996) study on the careers of twenty-five women outdoor leaders suggested that equal opportunity hiring policies and advancement tracks, support networks, and single-gender programmes for women and girls would stimulate equity in outdoor leadership positions.

A compelling question formulated from the scholarship on feminist leadership and pedagogy is whether tenets of this way of leading and teaching can or should direct how the entire field of outdoor study and practice will evolve.

Same-sex outdoor trips

Women who desire access to outdoor adventures have experienced constraints to participation. Gender role socialisation, motherhood and family obligations, financial priorities, lack of time, sexual harassment, lack of an outdoor companion, and fear are among the structural, interpersonal and intrapersonal factors preventing women from being fully engaged in outdoor adventure (Warren, 1985; Allin, 2003; Bialeschki, 2005). However, women's participation has continued to increase as women, in many cases, have negotiated these constraints in order to participate (Little, 2002b).

One avenue for adult women to overcome constraints to outdoor adventures is through participation in same-sex trips. Advocacy of single-sex outdoor trips for women in the 1970s and early 1980s caused an increase in women-only programmes, with subsequent analysis of their worth (Hornibrook et al., 1997). Benefits of these programmes were established and used for justification, while the idea of single-gender learning spaces on mixed-gender trips was also promoted (Warren & Rheingold, 1993). Philosophies that guide women's and girls' programmes include an ethic of care, cooperation and shared leadership, and reliance on conscious choice that resists subtle influences to conform to facilitator or programme values (Mitten, 1985; Tyson & Asmus, 2008).

Studies showed benefits of women-only outdoor adventure programmes to be connections to nature and wilderness, relational bonding, physical confidence and strength, competence, disengagement from traditional gender roles, overcoming fear and gaining autonomy (Loeffler, 1997; Boniface, 2006; Wedin, 2009; Myers, 2010; Libby & Carruthers, 2013). Further research could investigate whether these benefits can be attained on mixed-gender trips and what would need to change in current leadership and teaching in the outdoors to make this possible. Currently, critiques of women-only programmes suggest that dominant discourses of masculinity in all outdoor programmes are not addressed by the existence of these trips, thereby failing to create real social change (Lugg, 2003).

Girls in the outdoors

Groundbreaking research on girls' development (Brown & Gilligan, 1992) caused outdoor educators to consider how adolescent girls' experience of the outdoors might be unique, how outdoor programmes might benefit girls' development, and what accompanying modifications of existing outdoor programmes would meet the needs of young women. Authorities on girls' development found that adolescent girls tend to lose their voice in the transition from pre-teen to teenage years, and this silence predicates development problems stemming from acceptance of social stereotypes and notions of gender identity based on white, middle-class, heterosexual, male conceptions of what a women or girl 'should be'. Consequently, girls in their adolescent years are at risk for a decrease in physical activity, diminishing resilience, a disassociation with self, eating disorders, depression, decrease in self-worth and self-esteem, relational aggression and other risky behaviour (Humberstone & Lynch, 1991; Henderson & Grant, 1998; Gubitz & Kutcher, 1999; Sammet, 2010).

Outdoor educators with an interest in girls' development have identified benefits and constraints for girls in the outdoors. Culp (1998) identified constraints to adolescent females' participation in outdoor pursuits such as physical and safety concerns, lack of opportunity, differential opportunities for males and females, and negative peer influence. With the concern that girls suffer a diminished voice and sense of agency as they reach their teenage years, outdoor programing has been seen as a way for girls to gain beneficial attributes such as resiliency, positive identity formation (Gubitz & Kutcher, 1999), leadership, social skills, self-esteem (Wang, Liu &

Kahlid, 2006) and an increased ability to speak out (Whittington, 2006). Results of one study of several all-girl programmes found the benefits to be that 'all-girls programmes create a space for adolescent girls to feel safe, increase their connection with others, and provide freedom from stereotypes' (Whittington, Mack, Budbill & McKenney, 2011, p. 2). Other benefits include the reported feeling of self-confidence that solidified girls' belief in their own abilities (Allen-Craig & Hartley, 2012), perseverance, courage, resiliency and feelings of physical strength (Whittington & Budbill, 2013).

The concept of courage has been central to the philosophies of girls' outdoor programmes. In studying adolescent females, Rogers (1993) used the 13th century definition of courage 'to speak one's mind by telling all one's heart' and posited that this ordinary courage is lost as girls reach early adolescence. All-girls programmes arose to address these concerns, spearheaded by Outward Bound's Connecting with Courage programme (Porter, 1996). A voice-centred relational approach integrated into challenging outdoor activities was the basis of programming, with self-expression such as drama, journaling and art work being a key component as well.

Best practices for working with girls in outdoor programmes have been refined over the years to encompass a theoretical basis stressing strength-based approaches and an ethic of care as underpinnings (McKenney, Budbill & Roberts, 2008). Within this framework, authentic choice is emphasised and leadership provides positive role modelling. A strength-based approach, a programme philosophy that emphasises the positive attributes and efforts of the student to build on their natural talents rather than focus on their weaknesses (Passarelli, Hall & Anderson, 2010), is utilised to help girls maintain their innate strengths and resiliency in the face of social pressures that undermine the self-confidence of adolescent females. Prior friendships are honoured in the spirit of relationship building so that girls are encouraged rather than discouraged from sharing the outdoor experience with their friends (Porter, 1996). As Culp (1998) has suggested that peer relationships are pivotal to girls, outdoor courses offer opportunities for girls to have positive relationships with other girls (Whittington, 2006).

Constructions of gender in the outdoors

Insistence polarised conundrums in outdoor studies about the female body (feminine vs strong) (Newbery, 2003), nature (women aligned to nature vs men to culture), (Humberstone & Pedersen, 2001), and meanings of outdoor experience (social relationships vs physical risk) (Little, 2002a) must be continually challenged and demystified for liberatory gender relations and experience in the outdoors to hold promise.

While Henderson and Gibson (2013) noted the development of a nascent analysis of men's experience in the leisure literature, the outdoor adventure field has been slower in examining masculinity. Humberstone's (2000) writing on hegemonic masculinity in outdoor education is an exception where, making a comparison to sports, she posits that prevailing cultural messages 'celebrate the idealised form of masculinity at the same time as inferiorising the 'other'; women and forms of masculinity that do not conform' (p. 29). While being aware that men in the outdoors who resist dominant stereotypes are marginalised, expressions of alternative masculinities that contradict the prevailing ethos noted by scholars may help to reconstruct the male-dominated nature of the outdoor experience.

In addition to interrogating concepts of masculinity in outdoor studies there is a need to consider the intersectionality of oppressions with regard to gender (Henderson & Gibson, 2013). In a study of multiple-hierarchy stratification of constraints in outdoor recreation, Shores, Scott and Floyd (2007) found that identities such as gender, race/ethnicity, age and class interacted, with multiple disadvantageous statuses correlating to a higher likelihood of experiencing outdoor recreation constraints. Studying gender in the outdoors in isolation from other social identities belies the complexity of the lived experience of participants. Further, in the same way that much of the literature on outdoor education, adventure and recreation has implicitly been located in male experience, the writings on females in the outdoors often assume the experience of white, able-bodied, class-privileged, heterosexual women. Some attempts to make connections between intersectional experiences of privilege and oppression for women outdoors have shown up in scholarly work on the meanings and experience of women of colour (Roberts & Drogin, 1993; Roberts & Henderson, 1997). Understanding that women's outdoor adventure experience can continue through the life cycle is an underrepresented topic (Kluge, 2007), while socio-economic class can also influence engagement in the outdoors, with women questioning costly outdoor programmes while men report that time scarcity due to employment responsibilities constrains participation (Shores et al., 2007). Entry-level outdoor skills programmes for women have flourished as a way to gain outdoor competence without huge monetary commitments (Jones, 2007; Stenberg, 2007).

Heteronormative views proliferate in outdoor education, with the voices of lesbian and gay outdoor professionals virtually non-existent (Barnfield & Humberstone, 2008), leading to the proposition that by 'queering outdoor education' educators can interrupt the status quo of heterosexism and sexism (Russell, Sarick & Kennelly, 2003). Supported by homophobia, gay and lesbian baiting, the practice of labelling people as gay or lesbian no matter their sexual orientation, is used as a weapon of sexism to reinforce traditional gender role expectations (McClintock, 1996).

Dialogues about gender issues in the outdoors have traditionally adhered to a gender binary of dichotomous references of male and female within dialogue and practice. The range of transgender experience has been only recently explored in outdoor recreation and adventure (Grossman, O'Connell & D'Augelli, 2005; Mitten, 2012; Wilson & Lewis, 2012). As outdoor educators better understand the lived experience of transgendered people, the more likely it is that the gender binary might be challenged in the outdoor field and trans-sensitive practices to support transgender youth and adults be developed.

Additional studies of these intersections of locations of privilege and disadvantage in participants and leaders in the outdoors are needed as an answer to normalising white, middle-class, fit and able-bodied, youthful, heterosexual, male assumptions.

Conclusion

The future of outdoor studies rests on addressing some provocative questions that have previously been underrepresented in the dialogues about gender in the outdoors.

Can transgressive teaching and leading with attention to feminist values impact the entire field of outdoor education and recreation? How do dominant paradigms of masculinity in wilderness and adventure adversely affect men as well as women? Will acceptance of gender fluidity open up dialogues of women and men's issues in the outdoors to be less polarised? How can gendered outdoor messages be muted by an oppositional stance? Can the marginalisation of women and girls on mixed-gender outdoor adventures be mitigated so that the strengths of all participants can be recognised and affirmed? Can normalising of practices rooted in white, male, middle-class, heterosexual, able-bodied and youthful positions of privilege be a broadly contested site of resistance that challenges the paradigms of outdoor practice, thereby creating inclusivity?

This chapter has critically explored the gendered nature of outdoor education, recreation and adventure. Certainly, more scholarly work is necessary to address these dilemmas but, ultimately, the future rests not in *if* we will answer these questions but *when* and *how* – and, importantly, *who* will take the lead. While outdoor studies focused on gender have and continue to evolve, significant gaps, promising methodologies, alternative theoretical frameworks and the interrelationship of meanings are still to be explored.

References

Allen-Craig, S. & Hartley, C. (2012). Exploring the long-term effects for young women involved in an outdoor education program. *Journal of Outdoor Recreation, Education and Leadership, 4*(2), 88–92.

Allin, L. (2003). Women's reflections on a career in outdoor education. In B. Humberstone, H. Brown & K. Richards (Eds.) *Whose Journeys? The Outdoors and Adventure as Social and Cultural Phenomena* (pp. 229–239). Penrith, Cumbria: Institute for Outdoor Learning.

Barnfield, D. & Humberstone, B. (2008). Speaking out: Perspectives of gay and lesbian practitioners in outdoor education in the UK. *Journal of Adventure Education and Outdoor Learning, 8*(1), 31–42.

Bell, M. (1996). Feminists challenging assumptions about outdoor leadership. In K. Warren (Ed.) *Women's Voices in Experiential Education* (pp. 141–156). Dubuque, IA: Kendall/Hunt.

Bell, M. (1997). Gendered experience: Social theory and experiential practice. *Journal of Experiential Education, 20*(3), 143–151.

Bialeschki, M.D. (2005). Fear of violence: Contested constraints by women in outdoor recreation activities. In E. Jackson (Ed.) *Constraints to Leisure* (pp. 103–114). State College, PA: Venture Publishing.

Boniface, M. (2006). The meaning of adventurous activities for 'women in the outdoors'. *Journal of Adventure Education and Outdoor Learning, 6*(1), 9–24.

Brown, L. & Gilligan, C. (1992). *Meeting at the Crossroads: Women's Psychology and Girls' Development.* Cambridge, MA: Harvard University Press.

Cook, L. (2001). Differential social and political influences on girls and boys through education out of doors in the United Kingdom. *Journal of Adventure Education and Outdoor Learning, 1*(2), 43–51.

Culp, R.H. (1998). Adolescent girls and outdoor recreation: A case study examining constraints and effective programming. *Journal of Leisure Research, 30*(3), 356–380.

Denny, K.E. (2011). Gender in context, content, and approach: Comparing gender messages in Girl Scout and Boy Scout handbooks. *Gender & Society, 25*(1), 27–47.

Dingle, P. & Kiewa, J. (2006). Links between kayaking, fear, confidence and competence: Factors affecting women's participation in paddling in a tertiary outdoor education course. *Australian Journal of Outdoor Education, 10*(1), 46–53.

Frauman, E. & Washam, J. (2013). The role of gender as it relates to confidence among university outdoor programs' staff. *Journal of Outdoor Recreation, Education and Leadership, 5*(2), 119–123.

Glotfelty, C. (1996). Femininity in the wilderness: Reading gender in women's guides to backpacking. *Women's Studies, 25*(5), 439–456.

Grossman, A.H., O'Connell, T.S. & D'Augelli, A.R. (2005). Leisure and recreational 'girl–boy' activities – studying the unique challenges provided by transgendered young people. *Leisure/Loisir: Journal of the Canadian Association for Leisure Studies, 29*(1), 5–26.

Gubitz, K.F. & Kutcher, J. (1999). Facilitating identity formation for adolescent girls using experientially based outdoor activities. *TCA Journal, 27*(1), 32–39.

Haluza-DeLay, R. & Dyment, J.E. (2003). A toolkit for gender-inclusive wilderness leadership. *JOPERD – The Journal of Physical Education, Recreation & Dance, 74*(7), 28–32.

Henderson, K. (1996). Feminist perspectives on outdoor leadership. In K. Warren (Ed.) *Women's Voices in Experiential Education* (pp. 107–117). Dubuque, IA: Kendall/Hunt.

Henderson, K. & Grant, A. (1998). Recreation programming: Don't forget the girls. *Parks & Recreation,* (6), 34–41.

Henderson, K.A. & Gibson, H.J. (2013). An integrative review of women, gender, and leisure: Increasing complexities. *Journal of Leisure Research, 45*(2), 115–135.

Hornibrook, T., Brinkert, E., Parry, D., Seimens, R., Mitten, D. & Priest, S. (1997). The benefits and motivations of all-women outdoor programs. *Journal of Experiential Education, 20*(3), 152–158.

Humberstone, B. (2000) The 'outdoor industry' as social and educational phenomena: Gender and outdoor adventure/education. *Journal of Adventure Education & Outdoor Learning, 1*(1), 21–35.

Humberstone, B. & Lynch, P. (1991). Girls' concepts of themselves and their experiences in outdoor education programmes. *Journal of Adventure Education and Outdoor Leadership, 8*(3), 27–31.

Humberstone, B. & Pedersen, K. (2001). Gender, class and outdoor traditions in the UK and Norway. *Sport, Education & Society, 6*(1), 23–33.

Irish III, P.A. (2006). Gender-specific effects of muting on outdoor ropes challenge participation. *Journal of Experiential Education, 29*(2), 168–186.

Jones, J.J. (2007). Impact of 'Becoming an Outdoors-Woman' on self-efficacy, constraints and participation in outdoor recreation. Doctoral dissertation, Ohio University.

Jordan, D.J. (1992). Effective leadership for girls and women in outdoor recreation. *JOPERD – The Journal Of Physical Education, Recreation & Dance, 63*(2), 61–64.

Kluge, M.A. (2007) Re-creating through recreating: Using the personal growth through adventure model to transform women's lives. *Journal of Transformative Education, 5*, 177–191.

Libby, J. & Carruthers, C. (2013). Outcomes associated with a university outdoor adventures women's canoe trip. *Journal of Outdoor Recreation, Education and Leadership, 5*(3), 210–225.

Little, D.E. (2002a). How do women construct adventure recreation in their lives? *Journal of Adventure Education and Outdoor Learning, 2*(1), 55–69.

Little, D.E. (2002b). Women and adventure recreation: Reconstructing leisure constraints and adventure experiences to negotiate continuing participation. *Journal of Leisure Research, 34*(2), 157–177.

Loeffler, T.A. (1996). Leading the way: Strategies that enhance women's involvement in experiential education careers. In K. Warren (Ed.), *Women's Voices in Experiential Education* (pp. 94–103). Dubuque, IA: Kendall/Hunt.

Loeffler, T.A. (1997). Assisting women in developing a sense of competence in outdoor programs. *Journal of Experiential Education, 20*(3), 119–123.

Loeffler, T.A. (2000). The seasons of competency development for women. *Pathways: The Ontario Journal of Outdoor Education, 12*(4), 4–8.

Lugg, A. (2003). Women's experience of outdoor education: Still trying to be 'one of the boys'. In B. Humberstone, H. Brown & K. Richards (Eds.) *Whose Journeys? The Outdoors and Adventure as Social and Cultural Phenomena* (pp. 33–47). Penrith, Cumbria: Institute for Outdoor Learning.

Martin, B., Cashel, C., Wagstaff, M. & Breunig, M. (2006). *Outdoor Leadership: Theory and Practice.* Champaign, IL: Human Kinetics.

McClintock, M. (1996). Lesbian baiting hurts all women. In K. Warren (Ed.) *Women's Voices in Experiential Education* (pp. 241–250). Dubuque, IA: Kendall/Hunt.

McKenney, P., Budbill, N.W. & Roberts, N.S. (2008). Girls' outdoor adventure programs: History, theory, and practice. In K. Warren, D. Mitten & T.A. Loeffler (Eds.) *Theory and Practice of Experiential Education* (pp. 532–554). Boulder, CO: Association for Experiential Education.

McNiel, J.N., Harris, D.A. & Fondren, K.M. (2012). Women and the wild: Gender socialization in wilderness recreation advertising. *Gender Issues, 29*(1–4), 39–55.

Mitten, D. (1985). A philosophical basis for a women's outdoor adventure program. *Journal of Experiential Education, 8*(2), 20–24.

Mitten, D. (2012). Transgender and gender-nonconforming participation in outdoor adventure programming: Let's go mainstream. In B. Martin & M. Wagstaff (Eds.) *Controversial Issues in Adventure Programming* (pp. 235–240). Champaign, IL: Human Kinetics.

Mitten, D., Warren, K., Lotz, E. & d'Amore, C. (2012). The hidden curriculum in adventure education: A Delphi study. In *Proceedings of the 2012 Symposium on Experiential Education Research.* (pp. 37–40). Madison, WI: AEE.

Myers, L. (2010). Women travellers' adventure tourism experiences in New Zealand. *Annals of Leisure Research, 13*(1–2), 116–142.

Newbery, L. (2003). Will any/body carry that canoe? A geography of the body, ability, and gender. *Canadian Journal of Environmental Education, 8*, 204–216.

Newbery, L. (2004). Hegemonic gender identity and Outward Bound: Resistance and re-inscription? *Women in Sport & Physical Activity Journal, 13*(1), 36–49.

Passarelli, A., Hall, E. & Anderson, M. (2010). A strengths-based approach to outdoor and adventure education: Possibilities for personal growth. *Journal of Experiential Education, 33*(2), 120–135.

Porter, T. (1996). 'Connecting with Courage,' an Outward Bound program for adolescent girls. In K. Warren (Ed.) *Women's Voices in Experiential Education* (pp. 267–275). Dubuque, IA: Kendall/Hunt.

Roberts, N.S. & Drogin, E.B. (1993). The outdoor recreation experience: Factors affecting participation of African American women. *Journal of Experiential Education, 16*(1), 14–18.

Roberts, N.S. & Henderson, K.A. (1997). Women of color in the outdoors: Culture and meanings. *Journal of Experiential Education, 20*(3), 134–142.

Rogers, A. (1993). Voice, play, and a practice of ordinary courage in girls and women's lives. *Harvard Educational Review, 63*(3), 265–295.

Russell, C., Sarick, T. & Kennelly, J. (2003). Queering outdoor education. *Pathways: The Ontario Journal of Outdoor Education, 15*(1), 16–19.

Sammet, K. (2010). Relationships matter: Adolescent girls and relational development in adventure education. *Journal of Experiential Education, 33*(2), 151–165.

Shores, K.A., Scott, D. & Floyd, M.F. (2007). Constraints to outdoor recreation: A multiple hierarchy stratification perspective. *Leisure Sciences, 29*(3), 227–246.

Stenberg, K. (2007). Free life: A report from the 'Outdoor Life for Women' program in Sweden. *Pathways: The Ontario Journal of Outdoor Education, 19*(3), 29–33.

Tyson, L. & Asmus, K. (2008). Deepening the paradigm of choice: Exploring choice and power in experiential education. In K. Warren, D. Mitten & T.A. Loeffler (Eds.) *Theory and Practice of Experiential Education* (pp. 262–281). Boulder, CO: Association for Experiential Education.

Wang, C., Liu, W. & Kahlid, A. (2006). Effects of a five-day Outward Bound course on female students in Singapore. *Australian Journal of Outdoor Education, 10*(2), 20–28.

Warren, K. (1985). Women's outdoor adventures: Myth and reality. *Journal of Experiential Education, 8*(2), 10–15.

Warren, K. (2012). Paradigms of outdoor adventure and social justice. In B. Martin & M. Wagstaff (Eds.) *Controversial Issues in Adventure Programming* (pp. 120–125). Champaign, IL: Human Kinetics.

Warren, K. & Loeffler, T. (2006). Factors that influence women's technical skill development. *Journal of Adventure Education and Outdoor Leadership, 6*(2), 107–120.

Warren, K. & Rheingold, A. (1993). Feminist pedagogy and experiential education: A critical look. *Journal of Experiential Education, 16* (3), 25–31.

Wedin, B.M. (2009). Experiencing the wilderness. *Journal of Outdoor Recreation, Education and Leadership, 1*(2), 172–190.

Whittington, A. (2006). Challenging girls' constructions of femininity in the outdoors. *Journal of Experiential Education, 28*(3), 205–221.

Whittington, A. & Budbill, N. (2013). Breaking the mold: Impacts of adventure education on girls. *Journal of Outdoor Recreation, Education and Leadership, 5*(1), 37–53.

Whittington, A., Mack, E., Budbill, N. & McKenney, P. (2011). All-girls adventure programmes: What are the benefits? *Journal of Adventure Education and Outdoor Learning, 11*(1), 1–14.

Wilson, J. & Lewis, S. (2012). Transgender-specific programming: An oasis in the storm. In B. Martin & M. Wagstaff (Eds.) *Controversial Issues in Adventure Programming* (pp. 229–234). Champaign, IL: Human Kinetics.

Wittmer, C.R. (2001). Leadership and gender-role congruency: A guide for wilderness and outdoor practitioners. *Journal of Experiential Education, 24*(3), 173–178.

Wright, M. & Gray, T. (2013). The hidden turmoil: Females achieving longevity in the outdoor learning profession. *Australian Journal of Outdoor Education, 16*(2), 12–23.

36

Age and the outdoors

Mike Boyes

University of Otago

The outdoors is an ecosystem of places in the open air where older people connect to nature, to one another and to themselves. Activities in the outdoors range from walking, gardening and fishing through to adventure activities such as windsurfing and backpacking. Natural landscapes provide multiple opportunities for engagement that contribute to active lifestyles, increased life satisfaction and improved health for older people (Alves & Sugiyama, 2006). Both individual agency (e.g. motivation) and social structure (e.g. neo-liberalism) are seen to work in tandem to frame an outdoor lifestyle.

This chapter reviews the literature that connects older people to natural outdoor environments. Socio-cultural perspectives underpin the discussion. Contemporary discourses such as active ageing and successful ageing are influential lenses to critically examine the role of the outdoors. The outdoors is remarkably functional and I examine some of the perspectives drawing on older people's insights into their engagement in natural places. Healing gardens provide therapeutic places of refuge and recovery. Vegetable and flower gardens are sites of industry, beauty and appreciation. Relatively benign natural places are ideal for exploration and exercise by foot, boat, bicycle or ski. Adventure activities provide opportunities to engage in risk taking, thrill and uncertainty, and many outdoor adventure activities are enshrined in adventure tourism where older people are a targeted clientele (Patterson & Pan, 2007). Outdoor landscapes are sites of embodiment, personal development, environmental knowledge and social interaction. Engagement is representative of life chances provided by social structures. Discursive positions such as individualism are expressed through the consumption of goods such as adventure tourism packages, and outdoor clothing and merchandise. Some activities provide sites of embrace, escape and resistance to post-modernist notions of ageing.

Sociological approaches and dominant discourses

A number of influential writers, such as Bourdieu, Giddens and Biggs, espouse the importance of the interaction between individual experience and social and economic factors (see Katz, 2013). Bourdieu believed that the individual and social structures were merged. Hence experiences of ageing shape and are shaped by dominant social and cultural values. The word habitus encompasses the subjective and embodied experiences of individuals that emerge from living the beliefs, values and practices of social structures. Like Bourdieu, Giddens positions a 'duality of structure' to describe the interaction of human agency and social structure within late modern society (Giddens, 1991). The cultural contexts of late modernity 'have become increasingly indeterminate, future oriented, internally referential and reflexive' (Katz, 2013, p. 37). Individual reflexivity involves the active role of the individual in making choices and decisions from multiple and changing options. These options depend upon social structures that influence life chances and lifestyle identity. In contrast, Biggs (1999) sees the individual as having an inner self that has agency to negotiate the interface with social space. Like Giddens, Biggs identifies the fragmentation and pluralism of late modernity leading to identity being fluid and fragmented (Tanner, 2010). Of particular relevance to ageing populations is the notion that identity needs to be 'created and re-created by the individual in the face of changing experiences' (Tanner, 2010, p. 177).

Looking at the broader social picture, the demographics of an ageing world show a number of trends. The World Health Organization (WHO) (2002) considers population ageing as one of humanity's greatest triumphs but also one of the greatest challenges. The yin and yang of triumph and challenge are played out in the discourses that influence ageing. Older people are becoming more prevalent as health standards rise, medical knowledge expands and the 'baby boomer' generation (associated with the post-war peak in births) retires. Life expectancy is rising and there are growing proportions of older people to younger generations (WHO, 2002). The WHO Active Ageing Policy emphasises the importance of opportunities for health, participation and security to enhance quality of life. On the other hand, Franklin and Tate (2009) identify that 80 per cent of all American adults 65 years of age and older have at least one chronic health condition and 40 per cent suffer severe functional disabilities, e.g. heart disease. As a consequence, health-care systems are increasingly burdened.

Successful ageing and its comparable concepts such as active ageing, positive ageing, ageing well and healthy ageing, are dominant, contemporary discourses. These discourses are multidimensional and feature both individual agency and social structure. Research, however, has been dominated by a focus on the individual. As Fernandez-Ballesteros et al. (2008) identify, biomedical researchers focus on health and physical functioning; psychologists focus on subjective dimensions; and social scientists on socio-economic conditions and effects. The components of successful ageing have been identified from cross-cultural studies as: (i) physical health, e.g. free from chronic diseases; (ii) social health, e.g. having family and friends; (iii) psychological health, e.g. feeling good about oneself; and (iv) functional health, e.g. staying involved with the world and people (Fernandez-Ballesteros et al., 2010). Depp and Jeste (2009) confirmed that the most frequent definitions of successful ageing were: younger age, non-smoking, absence of chronic disease, greater levels of physical activity, more social contacts, better self-rated health, absence of depression, absence of cognitive impairment and fewer medical conditions. Many of these components have a biomedical or psycho-social base.

Expectations of ageing are changing as the successful ageing discourse gains ground and working life expectations change. As part of a neo-liberal agenda, there is a move to promote extended working lives through the Organisation for Economic Co-operation and Development (OECD) 'Live longer, work longer' campaign (OECD, 2006). The OECD acknowledges that the main driver is the cost to business and the economy of medical and social protection systems for retirees. It is also being sold as a health and wellbeing factor through the auspices of empowering individuals with flexible and personal choices in work, learning, leisure and care giving. The responsibility and the risks of ageing are being passed from the state to the individual.

The expectation of work continuation may be in conflict with the successful ageing expectations of an active and leisured phase of life (Moulaert & Biggs, 2012). Laslett's (1996) concept of the Third Age holds out the promise of a period of time around the retirement years when older people are healthy and active with time and money to spend on meaningful leisure, but positive experiences of ageing are not necessarily dependent on full physical and mental health (Hubble, 2011). The choice of continuing working lives may well increase the affluence and wellbeing of those who have employment and expensive leisure lifestyles (e.g. ski trips), however they will be time poor. As ageing workers work on, retirement may be hastened by poor health, with the corresponding impact on lifestyle choices. In effect, the state has maximised its extraction of value from the individual and minimised its outlay. For others with no employment prospects and few assets, time is plentiful but a quality retirement may be a more difficult proposition. Being deprived of the choice to continue working may enforce traditional stereotypes such as proposed by dependency and disengagement theory, where withdrawal from the mainstream becomes the norm. As Moulaert and Biggs (2012) suggest, there is a deeper debate here: 'the purpose of later life and the contribution of older citizens' and the 'legitimacy of certain practices concerning identity and retirement'.

A healthy lifestyle is seen as an effective strategy for successful ageing (Franklin & Tate, 2009). Lifestyle choices can impede or facilitate successful ageing and in neo-liberal times when the value of personal choice is promoted, it is implied that these factors are under personal control. On the face of it, moderate physical activity, making good friendships and sound nutrition are individual actions that may improve quality of life and extend the health span. These initiatives are reflected in the literature that focuses on health promotion and disease prevention. The key message from Franklin and Tate's overview (ibid.) is that the health span of older adults can be improved through individual lifestyle modifications, hence lifestyle leads to lifespan.

Consistent with Bourdieu and Giddens, lifestyle can also be seen as a nexus of individual agency and social structure. Katz (2013) believes the incorporation of lifestyle into successful ageing paradigms blunts the social and critical dimensions that influence choice. Undoubtedly, individuals determine how ageing is expressed and experienced. But, noticeably, the principles of choice and identity place less value on social and environmental determinants of health. A customary lifestyle built over years has been considerably influenced by the social circumstances, contexts and structures that create life's chances. Atchley's (1989) continuity theory suggests that individuals will maintain similar behaviours and preferences from their earlier lives in the face of an increasingly complex and fluid society. Some may have vastly reduced options created by changing circumstances like financial pressure, dependency and living with disabilities.

Natural environments as sites of ageing

In this section I begin by exploring how outdoor places have meanings that impact on the identity and lifestyle of older individuals. Then the benefits of outdoor immersion are explored from the rubric of physical activity and social connectedness. The benefits of nature-based experiences will be discussed in the subsequent section.

Rather than a blank slate, natural outdoor places are living constructs, inscribed with meaning. Meanings may be functional, symbolic and emotional, and are realised through the experiences people have in these places (Gesler, 2003). For instance, a river could be a site of low exertion and calm relaxation while fishing, or excitement and risk through canoeing. What is memorable may be the natural beauty or tranquillity of a place and/or the combination of rock, wave and eddy mediated through fishing or kayaking as leisure constructs.

The experiences are direct, sensory and embodied, more often shared with other individuals. Engagement produces knowledge and practices, and knowledge and practices produce discourse. For many outdoor enthusiasts the outdoors is a lifestyle reflective of their identities and a central organising concept in their lives. For instance, the older participants in Cosgriff, Little and Wilson's study (2010, p. 15) reported a deep connection with the outdoors in that nature was 'a part of me' and the 'preferred forum for their physical engagement'.

A good example of an outdoor lifestyle is Whitaker's (2005) group of older cyclists whose lives were liberated by getting outdoors on their bikes. They cycle three to seven times a week at the fast pace of 30 km per hour, clocking up 8000 to 12,000 km per year. Subsequently, physical fitness levels are high. To support their habit the cyclists exercise moderation in dietary and alcohol intake. An overall sense of wellbeing was commonplace 'that extends beyond the pleasant sensations during and after a ride to the perception of the self and its relation to the external world' (ibid., p. 23). The information on this group challenges established medical and cultural ideas about what the body is capable of doing as it ages.

There is considerable research evidence to link the separate entities of: (i) physical activity; (ii) social connectedness; and (iii) being in natural places, to the health and wellbeing of older people. Engagement in the outdoors takes the form of physical activity of the body generally moving through a natural environment. The activities involve slow rhythmic movements over extended time frames and are well suited to the older person. There is a large body of research supporting the importance of physical activity for the older person to functional health and wellbeing. The meta-analyses of Alves and Sugiyama (2006), and Chodzko-Zajko, Schwingel and Park (2009) look at physical activity in general and identify a range of benefits. These include improved sleep, illness prevention, improved functional ability, reduced chance of falling, greater strength, etc. In addition, physical activity has psychological benefits, e.g. improved cognitive performance; social benefits, e.g. meeting new friends; and effects on general wellbeing, e.g. maintaining an independent lifestyle.

For older persons, being socially connected to family and friends has been identified as a profoundly important predictor of successful ageing (Fernandez–Ballesteros et al., 2010). Being with others in the outdoors provides socialisation opportunities and keeps folk active in their communities. Opportunities abound to enjoy the camaraderie of friends and to develop new friendships (Wood & Giles-Corti, 2008). In so doing, interpersonal skills are exercised in meaningful contexts. In particular, trust, connection and reciprocity are observed (Boyes, 2013). The benefits of social engagement for physical and mental health are reported by Ziersch, Baum, MacDougall and Putland (2005). These benefits include reduced feelings of loneliness and alienation, and fewer cases of depression. I now move to explore the interaction between people and a wide range of natural environments.

Landscapes of outdoor leisure

An experience of a place is an 'embodied encounter in the cultural ideas that influence the interpretations we make of the experience' (Wattchow & Brown, 2011, p. x). Concomitant to the fluidity and fractured social nature of our modern world, the outdoors is remarkably utilitarian. The beliefs and values of dominant discourses are influential on the specific forms of outdoors leisure that are desirable. Advantages and disadvantages through prosperity and biological fortune are influential, hence exertion levels can be gentle supported walks through to activities requiring a high-energy output such as windsurfing or backpacking. The social contexts of engagement vary widely and in this section I explore different landscapes of outdoor leisure: (i) therapeutic and healing gardens; (ii) productive vegetable and flower gardens; (iii) outdoor exploration; (iv) adventure and adventure tourism. The context, process and outcomes inform the argument.

Therapeutic and healing gardens

No matter the landscape, exposure to nature can have restorative power through healing and recovery (Gesler, 2003). Certain places have reputations for therapeutic value; none more so than gardens linked to hospitals, rest homes, retirement villages and the like. These gardens provide opportunities for physical activity and social support, and give older people a sense of control over their environment (Marcus, 2014). Gardens of this ilk go back to the monastic infirmary gardens of medieval times (Gesler, 2003).

The gardens are tended by institutions, and designed for visual and embodied engagement. They are safe, sheltered and accessible, with non-toxic plants and non-injurious features. Their design features a variety of private areas and longer and shorter pathway loops for strolling and exercise. Semi-private niches, where a patient and visitor can converse in private, are desirable. Hence, well-designed gardens promote social support (Marcus & Barnes, 1999). Beauty and aesthetic pleasure through all of the senses is important. As Marcus (2014) identifies, 'A healing garden needs to provide a multisensory experience with colourful flowers, varying shapes and textures of green, the sights and sounds of water, elements that attract birds and butterflies, fragrances, and ornamental grasses . . . '. Water has long been linked to healing, especially through lakes, the sea and mineral springs (Gesler, 2003). Some hospital gardens are designed with features for specific populations such as calming herbs for those with depression and different walking surfaces for stroke patients. Other gardens provide opportunities for light exercise through gardening tasks and walking paths (Marcus, 2014). Gardens represent the recognition of nature-based therapy in health care (Marcus, 2014). The specific benefits of healing gardens – including better sleep quality, less illness, restorative effects, etc. – are well reviewed by Marcus and Barnes (1999) and Alves and Sugiyama (2006).

Vegetable and flower gardens

Vegetable and flower gardens are sites of industry, beauty and appreciation. They vary from individual ownership in a home space to shared gardens where social interaction is encouraged. The differences between hospital gardens and productive gardens are in ownership and identity, the need to engage in physical labour and the different levels of social engagement that emerge. Freeman, Dickinson, Porter and van Heezik (2012) note the idiosyncratic and multifaceted ways that people connect with nature through their gardens. In many countries, gardening attracts vast numbers of people. In the USA, gardening is the second most popular leisure activity next to walking, and the over-65 age group is more represented than others (Ashton-Shaeffer & Constant, 2006). Likewise in New Zealand, gardening is also the second-highest to walking in terms of participation levels across all sport and recreation. Of these participants, 52 per cent of the gardeners were over 50 years of age (Sport & Recreation New Zealand (SPARC), 2008). The physical labour of a garden necessitates regular, light to moderate exertion levels (ibid.; Park, Shoemaker & Haub, 2008).

Flower gardens are places of beauty and appreciation. The fragrance, shape and colour of flowers and ornamental plants are appreciated. Vegetable gardens also have aesthetic value to the beholder. Human wellbeing has been linked to those who feel connected to nature and also are emotionally attuned to nature's beauty (Zhang, Howell & Iyer, 2014). As well as beauty, vegetables and flowers have utility as decorations and food. A productive vegetable garden is a good way to get senior citizens eating more health-supporting vegetables and to enhance their quality of life (Sommerfield, Waliczek & Zajicek, 2010).

Gardens are important to older people's wellbeing, as supported by research outcomes that include: social interaction, intellectual stimulation, stimulus avoidance, physical fitness, skill development, creative opportunities (Ashton-Shaeffer & Constant, 2006), good physical and mental health (Park *et al.*, 2008), better personal health and higher levels of physical activity (Sommerfield *et al.*, 2010), self-rated health and happiness, and perceptions of control and mastery (O'Callaghan, 2011). Some liked gardening alone and valued the peace, solitude and stimulus avoidance. Others were motivated by the social motivations and friendship building that came from community gardens, or gardening as a common point of interest and the exchange of produce with others.

Outdoor exploration

Relatively benign natural places are ideal for exploration and exercise by older people where the individual can freely choose the activity, the duration, the intensity and the companions. Common activities are walking, fishing, hunting, food gathering, sailing, cross-country skiing and bicycle riding, among others. The benefits are physical, psychological, social and environmental through connections to nature. Of the activities, walking is the most popular. In the UK, USA and New Zealand, about 50 per cent of older people walked regularly and others walked occasionally (Eyler, Brownson, Bacak & Housemann, 2003; Knight & Edwards, 2008; Sugiyama, Ward Thompson & Alves, 2009). In the NZ study, 58 per cent described the exercise as moderate intensity, and 35 per cent of light intensity. Dog ownership is a factor in promoting regular walking by older people in the outdoors; 90 per cent of owners walk their dog once or twice a day, and report considerable physical, psychological and social benefits (Knight & Edwards, 2008). Dogs also serve as social catalysts to meet others.

Fishing, hunting and food gathering are significant activities that get older people outdoors. The SPARC survey (2008) listed fishing as attracting 16.6 per cent of the sample, with 30.2 per cent aged over 50 years. The exercise was described as light intensity with participation on two days out of seven. In contrast, in Zinn's (2003) study of 1014 older hunters (94 per cent male), 60 per cent had spent more than eleven days hunting in the prior year. The consumption of wildlife through tourism is noted by Lovelock (2008) especially activities such as fly fishing. Noticeable in the NZ context is the large number of Māori elders who engaged in harvesting food such as shellfish, flounder, mussels, fish, eels and kina from the sea and estuaries, often with other family members (Grant, 2010). Gathering wild fruit and berries is also common.

In New Zealand, mountain biking by the over-50 and over-65 year groups represents the fastest-growing sport and recreation activity in the last five years. Whitaker's (2005) study of older Italian cyclists captures the interaction between cyclists and their natural and social environments. Cross-country skiing is another activity with large numbers of older participants, especially in the Nordic countries and Canada. In a study of octogenarian cross-country skiers, Trappe *et al.* (2013) report aerobic capacity to rival that of people forty to fifty years younger. Sailing is also a popular activity for older people.

Outdoor adventure

Adventure landscapes provide older persons with opportunities to engage in risk taking and fun in environments that may be more hazardous and remote. Activities like rock climbing, backpacking, off-trail mountain biking and wind surfing are more challenging and effortful than the activities in the prior section, although clear overlaps exist. Sugarman (2003) provides a brochure example: 'a rugged lifestyle, canoeing to primitive campsites, cooking over the fire and sleeping in tents'. As an example of an active older person in nature, Humberstone (2012) writes an interesting narrative of a windsurfer tackling the embodied challenges that are entwined. It is apparent that increasing numbers of active older people are seeking authentic leisure experiences (McCormack, Cameron, Campbell & Pollock, 2008). For example, a notable event occurred in South Africa in 2013 when Mohr Keet made a 160 m bungee jump at 96 years old!

Adventures are attractive to the older person, especially emotional, social and environmental engagement through fun, excitement and pleasure (Boyes, 2013). Participants like the high interest levels, the excitement, the physicality, learning new skills and emotional highs. However, they need to feel safe and supported, and dislike being out of their comfort zones (ibid.). The natural environment is integral and defining of the experience, with participants liking sensory immersion into sights, smells and tactility. Most demonstrate a strong environmental ethos and value opportunities to accrue social capital (Boyes, 2013).

Many outdoor adventure activities are enshrined in adventure tourism where older people are a targeted clientele through adventure activities offered by outdoor centres and adventure tourism companies. Older adventure tourists are engaging in the consumption of adventure motivated by a desire for novelty, escape and authentic experiences (Patterson & Pan, 2007). In a survey of US adventure providers, 78 per cent indicated that they were offering adventure activities for older age groups (Sugarman, 2003). The programmes featured physically challenging and adrenaline-driven activities through forms of commodified adventure. Some programmes targeted the beginner by focusing on learning skills in a shorter duration and with less intensity. In contrast, advanced programmes involved travelling and camping in remote locations, with expectations of higher fitness and experience levels. The problem for the consumption of adventure through tourism is the sustainability of the practices once people have come home.

Conclusion

This chapter explores some of the unifying arrangements that bring together approaches to research on older people in the outdoors. Humans are part of nature, although through the life course may have become estranged from it. Others have always maintained a strong identification with an outdoor lifestyle. Regardless of life history, the outdoors presents a unique combination of beautiful natural places, opportunities for physical activity at the level of individual choice, and inherent social contexts that promote social connectedness. Positive research outcomes are clear for each of the domains although much less research explores the holistic integration of the components.

Most research focuses on the agency of the older individual to determine how ageing is expressed and experienced. Many active and successful ageing strategies identify with biomedical approaches that emphasise physical and functional health as prevention and rehabilitation from disease. Psychological approaches explore embodiment, personal development and social integration. The research into the effect of social structures is less pervasive and many opportunities exist here. Undoubtedly, life chances are mediated through education and employment opportunities, and cultural, class and ethnic values. The fluidity, pluralism and opportunity of late modernity also shape prospects. The influence of social structures like neo-liberalism build expectations that individuals will take more responsibility for their lives, will work longer, develop their individualism, and continue to consume the goods, products and services of free market economies. The outdoors is beginning to appear in these analyses. The further linking of the interaction of older people and nature to social theory would be desirable.

The landscapes of outdoor leisure are wide ranging, from healing and productive gardens to sites of exploration and adventure. Within these contexts there are wide-ranging activities requiring differing levels of exertion and knowledge. Through the landscapes, the outdoors has the potential to meet the needs of a wide range of people, whether the needs arise from individual agency or the impacts of life choices from social structures. Much more research is needed in these areas. Regardless, outdoor places are not unproblematic and may not appeal to all. For the devotees like the Italian cyclists and the Norwegian cross-country skiers, an outdoor lifestyle provides a source of commitment and identity that has implications for the individuals, their families and their culture. Broadly considering the different landscapes of outdoor leisure, a debate is opened about the flexibility of retirement practices incorporating the outdoors and the contribution of older citizens to society.

References

Alves, S. & Sugiyama, T. (2006). Inclusive design for getting outdoors: Findings for other researchers. Retrieved from: www.idgo.ac.uk/useful_resources/for_other_researchers.htm.

Ashton-Shaeffer, C. & Constant, A. (2006). Why do older adults garden? *Activities, Adaptation & Aging, 30*(2), 1–18.

Atchley, R.C. (1989). A continuity theory of normal ageing. *Gerontologist, 29*, 183–190.

Biggs, S. (1999). *The Mature Imagination*. Buckingham: Open University Press.

Boyes, M. (2013). Outdoor adventure and successful ageing. *Ageing & Society, 33*(4), 644–665.

Chodzko-Zajko, W., Schwingel, A. & Park, C.H. (2009). Successful aging: The role of physical activity. *American Journal of Lifestyle Medicine*, Jan/Feb, 20–28.

Cosgriff, M., Little, D.E. & Wilson, E. (2010). The nature of nature: How New Zealand woman in middle to later life experience nature-based leisure. *Leisure Sciences, 32*, 15–32.

Depp, C.A. & Jeste, D.V. (2009). Definitions and predictors of successful aging: A comprehensive review of larger quantitative studies. *Focus, 7*(Winter), 137–150.

Eyler, A.A., Brownson, R.C., Bacak, S.J. & Housemann, R.A. (2003). The epidemiology of walking for physical activity in the United States. *Medicine & Science in Sports & Exercise, 35*, 1529–1536.

Fernandez-Ballesteros, R.F., Abarca, D., Blanc, E., Efklides, A., Kornfeld, R., Lerma, A.J., Mendoza-Nuñez, V.M., Mendoza-Ruvalcaba, N.M., Orosa, T., Paúl, C. & Patricia, S. (2008). Lay concept of aging well: Cross-cultural comparisons. *Journal of American Geriatrics Society, 56*(5), 950–952.

Fernandez-Ballesteros, R.F., Abarca, D., Blanc, E., Efklides, A., Moraitou, D., Kornfeld, R., Lerma, A.J., Mendoza-Nuñez, V.M., Mendoza-Ruvalcaba, N.M., Orosa, T., Paúl, C. & Patricia, S. (2010). The concept of 'ageing well' in ten Latin American and European countries. *Ageing and Society, 30*, 41–56.

Franklin, N.C. & Tate, C.A. (2009). Lifestyle and successful ageing: An overview. *American Journal of Lifestyle Medicine* (Jan/Feb), 6–11.

Freeman, C., Dickinson, K.J.M., Porter, S. & van Heezik, Y. (2012). My garden is an expression of me: Exploring householders relationships with their gardens. *Journal of Environmental Psychology, 32*, 135–143.

Gesler, W.M. (2003). *Healing Places*. Oxford: Rowman & Littlefield.

Giddens, A. (1991). *Modernity and Self Identity. Self and Society in the Late Modern Age*. Cambridge: Polity Press.

Grant, T. (Producer) (2010). Mahinga kai. *Maori television on demand*, 14 December.

Hubble, N. (2011). Many pleasures to the fourth age. *Guardian*. Retrieved from: www.theguardian.com/society/2011/jul/01/pleasures-of-the-fourth-age.

Humberstone, B. (2012). Engagements with nature: ageing and windsurfing. In B. Watson & J. Harpin (Eds.) *Identities, Cultures and Voices in Leisure and Sport* (pp. 159–169). Eastbourne: Leisure Studies Association.

Katz, S. (2013). Active and successful ageing. Lifestyle as a gerontological idea. *Reserches Sociologiques et Anthropologiques, 44*(1), 33–49.

Knight, S. & Edwards, V. (2008). In the company of wolves. The physical, social and psychological benefits of dog ownership. *Journal of Aging and Health, 20*(4), 437–455.

Laslett, P. (1996). *A Fresh Map of Life*. Cambridge: Weidenfeld & Nicolson Ltd.

Lovelock, B (Ed.) (2008). *Tourism and the Consumption of Wildlife: Hunting, Shooting and Sport Fishing*. New York: Routledge.

Marcus, C.C. (2014). Landscape design: Patient-specific healing gardens. Retrieved from: www.world-healthdesign.com/Patient-specific-Healing-Gardens.aspx.

Marcus, C.C. & Barnes, M. (1999). *Healing Gardens*. New York: Wiley.

McCormack, C., Cameron, P., Campbell, A. & Pollock, K. (2008). 'I want to do more than just cut the sandwiches': Female baby boomers seek authentic leisure in retirement. *Annals of Leisure Research, 11*(1/2), 145–167.

Moulaert, T. & Biggs, S. (2012). International and European policy on work and retirement: Reinventing critical perspectives on active ageing and mature subjectivity. *Human Relations, 66*(1), 23–43.

O'Callaghan, A. (2011). Gardening – benefits for elderly. Retrieved from: ucanr.org/sites/camg2011/files/101993.pdf.

OECD (2006). Live longer, work longer. Retrieved from: www.oecd.org/employment/livelongerworklonger.htm.

Park, S., Shoemaker, C. & Haub, M. (2008). Can older gardeners meet the physical activity recommendations through gardening? *HortTechnology, 18*(4), 639–643.

Patterson, I. & Pan, R. (2007). The motivations of baby boomers to participate in adventure tourism and the implications for adventure tour providers. *Annals of Leisure Research, 10*(1), 26–53.

Sommerfield, A.J., Waliczek, T.M. & Zajicek, J.M. (2010). Growing minds: Evaluating the effect of gardening on quality of life and physical activity level of older adults. *HortTechnology, 20*(4), 705–710.

Sport & Recreation New Zealand (SPARC). (2008). *Sport, Recreation and Physical Activity Participation among New Zealand Adults*. Wellington, NZ: SPARC.

Sugerman, D. (2003). The relationship of age to motivation and skill development level in outdoor adventure programs for older adults. *Society and Leisure, 25*(2), 351–376.

Sugiyama, T., Ward Thompson, C. & Alves, S. (2009). Associations between neighbourhood open space attributes and quality of life for older people in Britain. *Environment and Behavior, 41*(1), 3–21.

Tanner, D. (2010). *Managing the Ageing Experience*. Bristol: The Policy Press.

Trappe, S., Hayes, E., Galpin, A., Kaminsky, L., Jemiolo, B., Fink, W., Trappe, T., Jansson, A., Gustafsson, T. & Tesch, P. (2013). New records in aerobic power among octogenarian lifelong endurance athletes. *Journal of Applied Physiology, 114*, 3–10.

Wattchow, B. & Brown, M. (2011). *A Pedagogy of Place. Outdoor Education for a Changing World*. Clayton, VIC: Monash University Publishing.

Whitaker, E.D. (2005). The bicycle makes me smile: Exercise, aging, and psychophysical well-being in older Italian cyclists. *Medical Anthropology, 24*, 1–43.

Wood, L. & Giles-Corti, B. (2008). Is there a place for social capital in the psychology of health and place? *Journal of Environmental Psychology, 28*, 154–163.

World Health Organization (2002). Active ageing: A policy framework. Retrieved from: www.who.int/ageing/publications/active/en/

Zhang, J.W., Howell, R.T. & Iyer, R. (2014). Engagement with natural beauty moderates the positive relation between connectedness with nature and psychological well-being. *Journal of Environmental Psychology, 38*, 55–63.

Ziersch, A.M., Baum, F.E., MacDougall, C. & Putland, C. (2005). Neighbourhood life and social capital: The implications for health. *Social Science & Medicine, 60*, 71–86.

Zinn, H.C. (2003). Hunting and sociodemographic trends: Older hunters from Pennsylvania and Colorado. *Wildlife Society Bulletin, 31*(4), 1004–1014.

37

Disability and the outdoors
Some considerations for inclusion

John Crosbie

INSTITUTE FOR OUTDOOR LEARNING

Introduction

There has been a long history of the involvement of people with disabilities (PwD) in the outdoors. There are records of children with disabilities involved in camp activities in the USA in the early 20th century, and sports activities started to be used as part of the formal rehabilitation process at Stoke Mandeville hospital, UK, for those with acquired spinal cord injuries during the Second World War (Brittain, 2010). Personal development is a frequently cited benefit of outdoor adventurous activities for PwD and this is the reason why many organisations work with this sector of the population. For the participants themselves, however, personal development per se is seldom the motivation for their involvement, which is no different from those without disabilities. Richardson (1986, p. 45) reminds us that:

> Disabled persons participate in outdoor adventure activities not for their therapeutic benefits but for the same reasons as do able bodied people – for enjoyment, a love of the natural environment, a feeling of accomplishment and the opportunity to overcome natural obstacles and test their own limits.

Although the intentions for participation may be similar, McAvoy and Lais (1999) suggest that the restricted opportunities for PwD to take part in outdoor activities can make the experiences of higher value to those with disabilities than to their non-disabled counterparts.

This chapter considers various models of disability; some philosophical reasoning behind the inclusion of PwD in the outdoors; some of the practical issues associated with their involvement; and suggests a range of alternative models for inclusion of PwD into outdoor programmes. The chapter goes on to outline recent research into the impact participation has on the lives of disabled people, and opportunities for further investigation.

Justification for the inclusion of people with disabilities into outdoor activities

Contemporary society has embraced in principle the concepts of social justice, equality and the inclusion of people with disabilities into mainstream society. This includes those with disabilities having access to the activities that non-disabled people have the opportunity to participate in. Nonetheless, the physical, intellectual and sensory requirements of a number of activities, especially those in the outdoor adventurous activities field, do not make the inclusion of many of those with disabilities an easy or natural occurrence.

For the majority of providers who do not work in the specialist fields relating to minority populations, the issues of inclusion of these populations are seldom core to everyday thinking. Even those who do work with these groups, their focus is invariably on only the minority population within their field of particular interest. For many years organisations working in the outdoors did not readily consider PwD for inclusion in their programmes. Nevertheless, there has been a long history of organisations working with specific disability groups although the participants' needs have usually been little different to those of their non-disabled counterparts, or alternatively the work has involved participants who required a specialist approach rather than those who required specialist facilities or adapted equipment. In addition, there have been a small number of specialist organisations working specifically with those with disabilities.

Changes in the law (for example, in the UK the Disability Discrimination Act/Equality Act, and in the USA the Americans with Disabilities Act) created a legal framework that required reasonable adjustments to be made to include PwD in any service offered to the public, and this included outdoor adventurous activities. In the UK, education policy moved away from pupils with disabilities being educated in segregated 'special schools' towards 'integrated schools' with a special unit or class for pupils with disabilities and 'inclusive schools' where pupils with disabilities were taught in the same classes as their non-disabled peers. The knock-on effect of this education policy was that all 'out of school activities' had to consider the needs of every pupil in the class, including those with disabilities. As a result outdoor education centres (especially those funded by an education authority) also had to accommodate pupils with disabilities.

The inclusion of PwD in the same activities as their peers offers those with disabilities a degree of normalisation (Wolfensberger, 1972) that helps reduce the stigmatisation of disabled people (Barg, Armstrong, Hetz & Latimer, 2010). The opportunities to participate in recreational activities that have a social aspect are particularly beneficial in assisting with the development of friendships between disabled and non-disabled people as there is an area of common interest (Tasiemski, Kennedy, Gardner & Blaikley, 2004; Crosbie, 2014). Where the activity involves real adventure or an experience of shared adversity the friendship bonds that can develop are frequently robust and require considerable force to break (Beames & Atencio, 2008). In addition, sports and physical activities provide opportunities for those with disabilities to demonstrate both capability and judgement, with the mastering of a challenging activity being an effective way for PwD to create a positive impression of their ability; in addition this challenges the prejudgements and attitudes of non-disabled people (Arbour, Latimer, Marlin Ginis & Jung, 2007). These positive attributes demonstrated through participation in activities can be carried over into other aspects of daily life, including the field of employment, thus assisting PwD to obtain work (McCleary & Chesteen, 1990). Hence, through participation in outdoor activities, the above benefits may be obtained, and these in turn may lead to those with disabilities being better included within wider society.

Inclusion of this nature is in accord with the 'social model of disability', which is the preferred view of disability by the disabled community. This is in contrast to the 'medical model of disability' that is seen by disabled people as a very negative approach to disability as it both devalues individual worth and stigmatises those with disabilities. These two models are briefly described below.

Models of disability

The medical model of disability

This view of disability asserts that disability lies within the impairment of the individual; that there is something 'wrong' with the person. The fact that the person cannot walk or cannot see is regarded as 'the problem' and it is the impairment that requires addressing or to be compensated for in order for the individual to fit in to everyday society (Office for Disability Issues, 2010). The individual is not accepted as a person with differences or limitations but as a patient who requires medical intervention in order to make them 'normal' and thus a functioning member of society.

The social model of disability

This view of disability turns the medical model on its head. This model asserts that, even though an individual may have an impairment, there is nothing 'wrong' with the individual. However, they are prevented from fulfilling a normal role in society (or disabled) by the attitude of others and the limitations imposed upon them by society (Office for Disability Issues, 2010). These limitations include poor architecture, failure to provided information in an accessible format, stigmatisation, and discrimination in the provision of services and in employment. The lack of employment of the majority of PwD places them at a financial disadvantage, which in turn impacts all other aspects of their lives (Louvet, 2007). From a social model viewpoint, it is not that an individual cannot walk that prevents them gaining access to a building but rather it is because the building is not designed to include all members of society (e.g. wheelchair users), in the same way a blind person is denied access to information not because they cannot see but because the information is presented in a written format (rather than verbally or in Braille). In employment situations it is the attitude or prejudice of the employer or the lack of willingness to make adjustments to the workplace that denies disabled people employment. From this viewpoint it is not the impairment, but society that creates the disability and, because of this, disability is a socially constructed phenomenon and a form of social oppression (Oliver, 1996).

Although it may be argued that the social model of disability rightly challenges society and the efforts that society makes to include those with disabilities, there are circumstances when this model makes little sense. Some aspects of being in the natural environment and partaking in sporting activities would fall in to this category. Although outdoor experiences that cater for the needs of all people may be considered the ideal, to design a programme that would enable *all* people with disabilities to take part is highly likely to affect the quality or nature of the experience for other participants (Richardson, 1986; Crosbie, 2010), and this itself is a justification for discrimination against disabled people allowed for under the UK Equality Act. Hence, if we are to include PwD in outdoor experiences, compromises will need to be made; this will be covered in the next section.

Approaches to provision

So far two approaches of engaging PwD into outdoor programmes have been alluded to, those of specialist provision and inclusive provision. However these are not the only options (Crosbie, 2010; Black & Stevenson, 2011) and a range of alternative options to providing outdoor education for PwD are described below.

Inclusive provision may occur where an individual takes part in mainstream activities as the nature of their disability does not require any (or only minor) adaptations to the programme.

Alternatively a provider may run a programme that is designed to include people with disabilities alongside non-disabled participants. In both cases the provision is likely to be restricted to certain types of disabilities or levels of impairment. Inclusive provision can also occur where a client group happens to contain a participant with a disability and the provider can design a bespoke programme or modify an existing one to enable all delegates to be fully involved. The advantages of inclusion are that the individual is not segregated in any way but it has the potential disadvantage of reducing the level of the activity and associated challenge to the non-disabled participants or restricting the range of people with disabilities who can be included.

Parallel provision, or activity, occurs when people with disabilities are included in the programme, however for those parts where an individual is unable to participate because of their disability, an alternative activity is provided. This could involve a different level of the same activity or a completely separate activity altogether (ideally, whichever is chosen should fulfil the same objectives as the mainstream activity). The advantages of this model are that those with disabilities are included in those parts of the programme where they can be involved, yet the non-disabled participants are not prevented from taking part in sections of the programme due to the disability of some group members. The disadvantages are that this may be seen as a cop-out from the failure of an inclusive programme to take into account the needs of all participants. In addition, the differences in ability are still being emphasised by the programme design.

Integrated provision involves participants with disabilities sharing the same facilities as non-disabled people but undertaking a separate programme that more closely meets their needs or intended outcomes. The advantages of integration are that disabled people are undertaking the same type of activity in the same location but are potentially working at a different level of intensity. This is the same as with any other streaming. The disadvantages are that there is segregation by ability, and that interaction between those with and without disabilities is restricted to social time and without the opportunities for shared experiences of the activities with the bonds and increased understanding between individuals groups that may arise from these.

Specialist provision usually occurs in a separate, segregated facility using staff with specialist knowledge and often using specialist equipment. The advantage of specialist provision is that the quality of the delivery and facilities should maximise the participation by those with disabilities, with the removal of any compromises in order to accommodate both disabled and non-disabled people. In such an exclusive environment, PwD do not become the subject of excessive attention, resentment as the cause of compromise or delay to the activity, or part of the problem to be overcome. Disadvantages are the obvious segregation, however once the adaptive techniques required for the activity have been learned and confidence gained in their own ability to perform, PwD may now be better equipped to participate alongside their non-disabled peers. The issue of inclusion can then be addressed at a later date with fewer negative connotations for the disabled participants and with greater potential for a more positive outcome.

Practical implications

As indicated above, the inclusion of PwD into an outdoor programme will invariably have an impact on that programme. Whether this impact is viewed as a positive or negative will depend on the philosophical stance of the observer and the intended outcomes of the programme (Crosbie, 2010). For example, those who regard the physical and emotional challenge in overcoming difficult tasks as key to the learning outcomes of a programme may find the reduction to the level of challenge within a programme, caused by the inclusion of those with disabilities, more difficult to accept compared to those who have the primary focus of their programme being mutual understanding, the acceptance of others or teamwork.

There are a number of potential difficulties in both including people with disabilities within a standard programme, as well as in running specialist programmes designed for PwD. The inclusion of those with disabilities is likely to widen the ability range within the group of participants. This could be the range of intellectual ability, motivation, mobility or physical fitness. The increased range will make the choice of the most appropriate type or level of challenge within the activity more difficult for the facilitator. In addition, consideration will need to be given to the style of presentation of information for participants taking part (instructions) as well as the equipment needed and any reviewing techniques to be used.

The type of problems that could be encountered may be emphasised by considering a 'mixed ability' group that, in addition to those without disabilities, also included the following participants: (i) a wheelchair user; (ii) someone who was blind; (iii) someone who was deaf; (iv) someone with a learning disability; (v) someone with ADHD; (vi) someone who experienced Grand Mal epileptic seizures. Contemplate the appropriate level of activity (in any particular field), presentation style and reviewing techniques that would be suitable for this group. Obviously such an eclectic mix would be unlikely, even in an organisation specialising in working with people with disabilities, but considering a group such as this does emphasise the need to take into account the appropriate medium for the presentation of information, the language used, the type and level of activity, the required staffing ratios and the acceptable degree of risk, as these are likely to differ markedly for each individual.

Although it may be argued that a participant-centred approach should be adopted for every programme, the extremes encountered in the above group would make it virtually impossible to cater for every individual's needs within a single session. In contrast, with a more homogenous disability group – for example, one consisting solely of those with hearing impairments – the availability of a sign language interpreter *may* be the only additional requirement that differentiates this group from others without disabilities (although this will be dependent on the activity undertaken).

In including PwD into the outdoors, the focus for adaptations and expenditure is often on the premises and buildings. This is understandable as there is a legal requirement to provide access and there are established standards for building design for disability access. In addition, without access to the premises it is unlikely that any activity could take place. Although great importance is often placed upon the residential experience within outdoor education provided by centres (Education Scotland, 2011), it is the activities that are the primary focus of the experience for the participants. In addition to ensuring that there is access to the premises, providers including those with disabilities need to carefully consider the quality of the outdoor experience they are offering these participants, and whether that experience will meet the needs of the individual and/or the intended outcomes of the programme. If a participant with a disability is merely a passive observer, or involved only in tasks not core to the activity (e.g. belaying someone else but without the opportunity to climb) they do not gain the same experience and the activity will further highlight the differences in ability between those with and without disabilities, so reinforcing the stereotypes that an inclusive activity sets out to diminish (Devine, 2004; Rankin, 2012). In the same way, including the person with a disability as part of the 'problem' (e.g. the task set is to get a wheelchair user to the top of the hill, across a rope challenge course element, or similar) has very negative connotations for the individual and will reflect poorly on the organisation's approach to disabled people. Ideal scenarios are those that enable PwD to make a meaningful contribution to the task, as opposed to their input being tokenistic or their involvement being regarded as a hindrance and the disabled person being 'excess baggage' (Thompson, 2002).

To have all participants 'buy in' to the aims of a programme is preferable in outdoor settings and this is particularly important when working with PwD, especially if a compromise to the nature of the activity has had to be made to accommodate those with a disability. Failure to do this may result in the person with a disability being 'blamed' by the other participants for the reduced quality of experience and this is likely to have a negative impact on the relationships within the group (Crosbie, 2010).

Full participation by those with particular disabilities can be markedly improved by equipment that best enables the individual to undertake the activity. Unfortunately the combination of the range of potential impairments together with the range of possible activities and the high cost of specialist equipment makes this difficult to achieve in all circumstances. Some adaptive pieces of equipment may be suitable only for a specific individual, and others, although providing access to a range of individuals, may be used so infrequently that it would be unreasonable to expect a provider to invest in these seldom used items, especially when they are often of high capital cost. The issue of high cost and low usage applies to the vast majority of equipment specifically designed for people with disabilities.

On the other hand, there is equipment on the market that may be used by non-disabled people but can also aid the involvement in an activity by a large number of PwD. A good example of this occurs in paddlesports. Open Canadian canoes offer greater ease of access, greater stability, the ability to have an assistant/support worker in the same boat and a less complex paddling movement when compared to kayaks. If kayaks are the appropriate craft for the operating environment, then sit-on-top craft offer greater ease of access, greater stability, and some models can be paddled by either one or two people. The choice of equipment that can be used by both disabled and non-disabled people (referred to as inclusive design) has a number of advantages. The principal ones being that expensive equipment is not lying idle, that disabled participants are not made to feel different by using specialist equipment, and that there is greater flexibility as to the number of disabled participants that may be accommodated at any one time (i.e. not limited by the numbers of specialist or adapted equipment available).

Unfortunately the capital nature of equipment and extended replacement cycles results in the replacement of standard equipment with alternatives that are more inclusive by design over a long lead-in time. In addition, the choice of equipment purchased is often not within the remit of the facilitators responsible for running 'inclusive' sessions. Decisions are often influenced by financial constraints, organisational traditions and the personal preferences of the decision makers, rather than the needs of a society that includes people with disabilities.

Purpose and benefits

As has been identified above, the motivation behind participation in the outdoors by PwD is probably the same as for non-disabled people. In the same way all the potential benefits for non-disabled people are also available to disabled participants. Having said that, it must also be recognised that the life experiences of many disabled people (especially those with congenital impairments) may be markedly different to those of their non-disabled peers (McAvoy & Lais, 1999), and with such a different starting point, the level of achievement is also likely to be different either globally or in certain areas that may relate directly to their disability. In addition, there are outcomes that are achievable by disabled people that cannot be achieved by non-disabled people or that work at a level that may not be considered as an outcome by those not specialising in this field (Crosbie, 2010). Examples of these are described below.

Normalisation

Through enabling a person with a disability to experience the same social, domestic, work or educational world that non-disabled people regard as 'normal', the social barriers between

383

disabled people and their non-disabled peers are reduced (Wolfensberger, 1972). As recreational activity plays a large part in social discourse, participation in a range of activities adds to the life experiences of disabled people and to their ability to engage in everyday conversations so helping to build friendships (Murray, 2002).

Socialisation

Due to their reduction in independent mobility, PwD often have reduced opportunities to meet others, especially those without disabilities, outside their immediate domestic, educational or hospital environment (a large majority of PwD are not in work) (Harrison & McGuire, 2008; Allsop, Negley & Sibthorp, 2013). Meeting others (with or without a disability) through outdoor activities, the residential setting of outdoor centres or other recreational situations, provides valuable opportunities to extend both the individual's social circle and their skills to operate in new social situations (Arbour et al., 2007; Crosbie, 2014).

Life skills and independence training

The institutionalisation and overprotectiveness of the domestic situations that many disabled people find themselves living in, denies an individual the opportunity to practise basic domestic skills or even make simple domestic choices (Zoerink, 1988). The altered environment found in the outdoor or residential setting, combined with the reduction in staffing ratios, can provide opportunities for an individual to practise or demonstrate a degree of domestic independence (Costa, Duarte, Pinto & Raposo, 2004).

Rehabilitation

For those with acquired disabilities, the outdoors can be used to provide an environment where certain life skills or activities for daily living can be practised or applied (Wise & Hale, 1999). The application is often to novel situations, and this can assist the individual in adopting a problem-solving approach to new situations, thus increasing the ability to adapt and remain as independent as possible (Hitzig, Alton, Leong & Gatt, 2012). Overcoming disability issues, and thus being able to perform tasks expected of a non-disabled person, is an essential part of rehabilitation, and leads to greater independence, employability and an increased ability to maintain relationships (Dattilo, Caldwell, Lee & Kleiber, 1998).

Inclusion

All of the above may assist an individual to be more involved in everyday activities with non-disabled people. This aids the inclusion of the individual into their community and, more generally, PwD into mainstream society (Borgman, 2002; Brodin, 2009).

Demonstration of ability

Outdoor activities, as well as other activities usually perceived to be outside the normal scope of PwD, can be used to demonstrate to both the individual and to wider society what that individual or disabled people generally are capable of achieving. This can have a positive impact on both the disabled community and wider society through the realisation of the abilities of those with disabilities and that any impairment is specific to particular activities rather than having a global effect (Arbour *et al.*, 2007; Barg *et al.*, 2010).

Freedom from disabling elements

Many outdoor activities have provided PwD with a sense of freedom from their disability or the trappings associated with disability. Examples of these include paddle or sail sports, where a wheelchair user has no need for their wheelchair in the activity and the nature of the activity provides little or no indication that the individual has a disability. Similarly, visually impaired people may find freedom from needing a guide or concern from harm in large hazard-free areas such as when cross-country skiing or skating on lakes. In segregated situations this feeling has included freedom from the attitude of non-disabled people and/or the pressures placed on the participant to perform in a manner expected by a non-disabled person (Goodwin & Staples, 2005; Crosbie, 2010).

Outcomes and impacts

As has been indicated above, the same outcomes from outdoor experiences may be achieved by both PwD and non-disabled people, however, due to their different life experiences, needs and expectations, the benefits for the majority of PwD may be at a more fundamental level. Recent research into a range of programmes run specifically for PwD in a group of UK outdoor centres identified independence, confidence, the opportunities to have new experiences, a realisation of the individual's ability and an improvement of social networks as the main outcomes identified by the participants themselves, and this was supported by those close to the participants (e.g. family, carers, teachers), as well as the visit organisers (Crosbie, 2014). It is considered that the acquisition of some or all of these attributes has the potential to increase the independence of participants, reducing their dependency on others, improving employability and so potentially helping to reduce the demand on social welfare budgets. These outcomes may also help the individual to be better included into everyday society.

Discussion and concluding remarks

Opportunities for future research may focus on a number of areas. These include a longitudinal perspective to investigate the role an outdoor experience may have on the lives of PwD beyond the short term that, through the practicalities of most research, is the focus of most studies. The value of outdoor experiences to PwD could be obtained by investigating the attitude to participation in outdoor activities by those who have never contemplated taking part. An alternative viewpoint on the impact of outdoors experiences on PwD in society could be gained by considering the attitude of employers and other influential members of society whose decisions have the potential to affect the lives of disabled people. The inclusion/segregation debate could be informed by a study that compared the outcome from specialist/segregated providers of outdoor experiences with those organisations who accommodate disabled people as part of an inclusive programme.

Experience has shown that a number of difficulties are likely to be encountered when attempting to conduct research into PwD as invariably a number of gatekeepers are encountered. Gatekeepers will exist within any outdoor project being researched, within any organisation that a participant is a part of, and with parents or significant others of the potential respondent. Although these gatekeepers do exist in other research situations, particularly when researching children, it would be unusual when researching non-disabled people to encounter

John Crosbie

the same number of gatekeepers, and they would not have the same degree of control over whether or not access is granted. In addition, conducting interviews with those with intellectual impairments requires the awareness of a set of skills and techniques not required with other populations. The quality of the responses from people with intellectual impairments may not have the same level of sophistication and, in addition, consideration must be given to whether the questions asked of participants with intellectual impairments have been fully understood and whether there is a degree of acquiescence in their responses (Finlay & Lyons, 2001).

Although the inclusion of PwD into outdoor activities has come a long way, there is still a considerable further distance to travel until full inclusion is reached. Whether this social ideal is either achievable, or even the optimum model, remains a matter for debate. The involvement of some PwD is likely to significantly change the nature of the activity for all participants (Richardson, 1986), and whether this change will impact on the outcomes, and whether this is detrimental or beneficial to participants must be carefully considered beforehand, and in conjunction with the aims or intended outcomes of the programme (Crosbie, 2010).

References

Allsop, J., Negley, S. & Sibthorp, J. (2013). Assessing the social effect of therapeutic recreation summer camp for adolescents with chronic illness. *Therapeutic Recreation Journal, 47*(1), 35–46.

Arbour, K., Latimer, A.E., Marlin Ginis, K.A. & Jung, M.E. (2007). Moving beyond the stigma: The impression formation benefits of exercise for individuals with a physical disability. *Adapted Physical Activity Quarterly, 24*, 144–159.

Barg, C., Armstrong, B., Hetz, S. & Latimer, A. (2010). Physical disability, stigma, and physical activity in children. *International Journal of Disability Development and Education, 57*(4), 371–382.

Beames, S.K. & Atencio, M. (2008). Building social capital through outdoor education. *Journal of Adventure Education and Outdoor Learning, 8*(2), 99–112.

Black, K. & Stevenson, P. (2011). The inclusion spectrum incorporating STEP. Retrieved from: www.sportdevelopment.info/index.php/browse-all-documents/748-the-inclusion-spectrum?catid=98%3Adisability-sport-a-physical-activity.

Borgman, M. (2002). Social integration through adventure programming. *New Zealand Journal of Outdoor Education, 1*(1), 14–23.

Brittain, I. (2010). *The Paralympic Games Explained*. London: Routledge.

Brodin, J. (2009). Inclusion through access to outdoor education: Learning in Motion (LIM). *Journal of Adventure Education & Outdoor Learning, 9*(2), 99–113.

Costa, É., Duarte, J., Pinto, J.F. & Raposo, T. (2004). Outdoor pursuits as a way of developing skills in the disabled population. Lda: G.C. Grafica de Coimbra.

Crosbie, J.P.G. (2010). Expeditions for people with disabilities. In S.K. Beames (Ed.) *Understanding Educational Expeditions*. Rotterdam: Sense.

Crosbie, J.P.G. (2014). The value of outdoor education for people with disabilities: An in depth case study into the Calvert Trust. Unpublished doctoral thesis, University of Edinburgh.

Dattilo, J., Caldwell, L., Lee, Y. & Kleiber, D.A. (1998). Returning to the community with a spinal cord injury: Implications for therapeutic recreation specialists. *Therapeutic Recreation Journal, 32*(1), 13–27.

Devine, M.A. (2004). 'Being a 'doer' instead of a 'viewer': The roles of inclusive leisure contexts in determining social acceptance for people with disabilities. *Journal of Leisure Research, 36*(2), 137–159.

Education Scotland (2011). Outdoor learning: Practical guidance, ideas and support Retrieved from: www.educationscotland.gov.uk/Images/OutdoorLearningSupport_tcm4-675958.pdf.

Finlay, W.M.L. & Lyons, E. (2001). Methodological issues in interviewing and using self-report questionnaires with people with mental retardation. *Psychological Assessment, 13*, 319–335.

Goodwin, D. & Staples, K. (2005). The meaning of summer camp experiences to youths with disabilities. *Adapted Physical Activity Quarterly, 22*(2), 160–178.

Harrison, M.M. & McGuire, F.A. (2008). An investigation of the influence of vicarious experience on perceived self-efficacy. *American Journal of Recreation Therapy, 7*(1), 10–16.

Hitzig, S.L., Alton, C., Leong, N. & Gatt, K. (2012). The evolution and evaluation of a therapeutic recreation cottage program for persons with spinal cord injury. *Therapeutic Recreation Journal, 46*(3), 218–233.

Louvet, E. (2007). Social judgment toward job applicants with disabilities: Perception of personal qualities and competences *Rehabilitation Psychology 52*(3), 297–303

McAvoy, L.H. & Lais, G.J. (1999). Adventure programs that include persons with disabilities. In J. Miles & S. Priest (Eds.) *Adventure Education*. State College, PA: Venture Publishing.

McCleary, I.D. & Chesteen, S.A. (1990). Changing attitudes of disabled persons through outdoor adventure programmes. *International Journal of Rehabilitation Research, 13*(4), 321–324.

Murray, P. (2002). *Hello! Are You Listening? Young Disabled People's Views on Leisure*. York: Joseph Rowntree Foundation.

Office for Disability Issues (2010). About us: The social model of disability. Retrieved from: www.gov.uk/government/organisations/office-for-disability-issues/about.

Oliver, M. (1996). *Understanding Disability: From Theory to Practice*. London: Macmillan.

Rankin, M. (2012). Exploring why disabled people and deaf people do and don't participate in sport. Retrieved from: www.efds.co.uk/assets/0000/3832/EFDS_qualitative_research_report_20110419_ER.pdf.

Richardson, D. (1986). Outdoor adventure: Programs for the physically disabled. *Parks and Recreation, 21*(11), 43–45.

Tasiemski, T., Kennedy, P., Gardner, B.P. & Blaikley, R.A. (2004). Athletic identity and sports participation in people with spinal cord injury. *Adapted Physical Activity Quarterly, 21*(4), 364–378.

Thompson, A. (2002). Outdoor education for people with disabilities in Aotearoa. *New Zealand Journal of Outdoor Education, 1*(1), 51–59.

Wise, J.B. & Hale, S.B. (1999). Strengthening and generalizing self-efficacy in a male with a spinal cord injury. *Therapeutic Recreation Journal*(4), 333–341.

Wolfensberger, W. (1972). *The Principle of Normalization in Human Services*. Toronto: National Institute on Mental Retardation.

Zoerink, D.A. (1988). Effects of a short-term leisure education program upon the leisure functioning of young people with spina bifida. *Therapeutic Recreation Journal, 22*(3), 44–52.

38

Spirituality and the outdoors

Paul Heintzman

UNIVERSITY OF OTTAWA

The English word 'spirituality' comes from the Latin *spiritus*, meaning 'breath of life', and can be traced to the Greek word *pneuma* used in the New Testament to describe a person's spirit guided by God's Spirit. Today, spirituality may be defined as 'the feelings, thoughts, experiences, and behaviors that arise from a search for the sacred' (i.e. divine being, Ultimate Reality or Ultimate Truth) (Larson, Swyers & McCullough, 1998, p. 21). Using the behavioural model of outdoor recreation this chapter synthesises empirical findings on outdoor activities and spirituality using a framework (Heintzman, 2010) that includes antecedent conditions, setting and recreation factors, and spiritual outcomes (see Figure 38.1).

This framework identifies factors that influence spiritual outcomes. Not all of the factors may be necessary or sufficient for spiritual outcomes; specific factors and combination of factors may vary.

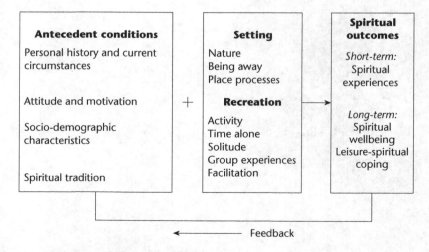

Figure 38.1 Outdoor activities and spirituality

Antecedent conditions

Antecedent conditions refer to people's characteristics prior to outdoor activity participation. Personal history and current circumstances may influence spiritual outcomes (Stringer & McAvoy, 1992; Fox, 1997; Elliot, 2010; Foster, 2012; Pond, 2013). For Elaine, a participant in an environmental education course, the course was a celebration:

> [The course] was a very positive experience for me and I think part of that has to do with the frame of mind in which I came . . . it was something I wanted to do to celebrate turning 50 . . . There were no demands upon me by my children, of work. It was a real gift for me to be able to just go off on my own. (Heintzman, 2007b, p. 3)

For a young married couple, the course occurred at a difficult time of relocation and moving from a very remote area to an urban centre. As the wife stated, 'the course was wrapped up in that context . . . we were both just really depressed at the beginning of the course . . . But the course allowed some space for me to figure some of that out' (Heintzman, 2007b, p. 3).

Closely related to personal history and current circumstances is the motivation and attitude that have also been associated with spiritual outcomes (Stringer & McAvoy, 1992; Heintzman, 2007a, 2007b; Moore, 2011). For example, in the quotation above from Elaine, she mentioned that the fact the course was a positive experience had to do with 'the frame of mind' with which she came to the course. She elaborated: 'I was very much in an attitude of having my hands wide open to just receive what came, so each experience was very full in that regard . . . '. Similarly, another participant mentioned the 'making of conscious choices to accept where I am, appreciate where I am'. A third participant also spoke about the attitude of the participant as being important, 'if the student were receptive spiritually, then . . . they can be learning . . . in any sort of situation' (Heintzman, 2007b, p. 4). While qualitative studies suggest some wilderness recreationists didn't experience spiritual outcomes because they didn't seek them (Stringer & McAvoy, 1992; Heintzman, 2007a), quantitative studies suggest many (46% to 82%) but not all wilderness/park visitors are motivated by spiritual outcomes (e.g. Brayley & Fox, 1998, p. 24; Lemieux et al., 2012, p. 77, respectively), although these outcomes may not be the most valued (Behan, Richards & Lee, 2001).

In regards to socio-demographic characteristics, spiritual outcomes have been associated more with women than men (Lusby & Anderson, 2010; Heintzman, 2012; Lemieux et al., 2012), are described more completely by women (Unruh & Hutchinson, 2011), increase with age (Heintzman, 2012), increase with education (Winter, 2007; Moore, 2011; Heintzman, 2012) and decrease with income (Heintzman, 2012; Lemieux et al., 2012).

Spiritual tradition may also influence spiritual outcomes during outdoor activities (Heintzman, 2008b; Cheung, 2011; Moore, 2011; Berkers, 2012; Foster, 2012; Hoover, 2012) as seen in Unruh and Hutchinson's (2011) study of the impact of gardening upon daily life and stressful life experiences. For example, one participant viewed gardening as significant to his spiritual journey, yet did not connect it to religion:

> . . . I wouldn't think of myself as a particularly religious person . . . I am perhaps a bit of a spiritual person. I am not quite sure what the spirit is . . . the closest (and I don't know how close that is) to come to grips with this spirituality has been through doing things like gardening . . . I think for me it has to do with nature, the world around us, our environment, how I fit in as a human being in that. (Unruh & Hutchinson, 2011, p. 571)

Gardening complemented or affirmed religious spiritual faith for other participants, as explained by one participant:

> I mean, creation just reminds you of God's creation and the wonderful things that he has done. I believe that God is creator . . . And when I look at the intricate designs in a flower or a leaf or the birds and all of these things, how can we not believe that there was a real intelligence behind it? You know, a creator. (Unruh & Hutchinson, p. 572)

Gardeners with religious views viewed their garden 'as an extension of their spirituality and a confirmation of their beliefs', while those with secular views tended to 'embed their spirituality in their relationship with nature as manifested in their garden' (Unruh & Hutchinson, p. 572).

In Snell and Simmond's (2012) study of spiritual experiences in nature, those from a religious spiritual tradition articulated a metaphysical framework in which their spiritual experiences in nature were viewed as purposeful and intelligible while those with non-religious spiritual perspectives struggled to come up with, or resisted interpretations of their spiritual experiences that gave any substantial meaning other than being pleasant or extraordinary psychological states. Snell and Simmonds speculated that 'Perhaps religious beliefs . . . serve to legitimize the subjective experience of the sacred by providing a language and metaphysical framework that make it more meaningful for long-term self-development and psychological well-being' (p. 332).

Setting factors

Factors related to setting, such as being in nature, going away to a different environment and place processes, may influence spiritual outcomes. Research has determined that leisure activities in nature are conducive to spiritual outcomes for a variety of reasons, as summarised by Heintzman (2010): nature elicits a sense of wonder, awe and amazement; helps some people connect with their God or higher power; provides a sense of peacefulness, calm, stillness and tranquillity; creates space to explore spirituality through reflection; and is powerful and therapeutic. For example, Elaine explained:

> Having that extended time in nature . . . being in the created world, outdoors. That really provided the setting for meditation, prayer. Just an enjoyment of the grandeur and the majesty of God's presence as I experience Him in nature . . . That my senses are heightened . . . I think in nature when you are confronted with the grandeur of sky, ocean, wind, sun, such variety of texture, smell, height, sound, all of that, is very stimulating for me . . . it is a transcendent experience . . . I'm just aware of God's greatness in the variety of what is seen visually of sights and smells and sounds and to think that God has created all that . . . I am given a larger perspective on existence. (Heintzman, 2007b, p. 7)

Going away to a different environment is conducive to spiritual outcomes (Sweatman & Heintzman, 2004; Heintzman, 2007a, 2007b, 2008b; Ellard, Nickerson & Dvorak, 2009; McDonald, Wearing & Ponting, 2009; Bobilya, Akey & Mitchell, 2011; Foster, 2012). Stringer and McAvoy (1992) observed that greater opportunities and enhancement of spiritual experiences in the wilderness were usually ascribed to the lack of constraints and responsibilities characteristic of everyday life. The following quote illustrates:

[My husband] and I get really connected, our spirits are connected on [canoe] trips . . . leaving everything behind, and getting down to basics and I think that's very meditative too because when we meditate we're just there with God, it's very simple and we don't need anything else really. And so when you go on a canoe trip or a camping trip, you just take a few things. And you . . . don't really need a lot of stuff especially for our spirits, for our spiritual growth or enhancement. (Heintzman, 2000, p. 50)

Various place concepts and processes during outdoor activities have been associated with spirituality: place identity (Anderson & Fulton, 2008); place attachment and sacred space (Fredrickson & Anderson, 1999); sense of place (Heintzman & Mannell, 2003); place meanings (Hutson & Montgomery, 2010; Salk, Schneider & McAvoy, 2010); and special place locations (Brown & Raymond, 2007). This concept is illustrated by the following response to whether any leisure settings were associated with spiritual growth:

Muskoka, it's where I grew up and it's very much a sense of that landscape having formed who I am and also formed my spirituality. It influences the images that I have of God, it influences images of all kinds of things, it is just very much a part of me, so Canadian Shield, water, trees, growing out of rocks along the water edge. I mean that's where I feel most at home. I don't live there anymore. I do have the capacity . . . in different settings of seeing the wonder there, but it comes most easily when I'm home. (Heintzman, 2000, p. 51)

Recreation factors

Participants in qualitative studies have identified numerous and diverse outdoor activities they associate with spiritual outcomes (Stringer & McAvoy, 1992; Heintzman, 2000, 2007b; Schmidt & Little, 2007; Berkers, 2012). Spiritual outcomes have also been documented in studies of climbing (Pond, 2013), dragon boat racing (Unruh & Elvin, 2004; Parry, 2009), gardening (Unruh & Hutchinson, 2011), four-wheel driving in the desert (Narayanan & Macbeth, 2009), snowboarding (Elliot, 2010), windsurfing (Humberstone, 2011), surfing and scuba diving (Moore, 2011), yacht cruising (Lusby & Anderson, 2010) and zoo visiting (Luebke & Matiasek, 2013). While activities that facilitate spirituality vary from person to person, research suggests activities that help people get in touch with themselves, and are compatible with who they are and their personality, are the ones that promote spiritual well-being (Heintzman, 2000).

Ontario Parks' visitors who spent most of their time at a park in more nature-oriented activities (e.g. viewing/photographing nature, guided hikes/walks) rated higher on the degree to which introspection/spirituality added to their satisfaction than did visitors who spent most of their time in activities such as biking and motor boating (Heintzman, 2012; see Table 38.1).

Similarly, Behan et al. (2001) found that spiritual benefits were valued more by foot travellers than by mountain bikers as it was easier for non-mechanised travellers to focus on nature. Nevertheless, four-wheel-drive travel in the Australian desert has been found to have a spiritual dimension, possibly due to viewing the journey to the desert as a pilgrimage to sacred space (Narayanan & Macbeth, 2009).

Challenging activities can facilitate spiritual outcomes (Fredrickson & Anderson, 1999; Marsh, 2008; Sharpley & Jepson, 2011). Schmidt and Little (2007) gave the following example:

Paul Heintzman

Table 38.1 Role of introspection/spirituality in satisfaction with park experience by activity participated for the most time while at the park

Activity	N	Mean	SD
1 Viewing/photographing nature	341	3.37	1.64
2 Guided hikes/walks	82	3.57	1.48
3 Visiting viewpoints/lookouts	83	3.60	1.55
4 Other	746	3.65	1.61
5 Trail hiking (non-guide)	1381	3.67	1.53
6 Canoeing	570	3.72	1.64
7 Swimming/wading	2742	3.89	1.47
8 Fishing	519	3.93	1.68
9 Attending staff presentations	39	3.95	1.43
10 Casual play (i.e. Frisbee)	506	3.96	1.43
11 Picnicking	168	3.96	1.51
12 Visiting historical/nature displays	44	3.98	1.82
13 Biking	478	3.99	1.49
14 Motor boating	153	4.01	1.50
15 Using playground facilities	96	4.10	1.37
Total	7948	3.81	1.54

Note: Mean scores based on scale 1 = Most strongly adds to satisfaction, 9 = Most strongly detracts from satisfaction

Source: Heintzman (2012, p. 301)

> It was a very hard walk, steep and what was running through my head was basically a lot of fear and a lot of nervous energy . . . Once we got there it was beautiful and so tranquil and the day was just so perfect and blue and I thought to myself, 'Lord, I'm really glad I'm here and I can see this beauty and vastness of the land.' It made me appreciative and the fear I felt on the way gave an added focus to the appreciation . . . and the connection that was there. (p. 238)

The type of spiritual outcome may also be influenced by the type of activity engaged in. Canoeists have had spiritual experiences focused on interconnections with people, while mountain hikers have described spiritual experiences involving appreciation of wilderness beauty (Stringer & McAvoy, 1992).

In the case of a structured or programmed outdoor activity, opportunity for free time may be a factor (Stringer & McAvoy, 1992; Fox, 1997). One residential youth camper explained how scheduled alone time during a solo was important: 'I think with the solo it was a time when you could really think . . . they kept throwing things at us all month, like stuff to learn and we finally had time to think about it, and catch up with yourself, so I think that helps with my spiritual development' (Sweatman & Heintzman, 2004, p. 27).

The importance for spirituality of solitude in the outdoors has been reported by several studies (Fox, 1997; Fredrickson & Anderson, 1999; Coble, Selin & Erickson, 2003; Sweatman & Heintzman, 2004; Heintzman, 2007a, 2007b, 2012; Marsh, 2008). A wilderness canoeist explained, 'being alone, it gives me that time and the opportunity just to try and work my own way through some of those issues of situations that . . . may be negatively affecting my spiritual well-being' (Heintzman, 2007a, p. 221). In quantitative studies, Ontario Parks' campers who visited a park alone rated introspection/spirituality higher than those who were with others (Heintzman, 2012).

Spirituality is linked to group experiences in the outdoors (Fox, 1997; Fredrickson & Anderson, 1999; Sweatman & Heintzman, 2004; Heintzman, 2007a, 2007b, 2008b; Pond, 2013). As one wilderness adventurer stated: 'just the people . . . trusting other people and loving them, and tolerating their weaknesses . . . That was the spiritual awakening for me, you know, the friendship' (Stringer & McAvoy, 1992, p. 18). Being part of a male-only or female-only group has also played an important role in spiritual outcomes (Fox, 1997; Fredrickson & Anderson, 1999; Heintzman, 2008b).

In some cases a balance of solitude and group experiences is helpful to spirituality (Heintzman, 2007a, 2007b; Sharpley & Jepson, 2011). A wilderness canoeist stated, 'I think I found some spiritual jewels, some spiritual treasures in all the social settings, being alone definitely, being around the fire with the entire group definitely, and just in one-on-one conversations with people' (Heintzman, 2007a, p. 221). 'There is a dynamic of tension between interaction and solitude: Both enable a spiritual meaning' (Marsh, 2008, p. 292).

Facilitation may play an important role in spiritual outcomes for outdoor activities that occur in a group or as a part of a programme. Lasenby's (2003) study of outdoor education participants concluded that, 'facilitation of an outdoor education program is a major factor in both allowing [spiritual] experiences to occur, and in assisting with the "meaning making" process that follows' (p. 4). Environmental education participants noted that what was most important was the way the facilitators put together the overall mix of activities, experiences and elements of the course as the holistic, 24-hour nature of the course led to spiritual impact (Heintzman, 2007b). Thus Deirdre, a course participant, found it difficult to identify specific course activities that enhanced her spiritual wellbeing 'because there were so many different experiences that contributed to the whole'. She described this holistic experience in terms of relationships:

> I really lived . . . in terms of the basics, I lived in relationships with people, I lived in relationship with God, I lived in relationship with creation, I lived . . . in a relationship with the world around me. I lived basically. (pp. 4, 5)

Research suggests that outdoor activities can be combined with explicit or overt spiritual activities to facilitate spiritual outcomes (Anderson-Hanley, 1996; LeDuc, 2002; Griffin, 2003; Daniel, 2007; Heintzman, 2007b; Bobilya et al., 2011) although this is not always the case (Heintzman, 2007a), depending on how interested participants are in the spiritual dimension of an activity.

Spiritual outcomes

The most common outcome studied is spiritual experience (Fox, 1997; Fredrickson & Anderson, 1999; Chiesura, 2004; Loeffler, 2004; Sweatman & Heintzman, 2004; Ellard et al., 2009; Humberstone, 2011; Luebke & Matiasek, 2013), which often includes affective dimensions (feelings such as peace, awe, love), cognitive processes (e.g. contemplation), transcendence of one's self and environment, and a high level of emotional intensity (Stringer & McAvoy, 1992). For example, a wilderness canoeist described his spiritual experience as:

> the wonderful sense of peace, the wonderful sense of connectedness to my world around me, to myself, . . . not a sense that something was wrong, or I needed to work on something, there was just a peace, there was a tranquility, there was acceptance, there was harmony and I really fondly remember those moments because I felt so good inside . . . (Heintzman, 2007a, p. 218)

Haluza-Delay (2000) criticised studies that focus exclusively on pleasant emotional states, and urged investigation of whether or not the experiences lead to life transformation. Lasenby

(2003) gave the term *hangover* to 'the short-term, immediate effects, which are all highly positive, but [do] not deal with the long-term transformational effects that spiritual experience
might have' (p. 62).

An outcome that reflects life transformation is spiritual wellbeing, which Hawks (1994)
defined as:

> A high level of faith, hope, and commitment in relation to a well-defined worldview or
> belief system that provides a sense of meaning and purpose to existence in general, and that
> offers an ethical path to personal fulfilment which includes connectedness with self, others,
> and a higher power or larger reality. (p. 6)

Using the concept of spiritual wellbeing, the longer-term impact of a wilderness canoe trip has
been associated with the memory and recollection of the experience (Heintzman, 2007a), and
the enhancement of deep, spiritually oriented friendships (Heintzman, 2008b). In quantitative studies, significant positive relationships have been found between spiritual wellbeing and
frequency of outdoor activity participation (Ragheb, 1993; Heintzman & Mannell, 1999), as
well as frequency of participation in picnicking, gardening, a day outing to the zoo or park, and
plant care; however, there was a negative relationship with adventure trekking (Heintzman &
Mannell, 1999). Doi (2004) discovered that the use of leisure-spiritual processes to achieve
spiritual wellbeing was significantly higher for college students that preferred outdoor activities compared to students who preferred sports. Lemieux *et al.* (2012) found that 73.4 per cent
of park visitors perceived spiritual wellbeing outcomes from connecting with nature, being
inspired by nature and seeking the meaning/purpose of life while visiting parks. In a study of
urban park experience, the spiritual component of wellbeing was enhanced by the stimulation
of a spiritual connection to nature that energised and enriched life (Chiesura, 2003).

Although not explicitly using the spiritual wellbeing concept, studies in outdoor settings
have found outcomes similar to dimensions of spiritual wellbeing: greater spiritual connection
to nature (Kellert, 1998); enhanced long-term awareness of God, nature and self (Daniel, 2007);
significant positive changes in spiritual beliefs (LeDuc, 2002) and spiritual development variables
(Cheung, 2011); initial positive change in closeness to God (Henderson, Oakleaf & Bialeschki,
2009); and enhanced sacredness of life, meaning and purpose, and transcendent dimensions of
spirituality (McDonald *et al.*, 2009). Spiritual outcomes have also been associated with environmentalism (Moore, 2011) and landscape preservation values (Hutson & Montgomery, 2010).

Another outcome is leisure-spiritual coping, which refers to the ways people receive help, in
the context of their leisure, from spiritual resources (e.g. higher power, spiritual practices, faith
community) during periods of life stress (Heintzman, 2008a). Leisure-spiritual coping through
outdoor activities has been helpful for those experiencing major life change (Fredrickson &
Anderson, 1999), cancer (Unruh & Elvin, 2000; Parry, 2009) and other stressful conditions
(Schneider & Mannell, 2006; Snell & Simmonds, 2012). For example, Unruh and Hutchinson's
(2011) study of gardeners concluded that the spiritual meanings of gardening might have a significant role in the reappraisal of life events as well as in meaning-focused coping with stressful
life experiences such as cancer. While for some participants, anxiety and uncertainty associated
with life stress or illness sometimes prevented the enjoyment associated with gardening, for
others the enjoyment of gardening facilitated hope and planning for the future in spite of uncertainty due to significant life stress. Profound experiences of enjoyment provided the reflective
space necessary for spiritual reflection and meaning-focused coping. Participants who experienced chronic health conditions found meaning through regular gardening tasks and occasional
special garden projects, such as creating ponds or building trails. Gardening connected the

participants to plants that they nurtured, to people that they shared gardening with, and to an inner sense of being untouched by stress and illness. These participants felt grounded and at peace in the garden. More significantly, gardening provided the opportunity to express hopes and losses in the present and for the future. The garden, as a living system, reflected life tensions. Thus gardening, as an outdoor activity that has diverse spiritual meanings, can be a resource for living with stressful life and health experiences.

Conclusion

The theoretical framework presented in this chapter (see Figure 38.1), based on extant empirical research, can serve as a guide in conducting future research on this topic, just as an earlier version (Heintzman, 2010) was used for research on surfing and scuba-diving (Moore, 2011). The framework provides a way to explore the processes that link outdoor activities with spirituality, and helps explain the complexity of the relationships between these two phenomena. Future research might focus on:

- determining the components of the framework that are most influential and whether there are additional components;
- spiritual behaviours and the long-term consequences rather than just the immediate spiritual feelings of outdoor activities;
- the social and environmental justice dimensions of spirituality in addition to personal spiritual benefits;
- more quantitative research, including the use of spiritual wellbeing and other scales, to determine whether qualitative findings can be generalised to larger populations;
- how outdoor activities repress as well as facilitate spiritual benefits;
- diverse population groups, as the experiences of spirituality are different among these groups.

Finally, the theoretical framework reminds practitioners that the relationship between outdoor activities and spirituality is complex and therefore all the components of the framework, and possibly others not included, need to be considered when implementing outdoor activities or managing outdoor facilities and resources for spiritual outcomes.

References

Anderson-Hanley, C. (1996). Spiritual well-being, spiritual growth and outward bound-type programs: A comparative study. Paper presented at the annual meeting of the Christian Association for Psychological Studies, April. St Louis, MO.

Anderson, D.H. & Fulton, D.C. (2008). Experience preference as mediators of the wildlife related recreation participation: Place attachment relationship. *Human Dimensions of Wildlife, 13,* 73–88.

Behan, J.R., Richards, M.T. & Lee, M.E. (2001). Effects of tour jeeps in a wildland setting on non-motorized recreationist benefits. *Journal of Park and Recreation Administration, 19*(2), 1–19.

Berkers, V. (2012). Religion, spirituality and leisure: A relational approach. The experience of religion and spirituality of Dutch New Christians and New Spirituals during leisure activities. Unpublished master's thesis, Utrecht University, Utrecht, Netherlands.

Bobilya, A.J., Akey, L. & Mitchell, D., Jr (2011). Outcomes of a spiritually focused wilderness orientation program. *Journal of Experiential Education, 33*(4), 301–322.

Brayley, R.E. & Fox, K.M. (1998). Introspection and spirituality in the backcountry recreation experience. In M.D. Bialeschki & W.P. Stewart (Eds.) *Abstracts from the 1998 Symposium on Leisure Research* (p. 24). Ashburn, VA: National Recreation and Parks Association.

Brown, G. & Raymond, C. (2007). The relationship between place attachment and place values: Toward mapping place attachment. *Applied Geography, 27*, 89–111.

Cheung, A.C.K. (2011). Spiritual development of adolescents in adventure-based programs in Hong Kong. *Journal of Experiential Education, 33*(4), 411–415.

Chiesura, A. (2004). The role of urban parks for the sustainable city. *Landscape and Urban Planning, 68*, 129–138.

Coble, T.G., Selin, S.W. & Erickson, B.B. (2003). Hiking alone: Understanding fear, negotiation strategies and leisure experience. *Journal of Leisure Research, 35*(1), 1–22.

Daniel, B. (2007). The life significance of a spiritually oriented, Outward Bound-type wilderness expedition. *Journal of Experiential Education, 29*(3), 386–389.

Doi, A.S. (2004). Spiritual well-being and leisure preferences in college students. Unpublished master's thesis, Springfield College, Springfield, MA.

Ellard, A., Nickerson, N. & Dvorak, R. (2009). The spiritual dimension of the Montana vacation experience. *Leisure/Loisir, 33*(1), 269–289.

Elliot, N.M.R. (2010). *'Soulriding' and the spirituality of snowboarding.* Unpublished doctoral dissertation, Kingston University, London, England.

Foster, I.M. (2012). Wilderness, a spiritual antidote to the everyday: A phenomenology of spiritual experiences in the Boundary Waters Canoe Area Wilderness. Unpublished master's thesis, University of Montana, Missoula, MT.

Fox, R.J. (1997). Women, nature and spirituality: A qualitative study exploring women's wilderness experience. In D. Rowe & P. Brown (Eds.) *Proceedings, ANZALS Conference 1997* (pp. 59–64). Newcastle, NSW: Australian and New Zealand Association for Leisure Studies, and the Department of Leisure and Tourism Studies, University of Newcastle.

Fredrickson, L.M. & Anderson, D.H. (1999). A qualitative exploration of the wilderness experience as a source of spiritual inspiration. *Journal of Environmental Psychology, 19*, 21–39.

Griffin, J. (2003). The effects of an adventure-based program with an explicit spiritual component on the spiritual growth of adolescents. *Journal of Experiential Education, 25*(3), 351.

Haluza-Delay, R. (2000). Green fire and religious spirit. *Journal of Experiential Education, 23*(3), 143–149.

Hawks, S. (1994). Spiritual health: Definition and theory. *Wellness Perspectives, 10*, 3–13.

Heintzman, P. (2000). Leisure and spiritual well-being relationships: A qualitative study. *Society and Leisure, 23*(1), 41–69.

Heintzman, P. (2007a). Men's wilderness experience and spirituality: A qualitative study. In R. Burns & K. Robinson (Comps.) *Proceedings of the 2006 Northeastern Recreation Research Symposium* (pp. 216–225) (Gen. Tech. Rep. NRS-P-14). Newton Square, PA: US Department of Agriculture, Forest Services, Northern Research Station.

Heintzman, P. (2007b). Rowing, sailing, reading, discussing, praying: The spiritual and lifestyle impact of an experientially based, graduate, environmental education course. Paper presented at the Trails to Sustainability Conference, Kananaskis, Alberta, Canada.

Heintzman, P. (2008a). Leisure-spiritual coping: A model for therapeutic recreation and leisure services. *Therapeutic Recreation Journal, 42*(1), 56–73.

Heintzman, P. (2008b). Men's wilderness experience and spirituality: Further explorations. In C. LeBlanc & C. Vogt (Eds.) *Proceedings of the 2007 Northeastern Recreation Research Symposium* (pp. 55–59) (Gen. Tech. Rep. NRS-P-23). Newton Square, PA: US Department of Agriculture, Forest Services, Northern Research Station.

Heintzman, P. (2010). Nature-based recreation and spirituality: A complex relationship. *Leisure Sciences, 32*(1), 72–89.

Heintzman, P. (2012). The spiritual dimension of campers' park experience: Management implications. *Managing Leisure, 17*(4), 370–385.

Heintzman, P. & Mannell, R. (1999). Leisure style and spiritual well-being. In W. Stewart & D. Samdahl (Eds.) *Abstracts from the 1999 Symposium on Leisure Research* (p. 68). Ashburn, VA: National Recreation and Park Association.

Heintzman, P. & Mannell, R. (2003). Spiritual functions of leisure and spiritual well-being: Coping with time pressure. *Leisure Sciences, 25*, 207–230.

Henderson, K.A., Oakleaf, L. & Bialeschki, M.D. (2009). Questions raised in exploring spiritual growth and camp experiences. *Leisure/Loisir, 33*(1), 179–195.

Hoover, M. (2012). Understanding national park visitor experiences through backcountry register content analysis. In J. Bocarro & M. Stodolska (Eds.) *Abstracts from the 2012 Leisure Research Symposium.* Ashburn, VA: National Recreation and Park Association.

Humberstone, B. (2011). Embodiment and social and environmental action in nature-based sport: Spiritual spaces. *Leisure Studies, 30*(4), 495–512.

Hutson, G. & Montgomery, D. (2010). Stakeholder views of place meanings along the Niagara Escarpment: An exploratory Q methodological inquiry. *Leisure/Loisir, 34*(4), 421–442.

Kellert, S.R. (1998). *A National Study of Outdoor Wilderness Experience*. Washington, DC: National Fish and Wildlife Foundation.

Larson, D.B., Swyers, J.P. & McCullough, M.E. (1998). *Scientific Research on Spirituality and Health: A Consensus Report*. Rockville, MD: National Institute for Health Care Research.

Lasenby, J. (2003). Exploring episode-type spiritual experience associated with outdoor education programs. Unpublished master's thesis, University of Edinburgh, Scotland.

LeDuc, J. (2002). The relationship between adventure-based programs and spiritual development in high school adolescents at a Christian camp. Unpublished master's thesis, University of California, Chico.

Lemieux, C.J., Eagles, P.F.J., Slocombe, D.S., Doherty, S.T., Elliot, S.J. & Mock, S.E. (2012). Human health and well-being motivations and benefits associated with protected area experiences: An opportunity for transforming policy and management in Canada. *Parks: The International Journal of Protected Areas and Conservation, 18*(1), 71–85.

Loeffler, T.A. (2004). A photo elicitation study of the meanings of outdoor adventure experiences. *Journal of Leisure Research, 36*(4), 536–556.

Luebke, J.F. & Matiasek, J. (2013). An exploratory study of zoo visitor's exhibit experiences and reactions. *Zoo Biology 32*, 407–416.

Lusby, C. & Anderson, S. (2010). Ocean cruising – a lifestyle process. *Leisure/Loisir, 34*(1), 85–105.

Marsh, P.E. (2008). Backcountry adventure as spiritual experience: A means–end study. *Journal of Experiential Education, 30*(3), 290–293.

McDonald, M.G., Wearing, S. & Ponting, J. (2009). The nature of peak experiences in wilderness. *Humanistic Psychology, 37*(4), 370–385.

Moore, C. (2011). Spiritual experiences and environmentalism of recreational users in the marine environment: New Zealand surfers and scuba divers. Unpublished master's thesis, Lincoln, New Zealand: Lincoln University.

Narayanan, Y. & Macbeth, J. (2009). Deep in the desert: Merging the desert and the spiritual through 4WD tourism. *Tourism Geographies, 11*(3), 369–389.

Parry, D.C. (2009). Dragon boat racing for breast cancer survivors: Leisure as a context for spiritual outcomes. *Leisure/Loisir, 33*(1), 317–340.

Pond, M.F. (2013). Investigating climbing as a spiritual experience. Unpublished master's thesis, Ohio University, Athens, OH.

Ragheb, M.G. (1993). Leisure and perceived wellness: A field investigation. *Leisure Sciences, 15*, 13–24.

Salk, R., Schneider, I.E. & McAvoy, L.H. (2010). Perspectives of sacred sites on Lake Superior: The case of the Apostle Islands. *Tourism in Marine Environments, 6*(2/3), 89–99.

Schmidt, C. & Little, D.E. (2007). Qualitative insights into leisure as a spiritual experience. *Journal of Leisure Research, 39*(2), 222–247.

Schneider, M.A. & Mannell, R.C. (2006). Beacon in the storm: An exploration of the spirituality and faith of parents whose children have cancer. *Issues in Comprehensive Pediatric Nursing, 29*, 3–24.

Sharpley, R. & Jepson, D. (2011). Rural tourism: A spiritual experience. *Annals of Tourism Research, 38*(1), 52–71.

Snell, T.L. & Simmonds, J.G. (2012) 'Being in that environment can be very therapeutic': Spiritual experiences in nature. *Ecopsychology, 4*(4), 326–335.

Stringer, L.A. & McAvoy, L.H. (1992). The need for something different: Spirituality and wilderness adventure. *Journal of Experiential Education, 15*(1), 13–21.

Sweatman, M. & Heintzman, P. (2004). The perceived impact of outdoor residential camp experience on the spirituality of youth. *World Leisure Journal, 46*(1), 23–31.

Unruh, A.M. & Elvin, N. (2004). In the eye of the dragon: Women's experience of breast cancer, and the occupation of dragon boat racing. *Canadian Journal of Occupational Therapy, 71*(3), 138–149.

Unruh, A.M. & Hutchinson, S. (2011). Embedded spirituality: Gardening in daily life and stressful experiences. *Scandinavian Journal of Caring Sciences, 25*, 567–574.

Winter, C. (2007). The intrinsic, instrumental and spiritual value of natural area visitors and the general public: A comparative study. *Journal of Sustainable Tourism, 15*(1), 599–614.

39

Outdoor education, environment and sustainability

Youth, society and environment

Geoff Cooper

INSTITUTE FOR OUTDOOR LEARNING

Young people are growing up in a society faced by increasing environmental concerns. Globally resources are being used up at an escalating rate. Habitats are changing, rainforests diminishing, deserts expanding, tens of species are lost each day, while the human population increases by more than a million each week. A far-reaching report on the state of the world's wildlife states that the Living Planet Index, which measures more than 10,000 representative populations of mammals, birds, reptiles, amphibians and fish, has declined by 52 per cent since 1970 (WWF, 2014). Most people in the industrialised world are removed from the land and the rhythms of nature. Many Westernised people exist in an insulated, cossetted world protected from the vagaries of the outdoors.

The dominant belief is that technology and commercialisation can solve these global concerns. However, the fragility of our Western political and economic system became all too apparent in 2008 with the failure of the banking system, which has led to rising unemployment, increasing poverty and inequality in many countries. The subsequent insecurity became the breeding ground for an ill-founded fear of threats from mass immigration and terrorism, which in turn may persuade many people to give up their human rights and possibly become more open to manipulation from central governments.

Poverty, homelessness, malnutrition and environmental degradation are all symptoms of an economic and political system rooted in competition, commercialisation and growth. Today's rapid consumption of resources is undermining the environmental resource base. It is exacerbating inequalities and the dynamics of the consumption-poverty-inequality-environment nexus are accelerating (United Nations, 1998). The question for outdoor educators and policy makers is should practice in outdoor education accept and reflect these values or should it provide the space to question dominant oppressive ideologies?

Positioning outdoor education

This debate over the role of education in either supporting the existing structures and values in society or challenging them is long standing (Huckle & Sterling, 1996). In rapidly changing lives many young people will work at jobs that may not yet exist and there is an ever greater need for a more relevant education that meets the needs of new challenges. Kushell (2014) argues that it is essential for young people to acquire the skills and values for this uncertain future. Formal education in schools in the UK has its roots still firmly bedded in satisfying the needs of a former industrialised era (Robinson, 2006) and has become increasingly restricted by a knowledge-based national curriculum that is directed towards a market philosophy and management culture (Ball, 1990, 2008).

Outdoor education is part of both the formal and non-formal sectors in the UK (as discussed below). Schools organise fieldwork as part of the geography and science curriculum, and outdoor education centres may offer programmes that relate to physical education, environmental education, and personal and social development. There are also opportunities in the less structured non-formal education sector through youth and community work and out-of-school outdoor activities (Becker & Schirp, 2008; Backman, Humberstone & Loynes, 2014). In some countries, such as Slovenia, outdoor learning is predominantly linked to the school curriculum, while in others, such as Iceland, it is mainly provided by the non-formal sector.

Arguably, outdoor education can be a powerful force for change. It can involve active learning in real-world situations outside the confines of the classroom. Outdoor education can incorporate the arts, sciences, social sciences and physical education. It cuts across subject disciplines and involves the cognitive, affective and psycho-motor domains. It does not have the constraints of timetables and curricula, and this greater flexibility and emphasis on active, hands-on learning provides the opportunity to question the dominant structures and values held in society. But in a neo-liberal society there are pressures from the marketplace for outdoor education to succumb to commercial values.

Commercialisation of the outdoors

Many outdoor educators question the trend, often perceived as emerging from the outdoor recreation industry, towards standardisation, programming and commodification infiltrating outdoor learning (Loynes 2007; Becker 2008; Beames & Brown 2014). Outdoor clothing, equipment and high-adrenaline adventures are marketed by the leisure industry, and some outdoor education providers are adopting commercial practices. The decline in public-sector provision in outdoor education in the UK and the growth of private operators has, for the most part, led to the packaging of activities where the emphasis is on fun, thrills and physical experiences, and learning becomes secondary or incidental. There are clear parallels between these experiences and the 'rides' in a theme park. They may use high-tech equipment, and activities tend to be competitive and task-centred, with the environment providing the arena or gymnasium. This packaging of experiences has become apparent with the growth of commercial outdoor activity centres and businesses (Cooper 2007).

This tendency reflects the dominant ideology, whose culture emphasises speed, glamour and self-centredness. This fits readily into a world of instant gratification, sound bites and the 'selfie'. It is at odds with most of the originating principles of outdoor education, which were based on exploration, nature, community, cooperation and reflection (Parker & Meldrum, 1973). More particularly, as with much neo-liberal practice, the importance of environment and sustainability is ignored, and with it an understanding of the significant contribution of outdoor education to environmental education and sustainability.

Towards outdoor pedagogies in tune with environment and community

The term environmental education was introduced in the 1960s in the UK but its development can be traced to earlier environmental thinking in natural science, rural studies, fieldwork, countryside conservation and urban studies. It is commonly accepted that environmental education should include opportunities for learning *about*, learning *in* or *through*, and learning *for* the environment (Sterling & Cooper, 1992). Based on an early definition (IUCN, 1970) environmental education is usually considered as process of learning that raises awareness, develops understanding and skills, clarifies attitudes and values and, crucially, leads to action for the environment.

In the UK, there have been four distinct approaches to environmental education, as identified below. Each has its own focus, methodology and proponents. Outdoor education makes an important contribution to all four.

Reconnecting with nature: aesthetic approaches

These approaches emphasise the importance of direct experiences of natural environments where individuals can explore feelings, consider how they are connected to the rest of life, express a sense of awe and wonder, and develop imagination and creativity. Artists and writers have often approached the environment in this way, as a source of inspiration. Their work can also raise awareness and emotions, and encourage individuals to make connections with nature. Some writers have suggested that emotional attachment to nature arises not simply through our senses but also through the movement of bodies, which may engage more of the senses holistically by walking, running, swimming and so forth (Humberstone, 2014). The senses and emotions are all interconnected and become embodiment in nature through movement. Outdoor educators may well be aware of how being active while in natural surroundings often influences our own moods and levels of interest and awareness (Cooper, 1998).

Environmental and outdoor educators such as Van Matre (1972), Cornell (1979), Henley (1989), Cooper (1998) and Knapp (1999) have stressed the value of direct contact with the environment and see this as a starting point in the process of environmental understanding. They offer many ideas and activities that can be used by outdoor leaders to encourage environmental awareness through engaging the senses. These sensory activities have become popular with outdoor educators across Europe and North America, particularly those working in the non-formal sector. Van Matre and the Institute of Earth Education have developed 'earthwalks' where short sensory activities are selected so that they flow from one to another as part of an environmental programme (Van Matre, 1990).

Writers from a variety of disciplines have stressed the importance of links with nature. Wilson (1984) put forward the concept of 'biophilia', arguing that humans have a cultural-genetic link with nature. He claims that people have a 'love of living things' that dates back millions of years to a time when the human species was in its earliest stages of evolution. Wilson believes that all people have a built-in genetic imprint that causes our inner need to commune with nature, which arguably with education can be reignited. Chawla (1986) describes how experience of 'ecstatic' or outstanding places can have a profound impact on a young person's creativity and development. Similarly, Cohen (1989) a pioneer in the field of nature-connected psychology offers a strong argument for the restorative and developmental qualities that result from experiencing nature. Nature can reach the hearts of people, but also produce clearer thinking and understanding. Louv (2006) argues that children's loss of connection with the natural world is producing a series of harmful mental and physical ailments, which he refers to as nature-deficit disorder.

Direct experiences in the outdoors are great motivators; they can unlock talents that remain hidden in more formal situations. Mortlock (1984) argues that direct contact with the natural environment through challenging situations can be inspirational and lead to feelings of 'oneness' with the Earth. Many will not have these intense challenges, but even in cities people find simple ways to connect with nature, as I found on my first visit to the town of Wigan:

> One wet May evening, I was driving home and got lost amidst an area of wasteland and factories. I suddenly came upon a stretch of canal packed with people, young and old, fishing. Some sheltered by the canal bank under large umbrellas, their attention fixed on their lines. What had brought so many people out on this damp evening? My first thought was that it was a competition. But I was wrong; these were individuals in their free time, sitting by a stretch of not too clean water for hours without necessarily catching a fish.

> So why were they there? I stopped to ask them and their replies were similar: 'It gives me a chance to get away from things, to relax, clear my head'. 'I like the peace and quiet', 'I've got time to think', 'I feel free'. This ability of fishing to induce a state of calm has been recognised and schemes to introduce young offenders to fishing have been developed in the UK.

Scientific and knowledge-based approaches

The two main traditions of outdoor education in the UK, field studies and outdoor adventure, emerged through two distinct routes. During the past sixty years these have developed as quite distinctive movements with their own particular philosophies (Drasdo, 1972; Cooper, 1999).

The early development of field studies was linked to the study of science, particularly biology, geography and geology. Fieldwork has been closely related to formal education through school and college curricula. The Field Studies Council was founded in 1943 and has continued to establish a range of centres throughout England and Wales. Since the 1960s many local education authorities have opened field study centres where students can learn about and through the environment (Ogilvie, 2013).

On an informal level, over recent years, outdoor citizen science has developed in the UK. The world's largest wildlife survey is organised each year by the Royal Society for the Protection of Birds (RSPB), when the public is asked to record the species of birds visiting their garden over a set period on a weekend in January. The Open Air Laboratories (OPAL) network has developed a range of UK-wide citizen science surveys including a Tree Health Survey, Bug Count and Soil Survey. The first aim of OPAL is to encourage 'a change of lifestyle to spend time outside observing and recording the world around us'. These national scientific surveys give valuable insights into the health and distribution of wildlife, and this can highlight issues such as habitat loss and climate change.

Such scientific field investigation involves observation, measurement, recording, analysis and hypothesis testing. It provides the knowledge for understanding the natural processes that relate us to other life on the planet. Of particular importance to environmental education are the key ecological concepts such as the water and nutrient cycles, food webs, habitats, ecosystems, adaptation, evolution and change over geological time. The understanding of ecosystems and our interrelationship with them can be a powerful lesson in appreciating our dependency on other life on our planet.

Social critical analysis

Arguably, there are no such things as environmental problems, rather the problems lie with the way individuals and societies make economic, social and political decisions that affect the environment. The critical analysis approach places people's attitudes, actions and values firmly at the centre of environmental considerations and concerns. Emphasis is placed on critical thinking and enquiry to understand and make sense of a particular issue. It is about clarifying one's own values, and learning how as individuals and members of society we can be actively involved in promoting change (see Öhman, 2008).

One approach to critical thinking is through a method known as Philosophy for Children (P4C). Based on the work of Lipman (1976), P4C uses a stimulus, for example a story, object or outdoor experience, to encourage young people to develop their thinking skills, and to raise a selection of deep or philosophical questions that have no one correct answer. The group decides and votes on the questions, and chooses one for in-depth dialogue. The leader facilitates the discussion and allows time for the group to reflect on the opinions and values raised. This method allows young people to think for themselves, appreciate others' views and to work out their own values. There is great scope for using these methods in outdoor learning (Rowley & Lewis, 2003).

Outdoor education offers many opportunities to introduce environmental issues through direct experience. Issues relating to land ownership, land use change, loss of habitats, recreational conflicts and access to the countryside are a few obvious examples (see Mansfield, Chapter 40 in this volume). Raising questions can promote important discussion around these issues. For example, when mountain walking one question might be, 'What is the future of our uplands in Britain?' or, more contentiously, 'Should we leave the uplands to re-wild?' These questions raise a host of issues and debating points such as: Do we want our uplands to provide more food or trees for fuel? Or do we want them for conservation and biodiversity? If the latter is the case are we happy for heather moorland to be managed for grouse shooting? Should our uplands be managed as a carbon sink or for renewable energy in the form of wind farms? And what about the wonderful opportunities the mountains and moorlands give us for recreation and outdoor education, and the mental and physical benefits that follow?

These are simple questions but they lead to complex choices and potential repercussions. Engaging in these dialogues, participants may begin to appreciate the range of opinions expressed by different interest groups, assess the arguments on each side before a personal judgment is made. It takes humans into the realm of considering what are society's current values and determining the values which need to be adopted for more sustainable lifestyles (Cooper, 2012).

Community action

The community action approach involves taking reflective action to improve the environment. It is about becoming a more environmentally conscious citizen. The action could include energy saving, recycling schemes, tree planting, renovating buildings, clearing litter, etc., but may also include campaigning on environmental issues. Many young people in the UK are introduced to the outdoors through practical conservation projects, which are often connected with creating or restoring wildlife habitats and making them accessible for visitors. The Conservation Volunteers, National Trust, National Park Authorities and Woodland Trust are some of the agencies that organise conservation work parties. Some recreational groups develop environmental action; Taylor (2007) talks of the development of environmentalism in the surfing communities of North America. Wheaton (2007) discusses the environmental activism of the Surfers Against Sewage organisation, which emerged from surfers' and windsurfers' concerns about sea pollution in the UK.

Environmental and other campaign groups are now using the internet to galvanise public opinion. The campaign launched by the organisation 38 Degrees in 2010 collected half a million signatures protesting about the proposed privatisation of vast areas of English national woodland. The government was forced to suspend sales of forest land due to the strength of feeling from all sections of society.

Outdoor leaders are in a privileged position to play a crucial role in encouraging good environmental practice through adopting programmes such as the John Muir Award, which incorporates conservation as one of its four challenges. Leaders often provide strong role models and their actions can be significant to young people. Furthermore they may raise awareness and promote environmental practice in their organisations.

Outdoor education clearly has a great deal to offer all four approaches to environmental education. It can address all aspects of environmental education, from awareness, understanding and the development of skills to the discussion of attitudes and values, and the ways in which action can be taken. It also has an important part to play in what has become known as education for sustainability.

From environmental education to sustainability

The term sustainable development has become increasingly important as a concept since the United Nations Earth Summit in Rio in 1992, when governments throughout the world drew up priorities for action on environment and development. There have been many attempts to define sustainable development. An early definition and one often quoted is: 'development that meets the needs of the present without compromising the ability of future generations to meet their needs' (World Commission for Environment and Development, 1987, p. 8). More recent definitions have stressed the importance of improving the quality of our lives without harming the ecosystems we depend upon.

Sustainable development is not just about conserving environments and maintaining biodiversity. It is also about the relationships between people on the planet and involves making connections between the natural, social, economic and political domains at local, regional and global levels. Education for Sustainability includes understanding the arguments for social justice, sharing resources more equitably and for improving the quality of our lives in terms of access to health care, education, justice, work, leisure and democracy (Magee *et al.*, 2013). It is about caring for people from all sections of society and countries of the world. It is concerned with both present and future generations (Jones, Selby & Sterling, 2010). It implies the need for an ethic based on cooperation rather than competition, quality of life rather than standard of living, and community rather than individual interest. It is therefore a broader concept than environmental education and includes aspects of personal and social education, citizenship, economic understanding, global awareness and ethical considerations (Sterling, 2001; Cooper, 2012).

Encouraging sustainability through the outdoors

There is sometimes a tension between outdoor education and the use of the environment (again see Mansfield, Chapter 40 in this volume). Some groups may simply use the environment as a backcloth for their own aims, treating it as a gymnasium for physical activity or a laboratory for scientific investigation. Four types of potential impact – physical, ecological, social and psychological – have been identified (Cooper, 2004). Ogilvie (2013) reports on the Adventure and Environmental Awareness Group's initiatives. This group was established in the early 1980s in the UK to raise awareness and to encourage collaboration among outdoor users, conservationists and land managers to draw up recommendations and disseminate good practice. National governing bodies, such as the British Mountaineering Council, have also contributed to this

Geoff Cooper

process by producing environmental guidelines and codes of practice. While these forms of environmental policy are important, there is a wider role for outdoor educators in encouraging sustainable lifestyles through questioning their own and their organisation's values, and considering how these are presented to groups through their philosophy, methodology, programmes and activities.

Values are those underlying beliefs and principles that shape our attitudes and behaviour. Currently the dominant value system in Western countries is based on economic growth, material possessions, social position and external appearance. There are, however, higher 'core' values recognised by many different cultures throughout the world, which form the basis for a more peaceful, cooperative and sustainable existence (see Öhman, 2008; New Economics Foundation, 2010). The Brahma Kumaris World Spiritual University has developed an international education programme called 'Living Values' (Brahma Kumaris, 1995). These include twelve higher values, common it suggests to all people: cooperation, freedom, happiness, honesty, humility, love, peace, respect, responsibility, simplicity, tolerance and unity. Such sets of values can be a useful starting point for some educators to explore their own values, but many outdoor leaders will be more comfortable for young people to reflect on and clarify their own values rather than be presented with a creed to be followed.

Researchers working in more than eighty countries have defined around sixty human values that occur across them (Schwartz et al., 2012). These form clusters, with some values related closely to one another, such as politeness and respect for tradition. Sharp contrast can be drawn between a cluster of 'intrinsic values', such as responsibility, equality, curiosity, associated with behaviours that benefit environment and community, and 'extrinsic values', such as social power and ambition, which lead to self-centredness (Blackmore, Underhill, McQuilkin, Leach & Holmes, 2013). The Real World Learning Network (Real World Learning, 2013) is a partnership of outdoor learning providers across Europe, which has adopted this values framework to explore ways of promoting more sustainable lifestyles.

Another European network of outdoor researchers and educators, the European Institute for Outdoor Adventure Education and Experiential Learning has, in its recent conferences (European Institute for Outdoor Adventure Education and Experiential Learning, 2013), begun to consider and raise the issues around outdoor learning and sustainability. There is a growing critique (see Wattchow & Brown, 2011) of outdoor pedagogies, which focus on adventure in remote areas and those that concentrate on the acquisition of personal skills, confidence building and self-esteem, and also the ways in which teacher–pupil interaction may not always attend to nature authentically (Humberstone & Stan, 2012). The former adventurous approaches are removed from everyday life, have little contact with community and are more associated with the extrinsic values mentioned earlier. Outdoor educators have, over recent years, expounded other more relevant pedagogies and traditions as a basis for their research and practice. *Friluftsliv*, place-based learning and global education offer values and methodologies that can encourage more sustainable living.

Friluftsliv, or outdoor nature life, developed in Scandinavia as part of a cultural tradition, living and travelling with family and friends in a simple way and in harmony with nature (Backman, 2007; Gurholt, 2008). Ideally, groups are kept small to encourage involvement, and activities are close to nature – for example, walking, ski touring, paddling an open canoe, sleeping out in a cabin or around a campfire. Equipment is simple and journeys are not rushed, allowing time for reflection and discussion (see Gurholt, Chapter 28 in this volume). Tellnes (1993) argues that *friluftsliv* can create a base for environmental consciousness, good health, higher quality of life and sustainable development. Repp (1996) also stresses the importance of 'good meetings with nature' in developing the whole person, physically, emotionally and intellectually. These experiences may not only lead to a rediscovery of nature, in a sensitive way, but may bring about changes in attitudes and a deeper understanding of oneself and other aspects of life. These approaches are not exclusive to Scandinavia: Henderson and Vikander (2007) have explored similar nature–life traditions in a selection of other countries.

Place-based learning has developed as a multidisciplinary approach (Gruenewald, 2003; Sobel, 2004), and has been applied to outdoor learning as an alternative to the dominant practice based on risk, adventure, and personal and social development (Wattchow & Brown, 2011). Orr (1992) argues that we have become 'deplaced' people for whom our immediate surroundings are no longer sources of food, water, livelihood, energy, materials, friends, recreation or sacred inspiration. Poorly designed, homogeneous development is discouraging a sense of connection and responsibility. Through a sense of place we can develop feelings of attachment based on knowledge and experience of being in an area that has its own distinctiveness in terms of landscape, wildlife, buildings, occupations, culture and traditions. This process helps to ground people, connect them to land and community (Beames & Ross, 2010). By raising feelings and knowledge of place, communities are strengthened, pride develops, heritage is celebrated and traditions restored. This emphasis on the local may act as an antidote to standardisation and commercialisation. It can generate more interest and activity in the community, which can lead to employment opportunities through support for local services and businesses, less outward travel and more sustainable lifestyles. Wattchow and Brown (2011, p. 180) propose a useful approach in the form of four 'signposts' to support their vision of making available place-responsive outdoor education.

Towards the bigger picture

Friluftsliv and place-based approaches deepen our knowledge and feelings for environment and community, and through this closer connection human beings are arguably more likely to develop values that are sensitive and caring. But do these pedagogies lead to a social critique of nature, place and community? Who makes the decisions that affect landscape, nature and housing? Many people, particularly those living in anonymous, run-down urban areas with high unemployment, may not have a strong affinity to place. How has this loss of relationship between people and place arisen? This inevitably leads to bigger questions of ownership, control and social justice.

Some outdoor adventure experiences are based on escaping from every day existence. Place-based learning questions these short-term, one-off experiences and adopts a slower pace to exploring the commonplace. But is this celebration of the local to the detriment of considering people living on other parts of the planet? Sustainability is about a bigger discourse, about sharing resources more equitably across the globe. In arguing that outdoor learning is a powerful and vital part of mainstream education, then, these issues should be addressed more directly.

'Valuing Places' was a curriculum project developed by the Geographical Association for 7–14 year olds in England and Wales from 2003–06. It explored how teaching about places, starting from the home and school, can develop students' understanding of global interconnections. It argued that place cannot be treated in isolation and that the character of a place can be understood only through its relations with the world beyond. Teaching resources were developed for the classroom and outdoor learning (Geographical Association, 2013).

Fishwick and Mullarkey (2008) provide several Global Learning Outdoors projects for young people. Major themes – 'Shelter', 'Water', 'Needs or Wants?' – are developed through journeys in the outdoors. Woodland activities, such as shelter building, fire lighting and simple outdoor cooking, are introduced and related to how people satisfy these basic needs in other parts of the world. Packing a rucksack for an overnight expedition leads to a discussion of what is essential and what luxuries are taken for granted. These powerful learning experiences through the outdoors are not isolated but can be related to the bigger picture of global awareness.

Working with communities and environment: a concluding story

Many of the ideas mentioned above on how outdoor educators can contribute to environmental education and sustainability are encapsulated and enacted in the following story:

> I met Rod Walker on his homestead, near Pucón in Chile in 2004. He's a British environmental educator who worked in Antarctica and returning home via Chile in 1965 had never quite made it back. As a consequence he set up the first outdoor education centre in Chile and since the 1990s has been working with local communities in central Chile close to the Cañi auracaria (monkey puzzle) forest.

> I was part of a small group of outdoor educators he'd invited to help with a community based eco-tourism project. At the time there had been rapid environmental change in Chile with pressure from commercial logging, new roads and electricity supply. There were few opportunities for the young, especially the indigenous Mapuche people and Rod had the vision to use their considerable knowledge and skills in their training as environmental guides for the Cañi sanctuary.

> Rod was keen for us to connect with this place by meeting a variety of local people and to listen to their stories. He introduced us to the sanctuary slowly, we shared examples of sensory activities, travelled barefoot and gained knowledge of the ecosystem and how forest plants are used by the Mapuche. With the help of local guides, our task was to explore the forest to identify routes for footpaths and to choose areas suitable for simple campsites for sustainable tourism. This project has now been realised and visitors can have guided visits to the Cañi, learning about this special ecosystem and the culture and traditions of the area.

This story, inspired by one person with a clear set of values based on sustainability and social justice, demonstrates how outdoor educators can engage with environment and community in a practical and ethical way. It is about a deep connection with people and place through emotions and knowledge. Built into the story is a social critique of the values of a commercial society and the need for remedial action to counteract its excesses. It is concerned with the interconnecting systems of environmental protection, community development and social justice – the very essence of sustainability. The story is about a particular group of people in a particular place, but the vision and practical action will resonate with many communities throughout the world.

References

Backman, E. (2007). *Teaching and Learning Friluftsliv in Physical Education Teacher Education*. Stockholm: Stockholm Institute of Education.

Backman, E., Humberstone B. & Loynes, C. (Eds.) (2014). *Urban Nature: Inclusive Learning through Youth Work and School Work*. Borås, Sweden: Recito Förlag AB.

Ball, S. (1990). *Politics and Policy Making in Education*. London: Routledge.

Ball, S. (2008). *The Education Debate*. Bristol: Policy Press.

Beames, S. & Brown, M. (2014). Enough of Ronald and Mickey: Focusing on learning in outdoor education. *Journal of Adventure Education and Outdoor Learning, 14*(2), 118–131.

Beames, S. & Ross, H. (2010). Journeys outside the classroom. *Journal of Adventure Education and Outdoor Learning, 10*(2), 95–109.

Becker, P. (2008). The European Institute for Outdoor Adventure Education and Experiential Learning: A report of the first decade. Retrieved from: www.eoe-network.eu.

Becker, P. & Schirp, J. (2008). *Other Ways of Learning*, Marburg: bsj Marburg.

Blackmore, E., Underhill, R., McQuilkin, J., Leach R. & Holmes, T. (2013). *Common Cause for Nature*. Machynlleth: Public Interest Research Centre.

Brahma Kumaris (1995). *Living Values: A Guidebook*. London: Brahma Kumaris, World Spiritual University.

Chawla, L. (1990). Ecstatic places. *Children's Environments Quarterly*, 7(4), 18–23.

Cohen, M. (1989). *Connecting with Nature, Creating Moments that Let Earth Teach*. Eugene, OR: World Peace University.

Cooper, G. (1998). *Outdoors with Young People*, Lyme Regis: Russell House Publishing.

Cooper, G. (1999). Changing roles for outdoor education centres. In B. Humberstone & P. Higgins (Eds.) *Outdoor Education and Experiential Learning in UK*. Luneburg: Universitat Luneburg.

Cooper, G. (2004). Outdoor education and the sustainable use of the environment. In P. Barnes & B. Sharp (Eds.) *The RHP Companion to Outdoor Education*. Lyme Regis: Russell House Publishing.

Cooper, G. (2007). Activity centres or outdoor education centres? *Horizons, 37*, 10–13.

Cooper, G. (2012). Outdoor learning, environment and sustainability. *Environmental Education, 100*, 28–31.

Cornell, J. (1979). *Sharing Nature with Children*. Watford: Exley.

Drasdo, H. (1972). *Education and the Mountain Centres*. Tyddyn Gabriel: Welsh Universal Press.

European Institute for Outdoor Adventure Education and Experiential Learning (2013) Retrieved from: www.eoe-network.org.

Fishwick, B. & Mullarkey, G. (2008). Going global outdoors. *Horizons, 42*, 24–25.

Geographical Association (2013). Retrieved from: www.geography.org.uk/projects/valuingplaces/.

Gruenewald, D. (2003). Foundations of place: A multi-disciplinary framework for place-conscious education. *American Education Research Journal, 40*(3), 619–654.

Gurholt, K.P. (2008). Norwegian friluftsliv and ideals of becoming an 'educated man'. *Journal of Adventure Education and Outdoor Learning, 8*(1), 55–70.

Henderson, B. & Vikander, N. (2007). *Nature First*. Toronto: Natural Heritage Books.

Henley, T. (1989). *Rediscovery: Ancient Pathways – New Directions*. Vancouver: Western Canada Wilderness Committee.

Huckle, J. & Sterling, S. (1996). *Education for Sustainability*. London: Earthscan.

Humberstone, B. (2014). Embodiment, nature and well-being: More than the senses? In M. Robertson, R. Lawrence & G. Heath (Eds.) *Experiencing the Outdoors: Enhancing Strategies for Wellbeing*. Rotterdam: Sense Publishers.

Humberstone, B. & Stan, I. (2012). Nature in outdoor learning – authenticity or performativity well-being, nature and outdoor pedagogies project. *Journal of Adventure Education and Outdoor Learning, 12*(3), 183–198.

IUCN (1970). International working meeting on environmental education in the school curriculum. Final report, IUCN.

Jones, P., Selby, D. & Sterling, S. (Eds.) (2010). *Sustainability Education*. London: Earthscan.

Knapp, C. (1999). *In Accord with Nature*. Charleston, West Virginia: ERIC/CRESS.

Kushell, J. (2014). Retrieved from: www.huffingtonpost.com/jennifer-kushell/.

Lipman, M. (1976). *Philosophy for Children*. Oxford: Basil Blackwell.

Louv, R. (2006). *Last Child in the Woods*. Chapel Hill, NC: Algonquin Books.

Loynes, C. (2007) Why outdoor learning should get real. In B. Henderson & N. Vikander (Eds.) *Nature First*. Toronto: Natural Heritage Books.

Magee, L., Scerri, A., James, P., Thom, J., Padgham, L., Hickmott, S., Deng, H. & Cahill, F. (2013). Reframing social sustainability reporting: Towards an engaged approach. *Environment, Development and Sustainability, 15*(1), 225–243.

Mortlock, C. (1984). *The Adventure Alternative*. Milnthorpe: Cicerone Press.

New Economics Foundation (2010). *The Great Transition*. London: New Economics Foundation.

Ogilvie, K. (2013). *Roots and Wings: A History of Outdoor Education and Outdoor Learning in the UK*. Lyme Regis: Russell House Publishing.

Öhman, J. (Ed.) (2008). *Values and Democracy in Education for Sustainable Development – Contributions from Swedish Research*. Malmo: Liber.

Orr, D. (1992). *Ecological Literacy: Education and the Transition to a Postmodern World*. New York: State University of New York Press.

Parker, T. & Meldrum, K. (1973). *Outdoor Education*. London: Dent.

Real World Learning (2013). Retrieved from: www.rwlnetwork.org.

Repp, G. (1996). Outdoor adventure education and friluftsliv seen from a sociology of knowledge perspective. *Journal of Adventure Education and Outdoor Leadership, 13*(2), 63–66.

Robinson, K. (2006). Retrieved from: www.ted.com/talks/ken_robinson_says_schools_kill_creativity.

Rowley, C. & Lewis, L. (2003). *Thinking on the Edge*. Bowness-on-Windermere: Badger Press.

Schwartz, S., Cieciuch, J., Vecchione, M., Davidov, E., Fischer, R., Beierlein, C., Ramos, A., Verkasalo, M., Lönnqvist, J., Demirutku, K., Dirilen-Gumus, O. & Konty, M. (2012) Refining the theory of basic individual values. *Journal of Personality and Social Psychology, 103*(4), 663–688.

Sobel, D. (2004). *Place-based Education: Connecting Classrooms and Communities*. Great Barrington, MA: The Orion Society.

Sterling, S. (2001). *Sustainable Education – Re-visioning Learning and Change*. Dartington: Green Books.

Sterling, S. & Cooper, G. (1992). *In Touch – Environmental Education for Europe*. Godalming: WWF UK.

Taylor, B. (2007). Surfing into spirituality and a new, aquatic nature religion. *Journal of the American Academy of Religion, 75*(4), 923–951.

Tellnes, A. (1993). Friluftsliv – outdoor nature life as a method to change attitudes. *Journal of Adventure Education and Outdoor Leadership, 10*(3), 12–15.

United Nations (1998). *Human Development Report 1998 Overview*. New York: United Nations Development Programme.

Van Matre, S. (1972). *Acclimatization*. Martinsville, IN: American Camping Association.

Van Matre, S. (1990). *Earth Education – A New Beginning*. Warrenville, IL: Institute for Earth Education.

Wattchow, B. & Brown, M. (2011). *A Pedagogy of Place*. Monash: Monash University Publishing.

Wheaton, B. (2007). Identity, politics, and the beach: Environmental activism in surfers against sewage. *Leisure Studies, 26*(3), 279–302.

Wilson, E. (1984). *Biophilia*. Cambridge, MA: Harvard University Press.

World Commission for Environment and Development (1987). *Our Common Future* (Brundtland Report). Oxford: Oxford University Press.

World Wildlife Fund (2014). *Living Planet Report*. Gland: WWF International.

40

Land management and outdoor recreation in the UK

Lois Mansfield

UNIVERSITY OF CUMBRIA

The relationship between outdoor recreationists and other land users in the United Kingdom has been, and continues to be, contentious. Why this exists in the UK is due to two main factors. First, is the influence of the historical development of land ownership patterns over the past ten centuries, where consequently now over half the land is owned by only 0.06 per cent of the population (Fairlie, 2009). Millions of outdoor recreationalists every year may unwittingly cross over land where private landlords guard their land rights closely. Second, practically every hectare[1] of land can be classified as multifunctional, the most obvious and predominant of which is combinations of primary food production and secondary outdoor recreation and nature conservation. This multifunctionality is fairly unusual globally: in North America and Australasia, for example, access to the outdoors is limited to areas deliberately set aside for recreational purposes or as wilderness for both biodiversity and recreation. This explains why National Parks in the UK are living, working landscapes, whereas in most other parts of the world National Parks are wilderness (e.g. Runte, 1987). That is to suggest land-scapes are largely devoid of most forms of economic exploitation, which consume resources for profit.

Inevitably, land ownership rights and multifunctionality have led to conflict between user groups, such as outdoor recreationalists. This chapter first explores the purposes of some of the main UK land users. It will then go on to consider the nature of conflicts between these purposes and outdoor recreation. Finally it will consider various approaches and management tools that have been successfully applied to mitigate conflicts between outdoor recreationalists and other land users.

The purposes of land use in the UK

Within the UK there are three primary rural land uses: agriculture, forestry and water supply (Khan, Powell & Harwood, 2012). Cutting across and sharing the same land are secondary land uses of conservation and outdoor recreation. The tensions between these primary and secondary groups has been continuous since about the 1860s, the underlying reason being varying incompatibility in terms of resource use.

Agriculture

Agriculture dominates land use, occupying 69.1 per cent of the land area. The primary aim of UK farmers is to produce food either for domestic consumption or export; few have additional objectives. The motivations of farmers are generally instrumental (i.e. to generate a satisfactory income) or intrinsic (i.e. farming is valued as an activity in its own right) (Mansfield, 2011). Few, if any, farmers perceive themselves as producers of public goods (i.e. landscape, biodiversity or habitats) and this is often the greatest area of conflict between them and other groups. UK agriculture is divided into upland enterprises (above 240 m asl),[2] producing livestock for lamb, beef or wool, and lowland, which is dominated by dairy and arable operations. Upland areas are also synonymous with high conservation value landscapes and those with the perception of providing the most 'wild' experience for outdoor enthusiasts.

As agricultural economics have changed and costs of production risen, lower profit margins have forced farmers to either intensify production, resulting in a range of environmental problems, or diversify their business activities to keep pace with reduced incomes (Mansfield, 2011). In the latter case, outdoor recreation experiences have benefited from farmers converting barns for holiday lets, setting up bunkhouses for walkers or developing recreation attractions. The ability of farmers to exploit the outdoor sector has had varying success, with those farms lying within a National Park or other visitor destinations gaining the most, followed by those on the land just beyond, and finally those in the wider countryside (Walford, 2001). At the same time, political changes in the European Union, along with pressure from the World Trade Organization, have led to modulation of farming support away from production towards environmental management (improving the environmental quality and public goods) and rural development (supporting farm diversification) (Council Regulation (EC) no 1257/99).

Forestry

In 1900, UK woodland equated to about 5 per cent of the land area as a result of hundreds of years of timber exploitation, agricultural clearance and urban expansion. With the outbreak of war in 1914, it became apparent how little woodland was left. Following the Acland Report, the state-funded Forestry Commission was tasked with expanding the forest area as rapidly as possible, to create a strategic stockpile for the nation, and 400,000 hectares were planted by 1934 (Starr, 2005). The Commission achieved this by buying up land and planting it with fast-growing coniferous plantations, which could be harvested for use in forty to sixty years, unlike hardwoods which take around eighty to 120 years to mature. Today forest and woods account for 3.1 million hectares of the UK (13 per cent of the land area) of which 46 per cent is broadleaf and 54 per cent coniferous, with approximately half accessible by the public (Forestry Commission, 2014).

Much of the land bought by the Commission was poor agricultural land of naturally high conservation value, which led to direct conflict between foresters and farmers and conservationists (Zuckerman, 1957). Fast-growing conifers do not generally sit well with the public either, due to their artificial aesthetics of what is generally thought of as 'miles and miles of trees on parade'. Furthermore, in the 1960s it was discovered that coniferous plantations were causing accelerated soil acidification leading to heavy metal release, which eventually reached water bodies rendering some biologically dead (Dudley, 1985). Over time the aims and objectives of the Forestry Commission changed. The management underpinning philosophy shifted from instrumental, monocultural activities to more intrinsic, multifunctional ones (Mather, 1998). By the late 1960s provision of employment in depressed rural areas and production of timber for domestic processing industries were replaced to encompass recreation, nature conservation and amenity, allowing more flexible planting regimes.

Today, Forestry Commission land is designed to provide timber, conservation, amenity and recreation as laid down by the Helsinki Accords in 1993 (Forest Europe, 1993). The car parks, walking trails, picnic areas and simple visitor centres of the early years have been replaced by more sophisticated outdoor facilities, such as mountain bike routes and sculpture trails. Following this lead, some of the larger private forestry companies operating in the UK, accounting for 60 per cent of afforested areas, now have extensive bike trails weaving across their land (for example, UPM Tilhill at Coed Llandegla in Wales) either using statutory or permissive rights of way. Running parallel has been the development of the Forest Schools movement in the UK (Knight, 2011). Forests are no longer seen as simply a timber resource, but multifunctional facilities for private and public use alike (Buttoud, 2002).

Water supply

Water bodies in the UK constitute natural lakes and rivers, and artificially impounded waters such as reservoirs and canals. Static water bodies like lakes and reservoirs cover 436 km^2 supported by network of 42,800 km of rivers and streams (Dill, 1993).

The organisation of water supply in the UK has evolved gradually since around 1800. Most water was supplied on a highly localised basis at first by local government authorities or small private companies, who would organise, fund and manage their own supplies. This included the construction of dams and reservoirs in areas of the country endowed with high annual precipitation. In this way, water expanses such as Thirlmere and Haweswater in the English Lake District came into being. After 1945, the system became more consolidated and streamlined, culminating in ten publicly owned authorities operating on a super-catchment[3] basis until 1989. It is during this period that most of the large landscape protection areas, such as National Parks and Areas of Outstanding Natural Beauty, were set up. Since 1989 these authorities have become privatised. Many of these companies own large areas of reservoir/lake catchments, allowing them management control with respect to water quality and quantity. The land itself is often farmed by tenants.

Similar to the situation of the Forestry Commission, the mid-20th century public ownership encouraged access for other purposes, such as recreation. While actual use of some water bodies is forbidden for personal safety reasons or contamination purposes, the surrounding land is used for quiet outdoor pursuits such as walking. Over the years the water authorities', and then companies', estates have expanded to provide locations for a plethora of outdoor activities. One such example is Kielder Water in northern England. Claimed to be the largest manmade lake in Northern Europe (1000 ha) and surrounded by 250 square miles of working forest (owned by the Forestry Commission), the site offers a wide range of outdoor activities (Kielder Water and Forest Park Development Trust, 2010).

Nature conservation

The UK supports a huge variety of habitats, most of which are plagioclimax communities.[4] These are produced through direct management. The key to maintaining a healthy ecosystem is to perpetuate the low-intensity use that has produced these habitats, rather than intensify it, which would remove what is left of the biodiversity. There is little natural habitat left in the UK islands, mainly consisting of a few areas of mire from the retreat of the last ice, montane (alpine) habitats and minuscule fragments of woodland from 8000 years ago, all inaccessible for exploitation.

In the UK, a network of conservation designations covering 1.7 million hectares exists to do this. The land these conservation areas occupy is either owned outright by government agencies charged with protecting the UK's natural heritage or is predominantly privately owned by a landowner. As a consequence, multifunctional land use is common, with blends of conservation, agriculture and recreational use typical. Quality is measured objectively using a wide range of data to determine if the habitat is in favourable condition, and any remedial work can be the landowner's financial responsibility. While primary rural land use functions are responsible for much of the damage, outdoor recreation is also a culprit, mainly through the degradation of access points and egress (Drewitt & Manley, 1997). The biggest culprit is footpath (trail) use, which has decimated many UK upland areas, notably montane (Holden, 1998) and moorland (Holden et al., 2007).

Beyond the statutory network, various environmental initiatives operate through national and European legislation, enabling grant funding for landowners to perpetuate land management practices that are more sympathetic with biodiversity needs. An example of this is the voluntary Environmentally Sensitive Areas scheme, which ran between 1986 and 2012, providing funds to farmers (Mansfield, 2011). Part of this scheme also catered for the inclusion of permissive rights of way for walkers and other path users over the life of an agreement.

Land ownership and access

Access is arguably the most contentious area of conflict between land managers and outdoor recreationalists in the UK. In order to understand why, an appreciation of the development of rural land ownership is needed because it provides some explanation of landowners' perspectives and actions towards those crossing their land today while engaging in outdoor sport and activities. Much scholarship has argued that this hegemony became embedded through the UK class system and historical materialism (Quinn, Fraser, Hubacek & Reed, 2010), and examines the historical power struggles between various social classes, property rights and land use patterns.

While the public has legal access to the 190,000 km of paths and trails in England – known as Rights of Way (RoW) – only recently have we gained access to the wider countryside. Historically, most land was unenclosed and cultivated as open fields until the 13th century or classified as waste – land no good for cultivation, and typically including mountains, moor, heath, downland (chalk grassland) and wetlands – those areas now largely most sought by outdoor recreationalists to experience 'wilderness'. Over the next 400 years land was enclosed piecemeal by prospecting owners, except for the poorer-quality upland Commons[5] in England and Wales, and the land traditionally controlled under the Scottish Clan system. From about 1760, about 2.8 million hectares of Commons and waste succumbed to enclosure by various Acts of Parliament (Overton, 1996). In Scotland, where there was no Common land, the controversial Highland Clearances and longer historical ownership has resulted in more than 50 per cent of the country being controlled by only 608 landowners, 10 per cent of which is held by eighteen individuals (Warren, 2002).

The mass privatisation of the UK countryside ran parallel to proletarianisation and migration into urban areas as the Industrial Revolution unfolded. In 1815 most people lived and worked in the countryside; by 1870 two-thirds were urbanised, most in squalid, cramped, unhealthy conditions. At the same time, the railway network expanded. Travel writing and landscape poetry became popular, spawning the Romantic Movement, and Victorian (1837–1901) philanthropists, such as Ruskin and Octavia Hill, sought to improve the wellbeing of the urban population (Lothian, 1999). These developments provided the impetus to encourage people to return the countryside, not to work there but to appreciate and enjoy clean air, landscape beauty and 'healthy' pastimes such as walking and, later, cycling.

However, the countryside had changed. The landowning gentry did not want the 'masses' wandering on their land citing crop and fishery damage, and disturbance of deer and grouse as the main reasons. As a result, there began a long power struggle between rural landowners and the public to win back rights to walk these areas again. Shoard (1999) gives a passionate account of the 'war', culminating in the famous mass trespass of Kinder Scout in England's Peak District in 1932. Nevertheless, it was only with the enactment of the National Parks and Access to the Countryside Bill 1949 and, later, the Countryside (Scotland) Bill 1967, that the first steps were taken to secure public access. Finally, in 2005, the Countryside and Rights of Way Act (CROW) 2000 came into effect across England, with 865,000 hectares of land being made accessible to the public (CROW, 2000). It is now possible for individuals to walk, run, climb and picnic freely on mapped areas of 'waste' without having to stick to RoWs.

While land access has pretty much been made available to the public, water bodies are much less accessible. There is no automatic right to access water, launch a boat or traverse a water body in England and Wales. Only about 4 per cent of waterways are legally accessible (66,000 km) in contrast to all other European countries, including Northern Ireland and Scotland. Denied access is underpinned by landowners guarding their lucrative fishing rights, closely supported by anglers, who accuse paddlers and boaters of catching lines and disturbing fish. As a result this is the main area of access campaign still ongoing, spearheaded by organisations such as the British Canoe Union (2014) and the Sport+Recreation Alliance (2014).

Cultural severance

There remains a lack of empathy between rural and urban populations, sometimes referred to as cultural severance (Rotherham, 2008), or a disenfranchisement of people from food production and wider rural activities. Arguably, there are three underlying factors creating this. Most land in the UK is agricultural; other main land users have been able to physically separate their primary functions from secondary recreation and, finally, the key resource use has been mainly one of public good rather than common, such as at Kielder.

Crop and livestock damage, and stock worrying by domestic dogs, legitimise access denial through the ignorance of 'townies' and their related behaviour. Loss of income and damage to business are often cited by farmers as reasons as to why their relationship with the public is at best muted (Mansfield, 2011). It could be argued that these are superficial and resolvable, supported by various simple management strategies. However, there are much deeper sociological issues. There is conflicting evidence as to whether the public understands that agriculture and other forms of rural land management are actually responsible for the UK outdoor landscape they enjoy (see Hall, McVittie & Moran, 2005, vs McVittie, Moran, Smyth & Hall, 2005). To make the situation more complex is the public's misunderstanding of public goods and commons. According to Hardin (1968) all environments contain elements that cannot have a financial value placed upon them, such as landscape, habitat, traditional skills and vibrant communities (see Spratt, Simms, Neitzert & Ryan-Collins, 2010). These types of non-market items can either be called public goods or commons, both difficult to charge for, but can be of benefit to all. Public goods are non-rivalrous; this means individuals can use them and they do not diminish; second, they are non-excludable – people can take advantage of them without intervention, regardless of whether they have paid for them or not. Flowing water in Scotland is an example of a public good. Resource commons, instead, are non-excludable but rivalrous – that is, they can be damaged with overuse; vegetation and soil being the most obvious. Because monetary value cannot easily be placed on either of them, governments refer to this as market failure and consequently intervene in public good or commons management in various ways, such as the establishment of national parks. Thus multifunctional UK landscapes have not only primary and secondary land uses operating within them, but also supply a range of market and non-market goods and services.

Among the conflict of interests between resource, public goods and commons, are the personal concerns of the farmers themselves. Overall, the agricultural community feel that there is a complete lack of empathy as to their role in wider society – to produce food for the table. According to Mansfield (2011), disconnect is unfortunately intensified by their own motivations, which undervalue external social relations. Furthermore most farmers resent the increasing interference by exogenous conservation and outdoor organisations, which are proliferated by employees with no farming background and a general ignorance about food production practicalities. Consequently, generally farmers feel increasingly disenfranchised from the policy-making centres of power. They are trapped in a position where they have little power in decision making and may feel manipulated. Conceptually they might sit on the lower rungs of the classic Arnstein's (1969: 220) 'ladder of citizen participation'. This undervaluing of farmers' knowledge and skills is further exacerbated by experts from other sectors, who largely repeatedly undervalue the management knowledge and skills of local people (Mitchell, 1989: 117).

The poor relationship between agriculture and the general public is exacerbated by physical observations of the impacts of farming operations on the environment by the public (Bunce, 1994). For most of the 20th century, UK and EU agricultural policy provided financial assistance for farmers to continue farming, while at the same time unwanted side effects such as environmental damage and overproduction were overlooked. The case of overgrazing on upland areas is probably the most extreme example, as it has affected large expanses of hill and mountain tops in some of the most iconic British landscapes, like the English Lake District. The idealised romantic perception of these landscapes continues to resonate even with today's public, and thus anything that threatens this world image must be curbed to maintain the 'preserved countryside' (Marsden, 1998). The popular press does little to build bridges of empathy between the visiting outdoor public and the indigenous farming population; instead presenting inaccurate accounts of what is a complex set of interrelated political, economic and social processes (Ilbery, 1998). While the causes of overgrazing are complex, the symptoms are not. Excessive grazing can eventually cross a threshold beyond which the vegetation or even the soil cannot recover, and only drastic management intervention can restore equilibrium. However, domesticated stock grazing is not the only cause of such damage, outdoor recreation is as culpable.

Exceeding carrying capacity

After a time, repeated footfalls or wheel pressure on vegetation will wear it away (Bayfield & Aitken, 1992). Research and professional literature forming part of the wider discipline of recreation ecology is copious regarding the environmental impacts of outdoor recreation and solutions to it (see Liddle, 1997). A central concept of recreation ecology is that of carrying capacity: the ability of a resource to absorb use without deterioration; once a certain threshold is reached damage occurs. First introduced in the 1920s in relation to livestock management (Hawden & Palmer, 1922, cited in Dhondt, 1988), carrying capacity principles are now widely applied to the effects of outdoor recreation in either a biophysical or perceptual way (see Plummer, 2009, pp. 169–206). Biophysical phenomena are damaged beyond natural recovery, the most classic example being footpath erosion. Bates (1935) began such investigations when the effects of trampling on chalk grassland were researched. Later on, Coleman (1981) conceptualised the relationship between biophysical factors and recreation. In contrast, perceptual carrying capacity refers to the point at which people begin to 'feel' an area is overcrowded. While there has been little research into this concept in the UK, much time and consideration has been given to it in North American National Parks and other protected areas (Manning, 2007; Plummer, 2009).

It is quite possible for a resource, say a footpath, to have multiple carrying capacities, and for individual people to have differing opinions as to where the threshold lies. More often than not there is a continuum of carrying capacities with that for agriculture being the highest, followed by recreation, and finally the lowest being for nature conservation. With outdoor recreationalists, sitting in the middle ground, they become the focus of conflict for both parties. For farmers, it is the threat to livelihood through lack of empathy and related access damage, for the nature conservationists it is vegetation damage and wildlife disturbance.

Management solutions

While, conceptually, carrying capacity provides insight into unwanted effects of outdoor recreation, it has been widely criticised as a redundant concept when it comes to practicalities of managing recreation impacts (e.g. Lindberg, McCool & Stankey, 1997). In response, two broad churches of management have evolved: those that directly regulate people's behaviour and those that are indirect, and subtly manipulate people's activities (Mitchell, 1989). Regulatory methods include tools such as zoning areas into those that receive higher or lower recreation use or by setting up restrictions on use intensity. In contrast, manipulative techniques include physical alterations and information dispersal, 'nudging' people to comply with management needs (Agate, 1996). Arguably, these two approaches are used in varying ways dependent on two factors: first, level of management control between strategic and operational decision making and, second, as to whether the land use is mono, dual or multifunctional.

In countries where land is under state control and expressly set aside for recreation with another use, the management tools are dominated by regulatory approaches. For example, the Department of Conservation in New Zealand, which administers the Abel Tasman National Park, has successfully zoned the park with visitor use controlled through paid trail permits and maximum-capacity camping sites (DoC, 2008). In the UK, regulatory control can be used only when a single landowner exists for a site, as in the case of afforested areas and water supply estates or, at the very highest level of statutory legislation, through the RoW network. These situations apply in all cases to strategic management; it is the overall approach an organisation wishes to take to resolve conflict.

Combined with management control is management activation, which can be either proactive or reactive. Proactive management is designed to enable recreation managers to pre-empt damage. It is based on carrying capacity, but uses more sophisticated frameworks that quantify damage in order to trigger management before set thresholds are breached (Manning, 2007). It relies totally on the manager's knowledge and their being able to quantify and, most importantly, have management control over all variables responsible for damage. For example, North American managers use tools such as Limits of Acceptable Change (LAC) or Visitor Experience and Resource Protection (see Stankey et al., 1985; Manning, 2001) in their parks. As a result, the manager can, if they wish, insert a new trail route with no recourse to any outside body, whereas in the UK the construction of a new path route is only possible if special legal dispensation can be gained. While knowledge and quantification of recreation pressure is fully understood in the UK by most academics and practitioners, there is not the level of management control required for proactivity, simply because of UK landownership and access history. One case where LAC has been applied in the UK is for ski management of privately owned Aonach Mor, part of the Ben Nevis range, NW Highlands of Scotland (Northern Ecological Services, 2014). In contrast, reactive management responds to actual observation of damage, such as vegetation deterioration, soil erosion or complete path failure. So, importantly, reactive management addresses the symptoms and not the causes of land misuse because there is no actual management control allowing proactivity.

Most UK land has multiple uses, with usually either a single landowner indifferent to access or a multiplicity of owners over distance. This is compounded by multiple access points by road or foot, which cannot be regulated to limit the amount of people entering outdoor environments. As a consequence, UK recreation managers are often limited to manipulative approaches to deal with operational recreational issues, focusing on the actual practicality of resolving a conflict. Path maintenance is perhaps the most common and effective approach for damage control. Pearce-Higgins and Yalden (1997) were able to demonstrate a reduction from 30 to 3.8 per cent of walkers straying into and damaging vegetation after path maintenance. However, path maintenance is expensive: it can cost up to £120 ($180/130€) per metre to put a path back in some upland environments. Consequently any recreational manager will use minimal path work in conjunction with the other, cheaper tools. These include: traffic diversion (e.g. SNH, 2002); facility clustering known as 'honey pots'; educational tools such as the British Mountaineering Council's (2014) Regional Access Database or codes of conduct; or interpretation designed to explain, engage and change an individual's behaviour (Veverka, 1994).

Concluding remarks

This chapter has explored the main UK rural land uses of agriculture, forestry and water supply. Overlying these primary uses are nature conservation and recreation, leading to land that is typically multifunctional. This multifunctionality has created much conflict, largely created through a unique system of land ownership and access, and underpinned by increasing cultural severance between those who own and manage the land and those who visit. Further exacerbating land degradation is the unavoidable damage outdoor recreation use causes the environment. While management control and management activation provide effective frameworks to resolve the consequential conflicts globally, multifunctional land use and ownership in the UK force managers in the UK to rely on broader goodwill and recognition of productive land use objectives by recreationalists.

Notes

1 Hectare = a unit of measurement 100 by 100 metres in size, roughly equivalent to 2.47 acres.
2 asl = above sea level, a term used in the UK as a geographical benchmark, not to be confused with Ordnance datum taken from Newlyn in Cornwall, used by the Ordnance Survey for mapping purposes.
3 Catchment = an area of land that drains into a lake or river at its lowest point. Super-catchments are made of up of several catchments that draw water into a major river system, such as the River Thames running through London.
4 Plagioclimax community = an ecological community halted at an earlier stage of succession as a result of human intervention.
5 Commons = land where individuals have the right to graze stock, take firewood or fish, or other recorded resources for their own use, but they do not own the land upon which the right exists. Today about 4 per cent of England and Wales is registered as Common land, focused mainly in upland areas. Commons are not be confused with resource commons (lower case) (see text).

References

Agate, E. (1996). *Footpaths: A Practical Handbook*. Wallingford, UK: BTCV.
Arnstein, S.P. (1969). A ladder of citizen participation. *American Institute of Planners, 35*, 216–224.

Bates, G.H. (1935). The vegetation of footpaths, sidewalks, cart-tracks and gateways. *Journal of Ecology, 23*, 470–487.

Bayfield, N.G. & Aitken, R. (1982). *Managing the Impacts of Recreation on Vegetation and Spoils: A Review of Techniques.* Banchory: ITE.

British Canoe Union (2014) River access campaign. Retrieved from: www.bcu.org.uk/about/campaigns.

British Mountaineering Council (2014) BMC regional access database. Retrieved from: www.thebmc.co.uk/modules/RAD/.

Bunce, M. (1994). *The Countryside Ideal Anglo-American Images of Landscape.* London: Routledge.

Buttoud, G. (2002). Multipurpose management in mountain forests: which approaches? *Forest Policy & Economics, 4*, 83–87.

Coleman, R. (1981). Footpath erosion in the English Lake District. *Applied Geography, 1*, 121–131.

Council Regulation (EC) 1257/99 on support for rural development from the European Agricultural Guidance and Guarantee Fund (EAGGF) amending and repealing certain Regulations.

CROW (2000) Countryside and Rights of Way Act 2000. Retrieved from: www.leglisation.gov.uk/ukpga/2000/37/contents.

Department of Conservation (2008). *Abel Tasman National Park Management Plan 2008–2018.* Retrieved from: www.doc.govt.nz/documents/about-doc/role/policies-and-plans/national-park-management-plans/abel-tasman/atnp-management-plan.pdf. Nelson, New Zealand: DoC.

Dhondt, A.A. (1988). Carrying Capacity: a confusing concept. *Acta Œcologica, 9*(4), 337–346.

Dill, W.A. (1993). Inland fisheries in Europe. EIFAC Technical Paper No. S2. Rome: FAO. Retrieved from: www.fao.org/docrep/009/t0798e/T0798E16.htm.

Drewitt, A.L. & Manley, V. (1997). The vegetation of the mountains and moorlands of England – national assessment of significance. English Nature Research Reports No. 218.

Dudley, N. (1985). *The Death of Trees.* London: Pluto Press.

Fairlie, S. (2009). A short history of enclosure in Britain. *The Land, 7.* Retrieved from: www.thelandmagazine.org.uk/articles/short-history-enclosure-britain.

Forest Europe (1993). Retrieved from: www.foresteurope.org/ministerial_conferences/helsinki1993.

Forestry Commission (2014). Forestry statistics 2013. Retrieved from: www.forestry.gov.uk/forestry/infd-9b8cf9.

Hall, C., McVittie, A. & Moran, D. (2004). What does the public want from agriculture and the countryside? A review of evidence and methods. *Journal of Rural Studies, 20*, 211–225.

Hardin, G. (1968). The tragedy of the commons. *Science, 162*, 1243–1248.

Holden, A. (1998). The use of visitor understanding in skiing management and development decisions at the Cairngorm mountains, Scotland. *Tourism Management, 19*(2), 145–152.

Holden, J., Shotbolt, L., Bonn, A., Burt, T.P., Chapman, P.J., Dougill, A.J., Fraser, E.G.D., Hubacek, K., Irvine, B., Kirkby, M.J., Reed, M.S., Prell, C., Stgal, S., Stringer, L.C., Turner, A. & Worrall, F. (2007). Environmental change in moorland landscapes. *Earth-Science Reviews, 82*(1/2), 75–100.

Ilbery, B.W. (1998). *The Geography of Rural Change.* London: Longman.

Khan, J., Powell, T. & Harwood, T. (2012) Land use in the UK. Retrieved from: www.google.co.uk/url?sa=t&rct=j&q=&esrc=s&frm=1&source=web&cd=1&sqi=2&ved=0CCEQFjAA&url=httpper cent3Apercent2Fpercent2Fwww.ons.gov.uk per cent2Fons per cent2Fguide-method per cent2Fuser-guidance per cent2Fwell-being per cent2Fpublications per cent2Fland-use-in-the-uk.pdf&ei=IXijVd HZK4u07gaH8YHQBA&usg=AFQjCNEX3J_lteBlLKf3A6FvARwtHqX3sg&bvm=bv.97653015,d. ZGU.

Knight, S. (Ed.) (2011). *Forest School for All.* London: Sage.

Liddle, M.J. (1997) *Recreation Ecology: The Ecological Impact of Outdoor Recreation and Ecotourism.* London: Chapman & Hall.

Lindberg, K., McCool, S. & Stankey, G. (1997). Rethinking carrying capacity. *Annals of Tourism Research, 24*(2), 461–465.

Lothian, A. (1999). Landscape and the philosophy of aesthetics: Is landscape quality inherent in the landscape or in the eye of the beholder? *Landscape & Urban Planning, 44*, 177–198.

Manning, R.E. (2001). Visitor experience and resource protection: A framework for managing the carrying capacity of national parks. *Journal of Park and Recreation Administration, 19*, 93–108.

Manning, R.E. (2007). *Parks and Carrying Capacity: Commons without Tragedy.* Washington: Island Press.

Mansfield, L. (2011). *Upland Agriculture and the Environment.* Bowness-on-Windermere: Badger Press.

Marsden, T. (1998). Theoretical approaches to rural restructuring: Economic perspectives. In B.W. Ilbery (Ed.) *The Geography of Rural Change* (Ch. 2). London: Longman.

Mather, A. (1998). The changing role of forests. In B.W. Ilbery (Ed.) *The Geography of Rural Change* (Ch. 6). London: Longman.

McVittie, A., Moran, D., Smyth, K. & Hall, C. (2005). Measuring public preferences for the uplands. Final report to International Centre for the Uplands, Hackthorpe, Cumbria.

Mitchell, B. (1989). *Geography and Resource Analysis*. London: Longman.

Natural England (2012). The Countryside Code, NE326. Retrieved from: www.gov.uk/government/uploads/system/uploads/attachment_data/file/338299/countryside-code.pdf.

Northern Ecological Services (2014) Retrieved from: www.northecol.co.uk/visitor.html.

Overton, M. (1996). *The Agricultural Revolution in England: The Transformation of the Agrarian Economy 1500 to 1850*. Cambridge: Cambridge University Press.

Pearce-Higgins, J.W. & Yalden, DW. (1997). The effect of resurfacing the Pennine Way on recreational use of Blanket Bog in the Peak District National Park, England. *Biological Conservation, 82*, 337–343.

Plummer, R. (2009). *Outdoor Recreation. An Introduction*. London: Routledge.

Quinn, C.H., Fraser, E.D.G., Hubacek, K. & Reed, M.S. (2010). Property rights in UK uplands and the implications for policy and management. *Ecological Economics, 69*(6), 1355–1363.

Rotherham, I.D. (2008). The importance of cultural severance in landscape ecology research. In A. Dupont & H. Jacobs (Eds.) *Landscape Ecology Research Trends* (pp. 71–87). USA: Nova Science Publishers, Inc.

Runte, A. (1987). *National Parks: The American Experience* (2nd edn). Lincoln, NE: University of Nebraska Press.

Shoard, M. (1999). *A Right to Roam*. Oxford: Oxford University Press.

SNH (2002). *Scottish Outdoor Access Code. Public Access to Scotland's Outdoors. Your Rights and Responsibilities*. Battleby: SNH.

Sport+Recreation Alliance (2014) Access and the environment. Retrieved from: www.sportandrecreation.org.uk.

Spratt, S., Simms, A., Neitzert, E. & Ryan-Collins, J. (2010) *The Great Transition: A Tale of How it Turned Out Right*. London: New Economics Foundation.

Stankey, G., Cole, D., Lucas, R., Peterson, M., Frissell, S. & Washburne, R. (1985). The Limits of Acceptable Change (LAC) system for wilderness planning. USDA Forest Service General Technical Report INT-176.

Starr, C. (2005). *Woodland Management – Practical Guide*. Ramsbury: Crowood.

Veverka, J. (1994). *Interpretive Master Planning*. Tustin, CA: Acorn Naturalists.

Walford, N. (2001). Patterns of development in tourist accommodation enterprises on farms in England and Wales. *Applied Geography, 21*, 331–345.

Warren, C. (2002). *Managing Scotland's Environment*. Edinburgh: Edinburgh University Press.

Zuckerman, S. (1957). *Forestry, Agriculture and Marginal Land: A Report by the Natural Resources (Technical) Committee*. London: HMSO.

Part 6

Transdisciplinary and interdisciplinary approaches to understanding and exploring outdoor studies

Introduction

Barbara Humberstone

Buckinghamshire New University

The study of human interaction within and with the environment or non-human world exists as a part of many social and natural science disciplines. Particular disciplines and sub-disciplines bring different perspectives and knowledges to the study of outdoor pedagogies and nature-based physical cultures. In this section, we transcend boundaries between disciplines by bringing together chapters that are informed by research and theories emerging from a variety of approaches prominent in different social science disciplines. This is not to infer that earlier chapters do not do this, rather here the particular emphasis is on paradigmatic permeability.

The concept of transdisciplinarity is much debated. Hirsch Hadorn *et al.* (2008, p. 29) maintain:

> there are about four core concerns which show up in definitions of 'transdisciplinarity' or related terms: first the focus on life-world problems; second the transcending and integrating of disciplinary paradigms; third participatory research; and fourth the search for unity of knowledge beyond disciplines.

They further argue that:

> While the first two concerns are widely shared, there is disagreement over whether, and to what extent participatory research is needed for taking into account societal views in investigation issues.

We would maintain that participatory research is vital in understanding and transforming human interaction within and with the environment or non-human world. We take Sparkes and Smith's (2014: 243) view that 'TDR (transdisciplinary research) is a collaborative knowledge generation process between researchers and stakeholders', and acknowledge that shared knowledge is a crucial ingredient of TDR and research and practice in the outdoors.

Hirsch Hadorn *et al.* (2008) also maintain that, '[T]here is even more disagreement about the importance of the search for unity of knowledge in addressing issues in the life-world.' Nevertheless, post-structuralist and post-modern perspectives maintain there can be no one 'truth' or unity of knowledge. Markula and Pringle (2006), whose influential work within sporting cultures engages with Foucault's work on the power/knowledge/self nexus, draws attention to notions of partiality. This conflict/ambiguity/tension around 'unity of knowledge' within environmental education dimensions of outdoor studies is explicated by Gough (2015) when he writes in 'Rewording the world. Narrative and nature after poststructuralism':

> Longing for 'one true story' drives the construction of narrative strategies in which fact and fiction are mutually exclusive categories: facts are equated with 'truth' (and fiction with lies), and 'scientific facts', especially, are privileged representations of a 'reality' that in principle is independent of human subjectivity and agency. But fact and fiction are culturally and linguistically closer than these narrative strategies imply. A fiction, from the Latin *fictio,* is something fashioned by a human agent. 'Fact' also refers to human action: a fact is the thing done, 'that which actually happened', the Latin *factum* being the neuter past participle of *facere,* do. Thus, both fact and fiction refer to human experience, but 'fiction' is an active form – the act of fashioning – whereas 'fact' descends from a past participle, which disguises the generative act. (Gough, 2015, p. 236)

In this section, we bring together writings that engage with the outdoors from diverse social science perspectives that are inter- and transdisciplinary. The authors approach their chapters through crossing knowledge borders theoretically and/or methodologically. The chapters engage with theoretical approaches prominent or emerging in cultural studies, mobile geography, experiential education, construction of risk, sports coaching, adventure tourism and eco-tourism, together with the theoretical and 'archaeological' perspectives of Bourdieu, Foucault and others.

Beard's chapter provides a broad analysis of the multidimensionality within the field of experiential education/learning that crosses a multitude of aspects of teaching and learning. Many strands of studies, particularly outdoor education/learning equate themselves with experiential education; learning through experience. Beard examines the broader historical basis of experiential learning, and its relationship with outdoor learning and other areas of education, moving the theoretical perspective, as a consequence of relational connectivity, to take account of complexity.

Engaging with cultural geographical perspectives to explore outdoor studies, Brown and Wattchow draw attention to the importance of place-responsiveness in outdoor studies, and its implications. They engage with the burgeoning work of place-sensitive educators and cultural geographers, particularly drawing upon social anthropologist Ingold to explore the relational concepts of 'enskilment' and 'dwelling' through which to highlight challenges to the traditional, sometimes pathological, early focus on personal and social development foundations of outdoor education. While Brown and Wattchow's chapter focuses on engagement with and analyses of landscape, Brown (2015) draws attention to the significance of seascapes and the ways in which the sea plays an integral part in shaping who we are.

This place-responsive turn in outdoor studies is indeed significant and has implications for further development of transdisciplinarity analyses. Brookes, in the following chapter, also highlights the importance of taking account of place when considering the events surrounding fatal and serious accidents involving participants on organised outdoor education events. While there has been some analysis of risk and outdoor studies from theoretical perspectives of Beck, Simmel (see Beedie's chapter), Brookes' chapter takes a realist/empirical approach revealing actual events and their antecedents to highlight the rarity of such events and the pertinence of being fully knowledgeable and informed of the location and environmental conditions into which people and groups venture.

Associated with Brookes' analysis regarding the safety and relevance of situated knowledges of the outdoors, Collins and Collins bring together dimensions from sport coaching and what constitutes skills (technical and communicative) assumed for outdoor leaders, emphasising the broader and different knowledges needed to lead/coach/teach groups/individuals in outdoor spaces from more 'traditional' sports. Their chapter stresses the need for adventure sport coaches to have a clear understanding of the context, place and environmental conditions in order to be able to make appropriate and safe decisions. In addition to refined pedagogic skills, adventure sport coaches, they argue, need specific judgement capabilities that differentiate them from coaches belonging to more 'traditional' sports, and other outdoor professionals. This chapter sheds some light on Drasdo's rhetorical question (Introduction p. 2–3) as to whether 'mountaineering' (or any adventurous physical culture) is a sport.

'Should they have been there?' is the question posed in Beedie's chapter, which is concerned with adventure tourism, citing the 1996 Everest tragedies. Like Collins and Collins, Beedie draws attention to similarities and differences between concepts and knowledges in the dominant/parent discipline, tourism and that of adventure. He argues that there is more to adventure tourism than the tourist 'gaze' because of its experiential dimension, but qualifies this by pointing out that decision making is largely made by a guide or instructor rather than participants. The chapter takes a critical social-cultural perspective, examining identity, commodification and consumption in the adventure tourism industry.

Also associated with tourism, Maher's chapter discusses ecotourism from Canadian perspectives, focusing on Polar cruising expeditions. The chapter highlights the paradox of ecotourism in which the commercial enterprise attempts to promote environmental sensitivities. Links, both epistemologically and practically, are explored between recent Canadian outdoor education programmes and specific forms of Polar expedition. While outdoor education programmes are for the most part directed at young people, these latter types of organised experience are undertaken by wealthier (semi)-retirees. Outdoor education practitioners may frequently move between these types of organisation for employment.

While Telford and Beames draw explicitly on Bourdieu's theory of social practice to critique and problematise the practice of present-day mountaineering, Becker examines the archaeology of the outdoor movement, largely but not solely from a German perspective. Both of these analyses draw inspiration from continental European theorists explicitly in Telford and Beames' chapter. Although the Foucauldian process of archaeology of knowledge provides the implicit inspiration for Becker's work, his analysis is located more in the traditional history of ideas movement. Through cultural theory of social practices, Becker examines the historical transformation of practice and interpretation of activities in nature, from the outdoors as alien to the bourgeoisie (since only the workers – hunters, shepherds – travelled in the hills) to its acceptability through examples of 'purification'. Telford and Beames point to the socio-political and spiritual factors that have influenced the ways in which humans perceive and have interacted with mountains from early civilisations. The subsequent diverse cultural lenses derive their antecedents from early Eurasian narratives, particularly the strong influence of Greek and Roman antiquity and, more recently, Romanticism. Both chapters emphasise cultural production and the influence of taste and aesthetics in human–nature relations.

In the final chapter, Olive synthesises a number of theoretical frameworks to explore localism through her experiences as a surfer in surfing physical cultures. She draws attention to the underresearched issues of localism and place-based pedagogies that engender exclusivity. Drawing on Probyn (1993), she links 'feminist and cultural studies theory, methods, ethics and reflexivity', in her embodied approach of 'think(ing) the social through ourselves', to explore non-local surfers' development of ecological sensibilities to place and community. Olive's chapter synthesises theories and draws on notions of intersectionality (see Henderson & Gibson, 2013) in her methodology, making significant connections. Olive's embodied narrative is initially inspired by exclusionary graffiti, which symbolised the hegemony of place-specific power relations.

Recent cultural studies analyses of outdoor physical cultures have drawn upon the notion of 'ecological sensibilities', as exemplified here by Olive, to refer to findings that suggest place-based pedagogies engendered through nature-based physical cultures may develop in participants ecological sensibilities – that is, strong awareness of and even positive action in relation to caring for the environment. Many chapters in this book have indicated that ecological awareness is one of the underpinning aims of environmental education, and of much outdoor education and learning. The importance of connecting notions of pedagogy across all forms of outdoor engagement has been highlighted in this *International Handbook of Outdoor Studies* and we have emphasised the interconnections with and fruitfulness of paradigmatic permeability.

References

Brown, M. (2015). Seascapes. In M. Brown & B. Humberstone (Eds.) *Seascapes: Shaped by the Sea. Embodied Narratives and Fluid Geographies* (pp. 13–26). Surrey, UK: Ashgate.

Gough, N. (2015). Rewording the world. Narrative and nature after poststructuralism. In M. Robertson, R. Lawrence & G. Heath (Eds.) *Experiencing the Outdoors: Enhancing Strategies for Well-being* (pp. 233–244). Rotterdam, The Netherlands: Sense Publications.

Henderson, K.A. & Gibson, H.J. (2013). An integrative review of women, gender, and leisure: Increasing complexities. *Journal of Leisure Research, 45*(2), 115–135.

Hirsch Hadorn, G., Biber-Klemm, S., Grossenbacher-Mansuy, W., Hoffmann-Riem, H., Joye, D., Pohl, C., Wiesmann, U. & Zemp, E. (2008) The emergence of transdisciplinarity as a form of research. In G. Hirsch Hadorn, H. Hoffmann-Riem, S. Biber-Klemm, W. Grossenbacher-Mansuy, D. Joye, C. Pohl, U. Wiesmann & E. Zemp (Eds.) *Handbook of Transdisciplinary Research. Proposed by the Swiss Academies of Arts and Sciences* (pp. 19–39). Heidelberg: Springer.

Markula, P. & Pringle, R. (2006). *Foucault, Sport and Exercise: Power, Knowledge and Transforming the Self.* London: Routledge.

Probyn, E. (1993). *Sexing the Self: Gendered Positions in Cultural Studies.* London: Routledge.

Sparkes, A.C. & Smith, B. (2014) *Qualitative Research Methods in Sport, Exercise and Health: From Process to Product.* London: Routledge.

41

Experiential learning

Towards a multidisciplinary perspective

Colin Beard

SHEFFIELD HALLAM UNIVERSITY

The doctrine or the wisdom?

The term 'experiential learning' is in common usage: it has been variously appropriated, constructed and reconstructed (Usher & Edwards, 1994) across the globe. Experiential learning (EL) has a lexicon of meanings, with foundational roots in many fields and disciplines: complex and multidimensional, the term is influenced by an evolving understanding of the human experience of learning. Partly because of its long lineage and its multidisciplinary nature, experiential learning is not easily defined, has no unified theory, and is a term that has escalating ideologies and problematic boundaries. A core issue that arises from definitional disputes often concerns the extent to which EL might embrace life itself (Fenwick, 2003, p. 87), suggesting that the concept has moved on to the point where the 'distinction between experience and non-experience becomes absurd' (Fenwick, 2003, p. ix). *Experience* and *learning* are sub-component terms that embrace not only practical everyday issues but also a diverse range of philosophical, ontological, epistemological and methodological explanations (Hager, 1999). Experience and learning are so closely intertwined that in many respects they mean the same thing and thus experiential learning might be considered a tautology.

This all suggests that, for this fluid, evolving term, any search for unanimity might be impracticable. Indeed 'one set of meanings of it is the meanings of all those who have contributed to the literature' (Moon, 2004, p. 107) and 'views of experiential learning differ widely' (Moon, 2004, p. 110) within and across disciplines. Experiential learning is further problematised by boundary incursions from overlapping fields such as experiential education, environmental education, adventure education and outdoor education. Thus boundary disputes surface, for example between experiential learning and experiential education: some writers argue that experiential learning is a sub-field of experiential education, possibly even redundant (Smith, Knapp, Seaman & Pace, 2011). A counter-position is that learning is much broader: in a phylogenetic sense it precedes human language, and expands beyond education.

The very creation of the term experiential learning implies something different, and conceived as special in some way. Experiential learning is said to have potential to liberate or domesticate, to oppress or emancipate: it always involves a direct encounter with experience, always therefore a site of struggle (Usher, 2009). Experience and learning are not static phenomenon, but shifting, multiphasic and subject to continuous reflective reconstructions. Indeed no matter how hard we try to homogenise these slippery concepts such as *experience* and *learning*, there will always be parts that elude the human grasp: it might then be helpful to accommodate conceptual fluidity. Michelson suggests there is a fruitful incoherence to experiential learning; with its roots in alternative practice it is 'liberatory precisely because it is unstable and provisional, because it is collective and not individual, because it always contains an insurgent element that resists categorisation and management' (1999, p. 142). This may partially explain why experiential learning is positioned as 'central to the theory and practice of adult education in the postmodern moment' (Usher, 2009, p. 169).

Experiential learning has thus resisted categorisation and labelling. This bequeaths benefits and difficulties: Eastern sages suggest that difficulties arise when inherent complexity confuses the signposts with the journey, and that we need to understand that the 'learning doctrine is not the same as practicing the wisdom the doctrine is intended to teach' (Stevenson, 2000, p. 17).

A brief perspective on the lineage of experiential learning

Eastern and Western philosophical perspectives on learning from experience emerged at a similar time. Ancient Greek philosophical contributions are said to have given rise to the 'West's first conceptual notion of experience' (Roberts, 2012, p. 17), and that Aristotle was the 'progenitor of [the] experiential learning cycle' (Stonehouse, Alison & Carr, 2011, p. 18). The well-known Confucian aphorism beginning with *I hear I forget*, underpins the 'Tell Show Do' Cone of Experience triangle developed by Dale in the 1940s. In the 1930s US educationalist John Dewey made a significant contribution (see Hunt, 1995). Rogers, applying therapeutic principles in the 1960s and 1970s, developed a humanistic, learner-centred focus for learning that remains a strong influence today (see Smith & Knapp, 2011). In the 1980s a significant appraisal of the multiplicity of meanings of experiential learning was made, and the notion of 'Four Distinct Villages' was derived from the global community that had gathered at a first major conference of practitioners (Weil & McGill, 1989). The work of Kolb emerged in 1984, with the creation of the now ubiquitous experiential learning cycle, and Cell published *Learning to Learn from Experience* (1984). Said to be the 'decade of emotions' (Sadler-Smith, 2008, p. 272), the 1990s witnessed important critical sociological perspectives from writers such as Usher and Edwards (1994) and Michelson (1998). By the mid-1990s experiential learning covered very diverse perspectives across a wide variety of disciplines and fields, including traditional education, alternative education, outdoor adventure education, career education, special education, therapy, social and cultural work, organisational development, team building and corporate training.

At the end of the 20th century a body of literature emerged exploring what Roberts (2012) refers to as 'neo-experiential'; the focus was on experiential marketing (Schmitt, 1999) and the experience economy (Pine & Gilmore, 1999), with experiential learning methods even moving into accounting education (Dellaportas & Hassall, 2013). The scope and diversity of experiential learning had broadened even further, with professionals from many fields outside the traditions of education continuing to examine experiential theory and practice. Some central assumptions underpinning experiential learning were being articulated: Boud, Cohen and Walker (1993) positioned: (i) experience as the foundation of, and the stimulus for, learning; (ii) learners as actively constructing their own experience; (iii) learning as a holistic process; (iv) learning as socially and culturally constructed; and (v) learning as influenced by the socio-emotional context in which it occurs.

Experience and *learning* have for centuries occupied a central position in philosophical deliberations about *being* and *knowing*. Bhaskar suggests that, 'for most of its recognised history, the philosophy of the human sciences has been dominated by dichotomies and dualisms' (1998, p. xiii). The implications for a multidisciplinary understanding of experiential learning are that the Socratic imperative 'Know Thyself' has ontological and phylogenetical imperatives, otherwise a fundamental disconnectedness exists, creating:

> an interlocking system of overlapping dualisms that guide our thought and actions in environmentally significant ways; and these include civilised/wild, modern/primitive, culture/nature, mind/body, and so on. In each case, the first term of each pair represents a preferred state or entity, whereas the second indicates something that we try to distance ourselves from, composing a value system that gives the impression of being based on 'factual' distinctions. (Kidner, 2001, p. 10)

In exploring a sociology of nature, Macnaghten and Urry (1997) contend that social scientists should decipher the social implications of the fact that nature has always been elaborately entangled and fundamentally bound up with the social. This cultural filter is said to present the 'world' as synonymous with 'social', 'experience' synonymous with 'environment' as though 'they were the same wherever one happens to be' (Pepper, 1984, p. 6). Benton and Redclift similarly critically examine the heritage of social theory in relation to the natural environment, arguing that sociology has made a slender contribution to the study of the environment, because:

> culture, meaning, consciousness and intentional agency differentiated the human from the animal, and effectively stemmed the ambitions of biological explanation . . . In one move the opposition between nature and culture (or society) made room for social sciences as autonomous disciplines distinct from the natural sciences, and undercut what were widely seen as the unacceptable moral and political implications of biological determinism. (Benton & Redclift, 1994, p. 3)

Experiential learning has to be understood as situated in, and interacting with, the dominant theories of human learning at any one time. At the beginning of 20th century behaviouralist and ethological studies were substantial. These were followed by cognitivist contributions, then humanist perspectives and finally, towards the end of 20th century, social constructivist viewpoints. These episodic developments had no hard-and-fast boundaries in reality, and were significantly influenced by numerous undercurrents. This persistent search for more complete understandings indicates a continuous deficit, with emergent new thinking suggesting further change. In this same manner experiential learning appears to be moving towards greater fluidity, holism and complexity, with undercurrents pointing towards a repositioning, within an ecological trajectory, to a new *revisionary post-modernism*.

Why multidisciplinary and transdisciplinary perspectives?

Dillon (2007) suggests that explorations across disciplines can generate creative and integrative activity, so as to open up a new theoretical space and create more integrative new thinking grounded in intra-disciplinary (within disciplines), inter-disciplinary (breaking out of the disciplinary boundaries), multidisciplinary (combination/researching in more than one simultaneously/juxtaposition) and transdisciplinary (across/beyond/unity of knowledge) understanding (Dillon, 2007). A central debate in experiential learning is the extent to which experience and knowledge are socially, culturally, psychologically, environmentally or otherwise constructed. Fenwick (2003, p. 13) suggests that learning experiences involve us 'physically, emotionally, sensually, mentally and perhaps spiritually'; this, and the following simple, holistic definition of experiential learning, suggests the necessity for a broader multi-disciplinary understanding:

> Experiential learning occurs when experience is the central foundation of, and stimulus for learning as a sense making process that actively and reflectively engages the inner world of the learner as a whole person (physical-bodily, intellectually, emotionally and spiritually) with the intricate, shifting 'outer world' human, and more than human, environment (environment, nature, place, social, cultural, political, cosmos). (Adapted from Beard & Wilson, 2006, p. 2)

Signs of change: an emerging unanimity of the core neglected areas

Over the last three to four decades constructivist and post-modernist interpretations of experiential learning have sought to 'search out and experiment with narratives that expand the range of understanding, voice, and the storied variations in human experience' (Lincoln and Guba, 2003, p. 285), albeit within a dismantling of grand narratives. The learner is seen as the 'central actor in a drama of personal meaning, as independent creators and constructors of knowledge, with varying capacity or confidence to rely on their own constructions' (Fenwick, 2003, p. 22), and post-modern readings of experiential learning often occur through the lenses of power, commodification, freedom and responsibility, so that people become, as advocated by Maxine Green, 'wide awake' (Frank, 2011, p. 65).

At the beginning of the 21st century further calls for change were gathering momentum around the globe. Kidner (2001) opens up a debate about psychology's betrayal of the natural world. He called for an integration of nature and psyche, and a reconfiguration of selfhood that is not solely constructed by discourse, and argues that nature is 'prior to human existence or activity – historically, ontologically, and materially' – and is a 'condition of social life rather than a consequence of it' (2001, p. 20). In outdoor education, Nicol (2003a, p. 115) calls for a new 'ecological ontology', suggesting greater 'interconnectedness and interdisciplinarity, drawing on both the social and natural sciences' (Nicol, 2003b, p. 16). Unifying calls from Loynes (2002), Payne (2002), Beringer and Martin (2003), Friese, Hendee and Kizinger (1998), and Burns (1998) all voice concern about the homocentric splitting and elevation of the learner from the more substantive 'pedagogy' of experience. Payne (2002, p. 19) argues for a reconciliation of the inner and outer world experiences as worthy of pursuing for critical outdoor learning, recommending a 'sorely needed reparation of first, human–environment, second, community/society–land/sea/town/cityscapes, and, third, culture–nature relations'. Stewart (2003, p. 311) similarly notes that the challenge facing experiential learning is the acquisition of a new multidisciplinary understanding of terms like 'environment/nature, experience and place'. Geographer Pepper (1984) likewise provides an important historical, philosophical and ideological contribution to this debate, arguing that the deeper experience of place has largely been ignored in education, including outdoor education. A comprehensive review of recent developments in outdoor education in Singapore similarly calls for a new environmental awareness, a new ecology of thinking (Ho, 2014).

Hager (1999, p. 71) argues that 'with the decline of the fortunes of the scientific approach in the late twentieth century, scientism seems to have been replaced by "discursivism" as its mirror image. Whereas scientism is the extreme view that all genuine understanding is scientific, then discursivism is the equally disputable view that language is the key to all understanding.' After the linguistic turn came the corporeal turn (Sheets-Johnstone, 2009) and new concerns surfaced about disembodiment, due to a 'concentration on talk and reflection' (Fenwick, 2003, p. 63). Burr (2003, p. 197) acknowledges that aspects of experience are difficult to translate into thought or language, and so suggests that 'we should regard such forms of experience and expression as "extra discursive", i.e. existing in a realm outside of language and discourse'. From a critical feminist perspective Michelson (1998, p. 218) notes the ambivalent relationship of experiential learning to this rejection of the body as a site of knowledge; she refers to the dualisms of skill–knowledge, reflection–experience and theory–practice as 'versions of the mind–body split and the privileging of mind over body', suggesting the theoretical underpinnings of experiential learning are 'socially over-determined' (op. cit., p. 227). Recent work by Gallagher (2005) uncovers valuable insights from neuroscience to shed further light on how the body shapes the mind.

Bodily perception, in evolutionary terms, is said to be the root source of our human 'consciousness', and Lakoff and Johnson (1999) argue that human thought is mostly unconscious. The interplay between the conscious and subconscious, the body and mind, becomes problematic for post-modern and post-structural accounts. Abram (1997) exposes the part played by human language in divorcing the human from the more-than-human world, developing the concept of 'perceptual reciprocity', as conceived by Merleau-Ponty, that recognises the complex inner–outer world relationality, and the role of the 'sensuous and sentient life of the body itself' (Abram, 1997, pp. 45–47). Established constructivist theories tend to simplify the complexity of the external world to 'raw materials' upon which knowledge is socially constructed. Illeris (2002, p. 119) similarly discounts nature, claiming that it is difficult to find 'untouched nature', and so the 'material is under submission to the more dominant social'. Environmental[1] and feminist literatures are often critical of such homocentric misrepresentations.[2] The concern, then, is the extent to which the experience of being a human and belonging in the more-than-human world is fully embraced.

Boler (1999) expresses concern over the splitting and privileging of the rational over the affective, explained to an extent by the inadequacy of the spoken and written word when describing movement, or emotionally laden events that move us (see Sheets-Johnstone, 2009). In the sense of an outdoor experience this is particularly well illustrated by Kull (2008) in attempting to articulate the experience of solitude for a PhD thesis. Living for a year in a remote area of Patagonia, the tension between 'education' and 'learning' surfaces through his struggle between experience and discourse:

> In conceptualising, organising, and thinking about these sensory impressions, the immediacy of experience can easily be lost. It requires patience and practice to soften this habitual activity by over and over *letting go of thought and analysis* to simply stay with the swirl of sound just as it is without trying to do anything with it. (Kull, 2008, p. 279, italics added)

Kull focuses on experience by not thinking too much. He recommends staying with the sensing–observing–feeling dynamic. He remarks how, at one stage, he tried to capture in writing, other significant experiences, but gave up, as, in his words:

> There is no dance between word and world. What I see and feel begs a sensuous tango, but my words march static and stiff in lines across the page. (Kull, 2008, p. 184)

Words fall into line, one word after another, in restrictive linearity. The one-dimensional form of written and spoken word increasingly creates a new site of struggle for humans as the discursive form labours in an attempt to formulate human experience.

Towards holism: revisionary post-modernism

Constructivist Gergen (1999, p. 138) suggests we may be 'on the verge of a major transformation in our way of conceptualising ourselves'. For Gergen it is important that we transcend what he calls the privileging of the social, and expand the concept of relational to include the non-social, and particularly the natural environment. This he argues will come about by spanning areas of enquiry such as physics, biology, neurology, economics, meteorology and psychology. 'Ecologists' and 'complexitivists' focus on these interrelationships, and the way sub-systems are intertwined with larger more complex systems. The relational expansion moves from the minute 'integrities (e.g. organs and cells) which are themselves subsystems of larger systems, with their own particular integrities (e.g. family, a community, a society) so that each of us is, all-at-once, a collective of wholes, a whole, and a part of a whole' (Davis & Sumara, 1997, p. 110). *Enactivisim*, for example, (Davis & Sumara, 1997, p. 110) is a theory of cognition that applies ecological metaphors to draw attention to the fact that 'both cognizing agent and everything with which it is associated are in constant flux, each adapting to the other in the same way that the environment evolves simultaneously with the species that inhabit it'.

These developments signpost what Sterling (2003) calls a revisionary post-modernism, a participatory worldview stance, which takes us beyond homocentric interpretations to present further opportunities for holistic expansion and interpretation, so that all contributing perspectives from a very diverse range of fields and disciplines are acknowledged and embraced. In this way all contributions move our understanding forward; a new way of thinking about experiential learning is called for, whereby 'meaning and mystery are restored to human experience (of learning), so that the world is again experienced as a sacred place' (Reason, 1994, p. 10, quoted in Sterling, 2003, p. 36). In exploring of the temporal and spatial multidisciplinary lineage of experiential learning, the emerging participatory worldview will now be elaborated upon.

Sterling explores *whole systems thinking* in education as a basis for paradigm change. Sterling suggests a 'revisionary or constructive postmodernism and ecological thinking as an emergent social paradigm that allows Western thinking and culture to both subsume and go beyond the limits of modernism and deconstructionism, towards a more holistic alternative' (Sterling, 2003, p. 34). He argues for more integrative way of seeing the world, and a shift away from reductionism towards holism. Strong social constructivism suggests idealism to the point that there is no independent reality other than that created in the mind. Sterling suggests relationalism, or a *panexperientialist* view that acknowledges ecological realism, which is fundamental to environmentalism, but fully acknowledges the role of perception, and of language, emphasised by idealists and constructivists.

These alternative metaphors, of 'ecologism', as whole systems thinking, and post-modern ecological worldview, embrace environmental/sustainability issues beyond the social into the more-than-human world, where 'other' views (behavioural, cognitive, humanistic, constructivist) are neither abandoned nor ignored, rather incorporated within a larger emerging framework of meaning and understanding, using both/and/or thinking.

Other significant scholars are calling for such an ecological worldview. In a substantive and seminal text on qualitative research Lincoln and Guba, in a section called a '*glimpse of the future*' (2003, p. 286; italics added), suggest that 'we stand at the threshold of a history marked by multivocality, contested meanings, paradigmantic controversies, and new textual forms . . . [and that] we may also be entering an age of greater spirituality . . . with an emphasis on enquiry that reflects ecological values . . . whilst promoting freedom and self-determination, with reflexivity that respects communal forms of living that are not Western'. Lincoln and Guba created a new fifth paradigm called 'participative', adding to positivism, post-positivism, critical theory and constructivism.

Similar calls appear in various guises, as 'co-evolutionary' (Norgaard, 1994), a 'living systems' approach (Elgin, 1997) and a 'postmodern ecological worldview' (Zweers, 2000). Jackson (2011), who underpins his thinking about *lifewide* learning with experiential learning, similarly calls for an ecological perspective that might transform education towards more organic

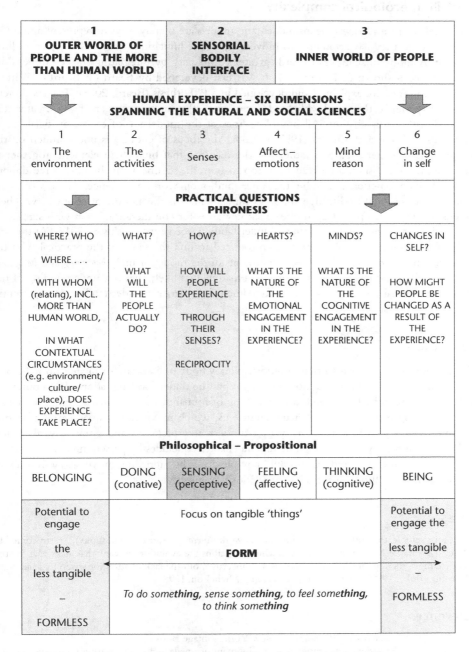

Figure 41.1 An evolving multidisciplinary modelling of the human experience

Source: Beard and Wilson (2013)

approaches. This increased sophistication of understanding has not been paralleled by correspondingly complex modelling: simplistic models (e.g. Dale, 1969; Kolb, 1984) continue to dominate the literature.

Modelling ecological complexity

The Greek word *paradeigma* means model, and models are merely ways to represent and interpret the world; they have potential to move beyond the limitations of words, but also to limit thinking. A model that moves towards greater complexity by integrating six key dimensions of experience is shown in Figure 41.1. It was first developed by Beard (in Beard & Wilson, 2002), and more fully explained and developed in a PhD thesis (Beard, 2008). The six dimensions of experience that are highlighted derive from the multidisciplinary body of literature explored within this chapter. All boundary lines of the model are of course artificial, as, in the words of Davis and Sumara (1997, p. 108), 'the focus of enquiry is not so much on the components of experience but, rather, on the relations that bind these elements together in action'. The model should be read from top to bottom, starting with the core three dimensions of human experience, notably the inner- and outer-world experience. These worlds are mediated by sensorial-bodily dynamics, so fundamental to the notion of reciprocity. These dimensions are then opened up to create six key areas for consideration, each with significant complexity requiring a multidisciplinary understanding (see Beard & Wilson, 2013). At the base of the model, philosophical language is introduced to link the sense of the practical with the theoretical-philosophical. The outer components of the model, namely *belonging* and *being*, are vastly complex, and less to do with form and matter. It is likely that our understanding of this complex relational connectivity will be fundamental to a greater understanding of experiential learning in the 21st century.

Conclusion

This chapter briefly explores a rich, multidisciplinary body of literature to suggest how the wisdom of the experiential learning doctrine might best be understood and adopted. A contextual backcloth of episodic, hegemonic understanding of human learning that has influenced experiential learning is exposed. Smaller undercurrents, which move experiential learning beyond constructivism into a new revisionary post-modern interpretation and point towards a new ecological complexity, are also identified. The chapter concludes by presenting a new working model that, to an extent, reflects this fluid complexity. The modelling moves away from existing simplistic illustrations towards a new relational connectivity.

Notes

1 See, for example, the 20th century philosophical work on *ecosophy* (or ecophilosophy), a term coined by Naess (1995), the Norweian philosopher, which questions the evolutionary view that 'man' is at the top.
2 For example, the feminist literature expressing concerns about the lack of attention given to *emotion* and learning (Boler, 1999) and the *body* and learning (Michelson, 1998).

References

Abram, D. (1997). *The Spell of the Sensuous*. New York: Vintage Books.
Beard, C. (2008). Experiential learning: The development of a pedagogic framework for effective practice. Unpublished PhD thesis, Sheffield Hallam University, UK.

Beard, C. & Wilson, J. (2002). *The Power of Experiential Learning: A Handbook for Educators and Trainers*. London: Kogan Page.

Beard, C. & Wilson, J. (2006). *Experiential Learning: A Best Practice Handbook for Educators and Trainers* (2nd edn). London: Kogan Page.

Beard, C. & Wilson, J. (2013). *Experiential Learning: A Handbook for Education, Training and Coaching* (3rd edn). London: Kogan Page.

Benton, T. & Redclift, M. (1994). Introduction. In M. Redclift & T. Benton (Eds.) *Social Theory and the Global Environment* (pp. 1–27). London: Routledge.

Beringer, A. & Martin, P. (2003). On adventure therapy and the natural worlds: respecting nature's healing. *Journal of Adventure Education and Outdoor Learning*, 3(1) 29–40.

Bhaskar, R. (1998). Introduction. In M. Archer, R. Bhaskar, A. Collier, T. Lawson & A. Norrie (Eds.) *Critical Realism: Essential Readings* (pp. ix–xxiv). London: Routledge.

Boler, M. (1999). *Feeling Power: Emotions and Education*. New York: Routledge.

Boud, D., Cohen, R. & Walker, D. (1993). *Using Experience for Learning*. Buckingham: Open University Press.

Burns, G. (1998). *Nature Guided Therapy: Brief Integrative Strategies for Health and Well-being*. Philadelphia, PA: Brunner/Mazel.

Burr, V. (2003). *Social Constructionism* (2nd edn). Hove: Routledge.

Cell, E. (1984) *Learning to Learn from Experience*. Albany, NY: State University of New York Press.

Dale, E. (1969). *Audiovisual Methods in Teaching*. New York: Dryden Press.

Davis, B. & Sumara, D.J. (1997). Cognition, complexity and teacher education. *Harvard Educational Review*, 67(1), 105–125.

Dellaportas, S. & Hassall, T. (2013). Experiential learning in accounting education: A prison visit. *British Accounting Review*, 45, 24–36.

Dillon, P. (2007). A pedagogy of connection and boundary crossings: Methodological and epistemological transactions in working across and between disciplines. Paper presented at Creativity or Conformity? Building Cultures of Creativity in Higher Education, University of Wales and the Higher Education Academy, Cardiff, 8–10 January.

Elgin, D. (1997). *Global Consciousness Change: Indicators of an Emerging Paradigm*. San Anselmo, CA: Millenium Project.

Fenwick, T.J. (2003). *Learning Through Experience: Troubling Orthodoxies and Intersecting Questions*. Florida: Krieger Publishing.

Frank, L. (2011). Maxine Green: The power of the possible. In T. Smith & C. Knapp (Eds.) *Sourcebook of Experiential Education* (pp. 64–85). New York: Routledge.

Friese, G., Hendee, J. & Kizinger, M. (1998). Wilderness experience programme industry in the US: Characteristics and dynamics. *Journal of Experiential Education*, May–June.

Gallagher, S. (2005). *How the Body Shapes the Mind*. Oxford: Oxford University Press.

Gergen, K. (1999). *An Invitation to Social Construction*. London: Sage.

Hager, P. (1999). Robin Usher on experience. *Educational Philosophy and Theory*, 31(1), 63–75.

Ho, S. (2014). The purpose outdoor education does, could and should serve in Singapore. *Journal of Adventure Education and Outdoor Learning*, 14(2), 153–171.

Hunt, J. (1995). Dewey's philosophical method and its influence on his philosophy of education. In K. Warren, M. Sakofs & J.S. Hunt Jr (Eds.) *The Theory of Experiential Education* (pp. 23–32). Dubuque, IA: Kendall/Hunt.

Illeris, K. (2002). *The Three Dimensions of Learning*. Florida: Krieger Publishing.

Jackson, N. (2011). *Learning for a Complex World: A Lifewide Concept of learning, Education and Personal Development*. Bloomington, IN: Author-House Publishing.

Kidner, D. (2001). *Nature and Psyche: Radical Environmentalism and the Politics of Subjectivity*. New York: State University of New York Press.

Kolb, D. (1984). *Experiential Learning: Experience as the Source of Learning and Development*. New York: Prentice-Hall.

Kull, R. (2008) *Solitude: Seeking Wisdom in Extremes*. Novato, CA: New World Library.

Lakoff, G. & Johnson, M. (1999) *Philosophy in the Flesh*. New York: Basic Books.

Lincoln, Y. & Guba, E. (2003). Paradigmatic controversies, contradictions, and emerging confluences. In Denzin, N. & Lincoln, Y. (Eds.) *The Landscape of Qualitative Research: Theories and Issues* (2nd edn) (pp. 253–291). London: Sage.

Loynes, C. (2002). The generative paradigm. *Journal of Adventure Education and Outdoor Learning*, 2(2) pp. 113–125.

Macnaghten, P. & Urry, J. (1997). Towards a sociology of nature. In P. McDonagh & A. Prothero (Eds.) *Green Management: A Reader* (pp. 6–21). London: Dryden Press.

Michelson, E. (1998). Re-remembering: the return of the body to experiential learning. *Studies in Continuing Education, 20*(2), 217–233.

Moon, J. (2004). *A Handbook of Reflective and Experiential Learning: Theory and Practice.* London: Routledge.

Naess, A. (1995). *Ecology, Community and Lifestyle.* New York: Cambridge University Press.

Nicol, R. (2003a). Pillars of knowledge. In B. Humberstone, H. Brown & K. Richards (Eds.) *Whose Journeys? The Outdoors and Adventure as Social and Cultural Phenomena: Critical Explorations of Relations Between Individuals, 'Others' and the Environment* (pp. 115–130). Barrow-in-Furness: Fingerprints.

Nicol, R. (2003b). Outdoor education: Research topic or universal value? Part three. *Journal of Adventure Education and Outdoor Learning, 3*(1), 11–28.

Norgaard, R. (1994). *Development Betrayed: The End of Progress and a Co-evolutionary Revisioning of the Future.* London: Routledge.

Payne, P. (2002). On the construction, deconstruction and reconstruction of experience in critical outdoor education. *Australian Journal of Outdoor Education, 6*(2), 4–21.

Pepper, D. (1984). *The Roots of Modern Environmentalism.* Beckenham: Croom Helm.

Pine, J. & Gilmore, B.H. (1999). *The Experience Economy, Work is Theatre and Every Business is a Stage.* Boston, MA: Harvard Business School.

Reason, P. (1994). *Participation in Human Enquiry.* London: Sage Publications.

Roberts, J. (2012). *Beyond Learning by Doing: Theoretical Currents in Experiential Education.* New York: Routledge.

Sadler-Smith, E. (2008). *Inside Intuition.* London: Routledge.

Schmitt, B.H. (1999). *Experiential Marketing: How to Get Customers to Sense, Feel, Think, Act, Relate to Your Company and Brands.* New York: The Free Press.

Sheets-Johnstone, M. (2009). *The Corporeal Turn: An Interdisciplinary Reader.* Exeter: Imprint Academic.

Smith, T. & Knapp, C. (Eds.) (2011). *Sourcebook of Experiential Education.* New York: Routledge.

Smith, T., Knapp, C., Seaman, J. & Pace, S. (2011) Experiential education and learning by experience. In T. Smith & C. Knapp (Eds.) *Sourcebook of Experiential Education* (pp. 1–11). New York: Routledge.

Sterling, S. (2003). Whole systems thinking as a basis for paradigm change in education: explorations in the context of sustainability. Unpublished PhD Thesis, University of Bath, UK.

Stevenson, J. (2000). *Eastern Philosophy.* New York: Alpha Publishing.

Stewart, A. (2003) Encountering landscapes: An exploration of environment specific learning on an extended journey. In B. Humberstone, H. Brown & K. Richards (Eds.) *Whose Journeys? The Outdoors and Adventure as Social and Cultural Phenomena: Critical Explorations of Relations Between Individuals, 'Others' and the Environment* (pp. 311–328). Barrow-in-Furness: Fingerprints.

Stonehouse, P., Allison, P. & Carr, D. (2011) Aristotle, Plato, and Socrates: Ancient Greek perspectives on experiential learning. In T. Smith & C. Knapp (Eds.) *Sourcebook of Experiential Education* (pp. 18–31). New York: Routledge.

Usher, R. (2009) Experience, pedagogy, and social practices. In K. Illeris (Ed.) *Contemporary Theories of Learning* (pp. 159–168). London: Routledge.

Usher, R. & Edwards, R. (1994) *Postmodernism and Education.* London: Routledge.

Weil, S. & McGill (Eds.) (1989) *Making Sense of Experiential Learning: Diversity in Theory and Practice.* Milton Keynes, UK: SHRE/Open University Press.

Zweers, W. (2000). *Participation with Nature: Outline for an Ecologisation of our Worldview.* Utrecht: International Books.

42

Enskilment and place-responsiveness in outdoor studies

Ways of life

Mike Brown

THE UNIVERSITY OF WAIKATO

Brian Wattchow

MONASH UNIVERSITY

Where are we?

We open this chapter with a scene familiar to many practitioners in outdoor studies. Imagine a group of students and their outdoor guide or teacher as they are about to embark on a journey. They form a circle and consult their maps. Through the transparent skin of their map cases they can see their compasses and the topographic maps neatly folded to show the country they will traverse in the day ahead. They pinpoint their position among the grid work of northings and eastings. Their guide points to a spot towards the edge of the map – their intended destination for the evening. It is an everyday scene, and learning to navigate through unfamiliar terrain is no doubt an important skill. Yet the social anthropologist Ingold raises serious questions about what such a scene reveals, and hides, about people's perceptions of landscape, and their attachments and detachments from outdoor places. Navigation, Ingold (2000, p. 235) argues, begins with the question 'Where am I?' How we attempt to answer this question reveals a great deal about our association with the places we live, work and travel within.

> For the map-using stranger, making his [*sic*.] way in unfamiliar country, 'being here' or 'going there' generally entails the ability to identify one's current or intended future position with a certain spatial or geographic location, defined by the intersection of particular coordinates on the map. (Ingold, 2000, p. 219)

Navigation through map use, according to Ingold, is synchronic and relies upon the ability to abstract (e.g. to 'see' and interpret the world from the perspective of a satellite and to imagine what will be required to leave one set of coordinates to reach another through a system of symbolic markings that indicate features in the terrain). By way of contrast, Ingold suggests that wayfinding relies upon inhabitants building familiarity with a place through time. This occurs through the recounting of historical narratives and personal experiences of places. In wayfinding, people 'feel their way' through places that are constantly 'coming into being through the combined action of human and non-human agencies' (Ingold, 2000, p. 155). Readers in Britain and Europe will be familiar with various ways and paths that trace historical routes, such as the El Camino Santiago (the Way of St James) – a long-distance pathway that crosses France and Spain, following a Christian pilgrimage route that has been walked since medieval times. Or a *way* may connect the 'old' paths between villages, such as the Spey Way in Scotland, which follows the River Spey. Every country has such pathways. Many modern walking paths or tracks, even those that pass through remote country, follow ancient walking routes that have been traversed for thousands of years (e.g. in New Zealand many high-country trails follow earlier Māori trading routes). The key point, Ingold argues, is that wayfinding, rather than navigating, reflects how humans experience and live in the world. Macfarlane's (2012) book *The Old Ways* explores many types of paths and ways, from the remote, to the ritualistic and the routine, and how the human body and mind are shaped through walking them. Reading his book reminds us of the enriching and intrinsic values of being attentive, skilful and purposeful – like the pilgrim. Even on a path we walk every day, if we are wayfinding, we are in a deep conversation with the place, its inhabitants and ancestors as we move and rest within it. For Ingold, wayfinding more closely represents storytelling than reading a map. For, as he reminds us, 'the map can be a help in the beginning to know the country, but the aim is to learn the country, not the map' (1993, p. 462).

Our purpose in this chapter is to consider the significance and potential of place-responsiveness in outdoor studies. Place-responsiveness has developed as a distinct theme in outdoor studies over the past decade or so, in particular with research findings and writings from authors in Scotland, Canada, New Zealand and Australia (Brookes, 2002; Stewart, 2004; Wattchow, 2005, 2007, 2008, 2013; Brown, 2008, 2012; Mullins & Wattchow, 2009; Harrison, 2010; Wattchow & Brown, 2011; Mannion, Fenwick & Lynch, 2013). The significance of this scholarship is that it challenges assumptions and beliefs relating to the philosophy, purpose and practice of outdoor studies. This body of literature poses serious questions about the aims of outdoor studies with regard to personal and social development outcomes and even global approaches to environmental problems and the universalisation of nature, especially 'wilderness'. Proponents of place-responsive approaches have also raised questions about overly simplistic experiential models of learning, and deeply held beliefs about the 'core' philosophy of outdoor learning with regard to risk, challenge and transferability of learning. Writers conversant with the literature on place-responsiveness have argued for more localised approaches to knowing, knowledge and practice.

Our aim is to extend this commentary by drawing upon insights from the social anthropologist Ingold (2000) on enskilment and taskscapes, as we believe these have the potential to further highlight what a place-responsive curriculum and pedagogy in outdoor studies might look like. For Ingold:

> A place owes its character to the experiences it affords to those who spend time there – to the sights, sounds and indeed smells that constitute its specific ambience. And these, in turn, depend on the kinds of activities in which its inhabitants engage. It is from this relational context of people's engagement with the world, in the business of dwelling, that each place draws its unique significance. Thus whereas with space, meanings are *attached* to the world, with the landscape they are *gathered from* it. (Ingold, 2000, p. 192)

One of the key ideas that we want to introduce is that to inhabit places requires purposeful and skilful practice. Study in and of the outdoors, through processes that involve rapid passage from one point to another, or reify abstract knowledge or skills divorced from context, provides a fragmented or partial image of the network of interconnected places that collectively constitute 'the outdoors'. That is, we will learn little about a place if all we do there is count, move, measure and record. Nor are we likely to learn much if our experience in an outdoor setting is based solely on the performance of outdoor activities when the local particularities of place, the lives of its inhabitants, and its subtle histories and stories, hold little or no significance for us. Similarly, our engagement with a place will be far from complete if we do no more than seek a subjective encounter, where we place emphasis on 'internalising' our experiences, such as our aesthetic response to the grandeur of wild and natural country. We may be moved to write poetry and create art, but we may be using nature as a mirror, to use Cronon's (1996) analogy, as our words and etchings become little more than reflections of our own desires. According to Ingold, the key that opens the door to place is to be found in what he calls 'the business of dwelling', and dwelling involves inhabitation, and inhabitation requires skill. In his view, 'skill is at once a form of knowledge and a form of practice, or if you will – it is both practical knowledge and a form of knowledgeable practice' (Ingold, 2000, p. 316).

Place, placelessness and the recovery of landscapes

Ingold builds on a strong tradition within place scholarship when he draws from the phenomenological philosophies of Heidegger and Merleau-Ponty. The influence of Heidegger and Merleau-Ponty inspired a reconsideration of the focus and work of human geography in the 1970s and 1980s (see, Tuan, 1977; Relph, 1976; Seamon, 1979; Seamon & Mugerauer, 1985; Massey, 1994; Mugerauer, 1995; Creswell, 2004).

While considerable differences with regard to definitions of both place and landscape are to be found among these authors, some commonalities help refine an understanding of place.

- Place is neither land nor location, nor is it nature.
- Place is not simply space that has been invested with human meaning by having values projected upon it.
- Place is phenomenal in character and is constantly in a state of becoming.
- Place develops by way of a reciprocal relation between inhabitants who dwell there and the characteristics of local country (landforms, life forms, seasons, etc.).
- Place and knowing is deeply linked with storying.

For Ingold, to know one's place is to have the 'ability to situate one's current position not within a set of abstract coordinates but within the historical context of journeys previously made – journeys to, from and around places,' and it is this 'that distinguishes the countryman [sic.] from the stranger' (Ingold, 2000, p. 219). This alternative view of place or landscape counters persistent and dominant ideas within Western knowledge systems. Daniels and Cosgrove (1988) typify the dominant belief when they state: 'a landscape is a cultural image, a pictorial way of representing or symbolising surroundings' (p. 1). Their position suggests that landscapes are best studied from the outside, and that human perception proceeds from some kind of privileged and external location. Ingold argues the opposite: perception and experience for humans, as it is with all animals, unfolds from within a landscape, along the pathways and in the centres of significance that make up places.

Outdoor pedagogies of place

Calls for a more place-based or place-responsive approach in outdoor studies have not occurred in isolation. Similar discussion and debates are to be found in the broader discourse of education studies and in social ecology. While place may be a nebulous concept to many educators (Orr, 1992) there have been notable exceptions. Examples include Smith (2002), who reviewed a number of place-based educational initiatives and summarised their pedagogic approaches. Similarly Gruenewald has argued for a multidisciplinary approach to place in education (2003a), and a critical pedagogy of place based on decolonisation and reinhabitation (2003b). Later these two authors combined to consider how place-based education initiatives reflected a broader movement in society towards a 'new localism' as a reaction against globalisation and corporate capitalism, and the pressures these placed on educational policy, curricula and practice (Gruenewald & Smith, 2008). These authors highlight the profound educational significance of place: 'Places, and our relationship with them, are worthy of our attention because places are powerfully pedagogical' (p. 143). In a similar vein, Ingold speaks of an 'education of attention' (2000, p. 37) that comes about through perception and action as one engages in the process of enskilment in particular places.

Several authors within outdoor education have written about, and researched, the philosophical and pedagogical potential of 'place'. Australian outdoor educators have been prominent in this emerging discourse. As early as 1994, Brookes (1994) raised concerns about pursuits-based outdoor programming, characterising it as 'short raids on the bush as strangers' rather than educational programmes that might aim to 'develop a sense of place' (p. 31). Although 'place' became an increasingly prominent term used by outdoor educators (Stewart 2004; Birrell, 2005; Wattchow, 2005; Payne & Wattchow, 2008) there had been little empirical research into place-responsive forms of practice in outdoor studies.

The last decade has seen a number of research studies, using a range of qualitative approaches, focusing on the role of place in outdoor education (Stewart, 2003; Preston & Griffiths, 2004; Wattchow, 2006; Mullins, 2007; Wattchow & Brown, 2011). Similar studies have been undertaken in New Zealand (Brown, 2012, 2013; Taylor, 2014) and Scotland (Harrison, 2010; Higgins & Wattchow, 2013; Mannion et al., 2013). It is possible to group these research studies into two categories. First, there are studies that report on how existing outdoor programmes are, or are not, responsive to place. Second, there are studies that report on programmes that have deliberately been constructed to promote place-responsiveness.

It is hard to generalise findings from these research studies, and that is as it should be. Each one reports on a particular group (or groups) of educators and learners in a particular place and time. They range across primary and secondary school age learners through to university undergraduates, with a few of the studies also focusing on place-responsive educators (Preston & Griffiths, 2004; Stewart, 2004; Wattchow, 2006; Mullins, 2007; Harrison, 2010; Wattchow & Brown, 2011; Brown, 2013; Higgins & Wattchow, 2013; Mannion et al., 2013). Settings for the studies range across the mountains and rivers of Australia and New Zealand to the Highlands of Scotland. This nascent body of research indicates:

- a shift in programming away from 'risky' outdoor pursuits with a narrow focus on 'context-free' personal and social development outcomes;
- a shift away from using outdoor pursuits centres that present 'pre-packaged' programmes;
- a shift away from 'one-off' visits to remote locations to repeated visits to accessible outdoor places;
- a move towards a holistic engagement with outdoor places, involving cross-curricula engagement and a celebration of embodied ways of knowing;

- a move towards engaging with local places, with some programmes commencing and finishing at participants' homes and schools;
- a move towards tracing participants' family and ancestral connections to particular places;
- a move towards gathering and telling multilayered stories about local land forms, life forms, historical events, indigenous and settler relationships with the land;
- a move towards descriptive writing and creative arts as a means of reflecting upon and representing place experiences.

One of the features of this research and writing into place-responsiveness in outdoor studies is the inclusion of detailed descriptions about local geography, ecologies, towns and peoples – the locations and socio-cultural context in which the research occurred. This is unusual as much research in outdoor studies (particularly that which is focused on outcomes) can be described as placeless – that is, where context, time and situation appear to be considered largely irrelevant by the researchers, discussion and findings from such research risks ending up sounding clinical, distanced and detached. As readers we may be left wondering about the local conditions from where the research participants' voices arose and the researcher's interpretations emanated. Or, as Ingold might argue, we hear a story but it is disconnected from its landscape. While there is scope for even greater descriptions of local histories and particularities, this emergent scholarship into place-responsiveness in outdoor studies, seems to have initiated a process of localisation and contextualisation. Our attention now turns to asking: what is required of outdoor educators, leaders and learners in terms of practical knowledge and knowledgeable practice in this new localism, or place-responsiveness? What specific pedagogic approaches might best serve the growth of attentive, skilful and purposeful learning in outdoor places?

From testing ground to taskscape

One of the most persistent and deeply held beliefs about the virtues of outdoor studies is that adventurous pursuits build character and that this personal development will transfer to other aspects of participants' lives. Brookes (2003a, 2003b) and Brown (2010) have questioned and dissected these beliefs at length. Our interest here has to do with the consequences of such beliefs for how educators and learners perceive landscapes and participate in outdoor places. Understanding the origins of a belief in the virtues of risky outdoor pursuits tells us much about the requirements and possibilities of alternative approaches – such as dwelling and place-responsiveness.

Macfarlane (2003) traces the rise of outdoor risk taking as a relatively late development within the Romantic response to nature in the 18th century. Prior to this, risks in the outdoors had more to do with the dangers of hunting, work and defending one's territory – and these risks were to be avoided, or minimised where possible. There were also risks associated with travel, particularly when traversing remote country between towns and cities. Rapid industrialisation saw a mass movement of the population from rural regions to industrial cities, and with the rise of rail transport and as the cities became more crowded and polluted, some sought a return to nature (Bate, 2000). This new breed of usually well-to-do, educated, outdoor travellers brought their pens and brushes with them to capture the beauties of the bucolic landscape, rendered as nostalgic scenes of a fast-fading agrarian age, and to record their experiences of wildness in the last vestiges of untamed country. Macfarlane (2007) has subsequently argued that, rather than inventing a love for wild places, they rekindled the 'first glimmerings of wild consciousness' (p. 14) that was founded in the monks, bards and pilgrims who travelled the ancient paths centuries before. But the Romantic approach differed in that it celebrated and actively promoted the sensation of 'pleasurable fear' (Macfarlane, 2003, p. 73). The Romantic ideal was to re-experience an intensity of life that had become dulled in modern society. Macfarlane (2003) argues that the pursuit of *pleasurable fear* required the outdoor landscape to be culturally constructed as a *testing ground*.

While it may be argued that the Romantics preserved a love and connection for the outdoors that was being severed by the rise of industrialisation and urbanisation, their ideas also cast a long shadow upon how we think outdoor landscapes should be encountered and experienced. When wild nature is universalised it no longer really matters where you are in the outdoors – as long as it is majestic, awe inspiring and wild. And, as our lives have become increasingly urbanised, the polarity of society and wild nature seems even greater. Outdoor studies and practice seem caught in a double bind. We seem to be required to travel further from home in our search for wildness, and when we arrive we frequently treat it as an arena to learn and test a new set of skills and knowledge that simultaneously embraces and manages risk.

In contrast, one of the things that place-responsive writers have urged us to do is to consider the pedagogical importance of place(s) and to ask the following questions (adapted from Berry, 1987) to assist with programme design rather than 'using' places as empty sites upon which we inscribe our desires. What is here in this place? What will this place permit us to do? What will this place help us to do? How is this place interconnected to my home place? These guiding questions help frame a different orientation to designing learning experiences in the outdoors which foregrounds the role of the particularity of place(s) in what might be learned.

In *A Pedagogy of Place: Outdoor Education for a Changing World* (Wattchow & Brown, 2011), we proposed four signposts to a place-responsive pedagogy: (i) The need to be present in and with a place; (ii) recognition of the power of place-based stories and narratives; (iii) the value of apprenticing ourselves to places; and (iv) the representation of place experiences. These guiding questions or signposts indicate a desire by educators to understand how learning and being are inextricably linked to places and our relationships with them. We find an interesting corollary in Ingold's notion of a taskscape, and the development of skills through dwelling and moving in and through landscapes.

Ingold (2000) refers to tasks as any 'practical operation, carried out by a skilled agent in an environment, as part of his or her normal business of life, in other words, tasks are the constitutive acts of dwelling' (p. 195). He stresses that the tasks interlock both technical and social aspects of life. He uses the term taskscapes to denote the connection between technical and social practices that are embedded in the process of dwelling. As he points out, 'The taskscape exists only so long as people are actually engaged in the activities of dwelling' (2000, p. 197). It is through dwelling and being in place(s) that people become skilled. As Ingold points out, and we alluded to earlier, when a novice studies 'something' they do not become skilled through 'the acquisition of rules and representations' (Ingold, 2000, p. 415), rather they are deemed skilful when they are able to dispense with the rules and attend to the specifics of their situation. Ingold (2000) highlights the following five dimensions of any kind of skilled practice.

First, intentionality and functionality are immanent in the practice itself, rather than being prior properties, respectively of an agent and an instrument. Secondly, skill is not an attribute of the individual body in isolation but of the whole system of relations constituted by the presence of the artisan in his or her environment. Thirdly, rather than representing the mere application of mechanical force, skill involves qualities of care, judgment and dexterity. Fourthly, it is not through the transmission of formulae that skills are passed from generation to generation, but though practical, 'hands-on' experience. Finally, skilled workmanship serves not to execute a pre-existing design but actually to generate the forms of artefacts. (p. 291)

Ingold's articulation of enskilment developed within a taskscape provides another perspective on learning in and through places. Mullins (2014) has suggested that enskilment provides valuable insights into the importance of skills in outdoor studies as it 'situates and shapes participants in relation to dynamic landscape features and environmental processes while involving complex social relations that build, challenge, and express individual, communal, and place meanings' (p. 11).

Ingold's conceptualisation of enskilment, within taskscapes, provides further support to the existing body of literature that argues for the pedagogical importance of place(s) in learning and being. Ross and Mannion (2012) have also highlighted how Ingold's account of dwelling can reshape how we think about curriculum making. They suggest that:

> Curriculum making (and indeed all being) is necessarily a process of living in and through the world, without recourse to mindful representation of it, so traditional or textual understandings of curriculum are rendered potentially incoherent. The second is that learning is a process of 'attunement' to the meanings that inhere in the relationships that make up the world, so there is significance in the diversity of places, materials and persons involved in curriculum making. (p. 304)

Dwelling in place(s) and being responsive to the socio-cultural context challenges conceptions of the outdoors as a testing ground on which we can impose prescribed activities with stated learning outcomes. Outdoor studies curricula should arise from the lived embodied experiences of educators and participants that arise in particular outdoor place(s).

Where are we? We are here!

We have previously presented four signposts to a place-responsive pedagogy (Wattchow & Brown, 2011). They were a distillation of our understanding and adaptation of a diverse body of literature, reflections on personal practices and conversations with experienced practitioners. We were concerned to provide an alternate perspective on outdoor learning that aligned with broader educational discourses rather than reverting to foundational beliefs that were proving to be increasingly problematic.

We continue to maintain that carefully facilitated outdoor studies that take place(s) as a focal point, can do more than impart knowledge about the world. As has been suggested earlier, a focus on personal and social development outcomes runs the risk of perpetuating the 'culture of acquisition' (Lave, 1990, p. 310) that disavows embodied ways of knowing, and favours abstract, context-free knowledge. As Ingold and others (see Brown, 2009) have argued, learning in and through places is 'a process of *enskilment*, in which learning is inseparable from doing, and in which both are embedded in the context of a practical engagement in the world – that is, in dwelling' (Ingold, 2000, p. 416). Having learned to be 'at home', to dwell, in outdoor places – it is our hope that outdoor educators might continue with their exploration of possibilities in their home places while also learning to travel afar with a renewed sensibility for outdoor places. Becoming place-responsive includes providing opportunities for students to 'recognize, acquire and enable the skills needed to interpret their surroundings and act for a better future' (Mullins, 2014, p. 329). We hope that this chapter might act as a map that provides an overview of place-responsiveness and its contribution to reshaping outdoor studies. But, like any map, it merely conveys a 'symbolic picture' of the field – the challenge is to embrace and implement a place-responsive orientation – to learn your places, to ever deepen your relationship with them and respond appropriately. This approach is more likely to be supportive of the needs of students in contemporary times than reverting to time-worn clichés and prescriptive formulas that advertise predetermined outcomes. For, as Ingold (2000) has pointed out:

> Ways of life are not therefore determined in advance, as routes to be followed, but have continually to be worked out anew. And these ways, far from being inscribed upon the surface of an inanimate world, are the very threads from which the living world is woven. (p. 242)

References

Bate, J. (2000). *The Song of the Earth*. London: Picador.

Berry, W. (1987). *Home Economics*. San Francisco, CA: North Point Press.

Birrell, C. (2005). A deepening relationship with place. In T. Dickson, T. Gray, & B. Hayllar (Eds.) *Outdoor and Experiential Learning: Views from the Top* (pp. 53–62). Dunedin: Otago University Print.

Brookes, A. (1994). Reading between the lines: Outdoor experience as environmental text. *Journal of Physical Education, Recreation and Dance*, October, 29–33.

Brookes, A. (2002). Lost in the Australian Bush: Outdoor education as curriculum. *Journal of Curriculum Studies, 34*(4), 405–425.

Brookes, A. (2003a). A critique of Neo-Hahnian outdoor education theory. Part One: Challenges to the concept of 'character building'. *Journal of Adventure Education and Outdoor Learning, 3*(1), 49–62.

Brookes, A. (2003b). A critique of Neo-Hahnian outdoor education theory. Part Two: 'The fundamental attribution error' in contemporary outdoor education discourse. *Journal of Adventure Education and Outdoor Learning, 3*(2), 119–132.

Brown, M. (2008). Outdoor education: Opportunities provided by a place-based approach. *New Zealand Journal of Outdoor Education, 2*(3), 7–25.

Brown, M. (2009). Reconceptualising outdoor adventure education: Activity in search of an appropriate theory. *Australian Journal of Outdoor Education, 13*(2), 3–13.

Brown, M. (2010). Transfer: Outdoor adventure education's Achilles heel? Changing participation as a viable option. *Australian Journal of Outdoor Education, 14*(1), 13–22.

Brown, M. (2012). Student perspectives of a place-responsive outdoor education programme. *New Zealand Journal of Outdoor Education, 3*(1), 64–88.

Brown, M. (2013). Teacher perspectives on place-responsive outdoor education. *Set, 3*, 3–10.

Creswell, T. (2004). *Place: A Short Introduction*. Oxford: Blackwell Publishing.

Cronon, W. (1996). *Uncommon Ground: Rethinking the Human Place in Nature*. New York: W.W. Norton & Company.

Daniels, S. & Cosgrove, D. (1988). *The Iconography of Landscape*. Cambridge: Cambridge University Press.

Gruenewald, D. (2003a). Foundations of place: A multidisciplinary framework for place-conscious education. *American Educational Research Journal, 40*(3), 619–654.

Gruenewald, D. (2003b). The best of both worlds: A critical pedagogy of place. *Educational Researcher, 32*(4), 3–12.

Gruenewald, D. & Smith, G. (2008). *Place-based Education in the Global Age*. New York: Lawrence Erlbaum Associates.

Harrison, S. (2010). 'Why are we here?' Taking place into account in UK environmental education. *Journal of Adventure Education and Outdoor Learning, 10*(1), 3–18.

Higgins, P. & Wattchow, B. (2013). The water of life: Creative non-fiction and lived experience on an interdisciplinary canoe journey on Scotland's River Spey. *Journal of Adventure Education and Outdoor Leadership, 13*(1), 1–18.

Ingold, T. (1993). Technology, language, intelligence. In K. Gibson & T. Ingold (Eds.) *Tools, Language and Cognition in Human Evolution* (pp. 449–472). Cambridge: Cambridge University Press.

Ingold, T. (2000). *The Perception of the Environment: Essays in Livelihood, Dwelling and Skill*. London: Routledge.

Lave, J. (1990). The culture of acquisition and the practice of understanding. In J. Stigler, R. Shweder & G. Herdt (Eds.) *Cultural Psychology: Essays on Comparative Human Development* (pp. 309–327). Cambridge: Cambridge University Press.

Macfarlane, R. (2003). *Mountains of the Mind: A History of Fascination*. London: Granta Books.

Macfarlane, R. (2007). *The Wild Places.* London: Granta Books.

Macfarlane, R. (2012). *The Old Ways: A Journey on Foot.* London: Hamish Hamilton.

Mannion, G., Fenwick, A. & Lynch, J. (2013). Place-responsive pedagogy: Learning from teachers' experiences of excursions in nature. *Environmental Education Research, 19*(6), 792–809.

Massey, D. (1994). *Space, Place, and Gender.* Minneapolis, MN: University of Minnesota Press.

Mugerauer, R. (1995). *Interpreting Environments: Tradition, Deconstruction, Hermeneutics.* Austin: University of Texas Press.

Mullins, M. (2007). Re-telling the Snowy River: Exploring connections between river guides, the experience of place, and outdoor education. Thesis for the award of Master of Education (Research), Monash University.

Mullins, M. & Wattchow, B. (2009). Re-telling the Snowy River: Exploring connections between river guides, the experience of place, and outdoor education. Paper presented at the Fourth International Outdoor Education Research Conference, Outdoor Education Research and Theory: Critical Reflections, New Directions, Beechworth, Victoria, 15–19 April.

Mullins, P. (2014). Conceptualizing skill within a participatory ecological approach to outdoor adventure. *Journal of Experiential Education, 37*(4), 320–334.

Orr, D. (1992). *Ecological Literacy: Education, and the Transition to a Postmodern World.* Albany, NY: State University of New York Press.

Payne, P. & Wattchow, B. (2008). Slow pedagogy and placing education in the post-traditional. *Australian Journal of Outdoor Education, 12*(1), 25–38.

Preston, L. & Griffiths, A. (2004). Pedagogy of connections: Findings of a collaborative action research project in outdoor and environmental education. *Australian Journal of Outdoor Education, 8(2),* 36–45.

Relph, E. (1976). *Place and Placelessness.* London: Pion Limited.

Ross, H. & Mannion, G. (2012). Curriculum making as the enactment of dwelling in places. *Studies in the Philosophy of Education, 31*, 303–313.

Seamon, D. (1979). *A Geography of the Lifeworld: Movement, Rest and Encounter.* New York: St Martin's Press.

Seamon, D. & Mugerauer, R. (Eds.) (1985). *Dwelling, Place and Environment: Towards a Phenomenology of Person and World.* Boston, MA: Martinus Nijhoff Publishers.

Smith, G. (2002). Place-based education: Learning where we are. *Phi Delta Kappan,* April, 584–594.

Stewart, A. (2003). Encountering landscapes: An exploration of environment specific learning on an extended journey. Unpublished master's dissertation, University of Tasmania.

Stewart, A. (2004). Decolonising encounters with the Murray River: Building place-responsive outdoor education. *Australian Journal of Outdoor Education, 8*(2), 46–55.

Taylor, C. (2014). Place responsive education: Student perspectives. Thesis for the award of Master of Sport and Leisure Studies, University of Waikato.

Tuan, Y. (1977). *Space and Place: The Perspective of Experience.* Minneapolis, MN: University of Minnesota Press.

Wattchow, B. (2005). Belonging to proper country. In T.J. Dickson, T. Gray & Hayllar, B. (Eds.) *Outdoor and Experiential Learning: Views from the Top* (pp. 13–27). Dunedin: Otago University Print.

Wattchow, B. (2006). The experience of river places in outdoor education: A phenomenological study. Thesis for the award of Doctor of Philosophy, Monash University.

Wattchow, B. (2007). Paddling, river places and outdoor education (Part 1): Playing with an unstoppable force. *Australian Journal of Outdoor Education,* 11(1), 10–20.

Wattchow, B. (2008). Moving on an effortless journey: Paddling, river-places and outdoor education (Part II). *Australian Journal of Outdoor Education, 12*(2), 12–23.

Wattchow, B. (2013). Landscape and a sense of place: A creative tension. In P. Howard, I. Thompson & E. Waterton (Eds.) *The Routledge Companion to Landscape Studies* (pp. 87–96). Routledge: London.

Wattchow, B. & Brown, M. (2011). *Pedagogy of Place: Outdoor Education for a Changing World.* Melbourne: Monash University Press.

43

Outdoor education, safety and risk in the light of serious accidents

Andrew Brookes

La Trobe University

Each serious incident in outdoor education (OE) and related areas potentially contributes to specific knowledge of how such incidents occur and how to prevent them. A serious incident can also become a lens to view not only particular programmes, but also the OE field. Fatalities, particularly multiple fatalities, have raised questions about aims and purposes (what were they doing there?) – and practice (why did they choose that activity in that location in those conditions?). In New Zealand a series of tragedies contributed to a decision to review commercial adventure activities (Department of Labour, 2010), and subsequent regulations (Mateparae, 2011; Gulley, 2013). In the UK the deaths of four teenagers on Lyme Bay, in 1993, led directly to changes in legislation (Bradford, 2002; Allison & Telford, 2005). This chapter examines OE through the lens of serious incidents. I consider some conclusions that can be drawn from an examination of past incidents, particularly in the light of what advances in technology have afforded, at least in some parts of the world. I consider why community responses to OE tragedies are likely to exhibit a clear pattern of strict aversion, rather than weighing risks against benefits, and some questions this poses for OE programmes and staffing.

In many industries serious incidents have been characterised by failures to learn lessons from past incidents (Toft & Reynolds, 1994). In the outdoor education field very few serious incidents are unprecedented, although potential lessons from precedents might be unknown to those involved because serious incidents are rare. Similar OE incidents might have occurred far away or long before, or might have involved a different type of organisation. When serious incidents are examined most involve kinds of hazardous situations that have been known and understood for decades. Exceptions, which I will not discuss in detail here, have tended to involve hazards in the wider community that have resulted in a catastrophe that happens to involve an OE group, for example aircraft crashes, mass murder, building fires or structural collapses. Natural hazards such as floods and tornados can also affect wide areas and might involve an OE group along with others. These exceptions are relevant to placing OE safety in a global context, and potentially affect OE conducted abroad, although I do not discuss that here.

Even if the OE field is very broadly conceived, incidents involving one or more fatalities are few. One of the studies this chapter draws on searched for every fatal incident involving school or youth group camps and excursions in Australia or involving an Australian group abroad over a period of fifty years, and found 102 incidents involving 146 deaths, including 20 per cent that occurred as a result of motor vehicle collisions en route or returning (Brookes, 2011b). In a second study, also defining OE as any kind of school or youth group camp or excursion, I searched for incidents anywhere having three or more deaths. That study sought incidents since 1900 that could be found using online searches in English. It found 93 incidents involving 684 deaths, not including travel-related incidents such as bus or aircraft crashes, and ferry disasters (Brookes, 2014).

Knowledge and insights from what is a thin scatter of serious incidents will not reliably accrue in the OE field as a matter of course, unless actively sought through studies such as those on which this chapter draws. This chapter provides tables that illustrate some key patterns in fatal incidents, and outlines some significant implications for the OE field.

Potentially fatal circumstances are distinct, and therefore knowable

Fatal incidents tend to occur in specific, narrow circumstances. Table 43.1 shows fatal incidents involving organised youth groups on lift-served ski slopes. Apart from some deaths on ski lifts that can be considered conventional workplace incidents, all of the on-slope deaths involved collisions with a fixed object, usually a tree. In contrast, the typical skiing accident is a fall resulting in injury to an extremity. Of 1404 injuries studied in an Australian study, only

Table 43.1 OE ski-slope fatalities, worldwide

Year	Victim	Cause	Location
1994	Canadian student	Collision with a tree	Frost Fire, USA
2000	16-year-old boy	Collision with a tree Novice	Thredbo, Australia
2005	10-year-old boy	Collision with a snowmaking machine Novice	Okemo Mountain, USA
2005	16 year old from Aarhus	Collision with a tree	Denmark
2007	18-year-old boy	Collision with a tree, no helmet	Breckenridge, USA
2009	17-year-old girl	Collision with a tree, helmet	Collingwood, Ontario
2009	13-year-old boy	Collision with tree, no helmet	Barrie, Ontario
2009	16-year-old girl	Advanced skier, black run, collision with tree, helmet	Perisher, Australia
2009	16-year-old girl	Inexperienced skier, blue run, collision with tree, helmet	Thredbo, Australia
2010	16-year-old boy	Collision with a tree, helmet	Panorama, Canada
2011	14-year-old boy, UK	Fell off ski lift, strangled	Chatel, France
2011	12-year-old girl	Slid off tow, lost helmet, hit pylon	Sion, Switzerland
2012	7-year-old boy	Unsupervised ski team children on chairlift, one fell 16m, helmet	Sugarbowl Resort, California, USA

Source: Brookes and Holmes (2014)

8 per cent were from collision with an object (Ashby & Cassell, 2007), including two deaths from collisions with a tree. While a victim's skiing inexperience is commonly a factor in skiing injuries (Langran & Selvaraj, 2002), victims of fatal incidents are more likely to be experienced (Tough & Butt, 1993), because experienced skiers ski faster and in less safe environments. Some OE deaths have occurred when a novice skier has collided with an object at speed.

Table 43.2 shows deaths from falls in Australian OE. All of the victims were young males who were either unsupervised or who had eluded supervision, even if momentarily. What makes the circumstances narrowly specific in each example is a combination of factors: skiing at speed, and the presence of fixed objects on a slope in one case, young males, steep ground, and ineffective supervision in the other. Similar patterns can be discerned in the other tables, and in sets of incidents I have not included in this chapter. For most programmes, in most locations, on most days the potential for a fatal incident is small, although some potential for drowning is omnipresent around water.

Table 43.2 OE falls, Australian fatalities

Incident	Deaths	Location	Brief description
Joffre Gorge 1976	M16	Joffre Gorge, Karijini NP WA	Fell approximately 30 m, body not recovered until next day. A 15-year old boy from the same school was seriously injured in a fall at nearby Weeno Gorge in August of the previous year (1975).
Tatachilla 1976	M11	Tatachilla Camp, McLaren Vale SA	4 teachers, 65 students at camp (old winery). One noticed missing (bed check). Found unconscious, died next day, severe head injuries. Extensive police interviews eventually established he fell while using a 1st-floor windowsill to get from one room to another during unsupervised play.
Barkly River 1979	M16	Barkly River Vic.	School club o/night bushwalk, 2 teachers, 2 ex-students, 9 students, 1 student from another school. (Sat.) 2 teachers and 6 students on day walk. In steep gully, camp in sight, 1 student allowed to take a different route alone, failed to reach camp. (Sun.) Search with own resources failed, (Mon.) police found body (dead) below 20 m cliff (spinal injuries).
Grampians 1979	M15	Grampians Vic.	1 staff, 12 students (cadets) abseiling. Activity ceased due to rain. 1 student climbed unsupervised up 8 m unroped to use walkie-talkie, large rock fell followed by the student, struck head (4.30 pm). Evacuation began, suspended (condition worsened). Breathing failed, ambulance arrived 6.30 pm.
Cathedrals 1983	M15	Cathedral ranges Vic.	3 teachers, 21 students walking as a group along 'Razorback' track. Girl fell 1 m, uninjured. Boy fell from same spot 1.5 m. Head injuries (around 3 pm). Evacuation began, 6 pm, suspended 8 pm (breathing failed), died 3.00 am on mountain.
Hawkesbury River 1986	M15	Hawkesbury River NSW	30 students on orienteering exercise. 1 student stepped on or over a loose rock, fell 1.5 m, rock landed on top of him. Attended by doctor, died at scene.

Freycinet 1987	M 15	Freycinet, TAS	During free time group of boys left campsite for a walk unsupervised. Two decided to climb a cliff. After 20 m became scared, but decided continuing up was easier. Both fell during an attempt to assist each other. Deceased fell 35 m.
Bungonia 1991	M16	Bungonia Gorge NSW	2 leaders, 4 juvenile offenders, canyoning. 1 fell 75 m during lunch break. Local police and homicide detectives investigated as possible suspicious death. Coroner unable to determine what caused the fall.
Boulder Falls 1992	M 20	Boulder Falls, Mersey River, TAS	51 students with unknown number of lecturers on 5-day bushwalk/geomorphology excursion. Deceased was a member of a smaller group who detoured from the track for a better view of the falls. Fell 45 m.
Bungonia 1994	M15	Bungonia NSW	2 leaders and senior student, 15 students, 5-day bushwalk. Students leading, not directly supervised, attempted to find a way down a cliff. 1 fell 20 m, died at scene.
Mount Sugarloaf 2003	M 16	Mount Sugarloaf, NSW	24 students on D of E orienteering exercise. Deceased with a smaller group. Became separated, fell 20 m. Severe head injuries.
Wadeville 2010	M 14	Hanging Rock Falls, QLD	End of season trip for teammates, family and friends. Observed to slip and fall 10 m into waterhole, did not resurface.

Source: Brookes (2011b)

OE-related incidents are not unique to OE

Even with adult groups excluded, the tabulated incidents show similar circumstances have resulted in similar incidents involving different kinds of organisations in different parts of the world. More detailed accounts than appear in the tables, where they exist, usually show how human and organisational factors led to a group encountering a particular hazard, but if anything the range of different ways of getting into the same kind of trouble, and the range of organisations involved, emphasises the importance of understanding underlying hazards. OE as such is not hazardous, but it sometimes occurs in hazardous situations. Inclusion of adult groups, which have suffered similar tragedies, would reinforce the point. There are strong reasons for separating youth groups from adult groups. As Cloutier (2003) observed in a report on the Connaught Valley incident (Table 43.3):

> . . . the tolerance for risk is much higher in a commercial trip than most parents would accept for a school trip. The philosophy held by an outdoor educator that risk is a necessary and worthwhile part of outdoor education is based on potential benefits and may not account for the real potential consequences . . . [x] has faced the reality of the consequences of this philosophy, and no parent, administrator, or board member spoken with would agree that educating students about backcountry skiing was worth the price that was paid on the trip in Rogers Pass on February 1, 2003. (p. 53)

447

Table 43.3 OE avalanche multiple fatalities, worldwide

Incident	#	Location	Description
Mt Baker 1939	6	Mt Baker, USA	Western Washington College of Education annual hike on Mt Baker, 25 students and 2 guides. Avalanche. 6 students died.
Mt Temple 1955	7	Mt Temple, Canada	A group of 22 schoolboys from the USA and two leaders climbing Mt Temple. One leader did not accompany the group; the other turned back and allowed the boys to continue. Avalanche swept 11 200 m down the mountain. 7 died.
Les Orres 1998	11	Les Orres, French Alps	Party of about 30 students, teachers and guides on snowshoe trek in extremely high avalanche danger. Avalanche caught the party, 21 injured, 9 seriously. 11 died.
Connaught Valley 2003	7	Rogers Pass, Canada	Relatively large group of outdoor education students ski touring in Connaught Creek, a known avalanche area in conditions of 'considerable' avalanche risk on the slopes high above the group. An unusually large avalanche buried 14. 2 nearby mountain guides assisted with the rescue of 7. 7 died.
Jungfrau 2007	6	Jungfrau mountain, Switzerland	Party of 14 Swiss defence recruits on week 17 of 21-week training programme. Avalanche killed 6. 8 rescued.
Valmeinier 2009	4	Valmeinier ski resort, France	7 school students and guide skiing off-piste near Valmeinier resort. Avalanche 900 m by 600m swept away all but one, who raised the alarm. 2 rescued, injured. 4 died.

Source: Brookes (2014)

In general the specific nature of potentially fatal circumstances leaves considerable room to conduct OE without risking death. The morphology of OE incidents might not be unique to OE, but an imperative to rigorously avoid deadly situations.

A fatality-free record is not proof of successful prevention

The very broad definition of OE I used, in a search for incidents across half a century in one study and over a century in another, was sufficient to elicit patterns of incidents but has nevertheless revealed few incidents. Most unsupervised boys near steep ground survive. Most groups who traverse avalanche terrain survive. Most fleets of small craft that venture on to open water (Table 43.4) emerge unscathed. Even though individuals and organisation might have accrued considerable experience of normal operations, and have a successful track record in dealing with more common, less serious incidents, most will not have experienced a fatal incident. It follows that most fatalities follow a previously fatality-free record. Experience alone is insufficient to guide fatality prevention. While serious OE incidents, particularly catastrophes, can in principle be attributed to failures to learn lessons from past incidents (Toft & Reynolds, 1994), such

Table 43.4 OE open-water small craft multiple fatalities, worldwide

Incident	#	Location	Description
Sheppey disaster 1912	9	River Thames, England	5 adults and 24 Scouts from the 2nd Walworth rowing down the River Thames from Waterloo Bridge to Leysdown, Isle of Sheppey. Cutter overturns in a violent squall. 9 Scouts die.
Big Pond Otis 1919	11	Big Pond, USA	27 campers, Springfield Boys Club, in two overloaded boats. One capsized in a squall. 11 drowned.
Balsam Lake 1926	12	Balsam Lake, Canada	1 adult and 15 campers in the middle of Balsam Lake, in a large canoe. Capsized. All clinging to canoe. Over the next 17 hours 11 boys drowned, as did the leader, who deliberately sacrificed himself.
Chazy School Picnic 1927	5	Chazy Lake, USA	Inter-class picnic for small high school. 5 students and 1 teacher on Chazy Lake in a rowing boat, caught by a sudden storm. Boat swamped. Teacher rescued unconscious, clinging to upturned boat. Children died.
Gardner Lake Tragedy 1936	12	Lake Gardner, USA	End of school year picnic at Lake Gardner, Maine. 16 children on a boat that was struck broadside by wind when it left a sheltered area, spilling the occupants into the water. 1 swam to shore, 3 were rescued. 12 drowned.
Baltic Sea 1948	23	Baltic Sea, Poland	23 Boy Scouts on the Baltic Sea, Poland, died when high waves capsized two boats.
'Wangle III' 1950	10	Off Calais, English Channel, France	Un-ballasted whaler, probably overloaded, with buoyancy tanks removed and replaced with vehicle inner tubes, attempted a return crossing of the English Channel with 8 Sea Scouts and 2 leaders. Difficult cross-sea conditions, wind against the tide. Lost at sea. 6 bodies found, 4 never recovered.
Oakville 1954	3	Oakville, Canada	4 cutters from Oakville Sea Scouts on Lake Ontario caught by a storm. Flotilla scattered. 3 cutters and crew brought to safety from 5 km offshore. Large disorganised search for the missing boat, 2 children and 1 leader found 2 bodies after several days. 1 never found.
Lake Hume 1963	7	Lake Hume, NSW, Australia	12 OB participants, 2-night canoe trip, 2nd morning. 1 canoe swamped, partly beached canoes. Resumed journey, hit by severe squall, water temp 9°C. Boats swamped. Two craft made shore, another's occupants climbed into a tree. Of 6 remaining in water, 1 survived after 4 hours in water clinging to a tree. 2 instructors arrived after the capsizes, also perished attempting rescue after assisting 2 in tree.
Timiskaming 1978	13	Lake Timiskaming, Canada	27 boys aged 11–13 and 4 leaders in 4 large canoes heading for James Bay on Lake Timiskaming, Quebec. Following wind and rough conditions. All craft capsized, 12 boys and 1 teacher died.

(continued)

Table 43.4 (continued)

Incident	#	Location	Description
Gulf of California 1978	3	Gulf of California, USA	OB unaccompanied kayaking trip off Punta Pulpito, Gulf of California, 9 students. Multiple capsize in high seas and high wind. Self-rescue failed, 6 went for help. 3 died.
Lake McNaughton 1982	6	Lake McNaughton, Canadian Rockies	29 Scouts in 5 patrols canoeing along Lake McNaughton, Canada. After 3 days wind and swells increased. 2 leaders and 4 Scouts from one patrol found floating in life jackets along the shore. Speculation that all succumbed to hypothermia while trying to empty canoes of water.
Lake Alexandrina 1987	4	Lake Alexandrina SA, Australia	11 Scouts and Venturers including 1 leader and 1 other adult, 2-night canoe trip. 2nd day hit by severe squall 1 km from land, water temp 10°C. 1 boat swamped, capsized, then others. 2 craft made it to shore, 1 survivor clung to craft for 2 hours before landing, 2 swam/waded to shore. Other 4 drowned. 2 survivors raised alarm, others rescued in the night, very cold.
Lyme Bay 1993	4	Lyme Bay England	8 novice kayakers, 2 outdoor centre staff, one a former cleaner on her first sea trip, and a teacher, on open-sea crossing in winter conditions in slalom kayaks without spray skirts. Offshore wind and tide. Group was wearing uninflated life jackets. Kayaks had insufficient buoyancy. No powerboat in support. Fleet carried out to sea in heavy swell, dispersed, some capsized, some sank. Delayed rescue. 4 teenagers died.
Camp MacDougall 2003	2	Lake Huron, Canada	9 Girl Guides in 4 aluminium canoes on Lake Huron. 1 canoe overturned, occupants taken in other canoes. Blown off course. 5 rescued, still in canoes. 4 found in water, hypothermic. 2 died.
Gulf of Mexico 2005	2	Suwannee, USA	8 children and 2 adults from the Darlington School in a mixed fleet of kayaks, canoes and motorised cataraft (pontoon boat) travelling along coast from Suwannee River. Motor cut out in deteriorating weather. 5 craft tied to the cataraft, but 1 canoe had become separated. Bodies of 2 14-year-old boys found 18 km offshore.
Southern Cross Beach 2008	3	Southern Cross Beach, South Africa	School excursion. 9 students in 4 inflatable boats (Crocs). 3 boats capsized in rough sea conditions. 6 students rescued, 3 drowned, including 1 who slipped out of life jacket when grabbed by rescue swimmer.
Præstø Fjord 2011	1 +	Præstø Fjord, Denmark	2 teachers and 13 students, aged 16–18, from Lundby Efterskole, were in a flat-bottomed dragon boat that capsized in Præstø Fjord. Water 2°C. Teacher died, 7 students were placed in artificial comas after suffering heart attacks from spending hours in the freezing water, many suffered brain damage. School and headmaster convicted of grievous bodily harm.

Source: Brookes (2014)

failures can be present on many occasions without a fatality ensuing. Longstanding successful programmes may harbour latent failures to prevent serious incidents.

Safety tends to be organised around activities, but incidents might not be activity related

Only some incidents are directly linked to an outdoor activity. The activity of skiing is causal for the on-slope deaths in Table 43.1, because skiing speed was a critical factor. Some of the deaths from falls in Table 43.2 involved organised rock climbing, but only indirectly – each such death occurred during downtime. Often, similar environmental circumstances have occasioned similar incidents involving a range of outdoor activities. Catastrophic open-water incidents in Table 43.4 involved canoes, kayaks, voyageur canoes, dragon boats, cutters and inflatables, all small craft on open water, but somewhat different activities. Avalanche incidents in Table 43.3 involved walking, snowshoeing, climbing, ski touring and alpine skiing in avalanche terrain. I have not included in the tables examples such as deaths from falling trees, or deaths on moving water in which an outdoor activity explained why the group was in an area, but otherwise was unrelated to an incident (Brookes, 2011b). If OE safety is conceptualised and organised around outdoor activities, as is sometimes the case, great care is required to ensure sufficient attention is focused on environmental hazards and all means that those hazards might be encountered. For example, a failure to sufficiently weight environmental hazards contributed to the Mangatepopo tragedy in New Zealand in which six children and a teacher drowned when caught by a flood in a gorge walk, in spite of extensive safety systems (Brookes, Corkill QC & Smith, 2009).

Weather conditions are critical, and knowable

In 70 per cent of the catastrophic incidents I considered (other than bus, ferry or aircraft incidents) weather or related conditions, such as water temperature, tides or snow conditions, were a critical factor, if not a cause. This large proportion is why approaches to OE fatality prevention must be transformed in the light of advances in weather forecasting, weather warnings and provision of information on weather-related conditions (see, for example, Silver, 2012). Incidents that at the time might arguably have been unpreventable due to uncertainties around the weather should now categorically be preventable. Incidents involving failures to locate shelter, long searches for missing groups or individuals, inability to communicate that a group is in trouble, or lack of field access to available weather information, all of which in the past came with the territory of OE, would also be mostly preventable due to cheap and accessible GPS devices and a gamut of communications devices, some of which are in everyday use. Adverse situations involving cold water (Table 43.4) or cold weather (Table 43.5) could in many cases have been retrieved had current location devices and communications been available. The pace of improvement in technology is such that use of technology to prevent fatalities probably must be reviewed at least every five years. Not all communications devices work in all geographic locations, but that is now just another consideration in choosing the safest available location.

Implications

OE fatalities must be understood in the context of changing community expectations. Youth mortality varies considerably between countries, with the highest rate almost four times the lowest in the Organisation for Economic Co-operation and Development (OECD) countries. Males in Iceland, Japan or Sweden are about twice as likely to survive childhood as males in

Table 43.5 OE adverse weather multiple fatalities, worldwide

Incident	#	Location	Description
Dachstein 1954	13	Dachstein massif, Austria	3 teachers and 10 students from the German town of Heilbronn set off from Obertraun for the Dachstein massif, against advice. Soaked with rain after 2 hours, but decided to carry on. After a massive search a body was found after 9 days. Last 2 victims found 43 days after search began. All died.
Wiesbachhorn Peak 1957	4	Wiesbachhorn Peak, Austria	Group of 11 students and a teacher from Vienna caught in a snowstorm on Wiesbachhorn Peak. 5 made their way back to a hut, 3 rescued, 3 students and the teacher died.
Old Baldy 1958	3	Madera Canyon – Mt Wrightson trail, USA	6 Scouts ages 12–16 set out to climb Mt Wrightson, Arizona, and camp overnight, against advice of Scoutmaster. 3 turned back, camped lower down. Rain overnight turned to heavy snow. Group camped lower rescued. Massive search in difficult conditions found the 3 bodies after 19 days.
Routeburn Track 1963	2	Harris Saddle, New Zealand	13 11–13 year-old children and 2 teachers walking Routeburn Track section, school excursion. Caught in blizzard. Teacher carried 1 to hut, returned to 2 left in sleeping bags. Both students died, teacher found in coma.
Four Inns 1964	3	Peak District, England	Rover Scouts' annual 'Four Inns Walk'. Forecast showers/fine but heavy rain and strong winds eventuated. 3, aged 19, 21 and 24, from two groups died. Large search for 2, last body recovered after 3 days.
Cairngorms 1971	6	Cairngorms, Scotland	6 students, 20-year-old student teacher and 18-year-old assistant on overnight walk. Caught in a blizzard overnight. Search and rescue in extremely difficult conditions. Leader and 1 student survived. 6 died about 200 m from a shelter.
Mt Hood 1986	9	Mt Hood, USA	2 adults and 11 children on a school ascent of Mt Hood in forecast poor weather. Descending in a blizzard, they built a snow cave for shelter, and lost some equipment. 2 left the group to seek help the next day. Rescuers found 3 bodies on the following day, and 2 days later found the cave. 9 died.
Mt Ruapehu 1990	6	Mt Ruapehu, New Zealand	2 instructors and 11 trainees on an Army adventure training course on Mt Ruapehu. Caught by a blizzard in snow shelters. Attempted to find emergency hut, about 400 m away, failed, could not relocate shelters. Classified report due for release in 2015. 6 recruits aged 18–23 died, hypothermia.
Antuco 2005	45	Antuco Volcano, Chile	475 poorly equipped teenage recruits on 28 km march caught in blizzard conditions. 45 died in blizzard that lasted 5 days.

Source: Brookes (2014)

New Zealand, Ireland or the USA (OECD, 2009). However, in most countries youth mortality has declined considerably from the second half of the 20th century (Viner *et al.*, 2011), increasing community expectations that youths will survive to adulthood. As cases of preventable OE deaths accumulate, and as online searches make such cases more accessible to anyone evaluating a new incident, OE practice will increasingly be expected to absorb lessons from past incidents. In wealthier countries, options for preventing many incidents have been enhanced by improvements in weather forecasting and associated data, communications and GPS location. The combined effect of these shifts is that, in many countries, OE programmes must exhibit strict aversion to any preventable fatal incident, rather than strike a balance between expected educational gains and the unlikely possibility of a tragedy.

The strict aversion standard, arguably manifest in enquiries into the Lyme Bay incident in 1993 (Table 43.4), Connaught Valley 2003 (Table 43.3) and Mangatepopo 2008 (Brookes, 2011a), is a distinct and important change to all forms of OE's social licence and logically comprises three distinct elements: (i) leaders or other decision makers must understand the nature of fatal risks in OE, which in turn requires knowledge of past incidents; (ii) decision makers must have sufficient knowledge and experience of the particular locations in which programmes are conducted to recognise potentially fatal hazards; and (iii) decisions made must exhibit strict aversion rather than weighing risks against benefits or expedience. Failure of any one of these three elements will not result inevitably in tragedy, but leaves open the possibility. Determining how such failures can occur opens debate about common practices and cognitive frameworks, which although unlikely to directly cause a serious incident, can be implicated in failures to prevent tragedy. For example:

- An assumption that normal operations and experience of common mishaps is sufficient to prevent fatalities. If anything the opposite is true, because fatality prevention requires specific, informed attention to hitherto latent possibilities.
- An educational philosophy based on personal transformation through a venture into the unknown (adventure). Fatality prevention emphasises knowing and recognising deadly hazards whenever possible, and requires local knowledge at least on the part of leaders. Valuing 'the unknown' potentially interferes with valuing local knowledge.
- Any overarching approach to risk broadly congruent with popular discourse about a soft generation. If lower-level risks such as risk of failure or discomfort are rhetorically bundled with deadly risks there is potential not to recognise specific situations that require aversion.
- An activity focus, as distinct from an environment focus. An activity focus does not rule out a deep and extensive understanding of environmental circumstances, but in practice can distract attention from hazardous situations not associated with any activity, and may generate epistemic structures which are relatively blind to environmental knowledge (Brookes, 2006).
- Competency-based approaches to staffing. While well suited to some dimensions of OE, competency schemes translate poorly from the built and engineered environments they were developed for to the specific location of any particular OE programme where knowledge, experience, and decision making can be more important than skills and procedural knowledge (Brookes, 2011a).

Concluding comments

Fatal incidents are not a distinguishing feature of OE. On the contrary, they are rare, albeit newsworthy events, related more to environmental circumstances than to OE as such. Potentially fatal circumstances form relatively narrow sets, leaving considerable scope to conduct OE programmes safely.

Fatal incidents are outlier events in OE, but nevertheless have and will continue to drive change in OE thought and practice. The light of community scrutiny shines brightly on OE in the aftermath of a tragedy. When tragedy does occur it tends to be preventable, it tends to have precedents, and it tends to bring into question not just the immediate circumstances but OE practices and purposes. Community standards for young persons' safety have shifted. Understanding of OE fatality prevention has improved. Technology has made prevention of many incidents more feasible. Deceptively simple requirements – aversion to fatal incidents, knowledge of past incidents and knowledge of the environments in which OE takes place – have potentially fundamental implications for how programmes are conceived and conducted. The OE field can expect diminishing community tolerance for programmes revealed by tragedy not to have considered those implications.

References

Allison, P., & Telford, J. (2005). Turbulent times: Outdoor education in Great Britain 1993–2003. *Australian Journal of Outdoor Education, 9*(2), 21–30.

Ashby, K. & Cassell, E. (2007). Injury in snow and ice sports. *Hazard, 66*, 1–24. Retrieved from: www.monash.edu.au/miri/research/research-areas/home-sport-and-leisure-safety/visu/hazard/haz66.pdf.

Bradford, J. (2002). From Lyme Bay to licensing. Retrieved from: www.aals.org.uk/lymebay01.html.

Brookes, A. (2006). Outdoor education safety guidelines and unfamiliar environments. A hidden curriculum? *Canadian Journal of Environmental Education, 11*, 195–206.

Brookes, A. (2011a). Preventing fatal incidents in outdoor education. Lessons learnt from the Mangatepopo tragedy. *New Zealand Journal of Outdoor Education, 2*(6), 7–32.

Brookes, A. (2011b). Research update 2010. Outdoor education fatalities in Australia. *Australian Journal of Outdoor Education, 15*(1), 37–57.

Brookes, A. (2014). Catastrophic incidents involving school or youth group camps and excursions since 1900. Paper presented at 18th National Outdoor Education Conference, Adelaide.

Brookes, A. & Holmes, P. (2014). Supervision of school and youth groups on lift-served ski slopes: A research perspective. Author abstract. *Australian Journal of Outdoor Education, 17*, 30ff.

Brookes, A., Corkill QC, B. & Smith, M. (2009). Report to Trustees of the Sir Edmund Hillary Outdoor Pursuit Centre of New Zealand. Mangatepopo Gorge incident, 15 April 2008. Turangi: OPC Trust. Copies available on request.

Cloutier, R. (2003). *Review of the Strathcona-Tweedsmuir School Outdoor Education Program.* Canada: Bhudak Consultants Ltd.

Department of Labour (2010). Review of risk management and safety in the adventure and outdoor commercial sectors in New Zealand 2009/10. Final Report. Wellington, NZ: Department of Labour.

Gulley, G. (2013). *Safety Audit Standard for Adventure Activities.* Wellington: New Zealand Ministry of Business, Innovation & Employment, pp. 1–18.

Health and Safety in Employment (Adventure Activities) Regulations (2011).

Langran, M. & Selvaraj, S. (2002). Snow sports injuries in Scotland: A case-control study. *British Journal of Sports Medicine, 36*(2), 135.

Mateparae, J. (2011). Health and Safety in Employment (Adventure Activities) Regulations. SR 2011/367. New Zealand Governor General in Council. Wellington. Retrieved from: www.legislation.govt.nz/regulation/public/2011/0367/latest/DLM3961552.html.

OECD (2009). *Doing Better for Children.* OECD Publishing.

Silver, N. (2012). *The Signal and the Noise: Why So Many Predictions Fail – but Some Don't.* Kindle Edition.

Toft, B. & Reynolds, S. (1994). *Learning from Disasters.* Oxford: Butterworth-Heinemann.

Tough, S. & Butt, J. (1993). A review of fatal injuries associated with downhill skiing. *American Journal of Forensic Medicine and Pathology, 14*(1), 12.

Viner, R.M., Coffey, C., Mathers, C., Bloem, P., Costello, A., Santelli, J. *et al.* (2011). 50-year mortality trends in children and young people: A study of 50 low-income, middle-income, and high-income countries. *The Lancet, 377*(9772), 1162–1174.

44

Challenges in adventure sports coaching

Loel Collins and Dave Collins

University of Central Lancashire

This chapter sets out to explore current knowledge regarding professional practice in an emerging sub-group of outdoor professionals, namely the adventure sports coach (ASC). This chapter will unearth the domain-specific mechanisms, challenges, context and dynamics of the Professional Judgement and Decision Making (PJDM) process in high-level ASCing. The literature-based findings of a series of previous positional and empirical papers (Collins & Collins, 2012, 2013, 2014; Collins, Collins & Grecic 2014) are summarised and implications considered. We have adopted an unconventional structure, on the assumption that readers will access these papers as providing the substance to our argument.

Our previous work: the basis for this chapter

Our previous studies, as listed above, utilised a thematic analysis to provide an in-depth investigation of the PJDM themes that occurred over a series of sessions in a group of ASCs. Based on data, interviews and video (cf. Rosenstein, 2002; Lyle, 2003; Muir & Beswick, 2007), we considered that the complexity of any coaching process lies in the judgements and decisions made by the coach pre, during and post activity. The video was used to stimulate the interview process and deepen the content and richness of the resultant data (cf. Cohen & Manion, 1994).

What is the adventure sports coach?

The ASC role has emerged in response to increased demand for performance development in AS. Collins and Collins (2012) conceptualise ASCing as an interacting sub-group of traditional coaching practice *and* of outdoor education. The ASC shares skills with coaching, guiding and educational colleagues; a similar if refined PJDM process (Collins & Collins, 2013) but, notably, an identifiably different epistemological framework (Collins et al., 2014) that is demonstrated in practice through a unique epistemological decision-making chain. The PJDM processes and epistemology serve to synergise those skills shared across outdoor education and coaching. Objective-wise, ASCing focuses on the individualised development of the skills (motor and cognitive) that enable independent effective participation in AS. Reflecting the average coach's personal construct of adventure, however, the actual focus often lies in the promotion and enablement of skilful and independent participation rather than high-level performance per se; another key difference to traditional sports coaching.

The emergent field of ASCing encompasses a multiplicity of combined roles and diversity of function that generates high cognitive loads in the coaching process. The ASC is unique in drawing on such a wide combination of skills, spanning areas such as risk management, risk–benefit exploitation, personal ability, pedagogic skills, leadership skills and domain-specific declarative knowledge in order to fulfil this complex and challenging role. The synergy of these skills and knowledge is facilitated via a refined PJDM (Collins & Collins, 2013) process that is centralised on a sophisticated epistemological belief (Collins et al., 2014) and an implicit but omnipresent attention to the management and implication of risk within the coaching process.

By necessity, but also frequently by design, the resulting coaching process is flexible and adaptive. The ASC encounters three highly variable factors that all interrelate – namely the environment, the individual and the task (Davids, Button & Bennett, 2008) – which must continuously be 'dynamically blended' to optimise the experience for the client. Based on a refined observation and questioning process, the ASC compares the performance/behaviour of the student against a mental model for the performance and potential development of each individual in the client group. The myriad of possibilities, evolving from the many possible permutations of environment, task and individual, drive the need for adaptability, flexibility and creativity in the coaching process.

There are other, intrapersonal factors that impact on the blending process. Factors such as fatigue, for example, are common in all sports but, additionally in outdoor education, the impact of tiredness on, say, perceptions of risk is harder to anticipate and accommodate in the ASCing process. A student may confidently be able to paddle and learn in a grade-three rapid if it has a large pool at its end. In contrast, however, a continuous stretch of grade three can be 'too much' for those students who need pauses in which to mentally 'regroup'. Conversely, another student in the same group will find the opposite and wants as much 'stimulation' as possible. A further complication emerges that this may alter over the duration of the session, either due to skill development or over-stimulation. Accordingly, it seems sensible to consider that creativity is required to accommodate new strategies to address new challenges within the coaching process *and* adaptability and flexibility to enable the utilisation of existing coaching 'tools' to address new challenges.

Risk utilisation within adventure sports coaching practice

Risk Benefit Analysis (RBA) (Collins & Collins, 2013) emerges as one process in which risk utilisation is aligned with the epistemological beliefs (Collins et al., 2014) and pedagogy of the ASC. The fundamental question underpinning this conundrum is 'Does the benefit to the student outweigh the risks in a potential course of action?' – an issue that lies at the heart of the PJDM process for the ASC. The explicit focus on benefit in relation to risk characterises this element of the broader PJDM process. In this respect, and significantly, risk is utilised as an element of the coaching process rather than being something to minimise. The levels of risk are managed, in part, by manipulation of the physical and learning environment. For example, different students may be given different lines in a particular rapid, in a deliberate attempt to vary levels of risk for that student and in this way proactively managing the arousal level of the performer. Clearly, however, simply increasing (or decreasing) the level of risk does not automatically equate to better learning (Wolf & Samdahl, 2005): consequently the PJDM focus is on maintaining a suitable learning context and level of arousal, rather than simply increasing the risk as performance improves. In particular, this interaction with the context/environment appears crucial in the PJDM process.

RBA operates at three levels within the PJDM process. First, in relation to risk management, a construct that is well researched (cf. McCammon, 2004; Ewert, Shellman & Glenn, 2006); second, in relation to the perception of benefit, as highlighted by Ball and Ball-King (2013); and, third, the interaction between risk and benefit itself, as proposed in Collins (2014). The result of overlooking the benefit to a particular action leads to user recommendations and actions being driven by a desire to minimise rather than to utilise risk as a pedagogic tool within the ASCing process. This action, in the process, loses contextual relevance and fails to develop the independent and self-controlled performance desired (Collins et al., 2014). Misjudging the potential benefit of a course of action clearly undermines the entire RBA process and is, in itself, a decision-making trap.

Reflection in relation to risk utilisation

Critically, this ability to recognise the short-, mid- and long-term benefits of a course of action relies on an expertise in decision making – in particular, the 'in and on action' reflective process (Schön, 1983, 1987) that facilitates the adaptability and flexibility required to respond to environmental and individual needs. Pertinently, Schön's original definitions (1983) and later modification (1987) have been described as lacking clarity (Court 1988; Moon 1999). Such issues are of doubtful relevance to the ASC role, however. Clearly, 'thinking on our feet' (Schön, 1983) appears part of the ASC's coaching practice in 'reflecting on the phenomenon before him' (Schön, 1983, p. 68). This is 'in context' and, in this respect, reflects the (1987) notions of 'time outs' from the 'action present', a condition that is clearly recognisable in ASCing and perhaps better suits the on action/in context conceptualisation.

Extending the application of Schön's original conceptualisations, both Killion and Todenem (1991) and York-barr, Sommers, Ghere and Montie (2001) recognise a need to create time for reflection 'in action'. Both the need for a pause and space are clearly recognisable in ASCing and reflect the extended nature of the coaching interaction and the highly dynamic, three-way environment, student and task interaction that creates a cognitive and practically 'congested' coaching environment. So, notwithstanding the criticism of Schön's definitions (1983, 1987), authenticity, plus breadth and depth of both experience and reflective skills, all contribute to the coach's ability to adapt in response to the individual student, environmental and combined constraints of student in that environment (a continual auditing process).

Of course, the decision-making process is clearly susceptible to some shortcomings. The heuristic traps identified by McCammon (2001, 2004) and Cox (2007), and the procedural traps (highlighted above) are both misinterpretations of the factors that influence a given decision. Notably, however, these traps (e.g. assuming a slope is safe to ski because others have done so or getting on a river when it is higher than expected because you've promised the group) are not confined to heuristic decision making and can be considered in any naturalistic decision-making process (cf. recognition primed and naturalistic decision making (Kahneman, 2011)). For example, patterns of particular conditions on the sea, for example wind against tide, will not produce the same sea conditions two weeks apart because the tide will be of a different size and the underlying sea state (swell, history and forecast) is different: accordingly, an assumption based on apparently the same conditions fails by assumption and misinterpretation of the significance of the tide in this case. These traps are further exacerbated by shortcomings in authenticity, breadth and depth of experience or reflective ability by the ASC and by institutional traps such as timetable or programme requirements that reduce potential for flexibility and adaptability.

The development of suitable and effective PJDM skills allows the maximisation of experience and so helps to avoid these traps. However, it does seem unlikely that such an explicit aspect of the risk management process could otherwise be overlooked. Learning from the experience of decision making becomes as significant to the ASC as learning and understanding the effectiveness of the coaching process.

Meta-skills, adaptability, reflectivity and flexibility

Beyond the utilisation of risk within the coaching process, 'in and on action' reflection (Schön, 1983, 1987) provides the mechanism for flexible and adaptive practice, coach development and pedagogic development via PJDM. The epistemological position held by the ASCs, together with the dynamic environment, obliges the ASC to operate in an adaptive and flexible way. An aspect of this process will be the construction of new usable schemas via meta-cognitive processes.

Schemas are stable, organised patterns of thought that the individual develops over time and experience: these patterns of thought or behaviour include the relationships between the components in complex situations such as coaching; these are known as interactional schema. The schemas act as a mental structure, a framework, for managing experiences and the knowledge that is generated from them. An individuals' awareness of these schema becomes significant as they also become models against which new information is referenced. Schemas help in comprehending experience and adapting to the rapidly changing environments associated with AS. Individuals can develop schemas quickly in situations that do not require complex thought. However, developing new schema that challenge existing ones presents greater challenges for the ASC and student – for example, placing a kayak on edge to assist turning: a sea kayak may be placed on an outside edge to turn if the water has no eddy line, however when crossing an eddy line the sea kayak will be edged to the inside of the turn. Whichever technique is learned first challenges the schemas developed in the different second context. If the context is not understood the schemas is challenged even more; however, when the context is part of the process (the interactional schemas) the edging technique can be used differently.

The ASC is beset with clearly different demands to his/her traditional sporting colleagues and fellow outdoor professionals, although the ASC does share some technical knowledge with his/her guiding and teaching colleagues. Crucially, however, the uniqueness of the ASC lies in the complexity of the interactional relationship between these shared and discrete components. In short, it is not so much the different skills required, but how those skills and other factors interact.

As mentioned earlier, schema develop to reflect the relationship between components in a process; in the case of AS, factors such as anxiety and arousal levels and, significantly, the physical environment. These interactional schema may provide a pragmatic explanation in which the interaction of the components of ASCing can be conceived. Interactional schema for coaching are cognitive structures that utilise both the knowledge schema (Tannen & Wallat, 1987) required for the face-to-face, interpersonal coaching encounters and an understanding of the interactional framing/context (Tannen & Wallat) in which those knowledge schema are applied. In this respect it provides the link between environment and coaching practice, and may provide a mechanism to link the relationships between the constraints in constraints-led theories of skills acquisition (Davids et al., 2008). The constantly changing practice (Collins & Kusch, 1998) of ASCing links this notion with concepts of both interactive expertise (Collins & Evan, 2002) and adaptive expertise (Hatano & Inagaki, 1986).

A schema utilised to assist a student running a rapid, for example – 'head towards this rock for the first half of the rapid and this tree for the second' – may work only in the context of small, narrow, low-volume whitewater rivers in which the banks are visible. In a high-volume, wide-river context in which the banks are not clearly visible or details are indistinct (heavily vegetated or obscured by large water features), such a schema now carries clear weaknesses. To proactively address these issues a more suitable initial schema would teach and utilise water features as markers; thus, 'enter the rapid, down the "V", facing river left, on the third wave crest turn right to paddle across the rapid to the downstream "V" on river right'. This schema would work on narrow, steep and low-volume rivers as well as the later high-volume, wide-river challenges that are appropriate progressions. Clearly the initial choice or ineffective communication of an unsuitable schema would result in the student getting lost in the rapid or, in the longer term, having to learn an entirely new set. In addition this water-based, interactional schema (volume, wave size and visibility of bank) could be transferred to overfalls (tidal rapids) in a sea kayak, which by definition have massive volume (waves), a single bank and are possibly offshore.

Notably, if the interaction can be made explicit, both the knowledge schema and interactional framework can be reflected and developed throughout the development of coaching skills. In practical terms, therefore, the interactional and knowledge schemas need to be developed alongside each other, with the interactional schema, somewhat counterintuitively and against current common practice, having primacy. This is because, once established, the interactional schema allows the knowledge schemas to be developed in relation to one another *and* to the context. As an example, a widely used approach in whitewater coaching is to consider all manoeuvres in terms of speed and angle to the current (Collins, 2002). This is a clear example of an interactional schema in which the relationship between the knowledge of how to generate, maintain and control speed and angle are dependent on the desired outcome (task), environment and, of course, the individual's capacity to perform those tasks. Depending on the result desired and the speed and current vector, boat speed and angle are adjusted to achieve the desired result. The student requires the knowledge schemas to generate and maintain speed and angle, and recognise the environmental constraints (cf. the affordances construct; Davids *et al.*, 2008). This is best considered against the analogy of mixing (interactional schema) of primary colours (the elements of basic knowledge or knowledge schema essential to the role) to create an infinite palette of colour, so representing a very broad range of approaches for use by the ASC. Recognition of a need for a wide spectrum of colours and the potential need to create new colours in response to the hyper dynamic nature of ASC creates a need for the interactional schema to be taught from the outset of the coaching process. In contrast, one can think of 'recipe coaching', which offers a more limited repertoire; the routine and pre-set combination of primary colours to produce a simple range of secondary colours; clearly strictly still a range of interactional schema, but much more limited.

The hyper-dynamic environments of ASCing require the full rainbow palette to respond to student, environment and task needs effectively, enabling the coach's skills to be as adaptive and flexible as possible. This contrasts against the routine delivery that produces a fixed premeditated response that only *may* match the challenges of the situation, such as the river example earlier. Of course, the use of a pre-set, smaller palette is easier to develop, and requires much less thought from the practitioner. In fact, this simplicity may account for the dominance of the limited, recipe approach to training and assessment. The question remains, however, what would an interactional schema 'look like' for an ASC, and this is certainly worthy of further empirical study.

A spectrum of solutions

Irrespective of the available palette, the ASC must cope with a variety of challenges. When encountering novel and poorly defined challenges, the ASC reconceptualises the challenges to align very broadly with a range of known strategies and approaches. These strategies are reconfigured, utilising meta-cognitive skills to generate new schema in order to address the novel problem. Font, Bolite and Acevedo (2010) proposed that this metaphoric thinking can enable coaches to anticipate, solve and address the novel problems that are encountered in the dynamic environment. The ability to operationalise the metaphoric thought is manifest in apparently creative, innovative and intuitive solutions to problems that may be better reconsidered as expert practice in broader coaching terms. The ASC is able to recognise and utilise links within the process, and these connections act as short cuts in the PJDM process, making it appear fast, intuitive and adaptive. Alignment with concepts of adaptive expertise (see Hatano & Ingaki, 1986) cannot be ignored on this basis.

By utilising meta-strategies to process the flow of information in each new/novel situation, this meta-skilfulness operates within a constant auditing cycle. These important meta-processes are essential elements of high-level practice; however, they cannot always be articulated by the ASC. Clearly, therefore, this knowledge is, at least in part, tacit and is a constituent of the intuitive element of the PJDM processes in high-level coaches (cf. Nash & Collins, 2006).

Undoubtedly, however, meta-cognition is important because it enables the active cognitive processing that is essential for deeper learning and, in the ASCing case, application and construction of useable knowledge. Meta-cognition enables the ASC to contextualise the knowledge provided in training, further optimising experience between training and certification. This, in turn, develops the interactional schema across elements of the coaching process. The interactional schema allow the PJDM processes to link episodic events with reality, potentially even recognising the 'conditions' that create those short cuts. These links and adaptive capacity are facilitated by the meta-cognitive skills that characterise the aforementioned adaptive expertise and therefore need to be generated in effective ASCs.

Implications for the education of adventure sports coaches

Changes in the use of and potential meaning of the term adventure (cf. commodification and 'sportification' process – Crum, 1991; Loynes, 1998; Brown, 2000) place new demands on the training and practices of the ASCs. Notably, however, a fundamental decision regarding the nature of good coaching and practice in ASCing has to be made if alignment between high-level practice, training of ASCs and training agencies is to be achieved. Establishing an epistemological position that reflects the unique elements of adventure, while also being inclusive of broader concepts of good coaching, may require some soul searching by the awarding bodies, while engagement with the experts in the field will avoid the potential epistemological void between practice, research and training. Successful alignments between ASCs, ASC educators and certifying authorities would be the start of a cohesive recruitment, training and accreditation process that meets the growing demand for ASCs.

In concert with this, consideration must be given to the epistemological and pedagogic underpinning of the ASC education process itself. An epistemological gap/void (Collins, 2012) between high-level practice and the content of training courses appears inevitable and begs the question, what is the educative process aiming to achieve? The ASCs examined in these studies (Collins & Collins, 2012, 2013, 2014) clearly operate as autonomous professionals (Paice, 2001) and have activity-specific and pedagogic skills to enable a practical and educational autonomy to operate in a range of environments and with a range of different students. The commitment to an individual's development is the focal point of the ASC's epistemological position and EC. The small Community of Practice (CoP) apparent between ASCs encourages collaboration with fellow professionals, exchange of approaches, and a clear drive for self-directed development that maintains a currency and validity in practice. Notably, the ASCs are self-regulated via their intrinsic motivations, in and on action reflective practices, and CoP involvement. However, the imposition of external regulation and accreditation (e.g. United Kingdom Coaching Certificate – UKCC), the commodification of adventure (Loynes, 1998; Brown, 2000) and the potential sportification of AS (Crum, 1991) make differing demands on the ASC education process. Specifically, the combination of regulation, commodification and sportification issues challenges long-held concepts of autonomy, independence, self-governance and ethics in practice that are a core part of AS. In short, personal ethics and values held within the CoP have been replaced (or at least challenged) by external rules, regulation and control from domains outside adventure. These accrediting bodies hold epistemological views that differ from the epistemological positions, political positions and models of practice to those within ASCing.

The assumption of transferability of pan-sport coaching theories may well be misplaced given the lack of attention to the process of transferability, especially given the extent to which the environment, tasks and motivation of the individuals involved vary between domains. More significantly, contextualising the application of those theories and assuming transferability and relevance will become a crucial aspect of ASC education, with potential weakness in relaying ad hoc translation by the ASC. The plethora of theory in practice-focused papers, books and articles is, by nature, contextual. It follows that the adventure context for practice must be explicitly addressed and itself generates a demand for further contextual investigation into ASC practice.

In the pursuit of accrediting practitioners via qualification routes that are generic, without considering the PJDM skills that are used to contextualise general theories or, even worse, relying on recontextualised theories in other domains, the potential for producing a truly autonomous professional becomes a matter of chance. Clearly, the ASC will require the meta-cognition and PJDM skills to develop the autonomy required for safe and appropriate operation in challenging environments. Stemming from this are two more fundamental needs: first, a reconsideration of the definition of expertise in dynamic fields such as education, rescue, military, medical coaching and, of course ASC; second, the outcome of the coach education process, namely to what extent is an ASC an autonomous professional or an accountable practitioner?

Conclusion

Pending further investigation, findings may be transferable to other domains of outdoor education and coaching practice. High-level ASCs have emerged as autonomous professionals who have a clear epistemological stance that is reflected in their practice; namely, a focus on the student's development, a desire for continual professional development and the emergence of a distinct sub-group that overlaps both outdoor education and coaching domains.

Significantly, however, adjustment to ASC education and training will be required if education is to address these needs. Pivotal to that is the generation of better thinkers in context, namely an adoption of PJDM as a central point for ASC practice. Clearly, as an emergent group of highly skilled practitioners, the practice of ASCing warrants further investigation and investment, as do the pedagogic approaches that may be applied to develop the adaptive expertise required for high-level practice.

References

Ball, D. & Ball-King, L. (2013). Safety management and public places: Restoring balance. *Risk Analysis, 3*, 763–771.

Brown, H. (2000). Passengers, participants, partners and practitioners. Working with risk to empower groups. *Horizons, 12*, 37–39. Retrieved from: www.outdoor-learning.org/.

Cohen, L. & Manion, L. (1994). *Research Methods in Education* (4th edn). London: Routledge.

Collins, H. (2012). Three dimensions of expertise. *Phenomenology and Cognitive Sciences, 12*, 253–273.

Collins, H.M. & Evans, R.J. (2002). The third wave of science studies: Studies of expertise and experience. *Social Studies of Sciences, 32*(2), 235–296.

Collins, H.M. & Kusch, M. (1998). *The Shape of Actions: What Humans and Machines Can Do*. Cambridge, MA: MIT Press.

Collins, L. (2002). *Top Tips for Coaches: Over 300 Top Tips and Handy Hints for Canoe and Kayak Coaches*. Plas y Brenin, Wales: National Mountain Centre.

Collins, L. (2014). Professional judgement and decision making in high level adventure sports coaches. Doctoral thesis, University of Centre Lancashire.

Collins, L. & Collins, D. (2012). Contextualising the adventure sport coach. *Journal of Adventure Education and Outdoor Learning, 12*, 81–93.

Collins, L. & Collins, D. (2013). Decision-making and risk management in adventure sports coaching. *Quest, 65*, 72–82.

Collins, L. & Collins, D. (2014). Integration of reflective practice as a component of professional judgement and decision making in high level adventure sports coaching practice. *Journal of Sports Science, 33*(6), 622–633.

Collins, L., Collins, D. & Grecic, D. (2014). The epistemological chain in high level adventure sports coaches. *Journal of Adventure Education and Outdoor Learning*. Manuscript submitted for publication.

Court, D. (1988). 'Reflection-in-action': Some definitional problems. In P.P. Grimmlett & G.L. Erickson (Eds.) *Reflection in Teacher Education* (pp. 143–146). New York: Teachers College Press.

Cox, L.A. (2007) Does concern-driven risk management provide a viable alternative to QRA. *Risk Analysis, 27*(10), 27–43.

Crum, B.J. (1991). 'Sportification' of Society and internal sports differentiation. *Spel en Sport, 1*, 2–7.

Davids, K., Button, C. & Bennett, S. (2008). *Dynamics of Skill Acquisition: A Constraints Led Approach*. Champaign, IL: Human Kinetics.

Ewert, A., Shellman, A. & Glenn, L. (2006). Instructor traps: What they are and how they impact decision making and judgement. Paper presented at Wilderness Risk Management Conference Proceedings, Killington, VT, October.

Font, V., Bolite, J. & Acevedo, J. (2010). Metaphors in mathematics classrooms: Analysing the dynamic process of teaching and learning of graph functions. *Educational Studies in Mathematics, 75*, 131–152.

Hatano, G. & Inagaki, K. (1986). Two courses of expertise. *Child Development and Education in Japan*, 262–272.

Kahnerman, D. (2011). *Thinking Fast and Slow*. London: Penguin.

Killion, J. & Todenem, G. (1991). A process for personal theory building. *Educational Leadership, 48*(6), 14–16.

Loynes, C. (1998). Adventure in a bun. *Journal of Experiential Education, 21*(1), 35–39.

Lyle, J. (2003). Stimulated recall: A report on its use in naturalistic research. *British Educational Research Journal, 29*, 861–878.

McCammon, I. (2001). Decision making for wilderness leaders: Strategies, traps and teaching methods. *Proceedings of Wilderness Risk Managers Conference*, Lake Geneva, WI, 16–29.

McCammon, I. (2004). Heuristic traps in recreational avalanche accidents: Evidence and implications. *Avalanche News, 68*(1), 42–50.

Moon, J. (1999) *A Handbook of Reflective and Experiential Learning: Theory and Practice*. London: Routledge.

Muir, T. & Beswick, K. (2007). Stimulating reflection on practice: Using the supportive classroom reflection process. *Mathematics Teacher Education and Development, 8*, 74–93. Retrieved from: www.merga.net.au/node/42.

Nash, C. & Collins, D. (2006). Tacit knowledge in expert coaching: Science or art? *Quest, 58*, 465–477.

Paice, E. (2001). Professional autonomy in professionals. CUBA Conference, University of London, September.

Rosenstein, B. (2002). Video use in social science research and program evaluation. *International Journal of Qualitative Methods, 1*(3), 22–43. Retrieved from: www.ualberta.ca/~ijqm.

Schön, D. (1983). *The Reflective Practitioner: How Professionals Think in Action*. Aldershot, UK: Ashgate.

Schön, D. (1987) *Educating the Reflective Practitioner*. San Francisco, CA: Jossey-Bass.

Tannen, D. & Wallat, C. (1987). Interactive frames and knowledge schemas interaction: Examples from medical examinations/interviews. *Social Psychologist Quarterly, 50*(2), 205–216.

Wolf, B. & Samdahl, D. (2005). Challenging assumptions: Examining fundamental beliefs that shape challenge course programming and research. *Journal of Experiential Education, 28*, 25–43.

York-barr, J., Sommers, W.A., Ghere, G.S. & Montie, J. (2001). *Reflective Practice to Improve Schools: An Action Guide for Educators*. Thousand Oaks, CA: Corwin.

45

Adventure tourism

Paul Beedie

University of Bedford

In his recent book concerning walking, climbing and the social construction of wild outdoor places, Macfarlane (2012, p. 323) suggests that one of modernity's enduring tensions is between displacement and mobility on the one hand and dwelling and belonging on the other: 'with the former becoming ubiquitous and the latter becoming lost (if it ever had been possible) and reconfigured as nostalgia'. This tension goes to the essence of tourism, which is, by definition, concerned with (temporary) displacement and seeking out alternative experiences. By touching on the 'other' through travel, particularly when the ambition of the journey is to engage with an outdoor experience, people are seeking a reconnection to place in keeping with the Romantic aspiration of locating a 'real' self through being in wild places (Solnit, 2001). If correct, this way of thinking helps understand the rise of adventure tourism. At one level adventure tourism is an oxymoron as 'adventure' is defined as uncertainty of outcome and 'tourism' as a systematic organisation of people's leisure time. But at another level, perhaps the desire for travel, encounters with novel and new cultures and places together with a human proclivity to feel safe, comfortable and 'anchored' in some way does make sense because this is what adventure tourism is about.

Adventure tourism has emerged for lots of reasons, notably: (i) the safety of everyday life makes engaging risk attractive; (ii) it has been suggested (Anderson, 1970; Mortlock, 1984) that humans have an exploratory instinct; and (iii) outdoor places provide an escapist option that creates a feeling of slowness and control as an antidote to the intensity and high speed of modern times. Simmel suggests: 'the adventure is a particular form in which fundamental categories of life are synthesised. Another such synthesis it achieves is that between the categories of activity and passivity, between what we conquer and what is given to us' (Simmel, 1911, in Frisby & Featherstone, 1997, p. 225). Among the adventure tourism themes to emerge in this chapter is the idea that activity is central but adventure experience is a social phenomenon, operating social rules that determine status: in adventure recreation status is earned through effort and achievement based on skills, judgement and determination but in adventure tourism, many of these virtues – which Simmel acknowledged are central to the experience – are compromised by the related processes of rationalisation and business productivity. Habermas (1962) explained this fundamental modern tension as the 'system world' of commerce and institutions infiltrating the 'life world' of the creative and cultural sphere. Loynes (2013 p. 137) argues that outdoor

Paul Beedie

adventure is increasingly controlled by commercial agendas that change activities and places, and adds: 'it is easy to slip into calling it an industry, which normalises uncritically what is only a recent colonisation'.

Kane (2012) reminds us that adventure tourism is built on the foundations of mythic journeys and famous first ascents – mostly of Western adventurers exploring, mapping and in many ways exploiting other cultures and place – and these are discursively anchored in a developed world perspective that connects to the attractiveness of risk activities and our curiosity about exploring outdoor places. Despite attempts to reconcile sustainability of the places we want to explore, culture creates iconic foci for adventure, which enhances the symbolic capital attached to such places and makes these more desirable locations to visit; the tourist infrastructure usually follows, as illustrated by the development of Namche Bazaar in Nepal as the stepping off point for a visit to and/or an ascent of Mt Everest – hotels, heated guest houses, internet connectivity and helicopter landing sites can all be found there today (Houston, 2006).

This example indicates that, despite the rhetoric of eco-tourism and its implicit agendas of authenticity and sustainability, these two ambitions are hugely difficult to achieve. Even when the physical activities of tourists are regulated and controlled there are still the carbon costs of flying from the developed world to the wilderness. The developed world perspective 'sees' the natural world as an adventure playground: in keeping with popular ideology, cliffs are places to climb and a gorge is a potential whitewater rafting descent. In this respect the 'seeing' is ideologically a mirror of the conditions of modernity and thus conquest, control and development remain the dominant ethos despite the ambition to use adventure tourism to 'slow down', to 'be at one with nature' and to locate an authentic self through active holiday choices.

Adventure tourism as a field of study

Adventure tourism is growing as an area of academic interest. Christiansen (1990) drew attention to what he called GRAMPIES – 'Growing Rich And Monied People In Excellent State'. He pointed to a healthy and ageing population (predominantly from the developed world) in good health, who projected their (educated, middle-class) values into their lifestyle choices and who understood that the accumulation of symbolic capital (visiting key places, climbing famous mountains, etc.) and its transfer into cultural and social capital was at least as effective as the accumulation of material possessions in demonstrations of status in the framework of conspicuous consumption. Additionally, opportunities to be active were recognised as important elements of healthy lifestyle choices. All this was happening at a time when travel opportunities (such as the emergence of budget airlines) were both diversifying and becoming more accessible to ordinary people, as well as greater levels of affluence.

However, as Swarbrooke, Beard, Leckie and Pomfret (2003) and others have shown, adventure tourism is not the exclusive domain of the educated, wealthy and middle aged. All ages are represented, but information concerning participants is limited and its access is complicated by the range of adventure tourism products available. Much of the existing theorising about adventure uses the (overly simplistic) model of 'hard' (e.g. ice climbing) and 'soft' (e.g. bird watching) adventure. However, there are several critical dimensions to the use of such a model and a brief mention of two is apposite. First, despite an assumption that 'risky' adventure might be the preserve of the young and thrusting, the picture is far from straightforward when octogenarians take on freefall parachuting and other adrenaline-rush activities, while young men and women in their twenties regularly sign up for the more sedate and 'deep immersion' activities such as wilderness trekking (Lintern, 2013); the 'categories' are therefore far from clear-cut (Beedie, 2003). Second, the age/gender/ethnicity patterns of participation have moved on since

464

Christiansen's analysis (Pike & Weinstock, 2013). Gender, for example, is a focus critique for Logan (2006) in her deconstruction of mountaineering dynamics on Aconcagua: 'The subversive nature of women's presence is stabilised by rendering them invisible, either by denying them access to high profile positions in the [adventure tourism] industry's infrastructure or by restricting them to traditional feminine work spaces' (Logan, 2006, p. 168). The adventure domain remains complex and contested.

The 'market' for activity holidays taps a deeply rooted need to feel secure (grounded, belonging to place) at the same time as a capacity to enjoy a sense of freedom and adventure. Whatever choices an individual makes, there are risks involved. The notion of 'adventure' has occupied debate throughout history. Simmel (1911, in Frisby & Featherstone, 1997, p. 222) sees adventure as connected to but detachable from everyday life: 'a foreign body in our existence which is yet somehow connected with the centre; the outside, if only by a long and unfamiliar detour, is formally an aspect of the inside'. Moreover, as articulated in his essay 'The Alpine journey' (Simmel, 1911, in Frisby & Featherstone, 1997, p. 219), he anticipated a diminishing return for adventurers commensurate with the infrastructure developments in the Alps (e.g. 'the railway line up the Eiger'), arguing for the educational experience of mountain activities when he says such facilitation: 'like all social averages this depresses those disposed to the higher and finer values without elevating those at the base to the same degree' (p. 219). Individual endeavour through physical effort does involve taking risks.

According to Lipscombe (2007) nothing in our lives is risk free, but to reduce risk in an adventure activity is to diminish the values central to the activity: 'The paradoxical relationship between adventure ideology and adventure practice becomes a concern when the element of adventure ceases to be the powerful learning tool it is because it has been made so safe so as to avoid possible litigation, it lacks the spontaneity, the stress and the hard earned achievements of genuine adventure' (Lipscombe, 2007, p. 13). Risk is connected to the essence of the adventure experience and has been explored using the concept of 'edgework' (Lyng, 2004). Lyng developed Mead's (1962) concepts of 'I' as the self and 'me' as the mediating voice of society that directs the spontaneous actions of the 'I'. For many people work is routinised and emotionally flat; Lyng argues that 'edgework' activities silence the 'me', and the 'I' has to respond to the activity challenge. 'What is left in place of these elements is a residual, "acting" self that responds without reflective consciousness. Thus risk takers describe their experience at the edge as self actualising or self determining, authentically real and creatively satisfying' (Lyng, 2004, p. 362). The key idea of exploring the 'boundary between chaos and order' (Laurendeau, 2006) works for individuals exploring the limits of their bodies, minds and adventure technologies (parachute, bike, kayak, etc.) as an adventure recreation choice, but becomes problematic when captured by a business selling adventure products.

There is inevitability that adventure tourism has developed risk management frameworks because of the need for tour operators, agencies and guides to protect themselves from what could go wrong when individuals make decisions about taking part in adventure activities. When people seek excitement they put themselves in a 'protective frame', which allows participants to come close to the metaphorical edge but not to fall into misadventure (Mortlock, 1984). This frame is built through accumulations of skill, training, preparation and appropriate equipment – it is evidenced, for example, in the traditional approach to mountaineering via many years of apprenticeship (Beedie, 2003). A core and fundamental issue in adventure tourism is that people with little or no practical experience of the risk activity they are choosing to engage with may believe, and be led to believe by popular ideology, they are operating in a protective frame when they are not. Krakauer's (1997) account of the tragedy on Mt Everest in 1996 when eight climbers, including guides, died in a storm high on the mountain on 9 May

465

is just one example of a tragedy catalyst for questions on the theme of 'Should they have been there?'

This key issue is where tourism and adventure tourism, which in terms of organisational mechanisms, temporary spatial and temporal displacement and aspirations for intrinsic and extrinsic reward are conceptually similar, can be seen as separate. Cloke and Perkins (1998, p. 189) draw attention to the experiential dimension of adventure tourism: 'active recreation participation . . . demands new metaphors based more on being, doing, touching *and* seeing, rather than just seeing'. This is essentially the difference between the tourist 'gaze' and the doing and performing of activity, however adventure activity remains an ambivalent term because in 'edgework' the locus of control is with the activist, in adventure tourism it is more likely to reside with the guide or instructor.

Despite the aspiration of many of us to live more 'slowly', many people who buy adventure tourism packages are money rich but time poor. As the market has grown so have the possibilities for diversification and geographical expansion; however, this is not without its issues. The following will develop three interconnected themes: identity, commodification and consumption. Underpinning these themes is the foundational concept of risk management. As Varley (2006) has shown through his adventure activity continuum, certain soft adventure activities are relatively easy to package and sell to tourists (e.g. wildlife safaris) because exposure to risk is controlled and the tourist is essentially passive as the experience is managed by guides. However, as the adventure (uncertainty) increases – for example, in making first ascents of mountains in remote regions – the 'product' becomes less saleable: 'when the industry and its expert instructors has control there is a trend towards less real risk and more perceived risk' (Beedie, 2013, p. 219).

Identity

One of the key elements of the modern world is identity (Jenkins, 1996; Pike & Weinstock, 2013); this essential concern derives its power from a ubiquitous desire to know who we are and what our place in the world is. Identity is becoming less stable as our lives accelerate and the possibilities for the identities we might construct become both multiple and more ephemeral (Ramsay, 2014). Adventure tourism has emerged as a 'location' that provides connections from the past to the present, and in doing so allows individuals to construct a sense of identity through a perceived proximity to famous adventurous explorers from history (Lindstrom, 2006). Anderson (1970) argues that individuals do this because many have an adventure instinct, which broadly connects exploration and survival. His tautological argument does not adequately encompass the potential accumulation of capital (Bourdieu, 1993) that derives from repeating historical adventure journeys and that makes a significant contribution to identity construction. What may be learned from history and the iconic images and rhetoric that surround adventure 'firsts' creates stories that in turn may shape people's personal ambitions. Humberstone (2009), drawing on the work of Brown (2000), suggests people use adventure as 'aesthetic signs' in identity construction and that when people are only 'participants' or 'passengers' in an activity, as opposed to 'partners' or 'practitioners', their dependence on guided expertise makes the construction of identity more shallow and inauthentic. However, the variety of activities and range of potential interactions between client and guide make the model less straightforward than it might seem. Adventures thus have a temporal and a spatial dimension but, crucially, they generate what Cater (2013) calls narrative capital. In this respect the imagination and its connections into our memories and past experiences become the building blocks of identity formation as narrative capital becomes absorbed.

Marschall (2012) investigates the intersections between memory and tourism, and argues: 'memory can be a more decisive factor in people's travel choices than the most aggressive advertisement' (2012, p. 323). She explains that developed countries have more educated tourists, which emphasises middle-class values and tastes. In particular, processes of enduring hardship ('travail') allow for 'experiential singularity' and 'communicative restaging and its ever new mental savouring'. Blogs, tweets and online diaries allow and support a discursive circulation of words and images that draw on, indeed even mimic, iconic images; e.g. when summiting a mountain a person may unconsciously adopt a victory pose reminiscent of that of Tenzing on top of Everest in 1953. Memory can connect adventure and tourism. The primary mechanism for this is nostalgia, the yearning for belonging to a different time and the 'slower rhythms of our dreams'. Semple (2013, p. 66) concurs: '[identity] emerges from the past as a creative process of drawing together previous encounters, fusing and forming new connections, re-framing the enacted roles and scripts of past events through an autobiographical memory system'. It is also noted that, by steering life stories in this way, people are creating imaginative anticipation of the next adventure: the most successful adventure providers build in progression for their clients so that a tourist might effectively develop an 'adventure career' by accumulating experiences and thereby reinforcing a sense of identity.

Commodification

It is the historical accounts of adventure that provide the raw material for the commodification of adventure: the process is an exchange mechanism between different forms of capital, notably economic (money), symbolic (an adventure journey) and social (status and networks). An important part of the 'doing' of adventure, it is suggested, is the opportunity to engage with something real and tangible. However, because of the historical time-lapse between exploration and repetition our contemporary experience of an adventure cannot be the same as that of the explorer: an authentic adventure experience today is much more elusive (Loynes, 2013). Authenticity becomes relative, as in 'it's new for me'. The difficulty in achieving an authentic experience is the result of the commercially mediated way that adventure is packaged. Mountaineering is a good example of this because the symbolic capital of a mountaineering ascent is location specific and easily quantifiable by height. Kane (2012) has researched the commodification of Mt Everest by studying websites and company blogs reflecting the inputs of paying clientele on Everest expeditions in the climbing season of spring 2010. The tourists he followed were both male and female. The mountain, he claims (2012, p. 281), 'provides objective authenticity in context and constructed authenticity through accounts of previous expeditions, while their claims of unique distinction proffer an existential authenticity'.

Everest has a status that has imbued the mountain with considerable symbolic capital, which has in turn been a catalyst for tourist development. Cohen (1988) acknowledges that commodification is a driver of tourism and that the passage of (outside) people through a location does have an impact upon the encountered culture. But, he argues, commercial development does not necessarily destroy cultural products, although it may change these and/or add new meanings. Adventure is such a malleable term, and its potential market so vast that it can exist in many different forms. The Everest Story is only one strand in the industry's growth, in which subsequent ascents by guided tourists reinforce mountaineering adventure mythology (Krakauer, 1997). Examples of products that contribute to this dynamic include the global 'slow' movement (e.g. the attractions of packages that demand switching off all communication devices), organic horticulture and cuisine (e.g. eating only locally sourced food), raising money for charitable causes (e.g. a sponsored ascent of Mt Kilimanjaro), being educated about global climate change (e.g. polar bear safaris inside the Arctic Circle) and technology-driven adventure activities (e.g. climbing walls and wake-boarding circuits).

At the other end of the spectrum are adventures such as bungee jumping and rafting on artificial waterways, which reinvent the adventure journey as a short-lived opportunity for instant gratification: 'these activities are stripped down to the bare bones of the thrill ride, which is not far removed from a theme park experience' (Loynes, 2013, p. 138). Bungee jumping was devised by Oxford University's student-led 'Dangerous Sports Club', and the initial 'demonstration' on Bristol's Avon Suspension Bridge in 1979 quickly led to arrests. McKay (2013) charts the subsequent history and then describes in more detail her research into the setting-up and successful running of the Orlando Towers bungee project in Soweto. The project evolved between 2001 and 2009 as various entrepreneurial interests and funding lines became available. Its success indicates how mainstream tourism (in the case of Soweto this includes conventional sightseeing tours to the Hector Petersen Memorial, the Mandela Museum and the former home of Archbishop Tutu) can be augmented with adventure activities. Moreover, it is white domestic tourists that make the bungee viable, which leads McKay (2013, p. 67) to conclude: 'it is in a location that for many represents adventure across a "social frontier"'. Her point is that adventure remains an ambivalent term perceived by individuals in different ways via different activities in different places at different times: an overseas tourist visiting Soweto might find the experience of being in such an infamous place surrounded by 'otherness' as challenging as a bungee jump.

Consumption

Consumption is directly connected to processes of commodification; the two are symbiotically dependent because there is no point in creating an adventure tourism product if people don't buy it (McGillivray & Frew, 2007). Crucial to processes of consumption is the market; adventure has become a commodity but one that is sensitive in both creating and responding to the adventure 'needs' of people: there are differences within any one activity focus. This is why adventure tourism works to both provide for a range of needs and construct other related needs for its business interests. Curtin and Wilkes (2005) look specifically at wildlife tourism, with a particular focus on the British Isles. The ambivalence of adventure, and its ideological relativism, is again illustrated by this reminder that the 'call' of the outdoors is not restricted to adrenaline activities. They suggest wildlife tourism exists on a continuum with the 'gentle environmental holiday maker' at one end and 'hard core wildlife chasers' at the other. There is clearly overlap and movement across, but to make the product (bird watching) attractive and the business sustainable the providers have to satisfy the comfort needs of the gentle group with the need to generate new and novel possibilities for the hard-core group.

Consumption, then, is sustained by striking a balance between retaining the edginess of the frontier while facilitating greater access and control, and the more atavistic experiences of being a long way from civilisation. Just as with the notion of emergent authenticity the strategy for providers is to retain the spirit of adventure while broadening the appeal of an adventure beyond the 'hard nuts', the youthful and idealistic existential tourists into more mainstream markets. When this logic is pursued, and when the impact of innovation and technology are factored in, it does make sense to take the adventure to where most of the people are – that is, urban areas (Beedie, 2005). Whitewater rafting is a good example. The more sublime and awe-inspiring descents of spectacular gorges in the Ecuadorian Andes, or the Shotover river in Queenstown New Zealand, will always draw in paying clientele, but if one does not have the time or the money to travel to exotic locations there are more local possibilities, such as at the Nene Whitewater Centre just outside Northampton, UK. This is an artificial site using a pump system to take water up from the

River Nene and release it down the concrete course. Rafts and kayaks use the facility, which is designed to maximise thrills and minimise adverse consequences of spills. There are two elements to the patterns identified (Beedie, 2005). First there is the market efficiency potential of bringing adventure to artificial settings; with skiing, for example: 'the designers of the infrastructure of the resort ensure that the place is commodified and very efficient at making money from the skiers, as the chair lifts, food, entertainment and accommodation are all controlled' (Loynes, 2013, p. 138). Second, there is the risk management potential as artificial technologies can be regulated and controlled, unlike elements such as the weather and distance from 'civilisation' in the great outdoors (Ball-King, Watt & Ball, 2013). Clearly, rationalisation in the form of management and control 'follows' adventure to the 'frontier' so that adventure, as in the original definition of uncertainty of outcome, can be retained only through an ongoing process of adjustment thus ensuring an ambiguity that, ironically, provides the potential for commercial operators to exploit (Beedie, 2005). Urban adventures that emerge from spontaneous activity such as 'parkour' (a combination of outdoor gymnastics and urban free running) are not immune to commercial, and therefore commodified, development (Atkinson, 2009).

Conclusions

Adventure tourism has developed because of the convergence of a number of key facilitators at the present time. Technological developments in transport (e.g. flying), communications (e.g. the internet), clothing (e.g. light, comfortable and functional garments that transcend tourism and fashion markets more generally) and mapping (e.g. GPS and other satellite systems) have combined with other social and cultural changes (e.g. greater affluence in the developed world) to create the conditions in which adventure tourism can be seen to be flourishing. Adventure tourism might be thought of as a more extreme form of escapism than mainstream tourism, and it offers, arguably, a more holistic experience by challenging the notion of the tourist gaze through the tourist engagement in activity. The emergent business model relies on discursive narratives of exploration and conquest to feed the market of aspirant adventurers that range from the young and enthusiastic who are especially interested in quick-fix adventures such as bungee jumping, to older, more considered participants whose engagement might be more gentle but more sustained as in wildlife tours and trekking.

The whole adventure tourism industry is risk managed and the resultant is two-fold: (i) that risk tends to migrate across a continuum from objective, real and serious to subjective, perceived and controlled; and (ii) the possibilities for authentic experiences (of wild places, of unmediated tactile experiences of the world) also migrate so that experiences take the form of emergent authenticity. Lastly, the ideology of adventure tourism remains ambivalent, which does not compromise anyone experiencing adventure(s) in their own way(s). This openness is clearly good for business. Adventure tourism is a social phenomenon with permeable walls so that processes of commodification, consumption and the ensuing implications for identity infiltrate, circulate and shape its structures and practices. There are many other connections that demonstrate this permeability. In this way of thinking, adventure tourism remains vibrant and attractive and can thus be expected to sustain and develop its possibilities.

References

Anderson, J. (1970). *The Ulysses Factor: The Exploring Instinct in Man.* London: Hodder & Stoughton.
Atkinson, M. (2009) Parkour, anarcho-environmentalism and poiesis. *Journal of Sport and Social Issues,* *32*(2), 169–194.

Ball-King, L., Watt, J. & Ball, D. (2013). The rise and fall of the regulator: Adventure sports in the United Kingdom. *Risk Analysis, 33*(1), 15–23.

Beedie, P. (2003). Adventure tourism. In S. Hudson (Ed.) *Sport and Adventure Tourism* (pp. 203–240). London: Haworth Press.

Beedie, P. (2005) Urban adventure tourism. *Journal of Travel and Tourism Marketing, 18*(3), 37–48.

Beedie, P. (2013) Managing risk: An analysis of adventure tourism in Britain. In M.C. Almeida (Ed.) *Turismo e Desporto Na Natureza* (pp. 203–223). Estoril, Portugal: ESHTE.

Bourdieu, P. (1993) *The Field of Cultural Production.* Oxford: Polity Press.

Brown, H. (2000). Passengers, participants, partners and practitioners. Working with risk to empower groups. *Horizons, 12*(Winter), 37–39.

Cater, C. (2013). The meaning of adventure. In S. Taylor, P. Varley & T. Johnston (Eds.) *Adventure Tourism: Meanings, Experience and Learning* (pp. 7–18). Abingdon: Routledge.

Christiansen, D. (1990). Adventure tourism. In J. Miles & S. Priest (Eds.) *Adventure Education* (pp. 433–442). State College, PA: Venture Publishing.

Cloke, P. & Perkins, H. (1998). Cracking the Canyon with the Awesome Foursome: Representations of adventure tourism in New Zealand. *Environment & Planning D: Society and Space, 16,* 185–218.

Cohen, E. (1988). Authenticity and commoditization in tourism. *Annals of Tourism Research, 15,* 371–386.

Curtin, S. & Wilkes, K. (2005). British wildlife tourism operators: Current issues and typologies. *Current Issues in Tourism, 8*(6), 455–478.

Frisby, D. & Featherstone, M. (1997) *Simmel on Culture.* London: Sage.

Habermas, J. (1962) *The Structural Transformation of the Public Sphere.* Cambridge: Polity Press.

Houston, D. (2006) Five miles out: Communion and commodification among the mountaineers. In L. Vivanco and R. Gordon (Eds.) *Tarzan Was an Eco-tourist and Other Tales in the Anthropology of Adventure* (pp. 147–160). Oxford: Berghahn Books.

Humberstone, B. (2009) Inside/outside the Western 'Bubble': The nexus of adventure, adventure sports and perceptions of risk in UK and Mauritius. In J. Ormond & B. Wheaton (Eds.) *On the Edge: Leisure Consumption and the Representation of Adventure Sports* (pp. 97–112). LSA Publication No. 66. Eastbourne: Leisure Studies Association.

Jenkins, R. (1996) *Social Identity.* London: Routledge.

Kane, M. (2012). Professional adventure tourists: Producing and selling stories of authentic identity. *Tourist Studies, 12*(3), 268–286.

Krakauer, J. (1997) *Into Thin Air: A Personal Account of the Mount Everest Disaster.* London: Macmillan.

Laurendeau, J. (2006) 'He didn't go in doing a skydive': Sustaining the illusion of control in an edgework activity. *Sociological Perspectives, 49*(4), 583–605.

Lindstrom, L. (2006) They sold adventure: Martin and Osa Johnson in the New Hebrides. In L. Vivanco & R. Gordon (Eds.) *Tarzan Was an Eco-tourist and Other Tales in the Anthropology of Adventure* (pp. 93–110). Oxford: Berghahn Books.

Lintern, D. (2013) Almost Alpine. *Summit, 72,* 42–46.

Lipscombe, N. (2007). The risk management paradox for urban recreation and park managers: Providing high risk recreation within a risk management context. *Annals of Leisure Research, 10*(1), 3–25.

Logan, J. (2006) Crampons and cook pots: The democratisations and feminisations of adventure on Aconcagua. In L. Vivanco & R. Gordon (Eds.) *Tarzan Was an Eco-tourist and Other Tales in the Anthropology of Adventure* (pp. 161–178). Oxford: Berghahn Books.

Loynes, C. (2013) Globalisation, the market and outdoor adventure. In E. Pike & S. Beames (Eds.) *Outdoor Adventure and Social Theory* (pp. 135–146). Abingdon: Routledge.

Lyng, S. (2004) Crime, edgework and corporeal transaction. *Theoretical Criminology, 8*(3), 359–375.

Macfarlane, R. (2012). *The Old Ways.* London: Hamish Hamilton.

Marschall, S. (2012). Personal memory tourism and a wider exploration of the tourism–memory nexus. *Journal of Tourism and Cultural Change, 10*(4), 321–335.

McGillivray, D. & Frew, M. (2007) Capturing adventure: Trading experiences in the symbolic economy. *Annals of Leisure Research, 10*(3) 54–78.

McKay, T. (2013). Leaping in to urban adventure: Orlando Bungee, Soweto, South Africa. *African Journal for Physical, Health Education, Recreation & Dance.* Supplement 2, 55–71.

Mead, G. (1962) *Mind, Self and Society.* Chicago, IL: University of Chicago Press.

Mortlock, C. (1984). *The Adventure Alternative.* Milnthorpe: Cicerone Press.

Pike, E. & Weinstock, J. (2013) Identity politics in the outdoor adventure environment. In E. Pike & S. Beames (Eds.) *Outdoor Adventure and Social Theory* (pp. 125–134). Abingdon: Routledge.

Ramsay, H. (2014) Reflective leisure, freedom and identity. In S. Elkington & S. Gammon (Eds.) *Contemporary Perspectives in Leisure: Meanings, Motives and Lifelong Learning* (pp. 173–184). Abingdon: Routledge.

Semple, T. (2013). The semiotics of slow adventure: Narrative and identity. In S. Taylor, P. Varley & T. Johnston (Eds.) *Adventure Tourism: Meanings, Experience and Learning* (pp. 63–75). Abingdon: Routledge.

Solnit, R. (2001). *Wanderlust: A History of Walking*. London: Verso.

Swarbrooke, J., Beard, C., Leckie, S. & Pomfret, G. (2003). *Adventure Tourism: The New Frontier*. London: Butterworth-Heinemann.

Varley, P. (2006). Confecting adventure and playing with meaning: The adventure commodification continuum. *Journal of Sport & Tourism, 11*(2), 173–194.

46

Ecotourism

Outdoor pedagogy at the periphery

Patrick T. Maher

Cape Breton University

Introduction

Ecotourism is a paradox; it is a commercial enterprise with a conscience. As an industry it is an ever growing global phenomenon. Academically it is also growing, with a variety of peer-reviewed journals, not-for-profit associations and even higher-education credentials dedicated to the subject. Ecotourism, it is claimed, is about appreciating nature and culture, sharing responsibility and promoting beneficial relationships between various stakeholders. Ecotourism attempts to create meaningful experiences that raise participants' awareness and create action through the development of ecological sensibilities. These outcomes are very similar to those envisioned by proponents of outdoor education. Outdoor education generally operates with experiential methods and endeavours to create meaningful relationships to nature. Outdoor education, covering related fields such as experiential education, ecological/environmental education and adventure education, is a much more typical segment of the outdoor studies landscape (see earlier chapters). This chapter explores the common ground and interdisciplinarity of ecotourism and outdoor education.

First, an overview of ecotourism from original discussions of the concept to its present-day conceptualisation is presented. Ecotourism is then compared with outdoor education to offer insights from these often segregated fields. A case study of expedition cruise tourism in the Polar regions gives illustrative examples of possible synergies in both theory and practice between ecotourism and outdoor education. The chapter will conclude with a number of anecdotal stories further illustrating the interconnectivity and interdisciplinarity of the two fields.

Ecotourism: past and present

With ecotourism, as with outdoor education, there is definitional confusion and complexity. Much of the growth in ecotourism happened following the discourse that began with the 1987 Brundtland Report. In that report, the World Commission on Environment and Development (WCED) defined sustainability as 'development that meets the needs of the present without compromising the ability of future generations to meet their own needs' (WCED, 1987, p. 43). Although the WCED definition of sustainability is used throughout the tourism industry, its use is a bit problematic and conflictual as tourism is clearly devised to satisfy wants, not meet

472

fundamental needs. Additionally, sustainable tourism or the use of many other terms, such as nature-based tourism, ecotourism, responsible tourism, is a judgement call; often a call made by the industry or an individual operator. Tourists are made up of a wide variety of people who constitute diverse subjectivities. Consequently, they enjoy a broad mix of products, activities and spheres of motivation, leading scholars to discuss aggregate terms such as NEAT (Nature, Eco-, and Adventure Tourism) (Buckley, 2000) or ACE (Adventure, Culture and Ecotourism) (Fennell, 2007). Nevertheless, I will stick with the term ecotourism, recognising that it does get used synonymously and in juxtaposition with many other terms.

The term ecotourism has been credited to consultant Héctor Ceballos-Lascuráin of Mexico. In the mid-1980s, before the Brundtland Report, he used the Spanish term 'turismo ecologico' to identify types of ecological tourism, which was later shortened to 'ecoturismo' (Wearing & Neil, 2009). Ceballos-Lascuráin stated that ecotourism 'involves travelling to relatively undisturbed or uncontaminated natural areas with the specific object of studying, admiring, and enjoying the scenery and its wild plants and animals, as well as any existing cultural aspects' (Weaver, 2005, p. 19). Thus, the two main facets of ecotourism in this context are: travel to unspoiled natural environments and travel where the predominant purpose is to experience the natural environment (Wearing & Neil, 2009). This definition, with some assumptions that ecotourism is undertaken in remote areas with only modest accommodations, has placed mass tourism and ecotourism at opposite ends of the tourism spectrum in some analyses.

Honey (2008, p. 33), has defined ecotourism as: 'travel to fragile, pristine, and usually protected areas that strives to be low impact and (often) small scale. It helps educate the traveller, provides funds for conservation, directly benefits the economic development and political empowerment of local communities, and fosters respect for different cultures and for human rights'. Whereas Fennell (2007, p. 24), states that, 'ecotourism is a sustainable, non-invasive form of nature-based tourism that focuses primarily on learning about nature first-hand, and which is ethically managed to be low-impact, non-consumptive, and locally oriented (control, benefits, and scale). It typically occurs in natural areas, and should contribute to the conservation of such areas.' These definitions differ in their inclusion of the imperative for improvement of local communities, but they do clearly indicate the need for connection to natural environments, and the critical role that learning plays.

Tourists' learning and interaction with the environment is posited to contribute to pro-conservation actions and attitudes (see Beaumont, 2001). Education is often provided in the form of interpretation, typically expected of any ecotourism operator. Qualified naturalists and guides provide interpretation and/or education about the places visited, before and during travel. Additionally, it is increasingly recognised that the industry operators are responsible for educating travellers about appropriate behaviour in unique and fragile areas (Wearing & Neil, 2009).

These two critical factors (the environment and learning) are what create linkages between ecotourism and outdoor education. The following section will outline outdoor education, from a Canadian perspective, and link the definitions and discourses in that sphere to ecotourism.

Outdoor education: a Canadian perspective

For a perspective on outdoor studies in Canada, one excellent starting point is the article by Henderson and Potter (2001). Similar to this chapter, Henderson and Potter struggled with the way in which many pieces of a field intersect: outdoor leadership, adventure studies, environmental education, experiential education, and so on. They settled finally on using the term outdoor education to encompass a broad suite of fields, recognising the varied nuances and

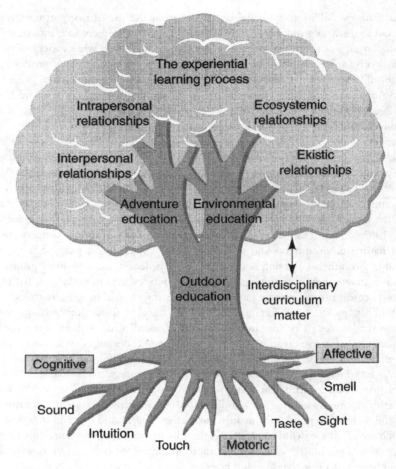

Figure 46.1 Priest's model of outdoor education

Source: Priest (1988); reprinted from Gilbertson, Bates, McLaughlin and Ewert (2006, p. 5)

perceived hierarchy of these different terms. This diversity of terminology is highlighted in a number of chapters in this Handbook.

In many ways, Canadian outdoor education is similar to that found in the United States in terms of philosophical development and delivery, but it is just different enough that I have decided this section is best labelled a Canadian perspective and not a North American one. Henderson and Potter (2001) argue that Canada's exploration history and geographical breadth distance it from some of the US and UK debates regarding education 'for' and 'about' the outdoors. Increasingly Canadian outdoor education includes respecting Indigenous perspectives and education 'in' and 'with' the outdoors. A simple understanding of North American outdoor education might be aligned with Priest's (1988) model. Figure 46.1 shows outdoor education in relation to the critical relationships and varied curriculum/sensory connections involved.

Experiential learning, starting with the conventional Kolb model (1984), offers the method found in most Canadian outdoor education programmes (see Beard, Chapter 41 in this section). Programmes offer an experience and reflective time whereby the student may then generalise their learning and potentially apply it when they return home. For critiques of the Kolb model, see Seaman (2008) and Schenck and Cruickshank (2015). As a pedagogical method this is directly in line with the thinking of Kurt Hahn, a key figure in the development of outdoor/ experiential education globally through organisations such as Outward Bound, United World Colleges and the Duke of Edinburgh Award Scheme. Hahn was described as having a key interest in 'putting students in motion . . . to come to grips with the healing powers of direct experience' (James, 1995, p. 37). In Canada this model appears quite common. Canadian outdoor education offers activities that are, according to Henderson and Potter (2001, p. 231), 'enjoyable, provide a sense of well-being, and likely teach some physical and technical skills along the way', all set in a milieu of exploration and where the activities themselves are very much set up as a means to an end versus recreational or skill development (e.g. rock climbing is used as a means to increasing self-esteem more than learning to actually rock climb). Henderson and Potter (2001) also note that Canadian outdoor education has five key avenues: youth camps, schools, higher education (colleges and universities), community programmes, and commercial programmes (largely operations that could be considered ecotourism). Three of these have a Hahn-esque building block among them. In particular schools, Outward Bound Canada (OBC) had a long history, e.g. the Canadian Outward Bound Wilderness School, and then Outward Bound Canada College. OBC also influences the many schools it contracts to, particularly the private schools in the Greater Toronto area.

Outward Bound Canada has also had a broad scope of influence on newer outdoor programmes and centres, which operate in a model that many would say is Outward Bound based. In addition, for a time Outward Bound Canada operated a youth camp, and was thus integrated into that grouping of camp organisations. Gilbertson *et al.* (2006, p. 5) conclude that outdoor education is 'the combination of learning in and through the natural world'. However, they do state that there are three primary subject areas: ecological relationships, developing physical skills and interpersonal relationships. They offer a blended model, which also includes ecotourism (see Figure 46.2).

Once again, the uniquely Canadian connection here is a connection to exploration and culture. Henderson and Potter (2001, p. 240) note that, 'the Canadian quest for the educational setting of the "country way back in" – is the seeking, no matter how illusory, the "pristine." Whether it really be there or not, we Canadian outdoor educators cling to notions of uncorrupted, unnamed, uncultivated.' Currently critical scholars question the romanticism of such statements and the cultural disconnection of the manner that conventional outdoor education treats Indigenous knowledge (see Mullins, 2009; Root, 2010).

Henderson and Potter (2001) finally note a number of commercial programmes offering outdoor education. Some of the programme operators are clearly placed in the sphere of ecotourism and this is where the drift into the similarity between outdoor education and ecotourism begins. Another prominent Canadian programme is Students on Ice (SOI). SOI is a programme for high-school and university students, which takes them to the 'ends of the earth' – the Arctic and Antarctic. Founded by Geoff Green (see Green, 2010), it is a ship-based programme designed to share knowledge, foster respect and encourage creative ways for students to conceptualise the way they can assist in the protection/conservation of the planet. SOI's educational programme is clearly designed to create an engaged citizenry, a corps of Polar ambassadors, which have realised the critical state of these regions at an early age, unlike the participants who engage in typical ecotourism to those regions. However, an organisation such as SOI gives an excellent look into the 'muddiness' of the ecotourism–outdoor education overlap.

Quite clearly, SOI can be identified as an outdoor education programme. Its programmes engage certified teachers and university professors to lead the activities; as per Gilbertson *et al.*'s

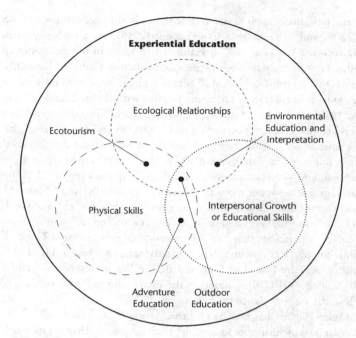

Figure 46.2 Outdoor education as a blend of subject areas
Source: Adapted from Gilbertson *et al.* (2006, p. 6)

(2006) definition, they allow students to learn in, and through, nature. However, it is correct to say that the programmes may also constitute ecotourism. The values and principles mirror those noted by Ceballos-Lascuráin, Fennell and Honey, and SOI operates in a manner consistent with what Wearing and Neil state is the norm for ecotourism: learning through interpretation, before and during the voyage. Green (2010) documents students' success following their expeditions producing a corps of Polar ambassadors, which is a key message of the International Association of Antarctica Tour Operators (IAATO, the industry association for Antarctic tourism based largely around expedition cruising – ecotourism). As stated by Landau (2002, p. 35), this ambassadorship philosophy stems from Antarctic tourism pioneer Lars-Eric Lindblad, who said: 'You can't protect what you don't know', and according to IAATO, it is 'creating ambassadors to the last great continent' (Denise Landau, personal communication, 29 April 2004).

SOI is one obvious example of the interconnections between outdoor education and ecotourism. SOI has demographic links to the typical outdoor education programmes mentioned by Henderson and Potter (2001) – those of kids and youth. However, this might also engage other age ranges up to retirement; after all, the latter is the typical age of expedition cruise passengers.

Case study: expedition cruising in the Arctic (and Antarctic)

Expedition cruise ships bring people to locations 'off the beaten path', offering access to remote parts of the world that may only be possible by sea. Walker and Moscardo (2006) and Ellis and Kriwoken (2006) offer insightful overviews of the expedition cruise ship market. Smaller ships, fewer passengers, and a central focus on education and interpretation differentiate expedition cruising from the larger cruise industry (Walker & Moscardo, 2006). These same characteristics also make this segment of ecotourism much closer to the Canadian perspective on outdoor education. The smaller ships do not require the infrastructure of conventional cruising such as wharves as shore access is typically by zodiac (inflatable rubber boat).

The ships carry between one hundred and one hundred and fifty passengers (Smith, 2006; Walker & Moscardo, 2006) and, typically, experiences follow 'the Lindblad pattern', named so for the pioneering work of Lars-Eric Lindblad, which began in the 1960s (Maher, 2012a). According to Crosbie and Splettstoesser (2011, p. 106),

> the Lindblad pattern of cruising emphasizes exploration and education. Experiences take three forms: using the ship as an observation platform (e.g., for whale watching), small boat cruising (e.g., along scenic coastlines, to view icebergs) and landings ashore. Throughout the cruises, both afloat and ashore, experienced staff and naturalists guide passengers, with lectures given en route between destinations. The guides also ensure visitors behave in a way that causes minimal or no disturbance to the natural environment.

Once again, this is the model used by SOI, and although it has developed apart from the standard theories of experiential and outdoor education the messages are quite similar. One key difference is that the passengers on expedition cruises are generally of more advanced years, as noted earlier. They are 'baby boomers' (see Boyes, Chapter 36 in this Handbook) and newly or near retirement, well educated, well travelled, in good health, having had highly successful careers, and therefore having high levels of disposable income (Jones, 1999; Smith, 2006). Expedition cruising appeals to them because they are typically interested in 'finding new unspoilt, previously unvisited locations with a strong natural or cultural appeal' (Ellis & Kriwoken, 2006, p. 251). Once again, the motivation is highly connected to the norms for outdoor education in Canada, the difference being the costs, but that is not to say typical outdoor education programmes (summer camps or thirty-day wilderness canoe trips) are cheap.

The major feature of expedition cruising, and a key component to its marketing, is the central role of guides in providing interpretation and education (Scherrer, Smith & Dowling, 2011). Expedition team members, local guides and park rangers may all be involved in providing interpretive and educational programmes based on the natural or cultural attractions of the destination; just as they are with SOI, and just as might happen in an outdoor education programme canoeing in Algonquin Park in central Canada. On-board activities such as lectures, background briefings and printed materials complement guided walks ashore, zodiac tours and site-specific activities such as guided snorkelling (Walker & Moscardo, 2006; Scherrer, Smith & Dowling, 2008). A similar depth of background details might be found for outdoor education programmes.

The guide's role in interpretation and education enhances the tourism experience by providing information and informing behaviour (Ham & Weiler, 2002). During expeditions, guides generally inform visitors of cultural and environmental issues, which can break down cultural stereotypes and environmental misconceptions. Changes afoot in outdoor education in Canada indicate that more programmes are adopting social and environmental justice aims. For example, more youth camp programmes are working with local Indigenous groups in a respectful way, more college or university programmes are choosing to eat 'locally' on wilderness trips rather than bringing all their food from their southern homes. Within expedition cruising, such understanding of issues fosters more appropriate visitor behaviour, benefits group management, increases safety, increases the quality of the experience and provides visitors a lasting impression (Scherrer et al., 2008, 2011). Factors such as staff knowledge and demonstration, group size, relevance and timing of information, reinforcement and information resources all have an influence on the overall visitor experience and the impact on local sites (Scherrer et al., 2008).

According to Walker and Moscardo (2006), passengers are drawn to dedicated, enthusiastic and knowledgeable staff, and Ham and Weiler (2002) found that passengers valued guides who were passionate, insightful, enjoyable, relevant and easy to follow, had local experience, and good time- and group-management skills.

In a study of expedition cruise tourists in the Ross Sea region of Antarctica, Maher (2010a) collected narratives on their experience and the educational component. These have also been reported on in Maher (2010b, 2011). These quotes come from separate tourists – all clients of a single expedition cruise operator. In addition to the Antarctic, the operator also works in the Canadian Arctic and has a twenty-four-year expeditionary relationship with the places it visits.

> What we got to do was amazing . . . Our staff was so incredibly competent that we made all our scheduled landings and extras. Capable ship, capable crew. Major emphasis on 'taking care of the environment' – treading lightly, not disturbing animals, respect critical areas. (Respondent Q127)

> I felt very at home and comfortable throughout the whole trip. I got to go out and do more things than I'd ever expected, I met some amazing people who will become lifelong friends and colleagues. (Respondent Q128)

Here the guides and the company seem to have played a major role in the success of an experience, which was already seen as incredible simply because of the location. The respondents recognised the educational emphasis, and the company and guides achieved what most outdoor education programmes hope to do – pushed participants just enough, but still kept them comfortable. The respondents made not just relationships with the natural world, but also interpersonal connections.

> The whole experience was just one huge fabulous perfect reward for the rest of my life. I'll be able to cast my mind back to a thousand tiny incidents and smile and feel completely happy. (Respondent Q49)

> Seeing the vast expanse and power of nature. It gives me hope that the world might survive the abuse we throw at it. (Respondent Q36)

> This visit has far exceeded what I had expected. Books and photos don't really do justice to this unique world . . . I didn't expect the lectures to be so well presented and informative. The whole expedition was geared to us experiencing everything possible and more. (Respondent Q59)

> The care of the team – to protect the environment by educating us how best to enjoy the experience –without disturbing wildlife or nature. (Respondent Q119)

Ecotourism operators and outdoor education providers would be pleased with the general outcomes expressed above: smiling participants, leaving with a sense of responsibility and a respect for why the programme operated as it did. To further the outdoor education/ecotourism connection is one participant's thoughts on physical skill – the third broad area noted by Gilbertson et al. (2006):

> Our trip fell into three sections; a week travelling to Cape Adare via the NZ sub-Antarctic islands; a little over a week in the Ross Sea area; and a week travelling home via Macquarie Island. The outward journey passed in a flash, as the whole experience was new, our fellow

travellers were becoming acquainted, and our expeditions leaders gave fascinating educational lectures and trained us in the skills we would need. The trip home was a little more tedious, as we did not have the expectancy that comes with journeying into the unknown. (Respondent Q32)

The final sentence also reveals a common end to many Outward Bound-type programmes: participants who begin to 'tune out' of the experience early – often referred to as 'barn storming' – because they are already back in the mindset of their everyday lives.

Discussion

Ecotourism activities and many outdoor education programmes generally seek to connect participants to nature, less so in conventional outdoor education, which was more concerned with personal development. Where connecting to nature is an aim, this is thought to be achieved through direct contact and assisting participants in their development of key values that shape the relationships (e.g. Leave No Trace principles, or discussion of larger environmental issues such as climate change). Beaumont (2001) questions the aims of ecotourism, suggesting that some sense of ecological sensitivities is already present in participants. Ryan (2003, p. 327) argues that, 'There exists neither a political will nor public willingness to change patterns of life . . . movements [to an ecotour in the Galapagos Islands or an outdoor education programme at a local field study centre] are simply commodifications wherein [participants] justify their explorations in terms of assuaging guilt rather than a serious concern about environmental issues.' Arguably, participants on holiday or in a unique outdoor situation may not recognise or have the desire to consider environmental issues that are local and global. Ecotourism and outdoor education are integrated into an increasingly mobile world. Maher (2010a) and Uriely (2005) agree that the tourism experience cannot to be divorced from everyday wider life events and circumstances. The transference of learning from experiences out of doors is an issue discussed across outdoor education (see Maher, 2012b).

Larsen, Urry and Axhausen (2007) have discussed a mobile social life and the networks of tourism, suggesting that tourism research has been marginalised because it is seen as exotic, while the experience itself has become more centre stage to people's lives. Larsen *et al.* (2007) suggest that tourism research might usefully focus on how tourism has moved into assisting with people's friendships and reproducing their social relations. Much outdoor education research has been concerned with just these issues.

Larsen *et al.* (2007) argues that tourists are not necessarily searching for lost difference, but rather distant connections. Outdoor education, it can be argued, is likewise trying to allow for better connections; certainly to nature, increasingly to place and culture. One of Maher's (2010a) respondents sums it up: 'Antarctica strikes me as not much different than anywhere we live. It's up to you to get out and experience it.' Thus, local nature, one's own local city park for example, should be explored because it offers educational value, and without direct contact one may not act to protect or conserve it when required.

Ecotourism and outdoor education are for the most part embedded in separate disciplinary silos. However, as has been argued, these disciplines have much in common and are two sides of the same coin. While interdisciplinarity and integration of ecotourism and outdoor education are only recently emerging academically, in practice there has been much overlap. From my experiences of more than fifteen years of teaching and researching in higher education in numerous countries around the world it is evident that students want to work across these fields, and that many practitioners already do. For example, when teaching on a Transcultural

European Outdoor Studies programme in Norway, a programme focused primarily around outdoor education and connections to nature (*friluftsliv* in Norwegian; see Gurholt, Chapter 28 in this Handbook), most students saw their careers to be within a commercial, tourist guiding enterprise. Many practitioners appear to combine employment in ecotourism with employment in outdoor education. For example, practitioners might instruct for an outdoor education provider such as Outward Bound one season, and then guide for an ecotourism operator such as Quark Expeditions (a well-known expedition cruise company) the next. Typically the opportunities for advancement and greater pay scale are better in ecotourism.

Universities are one pathway to career engagement in the outdoors. A number of higher-education institutions already combine these fields in their degrees: Mount Royal University in Canada has an ecotourism and outdoor leadership programme. Charles Sturt University in Australia offers an outdoor recreation and ecotourism programme. Pedagogically, ecotourism is aligned in many ways to outdoor education. In practice they may be separated only by the stereotypical demographics they serve (outdoor education for youth, ecotourism for retirees), but clearly they may even operate in the exact same remote locations. Outdoor education may be peripheral to other educational disciplines, while arguably ecotourism is at the forefront of tourism growth.

Conclusion

To conclude, outdoor education and ecotourism are not that different at all. Conventionally, ecotourism may be seen as having a more commercial lens, but in reality many outdoor education operators are now extremely conscious of the bottom line – this may be a change in recent years as more outdoor education programmes have developed so there is increased competition and these programmes are now less uniformly based on personal growth for youth; a segment that often has to be subsidised. Both ecotourism and outdoor education value direct contact with nature, and expect that pedagogical inputs will create long-lasting results. As shown with Students on Ice, and across expedition cruising, outdoor education is, and for the most part always has been, a part of the experience – simply discussed more as the 'Lindblad pattern' versus the Priest or Kolb model.

References

Beaumont, N. (2001). Ecotourism and the conservation ethic: recruiting the uninitiated or preaching to the converted? *Journal of Sustainable Tourism, 9*(4), 317–341.
Buckley, R. (2000). Neat trends: Current issues in nature, eco- and adventure tourism. *International Journal of Tourism Research, 2,* 437–444.
Crosbie, K. & Splettstoesser, J. (2011). Antarctic tourism introduction. In P.T. Maher, E. Stewart & M. Lück (Eds.) *Polar Tourism: Human, Environmental and Governance Dimensions* (pp. 105–120). Elmsford, NY: Cognizant Communication.
Ellis, C. & Kriwoken, L.K. (2006). Off the beaten track: A case study of expedition cruise ships in south-west Tasmania, Australia. In R.K. Dowling (Ed.) *Cruise Ship Tourism* (pp. 251–258). Wallingford, UK: CABI.
Fennell, D.A. (2007). *Ecotourism: An Introduction* (3rd edn). New York: Routledge.
Gilbertson, K., Bates, T., McLaughlin, T. & Ewert, A. (2006). *Outdoor Education: Methods and strategies.* Champaign, IL: Human Kinetics.
Green, G. (2010). Students on ice: Learning in the greatest classrooms on Earth. In M. Lück, P.T. Maher & E.J. Stewart (Eds.) *Cruise Tourism in Polar Regions: Promoting Environmental and Social Sustainability?* (pp. 93–105). London: Earthscan.
Ham, S. & Weiler, B. (2002). Toward a theory of quality in cruise-based interpretive guiding. *Journal of Interpretation Research, 7,* 29–49.

Henderson, B. & Potter, T. (2001). Outdoor adventure education in Canada: Seeking the country way back in. *Canadian Journal of Environmental Education, 6*, 225–242.

Honey, M. (2008). *Ecotourism and Sustainable Development: Who Owns Paradise?* (2nd edn). New York: Island Press.

James, T. (1995). Kurt Hahn and the aims of education. In K. Warren, M. Sakofs & J.S. Hunt Jr (Eds.) *The Theory of Experiential Education* (pp. 33–43). Dubuque, IA: Kendall Hunt Publishing.

Jones, C. (1999). Arctic ship tourism: An industry in adolescence. *The Northern Raven, 13*(1), 28–31.

Kolb, D.A. (1984). *Experiential Learning*. Englewood Cliffs, NJ: Prentice Hall.

Landau, D. (2002). Addressing cumulative environmental impacts of ship-based tourism in the Antarctic Peninsula region. In S.M. Huston & E.J. Waterhouse (Eds.) *Ross Sea Region 2001: The Next Steps. Proceedings of a Workshop to Build on the first Antarctic State of the Environment Report, Victoria University of Wellington 28–29 May 2002* (pp. 35–38). Christchurch: Antarctica New Zealand.

Larsen, J., Urry, J. & Axhausen, K.W. (2007). Networks and tourism: Mobile social life. *Annals of Tourism Research, 34*(1), 244–262.

Maher, P.T. (2010a). Footsteps on the ice: Visitor experiences in the Ross Sea Region, Antarctica. Unpublished doctoral dissertation, Canterbury, Lincoln University.

Maher, P.T. (2010b). 'Awesome size . . . magnitude of the place . . . the incredible beauty . . . ': Visitors' onsite experiences in the Ross Sea region of Antarctica. In C.M. Hall & J. Saarinen (Eds.) *Tourism and Change in the Polar Regions: Climate, Environments and Experiences* (pp. 215–235). Abingdon: Routledge.

Maher, P.T. (2011). Ambassadors for the experience: Perspectives from the Ross Sea Region. In P.T. Maher, E.J. Stewart & M. Lück (Eds.) *Polar Tourism: Human, Environmental and Governance Dimensions* (pp. 121–141). Elmsford, NY: Cognizant Communications Corp.

Maher, P.T. (2012a). Expedition cruise visits to protected areas in the Canadian Arctic: Issues of sustainability and change for an emerging market. *Tourism: An International Interdisciplinary Journal, 60*(1), 55–70.

Maher, P.T. (2012b). Transitions and transference: The 'ins and outs' of wilderness educational expeditions. *Pathways – The Ontario Journal of Outdoor Education, 24*(4), 9–13.

Mullins, P.M. (2009). Living stories of the landscape: Perception of place through canoeing in Canada's North. *Tourism Geographies, 11*(2), 233–255.

Priest, S. (1988). The ladder of environmental learning. *Journal of Adventure Education and Outdoor Leadership, 5*(2), 23–25.

Root, E. (2010). This land is our land? This land is your land: The decolonizing journeys of white outdoor environmental educators. *Canadian Journal of Environmental Education, 15*, 103–119.

Ryan, C. (2003). *Recreational Tourism: Demand and Impacts*. Clevedon, UK: Channel View Publications.

Schenck, J. & Cruickshank, J. (2015). Evolving Kolb: Experiential education in the age of neuroscience. *Journal of Experiential Education, 38*(1), 73–95.

Scherrer, P., Smith, A. & Dowling, R. (2008). *Tourism and the Kimberley Coastal Waterways: Environmental and Cultural Aspects of Expedition Cruising*. Gold Coast: Cooperative Research Centre for Sustainable Tourism.

Scherrer, P., Smith, A. & Dowling, R. (2011). Visitor management practices and operational sustainability: Expedition cruising in the Kimberley, Australia. *Tourism Management, 32*, 1218–1222.

Seaman, J. (2008). Experience, reflect, critique: The end of the 'learning cycles' era. *Journal of Experiential Education, 31*, 3–18.

Smith, V. (2006). Adventure cruising: An ethnography of small ship travel. In R.K. Dowling (Ed.) *Cruise Ship Tourism* (pp. 240–250). Wallingford, UK: CABI Publishing.

Uriely, N. (2005). The tourist experience: Conceptual developments. *Annals of Tourism Research, 32*(1), 199–216.

Walker, K. & Moscardo, G. (2006). The impact of interpretation on passengers of expedition cruises. In R.K. Dowling (Ed.) *Cruise Ship Tourism* (pp. 105–114). Wallingford, UK: CABI.

Wearing, S. & Neil, J. (2009). *Ecotourism: Impacts, Potentials and Possibilities*. Oxford, UK: Butterworth-Heinemann.

Weaver, D.B. (2005). Mass and urban ecotourism: New manifestations of an old concept. *Tourism Recreation Research, 30*, 19–26.

World Commission on Environment and Development (WCED) (1987). *Our Common Future*. Oxford: Oxford University Press.

47

Bourdieu and alpine mountaineering

The distinction of high peaks, clean lines and pure style

John Telford and Simon Beames

UNIVERSITY OF EDINBURGH

If one were asked to call to mind the world's iconic mountain, it is likely that an image of Everest, the Matterhorn, the Eiger or similar would be projected into our imagination. More than likely the image projected would have a composition that suggested grandeur, enticement, graceful immensity and wistful foreboding. Illuminated in soft moonlight, it might seem spectral, floating dreamily in the distance. Light and shadow, snow and rock, contrast to convey the nuanced complexity of a place that stands above and removed from the day-to-day banalities of humanity. Mystery, questfulness, exploration, revelation, transcendence, catharsis, perspective, clarity, endeavour, heroic tragedy, ecstasy, spirituality and discovery are but a few of the emotions and ideals that such images tend to provoke. This is not, however, the relationship that human beings, in Western Europe at least, have always experienced with regard to the Earth's most prominently protruding landscape features. This chapter uses Bourdieu's theory of social practice to explore the changing cultural interpretations of mountains, the effect of this on the practice of mountaineering, and participation in mountaineering as an act of social distinction (Bourdieu, 2010). By exploring mountaineering as a field of cultural production, and the notion of tastes and aesthetics within that field, the authors aim to deepen collective understandings of dominant human–mountain cultural relations.

Human–mountain relations

A complex array of socio-political factors has shaped, in a range of contrasting ways, the cultural lens through which human beings have perceived mountains and mountainous regions (Schama, 1995). In the narratives of the Jewish, Assyrian, Persian, Babylonian and other Eurasian peoples, mountains were holy places to be treated with extreme reverential awe (Kirchner, 1950, p. 412). Mountains' defensive morphology and meteorological vagaries were interpreted as clear communicative devices of the divine, and human beings understood that approaching such places, much less ascending them, should be undertaken only by a select, priestly few. The two strongest societal influences on contemporary Western culture – the Greeks and the Romans of classical antiquity – maintained a predominantly prosaic and pragmatic attitude towards the material world (Kirchner, 1950, p. 415). Hyde (1915) suggests that, in Ancient Greece, 'the love of the elemental, the unhumanized, the wild and savage, was . . . only embryonic' (p. 72). It is true that the Greeks held a particular reverence for the wild fecundity of nature embodied in Pan and their Arcadian foundational myth. However, their earthly aspirations were of a much more ordered, agricultural ideal (Schama, 1995, p. 527). The expansion of Christianity that grew out of the Roman Empire added a spiritual framework to the pragmatic disinterested-ness of the Romans and humanist idealism of the Greeks. Although echoes of more culturally intimate and spiritually connected relationships with mountains were never entirely erased in Europe, the increasingly dominant Christian worldview enthusiastically promoted an active distrust of what it considered to be a corrupted material world.

The English monk, John de Bremble, on crossing the Grand St Bernard pass in 1188, is reported to have expressed the dominant feeling of the day in saying, 'Lord, restore me to my brethren, that I may tell them that they come not to this place of torment' (Hyde, 1915, p. 107; Braham, 2004, p. 5). Thomas Burnet (1635–1715), theologian and author of *Sacred Theory of the Earth*, was appalled and troubled by the reality of the European Alps following his Grand Tour in 1671. His unease was not assuaged until he could theorise the origins of a landscape that seemed so antithetical to a divinely ordained world in such a way as to explain their compatibil-ity within the Creator God's design (Schama, 1995, pp. 428, 451). However, despite the thaw-ing of the ecclesiastical disengagement with the natural, or more-than-human (Abram, 1996), world, mountains in 17th and early 18th century Europe were still commonly regarded as unappealing, agriculturally unproductive, aesthetically revolting, disruptive to a healthy mental equilibrium, reminiscent of female genitalia, and – not unrelated to the latter – just downright dangerous (Macfarlane, 2003, pp. 14–15). In short, apart from ascetic hermit abodes, mountains had little if anything to offer humanity. This period of human interaction with mountains, from the sources available to us, represents a human relationship with mountains characterised by dread, distaste and awed respect.

However, mountains would shortly come to be commonly considered as objects of aesthetic beauty and, as Schama (1995) so lyrically states, admitted to the 'universe of blessed nature' (p. 426). The change in the way mountains were perceived is intimately connected with a cultural shift that Berlin (2000) describes as 'the greatest transformation of Western conscious-ness . . . in our time' (p. 20). That transformation was Romanticism. The following section charts the emergence of Romanticism and the enduring influence of this cultural transformation on contemporary mountaineering.

Romantic foundations of modern mountaineering

From the 1400s onwards, scientific discoveries based on rational, logical processes increasingly challenged religious dogma as a means of explaining and understanding the material world. Every sphere of life became a legitimate arena of scientific investigation, and inevitably this extended into and onto the high mountains (Kirchner, 1950, p. 428; Bainbridge, 2012, p. 4). During the earliest forays, no self-respecting Alpine explorer omitted to gather data on mete-orology, geology, botany or any other aspect of this new frontier. However, with the emer-gence of Romanticism in the late 17th century, the notion of a different and less scientifically instrumental relationship with the mountains became increasingly prevalent. Bainbridge (2012) provides a detailed and revealing account of the intimate relationship between mountaineer-ing and Romanticism: 'The Romantic period, then, saw the emergence of a new activity – mountaineering – and a new identity – the mountaineer – and both, I want to argue . . . are crucial to Romanticism, to the writers' sense of their identities and to their literary outputs' (pp. 1–2). Bainbridge (ibid.) draws attention to the fact that Coleridge makes the first recorded use of the term *mountaineering* in 1802 (Griggs, 1956–1971). Additionally, at this time, the meaning of the proper noun, *mountaineer*, is in the process of changing from specifically denoting someone who lives in a mountainous region to also include a description of someone who engages in mountain climbing. These two linguistic developments are significant events as they have direct and inevitable implications with regard to the way in which English speakers are able to make meaning of mountains in the social world (Bourdieu, 2010, p. xxv). Bainbridge (2012, p. 2) makes the important point that many of the major male Romantic poets were active and dedicated mountaineers, and most of those that were not at least attempted to present themselves as such. The Romantic poets developed something of a symbiotic relationship with mountains, the literary expression of which was then publicly communicated. As a result, their perspective has provided an enduring and highly influential lens through which mountains are perceived. Wordsworth, Coleridge, Shelley, Keats, Scott and Byron all participated in this new activity known as mountaineering, which was distinctly different from more Enlightenment-inspired, scientifically motivated explorations of high places. The new form of mountaineering was not motivated by the prospect of new scientific knowledge. Indeed, the visceral, embodied, quasi-mystical relationship of the poets with mountains – consider Byron's *Manfred*, for example – was in many ways antithetical to earlier rational, humanistic experiences.

Although it is impossible to give an absolute definition of Romanticism (Berlin, 2000, p. 1), several characteristics with which it is commonly associated are recognisable within modern mountaineering culture. First, there is the veneration of nature and the exploration of the relationship between humans and nature that commonly enter into spiritual, though not necessarily religious, territory. Second, there is the notion of the sublime. This is a concept that relates to the immeasurable greatness of the mountains in all spheres: physical, emotional, spiritual, metaphysical. It refers to the immensity of the landform and the feeling of its imposing power that draws one in – a sort of pleasurable horror. The counterposing of terror and joy, of purposefully seeking awe-full emotional sensation, is characteristic of Romanticism, which combined an intellectual scepticism of religious dogma and a suspicion of the limits of understanding offered by Enlightenment disembodied rationality (Schama, 1995, p. 49). Third, there is the notion of doing something for its own sake (Berlin, 2000); a commitment to an ideal, whatever that ideal might be. When, therefore, we consider Mallory's famous response to the question of why climb Everest, we might entertain the possibility that he was speaking neither with impatience nor with imperial anthropocentrism, but from the wellspring of a cultural understanding of being in the world; to have a goal, passion or desire, whatever that might be, is pure and legitimate and requires no further explanation. Last, there is the idea of exploring the human–nature connection and in so doing revealing dimensions of the self as a result of the purifying mountaineering endeavour. There is overlap here with the previously mentioned notions of the sublime and aesthetic beauty so splendid that it invokes spiritual sensations. Mountaineering brings these aspects together in one physically embodied enterprise and opens the door to transcendent experiences occurring.

Cultural distinction via cultural appropriation

As previously mentioned, while Coleridge is credited with the first recorded use of the verb 'mountaineering' (Bainbridge, 2012, pp. 1–2), the notion of a 'mountaineer' had long been in existence. Mountains and their environs had always been places where people made a living from practices such as hunting and animal pasture. The ready availability of local mountain dwellers who could offer their skills as 'pathfinders' to paying clients during the boom of early mountain exploration in the 18th and 19th centuries is testament to this fact (see de Bellefon, 1983; Cousquer & Beames, 2014). Nevertheless, in contemporary English, the noun form of the word no longer denotes someone who lives in or makes a living from mountains.[1] The identity associated with being a mountaineer has been entirely re-inscribed in our culture. Indeed, historically, cultural appropriation by social elites is a common social phenomenon (Bourdieu, 1978, p. 823). The most powerful and influential members of society borrow from the culturally specific practices of lower social classes, and transform them into higher-order social practices that carry different meanings and social purposes. Consider the transformation of association football from a traditional village game where innumerate participants competed in a raucous and unregulated manner with the aim of transporting the ball, often by any means necessary, to one end of the village or the other (FIFA, 2014). Over time, the codification of the game and subsequent elimination of local variations, the separation of the game from specific occasions in the folk calendar, and its establishment as a *sport* rather than a game, distinguished it and its participants from the popular – for which read *vulgar* (Bourdieu, 1978, p. 823) – roots of its origin. In addition, the development of the decorous notion of 'fair play' communicated that the participants were not so invested as to forget that it was 'only a game' (Bourdieu, 2010, p. 214). In doing so, the social activity was transformed and legitimised as a respectable pastime for the dominant classes, and distinct from and superior to the original form. The game's adaptations ensured that the colonising fraction was, 'defined . . . by everything which distinguishes it from what it is not and especially from everything it is exposed to; social identity is defined and asserted through difference' (Bourdieu, 2010, pp. 166–167). Clearly, in the more than one hundred years since the establishment of association football, the cultural meanings attached to the sport have evolved significantly and have quite different contemporary iterations. Still, the basic principle that dominant social fractions colonise social practices remains.

It is possible to read the evolution of modern mountaineering in a similar way. The gradual encroachment of the middle and upper classes into the mountain environment catalysed a transformation in the way that mountains were perceived in society more generally. Mountains were re-narratised in cultural consciousness. The following excerpt recounts an interaction between Joseph Budworth, a travel writer and poet at the turn of the 18th century, and his mountain guide, Paul Postlethwaite:

> Paul Postlethwaite sat down by me, and, after answering my questions, thought he had a natural right to make his own:
> *P.P.* Ith' neome oh fackins, wot a broughtin yoa here?
> *Rambler.* Curiosity, Paul.
> *P.P.* I think yoa mun be kurious enuff; I neor cum here bu after runnaway sheop, an I'me then so vext at um, I cud throa um deawn th' Poike. (Budworth, 1810, p. 269)[2]

For Postlethwaite, who makes his living in the mountains, the intellectualised endeavour provoked simply by curiosity is incomprehensible. Postlethwaite's question regarding what on earth motivated Budworth to want to climb to the top of Langdale Pike arises from a working-class habitus that prioritises function over form (Bennett, 2010, p. xxi), and generates the conclusion that the only thing worthy of curiosity is Budworth himself. For Postlethwaite, the high landscape is a vexing snare for errant sheep, not an arena of aesthetic enquiry with the power to provoke new and altered forms of consciousness. This exchange perfectly illustrates the coming together of two contrasting cultures of mountaineering that are occupying the same social space at this point. Budworth has no reason beyond intellectual inquisitiveness to climb to the top of the Pike: Postlethwaite's livelihood, and that of any of his dependants, is contingent upon his interaction with the mountain landscape. Bourdieu (2010) suggests that the Kantian principle of disinterestedness is key to understanding the way in which the engagement of the dominant social class in social practices showcases its distinctiveness and distinction. Disinterest refers not to a lack of willing, conscious involvement, but rather to the absence of utilitarian necessity as a motivating force for involvement. As the Romantic turn gathers momentum, we witness a marked shift in emphasis regarding the nature of human–nature interactions in mountain environments from function (dependence, reliance) to form (intellectualised, aestheticised, separate). The working relationship of Postlethwaite that is intimately tied to survival is superseded in the cultural hierarchy by an aesthetically inspired relationship that is separated from survival reliance or need. As the Romantic cultural interpretations of mountains and mountaineering were communicated through writings and paintings, so were the high places as a space in the social world increasingly colonised by society's dominant class.

With reference to art, Bourdieu (2010) proposes that there is no such thing as the 'pure' gaze of the observer or the pure intention of the artist. He proposes instead that it is a manufactured concept: 'The detachment of the pure gaze cannot be dissociated from a general disposition towards the world which is the paradoxical product of conditioning by negative economic necessities – a life of ease – that tends to induce an active distance from necessity' (p. xxviii). The notion of a pure gaze relates to Kant's morally agnostic aesthetic philosophy (Jenkins, 2002, p. 129) of an objective standard to which all art can be related and by which it can be judged. What logically follows is that there will be some people – those with a refined understanding, or 'taste' – who are able to, first, recognise and, second, appreciate this pure standard. Bourdieu completely refutes this position and suggests instead that 'taste' in terms of the pure gaze is a cultivated stance. Its defining disinterest is a learned disposition, born of affluence, which, by its very nature, ensures the continuity of that affluence by communicating the superiority of the gazer. If we consider the exchange between Budworth and Postlethwaite in this light, Budworth's interaction with the mountains is not representative of a refined aestheticism that justifies his somewhat condescending tone with regard to his guide. It is merely an arbitrary cultural construction generated (mostly unconsciously) within the affluent, dominant social class for the purpose of displaying the distinction of its members.

Peaks of distinction

Bourdieu (1990, p. 22) posits that struggles for reputation and prestige are a fundamental feature of social life. From this perspective, then, the development of modern mountaineering as a pursuit steeped in Romantic associations of aesthetic beauty, the sublime, sensorial fascination and quasi-spiritual existential insight, is neither accidental nor an inevitable developmental expression of human progress (Winthrop Young, 1936). This provokes the question as to why the dominant class should choose mountains as a means of displaying distinction. In *Distinction: A Social Critique of the Judgement of Taste*, Bourdieu (2010) asserts that:

> To distance themselves from common amusements, the privileged once again need only let themselves be guided by the horror of vulgar crowds which always leads them elsewhere, higher, further, to new experiences and virgin spaces, exclusively or firstly theirs, and also by the legitimacy of practices, which is a function of their distributional value, of course, but also of the degree to which they lend themselves to aestheticization, in practice or discourse. (p. 214)

This passage could have been written with mountaineering specifically in mind. Mountains fulfil the function of geographic or spatial separation in both the horizontal and vertical planes, and have the added benefit of doing so from both a literal and metaphorical perspective. The analogy between the physical ascent and spiritual ascent is easily made. The intellectualisation and, even more importantly, the aestheticisation of mountaineering imbue it with significant distinguishing potential. Mountaineering also fulfils other characteristics of social distinction outlined by Bourdieu (2010), perhaps most significantly in that mountaineering demonstrates its refined and elevated status by dint of substituting, 'man's [*sic.*] solitary struggle with nature for the man-to-man [*sic.*] battles of popular sports' (Bourdieu, 2010, p. 214). In almost every respect, mountaineering fits neatly with social practices that Bourdieu claims bestow social distinction.

Contemporary manifestations of distinction within the mountaineering community

Through the cultural appropriation of the social space of mountainous environments and the way in which mountaineering distinguishes its practitioners from other social agents, it is possible to recognise in mountaineering, 'the emergence of its object as a specific reality irreducible to any other . . . irreducible to a mere ritual game or festive amusement' (Bourdieu, 1978, p. 821). In Bourdieu's terms, we might reasonably define it as a sub-field of a larger social field of sport and recreational activities. A social field (Wacquant, 1989, pp. 37–41) is defined by the positions taken up by the individuals and institutions who inhabit the space and by the relations of power that exist between those positions. Every field has its own customs, logic, and accepted ways of thinking, rationalising, valuing and behaving. Business, music, law and education are all examples of cultural fields. Positions of power within a field are directly proportionate to the possession of whatever stakes are held by the field to be valuable. These stakes can be categorised under four headings: economic capital, social capital, cultural capital and symbolic capital (Bourdieu, 1986). Accepting mountaineering as a field leads us to consider within it the, 'existence of specific stakes and interests: via the inseparably economic and psychological investments that they arouse in the agents endowed with a certain habitus, the field and its stakes . . . produce investments of time, money and work' (Bourdieu, 1990, p. 87). The following vignette provides a point of entry into a consideration of the ways in which mountaineers invest time, money and work in order to accumulate particular forms of capital that increase their relative position in the field (Swartz, 1998, p. 121; Jenkins, 2002, p. 85; Beames & Telford, 2013).

> With the summer sky darkening and evening drawing near, a VW camper van is parked in front of the Great Wall of the Squamish Chief, with the boot door wide open. Two climbers sit on the tailgate relaxing after a day's climbing. They thumb through a dog-eared guide book, discussing the day's climbing, evaluating their achievements and making plans for the following day. Their language is replete with terms such as, 'clean lines,' being 'gripped,' taking 'whippers', and having 'epic' experiences. Arranged inside the van are the bare necessities of mountaineering life. Foodstuffs, coffee, a stove, a collection of plates, mugs, and cutlery nestle comfortably in what looks to be a self-made, wooden cabinet. Further inside, clothes and climbing gear are strewn across a sleeping platform. Yet, despite an appearance of cramped disorganisation, something about the display suggests a certain ascetic single-mindedness and focus. The van itself has seen better days. However, despite a faded paint job and the irregular edges of rust-decayed corners, this mobile home seems to fit the atmosphere of the scene perfectly. A pile of guidebooks to other mountain areas suggests that the two climbers are living an itinerant lifestyle that allows them to explore freedom in the vertical and horizontal planes.

This vignette is entirely fictional in its particularity, but anyone familiar with the mountaineering or climbing community will recognise its generality. Were it a photograph, it might well be entitled, 'Living the dream.' Every nuance of the image tells us something about the two climbers and their standing in the field: counter-cultural rebels, university of life philosophers, serendipitous wanderers and, somewhat jarringly, territorial colonisers (after all, they 'claim' and name new lines and 'tick off' iconic routes). As other climbers tramp past the van on their way home, they decode the ciphers. Were the two climbers to be sitting on the tailgate of a Mercedes-Benz sports car, or had they booked into a local bed and breakfast, the message would be very different. Neither of the latter have the kind of value attached to them that affords high amounts of cultural capital in the field of mountaineering.

Many of the forms of symbolic capital associated with mountaineering today can be traced directly back to mountaineering's roots in Romanticism. For example, the prestige (symbolic capital) attributed to those who demonstrate total commitment to the climbing 'lifestyle' harkens back to the revolutionary 18th century concept of dedication to an ideal, no matter what that ideal might be (Berlin, 2000, pp. 8–9). In a recent elegy to a departed friend, Leo Houlding (2014) wrote the following words: 'He was known locally as much for his organic gardening and deep philosophising as his sporting prowess. An experienced kayaker, skydiver and skier, when not living the dirtbag dream he worked as a rigger installing cameras on elaborate motorised cable systems to film major league American football' (p. 15). It is not difficult to contrast warm praise of 'dirtbag dream' with the condescending tones of 'weekend warrior' or 'armchair mountaineer' that one might hear at a crag in order to illustrate the distinguishing hierarchical processes at play. Bourdieu (1990) suggests that, 'struggles for recognition are a fundamental dimension of social life and what is at stake in them is an accumulation of a particular form of capital, honour in the sense of reputation and prestige, and that there is therefore, a specific logic behind the accumulation of symbolic capital' (p. 22). In other words, the tastes and preferences that mountaineers display with regard to clothing, food, accommodation, hair cuts, forms of transport, other forms of employment, and language used are all ways of making claims to honour and prestige – symbolic capital. Tastes and preferences are both a product and a function of the struggle for status in the social fields (Jenkins, 2002, p. 129), hence the recognisable cultural homogeneity within individual fields. If it were otherwise, if there were no common currency, how would it be possible to know who possesses what quantity of capital?

Themes of purity run through the field of mountaineering: the pure connection engendered when two people are joined by a single rope; the historical reluctance to use oxygen or crampons (as these were considered by some to be forms of cheating) (Davis, 2012, p. 384; Goodwin, 2004, paras 15–16); the debate over navigation cairns on Ben Nevis (Howett, 2004); ethical debates regarding the use of climber-placed protection and bolted protection; the ongoing debates regarding the commodification of adventure generally and certain routes specifically (Parnell, 2014, p. 3); and dominant vocabulary such as, 'clean lines', 'free ascents' and 'integrity' (Piolets d'Or, 2014). Mountaineers who commit to climbing in ways that are associated with these ideals of purity are able to accumulate the associated prestige and symbolic capital. 'Alpine style', for example, has become the gold standard of mountaineering; its uncluttered form, free of any ties to base camp via fixed ropes, permits easy analogy with notions of transcendental experiences of self-discovery. Climbing in this manner is more akin to a monastic pilgrimage than the industrial shift work of relaying hauled supplies. Alpine free climbing also provides greater scope for the embodied physicality of climbing itself to metamorphose into ever more aesthetic presentational forms. Ueli Steck's free solo speed ascents or Catherine Destivelle's balletic endeavours emphasise that there is much more capital at stake than that gained by simply reaching a summit.

In addition, as dynamic sites of struggle, fields do evolve. For example, the 'dirtbag' manner in which the climbers in the vignette present themselves to the world contrasts sharply with mountaineers of earlier eras, who often had significant baggage trains of porters carrying food and drink of choice delectation. As the accessibility of mountaineering has increased, particularly since the 1950s, the changing demographic of the field of mountaineering has impacted upon the forms of legitimate capital. Bourdieu (2010) draws attention to the potential for the 'symbolic subversion of the rituals of bourgeois order by ostentatious poverty', which manifests itself in an affectation of 'casualness towards forms and impatience with constraints, which is first marked in clothing or cosmetics since casual clothes and long hair – like the minibus or camping-car . . . are challenges to the standard attributes of bourgeois rituals' (p. 220). Noodles in a mug carry much stronger symbolism today than quails' eggs and foie gras.

Into the future

The desire to reach a summit is an expression of culture, as is the choice of route to get there, as is the manner in which the scaling is done, as is the interpretation of the experience by the individual. Applying Bourdieu's concepts of distinction and field helps us to deconstruct and reconsider taken-for-granted aspects of mountaineering. The dominant narrative that pervades mountaineering today is one bequeathed by individuals from a very narrow section of society that is located in a particular socio-historical context. The idea of mountaineering as a pure and sublime experience bound up in notions of ascendance and transcendence continues to perpetuate often unchallenged cultural understandings and practices within the field itself. However, the tastes and preferences associated with forms of capital within the field are all socio-cultural creations: their existence, their characteristics and mountaineers' appreciation of them are learned dispositions (Jenkins, 2002, p. 132). Many questions follow from drawing attention to this simple observation. If we liberate mountaineering from these subjective values for a moment, how else might it look? How else might people feel free to engage with mountain environments and how might this influence human interactions with the natural world? To what other forms of mountaineering might we ascribe legitimacy and value? What effect does the veneration of the hardest, highest routes have on the perceived accessibility of mountaineering, and whom does this veneration benefit? How should we respond to the received wisdom of transcendent mountain experiences when it would appear that they are a cultural invention of the last 300 years? How does the status quo impact upon women's experiences or the experiences of working-class climbers?

There are human–mountain histories that we have not had the space to explore in this chapter, for as with the voices of Postlethwaite and other pre-Romantic mountaineers, they have been muted within contemporary Western understandings of mountaineering. While this chapter focuses specifically on mountains and mountaineering, there are clear possibilities for applying the same analysis of socially constructed distinction and taste to other landscapes (and seascapes, skyscapes or spacescapes) and to other forms of outdoor adventurous sports.

Notes

1 Vestiges of the original meaning do remain, such as in the lyrics of the theme song of *The Beverly Hillbillies* television show (1962–1971), the first verse of which invites viewers to, 'Come and listen to a story about a man named Jed, A poor mountaineer, barely kept his family fed.' The French language, by contrast, allows the use of 'montagnard' and 'alpiniste' to differentiate between an inhabitant of the mountains and a climber mountaineer.
2 Bainbridge (2012) is acknowledged here for bringing this excerpt to the authors' attention.

John Telford and Simon Beames

References

Abram, D. (1996). *Spell of the sensuous*. New York: Pantheon.

Bainbridge, S. (2012). Romantic writers and mountaineering. *Romanticism, 18*(1), 1–15.

Beames, S. & Telford, J. (2013). Pierre Bourdieu: Habitus, field, and capital in rock climbing. In E. Pike & S. Beames (Eds.) *Outdoor Adventure and Social Theory* (pp. 77–87). London: Routledge.

Bennett, T. (2010). Introduction to the Routledge Classics edition. In Pierre Bourdieu, *Distinction: A social critique of the judgement of taste* (pp. xvii–xxii). London: Routledge.

Berlin, I. (2000). *The Roots of Romanticism*. London: Pimlico.

Bourdieu, P. (1978). Sport and social class. *Social Science Information, 17*(6), 819–840.

Bourdieu, P. (1986). The forms of capital. In J. Richardson (Ed.) *Handbook of Theory and Research for the Sociology of Education* (pp. 241–258). New York: Greenwood.

Bourdieu, P. (1990). *In Other Words: Essays Towards a Reflexive Sociology*. Stanford, CA: Stanford University Press.

Bourdieu, P. (2010). *Distinction: A Social Critique of the Judgement of Taste*. London: Routledge.

Braham, T. (2004). *When the Alps Cast their Spell. Mountaineers of the Alpine Golden Age*. In Pinn.

Budworth, J. (1810). *A Fortnight's Ramble to the Lakes* (3rd edn). London.

Cousquer, G.O. & Beames, S. (2014). Professionalism in mountain tourism and the claims to professional status of the international mountain leader. *Journal of Sport & Tourism, 18*(3), 185–215.

Davis, W. (2012). *Into the Silence. The Great War, Mallory and the Conquest of Everest*. New York: Alfred A. Knopf.

de Bellefon, R. (2003). *Histoire des Guides de Montagne: Alpes et Pyrénées (1760–1980)*. France: Cairn.

FIFA (2014). Retrieved from: www.fifa.com/classicfootball/history/the-game/Britain-home-of-football.html.

Goodwin, S. (2004). The Alpine journal: A century and a half of mountaineering history. *The Himalayan Journal, 60*. Retrieved from: www.himalayanclub.org/hj/60/1/the-alpine-journal-a-century-and-a-half-of-mountaineering-history/.

Griggs, E.L. (Ed.) (1956–1971). *Collected Letters of Samuel Taylor Coleridge* (6 vols). Oxford: Clarendon Press.

Houlding, L. (2014). Sean Stanley obituary. *Climb*, March, 27.

Howett, K. (2004). Talking point. Big issues – big debates: A report of the MCofS 2004 Annual Gathering. *Scottish Mountaineer, 24*. Retrieved from: www.mcofs.org.uk/mag_sm24_page2.asp.

Hyde, W.W. (1915). The ancient appreciation of mountain scenery. *Classical Journal, 11*(2), 70–84.

Jenkins, R. (2002). *Pierre Bourdieu*. London: Routledge.

Kirchner, W. (1950). Mind, mountain, and history. *Journal of the History of Ideas, 11*(4), 412–447.

Macfarlane, R. (2003). *Mountains of the Mind: A History of a Fascination*. London: Granta Books.

Parnell, I. (2014). Editorial. *Climb*, March, 3.

Piolets d'Or (2014). Retrieved from: www.pioletsdor.com/index.php?lang=en.

Schama, S. (1995). *Landscape and Memory*. London: HarperCollins.

Swartz, D. (1998). *Culture and Power. The Sociology of Pierre Bourdieu*. Chicago, IL: University of Chicago Press.

Wacquant, L.D. (1989). Towards a reflexive sociology: A workshop with Pierre Bourdieu. *Sociological Theory, 7*(1), 26–63.

Winthrop Young, G. (1936). Introduction. In L. Stephen (Ed.) *The Playground of Europe* (pp. vii–xiii). Oxford: Blackwell.

48

The archaeology of the outdoor movement and the German development

In the beginning was the curiosity about the sublime

Peter Becker

Philipps University of Marburg

Translated by Gudrun Vill-Debney

I

Whoever wants to clearly understand the present needs to know the past that has led to it. This is why an '*International Handbook of Outdoor Studies*' cannot avoid investigating the historical conditions, even if they seem a little outdated, which have contributed to the development of the cultural pattern of 'Natursuche' (the quest for nature), which can be seen as one of the most important roots of the outdoor movement.

Due to the complexity of its historical origins, I cannot be comprehensive but will have to limit myself especially to considering those ideas and discourses that in Europe led to the situation of change that also promoted and facilitated the gradual development of this cultural pattern.[1] This process, fed equally from the sources of (popular) philosophy, fine arts, literature, garden architecture and music in the course of the 17th, and especially in the 18th century, gained so much driving force that more and more people gave up their fear of untamed, wild nature and increasingly went to seek out nature and natural landscapes in quest of 'new' and surprising experiences.

II

Putting the origins of a new nature feeling into the 18th century goes against the canonised explanation, which holds that the aesthetically self-sufficient approach to nature goes back to a kind of proto-scene that happened at the threshold between the Middle Ages and modern times. The scene here, in short: On 26 April 1336, in a letter to his father confessor, Dionigi, the Italian poet Petrarca describes his arduous climb up Mount Ventoux, which, however, was amply rewarded by an aesthetically overwhelming, unlimited panoramic experience on the summit. However, the, at that time not yet crowned, poeta laureatus does not indulge in his emotional rapture of nature but quite accidentally opens the *Confessiones Augustines* he happened to have on him, on a page that evoked a great moral conflict in him. The passage brought home to him that he was about to endanger his spiritual welfare in favour of sensuous, worldly emotional fervour. Instead of taking care of his internal world, he had indulged – however briefly – in awed admiration of the external world. Aware of this contradiction, he begins the descent, during which the fascination of the mountain gradually fades.

While one group of interpreters celebrates this letter as the time of birth of modern nature experience, others believe that the aesthetic description of nature is meant only to serve as a metaphor for everything earthly, as a reminder of the real issue: the human quest for salvation (Groh & Groh, 1991, 1996). If one follows this interpretation, which is also supported by the fact that, in Petrarca's other works, no description of autonomous worldly emotional rapture can be found (Stierle, 2003), it takes another 300 years before a historical situation occurred that allowed the modern aesthetic approach to nature to develop, where the extremely negative picture of nature was overcome that had prevented people from seeking out nature freely.

Part of this picture, which was called *natura lapsa* (fallen nature), whose mythological origin can be found in *Genesis*, was the idea that nature was not only a place of horror but also in a process of permanent decay. Nature was seen as the result of God's act of punishment, which expelled human kind from paradise for having eaten from the Tree of Knowledge. Since then human kind has been burdened with this original sin. It has had to live in and with nature, which had now lost its original state of harmony. It had slipped into disorder, and thus offered a terrifying aspect and posed a constant fear and anxiety-causing danger. Hailstorms, earthquakes, pests, famines, floods, conflagrations, volcanic eruptions, were interpreted as expressions of divine wrath, as reminders of the Fall.

The Alps, for example, were likened to ruins, piles of rubble or wreckage. The German scholar Winckelmann perceived them as so alarming that he had the curtains of his coach drawn closed (Koschorke, 1990). Coastlines, which formed the border of the unrestrained, turbulent and lawless ocean, were also seen as expanses of rubble. Dominated by the chaos of storms, it destroyed ships and brought misfortune to the crews (Corbin, 1990). The natural scientist Scheuchzer, who otherwise fought against the death penalty for witchcraft, firmly believed that the Alps were haunted by dragons, which he carefully classified (Raymond, 1993). The impenetrable forest was said to be inhabited by witches and wild men and women (Termeer, 2005). The depths below the restless surface of the ocean were supposed to be terrorised by merciless monsters, such as sea snakes, krakens and sea demons (Corbin, 1990). In particular, the night, governed by the cold moon, was thought to be the domain of hell, of ghosts and the spirits of the dead. The night air, filled with toxic vapours by the moon, was said to be populated by demons.

Nature was seen as beautiful and useful where people had it under control and made improvements, such as in fruit growing or in baroque gardens, where nature was given a geometrical order, showed an aspect of regularity, harmony and symmetry, where the gardener gave trees and bushes an ornate shape and ordered them in lines. Beauty excluded chaos. It transformed it into harmony for the pleasure of mankind. Water, for instance, the element that is hostile to order, keeps breaking out and loses its temper easily, is tamed in baroque gardens. It lies smoothly in well-shaped basins, is pressed upwards in jets, or cascades down gently gurgling in a steady stream and thus this wild element is tamed into the 'living soul of the garden'.

It is understandable that such repulsive nature, governed by supernatural powers, obscure and full of dangers, could not be controlled. It did not tempt people to spend more time in it than absolutely necessary. Fear, not the quest for aesthetic delight, seemed the appropriate attitude towards it. Only woodcutters, hunters, herdsmen or seamen and trades people overcame their fear of terrible nature because of their working conditions. But before a different relationship with nature could develop, nature had to lose its terror, it had, first of all, to be de-demonised. This was achieved by science and theology, which supplied the necessary changes in interpretation.

III

Through the Scientific Revolution the model of *natura lapsa*, of fallen, fear-producing nature, lost its persuasive power. Cartesian philosophy suggested a strict separation between mind and matter, and thus took the soul out of nature and reduced things to their external form. Once plants, animals, stones, rivers, mountains, etc., were not considered to be influenced and governed by supernatural powers any more, nature could be ordered and objectified through the laws of mechanics and mathematical logic (Kittsteiner, 1991). The more nature behaved according to the rational laws of mathematics and mechanics, the less room there was, by necessity, for elves, witches, fairies, sorcerers and demons.[2] This rational attitude to nature was also supported by biblical references,[3] and thus theologians, instead of a vengeful God, found a God who had constructed nature, or rather the world, according to his own ingenious designs. Thus divine design was searched for and recognised in all areas of nature.

Positive functions, designed by God, were found for the ugly and terrifying features. Thus the awful mountains with their deeply fissured glaciers were turned into a useful natural space, supplying people with fresh water, clean air, minerals, medicinal herbs and timber (Groh & Groh, 1996). Even fire-spewing volcanoes acquired a practical use as air holes that relieved the pressure of the Earth's core and thus prevented earthquakes (Zelle, 1987). Ocean winds cleaned the water, sea salt prevented the development of mould and prevented the formation of ice, so people could fish all year round. In the same way that the Alps were seen as a protective wall for lovely Italy, the sea had the same function for England. Cliffs were no longer seen as rubble but as protective coastal fortifications (Corbin, 1990).

Terrible nature began to loose its forbidding quality, since it was proven useful and one could take an interest in it. Scientific quests for knowledge and theological reinterpretation were followed by aesthetic perception and experience gathering.

Locus classicus for this new evaluation of nature, which was going to keep philosophers and artists, as well as interested amateurs, busy for the next century or more, especially in England, France and Germany, is a letter of the year 1688, in which the English literary critic John Dennis writes about his crossing of the Savoy Alps. Describing an ascent it says:

> . . . the unusual height in which we found our selves, the impending Rock that hung over us, the dreadful Depth of the Precipice, and the Torrent, that roar'd at the bottom, gave us such a view as was altogether new and amazing . . . In the very same place Nature was Severe and Wanton. In the mean time we walk'd upon that very brink in a litteral sense, of Destruction; one stumble, and both Life and Carcass had been at once destroy'd. The sense of all this produc'd different motions in me, *viz.* a delightful Horrour, a terrible Joy, and at the same time, that I was infinitely pleas'd I trembled. (Dennis, 1943, pp. 133f.)

The last sentences was especially epoch-making. The traveller is overrun by a peculiar mixture of paradoxical feelings. Although the 'craggy Cliffs' give him an enormous fright, he does not find this fright repulsive, but pleasant and attractive. The residue of the old feeling of impotence in the face of wild nature is kept in check by the simultaneous feeling of fascination.

This might be the point where the budding confidence of a new enlightened approach to nature asserted itself – no more running away from the resistances emanating from nature. Instead it begins to endure them aesthetically and even tries to deal with them in practical ways.

This development of a new sense of sovereignty can be seen especially clearly in the reaction to thunderstorms. When interpreted as God's voice and wrath (*natura lapsa*), people had great fear and tried to appease him with prayer before, during and after a thunderstorm, ringing of bells, penitential sermons, firing cannons against the clouds. Although this fear could partly be mitigated by physico-theological considerations of utility, it was not before Franklin's practical invention of the lightning rod that people felt safe enough to face thunderstorms without fear. Conducting the lightning into the earth also takes away the wrath. God's voice can turn into a sound of nature, which then can become an aesthetic experience. Once safety has been procured, there is no need for prayers, but one can indulge in this new emotional mix of 'pleasant horror'.[4] For the literary scholar Alewyn (1974), what is happening here is anthropological change: the fear of fear is turned into the desire for fear.

IV

Under the term of the sublime, this emotional blend gives considerable momentum to contacts with and feelings about nature in a Europe that is going through the process of enlightenment. Its deep emotional effect suddenly makes the category of beauty seem pale and insignificant. Although beauty evokes feelings of pleasure and delight, it lacks the dynamics of the sublime thrill. John Dennis had also noted this in his letter when perceiving the lack of being moved by beauty of 'Flowry Meadows and murmuring Streams'. The sublime goes for what is exceptional, wild, irregular, immoderate, disharmonic, bleak, impetuous, an intensity that beauty excludes. The German philosopher of the Enlightenment Moses Mendelssohn (2006, p. 157) later described this conflict of aesthetic effect very accurately.

> The singular character of these mixed feelings is that they may not be so tender as pure pleasure, but they penetrate deeper into the heart and also seem to remain there longer. What is only pleasant may soon lead to satedness or, finally, nausea. . . . By contrast, something unpleasant mixed with something pleasant catches our attention and prevents that we are sated too early.

How beauty was de-throned by the sublime can be demonstrated by the example of the rapidly changing garden design. Geometrical design and axial symmetry were abandoned. Through a purposeful arrangement of rock formations, grottos and caves, combinations of tree types and leaf colours, light–shade contrasts, the creation of sounds, combinations of colour and scent, a natural drama of the sublime was staged that took visitors on guiding paths through individual natural scenes designed to provoke surprise, a sense of mystery, cause them to shiver, be horrified, in awe, etc.

This exciting new feeling towards nature is also reflected in painting, considered the 'most intimate sister of landscape design' (Hirschfeld). William Turner, Anton Koch, Joseph Vernet, Christian Dahl, Alexander Cozens, Caspar David Friedrich, Philipp Loutherbourg, to name a few, covered canvas over canvas with thunderstorms, rocky abysses, moonlit nights, storms, rock formations, waterfalls, shipwrecks, roaring breakers and glacier landscapes. People, if depicted at all, seemed insignificantly small. Those who wanted to step into the shoes of these small people and understand their emotional state, could follow Diderot's recommendation and go on an imaginary walk through the painted landscapes (Bätschmann, 1989).

The composers of the age provided the soundtracks for the painted turmoil of the elements. From Telemann's thirsty nature to Mendelssohn Bartholdy's thundering waves off the Hebrides or off Fingal's Cave, the musical descriptions of storms and thunderstorms, of violent storms in operas, of sunrises, earthquakes and rainbows of Bach, Beethoven, Haydn and other composers evoked impressions of powerful nature (Schleuning, 1998).

The interest in this new fascination for nature was probably also further spread by the Moralischen Wochenschriften (weekly ethical publications) and other periodicals, which played an essential role in the establishment of the emerging middle-class public. Addison, for example, published his reflections on the joys of imagination or his views on taste in the *Spectator*, whose express purpose was to discuss aesthetic questions. Since the *Spectator* was also translated into German, the topics published in this magazine were discussed widely not only in England but also in the reading societies in Germany that existed even in small towns and to which not only middle-class people had access. And they were also carried into coffeehouses and pubs, where Addison, for example, had to defend his views against a large audience (Deschner, 1972).

V

Neither discussions nor visits to galleries or concerts, however, could replace real experiences on location. For this, people had to leave the protected spheres of the coffeehouses in London, the salons in Paris or the reading societies in Berlin, and seek out wild nature. Where people set out, they expected to find outside the corresponding features to the fictitious ones.

The act of emotionally and aesthetically freeing the mind from horror was now completed by physically setting out from the libraries and study chambers of middle-class homes. In other words, it was not a departure enforced by the needs of everyday life but it was stimulated by curiosity about the unknown and unfamiliar natural space. Enlightenment did not only grip the mind but also the body. One could also say that, without the physical practices of movement, sublime nature would have remained an indoor phenomenon of the mind and its favoured locations of discourse. This physical urge to seek out undisguised nature, thus triggered, at the same time constitutes the take-off point of the European outdoor movement. Free from the burden of coping with everyday life, people no longer simply pass through nature but intentionally seek to encounter it.

VI

Those who did not yet trust their own eyes and ears in their search for this new feeling, for free nature and the pleasure in fear, used the templates offered by the arts, even if this did not quite agree with the principles of self-determined enlightenment. Since music and paintings could not be taken along, assistance in the search for the right places and appropriate natural experiences could be found in poetry and narratives. Rousseau was one of those who drew people out of their houses and into nature. His novel, *Julie, or the New Heloise*, lured them into the Alps, following the trail of its hero Saint-Preux. The fake songs of Ossian, the Celtic bard, created by McPherson, caused a veritable fevered rush to the north in search of the sublime. These people in quest of the sublime believed they could perceive the eerie atmosphere of the Ossian storm on the Caledonian west coast as it was described so stirringly by Corbin (1990, S. 172):

> Although numerous islands and reefs break the mighty power of the northern waves they provoke exceptional fear in people. . . . The soaring waves thrash against a coast lined by echoing reefs, resounding with the wind caught in their grottos. The wailing of the gale in the island labyrinth, the whistling of the winds between the moss-covered arcades of the ruins on the off-shore hills join in with the sound of the bard's harp.

The poetry of the time served as model not only for nature exploration on foot or for passive indulgence in ephemeral natural phenomena, such as storms, sunrises and sundowns and moon-lit nights, but it also provided suggestions for activities in which people could free their bodies from only being the container of the mind and theoretical knowledge in confrontation with sublime nature (see, for example, Lord Byron). This Byron chap – as the elderly Goethe called him – and whom he admired because he went sailing, canoeing and horse riding (Ross, 1968), this chap in his epic poem *Childe Harold's Pilgrimage* writes the lines:

> And I have loved thee, Ocean! And my joy
> Of youthful sports was on thy breast to be
> Borne, like they Bubbles, on word: from a boy
> I wanton'd with thy breakers – they to me
> Were a delight; and if the freshening sea
> Made them a terror – 'twas a pleasing fear
> For I was as it were a child of thee . . .
> (Byron 2014/1818, p. 95)

In contrast to Byron, who sought his experience of sublimity in approaching breakers and waves, Goethe was content with the sublimity radiated by the shining reflection of the moon on the water's surface when he went swimming in the Ilm at night. Both poets actively overcame their fear of terrible nature through swimming. Water, which can bring death through drowning, seemed to have been defeated by superior man. But in their sublime feeling still is retained a sense of the originally felt deadly threat.[5] The risk of death and the joy of self-assertion lie side by side.

This exemplary effect of fiction was not the only factor that allowed the new outdoor practice to become a middle-class one. Before these practices could be carried out with such superior ease, as shown by Byron and Goethe, before they could become an integrated part of the middle-class physical habitus, they had to be stripped of some of their wayward attributes.[6] The practices that were used in order to climb mountains, to sail along coastlines, to walk through forests and over hills, swimming in lakes and rivers, did not have to be newly invented. They all existed already as practices to cope with the necessities of everyday life; sailors sailed the sea, even had to swim if their ship sank; hunters and shepherds climbed mountains; craftsmen, day labourers, traders and itinerant folk travelled the roads on foot. In order to develop into an aesthetic practice of contemplative or active encounter with nature, the activities had to be separated from their work-related context and be invested with new meaning.

This process of change, which has been described by von Mallinckrodt (2008), was a somewhat obstructive one in the case of swimming, since middle-class status awareness at first rejected the imitation of unrestrained pleasure activities of lower classes or of people of doubtful status, such as sailors and boatmen, or even of savages. This violation of class norms was rectified by a series of papers on swimming. The fact alone that swimming became an object open to rational discussion that was worthy of publication increased its value. As an art that could be taught systematically in methodical steps on the basis of scientific analysis, and that could even save lives, swimming was granted access to the middle-class educational programme and to the middle-class culture of exercise.

VII

The 'original practice' of the outdoor movement – hiking – also had to undergo such a process of purification and reinterpretation from the necessity of craftsmen to travel to the joy of hiking of the bourgeoisie. However, this seemed somewhat easier, probably partly because the discourse of the Enlightenment, which was closely connected with the rise of the bourgeoisie, borrowed metaphors from the area of walking when presenting its principles. The criticised lack of personal autonomy was described in terms referring to 'apron strings', 'baby walker', 'ankle shackles', 'being led', 'anxiously clinging to', and the desired autonomy was referred to as 'free movement', 'going alone', 'finally learning to walk', 'trying out one's own powers' (Warneken, 1989, 1990).

At the same time as enlightened bourgeois in the second half of the 18th century developed into pedestrians, hiking was included in the philanthropic repertoire. Thus the new philanthropic model school, which was committed to the Enlightenment, welcomed the new school activity with the arguments already known. Hiking was to free children from the apron strings of school textbooks. The schoolboy is encouraged to 'take his own steps . . . to go ahead by himself, and to observe everything around him with his own eyes and evaluate it himself' (Salzmann, quoted in Althans, 1999, p. 37).[7]

Going on hikes opens up the narrow confines of the school, connects with reality and turns nature into a sphere of experience. It was quite common even fifty years later in other educational institutions, e.g. in the Bendersche Institute, to set out early to experience the sublime moment of the sunrise. It seems that, in this philanthropic practice of hiking, everything that attracted the interest of the pupils could be discussed without using any specific textbooks on the subject. Even the middle-class virtues of discipline, endurance, order and deferred gratification could be practised on the arduous marches.

Even the universities, which were undergoing far-reaching reforms around 1800, discovered hiking. A study guide in 1792, for example, recommended, after praising the independence and freedom of hiking, that students go on two hikes a year to test the knowledge laid down in books against reality (Bosse & Neumeyer, 1995). Evidently such recommendations were followed because the first travel guides are expressly addressed to students (ibid.). The kind of hiking that was very popular among the Musensöhne (students) was different from the philanthropic kind or that of craftsmen in that it did not have to follow a school curriculum or any guild regulations. It shed the constraints of school education or vocational training, and thus was able to enter into a relationship with the ideal of self-determined education. It freed itself from the dominance of narrow, specialised fields, and directed its attention to the balanced development not only of the mind and spirit, but also of the imagination, the powers of the senses and of the body. This education represented a fundamental attitude to oneself and the world, which, although it was practised in the study moratorium, remained a lifelong asset.

As a representative example, Bosse (2011, p. 88) quotes the Romantic writer Eichendorff, who called the 'apparently unattached and untroubled freedom of students' the 'still healthy and unscarred' life-phase in which they can test their life concept of continuous renewal. Hiking as inquisitive, self-determined as well as carefree departure into the open, the strange and unknown and the independent management of the obstacles that may arise on the way, was the physical symbolisation of a life-form that is focused on self-education (Bildung). Being bodily on the way is equivalent to being on the way mentally. In these student hikes, there is obviously a shift from the virtues of discipline, endurance and postponement of gratification to openness, willingness to take risks, optimistic self-confidence and confidence in the future.

Occasionally, hiking students were taken for vagabonds, were suspected of begging, and were expelled from the town or region (Bosse & Neumeyer, 1995). What for students were occasions of amusement was horror for the status-conscious bourgeoisie. Even when hiking they were haunted by their need for distinction. They feared they may be mistaken for members of the lower orders or for travelling folk. To protect against this they even thought of making the distinction clear through specific clothing (Althans, 1999). This petty need for marking status distinctions at first also hampered the introduction of the rucksack. A physical posture that was bent through carrying weight did not only remind the bourgeois of work situations of the lower classes, it also contradicted the elegant upright posture that he had only just acquired and trained through going for walks.[8]

Upright carriage was also a symbol of distinction, from the nobility and courtly culture, whose members travelled on horseback or in carriages, or were carried in sedan chairs and thus could not move without outside help. Seen from this point of view, hiking under one's own steam was an act of criticism of the feudal ways of locomotion; it was directed against the parasitical refusal of putting in any personal effort, which manifested itself in being carried.

The bourgeois in the late Enlightenment did not walk through nature in the same way their grandfathers had done, who, lured by this new and open nature divested of its horrors, followed their curiosity to explore it extensively. They did not have to break new ground as their grandfathers had to. While their younger sons had to acquire bourgeois virtues through walking under philanthropist guidance and their elder sons could acquire an open attitude to the world at the university through walking, their hiking fathers sought out nature to heal the slowly emerging cracks in bourgeois culture. In this process, external nature, in combination with the self-determinateness of hiking, helped internal nature by providing a temporary, non-alienated, simple and deeply emotional form of life, which was lost when the bourgeois everyday life became subject to the laws of the economy. In this connection and in the face of the considerably increasing yearning for nature of the age Schiller (2002/1795) asked the bourgeoisie what they thought was better, to regress into mother nature or to reignite the flame of the ideal. This question is yet to be answered.[9]

Notes

1 In order to give a comprehensive picture of the beginnings of this new cultural pattern, the chosen history-of-ideas approach needs to be complemented by further approaches, such as those of socio-economics or geographical structures. More specifically this might be, for example, an analysis of the processes of industrialisation and their effects on work and life organisation, on contemporary circumstances and on habitus formations, as well as an analysis of the economisation of natural spheres, such as large-scale soil and water improvement and redesign of landscapes for the better exploitation, as was done, for example, with the measure of enclosure.

2 The Romantic writer E.T.A. Hoffmann has described this process of de-mystification in his narrative 'Klein Zaches' as expulsion of sorcerers and witches to Dschinnistan. However, witches could win their right to remain in the enlightened world by knitting woollen socks for soldiers.

3 Groh and Groh (1991, p. 61) point out that the idea of God as craftsman or master builder, who created the world on the basis of numerical ratios, goes back to a Bible verse saying 'though hast ordered all things in measure and number and weight' (*Wisdom* 11, 20). This reference also served as justification for actions using technology and for building technical machinery, and thus for technical control of nature, as in the straightening of rivers and the building of dams.

4 In Rousseau's 'Confessions' (1996, p. 175) there is a place that mentions this practical safety as prerequisite for enjoying nature. 'In order to prevent accidents, the road had been given a parapet; therefore, I could look right down to the bottom and allow myself to be gripped by the dizziness to my heart's content;

because the enjoyable part of my predilection for steep slopes is that they make me dizzy and that I find this dizziness very pleasant as long as I am safe.'

5 This new playful but at the same time very serious cultivation of the body, which developed from the self-confident engagement with threatening nature, is also brought across in Klopstock's ode, in itself a sublime form of poetry, 'Der Eislauf' (ice skating). In order to run one's circles on the white crystal surface despite the frosty crackling of the 'death-throne' one has to leave the safe philistine warmth of the fireplace.

6 Byron, and even more so Goethe, who did not only swim regularly in lakes and rivers, but who went hiking, climbed mountains, went ice skating and horse riding, succeeded in integrating such different areas as intellectual productivity and physical experience into their lives. They made them fruitful for their own educational and spiritual development. The bourgeois who admired them were still a long way from being able to overcome their inhibition in the face of the cultural barrier between body and mind.

7 Rousseau, the shining example for philanthropists, had already ennobled the art of walking. In 'Emile' (1997, pp. 543f.) its advantages are praised: 'One can observe the whole country . . . one can explore everything that takes one's fancy, one can take a break at all viewing points. . . . I depend neither on paths nor on postilions. . . . I can see everything a human being can see; and since I only depend on myself I enjoy all the freedom there is for a human being to enjoy.'

8 Going for a walk as a cultural art was spreading around 1800. While hiking meant seeking out unknown natural spaces, walking was done outside the gates of the town for all to see. Here the bourgeois need for distinction could be satisfied in executing the posture and gait that conformed with their status. Through walking, the bourgeois learned to walk in a bourgeois manner: natural and casual, harmonious and self-confident, length of stride and speed carefully measured, not too fast, as that would not be appropriate to the bourgeois habitus and would remind them of errant boys and other below-status occupations (König, 1996). It was hard to make this look natural because watching others in the constant worry of observing distinction reflected on their own behaviour, which, being under constant scrutiny, could never become free and easy.

9 Ironical critics of the age also did not miss this enormous departure into nature. Romantic writer Ludwig Tieck considered this onslaught of hikers as caused by the lineage of nature hunters. Whom he meant were 'those . . . , who go on a veritable hunt for sunrises and sundowns on high mountains, for waterfalls and natural phenomena, and who spoil many a morning for others in expectation of a delight which often fails to materialise and which they afterwards have to feign' (Tieck, 1985, p. 111).

References

Alewyn, R. (1974). *Probleme und Gestalten*. Frankfurt/M.: Insel.
Althans, H.-J. (1999) Bürgerliche Wanderlust. In W. Albrecht & H.-J. Kertscher (Eds.) *Wanderzwang Wanderlust* (pp. 25–43). Tübingen: Niemeyer.
Bätschmann, O. (1989). *Entfernung der Natur*. Köln: Dumont.
Bosse, H. (2011). Musensohn und Philister. In R. Bunia *et al.* (Eds.) *Philister* (pp. 55–100). Berlin: Akademie Verlag.
Bosse, H. & Neumeyer, H. (1995). *Da blüht der Winter schön*. Freiburg: Rombach.
Corbin, A. (1990). *Meereslust*. Berlin: Wagenbach.
Dennis, J. (1943). Miscellanies in verse and prose. In *Critical Works, vol. II*. Baltimore: Johns Hopkins University Press.
Deschner, G. (1972). *Ursprünge der Rheinromantik in England*. Frankfurt/M.: Klostermann.
Groh, R. & Groh, D. (1991). *Weltbild und Naturaneignung*. Frankfurt/M.: suhrkamp.
Groh, R. & Groh, D. (1996). *Die Außenwelt der Innenwelt*. Frankfurt/M.: suhrkamp.
Kittsteiner, H.D. (1991). *Die Entstehung des modernen Gewissens*. Frankfurt/M.: Insel.
König, G.M. (1996). *Eine Kulturgeschichte des Spaziergangs*. Wien: Böhlau.
Koschorke, A. (1990). *Die Geschichte des Horizonts*. Frankfurt/M.: suhrkamp.
Lord Byron (2014/1818). *Childe Harold's Pilgrimage*. Free Download & Streaming: Internet Archive.
Mallinckrodt, R.v. (2008). Oronzio de Bernardi und die Schwimmkunst im 18. Jh. In Dies. (Eds.) *Bewegtes Leben* (pp. 231–245). Wiesbaden: Harrassowitz.
Mendelssohn, M. (2006). *Ästhetische Schriften*. Hamburg: Meiner.
Raymond, P. (1993). *Von der Landschaft im Kopf zur Landschaft aus Sprache*. Tübingen: Max Niemeyer.
Ross, W. (1968). Vom Schwimmen in Seen und Flüssen. In *Arcadia* (pp. 262–291).
Rousseau, J.J. (1996). *Bekenntnisse*. München: Winkler.

Peter Becker

Rousseau, J.J. (1997). *Emile oder von der Erziehung.* Düsseldorf: Artemis & Winkler.

Schiller, F. (2002/1795). Über *naive und sentimentalische Dichtung.* Stuttgart: Reclam.

Schleuning, P. (1998). *Die Sprache der Natur.* Stuttgart: Metzler.

Stierle, H. (2003). *Francesco Petrarca.* München: Hanser.

Termeer, M. (2005). *Verkörperungen des Waldes.* Bielefeld: Transcript.

Tieck, L. (1985). *Phantasus.* Frankfurt/M.: Deutscher Klassiker Verlag.

Warneken, B.J. (1989). Bürgerliche Gehkultur in der Epoche der Französischen Revolution. *Zeitschrift für Volkskunde, 85,* 177–187.

Warneken, B.J. (1990). Biegsame Herkunft und aufrechter Gang. In Ludwig-Uhland-Institut (Ed.) *Der aufrechte Gang* (pp. 11–23). Tübingen.

Zelle, C. (1987). *Angenehmes Grauen.* Hamburg: Meiner.

49

Surfing, localism, place-based pedagogies and ecological sensibilities in Australia

Rebecca Olive

THE UNIVERSITY OF WAIKATO

In 2013, the Australian government identified participation in lifestyle sports such as surfing, snowboarding, skateboarding and rock climbing as a significant trend in Australia (Hajkowicz, Cook, Wilhelmseder & Boughen, 2013). This growth reflects similar patterns in participation across much of the world, which Gilchrist and Wheaton (2011) argue might be much higher than the figures suggest. With participation in many of these sports requiring access to nature-based spaces that are often outside cities, questions of access to, responsibility for and sustainability of places are increasingly key in making sense of changes in our knowledge and resource management of recreational lifestyle sport and physical cultures. This includes a number of coastal surf sports such as surfing, body-boarding, wind-surfing, kite-surfing and ocean-swimming, which contribute to continued significance of the coast in recreational and cultural life in Australia (Pearson, 1979; Booth, 2001; Maguire, Miller, Weston & Young, 2011). Management of these spaces to sustainably cater for diverse populations, while at the same time encouraging increased access, creates tensions among local, resident coastal populations who feel the most invested in these areas (Evers, 2008a; Franklin, Picken & Osbaldiston, 2014). In Australia, 'local' knowledge of place and community is privileged as the most authentic, yet critical numbers of coastal users live in cities and experience the coast as an extension of their everyday lives (Goggin, 2002; Maguire *et al.*, 2011). Currently we have little understanding of how city-based surfers impact on and develop relationships with, the beaches and coasts they have come to love and care for (Urry, 1995; Franklin, 1998; Macnaghten, 2003; Wattchow & Brown, 2011).

This chapter is a response to the emphasis on 'the local' in research about the development of ecological sensibilities through nature-based lifestyle sports, instead suggesting that such sensibilities are equally possible through physical cultural connections, knowledges and relationships. This argument is a delayed response to graffiti I saw in 2009 at Broken Head – an Australian beach on the north coast of NSW, Australia – a beach I grew up on and where I still regularly surfed, despite living two hours north in Brisbane. The graffiti read 'SAVE BROKEN. STAY IN BRISBANE.' This text juxtaposed my local and non-local identities. This discussion will draw on my own experiences and relationships within surfing culture to illustrate that 'non-locals' can develop strong ecological sensibilities relating to place and community. Inspired by Elspeth Probyn (1993, 2003), the discussion takes an embodied approach to questioning this idea by thinking the idea of localism through my own embodied experience of both local and non-local relationships to surfing places. Linking feminist and cultural studies theory, methods, ethics and reflexivity, Probyn (1993) suggests that I may 'conceive of thinking the social through myself' (p. 3) by not only using my own experiences but other surfers' as well. This approach accounts for how experiences both challenge and support the discourses that help shape us – one cannot be discounted against the other. When we 'think the social through ourselves', we allow for a way of knowing that is unavoidably mediated through our subjectivity, revealing contextual specificity in terms of time and place, as well as sex, gender, race, ethnicity, sexuality, ability, age, class, and so on. This research approach acknowledges that experiences are specific to individual subjectivities, which may reproduce, resist or disrupt more generalised and normative understandings of cultures, and promote the role of the intersections of subjective self with others and with space. Such intersections are key to understanding the embodied and relational nature of subjective experiences.

> The body . . . becomes a site for the production of knowledge, feelings, emotions and history, all of which are central to subjectivity [yet] the body cannot be thought of as a contained entity; it is in constant contact with others. (Probyn, 2003, p. 290)

We experience our subjectivities in terms of how we are positioned as contextualised subjects, highlighted by a range of voices of cultural authority, all of whom impact us to varying degrees, depending on our relationships to the people and contexts around us (Rose, 1996). As Probyn asks, 'How can it be otherwise, given that our bodies and our sense of ourselves are in constant interaction with how and where we are placed?' (2003, p. 290). Approaching research in this way has a risk of centralising the self over others. Importantly, as Couldry (1996) cautions, this approach 'is *not* a licence for a subjective, overpersonalized form of writing; it should, rather, incite a re-examination of critical vocabulary' (p. 317). That is, I need to think through my subjective position without privileging it. This approach to research allows for a subjective, personalised, contextualised account of an experience, feeling, space or place. My work centralises lived, subjective, empathetic bodies as a tool for doing research (Davis, 1997). This approach continues to privilege the surrounding social and cultural world *and* the perspectives of cultural participants, while reflexively accounting for the limitations of the researcher's position within that.

Starting with a definition of ecological sensibilities and how these relate to lifestyle sports, this discussion will 'think the social through myself' to question why 'local' lifestyle nature-based sports participants continue to be positioned by cultural participants and researchers as possessing the most authoritative knowledge about their sporting cultures, community, place and environments. The discussion will draw on a range of research from cultural studies, cultural geography, history, outdoor education and sport sociology to explore the various intersections, understandings and pedagogies of place as negotiated by subjectivities and culture, and to imagine how these can be productive.

Surfing, localism and ecological sensibilities

Increasing scholarship is highlighting the environmental knowledges and relationships that sport and physical recreation can help develop. Scholars in outdoor education (Humberstone, 1998; Wattchow & Brown, 2011; Hill & Brown, 2014), cultural geography (Whatmore, 2002; Waitt & Cook, 2007; Anderson, 2009, 2014; Waitt, Gill & Head, 2009; Church & Ravenscroft, 2011), tourism studies (Franklin, 1998, 2014; Weiss, Norden, Hilscher & Vanreusel, 1998), sociology/sport sociology (Macnaghten, 2003; Wheaton, 2007; Mansfield, 2009; Erickson, 2011; Mansfield & Wheaton, 2011; Thorpe & Rinehart, 2012), and my disciplinary home of cultural studies (Satchell, 2007, 2008; Evers, 2009), have been exploring the potential for lifestyle sport and activities to sensitise people to environments and ecologies, the impacts on these of human relationships, and the need for sustainability in the ways we engage with community and nature. They all conceive of nature-based sports recreation as making available opportunities for individuals to experience the interconnectedness, the more-than-human-ness, of the environment and to develop a sense of themselves as a part of that (Evers, 2009; Wattchow & Brown, 2011; Hill & Brown, 2014; Hunter, 2014). As Humberstone (2011) describes it, 'the very fluidity of movement "through" nature brings forth continuously changing perceptions and awareness' (p. 497).

In all of these approaches place is clearly central. Discussing the pedagogical potential of outdoor education in learning about environmental sustainability, Hill and Brown (2014) suggest that,

> . . . the development of connections to place and learning about one's relationship with place, can help students to understand the nature-society system within which they operate and how their worldview, attitudes and actions impact upon that system. This can potentially lead to deeper reflection and understandings about how one's relationship with place is contingent on both current (intra-generational) and future (inter-generational) justice and how sustainability-based ethics might guide action towards solving the sustainability problem. (pp. 227–228)

Recent cultural studies research has described the process of developing individual 'sustainability-based ethics' as ecological sensibilities, which refers to the development of an eco-centric perspective that 'transcends the narrow sense of self and human superiority' (Satchell, 2008, p. 110). Ecological sensibilities operate through relationships and connectivity, 'whereby emotive responses to environmental conditions are attributed a deterministic ethical power: if we feel, we will act in a productive way' (Potter, 2005, p. 2; see also Rodman, 1998, p. 422). That is, human relationships to place, culture and experience manifest in individual ethical decisions about lifestyle choices and responsibilities relating to the environment. This approach takes an individualised approach to imagining sustainability, whereby 'the environment becomes acutely significant in terms of how it confronts the individual, when it meets "me", "head on", "in here"' (Macnaghten, 2003, p. 68). With a sense of individual connectivity and experience so key to the development of ecological sensibilities, nature-based sport and physical cultures offer productive and potential space in terms of environmental sustainability. Yet this is not without its tensions, a key one being the sense of ownership and entitlement that a sustained relationship to place can bring, coupled with the growing numbers of people participating in recreational nature-based and lifestyle sports and activities. In surfing culture, this issue is understood in terms of localism.

Evers (2009) describes the cumulative relationships that surfers develop to surfbreaks as 'an acute embodied sense of connectivity' (900). For Evers, surfing doesn't just involve surfers and waves. Instead, 'it is more than human. Dolphins, storms, driftwood, jellyfish, birds, fish, turtles, surfboards, shells, seaweed' (Evers, 2009, p. 898) are all part of the experienced surfing ecology. Satchell argues that these experiences and relationships open 'possibilities for an "eco-politics" deriving from a close analysis of the vicissitudes of belonging, the contested spaces of everyday life and the performance of care and creativity in an alternative teleology of emplaced encounters and returns' (Satchell, 2007, p. 3). Through these embodied place-based pedagogies and connections, 'surfers become participants in and advocates for their surf–shore territory', despite 'their ambivalence to organisation' (Anderson, 2014, p. 5). In all of this, place – whether, for example, a surfbreak, a coastline or a wave itself – is central, and the majority of researchers argue that repeat visits that establish relationships to one place are especially productive in developing ecological sensibilities (Satchell, 2008; Evers, 2009). In discussions of surfing, 'locals' have been afforded the most power and authority, both in terms of cultural participation and environmental understandings.

The intimate connection between surfing bodies and ecologies is most often framed in terms of 'being local'. That is, local surfers protect or save their breaks and coastlines, a positioning that suggests a sense of privilege and authority in 'their' coastal spaces. Local surfers commonly claim this kind of privilege over others because being local to a surfbreak carries a status that affords local surfers priority. In some ways, local status is developed through knowledge and skills specific to a place and its waves – knowledge such as how the wave breaks, where the rocks are, how the tides affect the break and so on, and 'Visiting surfers can tell who is part of this local crew by their confident body language and their knowledge of the wave' (Evers, 2008a, p. 411). In the surf, 'local' is something that is performed and recognisable.

In many busy surfbreaks around the world, expressions of 'being local' are manifested culturally through the line-up, and physically through acts of exclusion, including threatening graffiti and actual violence. This violence is sometimes expressed as 'localism' and 'surf rage', which acts as a form of cultural pedagogy to regulate ways of being a surfer in local terms (see Young, 2000; Preston-Whyte, 2002; Daskalos, 2007; Evers, 2008a). Systems of localism privilege skilled and/or local surfers over less skilled surfers and surfers from other towns, places and surfbreaks, delineating the distinction between who belongs and who does not. Such ideas, understandings and behaviours show how surfing experiences and relationships can be limited through exclusionary place-based pedagogies (Preston-Whyte, 2002; Wattchow & Brown, 2011). However, as Garbutt (2011) explains, being local is also associated with relationships to place developed through history and genealogy. Garbutt argues that people who are local in this way use their established historical relationships to assert themselves as knowing 'their' place best. Such people engage with their place 'from an inside that is spoken for, and for which the locals have the right to speak and act. The right . . . comes through a long association and knowledge of a place, its names and its history' (p. 127). For surfers, these rights manifest through relationships of longevity and commitment to place and specific surfbreaks. Carroll (2000) writes that, when it comes to waves, surfers can take these rights very seriously:

> This idea – that a surfer or surfers can claim ownership over a surfbreak – goes to the very heart of our moral Code. Nobody owns the waves, it is said. . . . [But] Many surfers who've spent years of their lives learning the curves and moods of a powerful and alluring surf spot feel a sense of ownership that makes land-based property rights seem feeble in comparison. (p. 60)

Coupled with the often dominating place surfing takes in a surfer's identity, these intense feelings of local-based 'rights' and 'ownership' over a surfbreak or place can create feelings that 'Newcomers . . . threaten to trouble the places locals have quietened and made their own' (Garbutt, 2011, p. 127). Evers (2008a) uses similar language to describe the tensions between locals and newcomers in the surf:

> Newcomers become confused. This means they regularly transgress rules and upset the local surfers who expect order at their break. . . . By claiming the responsibility of safety for themselves and others, local surfers have priority with waves and a sense of entitlement. (p. 412)

With Indigenous, settler and multicultural populations shaping colonial societies such as Australia, tensions surrounding whose voices carry authority in discussions about how we take care of our environment carry extra complexity and significance. For example, in Australia, white Australian surfers consistently ignore and exclude the historical, cultural and genealogical relationships to country of Aboriginal Australians, while 'newcomer' migrant knowledges remain largely excluded (McGloin, 2007; Evers, 2008a, 2008b, 2009; Garbutt, 2011).

The privilege so problematic in these social tensions also highlights the focus that existing research about sport and physical recreation has maintained on local surfing relationships to place as the most productive in terms of developing relationships of 'emplaced encounters and returns' (Satchell, 2007, p. 3). In Australia, large numbers of committed surfers live in metropolitan areas away from the coast and are not able to claim a 'local' surfing identity. Discussing British surfing, Anderson (2014) argues that, beyond the local surfbreak hierarchies, non-local surfers are characterised by 'locals' as 'oblivious to the cultural traces existing in the land and littoral to which they travel to' (p. 7), with their presence 'commonly framed as a threat' (p. 8). Anderson is describing 'mobile surfers' who are travelling away from their home break – that is, surfers who are 'local' elsewhere. Similar to the ways surfers ignore Indigenous histories and relationships to country, in emphasising 'time' as significant to their status they forget the migration of surfers along Australian coasts from the 1950s onwards. In the 1960s and 1970s, surfers were also characterised by 'locals' in the places they visited and relocated to as 'oblivious to the cultural traces existing in the land and littoral' (Anderson, 2014, p. 7) with their presence 'commonly framed as a threat' (p. 8; see also Pearson, 1979; Booth, 2001). In discussing issues of localism in the context of potential of place-based pedagogies, sport and environmental sustainability, it is important to keep in mind the historical context of places and communities.

Engaging with research across various disciplines – cultural studies, cultural geography, gender studies, history, outdoor education, sport sociology – has helped me think and rethink issues of place-specific power relations and pedagogies by reminding me of the various conceptual intersections that impact what we can know. The rest of this chapter will draw on my own lived experiences of surfing, local and non-local relationships to place, and ecological sensibilities. The idea that the personal is political is far from new, but in discussions of place-based pedagogies such as those presented here, it remains a powerful notion. Indeed, I have found that my personal experiences of place, surfing, and being local and non-local have been productive in helping me problematise the assumptions I have made about my own surfing relationships to place, and the authority allocated to me in various places and contexts. They have also helped me rethink the assumptions that my various positions have led me to in my research about surfing. In the case of this chapter, by being simultaneously positioned as both local and non-local to Broken Head by the graffiti I described earlier, I was able to experience the tensions of each position through an empathy for them both.

The Broken pipe

As I walked along the beach towards the headland, the black lettering on the stormwater pipe screamed out at me. SAVE BROKEN. STAY IN BRISBANE. The message (no longer there) was a message from locals to non-locals who use the beach for beach walks, surfing or picnics, all activities that 'locals' enjoy there regularly as well. Having grown up on this beach, the effect of the graffiti would usually be minimal on me – perhaps I would laugh or not really notice it. But on this occasion it resonated. For over a year I'd been living in Brisbane, the state capital in Queensland, to the north of my home. I'd moved to Brisbane in 2008 for my PhD candidature, leaving behind my everyday access to waves in my beachside hometown (Olive, 2013a). Living in Brisbane put me at least an hour and a half drive from any break that I wanted to surf, but the chance to research women's experiences of recreational surfing was worth the compromise. And anyway, my fieldwork was at home, so I got to spend plenty of time there. Nonetheless, a lot of the time I was city-bound, and writing, teaching, reading, working and living on a student budget made it tough affording the time and money to drive to the beach to surf. It was frustrating.

SAVE BROKEN. STAY IN BRISBANE.

I was living away from the sea in Brisbane, but Broken Head is a place where I spent childhood weekends, where I would go for a run after school, where I made out with boys as a teenager, where I've celebrated birthdays and attended barbeques, where I have taken countless afternoon walks alone or with my mum, sisters and aunt, where I have surfed waves big and small in conditions sunny and stormy, where I have had encounters with birds, dolphins, whales and echidnas, where I often feel afraid of the presence of unseen sharks, and where I have watched the introduced plant species, bitou bush, take over the sand dune system by killing away the sea grass and native trees holding the dunes together. This is a place dear to me, a place in my bones. But in the terms spelled out in this scrappy message by an unknown author, as a resident of Brisbane I was now a threat to the wellbeing of Broken Head. How was I supposed to respond? I laughed it off and wrote a blog post about it, which at the time was my response to everything (Olive, 2009, 2013b). But the words stayed with me, and I found them filtering into my thinking and writing over the years (Olive, 2013c).

SAVE BROKEN. STAY IN BRISBANE.

In 2010 I joined the Brisbane Boardriders – a group of surfers who mostly live in Brisbane, but who make time to surf most weeks. They check conditions for days ahead, pick one another up and drive together, bring packed lunches, take and post photos on social media, and share the experience of surfing. Each year, they design and produce a Brisbane Boardriders T-shirt that they wear with pride, and rent a beach-side apartment to share for the Noosa Festival of Surfing and again for a week in summer. Every month they get together at a pub in the inner city for dinner and surf talk. I was stoked to become a part of their club. At these meetings we would exchange surf stories, swap magazines and DVDs, boast about new boards, update knowledge on sandbars, and discuss surfing to our hearts' content. Whether it's history, shops, films, events, exhibitions, performances, festivals, public talks or book launches, if you want to be dialled in to all things surf in Brisbane, these are your people. Some of these guys have been surfing longer than I've been alive, and they continue to keep it in their life by driving north and south to beaches an hour and a half or more away as often as they can. Their knowledge of the different beaches is encyclopaedic – how the beaches have changed, memories of waves they enjoyed and shared during past epic swells. They know the history of surfing in Brisbane and how surfing culture in Brisbane intersects with surfing on the coast. And what blows me away is how generous they are in sharing this knowledge of and love for surfing with others – unlike coastal locals, these guys don't see newcomers as a threat.

Knowing how much the Brisbane Boardriders love and care for the breaks they surf, the memory of the graffiti I found at Broken Head stings me even more. It's aimed at my kind, welcoming, generous, stoked friends, who I know mean and do no harm at all, who I know love surfing and the coast as much as the surfers who live there, but who in no way take these places for granted and so, perhaps, have an even deeper understanding of how precious they are. I have learned a lot from my surfing friends in the city. A lot about balance, compromise and keeping the coastal connection alive, even when you are away for extended periods due to work, family and other responsibilities. They've shown me what it means to be committed to surfing and to the coast, about how to be invested in the wellbeing of places and communities without claiming ownership over them, and without marginalising the relationships of others. I am proud and very grateful to count myself among their number.

These days, I live by the beach in New Zealand, where tensions about 'being local' are framed by Maori, Pakeha[1] and more recent, increasingly diverse migrant populations. Despite differences in politics of colonisation and globalisation, at the breaks where I live and surf in NZ I see and hear the same kinds of exclusionary narratives about invading surfers from the city taking over 'their' breaks on the weekends. I've had a Pakeha local from here, tell me that I can't be local to Byron because no one is. I shrugged when he said that – the insinuated insult means little to me now. But of the people I've encountered through surfing, it is the surfers from Auckland or who are relatively new to the town that have been the most friendly, grateful and welcoming. They've chatted to me in the surf, given me their phone numbers, told me about books that describe various breaks around New Zealand, taken me out at breaks for the first time, offered to teach me how to negotiate the rocky coast that so greatly intimidates me, and invited me to join their Boardriders clubs up the coast. Only one local family has been generous in this way, and they are people I already knew from when they lived a while in my hometown.

This is not to say that visiting surfers aren't thoughtless. Many do act in ways that are oblivious to existing ways of doing things, of existing processes, hierarchies and orders. Some do arrive en masse and take over a space in ways that are momentary, confusing and damaging, while at the same time claiming rights as money-spending tourists. As well as crowding the surfbreak, visitors take up usually available car spots, usually available picnic spots, fill cafe tables, lengthen coffee queues, empty grocery store shelves, dominate rate payer-funded facilities like toilets, showers and barbeques, leave litter on the sand, stomp through fragile dunes when paths are close by, and then drive away leaving little that contributes to the wellbeing and sustainability of community and place (Summers, 2009). These issues are real and they are complicated and they upset me too, and in the past I have contributed my own voice through a published letter to the editor of the local paper, which led to a longer article the following week (see Gilbert, 2009). These days, I still feel my hackles rise when I see newcomers litter or transgress established rules. I'm learning to negotiate a path between caring for place and feeling a sense of place-based entitlement and authority, but this is still mediated through my White Australian history and assumptions.

Ecological sensibilities and place-based pedagogies through nature-based sport

To date, cultural studies, sports sociology, cultural geography and outdoor education scholars have convincingly theorised the *potential* of ecological sensibilities that outdoor sports participants can develop through their experiences of and relationships to nature and place (Franklin, 1998; Humberstone, 1998; Satchell, 2008; Anderson, 2009; Wattchow & Brown, 2011; Hill & Brown, 2014). For example, Jon Anderson (2014) argues that 'surfers become participants in and advocates for their surf–shore territory' (p. 5), thus contributing to the sustainability of their coastal community and environment through community and online spaces (see also Satchell, 2008). Yet while the impacts of these relationships have been explored in terms of organised environmental activism (Wheaton, 2007; Heywood & Montgomery, 2008; Anderson, 2009; Thorpe & Rinehart, 2012), very little empirical research considers how these relationships translate into everyday lifestyle choices outdoor sports participants make when they leave the field and are at home away from the activity (Franklin, 1998; Macnaghten, 2003). Empirically, this might be tricky to capture.

The continuing emphasis on surfing 'locals' ignores the many marginalised 'weekend' surfers living away from the coast. Surfers like my friends in the Brisbane Boardriders do have committed and caring relationships to the wellbeing and sustainability of coastal places. In the face of growing non-local participation, understandings of how ecological sensibilities can be inspired through recreational nature-based lifestyle sports take on a deeper tension when it comes to locating who gets to speak in defence of the management, protection and sustainably of coastal places. And this has implications for what researchers can do to contribute to change. As Hill and Brown (2014) argue:

> If the long-term sustainability and well-being of planetary ecosystems and social communities is the key goal of transformations, then there must be robust frameworks by which this transformation can be guided and practiced. We believe the exploration of how such frameworks might intersect with pedagogical practice, such as place-responsiveness, is important. (p. 221)

While I agree with this point about pedagogical frameworks, I recognise the difficulty in contributing to frameworks of pedagogies of place-responsiveness in *recreational* outdoor sport and physical activities, which lack structures within which to implement frameworks. Nonetheless, the potential Hill and Brown describe presents new challenges and opportunities relating to the capacity of researchers to engage with and contribute to cultural change in ways that connect with disparate groups of lifestyle and nature-based sporting participants in the context of complexities and tensions in indigenous, colonial and globalised relationships to place. Such an approach will help us explore what place-based pedagogies are in process and begin to imagine how researchers can make a 'contribution to the public good' (Turner, 2012, pp. 6–7).

Note

1 Pakeha is a Maori word used to describe people with European heritage.

References

Anderson, J. (2009). Transient convergence and relational sensibility: Beyond the modern constitution of nature. *Emotion, Space and Society*, 2(2), 120–127.
Anderson, J. (2014). Surfing between the local and the global: Identifying spatial divisions in surfing practice. *Transactions of the Institute of British Geographers*, 39(2), 237–249.
Booth, D. (2001). *Australian Beach Cultures: The History of Sun, Sand and Surf*. London: Frank Cass.
Carroll, N. (2000). Defending the faith. In N. Young (Ed.) *Surf Rage: A Surfer's Guide to Turning Negatives into Positives* (pp. 54–73). Angourie, NSW: Nymboida Press.
Church, A. & Ravenscoft, N. (2011). Politics, research and the natural environment: The lifeworlds of water-based sport and recreation in Wales. *Leisure Studies*, 30(4), 387–405.
Couldry, N. (1996). Speaking about others and speaking personally: Reflections after Elspeth Probyn's 'Sexing the self'. *Cultural Studies*, 10(2), 315–333.
Daskalos, C. (2007). Locals only! The impact of modernity on a local surfing context. *Sociological Perspectives*, 50(1), 155–173.
Davis, K. (1997). Embody-ing theory: Beyond modernist and postmodernist readings of the body. In K. Davis (Ed.) *Embodied Practices: Feminist Perspectives on the Body* (pp. 1–23). London: Sage.
Erickson, B. (2011). Recreational activism: Politics, nature, and the rise of neo-liberalism. *Leisure Studies*, 30(4), pp. 477–494.

Evers, C. (2008a). The Cronulla riots: Safety maps on an Australian beach. *South Atlantic Quarterly, 107*(2), 411–429.

Evers, C. (2008b). Rethinking gubbah localism. *Kurungabaa: A Journal of Literature, History and Ideas from the Sea,* April, *1*(1). Retrieved from: http://kurungabaa.net/2008/07/05/issue-1-commentary-rethinking-gubbah-localism/.

Evers, C. (2009). 'The Point': Surfing, geography and a sensual life of men and masculinity on the Gold Coast, Australia. *Social and Cultural Geography, 10*(18), 893–908.

Franklin, A. (1998). Naturalizing sport: Hunting and angling in modern environments, *International Review for the Sociology of Sport, 33*(4), 355–366.

Franklin, A. (2014). On why we dig the beach: Tracing the subjects and objects of the bucket and spade for a relational materialist theory of the beach. *Tourist Studies,* published online 25 June. DOI:10.1177/1468797614536331.

Franklin, A., Picken, F. & Osbaldiston, N. (2014). Conceptualizing the changing nature of Australian beach tourism in a low carbon society. *International Journal of Climate Change: Impacts and Responses, 5*(1), 1–10.

Garbutt, R. (2011). *The Locals.* Bern: Peter Lang.

Gilbert, J. (2009). Byron trashed by the crass in vans. *The Byron Shire Echo, 23*(32), 20 January, p. 7. Retrieved from: www.echo.net.au/downloads/byron-echo/volume-23/byronecho2332.pdf.

Gilchrist, P. & Wheaton, B. (2011). Lifestyle sport, public policy and youth engagement: Examining the emergence of parkour. *International Journal of Sport Policy and Politics, 3*(1), 109–131.

Goggin, G. (2002). Conurban. *M/C Journal, 5*(2), May. Retrieved from: http://journal.media-culture.org.au/0205/conurban.php.

Hajkowicz, S.A, Cook, H., Wilhelmseder, L. & Boughen, N. (2013). *The Future of Australian Sport: Megatrends Shaping the Sports Sector over Coming Decades.* Consultancy report for the Australian Sports Commission. CSIRO: Australia.

Heywood, L. & Montgomery, M. (2008). Ambassadors of the last wilderness? Surfers, environmental ethics, and activism in America. In M. Atkinson & K. Young (Eds.) *Tribal Play: Subcultural Journeys through Sport. Research in the Sociology of Sport* (Vol. IV, pp. 153–172). Bingley: Jai.

Hill, A. & Brown, M. (2014). Intersections between place, sustainability and transformative outdoor experiences. *Journal of Adventure Education and Outdoor Learning, 14*(3), 217–232.

Humberstone, B. (1998). Re-creation and connections in and with nature: Synthesizing ecological and feminist discourse and praxis? *International Review for the Sociology of Sport, 33*(4), 381–392.

Humberstone, B. (2011). Embodiment and social and environmental action in nature-based sport: Spiritual spaces. *Leisure Studies, 30*(4), 495–512.

Hunter, L. (2014). Seaspaces: Surfing the sea as pedagogy of self. In M. Brown & B. Humberstone (Eds.) *Seascapes: Shaped by the Sea* (pp. 41–54). Surrey, England: Ashgate.

Macnaghten, P. (2003). Embodying the environment in everyday practices. *The Sociological Review, 51*(1), 63–84.

Maguire, G.S., Miler, K.K., Weston, M.A. & Young, K. (2011). Being beside the seaside: Beach use and preferences among coastal residents of south-eastern Australia. *Ocean & Coastal Management, 54,* 781–788.

Mansfield, L. (2009). Fitness cultures and environmental (in)justice? *International Review for the Sociology of Sport, 44*(4), 345–362.

Mansfield, L. & Wheaton, B. (2011). Leisure and the politics of the environment. *Leisure Studies, 30*(4), 383–386.

McGloin, C. (2007). Aboriginal surfing: reinstating culture and country. *International Journal of the Humanities, 4*(1), 93–100.

Olive, R. (2009). The broken pipe. Blog post on *Making Friends With the Neighbours,* 15 July. Retrieved from: http://makingfriendswiththeneighbours.blogspot.co.nz/2009/07/broken-pipe.html.

Olive, R. (2013a). Blurred lines: Women, subjectivities and surfing. Unpublished doctoral thesis, School of Human Movement Studies, University of Queensland.

Olive, R. (2013b). 'Making friends with the neighbours': Blogging as a research method. *International Journal of Cultural Studies, 16*(1), 71–84.

Olive, R. (2013c). Tales from the city. *White Horses, 4,* no page.

Pearson, K. (1979). *Surfing Subcultures of Australia and New Zealand.* St Lucia, QLD: University of Queensland Press.

Potter, E. (2005). Ecological consciousness in Australian literature: Outside the limits of environmental crisis. Hawke Research Institute for Sustainable Societies, Working Paper Series, No. 29. Retrieved from: www.unisa.edu.au/Documents/EASS/HRI/working-papers/wp29.pdf.

Preston-Whyte, R. (2002). Constructions of surfing space at Durban, South Africa. *Tourism Geographies*, *4*(3), 307–328.

Probyn, E. (1993). *Sexing the Self: Gendered Positions in Cultural Studies*. London: Routledge.

Probyn, E. (2003). The spatial imperative of subjectivity. In K. Anderson, M. Domosh, S. Pile & N. Thrift (Eds.) *Handbook of Cultural Geography* (pp. 290–299). London: Sage.

Rodman, J. (1998). Four forms of ecological consciousness. In R.G. Botzler & S.J Armstrong (Eds.) *Environmental Ethics: Divergence and Convergence*. Boston, MA: McGraw-Hill.

Rose, N. (1996). Identity, genealogy, history. In S. Hall & P. Du Gay (Eds.) *Questions of Cultural Identity* (pp. 128–150). London and Thousand Oaks, CA: Sage.

Satchell, K. (2007). Shacked: The ecology of surfing and the surfing of ecology. *Online Proceedings*, *'Sustaining Culture', Annual Conference of the Cultural Studies Association of Australia*, University of South Australia, Adelaide, 6–8 December.

Satchell, K. (2008). Reveries of the Solitary Islands: From sensuous geography to ecological sensibility. In A. Haebich & B. Offord (Eds.) *Landscapes of Exile: Once Perilous, Now Safe*. Bern: Peter Lang.

Summers, L. (2009). Surf rage heats up in a Byron summer. *Byron Shire Echo*, *23*(32), 20 January, 9. Retrieved from: www.echo.net.au/downloads/byron-echo/volume-23/byronecho2332.pdf.

Thorpe, H. & Rinehart, R. (2012). Action sport NGOs in a neo-liberal context: The cases of Skateistan and Surf Aid International. *Journal of Sport and Social Issues*, *37*(2), 115–141.

Turner, G. (2012). *What's Become of Cultural Studies?* London: Sage.

Urry, J. (1995) *Consuming Places*. London: Routledge.

Waitt, G. & Cook, L. (2007). Leaving nothing but ripples on the water: Performing ecotourism natures. *Social and Cultural Geography*, *8*(4), 535–550.

Waitt, G., Gill, N. & Head, L. (2009). Walking practice and suburban nature-talk. *Social and Cultural Geography*, *10*(1), 41–60.

Wattchow, B. & Brown, M. (2011). *A Pedagogy of Place: Outdoor Education for a Changing World*. Melbourne, Australia: Monash University Press.

Weiss, O., Norden, G., Hilscher, P. & Vanreusel, B. (1998). Ski tourism and environmental problems: Ecological awareness among different groups. *International Review for the Sociology of Sport*, *33*(4), 367–379.

Whatmore, S. (2002). *Hybrid Geographies: Natures, Cultures, Spaces*. London: Sage.

Wheaton, B. (2007). Identity, politics and the beach: Environmental activism in Surfers Against Sewage, *Leisure Studies*, *26*(3), 279–302.

Young, N. (Ed.) (2000). *Surf Rage*. Angourie: Nymboida Press.

Index

Abe, O. 308
Aboriginal Australians 505
Abram, D. 429
accidents 444–454; *see also* fatalities
accountability 143, 149, 214
accreditation 145–146, 154, 155, 178, 180–181, 182–186, 461; *see also* certification
Acevedo, J. 460
action-reflection cycle 41, 43
adaptive dissonance 63
Addison, Joseph 495
adventure 2, 7; benefits to the community 26–27; certification 194–195; commodification of 460, 461, 467–468, 488; crises 25; developmental stages 28n6; educational camps in Brazil 329, 330, 331; Germany 21; higher education in the UK 131, 132–133; impact of programs 141; Norway 289, 294–295; older people 369, 374–375; roots of the word 291; teacher education 122–123, 126, 127
Adventure Activities Licensing Authority (AALA) 144–145
Adventure and Environmental Awareness Group 403
adventure education 2, 12, 85, 207–216, 278; Adventure Learning Schools 146; as collective good 221–222; cultural differences 272–273; defining 207–208; Japan 312; militarism 13; Norway 291–292; peace building 321, 323; personal development 321; research on 156; teacher education 121, 122–123; UK curriculum 142
Adventure Learning Schools (ALS) 146, 148
adventure playgrounds 245
adventure sports coaching 423, 455–462
adventure therapy 251–259
adventure tourism 132–133, 375, 423, 463–471
advertising 361

aerial adventure parks 217, 219, 220, 223, 224, 225
aesthetic experience 43, 44, 45, 46, 289
'affective thinking' 43, 44
affordances 83, 97, 110
Africa 271, 273, 275, 316–324
after-school programmes 153, 214
ageing 369, 370, 372, 375
agency 370, 375
agriculture 357, 409, 410, 412, 413, 414, 415
Aitchison, C. 338
Alderson, P. 204
Alewyn, R. 494
Allen, G. 105
Allin, Linda 155, 159–167, 362
'Alpine style' 488
Alps 492, 493
'alternative' development 31, 32, 35, 36
Alves, S. 372, 373
American Camp Association (ACA) 229, 230, 312
American National Standards Institute (ANSI) 222–223
Ananthapadmanabhan, G. 353
Anantharaman, Latha 336, 337, 351–359
Anderson, Jon 504, 505, 507
Anderson, J.R.L. 466
anonymity 199, 203–204
Antarctica 478, 479
apps 135, 213
Araki, E. 309
Arctic expeditions 423, 476–479
Aristotle 24, 32, 426
Arnstein, S.P. 414
Arokiasamy, P. 352
art 486, 494–495
Arthur, M.B. 160–161, 164
Ashcroft, R. 202
Ashida, S. 312
Ashworth, Letty 157, 198–206

Index

Askeladden 291, 292, 294–295
Askins, K. 343
aspirational ethics 204
assessment 134, 230; *see also* evaluation
assimilation 343
Associação Brasileira de Acampamentos
    Educacionais (ABAE) 326, 327
Association for Challenge Course Technology
    (ACCT) 219, 222–223
association supported certification 190–191
Atchley, R.C. 371
Atencio, Matthew 271, 277–287
attainment 143
Attarian, Aram 155, 156, 157, 189–197, 217,
    224, 225
attention restoration theory 63–64
Australia: adventure therapy 253; camps 228;
    certification 191, 192, 193; challenge
    courses 223; curriculum change 277;
    DEDICT model 124; ecotourism 480;
    fatalities 444–447, 449, 450; lifestyle sports
    501; local culture 82; outdoor education 278;
    Outdoor Education Australia guidelines
    114; PE 122; place-responsiveness 436, 438;
    sail training 238, 240; surfing 505–507; teacher
    education 123, 125
Austria 452
authenticity 467, 468, 469
(auto)ethnography 69, 72–73, 75
autonomy 62, 179, 209, 363, 461
avalanches 448, 451
awards 137
Axhausen, K.W. 479

Backman, Erik 81, 82, 121–130
Bacon, S.B. 64, 263
Baden-Powell, Robert 11, 12, 15, 33, 50, 298
Bainbridge, S. 483–484
Ball, D. 457
Ball-King, L. 457
Bandura, A. 320
Barnes, M. 373
Barnes, P. 160, 161, 182
Barret, J. 321
Barton, J. 65
Bates, G.H. 414
Baum, F.E. 372
Beames, Simon 282, 423, 482–490
Beard, Colin 422, 425–434, 464
Beaumont, N. 479
Becker, Peter 7, 8, 20–29, 423, 491–500
Beedie, Paul 423, 463–471
Behan, J.R. 391
behaviourism 127, 427
being 43, 44, 45, 46–47, 52
Bell, M. 361–362
Benjamin, Walter 22

Bennett, Troy 156, 227–235
Benton, T. 427
Beringer, A. 428
Berlin, I. 483
Berns, G.N. 164
Berry, W. 64
Bhaskar, R. 426–427
Bialeschki, M. Deborah 156, 157, 227–235
Biggs, S. 369, 370, 371
Bildung 8, 24, 26, 27, 28n4, 292, 293, 497
Binker, A.J.A. 265
biodiversity 344–345, 409, 411, 412
biomedical model 157, 370, 375
biophilia 63, 247, 400
Birch, M. 201
Bird, W. 279–281
Blackfeet 52
Blee, K.M. 204
Blenkinsop, S. 83, 126
boating 392, 413; fatalities 449–450; *see also*
    canoeing; kayaking
Bocher, B. 263
Bochner, A. 72
body 337, 364, 429, 502
Boler, M. 429
Bolite, J. 460
Boniface, M. 123
Bookout, V. 122
boot camps 14–15
Borton, T. 262, 265
Bosse, H. 497
Bottomley, K. 239
Boud, D. 263, 426
boundaryless careers 159, 160–161, 162,
    163, 165
Bourdieu, Pierre 108, 126, 369, 371, 423, 482,
    485–489
bourgeoisie 498, 499n6, 499n8
Bowdridge, M. 83, 126
Bowker, J.M. 172
Boyes, Mike 126, 239, 337, 369–377
Brahma Kumaris World Spiritual
    University 404
brain development 248
Brandon, K. 345
Brat Camp (TV show) 14–15
Brazil 271, 275, 325–332
Brenig, M. 318
Breunig, Mary 155, 168–177
Bricker, K.S. 273
Bridging the Gap 55
British (Schools) Exploring Society 13
British Mountaineering Council 403–404, 416
Brocklehurst, M. 164
Bronfenbrenner, U. 60, 83, 103
Brookes, Andrew 7–8, 11–19, 87, 422, 438, 439,
    444–454

Brown, Heather 2, 155, 157, 178–188, 466
Brown, Mike 75, 87, 88–89, 123, 210, 285, 372,
    405, 422, 435–443, 503, 508
Brown, P.C. 263
Bruce, M. 318
Buckle, J.L. 201
Budbill, N. 364
Budworth, Paul 485–486
Building Learning Power (BLP) 246
bungee jumping 317, 375, 468, 469
Bunting, C.J. 320
Bunyan, P. 123
Burke, R.J. 164
Burkhart, B.Y. 52, 53
Burnet, Thomas 483
Burns, G.W. 253, 428
Burr, V. 429
bushwalking 192
Byrne, J. 342, 344, 347–348
Byron, George Gordon 484, 496, 499n6

Cahsel, C. 318
Cain, J. 263
Caine, G. 262, 263
Caine, R.N. 262
Cajete, G. 49, 52, 54
Camargo, L.O. de L. 327
cameras 135, 136
Cameron, J. 88
Campaign for Adventure 16
camps 2, 17, 50, 227–235; Brazil 271,
    325–332; Canada 475; Czech Republic 298,
    299; Japan 308, 309–310, 312; Scotland 113
Canada: camps 227, 231, 232; challenge courses
    223; ecotourism 423, 480; ethnic minorities
    343; fatalities 445, 448, 449, 450; Indigenous
    knowledge 50, 52, 55; national parks 51; older
    people 374; outdoor education 473–476, 477;
    PE 122; place-responsiveness 436; sail training
    238; teacher education 121
canoeing 23, 55, 138, 371; Brazil 330; Canada 50;
    certification 190; coaching qualifications 181;
    Czech Republic 297, 298, 299, 300; disabled
    people 383; fatalities 449, 450, 451; Norway 290;
    rights of access 413; spirituality 392, 393, 394;
    teacher education 124, 125; see also kayaking
canopy tours 217, 219–220, 223, 224, 225
capitalism 84, 221, 328, 332, 438; see also neo-
    liberalism
careers 159–167, 362, 480
Carlson, T.B. 123, 124
Carnicelli, Sandro 272, 274, 275, 325–332
Carpenter, Cathryn 7, 9, 59–68
Carr, D. 179
Carroll, N. 504
carrying capacity 414–415
Casey, E. 85, 86, 88, 92

caste 336, 352
Cater, C. 466
Ceballos-Lascuráin, Héctor 473, 476
Cell, E. 426
certification 154, 155, 189–197, 222, 225; see also
    accreditation
challenge courses 190, 217–226
Chamlian, L.A. 327, 329
character 15, 86, 104, 439; colonial perspective 50,
    51; Outward Bound movement 13, 211, 237;
    Singapore 283
Charles, V. 200
Chavez, D.J. 174–175
Chawla, L. 400
Cheung, A. 272
Chick, G. 157
childminders 106, 107
Chile 406, 452
China 238, 262, 272–273
Ching, Chew Ting 271, 277–287
Chodzko-Zajko, W. 372
Chomik, T. 60
Christianity 483; Brazil 325, 329; Outward Bound
    movement 13, 15; Protestant ethics 21, 289
Christiansen, D. 464–465
Christie, Beth 81, 82, 113–120, 143
Chróinín, D.N. 122
class 163, 173, 336; cultural appropriation
    485; educational camps in Brazil 329, 331;
    intersectionality 364–365; land ownership 412;
    sail training 238; social distinction 486–487,
    498, 499n8; social justice 170, 174; swimming
    496–497
classroom interaction 70, 71
Claxton, Guy 148, 246
climate change 31, 32, 117, 242, 358,
    467–468
climbing 23, 73–74, 281, 496; 'Alpine style' 488;
    Brazil 330; certification 190; educational camps
    in Brazil 331; fatalities 451; India 356; Kenya
    317; Macmillan Academy 147; NGB awards 137;
    Norway 290; older people 374; Singapore 285;
    spirituality 391; UK curriculum 142; see also
    mountaineering
Cloke, P. 466
Cloutier, R. 447
coaching 423, 455–462
coastlines 492
Coates, Emily 7, 61, 69, 73–74
cognitive behavioural therapy 254
cognitive dissonance 63
cognitivism 427
Cohen, E. 467
Cohen, M. 400
Cohen, R. 426
Coleman, R. 414
Coleridge, Samuel Taylor 484

Collins, Dave 423, 455–462
Collins, Di 336, 337, 351–359
Collins, Loel 423, 455–462
colonialism 49, 50–51, 55
Comenius, Johan Amos 33, 297, 303
Comité Européen de Normalisation (CEN) 222, 223
commercialisation 156, 194–195, 336, 398, 399; challenge courses 220–221, 222; educational camps in Brazil 328–329
commodification 460, 461, 466, 467–468, 469, 488
commons 413–414, 416n5
communities of practice (CoP) 164, 460–461
community action 402–403
community engagement 345–346
competencies 160–161, 162–163, 164, 189, 453; see also skills
competency-based eduction (CBE) 172–173
confidence see self-confidence
confidentiality 199, 202, 205
connection 267
Connell, R.W. 336
conservation 31, 409, 411–412; carrying capacity 415; community action 402; ecotourism 473; environmental education 36; forests 410–411; John Muir Award 403
constructivism 427, 428, 429, 430
consumerism 337
consumption 21, 369, 398, 466, 468–469
continuous professional development (CPD) 181, 183
Cook, L. 360
Cooper, Geoff 81, 337, 353, 358, 398–408
Corbin, A. 495–496
Cordova, V.F. 54
Cornell, J. 264, 400
corporate manslaughter 180
Cosgriff, M. 125, 372
Cosgrove, D. 437
cotton wool culture 181
Couldry, N. 502
Coulter, M. 122
Council for Learning outside the Classroom (CLOtC) 141, 145, 185
counselling 251, 252–253, 254, 255
counsellors 327–328, 330–331
courage 364
Cox, L.A. 457
craft orientation 127
creative analytic practice (CAP) 74
creativity 149
crises 25–26, 27, 28n6
critical inquiry 127
Critical Race Theory (CRT) 343, 347
critical theory 86, 241
critical thinking 401–402
Cronon, W. 437

Crosbie, John 337, 378–387
Crosbie, K. 477
cross-disciplinary research 7; see also transdisciplinarity
Crow, G. 200
Culp, R.H. 363, 364
cultural appropriation 485, 487
cultural capital 487, 488
cultural competency 155, 171, 172–173, 175
cultural density 82, 103, 108–110
cultural issues 3, 82, 271–272; camps 231; cultural aspects of early years practice 107–110; language 272–273; nature-culture dichotomy 8, 51, 55
cultural severance 413–414
cultural studies 423, 424, 502, 503, 507
Cummings, M. 263
CUREE 142–143
curiosity 24, 26, 28n6, 110, 289, 291, 464
curricula 81, 83, 107; accreditation of instructors 146; Adventure Learning Schools 146; curriculum making 441; early childhood education in Scandinavia 96–97; evidence-based 213; knowledge-based 399; Macmillan Academy 148; place-responsive 436; Scotland 113, 115–117; Singapore 277–285; social justice 172; United Kingdom 141–143, 180
Curriculum for Excellence (CfE) 114, 115–117, 142
Currier, A. 204
Curry, N. 345
Curtin, S. 468
Curtner-Smith, M.D. 122
cycling: adventure education 208; Czech Republic 297, 298, 299, 301; Norway 290; older people 372, 374; spirituality 392; United Kingdom 412; see also mountain biking
Czech Republic 271, 273, 274, 297–306

Dalla-Longa, A. 163
Daniels, S. 437
Dante Alighieri 291
data security 199, 201
Davies, B. 83
Davis, B. 432
debriefing 261, 262–263, 265, 319
decision making 25, 457, 458
decolonisation 56
DEDICT model 124
Dedman, M. 13
deep ecology 32, 247, 292
DeFillippi, R.J. 160–161
Defoe, Daniel 291
Deloria, V.J. 53
Denison, J. 74
Denmark: camps 231; early childhood education 95–96, 97–98; fatalities 450; Forest School 244, 245; sail training 238

Dennis, John 493–494
Denny, K.E. 361
Denscombe, M. 199, 203
Denzin, N. 69, 73–74, 75
Depp, C.A. 370
depression 154, 251, 363, 370, 373
DeRoche, K. 204
Derr, V. 320
Destivelle, Catherine 488
developmental cascades 211, 233
developmental stages 28n6
Dewey, John 8, 63, 86, 246, 299, 426; experience
    40, 41–47; local environment 281–282;
    'occupations' 87, 90; progressive education 33,
    169, 228; reflection 262
Dewing, C. 185
Dibben, M. 329
Dickinson, K.J.M. 373
Dillon, P. 427
Dilthey, Wilhelm 21
disabilities 230, 337, 370, 371, 378–387
disclosure 199, 201, 202
discrimination: disabled people 380; gender 362;
    Kenya 318; parks 344; racial 348; social justice
    170, 171, 172; unconscious 155
disinterestedness 486
distinction 486–487, 489, 498, 499n8
diversity 170–171, 342, 345, 347; adventure
    education 123, 211–212; early years outdoor
    learning 109; peace initiatives 319; sail training
    240; teacher education 127–128; training for
    172
divine design 493
Dobson, A. 335
dog ownership 374
Doherty, K.L. 263
Doi, A.S. 394
doing 43, 45; learning by 41, 229, 230
Down, B. 108
Doyle, L. 86
dramaturgy 274, 301–304
Drasdo, H. 2–3, 423
Dryden, W. 252
Dubbert, P.M. 61
DuFour, J. 53
Duke of Edinburgh Award Scheme 11, 138, 475
Dustin, D.L. 273
Dyer, G. 14
Dyson, B. 123

early childhood education and care (ECEC)
    95–102
early years outdoor learning 83, 103–112, 245–246
'earthwalks' 400
eating disorders 255–257, 363
Ebashi, S. 308
ecofeminism 335, 336, 338

ecological framework 60, 83, 103–104
ecological realism 430
'ecological sensibilities' 424, 472, 503, 504, 507–508
ecology 247, 292; deep 32, 247, 292;
    fact-based environmental education 34; human
    37; participatory 55; shallow 32
economic sustainability 157
economisation 20–21, 126
eco-psychology 253
ecotourism 195, 224, 423, 464, 472–481
'edgework' 465, 466
Edginton, C.R. 319
EDICT model 124
education 2, 81–84, 398–399; Bildung distinction
    27n2; camps 228, 230,
    231–232; challenge courses 218, 220, 221, 222,
    224, 225; Dewey's definition of 46; disabled
    people 379; ecotourism 473, 477, 478, 479,
    480; educational camps in Brazil 325–332;
    experiential 7, 8, 45–46, 86–87, 222, 262–263,
    422, 425; Forest School 155, 157, 244–250,
    411; formal curricular initiatives in the UK
    141–150; Indigenous knowledge 49, 51, 55–56;
    as instrument of peace 316; Japan 308–309;
    non-formal 2, 3, 153–158, 168, 169, 172–175,
    399; sail training 240; Singapore 277–287; for
    sustainability 403; see also adventure education;
    environmental education; higher education;
    learning; pedagogy
Education Outside the Classroom (EOtC) 114,
    122
Education Scotland 115, 116, 118, 119n11
Edwards, R. 426
Ellis, C. 72, 476
Else, P. 245
Emanuel, E. 199
embodiment 369, 371, 372, 400, 502
Emerson, R.W. 262
emotions 24, 28n5
Enache, M. 161
enactivism 430
English language 272, 313–314
Enhancing Fieldwork Learning project 136
enskilment 436, 440–441
environmental control 31, 32, 34, 36
environmental education 2, 7, 8, 33–36, 337,
    399–403; camps 228; Indigenous knowledge
    55; Japan 308, 312, 313; place and 86; race and
    ethnicity 347; spirituality 393; teacher education
    82, 121, 125, 127
environmental justice 3, 335, 338, 344; Canada 477;
    place-responsive manifesto 91; sail training 242
environmental mastery 62
Environmental Sensitive Areas 412
environmentalism 30–39, 292, 353, 398; ecological
    realism 430; India 358; spirituality 394;
    wilderness protection 51

epistemology 174
equality 336, 338, 352, 358; adventure education 123; disabled people 378; educational camps in Brazil 331, 332
equipment 383
equity 91, 123, 347
Eraut, M. 180, 184
Erlebnispädagogik 8, 20, 23
Erlebnisse 8, 21–23, 26, 27, 293–294, 295
escapism 463, 469
ethics: adventure sports coaching 461; certification 190; challenge courses 222; codes of 180, 186, 193, 203; colonial legacy 55; educational camps in Brazil 329; environmental 125; Indigenous knowledge 53; non-formal education 154; professions 179; relational 37; research 157, 198–206; sustainability-based 503
ethnicity 163, 336, 341–350; ethnic identity 164, 322; intersectionality 364–365
ethnography 69, 70–71, 72–73, 74, 75, 241
Europe: challenge courses 223; ethnic minorities 341, 342–343; sail training 238; teacher education 121
European Institute for Outdoor Adventure Education and Experiential Learning 404
European Ropes Course Association 217
evaluation 142–144, 213, 214; camps 230; Japan 312; Macmillan Academy 148
Evans, J. 83, 103
Everest 423, 464, 465–466, 467, 482, 484
Evers, C. 503–504
Every Child Matters 142, 144
evidence-based curricula 213
evolutionary psychology 249
Ewert, A.W. 169, 207, 210, 313
exclusion 352, 504
exercise 61; *see also* physical activity
Exeter, David 81, 82, 141–150
existential perspective 37
expeditions 136, 208; Kenya 318, 319; Macmillan Academy 147; Polar 423, 476–479
experience 40–48, 292–293, 425–426, 429
experience-based knowledge 36–37
experiential education 7, 8, 45–46, 86–87, 222, 422; debriefing 262–263; experiential learning distinction 425
experiential learning 2, 8, 45, 141, 422, 425–434; benefits of 185; camps 233; Canadian outdoor education programmes 474–475; cycle of 171; Dewey 41, 46; Kenya 319; Macmillan Academy 148; models 263, 264; place-responsiveness 85, 436; research ethics 200, 205; Scotland 114, 115; Singapore 282; social context 62
exploration 97, 291–292, 374, 399, 475, 477
extreme sports 2

Faarlund, N. 302
fact-based environmental education 34, 36
falls, fatal 446–447, 451
fatalities 14, 16–17, 144, 180, 192, 423, 444–454, 465–466
fatigue 456
fear of nature 492, 493, 494
feedback 209, 210, 262, 266
Feltham, C. 252
femininity 163, 289, 361
feminism 335, 336, 360, 362, 365, 423, 429, 432n2; *see also* gender; women
Fennell, D.A. 473, 476
Fenwick, A. 89, 90
Fenwick, T.J. 425, 427–428, 429
FERAL model 124–125
Fernandez, V. 161
Fernandez-Ballesteros, R.F. 370
fidelity of programme implementation 156
field experience 195–196
Field Report (2010) 105
fields 126, 487, 488, 489
fieldwork 82, 83, 85, 134–136, 399, 401
Fine, Stephen M. 156, 227–235
Finland 231
fishing 371, 374, 392, 401, 413
Fishwick, B. 405
Fjørtoft, I. 281
Fleming, P. 11
'flow' 44, 303
flower gardens 369, 373–374
Floyd, M.F. 347, 364–365
Foglar, Jaroslav 299, 303
Font, V. 460
football 485
footpaths 412, 414, 415, 416
foraging 290, 301, 374
Forest School 155, 157, 244–250, 411
forestry 409, 410–411
Forsyth, D.R. 63
Foucault, Michel 73, 74, 126, 422
foundation myths 11, 12, 14
Foundation Stage 107, 108
Fox, Karen 8, 49–58
France 220, 223, 445, 448, 449
Frank, A. 72
Frankish, C.J. 60
Franklin, N.C. 370, 371
Fraser, M. 60
Freeman, C. 373
Freeman, M. 13, 15
Freire, P. 169, 185, 262
Friese, G. 428
friluftsliv 2, 82, 297, 404–405; adventure education 211; early childhood education in Scandinavia 96; feminist critique 336;

Forest School 246; Norway 271, 273, 275, 288–296; teacher education 121, 123
Frontier Adventure Projects 309
Frost, Robert 260
Fujii, E. 312
funding: adventure education 214; evidence-based research 73; Kenya 323; Macmillan Academy 146, 147; non-formal education 154; paucity of 141; Paul Hamlyn Foundation 142; research ethics 200–201; sail training 241
Furnass, B. 60

Gaard, G. 335
Gadamer, Hans-Georg 293
Gadgil, M. 353, 358
Gaia principle 249
Gallagher, S. 429
Galtung, J. 319
games 299, 301, 303–304, 329, 331
Garbutt, R. 504
gardening 373–374, 389–390, 391, 394–395
gardens: garden design 494; healing gardens 369, 373; vegetable and flower gardens 369, 373–374
Garvey, D.E. 263
Gass, M.A. 123, 124, 162, 253, 254, 263, 321
Gassman, J. 319
gatekeepers 385–386
gay people 365
Geike, Archibald 113
Geist, M. 204
gender 336, 360–368; adventure tourism 464–465; anxiety about masculinity 15–16; camps 231; careers 159, 161–162, 163, 164; climbing 73; educational camps in Brazil 330; friluftsliv 289; maternal overprotectiveness 16, 17; Norway 290; Outward Bound 12; skills 163; social justice 170, 172, 173; see also masculinity; women
General Teaching Council Scotland (GTCS) 114, 117–118, 118n2
Gentin, S. 341, 342–343
geography, earth and environmental science (GEES) 134
Gergen, K. 430
Germany 8, 20–29, 219, 238, 495
Ghere, G.S. 457
Gibson, E.J. 97
Gibson, H.J. 364
Giddens, A. 369, 370, 371
Gilbert, J. 89
Gilbertson, K. 475–476, 478
Gilchrist, P. 501
Gill, T. 16
Gillis, H.L. 220, 223–224
Gillis, L.M. 253, 254, 263
Gilmer, D.G. 320
Gintel, Allan 301
Global Learning Outdoors projects 405–406

globalisation 242, 272, 274, 438
Glotfelty, C. 361
Glover, R.D. 316
goals 208, 209
Goethe, Johann Wolfgang von 291, 496, 499n6
Golins, G. 63
Good for Woods 244
Goodale, T. 169
Goodenough, T. 202
Goodley, D. 74
Goodman, D.J. 173
Gopal, V. 353
Gordon, S. 239
Gorsuch, A.J. 319
Gough, N. 422
government, role of 155–156
Grady, C. 199
Graglia, P. 204
Gramann, J.H. 342
'GRAMPIES' 464
grazing 414
Greeks, ancient 482–483
Green, Geoff 475, 476
Green, L.W. 60
Green, Maxine 428
Greenaway, Roger 155, 260–268, 321
Greene, M. 169, 175
Grocott, A.C. 239
Groh, R. and D. 498n3
groups 62–63, 70–71, 208, 321–322; reviewing 261, 262, 266; spirituality 393
Gruenewald, D. 87, 438
Guba, E. 428, 430
Guha, R. 353, 358
Gurholt, Kirsti Pedersen 273, 288–296, 336

Habermas, J. 463
habitus 108–109, 369–370, 485
Hadjistavropoulos, T. 200
Hagen, Trond Løge 81, 82, 95–102
Hager, P. 428
Hahn, Kurt 11–12, 15, 22–23, 82, 123, 146, 211, 218, 475
'halo effect' 12
Haluza-Delay, R. 393
Ham, S. 478
Hamilton, J. 239
Hamilton, Robin 143
Hammel, H. 263
Hammerman, D.R. 121
Harcourt-Smith, K. 239
Hardin, G. 413
Hargreaves, Alison 73
Harper, Nevin 7, 9, 59–68, 255
Harris, Ian 155, 178–188
Hashimoto, K. 312
Hattie, J. 11–12, 141, 210, 319–320

Hawks, S. 394
Hay, D. 64
Hay, K. 239
Hayhurst, J. 239
healing gardens 369, 373
health 9, 59–68, 83, 106, 154, 248; broad
    conception of 273; camps 233; early childhood
    education in Scandinavia 96; evolutionary
    psychology 249; Forest School 247; older people
    370, 371, 372, 374, 375; physical activity 279;
    racial minorities 346–347, 348; Singapore
    274–275, 279–281
health and safety 104, 136, 144–145, 162, 245; see
    also safety
Heath, S. 200
Hébert, George 218, 219
Hegel, G.W.F. 246
hegemonic masculinity 364
Heidegger, Martin 8, 40, 43–44, 45, 87, 437
Heintzman, Paul 337, 388–397
Helstein, M.T. 73
Hendee, J. 428
Henderson, B. 473–474, 475, 476
Henderson, Karla A. 1–4, 153–158, 271–275, 338,
    364
Henley, T. 400
Henze, R.C. 54
hermeneutics 25, 88, 292
heterosexism 365
Hetherton, J. 61
Hibbler, D.K. 348
Higgins, Pete 81, 86, 113–120, 125, 142, 143
higher education 81, 181, 195; Canada 475; Czech
    Republic 300, 301; ecotourism 479–480; Japan
    310–311; Kenya 322; Norway 292; United
    Kingdom 82–83, 131–140; see also education
hiking 23, 25, 497–498; adventure education 208;
    Czech Republic 297; Japan 307–308; Kenya
    317; Norway 288, 290, 292, 294; Scandinavia 96,
    100; spirituality 392; see also walking
Hill, A. 88, 503, 508
Hirano, Y. 312
Hirsch Hadorn, G. 421
Hitchin, P. 263
Ho, Susanna 271, 273, 277–287
Hobbs, W. 194
Hoberman, J. 12
Hockley, Alan 7, 69, 71–73
Hoffman, E.T.A. 498n2
holistic knowledge 53–54
holistic systems approach 211
Holland, C. 247
Holland, M.B. 345
Holland-Smith, D. 160, 161, 162
Hollenhorst, S.J. 169
Holt, Alfred 237
Holtz, A. 63

Homer 291
Honey, M. 473, 476
Honneth, A. 21
Hopkins, David 146
Hoshino, T. 308
Houlding, Leo 488
Houston, W.R. 262
Hoyle, E. 180, 184
Hreniuk, Darren 219
Hughes, Everett 160
human ecology 37
human-environment interaction 1, 4, 49, 83, 89,
    253, 484, 486
humanism 254, 426, 427
Humberstone, Barbara 1–4, 7, 335–339, 421–424,
    503; careers 159, 163, 164, 165; hegemonic
    masculinity 364; identity construction 466; older
    people 374–375; research perspectives 9, 69–77;
    sail training 237; values 182
Hunt, J. 263
Hunter, J.A. 239
hunting 374
Hutchinson, S. 389–390, 394
Hyde, W.W. 483
Hytten, K. 169

I'Anson, J. 90
Ibsen, Henrik 289, 291
Iceland 399, 451
identity 182, 370; adventure tourism 466–467;
    career 162; cultural 274; ethnic 322; gender
    363; Indigenous 52, 53; older people 371, 376;
    professional 116
Iida, M. 308–309
Illeris, K. 429
immigrants 343, 345, 348
Imura, H. 311
incentives for research participants 200
inclusion 336, 347, 352, 353, 358; adventure
    education 123; cross-cultural leadership training
    172; disabled people 378–379, 380–381, 382,
    384, 385–386; non-formal education 154;
    scholarships 174
India 262, 336, 351–359
Indigenous knowledge 8, 49–50, 51–56, 474, 475,
    477
individualism 104, 169, 221, 341, 361, 369, 375
industrialisation 30–31, 50
inequality 338, 352–353, 398
informal learning 109, 153; see also
    non-formal education
informed consent 199–200, 203
Ingold, Tim 55, 72, 89, 289, 422, 435–436, 437,
    438, 440–442
Inkson, K. 164
Institute for Outdoor Learning (IOL) 181, 182,
    184, 185, 186

institutional habitus 108–109
instructors 137, 146, 163, 195, 208–209, 304; *see also* certification; leadership; training
integrated provision 381
intellectual impairments 386
interactive schema 458, 459
International Association of Antarctica Tour Operators (IAATO) 476
internationalisation 211
Interpersonal Process Recall (IPR) 255–257
interpretive research 69, 73–74, 156, 240, 241
intersectionality 364–365, 424
Inuit 52
iPads 133, 135, 136
Ireland 343–344, 453
Irwin, F.L. 228
Isayama, H.F. 327, 328

Jackson, N. 431–432
James, A. 239
James, T. 261
James, William 12, 63
Japan 238, 271, 273–274, 307–315, 451
Japan Outdoor Network (JON) 310
Jay, M. 348
Jeal, T. 12
Jeste, D.V. 370
Jie, Y. 171
John, P. 180, 184
John Muir Award 403
Johnson, C.W. 73
Johnson, C.Y. 172
Johnson, M. 429
Jojola, T. 52, 53
Jones, J.E. 262, 264
Jones, T. 185
Joplin, L. 41, 262–263
Junák 299–300, 304

Kafka, S. 239
Kahn, P. Jr. 249
Kane, M. 464, 467
Kant, Immanuel 486
Kaplan, S. 63–64
Karabinas, A. 239
Kårhus, S. 126
Katz, S. 371
Kaviti, L. 316, 321, 322, 323
kayaking 138, 337, 371; adventure education 208; Brazil 330; certification 190; disabled people 383; fatalities 450, 451; schema 458–459; Singapore 285; teacher education 124; *see also* canoeing
Keet, Mohr 375
Kellert, R.S. 320
Kellert, S. 63, 249
Kennedy, Donald 326

Kent, J. 202
Kenya 274, 316–324
Kenya School of Adventure and Leadership (KESAL) 317, 318
Keogh, R. 263
Khapova, S.N. 164
Kidner, D. 427, 428
Kielder Water 411, 413
Killion, J. 457
Kilpatrick, William H. 228
Kimball, R.O. 64
Kimmerer, R.W. 54
kinetic empathy 337
Kirk, G. 125
Kizinger, M. 428
Klimek, K. 262
Knapp, Clifford E. 155, 260–268, 400
Knight, Sara 244–250
knowing 43, 45, 46–47
knowledge: adventure sports coaching 456; experience-based 36–37; experiential learning 429; farmers 414; local 453; schema 458, 459; sharing 185; Western 54
Kolb, D.A. 171, 264, 319, 426, 474–475, 480
Korpela, K. 65
Krakauer, J. 465–466
Kraus, R.G. 330
Kriwoken, L.K. 476
Krouwel, W. 302
Kull, R. 429
Kurosawa, T. 309
Kushell, J. 399
Kvale, S. 201

Ladson-Billings, G. 170
Lahman, M. 204
Lais, G.J. 378
Lakoff, G. 429
land ownership 409, 411, 412–413, 415
land use and management 409–418
Landau, D. 476
landscape 25, 28n5, 422, 437; cultural diversity 342; spatial relations 38; urban 282; walking 71–73
language 272–273, 313–314, 429
Larsen, J. 479
Larson, C. 60
Larsson, L. 123, 126
Lasenby, J. 393–394
Laslett, P. 370–371
Latey, M. 352
leadership 2; adventure education 209, 211; adventure sports coaching 456; camps 229, 230; career paths 160; certification 190; cross-cultural leadership training 172; gender issues 361–362, 363; Japan 310–311, 313; non-formal education 154, 155, 168; *see also* training

learning: adventure education 207, 208, 209, 210, 214; brain development 248; camps 227, 228, 231, 232, 233; counselling 252; cycles 264; discovery 109–110, 124; by doing 41, 229, 230; early childhood education in Scandinavia 97; enskilment 441; environmental education 34; exploratory 109–110; higher education in the UK 133–134; informal 109, 153; Macmillan Academy 147, 148; in nature 33; place-responsive education 90, 92, 405; professional 178–179; Scotland 83, 114, 115; situated 9; student-centred 115, 124; tree of outstanding 144, 145; *see also* education; experiential learning
Learning and Teaching Scotland (LTS) 113, 117, 118
Learning Away initiative 142–143, 149
Learning for Sustainability 82, 114, 117, 118, 125
Learning outside the Classroom Quality Badge 145, 148
learning resource centres (LRCs) 133
Leave No Trace (LNT) 313, 319, 479
Leberman, S.I. 303
Leckie, S. 464
Lee, A. 171
Lee, Y.P. 232
legislation: disabled people 379, 380; Japan 310; Norway 246, 288, 295; Scotland 113; United Kingdom 83, 144, 180, 181, 413; *see also* policies; regulation
leisure, access to 331–332
leisure yachting 238
leisure-spiritual coping 394
Lemeiux, C.J. 394
Leopold, Aldo 33
lesbians 168, 365
Lester, S. 178–179
Lettieri, F. 327
liability issues 193, 194
licensure 190, 192
lifelong learning 153
lifestyle choices 371
Lightning, W.C. 52, 54
Limits of Acceptable Change (LAC) 415
Lincoln, Y. 69, 73–74, 428, 430
Lindblad, Lars-Eric 476, 477, 480
Linnaeus, Carl 33
Lipman, M. 402
Lipscombe, N. 465
litigation 223
Little, D.E. 372, 391–392
Liverpool John Moores University (LJMU) 131, 134, 135, 137
localism 423, 438, 439, 501–502, 503, 505
Locke, John 246
Loeffler, T.A. 163, 164, 362
Logan, J. 465
Lorde, A. 175

Lorimer, R. 160, 161, 162
Louv, Richard 16, 154, 279, 400
Lovelock, B. 374
Lowan-Trudeau, Gregory 8, 49–58, 172
Lowy, S. 122
Loynes, C. 221, 428, 463–464, 469
Luckner, J.L. 263, 265
Lynch, Jonathan 81, 82, 85–94
Lynch, P. 329
Lyng, S. 465

MacDougall, C. 372
Macfarlane, R. 436, 439–440, 463
Mack, E. 364
MacLeod, A.K. 61
Macmillan Academy 146–149
Macnaghten, P. 427, 503
Maher, Patrick T. 55, 423, 472–481
Mainiero, L. 161
Maizell, R.S. 265
Mallinckrodt, R. von 496
management solutions 415–416
Manifesto for Education outside the Classroom 141
Mannion, Greg 81, 82, 85–94, 441
Mansfield, Lois 338, 409–418
Maori 52, 55, 374, 436, 507
maps 13–14, 435–436
Marcellino, N.C. 328, 331
March, B. 193
Marcus, C.C. 373
Marker, M. 54
Markula, P. 74, 421–422
Marmarosh, C. 63
Marschall, S. 467
Marsh, H.W. 141, 210, 319–320, 321
Marsh, P.E. 393
Martin, Andrew J. 2, 274, 297–306
Martin, P. 159, 180, 278, 281, 283, 353, 358, 428
masculinity 12, 336, 360, 361, 363; anxiety about 15–16; *friluftsliv* 289; hegemonic 364; technical skills 163; wilderness programmes 169
Mason, B. 228
maternal overprotectiveness 16, 17
Mattu, L. 86
Maynard, Lucy 157, 198–206
Mbeki, Thabo 322
McAvoy, L.H. 378, 390
McBride, R. 122
McCammon, I. 457
McClintic, C. 262
McCoy, M. 87
McCulloch, Ken 156, 157, 236–243
McDaniel, M.A. 263
McDermott, H. 161, 162
McGowan, M.L. 193, 194
McInerney, P. 108

McIntosh, P. 174
McKay, T. 468
McKeen, C.A. 164
McKendrick, J.H. 328
McKenna, P. 123, 124
McKenney, P. 364
McKenzie, M. 15, 87, 88
McLaughlin, P. 143
McLeod, J. 252
McMillan, Margaret and Rachel 245
McNamee, J. 124, 281
Mead, G. 465
medical model of disability 379, 380
memory 467
Mendelssohn, Moses 494
mental health 61, 63, 248; adventure therapy 253;
    therapeutic interventions 251, 252; see also
    wellbeing
mentoring 163–164
Merleau-Ponty, M. 429, 437
meta-cognition 460, 461
Métis 49, 50
Metzner Free School 299
Michelson, E. 426, 429
Midura, W.D. 316
militarism 12, 13–15
Miller, D. 263
Miller, T. 201
Mitten, D. 182
Miyashita, K. 308
mobile technologies 133, 135, 212
modernisation 22, 31
Monaghan, B. 239
monism 307
Montie, J. 457
Moon, J. 425
Morgan, Bernard 238
Morony, S. 232
Morrow, V. 204
Mortlock, C. 86, 182, 262, 264, 294, 336, 400
Moscado, G. 476, 478
Mosely, C. 122
motivation 110, 149, 369; camps 231; careers 161;
    sail training 239; spirituality 389
Moulaert, T. 371
mountain biking: educational camps in Brazil 331;
    forests 411; Kenya 317; older people 374; PE
    teachers 281; teacher education 124; see also
    cycling
Mountain Instructor's Award
    (MIA) 137
Mountain Leader Award 136, 137
mountaineering 3, 423, 465, 467, 482–490;
    certification 190, 191; colonialism 50; Czech
    Republic 297; Norway 292; see also climbing
movement 98–99, 123, 124, 266, 400
Mullarkey, G. 405

Mullins, M. 441
Mullins, Philip 7, 8, 49–58
multidisciplinarity 75, 204, 427–428, 431, 432, 438;
    see also transdisciplinarity
multifunctionality 409, 412, 414, 416
Munir, F. 161, 162
Muñoz, S.-A. 279–281
Murphy, B. 60
Muthomi, Helen N. 273, 274, 316–324
Mzalendo, K.N. 322–323

Nada-Rajah, R. 335
Nadler, R.S. 263, 265
Naess, Arne 32, 247, 292, 432n1
Nakagawa, M. 309
Nakamura, M. 308
Namche Bazaar 464
Nansen, Fridtjof 289, 291, 292, 294
narrative 72
narrative capital 466
Nash, Roderick 341
national governing bodies (NGBs) 137, 181, 184,
    186, 403–404
National Outdoor Leadership School (NOLS)
    169, 191, 195, 212, 213, 274, 317, 318
National Parks 51, 115, 192, 345–346,
    409–411, 415
National Socialism 20, 23
natura lapsa (fallen nature) 492, 493, 494
nature: access to 154; adventure therapy 253;
    Czech Republic 299, 300; disconnection from
    351, 353; distanced relation to 30–32; early
    childhood education in Scandinavia 96, 97,
    98, 101; ecotourism 472, 479; environmental
    education 33–34, 35–36, 400–401; experience-
    based knowledge of 36–37; as fosterer 30, 32–33;
    Gaia principle 249; 'good meetings with' 404–
    405; health and wellbeing benefits 64, 65–66;
    India 353, 354–359; nature-culture dichotomy
    8, 51, 55; Norway 288, 289–290, 295; obstacles
    25; peace building 321–322; Romanticism 484;
    sensory experience of 279; spirituality and 337,
    390, 394; therapeutic benefits 373; use of the
    term 351–352; see also ecology; landscape
nature deficit disorder 16, 154, 400
nature protection 31, 34, 36
Naughton-Treves, L. 345
navigation 137, 435–436
neglect 16
Neil, J. 476
Neill, J. 141, 210, 319–320, 321
Nene Whitewater Centre 468–469
neo-liberalism 83–84, 147, 240, 336, 369, 399;
    challenge courses 218, 221, 224; commercial
    values 399; extended working lives 370;
    individual responsibility 375; personal choice
    371

Nepal 464
networks 163–164
Neuman, Jan 2, 274, 297–306
New Zealand: certification 191, 192; challenge courses 223; curriculum change 277; Education Outside the Classroom guidelines 114; fatalities 14, 444, 451, 452; gardening 373; Indigenous knowledge 52, 55; land management 415; older people 374; outdoor education 278; PE 122; place-responsiveness 436, 438; sail training 238; surfing 507; teacher education 125; walking paths 436; youth mortality rate 453
Newberry, L. 173–174
Newell, P.B. 343–344
Nicol, Robbie 8, 81, 113–120, 142, 337–338, 428
Nilsen, R.D. 96
Nishida, J. 312
non-formal education 2, 3, 153–158, 168, 169, 172–175, 399
non-governmental organisations 153, 154, 190, 193
normalisation 383–384
normative environmental education 34–35, 36
Northern Ireland 142, 413
Norway: adventure education 211; early childhood education 95–97, 98–99, 100; feminist critique 336; *friluftsliv* 271, 273, 275, 288–296; influence on Forest School 246; sail training 238; teacher education 123–124, 126; tourist association 33; Transcultural European Outdoor Studies programme 479–480
novelty 110, 208, 253
Nugent, C. 90
'numinous' experiences 64
nurseries 106–108

obstacles 25, 26, 281
Ocean Youth Club 238
Oevermann, U. 8, 24, 25
offenders 239
Office for Standards in Education (Ofsted) 143–144, 147
Ogilvie, K. 83, 403
Öhman, Johan 7, 8, 9, 30–39
Okamura, Taito 272, 273, 274, 307–315
older people 337, 369–377, 469
Olive, Rebecca 423–424, 501–510
Ontario Parks 391, 392
ontology 89, 92, 428
Ooko, Shikuku W. 273, 274, 316–324
Open Air Laboratories (OPAL) 401
opplevelse 293–294, 295
optimism, structural 24
Organisation for Economic Co-operation and Development (OECD) 370, 451
orienteering 124, 142, 181
Orr, D. 405
O'Sullivan, M. 123

Otto, R. 64
Outdoor Education Advisers' Panel (OEAP) 144
Outdoor Journeys 281
outdoor pre-schools 98
outdoor studies: definition of 2; documenting the impact of 273–274; environmental education 33–34, 35–36; experience 40–41, 45–47; gender in 360–368; ideological role 37; Japan 311–313, 314; nature as fosterer 32–33; place-responsiveness 436, 438–439; Scandinavia 82; *see also* research
Outward Bound 11–12, 13, 22, 123, 207, 212, 480; Adventure Learning Schools 146; camps 228; Canada 475; challenge courses 218, 219; Connecting with Courage 364; Czech Republic 302; Indigenous knowledge 55; influence on non-formal programmes 157; internationalisation 211; Kenya 317; masculinity 15, 169; reviewing 263; sail training 237; training 195
overprotectiveness 16, 17, 28n6

Paariaqtuqtut 52
packing 24
paddlesports 137, 383, 385; *see also* canoeing; kayaking
Paisley, K. 162
Palhares, Marcelo Fadori Soares 272, 274, 275, 325–332
panels, ethics 203
parallel provision 381
Park, A. 347
Park, C.H. 372
Parker, P. 164
parks: ethnic minorities 342, 344, 345–346, 347, 348, 349; Singapore 282; spirituality 391, 394; *see also* National Parks
Parry, D.C. 73
participatory research 3–4, 421
Pasanen, T. 65
Pathways to Peace 316–317, 318, 323
Paul, R. 265
Paul Hamlyn Foundation (PHF) 142–143, 149
Paylor, I. 239
Payne, P. 428
peace 273, 274, 275, 316, 318–319, 320, 321, 322, 323
Pearce-Higgins, J.W. 416
pedagogy: critical 126; cultural density 110; gender-sensitive 362; Germany 8, 22, 23; higher education in the UK 131, 133; place-responsive 88–89, 92, 436, 440, 441, 508; 'reform pedagogics' 33; 'school readiness' 105; socio-ecological 88; student-centred 82, 96, 123, 126; teacher education 126, 127; ways of knowing 8
Peeters, L. 254
Penny, D. 285

people with disabilities (PwD) 230, 337, 370, 371, 378–387
Pepper, D. 428
perception 28n5
performativity 81–82, 104–105, 106, 110
Perkins, H. 466
Perry, Donald 219
Perry, E.I. 17
personal and social development 62, 86, 123, 369, 399; adventure education 210, 211, 214, 321; adventure linked to 291; adventure therapy 251, 254; camps 233; 'context-free' 438; disabled people 378; expeditions 136; older people 375; Singapore 283; teacher education 126, 127; transferable benefits 439; UK curriculum 143
personalism 127
personality 22
Petrarch, Francesco 291, 492
Petzoldt, Paul 191, 318
Pfeiffer, J.W. 262, 264
phenomenology 45, 75, 87, 241, 292, 437
philanthropy 497
Phillipson, D. 237, 238
philosophy 40, 41, 307, 426–427, 493
Philosophy for Children (P4C) 402
photographs 135
physical activity 278–281; camps 229, 233; disabled people 379; early childhood education in Scandinavia 98, 99, 100; gardening 373, 374; girls 363; health and wellbeing 61, 65, 66; kinetic empathy 337; Norway 288; older people 370, 371, 372, 374, 375
physical education (PE) 81, 399; Japan 308, 310; Macmillan Academy 148; Singapore 278–285; UK curriculum 142
physical education teacher education (PETE) 82, 121, 122, 123–124, 126–128
physical skills 163
Pivovarov, V. 316, 319
place 85–94, 105, 110, 247, 437, 503; cultural density 110; 'ecological sensibilities' 504; Forest School 245–246; navigation 435–436; outdoor pedagogies of 438–439; place-responsive education 82, 83, 85, 87, 88–92, 405, 422, 436–442; Singapore 279, 280, 281–282; spirituality and 391; surfing 504, 505
planning 90–91
play 83, 106, 303; early childhood education in Scandinavia 96–99, 100, 101; restriction of freedom to 105
playgrounds 99, 107, 245, 392
playgroups 106
playscapes 281
playwork 245
pluralistic environmental education 35–36
poetry 484, 495–496
Poland 238, 240, 449

Polar expeditions 423, 476–479
policies: agricultural 414; disabled people 379; Scotland 113–114, 115–118; Singapore 277; United Kingdom 103, 105, 106, 143; see also legislation; regulation
Pomfret, G. 464
Porter, Stephan 373
Porter, Su 155, 178–188
Portugal 231
positionality 173
positive relationships 62
positivistic research 73, 156, 240
Postlethwaite, Paul 485–486, 489
post-modernism 421, 426, 427, 428, 429, 430
post-phenomenological approach 87–88
post-reflective experience 42
post-structuralism 87, 88, 89, 127, 421, 429
Potter, E. 503
Potter, T. 473–474, 475, 476
power 49, 505; feminist perspective 362; fields 487; teacher education 125–126, 127
pragmatism 33, 86, 87, 246, 289, 292
Pratt, N. 87
pre-reflective experience 42
pre-schools 98
Preston, L. 122, 125
Pretty, J. 65
Priest, S. 162, 239, 263, 321, 474, 480
primary education 107, 108, 118
Prince, Heather 1–4, 7–9, 81–84, 141–150, 160, 161
Pringle, R. 421–422
private sector 153, 154, 220–221, 271, 310, 399
privatisation 156, 157, 336, 402–403, 411, 412
privilege, recognition of 173–174
proactive management 415
Probyn, Elspeth 423, 501–502
process ethics 203–204
processing 261, 263, 265
Professional Ropes Course Association (PRCA) 219, 222–223
professional development 181, 183, 184, 186; adventure sports coaching 460–461; Brazil 327; challenge courses 222; Singapore 284; see also training
Professional Judgement and Decision Making (PJDM) 455–458, 460, 461
professions 178–180
programme proliferation 212–213
progressive education 22, 23, 33, 40–41, 169, 228
Project Adventure 123, 219
Protestant ethics 21, 289
psychoanalysis 254
psychotherapy 251, 252–253, 254, 255, 257
public goods 413–414
purpose in life 62
purpose of research 199, 200–201
Putland, C. 372

qualifications 137, 155, 162, 178, 181, 182, 186, 189; *see also* certification
'qualitative thought' 43, 44
Quark Expeditions 480
Quay, John 7, 8, 40–48, 86, 87
questioning 264–265, 266
Quinsland, L.K. 263

race 336, 341–350; intersectionality 364–365; social justice 170, 172, 173, 174; *see also* ethnicity
racism 12, 335, 336, 343
Raffan, J. 53
rafting: adventure education 208; adventure tourism 464; Brazil 330, 331; certification 190; India 352, 356; Kenya 317; Nene Whitewater Centre 468–469; Norway 290
Ratner, P.A. 60
reactive management 415–416
Real World Learning Network 404
'recipe coaching' 459
reciprocity 53, 56, 89
recreation 7, 156, 338, 409; challenge courses 220, 221, 224, 225; environmental impact of 414–415; forests 411; higher education in the UK 131, 132; Indigenous knowledge 49, 51, 55–56; management solutions 415–416; multifunctional land use 412; Scandinavia 96; spirituality and 391–393; water bodies 411; *see also* sport
Redclift, M. 427
Rediscovery 55
reflection 260–268, 399; dramaturgy 302, 303, 304; 'in and on action' 457, 458; narrative 26; peace education 320; spirituality 390
reflective experience 41–42, 43, 44, 45
reflective practice 181–182, 184, 186
'reform pedagogics' 33
regulation 156, 415; *see also* legislation; policies
rehabilitation 384
Reich, B. 316, 319
Reid, W.A. 282
Reinke, K. 122
relational ethics 37
relationality 52
relationships 62–63, 475; camps 229; careers 161; continuum of 169, 170; early childhood education in Scandinavia 98; educational camps in Brazil 329, 331; girls 364; non-formal education 155; older people 372; spirituality 394
religion 307–308, 325, 329, 337, 388, 390, 493; *see also* Christianity
Repp, G. 404–405
research 9, 69–77, 156–157, 273; adventure education 213–214; camps 229–231; careers 159; challenge courses 223–224, 225; cross-disciplinary 7; ethics 157, 198–206; India 353–359; Japan 311–313; participatory 3–4, 421; sail training 239–242; spirituality 389; tourism 479
residential outdoor learning 117, 143; budgetary constraints 149; disabled people 384; Macmillan Academy 148; Scotland 114
resilience 278, 279, 283, 363, 364
respect 169, 331
Reti, H. 53
reviewing outdoor experiences 260–268
Richards, G.E. 141, 210, 319–320, 321
Richards, Kaye 2, 155, 157, 251–259
Richardson, D. 378
Richmond, Dan 156, 157, 207–216
Rickinson, M. 70, 321
rights of access 246, 288, 357, 412–413
Ringer, M. 220, 254
Rippin, A. 11
Rishbeth, C. 342
risk 2, 16, 83, 369, 439; adaptive dissonance 63; adventure education 207, 208, 209; adventure linked to 291; adventure sports coaching 456–457; adventure therapy 253; adventure tourism 463, 464, 465, 466, 469; China 272–273; cost-benefit analysis 108; early years outdoor learning 104, 105–106; Forest School 245; games and play 303; generalised attitudes towards 17; hiking 498; Macmillan Academy 147; Norway 289, 294; older people 374; place-responsiveness 436; removal of 186; research 156; risk assessment 105, 136, 144, 181, 279, 280, 281; risk management 465, 466, 469; risk of harm to research participants 201–202; strict aversion standard 453; teacher education 122–123; tolerance for 447; *see also* fatalities
Risk Benefit Analysis (RBA) 456–457
Roberts, J. 86, 426
Roberts, Nina S. 174, 336, 341–350
Robinson, V. 73
Rodriguez, K. 204
Roediger III, H.L. 263
Rogers, A. 364
Rogers, Carl 426
Rogers, S. 103
role play 105
Rollins, R. 194
Romans 482–483
Romanticism 412, 439–440, 463; critique of civilisation 32; experiential education 86; *friluftsliv* 289, 292, 293–294; mountaineering 423, 483–484, 486, 488
Roosevelt, Eleanor 323
Root, E. 55
ropes 190, 217–226; Brazil 330; certification 190; Singapore 285; therapeutic practice 254–255, 256–257; *see also* challenge courses
Rosenthal, M. 12

Ross, H. 89–90, 142, 282, 441
Rousseau, Jean-Jacques 32–33, 495, 498n4, 499n7
routines 24–25, 26, 28n6
Rowe, D. 272
rowing 23, 298, 299
Royal Navy 237–238
Royal Society for the Protection of Birds (RSPB) 401
rucksacks 24, 498
rules 331
running ethics 203–204
rurality 343, 352
Russell, K.C. 253
Russia 231, 238
Ryan, C. 479
Ryff, C.D. 61
Rylander, Elyse 155, 168–177

safety 156, 180–181, 444–454; *see also* health and safety
sail training 157, 236–243
sailing 23, 208
Salem 23
Sallan, J.M. 161
Samdahl, D.M. 156, 224
same-sex outdoor trips 363, 364
Samuels, J.B. 194
Sandell, Klas 7, 8, 9, 30–39
Sandseter, Ellen Beate 81, 82, 95–102
Sankey, K. 86
Satchell, K. 503
Scandinavia 82, 95–102
Scanlin, M.M. 330
Schama, S. 483
schema 458–459, 460
Schiller, F. 498
Schmidt, C. 391–392
Schoel, J. 265
scholarships 174
Schön, D.A. 457
'school readiness' 105, 106, 110
schools: Czech Republic 300; Dewey's critique of traditional schooling 46–47; Germany 22–23; Japan 308, 309; Kenya 322
Schottenbauer, M. 63
Schraml, U. 348
Schwab, K.A. 273
Schwartz, G.M. 328
Schwingel, A. 372
science camps 231–232
Scotland 82, 83, 113–120, 142; fatalities 452; land management 412, 415; natural heritage places 248; *Outdoor Journeys* 281; place-responsiveness 436, 438; rights of access 413; teacher education 125
Scott, D. 364–365
Scouting Movement 11, 12, 17, 33, 50; camps 228, 231; Czech Republic 297–298, 299–300, 304;

gender issues 361; Japan 308, 309; masculinity 15; militarism 13
screen-based society 249
Scrope, K. 239
Seaman, Jayson 7, 8, 40–48, 86, 264
seascapes 337–338, 422
secondary education 116, 118
Seifert, Miloš 299
Sekine, A. 312
self-acceptance 62
self-actualisation 12, 465
self-awareness 173, 174, 186, 253, 266
self-confidence 26, 404; camps 229, 232; challenge courses 220; hiking 498; sail training 236, 239, 240; UK curriculum 142, 143; women and girls 363, 364
self-efficacy 232, 318, 320–321
self-enlightenment 26
self-esteem 63, 65, 297, 404; girls 363; sail training 236, 239; UK curriculum 142
self-realisation 21, 61
self-reflection 55–56, 155, 156, 185, 230, 295
self-regulation 155, 194, 210, 211, 222, 223, 461
Semple, T. 467
Senegal 343–344
senses 74–75, 279, 375, 400
Service Civil International 322
service-learning 171
Seton, Ernest Thompson 33, 50, 299
sexism 335, 336, 362, 365
Sexton, N.R. 344–345
sexuality 170, 172, 173, 175
Sharp, B. 163
Sharp, L.B. 308
Shaw, M.A. 171
Sheptycki, J.W.E. 239
Shibata, T. 308
Shinew, K.J. 348
Shiva, V. 353
Shoard, M. 413
Shooter, W. 162
Shores, K.A. 364–365
Sibthorp, Jim 156, 157, 162, 207–216
Silva, R. 326, 328, 331
Simmel, Georg 294, 422, 463, 465
Simmonds, J.G. 390
Simo, P. 161
Simpson, B. 203, 204
Simpson, S. 263, 265
Singapore 122, 271, 273, 274–275, 277–287, 428
Singer, B.H. 61
Single Pitch Award (SPA) 137
situated learning 9
skiing: certification 190; commodification 469; Czech Republic 297, 298, 299, 300; disabled people 385; fatalities 445–446, 451; Japan 308,

311–312; NGB awards 137; Norway 290; older people 374; teacher education 124
skills: accreditation 182, 184, 186; adventure education 208, 209; adventure sports coaching 455–456; camps 229–230, 231, 233; Canadian outdoor education programmes 475; certification 189, 190, 193; disabled people 384; educational camps in Brazil 328; enskilment 440–441; higher education in the UK 136–137, 138; Macmillan Academy 147–148; pluralistic organisations 175; Singapore 279, 280; social 321, 363; teacher education 123–124, 126, 127; technical 162–163, 181, 186, 189, 193, 209, 285, 362; transfer of 210; women 362, 365
Skills Active 160
Slovakia 231
Slovenia 399
smartphones 135, 213
Smith, B. 69, 75, 203, 204, 421
Smith, D. 239
Smith, G. 438
Smith, J.W. 347
Smith, W.W. 124
Smyth, J. 108
Smythe, W.E. 200
Snell, T.L. 390
social capital 163, 236, 375, 464, 487
social change 332, 338, 360
social constructionism 71
social constructivism 427, 429, 430
social context 62–63
social critical analysis 401–402
social distinction 486–487, 489, 498, 499n8
social fields 487, 488
social justice 3, 335, 336, 338, 406; Canada 477; critical theory 241; disabled people 378; gender 360; non-formal education 155; place-responsive manifesto 91; teacher education 127–128; training 168–177
social model of disability 379, 380
social practices 423, 485, 486
social science 427
social skills 321, 363
social structure 370, 375
social sustainability 157
socialisation: disabled people 384; gender 163, 360, 361, 363; habitus 108, 109; kinship 322
socio-cultural approaches 2, 71, 85–86, 87, 328, 369
socio-ecological approaches 60–61, 62, 63, 64, 88
socio-historical tradition 87
sociology 2
Socrates 262, 265
Sokol movement 298, 299, 300, 304
solitude 392, 393
Somerville, M. 87, 88, 89
Sommers, W.A. 457

South, G. 182
South Africa 345, 375, 450, 468
Sparkes, A.C. 69, 72, 73, 75, 203, 204, 421
spatial relations 38
special educational needs 109
specialist provision 381, 382
Speelman, E. 223–224
spirituality 64, 337, 352, 388–397, 484
Splettstoesser, J. 477
sport 2, 3; adventure sports coaching 423, 455–462; coaching qualifications 181; Czech Republic 298, 299, 302; disabled people 379; educational camps in Brazil 329; football 485; higher education in the UK 131, 132; Japan 310; lifestyle 501, 503, 508; surfing 501–510; see also recreation
sportification 460, 461
Squirrell, G. 199, 203
Srinivas, K. 353
Stan, Ina 7, 69, 70–71
Stanchfield, J. 263
standardisation 20
standards: challenge courses 222–223, 225; Scotland 117
Stankov, L. 232
Steck, Ueli 488
STEM camps 231–232
Sterling, S. 430
Stern, J. 204, 205
Stevenson, J. 426
Stewart, A. 87, 428
Stodolska, M. 343
Stoppa, E.A. 328
Štorch, Eduard 299–300
storytelling 247–248, 356, 439
Stott, Tim 82, 83, 131–140, 161
strength-based approach 364
stress 63–64, 154, 233
strict aversion standard 453
Stringer, L.A. 390
structural optimism 24
Stuart, Karen 157, 198–206
student-centred pedagogy 82
Students on Ice (SOI) 475–476, 477
Stuerm, F.H. 299
subjectivities 502
the sublime 484, 486, 494
suffering 27
Sugarman, D.A. 263, 374
Sugiyama, T. 372, 373
Sullivan, S.E. 161
Sumara, D.J. 432
summer camps 17, 227; Brazil 325–332; Canada 50; Czech Republic 298, 299; Japan 310; see also camps
Summers, A. 13, 17
Sunchild 53–54

Sunderland, M. 248
Surfers Against Sewage 402
surfing 501–510
sustainability 399, 404, 405, 406; adventure tourism 464; coastal communities 507, 508; definition of 472–473; education for 403; Forest School 248; India 358; Learning for Sustainability 82, 114, 117, 118, 125; non-formal education 157; sustainability-based ethics 503; teacher education 125
sustainable development 8, 31, 32, 36, 82; challenge courses 224; definition of 403; existential perspective 37; Scotland 114, 117, 118; spatial relations 38
Svojsík, A.B. 299
Swarbrooke, J. 464
Swayze, N. 55
Sweden: early childhood education 95–96, 97; environmental education 34, 36; parks 345; PE 122; teacher education 126; youth mortality 451
Swiderski, M. 162
swimming 308, 496–497, 499n6
Switzerland 445, 448
symbolic capital 464, 467, 487, 488

Tacey, D.J. 64
Tachibana, N. 311, 312
Taiwan 211
Tan, Yuen Sze Michelle 271, 277–287
Tanii, J. 312
Tapley, Earnest 218, 318
taskscapes 436, 440–441
Tate, C.A. 370, 371
Taylor, B. 337, 402
Taylor, M. 186
teacher education 82, 121–130; early childhood education in Scandinavia 97–98; Japan 311; Scotland 114; Singapore 285; see also training
teachers 116, 146, 282–285
technical skills 162–163, 181, 186, 189, 193, 209, 285, 362
technology 133–134, 135, 136, 398; adventure education 212, 213; adventure tourism 469; prevention of fatalities 451, 454; sail training 242
teenagers 330, 331, 363
Telford, John 423, 482–490
Tellness, A. 404
therapeutic benefits: adventure therapy 251–259; challenge courses 220, 221, 224, 225; healing gardens 373; of nature 248; wilderness therapy 64
therapeutisation 21
Third Age 370–371
38 Degrees 402–403
Thomas, G. 124–125
Thomas, J. 125
Thoreau, Henry David 33, 64

Thrift, N. 337
Tickell, C. 105
Tieck, Ludwig 499n9
Timken, G.L. 124, 281
Tinning, R. 126, 127
Todenem, G. 457
Tokuda, M. 313
Tolbert, P.S. 161
tolerance 168, 169, 172; educational camps in Brazil 329; sail training 239, 240
tour guides 193, 195, 477–478, 480
tourism: adventure tourism 423, 463–471; certification 194–195; challenge courses 219–220, 224; Czech Republic 297; ecotourism 195, 224, 423, 464, 472–481; Germany 27n4; higher education in the UK 131, 132–133; nature-based 33; older people 369, 374, 375
Toyota 310
tradition 22
traditional/craft orientation 127
training: accreditation 182–186; adventure sports coaching 460, 461; certification 189, 191–192, 195, 196; competencies 162; Japan 307, 310, 313; Kenya 318; Scotland 114; Singapore 284–285; social justice 168–177; technical skills 181; see also professional development; teacher education
tramping movement 297–298
transdisciplinarity 3, 421, 422, 427–428; see also multidisciplinarity
transferable benefits 156, 210, 439
transgendered people 365
Trappe, S. 374
traps, heuristic and procedural 457
traumatic crises 25, 27, 28n6
tree of outstanding learning 144, 145
tribal cultures 247–248
Tsukuhara, M. 308
Tuck, E. 87
Tucker, M.E. 64
Tudge, C. 321
Turčova, I. 2, 261, 274, 297–306
Turistický club 298, 300, 301, 304
turistika 297, 298, 300, 302, 304
Turner, G. 508
turning points 233
Tutu, Desmond 321
'Two-Eyed Seeing' 54
Tyrš, Miroslav 298
Tyrvainen, L. 65

Uhlendorf, K.J. 123, 124
Ukai, E. 308
United Kingdom: accreditation 155, 178, 180–181, 182–186; careers 160, 161; certification 191; curriculum change 277; disabled people 379; early years outdoor learning 103–112; EDICT model 124; environmental education 399–403;

ethnic minorities 342, 346–347; fatalities 180, 192, 444, 449, 450, 452; Forest School 244–250; formal curricular initiatives and evaluation 141–150; gender 360; higher education 82–83, 131–140; knowledge-based curriculum 399; land use and management 409–418; Manifesto for Learning Outside the Classroom 114; Nene Whitewater Centre 468–469; neo-liberalism 83; older people 374; outdoor education 83, 278; parks 345; PE 122; performativity 81–82; rurality 343, 352; sail training 237–238, 240, 241; teacher education 123; 'Valuing Places' project 405

United States: adventure education 123; anxiety about masculinity 15; boot camps 14; camps 17, 227, 228, 229, 230; careers 160; certification 189–195; challenge courses 217, 218–219, 223; child mortality 16–17; disabled people 378, 379; diversity 211–212; ethics 198; ethnic minorities 343, 346, 348; fatalities 445, 448, 449, 450, 452; favourite places 343–344; gardening 373; influence of programmes 274; influence on Japan 307, 308; national parks 51; older people 370, 374, 375; outdoor education 278; parks 347; PE 122; popular literature 341; sail training 238, 240; social justice 172; teacher education 121, 123, 124; US programmes in Germany 20; youth mortality rate 453

United World Colleges 11–12, 475
Unruh, A.M. 389–390, 394
urban landscapes 282
urbanisation 31, 50, 185, 245, 357, 358, 412, 439–440
Uriely, N. 479
Urion, C.A. 54
Urry, J. 427, 479
Usher, R. 426

Vacation School Lipnice (VSL) 301–303
Valcour, P.M. 161
values 21, 81, 182, 404, 406; adventure 27; adventure education 123; careers 161; consumerist 337; early childhood education in Scandinavia 96, 101; economic 126; educational camps in Brazil 328–329, 331; environmental education 402; pluralistic environmental education 35; teacher education 128
'Valuing Places' project 405
Van Ginkel, A. 263
Van Heezik, Y. 373
Van Matre, S. 400
Van Slyck, A.A. 17
Vanett, L. 54
Varley, P. 466
vegetable gardens 369, 373–374
vendors 190, 191, 194, 195
virtual field guides (VFGs) 134

virtual learning environments (VLEs) 133, 134
virtue ethics 204
Vivolo, Affonso Maurício 326
Voltaire 246

Wagar, J.V.K. 191
Wagstaff, Mark 155, 156, 217–226, 318
Waite, Sue 81, 82, 87, 103–112
Wales 142
Walker, A. 265
Walker, D. 263, 426
Walker, K. 476, 478
Walker, Rod 406
walking 71–73, 192, 496, 497, 499n8; Czech Republic 297, 301; Environmental Sensitive Areas 412; historical pathways 436; Norway 290; older people 374; path maintenance 416; Rousseau on 499n7; spirituality 392; United Kingdom 412, 413; see also hiking
Waller, T. 247
Walsh, V. 63
Walter, P. 249
Wandervogel 23, 27, 297–298, 299
Warren, Karen 163, 172, 336, 360–368
water 492, 496; water bodies 409, 411, 413; water-based fatalities 449–450, 451
Waters, A. 52
Wattchow, Brian 87, 88–89, 372, 405, 422, 435–443
wayfaring 71–73, 288, 289, 293, 294, 295; see also friluftsliv
wayfinding 13–14, 436
ways of knowing 8, 438
Wearing, S. 476
weather-related fatalities 451, 452
Webel, C. 319
Weber, Max 22
Weiler, B. 478
Weiss, C.H. 202
wellbeing 9, 59–68, 83, 106, 186, 273, 278; adventure therapy 246, 257; camps 233; challenge courses 220; early childhood education in Scandinavia 96, 98, 100; evolutionary psychology 249; Forest School 247, 248; gardens 373; older people 372; psychological 253; Singapore 279–281; spiritual 394; see also health
Wendler, D. 199
Wertheimer, Max 265
West, Amanda 155, 159–167
Western perspectives 50–51, 54, 55
Wheaton, B. 402, 501
Whitaker, E.D. 372, 374
whitewater rafting see rafting
Whitt, L.A. 53
Whittington, A. 360, 364
whole systems thinking 430

whole-school approaches 116, 117
wilderness 64, 169, 409; Adventure Learning
Schools 146; certification in wilderness
medicine 190; Japan 313; Kenya 318, 319, 320;
spirituality 392; teacher education 127; training
course 168; Western perspectives 51, 54, 55
Wilderness Education Association 191, 274, 307
Wilderness Education Association of Japan (WEAJ)
307, 313
Wilderness First Responder (WFR) 194, 195
Wilderom, C.P.M. 164
wildlife tourism 374, 466, 468, 469
Wiles, R. 200
Wilkes, K. 468
Williams, R.D. 171
Williamson, E. 202
Wilson, E. 372
Wilson, E.O. 247, 400
Wilson, J. 428
Wilson, M. 86
wind surfing 374–375, 391
Winton, S. 15
Wolch, J. 342, 344, 347–348
Wolfe, B.D. 156, 224
women 336, 360–368; adventure education 212;
careers 159, 161–162, 163, 164; India 353, 356,
358; mountaineering 465; Norway 290; social
justice 168, 175; spirituality 389; wayfinding
13–14; *see also* feminism; gender
Woodcraft Indians 33, 50, 297–298, 299
World Commission on Environment and
Development (WCED) 472
World Health Organization (WHO) 59, 370
Wylie, J. 72

Xiang, P. 122

yachting 238, 299, 391
Yalden, D.W. 416
Yamada, M. 312
Yamaoka, H. 308
Yanagi, H. 312
Yasunami, Y. 312
YMCA 228, 303, 308, 309–310, 325, 326
Yoneyama, K. 309
York-barr, J. 457
Yoshida, A. 308
young offenders 14, 239

Zelizer, V.A.R. 16–17
Zest for Living Scale 312
Ziersch, A.M. 372
Zinn, H.C. 374
ziplines 190, 195, 217, 219–220, 223, 224, 225